ENCYCLOPEDIA
OF
CORPORATE MEETINGS, MINUTES, AND RESOLUTIONS
THIRD EDITION

NOTE

Some of the materials used throughout this edition are adapted from Prentice-Hall's Corporation Service and Corporation Forms Service. We wish to acknowledge and thank the editors for use of these materials.

ENCYCLOPEDIA
OF
CORPORATE MEETINGS,
MINUTES, AND RESOLUTIONS
THIRD EDITION

William Sardell,
Revisor

VOLUME II

PRENTICE-HALL, INC.
Englewood Cliffs, New Jersey

Prentice-Hall International, Inc., *London*
Prentice-Hall of Australia, Pty. Ltd., *Sydney*
Prentice-Hall Canada, Inc., *Toronto*
Prentice-Hall of India Private Ltd., *New Delhi*
Prentice-Hall of Japan, Inc., *Tokyo*
Prentice-Hall of Southeast Asia Pte. Ltd., *Singapore*
Whitehall Books, Ltd., Wellington, *New Zealand*
Editora Prentice-Hall do Brasil Ltda., *Rio de Janeiro*
Prentice-Hall Hispanoamericana, S.A., *Mexico*

10 9 8 7 6 5 4 3

Library of Congress Cataloging in Publication Data
Main entry under title:

Encyclopedia of corporate meetings, minutes, and
   resolutions.

   Includes index.
   1. Corporate meetings—Law and legislation—
United States. 2. Corporation law—United States.
3. Corporation law—United States—Forms.
4. Corporate minutes—United States. I. Sardell,
William.

KF1414.E48	346.73'06645	85-9484
	347.3066645	

ISBN 0-13-275280-8

Printed in the United States of America

PREFACE TO THE THIRD EDITION

Corporate officers, directors, and practitioners have to keep on top of an ever-changing and dynamic body of laws, rules, and cases. They must be constantly fully aware of what these changes mean and their impact on the corporation and its functioning. Thousands of corporate directors, officers, and practitioners have long relied on Prentice-Hall's *Encyclopedia of Corporate Meetings, Minutes, and Resolutions* to help them do just that and to assure them that they are doing the job they are responsible for.

The *Encyclopedia,* consisting of two volumes, is structured quite simply. Each subject chapter is followed by a chapter that contains all the forms relating to the previous chapter. Odd-numbered chapters present the basic principles of law applicable to the specific area of corporate affairs. The textual portion deals with the basic statutes that affect the particular area, both state and federal, with full citations to the leading cases that interpret those statutes. This gives the user the necessary background to help him or her understand the context in which the forms apply.

Even-numbered chapters provide a host of carefully drawn forms that implement the principles given in the subject chapter. These forms have been taken from court opinions, records of cases on appeal, records of investigating committees, but always after careful checking and, if necessary, editing. The forms included throughout the volumes have been tested in actual practice. In addition, many alternate forms are included to enable the practitioner to use the one most suitable to the specific situation with which he or she is confronted. The forms include resolutions and minutes—both for directors and stock-holders—affidavits, notices, proxies, reports, and a host of others to assure that every aspect of corporate meetings and minutes is covered.

The *Encyclopedia* covers all these areas of corporate practice: stockholders' meetings; directors' and committee meetings; minutes of meetings; organization meetings; management of the corporation; compensation of directors, officers, and employees; subscription to capital stock; issuance and sale of capital stock; rights to subscribe to stock, stock purchase warrants, and options to purchase stock; calls for payment of stock and assessments; transfer of stock; dividends; amendment of charter and by-laws; borrowing and lending; purchase, sale and lease of assets; consolidation and merger; and reorganization, liquidation, and dissolution.

This new edition is based on a substantially revised text that includes many new principles and trends, plus a host of new cases illustrating those principles. The *Encyclopedia* includes:

(1) New law on corporate liability to innocent purchasers for issuing more than its authorized number of shares;
(2) A shareholder's right to rescind his or her purchase of stock when the corporation fails to deliver a stock certificate for the shares;
(3) Usury as a defense to corporate liability;
(4) The personal liability of a creditor for an illegal loan to a shareholder, even though the creditor became such after the director's resignation;
(5) The right of a director, officer, or shareholder to foreclose on a lien the corporation gave to secure a loan;
(6) Dividends on multiple classes of stock;
(7) The proper publicity when action is taken on a dividend;
(8) The right of minority stockholders to object to "short form" mergers;
(9) Liability of directors and officers when a corporation dissolves without giving the notice required by law;
(10) Liability of directors and officers even after all the assets of a dissolved corporation have been distributed.

New forms have been added and many forms changed where necessary to reflect changes in corporate practice. Here are just some of the many forms provided:

(1) Notice of stockholders' meeting for a public corporation, along with a proxy statement and proxy card;
(2) Directors' resolution ratifying payment of compensation to vice-president and merger, authorized by president;
(3) Directors' resolution authorizing gift to widow of executive;
(4) Stockholders' resolution applying a stock bonus plan;
(5) Resolution of directors authorizing release or partial release of subscriber, and stockholders' resolution ratifying such release;
(6) Assignment of stock required by the New York Stock Exchange;
(7) Directors' resolution authorizing sale and leaseback of real property owned by corporation;
(8) Notice of special meeting of stockholders to vote on recapitalization;
(9) Letter accompanying notice outlining plan of recapitalization;
(10) Statement to be sent to stockholders giving reasons for stock split.

The revisor is sincerely indebted to the editors of the original edition, Edith J. Friedman and the late Lillian Doris, for their careful planning and presentation that expedited the preparation of this revision.

William Sardell

CONTENTS—VOLUME I

CONTENTS—VOLUME II

Chapter 21

TRANSFER OF STOCK

Contents—Chapter 21

Right of stockholder to transfer his stock. A stockholder has the right to transfer his shares of stock without interference by the corporation.[1] This right is based upon the inherent power of a person to dispose of his property.[2] It is a continuing right, existing from the time the subscription to the stock is made until the corporation is dissolved. A stockholder can sell his stock to another stockholder or to a stranger; he does not need to know the character or responsibility of the buyer.[3] In general this is also true even if the stockholder is a majority holder. As far as selling that stock is concerned, majority holders, whether one or a group, have no fiduciary relation to other stockholders, merely by virtue of ownership of stock.[4] Nevertheless, the right to alienate a majority of stock is subject to some restriction. For example, in selling his stock a majority stockholder cannot legally dominate, interfere with, or mislead other stockholders.[5] Nor can majority stockholders legally sell their holdings to persons who intend to loot the treasury or mismanage the corporation to its injury.[6] If the majority holders actually control and manage the corporation they cannot use their power to damage the corporation or injure minority interests.[7]

A stockholder who is a director has the same right as other stockholders to transfer his stock, provided of course, that the transfer is not fraudulent or in breach of any trust. The fiduciary responsibility of directors to all of the stockholders will prevent their selling a controlling interest in the corporation, to the injury of the corporation, either knowingly or with negligent failure to investigate as to the possibility of such injury.[8]

---

[1]Farmers' Loan & Trust Co. v Chicago P&SRRR, (1896) 163 US 31, 16 S Ct 917; Bd. of Comm'rs v Reynolds, (1873) 44 Ind. 509. See also Sterling Midland Co. v Chicago-Williamsville C. Co., (1929) 336 Ill. 586, 168 NE 655; Trisconi v Winship, (1891) 43 La. Ann 45, 9 So 29.

[2]Howe v Roberts, (1923) 209 Ala. 80, 95 So 344; Hague v DeLong, (1937) 282 Mich. 330, 276 NW 467; Gerdes v Reynolds, (1941) 28 NYS2d 622.

[3]Curtis v Beckett, (1943) 114 Ind. App. 221, 50 NE2d 920; Levy v American Beverage Corp., (1942) 265 App. Div. 208, 38 NYS2d 517; Gerdes v Reynolds note 2 supra.

[4]Levy v American Beverage Corp. See note 3 supra; Gerdes v Reynolds note 2, supra.

[5]Roby v Dunnett, (1937) 88 F2d 68, cert denied, 301 US 706; 13 Fletcher, Corporations §5805.

[6]Gerdes v Reynolds. See note 2 supra; Insuranshares Corp. v Northern Fiscal Corp., (1940) 35 F Supp 22.

[7]Lebold v Inland Steel Co., (1941) 125 F2d 369, cert denied, 316 US 675, 62 S Ct 1045; Kavanaugh v Kavanaugh Knitting Co., (1919) 226 NY 185, 123 NE 148; Levy v American Beverage Corp., (1942) 265 App. Div. 208, 38 NYS2d 517.

[8]Perlman v Feldman, (1955) 219 F2d 173 (Ind. law); Soderstrom v Kungsholm Baking Co., (1951) 189 F2d 1008; Benson v Braun, (1956) NYS 2d 622. See also Southern Pacific Co. v Bogert, (1919) 250 US 483; 39 S Ct 533. Contra: Insurance Agency Co. v Blossom; (Mo. App. 1921) 231 SW 636.

Here are some examples of majority stockholder's fiduciary duty:

A bank that was majority stockholder of a corporation was liable for breach of duty to minority stockholders when it secretly sold its stock to a purchaser who wasted the corporate assets. The bank could have reasonably anticipated the purchaser's acts and so it breached the duty of care it owed to the corporation and to the minority.[9]

The president and chairman of the board of directors who owned 74 percent of a corporation's shares jointly with her husband, breached her fiduciary duty to the corporation and its shareholders when she planned to financially destroy the corporation by lending it money from a joint account she had with her husband and then demanding immediate payment, since her motive was to deprive her husband of the use of such account and remove him from directorship. This was not done to promote the interest of the corporation and the shareholders.[10]

A corporation that was a majority stockholder could not use attorney-client privilege as a defense to a motion to compel production of documents in a securities law action by minority stockholders on the ground that documents resulted from studies made by its counsel; the majority stockholders owed a fiduciary duty to minority and privilege could not be used to block the required disclosure.[11]

Utilization of corporate profits to cover costs of unreasonable salary and living expenses of majority stockholder was breach of the fiduciary obligation owed by such shareholder to the corporation. The burden of proving unreasonableness lies with the minority stockholder.[12]

A majority stockholder breached his fiduciary duty to minority stockholders when he arranged to sell all the corporation's stock without telling the minority that the sale was conditioned on the purchase of all the stock, since that was relevant to the value of minority's shares.[13]

In an analogous situation, the majority shareholder breached his purchase agreement with the minority shareholder when he failed to sell minority's shares along with his own in a private offering; the court based the damages on the last over-the-counter market price.[14]

---

[9]De Bann v First Western Bank & Trust Co. (Cal. App. 1975) Civ. No. 43994, 3–31–75.
[10]Thrasher v Thrasher (Col. App. 1972) 27 CA2d 23.
[11]Valente v Pepsico, Inc. (D Del. 1975) Civ. Action 4537, 8–25–75.
[12]Cole Real Estate Corp v Peoples Bank and Trust Co. (Ind. App. 1974) 310 NE2d 275.
[13]Blakesley v Johnson (Kan. S Ct 1980) 608 P 2d 908.
[14]Levine v Joseph (App. Div. 1983) 469 NYS 2d 113.

On the other hand, here are some examples contra:

A majority stockholder-director was not liable to a corporation's minority stockholders for breach of fiduciary duty when he sold his stock to a buyer who then looted the corporation, since at the time of sale no facts existed that would have put a prudent man on notice that the buyer's intentions were anything but honorable. Even the seller's continued position as director and his continued financial stake in the corporation did not charge him with knowledge of what the buyer was doing.[15]

A majority shareholder who was paid a premium for his stock because of the control that went with it had no duty to the corporation or minority shareholders to account for such additional profit.[16]

No breach of fiduciary duty occurred when the owners of 14 percent of the stock sold their shares to the owner of 20 percent, since that did not amount to the sale of a controlling block.[17]

Minority stockholders cannot hold the purchaser of control stock liable for its failure to share the control premium with them, when there is no showing of any conspiracy between the purchaser and the seller of the majority shares to defraud the minority.[18]

Sellers who sold control of a corporation at a premium price did not violate any fiduciary duty to the minority merely because they structured the transaction in such a way as not to trigger rights that the minority might have had to obtain a higher price than he in fact received.[19]

A parent corporation as majority stockholder did not breach its fiduciary duty to a subsidiary's minority stockholders, even though tax election made in distributing gains after liquidating the subsidiary postponed the capital gains tax on the parent's gains while allotting a pro rated share of the tax to minority stockholders. This is so, since tax liability remained the same and the parent should not be compelled to overlook income tax advantages.[20]

When the price paid to the controlling stockholder does not reflect any premium for the delivery of the board of directors, the buyer of such stock cannot void the purchase by claiming it included delivery of the board.[21]

---

[15] Harman v Willbern (CA–10 1975) 520 F2d 1333.
[16] Thompson v Hambrick (Tex. App. 1974) 508 SW2d 949.
[17] Kings County Development Co. v Buell (CA–9 1983) No. 81–5660 4–6–83.
[18] Doleman v Meiji Mutual Life Insurance Company (CA–9 1984) 727 F2d 1480.
[19] National Bank of Detroit v Whitehead and Kales Co. (CA–6 1984) No 82–1069 3–23–84.
[20] Grace v Grace Nat'l Bank of New York, (CA–2 1972) 465 F2d 1068.
[21] Goode v Powers (Ariz. S Ct 1965) 397 P2d 56.

Where the question of harm to the corporation is not present, the tests applied are those of good faith and reasonable care. If both are met, the holders of a majority of the stock are under no more restraint as to its transfer than holders of minority interests.[22]

Stockholders can transfer their stock when the corporation is in the hands of a receiver or in the process of liquidation.[23] The transfer carries with it any right that might accrue to the original owner.[24] Although shares cannot be transferred after dissolution, the stockholder may assign his right to share in the assets of the corporation, subject to any claims the corporation may have against the transferor.[25]

The situation referred to above in which the fiduciary duty of controlling stockholders comes into important play is when the controlling stockholders agree to deliver the board of directors to the buyers. There is no all-encompassing rule to delineate when this can be done.

In one case, the seller agreed to sell his 28 percent block of stock at a premium. But the buyer wanted control of the corporation, and said he would not take the stock unless the seller delivered the resignations of a majority of the board and caused the nominees of the buyer to be elected in their place. For an unrelated reason, the seller refused to go through with the sale. When the buyer sued for breach of contract, the trial court gave summary judgment to the seller on the ground, among others, that the agreement to deliver the board was illegal. The United States Court of Appeals, however, reversed the decision and sent the case back to the trial court to decide several issues, including the agreement to transfer control. It said that the *sale* of a corporate office is illegal, but the *transfer* of a corporate office, or even control of a corporation is not always illegal. If, for example, the *majority* stock is sold, there is nothing wrong in arranging for the resignation of the majority directors and filling the vacancies with the buyer's nominees. This, said the court, is simply a convenient way of accomplishing a foregone result. The trouble comes when, as here, less than a majority

[22]Nelson v Northland Life Ins. Co., (1936) 197 Minn. 151, 266 NW 857; Smith v Gray, (1926) 50 Nev. 56, 250 P 369; Levy v American Beverage Corp., (1943) 114 Ind. App. 221, 50 NE2d 290; Adams v Mid-West Chevrolet Corp., (1947) 198 Okl. 461, 179 P2d 147; Tryon v Smith, (1951) 191 Ore. 172, 229 P2d 251.

[23]Holingsworth v Multa Trina Ditch Co., (1931) 51 F2d 649; People v California Safe Deposit & Trust Co., (1912) 18 Cal. App. 732, 124 P 558; Curtis v Beckett, (1943) 114 Ind. App. 221, 50 NE 2d 920

[24]Holingsworth et al, note 23 supra.

[25]James v Woodruff, (1844) 10 Paige (NY 541) aff'd 2 Denio (NY) 574.

of the stock is sold. On this point, the three judges went separate ways.[26]

Minority stockholders have been able to bar majority stockholders of a corporation with shares listed on the New York Stock Exchange from issuing a new class of non-voting common stock. This is so, even though state law permitted the new class of stock, when its issuance would have resulted in the corporation's losing its listing, and the only purpose of the new class of stock was to keep the majority in control.[27]

Although the right to dispose of property is recognized by the courts, reasonable restrictions on that right have been upheld where the restrictions were imposed (1) by the certificate of incorporation, the by-laws, the contract of subscription, or any other contract between the corporation and the stockholder or among the stockholders themselves; (2) directly by statute; or (3) by the corporation under power given to it by statute.

Transfer of subscriptions to stock. A subscriber who has become a stockholder by the corporation's acceptance of his subscription has the right to transfer his subscription even before any payment has been made on the contract, whether or not a certificate has been issued to him, unless the statute, the charter, or the agreement between the subscriber and the corporation provides to the contrary.[28] In order to make the assignment effective, it must be accepted by the corporation and recorded upon its books. Until such acceptance and recording, the original subscriber continues liable for all calls made for the unpaid subscription.[29]

Usually, if the transfer is made by an original subscriber who is an incorporator and signer of the articles of incorporation, immediately after the corporation has received its charter, the acceptance by the corporation of the transferee as a subscriber in place of the original subscriber is voted toward the close of the meeting of the incorporators and is recorded in the minutes of the meeting. The acceptance may take place at any directors' meeting. It is not essential, however, that the acceptance of a transferee in place of the original subscriber be made

[26]Essex Universal Corp. v Yates (CA-2 1962) 305 F2d 572.
[27]United Funds, Inc. v Carter Products, Inc. (Md. Cir Ct 1963) Balto Daily Rec 9-23-63, p. 2
[28]Roosevelt v Hamblin, (1908) 199 Mass. 127 85 NE 98.
[29]Butts v King, (1924) 101 Conn. 291, 125 A 654. See also Webster v Upton, (1875) 91 US 384; Cambell v American Alkali Co., (1903) 125 F 207; Geary St. P&ORR v Bradbury Estate Co., (1918) 179 Cal. 46, 175 P 457; Sigua Iron Co. v Brown, (1902) 171 NY 488, 64 NE 194.

by formal action of the corporation expressed in voting or otherwise. It may be implied from the acts and course of conduct of the corporation, and the continuing recognition of the substitution of the transferee in place of the original subscriber.[30]

Right of stockholder to transfer shares before payment. Even stockholders who have not paid in full for their stock have a right to sell and transfer their shares. The one restriction on such a sale is that a shareholder in an insolvent corporation, with actual or implied knowledge of such insolvency, cannot sell his shares to an insolvent or irresponsible person in order to escape liability on the stock.[31] Title to the stock passes to the transferee at once and is not affected by the subsequent action of the corporation in recognizing or refusing to recognize his title.[32]

Effect of transfer of stock upon liability for calls and assessments. A person who makes an absolute transfer of his stock in good faith is relieved of further liability for calls upon an unpaid subscription, provided the transfer is duly recorded on the books of the corporation.[33] In most states it is held, either under common or statutory law, that the transferee of the stock is liable for all calls made after the transfer, but not for those made prior thereto.[34] The law of the state in which the corporation is organized governs, and not the law of the state in which the transferee resides.[35] Under common law, the liability of the transferee is based on "novation," that is, on a substitution of the transferee for the transferor as the debtor of the corporation for the balance unpaid on the stock.[36] The date of the call, not the date when it becomes payable, determines liability as between the transferor and transferee.[37]

A stockholder must act in good faith in order to be relieved of liability for calls by a transfer of his shares of stock.[38] If the transfer is

---

[30]Butts v King, note 29 supra.

[31]Banta v Hubbell, (1912) 167 Mo. App. 38, 150 SW 1089; Fletcher, Corporations §6103, §6371.

[32]Manchester St. Ry. v Williams, (1902) 71 NH 312, 52 A 461; 14 CJ §921.

[33]Webster v Upton, (1875) 91 US 384; Shaw v Green, (1937) 128 Tex. 596, 99 SW2d 889.

[34]Geary St. P&ORR v Bradbury Estate Co., (1918) 179 Cal. 36, 175 P 457; Sigua Iron Co. v Brown, (1902) 171 NY 488, 64 Ne 194.

[35]Black v Zachary, (1845) 44 US 527; Priest v Glenn, (1892) 51 F 400; McConey v Belton Oil & Gas Co., (1906) 97 Minn. 190, 106 NW 900.

[36]Campbell v American Alkali Co., (1903) 125 F 207; West Nashville Planning-Mill Co. v Nashville Sav. Bank, (1888) 86 Tenn. 252, 7 SW 340.

[37]Campbell v American Alkali Co., (1903) 125 F 207.

[38]Rochester & K. F. Land Co. v Raymond, (1899) 158 NY 576, 53 NE 507.

made for the sole purpose of avoiding liability, the transferor remains liable; such a transfer is fraudulent and void.[39] The transferor also remains liable unless the transferee accepts the transfer.[40] It has been held that the transferor remains liable after transfer to a minor.[41] A transferee has the right to assume that stock issued as fully paid is as represented, and is not subject to call, unless he has knowledge that the stock is watered.

If paid-up stock is assessable, the transferee is liable for assessments on the stock made after its transfer.[42] Generally, however, the statutes provide that a transferee is not liable for an assessment unless the power of assessment is stated on the face of the stock certificate.[43] If the transferee fails to have the stock transferred on the corporate record, he is liable to the transferor for any assessments the latter is compelled to pay after transfer.[44] A pledgee who has the stock transferred on the books to his name is liable.[45] A transfer of shares may be made even if there are unpaid assessments against the stock.[46]

In many states there are statutes giving the corporation remedies for the enforcement of unpaid subscriptions upon the failure of the subscribers to pay in response to a call for payment. Either under these statutes, or in their absence, at common law, the corporation generally has some or all of the following remedies:

(1) Bring an action at law for the amount of the unpaid call;
(2) Sell at public auction such part of the shares as will pay the call due plus expenses;
(3) Sell the shares in satisfaction of the amount of the call and expenses and refund any excess to the subscriber;
(4) After sale, as in 2 or 3, sue the subscriber for any deficiency existing;
(5) Forfeit to the company the shares and all previous payments made thereon; and
(6) Purchase the shares itself through its secretary, president, or a director if the amount of the call and expenses cannot be obtained by sale as in remedy 2 or 3.

---

[39] Bowden v Johnson, (1882) 107 US 521; Nat'l Bank v Case, (1878) 99 US 628.
[40] Russell v Easterbrook, (1898) 71 Conn. 50, 40 A 905.
[41] Hood v North C. Bank & Trust Co., (1936) 209 NC 367, 184 SE 51.
[42] Porter v Gibson, (1945) 25 Cal. 2d 506, 154 P2d 703; Libby v Tobey, (1890) 82 Me 397, 19 A 904.
[43] Wilson v Cherokee Drift Mining Co., (1939) 14 Cal. 2d 56, 92 P2d 802.
[44] Gaffney v People's Trust Co., (1920) 191 App. Div. 697, 182 NY Supp 451, aff'd, memo dec, (1921) 231 NY 577, 132 NE 895; Bell v O'Connor's Executors No. 2, (1940) 40 D&C (Pa) 353.
[45] Greutzmacher v Quevli, (1929) 208 Iowa 537, 226 NW 5.
[46] Craig v Hesperia Land & Water Co., (1896) 113 Cal. 7, 45 p. 10.

In some states the corporation may, by by-law provision, determine the manner of selling or forfeiting shares for non-payment of calls. Remedies for non-payment of calls may also be provided by the corporate charter or by the subscription contract.

Statutory, charter, or contract remedies are generally held to be in addition to, and do not abrogate appropriate common law remedies.[47]

Example: A corporation has the right to sue for the amount of the call although by statute, charter, or contract, it may also have the right to sell or forfeit the shares.[48]

Unless the right to do so is given by statute,[49] the corporation cannot sue at law for the amount of the call after it has availed itself of the remedy of forfeiture.[50]

A corporation must deliver stock certificates to a person designated in articles of incorporation as a 50 percent stockholder upon payment of the purchase price, when the corporation had not used statutory means to dispose of unpaid stock.[51]

Contractual restrictions on transfer of stock. Provisions in the charter or by-laws of the corporation, or in the stock certificates themselves, restricting the transfer of stock are enforceable as contracts between the corporation and the stockholder.[52] The right of a stockholder to alienate his property is, however, a matter of public policy and a stockholder is not free to contract away his privilege to any extent that he chooses. The restrictions agreed upon by the stockholder must be reasonable in order to be binding, and they are strictly construed.[53]

For example, transfer restrictions imposed by corporate articles on class A stock and requiring withdrawing stockholders to first offer stock to members of class, created first option rights and were not

---

[47]Campbell v American Alkali Co. (CA–3 1903) 125 F 207; State v Associated Packing Co. (Iowa S Ct. 1929) 277 NW 627; Mills v Stewart, (1869) 41 NY 384; Ohio Valley Industrial Corp. v H.L. Seabright Co., (1931) 111 WVa 55, 160 SE 300.

[48]Nashua Sav. Bank v Anglo-American Land, Mortg. & Agency Co., (1903) 189 US 221, 23 S Ct 517; Imperial Land Stock Co. v Oster, (1917) 34 Cal. App 776, 168 P 1159.

[49]Mandel v Swan Land & Cattle Co., (1895) 154 Ill. 177, 40 NE 462.

[50]Buffalo & NY City RR Co v Dudley, (1856) 14 NY 336.

[51]Scobes v Continental Hotel Corp. (La. Ct of App. 1970) 242 So2d 610.

[52]Vanucci v Pedrini, (1932) 217 Cal. 138, 17 P2d 706; Lawson v Household Finance Corp., (1929) 17 Del. Ch 1, 147 A 312; New England Trust Co. v Spaulding, (1941) 310 Mass. 424, 38 NE2d 672; Penthouse Properties, Inc. v 1158 Fifth Ave, (1939) 256 App. Div. 685, 11 NYS2d 416.

[53]In re Trilling and Montague, (1956) 140 F Supp 260; McDonald v Farley & Loetscher Mfg. Co., (1939) 226 Iowa 53, 283 NW 261; Guaranty Laundry Co. v Pulliam, (1947) 198 Okla. 667, 181 P2d 1007; Citizens State Bank v O'Leary, (1942) 140 Tex. 305, 167 SW2d 719; Pelton v Nevada Oil Co. (Tex. Civ. App. 1948) 209 SW2d 645.

prohibited by law as resulting in a buy-sell agreement between more than 20 members of class, since provision in articles did not amount to agreement among members of class. Nor was incorporation of New York Stock Exchange rules on transferability of shares unreasonable, when the corporation was a member of that exchange.[54] Absolute restrictions upon the sale of or transfer of stock, as distinguished from reasonable conditions precedent to transfer, will not be enforced.[55]

A distinction is sometimes drawn between restrictions imposed by charter and restrictions imposed upon an unwilling minority of stockholders through the by-laws. A provision that no stock shall be sold or transferred to a competitor was declared invalid as a provision in the by-laws, although the court held that such a by-law might have been valid if expressly authorized by the charter.[56] A provision in the certificate of incorporation that prohibited transfer of shares without first offering them to the corporation was valid; however, it was intended for the benefit of the corporation. So it cannot be enforced by a single stockholder acting in his individual capacity, but these restrictions were waived by resolution of the directors and the transfer was valid.[57] Where, however, the by-law restriction has been adopted by the unanimous vote of stockholders, a reasonable restriction is usually upheld, particularly where the question arises among the original stockholders.[58] Even if a restriction is void when considered strictly as a by-law, it may be enforced as an agreement entered into between the interested parties.[59]

Restriction requiring stockholders to give corporation option to purchase. A common contractual restriction on the transfer of stock is one requiring a stockholder to give to the corporation or to the other stockholders a first option to purchase her stock if the stockholder desires to sell it. That kind of provision is not an invalid restraint upon the alienation of corporate stock,[60] nor is it invalid as against public

[54]Ling and Co., Inc. v Trinity Savings and Loan Ass'n. (Tex. S Ct 1972) 482 SW2d 841, reversing (Tex. Ct of Civ. App. 1971) 470 SW2d 441.
[55]In re Laun, (1911) 146 Wis. 252, 131 NW 366.
[56]Kretzer v Cole Bros. Lightning Rod Co., (1916) 193 Mo. App. 99, 181 SW 1066.
[57]First Nat'l Bank of Boston v Sullivan (Mass. Ct of App. 1974) 314 NE2d 149.
[58]Krauss v Kuechler, (1938) 300 Mass. 346 15 NE2d 207; Weiland v Hogan, (1913) 177 Mich. 626, 143 NW 599; In re Laun, (1911) 146 Wis. 252, 131 NW 366.
[59]Palmer v Chamberlin, (1951) 191 F2d 532; Krauss v Kuechler, note 58 supra; Weiland v Hogan, note 58 supra.
[60]Warner & Swasey Co. v Rusterholz, (1941) 41 F Supp 498; Lawson v Household Finance Corp., (1929) 17 Del Ch. 1, 147 A 312; McDonald v Farley & Loetscher Mfg. Co., (1939) 226 Iowa 53, 283 NW 261. Albert E. Touchet, Inc. v Touchet, (1928) 264 Mass. 499, 163 NE 184; Model Clothing House v Dickinson, (1920) 146 Minn. 367, 178 NW 957; Peets v Manhasset Civil Engineers, (1946) 68 NYS2d 338; Wright v Iredell Tel. Co., (1921) 182 NC 308, 108 SE 744; First Nat'l Bank v Shanks, (1947) (Ohio Com Pls) 73 NE2d 93.

policy.[61] If for some reason the stock is issued in the name of a person other than the true owner, a restriction of this kind does not prevent a transfer of the stock to the true owner;[62] nor does it prevent a stockholder from selling his stock to another stockholder in the same corporation,[63] or disposing of it by will.[64] However, when a charter provision permitted transfer only back to the corporation, an agreement to transfer the stock to another stockholder did not transfer the right to vote it.[65]

The courts differ as to the validity of a by-law providing that stockholders must offer their stock to the corporation and other stockholders before selling it to outsiders, where the statute and the charter make no provision for the passage of such a by-law. Some courts have held a by-law passed for this purpose to be invalid, while others have held it to be valid.[66] The by-laws themselves have been interpreted in various ways in their application to stock transfer restrictions. Thus, a corporation whose by-laws restricted sale of its stock by giving its own stockholders the first option to buy could not prevent a stockholder's transfer of stock to his daughter as part of a divorce settlement. Such transfer was a gift, not sale, and did not violate the by-law.[67]

Note that restrictions of this type apply only to voluntary sales; awards by a court, like an award of the stock to a spouse in a divorce proceeding, are involuntary and not within the ambit of the restrictive provision.[68]

Further, the president of a close family corporation could not prevent transfer of stock to a present stockholder on the ground that such transfer violated a by-law restriction that the corporation had

---

[61] In re Trilling and Montague, (1956) 140 F Supp 260; Kromer v Koepge, (1952) 118 F Supp 571, aff'd, (1953) 217 F2d 655; State v Sho-Me Power Co-operative, (1947) 356 Mo 832, 204 SW2d 276; Allen v Biltmore Tissue Corp., (1957) 2 NY2d 534, 141 NE2d 812; Wright v Iredell Tel. Co., (1921) 182 NC 308, 108 SE 744.

[62] State ex rel Cabral v Strudwick Funeral Home (La. App. 1941) 4 SO2d 760.

[63] Talbott v Nibert, (1949) 167 Kan. 138, 206 P2d 131.

[64] Stern v Stern, (1945) 146 F2d 870. Although by-law is valid, it will be strictly construed and held applicable only to voluntary sale. Hence legatee can force transfer on books. Taylor's Administrator v Taylor (Ky. 1957) 301 SW2d 579.

[65] Groves v Rosemound Improvement Ass'n, Inc. (La. App. 1982) 413 S 2d 925.

[66] *Invalid:* Brinkerhoff-Farris Trust & Sav. Co. v Home Lumber Co., (1893) 118 Mo 447, 24 SW2d 129; First Nat'l Bank v Shanks (Ohio Com Pls 1947) 73 NE2d 293

Valid: Sterling Loan & Inv. Co. v Litel, (1924) 75 Col. 34, 223 P 753; Evans v Dennis, (1948) 203 Ga. 232, 46 SE2d 122; Nicholson v Franklin Brewing Co., (1910) 82 Ohio St 94, 91 NE 991.

[67] McLeod v Sandy Island Corp. (S C S Ct 1975) 216 SE2d 746.

[68] Castonguay v Castonguay (Minn. S Ct 1981) 306 NW 2d 143; Durkee v Durkee-Mower, Inc. (Mass. S Jud Ct 1981) 428 NE 2d 139.

first option to the stock, when he did not show that transferee had knowledge of such restriction.[69] A close corporation's by-laws saying that shareholders can only transfer their shares to blood descendants, does not keep stock in the family, when a stockholder in a testamentary disposition makes no mention of shares. They are part of his residuary estate and go to the trustee for charitable purposes along with the rest of his property.[70] Also, a stock transfer from one stockholder-director of a close corporation to another is valid when, as by-laws required, the stock was first offered to the corporation and to other stockholders-directors at an informal meeting of all stockholders-directors. Allegations that by-laws did not allow transfer of the stock to just one stockholder-director fails when such a restriction was not specifically stated in the by-laws.[71]

In many cases, the courts have not considered whether the by-law is technically valid, but have decided the question on the ground that the terms of the by-law, printed on the face of the certificate, became a contract between the corporation and the subscriber for its stock.[72] An amendment of the by-laws to make all subsequent transfers subject to the restriction has no force unless printed on the face of the certificate.[73] The provisions of a consent decree supersede by-law restrictions on the transfer of stock.[74]

A by-law can validly require a corporation to buy the shares of a stockholder seeking to sell, when there is no outside market, and can let the directors fix the book value.[75] And a by-law restriction on transfer to "aliens" does not apply to shares issued or outstanding before the by-law was adopted, even though the restriction appears on the face of the certificates.[76]

A sale or transfer of stock made in violation of a valid provision giving the corporation a prior option to purchase is void.[77] Directors may waive a provision of the by-laws requiring that stock be offered to the corporation before sale,[78] and a majority stockholder may vote his

---

[69] Norman v Jerick Corporation (Ore S Ct 1972) 501 P2d 305.
[70] In re Estate of Martin (Ariz. App. 1971) 490 P2d 14.
[71] Remillong v Schneider (ND S Ct 1971) 185 NW2nd 493.
[72] New England Trust Co. v Abbott, (1894) 162 Mass. 148, 38 NE 432; Hassel v Pohle, (1925) 214 App. Div. 654, 212 NY Supp 561; First Nat'l Bank v Shanks (Ohio Com Pls 1947) 73 NE2d 293.
[73] Peets v Manhasset Civil Engineers, (1946) 68 NYS2d 338.
[74] Weber v Lane, (1946) 315 Mich. 678, 24 NW2d 418.
[75] Rowland v Rowland (Ida. S Ct 1981) 633 P 2d 599.
[76] Joseph E. Seagram & Sons, Inc. v Conoco, Inc. (D Del. 1981) 519 F Supp 506.
[77] Hassel v Pohle, (1925) 214 App. Div. 654, 212 NY Supp 561.
[78] Blabon v Hay, (1929) 269 Mass. 401 169 NE 268.

stock to prevent the corporation from making a purchase of stock under such a by-law provision.[79] When the by-law requirement is not observed over a period of years, a transfer without complying with it may be valid on the ground that the requirement is waived.[80] Some courts hold that a by-law restriction may not be repealed without the consent of the minority.[81] On the other hand, courts have held that, while a transfer in violation of a provision that an offer must first be made to the corporation is invalid, that invalidity can be cured by stockholder ratification.[82]

Contractual restrictions held to be valid. The following contractual restrictions have been declared valid:

A by-law provision that all shares of stock are freely assignable, but that no owner shall sell to one who is not a stockholder without first offering the stock for sale to other stockholders.[83]

A by-law provision requiring stockholders to offer their stock first to the corporation at a price set by appraisers.[84]

A provision in the stock certificate, or the charter, that shares will not be transferred until all debts to the corporation from the record holder are paid.[85]

A contract between stockholders whereby they take out life insurance payable to a trust fund, so that if one dies, the stock shall be turned over to the surviving stockholders, or to the corporation, and paid for out of the insurance.[86]

A corporation that entered into an agreement with stockholders to remove restrictions on their shares and to include such unrestricted shares in a public offering had to issue to them new certificates without the restrictive legend and pay damages, plus accrued interest, occasioned by breach of agreement to include their shares in the public offering.[87]

---

[79]Kentucky Package Store v Checani, (1954) 331 Mass. 125, 117 NE2d 139.

[80]Pomeroy v Westaway, (1947) NY Misc 307, 70 NYS2d 449; Elliott v Lindquist, (1947) 356 Pa 385, 52 A2d 180.

[81]Bechtold v Coleman Realty Co., (1951) 367 Pa 208, 79 A2d 661.

[82]Stough v 501 Ranch, Inc., (La. App. 1982) 421 S 2d 1154.

[83]Deardon v Deardon, (1948) 360 Pa. 225, 61 A2d 348; In re Garvin's Estate, (1939) 335 Pa 542, 6 A2d 796; Rychwalski v Milwaukee Cando Co., (1931) 205 Wis. 193, 236 NW 131. See also Lewis v H.P. Hood & Sons, Inc., (1954) 331 Mass. 670, 121 NE2d 850.

[84]Shumaker v Utex Exploration Co., (1957) 157 F Supp 58, holding such a by-law provision is not invalid as an illegal agreement to arbitrate future disputes.

[85]Elson v Schmidt, (1941) 140 Neb. 656, 1 NW2d 314.

[86]Bohnsack v Detroit Trust Co., (1940) 292 Mich 167, 290 NW 367; Welchman v Koschwitz, (1952) 21 NJ Super. 304, 91 A2d 169; Greater NY Carpet House, Inc. v Herschmann, (1940) 258 App. Div. 649, 17 NYS2d 483.

[87]Bjork v April Industries, Inc., (Utah SCt 1977) No. 14620; 1–24–77.

A deceased stockholder's executrix could not have a corporation's repurchase option nullified on the ground it was an adhesion contract imposed on the deceased stockholder by the corporation's allegedly superior bargaining position. The option was proper since it protected the corporation against outside control.[88]

A corporation could repurchase stock from a former employee who was discharged after 19 months of employment, when they agreed that the corporation would sell him stock at a nominal price, but that it could repurchase the stock at the same price if he failed to continue working for three years.[89]

A transfer of stock was valid as between the parties, even though made without the directors' approval required by the by-laws, since beneficial ownership passed.[90]

Contractual restrictions held invalid. The following contractual restrictions have been declared invalid:

A by-law giving directors the right to refuse a transfer by one stockholder to another.[91]

A by-law giving directors power to refuse a transfer because they object to the transferee, or for any other reason.[92]

A provision in the certificate that stock may be transferred only to some person approved by the directors.[93]

A by-law prohibiting the transfer of certificates of stock except to the corporation.[94]

An agreement that no stockholder could buy or sell any share of stock in the corporation without the written consent of all the stockholders unless the sale was made between the stockholders themselves.[95]

A by-law declaring invalid a sale of stock to a competitor.[96]

A by-law authorizing directors and officers to refuse a transfer if they believed the transfer was sought in furtherance of a fraudulent scheme.[97]

---

[88] Yeng Sue Chow v Levi Strauss & Co., (Ct of App. 1975) 122 Cal. Rep 816.
[89] Waldorf v K.M.S. Industries, Inc., (Mich. Ct of App. 1970) 181 NW2d 85.
[90] Jones v Central States Investment Co., (Wyo. S Ct 1982) 654 P 2d 727.
[91] Morris v Hussong Dyeing Mach. Co., (1913) 81 NJ Eq. 256, 86 A 1026.
[92] Petre v Bruce, (1928) 157 Tenn. 131, 7 SW2d 43.
[93] Douglas v Aurora Daily News Co., (1911) 160 Ill. App. 506.
[94] Steel v Farmers' and Merchants Mut. Tel. Ass'n, (1915) 95 Kan. 580, 148 P 661; Herring v Ruskin Co-operative Ass'n (Tenn Ch App 1899) 52 SW 327.
[95] People ex rel. Malcolm v Lake Sand Corp., (1929) 251 Ill. App. 499.
[96] Kretzer v Cole Bros Lightning Rod Co., (1916) 193 Mo. App. 99, 181 SW 1066.
[97] Pelton v Nevada Oil Co (Tex. App. 1948) 209 SW 645.

A prohibition against an intra-family transfer of stock without permission of each shareholder was unduly restrictive and unreasonable. The test of reasonableness is whether restraint is so necessary to the enterprise as to justify the overriding general policy against restraints on alienation.[98]

An agreement requiring an employee, upon his discharge for cause, to offer his shares back to the company at the price he paid for them, violated a statute, since it unreasonably restrained the transfer of shares and permitted the company to repurchase at an unfair price.[99]

A repurchase agreement clause that stated "The Company, it officers, and/or subsidiaries agree to purchase from the purchaser. . . ." was unclear as to whether corporate officers could be held personally liable when the corporation failed to buy back. A full-scale trial would have to determine the intent of parties in making the contract.[100]

A by-law of a membership corporation requiring the surrender of certificates on the death or withdrawal of a member, but only because the membership had dwindled to such a degree that the purpose had failed.[101]

A buyout agreement provision that the corporation would buy life insurance on stockholder and use the proceeds to buy out his stock was invalidated when the life insurance policy was eliminated.[102]

Important considerations in drafting agreement. The above outlined cases indicate the guidelines that should be followed in drafting a buy-and-sell agreement. The following are the more important questions that must be answered:

(1) Shall the remaining stockholders or the corporation buy the stock?
(2) How shall the agreement be funded?
(3) If the agreement is funded by life insurance, who shall own the policies, pay the premiums and be the beneficiaries?
(4) Should the agreement be administered by a trustee?
(5) How should the stock be valued for the purposes of the agreement?

Pitfalls to watch. There are some pitfalls that can be avoided if you follow these suggestions when entering into a buy-and-sell agreement:

[98] Fayard v Fayard (Miss. S Ct 1974) 293 So2d 421.
[99] Systematics, Inc. v Mitchell (Ark. S Ct 1973) 253 Ark Rep 848.
[100] Hokama v Relinc Corporation (Hawaii S Ct 1977) 559 P 2d 279.
[101] Quinn v Stuart Lakes Club, Inc., (1981) 80 AD 2d 350, 439 NYS 2d 30.
[102] Keystone Printed Specialties Co., Inc. v Fischer (Pa. Super. Ct 1981) 430 A 2d 650.

(1) Make sure the agreement has a clause binding the stockholder's executor or other legal representative; otherwise, the provisions against transferring the stock may not bind them when the stockholder dies.[103]

(2) Whenever possible, make the restrictions against transfer of the stock part of the articles and by-laws; that way future stockholders and their successors will also be bound even though they are not parties to the agreement.[104]

(3) Make the corporation a party to the agreement; if you don't, a stockholder may later claim there was no consideration for the buy option to the corporation.[105]

(4) When you make provision for a retiring stockholder to offer his shares to the remaining ones in proportion to their respective holdings, include a clause that if any of the remaining stockholders don't elect to buy their shares, any of the other stockholders may do so. Failure to do so imposes a risk of the sale of such shares to outsiders.[106]

Necessity for stating restriction on certificate of stock. Under the Uniform Stock Transfer Act,[107] no restriction upon the transfer of stock was recognized unless the restriction was stated on the certificate of stock.[108]

A resolution passed by the board of directors placing restrictions on transfers, which were not printed on the certificates, would not be enforced.[109] A resolution or by-law of this type would not, by itself, justify the corporation in refusing to transfer on its books stock purchased in violation of the resolution or by-law, whether or not the restriction was reasonable,[110] and even though the transferee had notice of it.[111]

---

[103] Kolmer-Marcus, Inc. v Winer, (1970) 26 NY2d 795, 309 NYS2d 220; Vogel v Melish, (1964) 196 NE2d 402.

[104] Tu-Vu-Drive-In Corp. v Ashkins, (1964) 38 Cal. Rptr. 348; Peets v Manhasset, (1946) 68 NYS2d 335.

[105] Black & White Cabs of St. Louis, Inc. v Smith, (1963) 370 SW2d 669.

[106] Helmly v Schultz, (1963) 131 SE 2d 924.

[107] The Uniform Commercial Code, rather than the Stock Transfer Act, is now in effect in all states except Louisiana. However, it has not changed the former requirements of the Uniform Stock Transfer Act that restrictions be stated on stock certificates.

[108] Weissman v Lincoln Corp (Fla 1954) 76 So2d 478; Weber v Lane, (1946) 315 Mich. 678, 24 NW2d 418; Costello v Farrell, (1951) 234 Minn. 453, 48 NW2d 557. In Doss v Yingling, (1930) 95 Ind. App. 494, 172 NE 801, a restriction was binding on the president of the corporation, although it was not printed on a certificate he received after adoption of the Uniform Stock Transfer Act. Note that while the Uniform Stock Transfer Act was intended to make restrictions ineffective as to persons without notice, failure to note the restriction is no bar to enforcement against persons with actual notice. Erwin v West End Development Co. (CA-10 1973) 481 F2d 34.

[109] Travis v Del State Bank (Okla S Ct 1976) 553 P 2d 486.

[110] Age Publishing Co v Becker, (1943) 110 Col. 319, 134 P2d 205.

[111] Sorrick v Consolidated Tel. Co., (1954) 340 Mich 463, 65 NW2d 713.

When the certificates were not legended, an officer of a family corporation was not held to have knowledge of a by-law restriction when she was wife of president and was not active in the corporation's affairs.[112] However, while a by-law restriction that gave the corporation a first option applied to the division of community property, a wife was not a "transferee" with standing to set aside the restriction on the ground it was not stated on the stock certificates.[113]

Even though the certificates were never legended, the owner of stock was held to notice of a charter amendment that gave the corporation a first option to buy at a price set in the charter.[114] Similarly, a court could impose a constructive trust on shares obtained by the transferee in breach of fiduciary duty, even though not legended.[115]

Under Section 8-306(2)(c) of the Uniform Commercial Code, which provided that the transferor warrants that he knows no facts that might impair the validity of the security, only the immediate transferee is protected, so that a later purchaser could not hold the original owner for his failure to legend the stock.[116]

Effect of contractual restrictions on transferees. Valid restrictions on the transfer of stock are binding not only as between the corporation and the original stockholders, but also as against transferees with notice.[117] The restrictions are also binding on pledgees who accept stock as security with knowledge of the restrictions.[118] A provision in the stock certificate that shares will not be transferred until all debts due to the corporation from the record holder have been paid was held to be binding not only on the record holder, but also on his assignee.[119] A consent decree that restricts the transfer of stock is binding on the owner's assignee; the assignee is not entitled to a new

---

[112]Norman v Jerick Corp. (Ore. S Ct 1972) 501 P 2d 305.

[113]Monitor Technology, Inc. v Hetrick (Cal. App. 1978) 141 Cal. Rptr. 711.

[114]B & H Warehouse, Inc. v Atlas Van Lines, Inc. (N D Tex. 1972) 348 F Supp 517, rev on other grounds (CA-5 1974) 490 F 2d 818.

[115]Irwin v West End Development Co. (CA-10 1973) 481 F 2d 34.

[116]Ford v Cannon (M D Fla. 1976) 413 F Supp 1393.

[117]Ehrlich v Nyberg, (1979) 78 Ill. App. 3d 500, 396 NE 2d 1273; Warner & Swasey Co. v Rusterholz, (1941) 41 F Supp 498; Citizens State Bank v O'Leary, (1942) 140 Tex. 305, 167 SW2d 719. See also Musler v Homestead Bldg. & Loan Ass'n (Mo. App 1934) 66 SW2d 152. A reasonable restraint on alienation, inserted in the by-laws, is also valid against an undisclosed principal for whom the stock was purchased by an agent. Barrett v King, (1902) 181 Mass 476, 63 NE 934.

[118]Estate Funds, Inc. v Burton-Fifth Ave. Corp., (1952) Ill. NYS2d 596; First Nat'l Bank v Shanks, (1947) (Ohio Com Pls) 73 NE2d 293. See also Musler v Homestead Bldg. & Loan Ass'n, note 117 supra.

[119]Jennings v Bank of California, (1889) 79 Cal. 323, 21 P 852.

certificate that does not include the condition imposed by the consent decree.[120]

An agreement between the original stockholders, restricting the sale of stock to them, is not binding on the corporation when the certificate of incorporation, the by-laws, and the certificates of stock are all silent as to the restriction. Under such circumstances, a transferee of treasury shares is not bound by the restriction, even if she knew about the agreement.[121]

Lien of corporation on shares of stock. A corporation has no lien on its shares of stock merely because the stockholder is indebted to the corporation, in the absence of statutory, charter, or by-law provision creating this lien.[122] In some states a by-law attempting to create a lien in favor of the corporation is invalid, unless the statutes or articles of incorporation give express authority to adopt such a by-law.[123] Stock may, however, be impressed with a lien in favor of the corporation by statute or contract, for debts owing to it.[124] Under the Uniform Stock Transfer Act, there was no lien in favor of the corporation unless the right of the corporation to a lien was noted on the stock certificate.

If the owner of the stock transfers it to a bona fide holder who has no notice of the lien of the corporation, the corporation cannot refuse to transfer the stock to the name of the transferee.[125] The courts are not in agreement as to what constitutes notice to the transferee. It has been held that the purchaser of shares is chargeable with notice of liens created under the statute or charter, but not with those arising under the by-laws of the corporation or under the custom of dealing between the corporation and its stockholders.[126] Notice of a lien imposed by a by-law must appear on the face of the certificate.[127] A notation on the

[120]Kund v Fort Bedford Inn Co., (1942) 46 D&C Pa. 394.

[121]Peets v Manhasset Civil Engineers, (1946) 68 NYS2d 338. *Contra:* Thibodeaux v Pioneer Land Development & Realty Corp. (La. App. 1982) 420 S 2d 1162.

[122]Central Sav. Bank v Smith, (1908) 43 Col. 90, 95 P 307; Danron v Denny, (1919) 149 Ga. 280, 99 SE 851; Iowa-Missouri Grain Co v Powers (Iowa 1923) 191 NW 363; Gemmell v Davis, (1892) 75 Md. 546, 23 A 1032; Boyd v Redd, (1897) 120 NC 335, 27 SE 35.

[123]McKinney v Mechanics' Trust and Sav. Bank, (1927) 222 Ky. 264, 300 SW 631.

[124]Bank of Searcy v Mechants' Grocer Co., (1916) 123 Ark. 403, 185 SW 806; Sproul v Standard Plate Glass Co., (1902) 201 Pa. 103, 50 A 1003; First State Bank v First Nat'l Bank (Tex Civ App 1912) 145 SW 691; United Cigarette Mach. Co. v Brown, (1916) 119 Va. 813, 89 SE 850.

[125]See Kress v Tooker-Jordan Corp, (1930) 103 Cal. App. 275, 284 P 685. A provision on the stock certificate's face that the stock is transferable only on the company's books in accord with the by-laws is not sufficient notice to a transferee of the existence of a lien imposed by the by-laws. Chandler v Blanke Tea & Coffee Co., (1914) 183 Mo. App. 91, 165 SW 819.

[126]Bankers Trust Co v McCloy, (1913) 109 Ark. 160, 159 SW 205.

[127]Bank of Culloden v Bank of Forsyth, (1904) 120 Ga. 575, 48 SE 226.

face of the stock certificate of the existence of a lien has been held sufficient notice to a purchaser to put him on inquiry.[128]

When stock is sold or pledged, but the transferee does not have the transfer recorded on the corporation's records before the indebtedness of the record holder to the corporation accrues, the corporation's lien is valid. It is superior to the rights of the purchaser or pledgee.[129]

Restrictions on rights of indebted stockholder to transfer his shares. Even if a lien is created in favor of the corporation, the stockholder has a right to assign his shares subject to the lien.[130] Limitations on the right of an indebted stockholder to transfer his stock have been upheld as contractual restrictions, where such restriction was provided in the charter[131] or by-laws of the corporation.[132] The statutes in some states also specifically provide such restriction. A bona fide purchaser of the stock, without notice of the restriction, has been held not to be bound by it.[133] Regardless of the restriction, the transfer of stock may be made to the executor or representative of a deceased stockholder.[134] However, the corporation can refuse to consent to a transfer by the representative while the stockholder's indebtedness remains unpaid.[135]

Statutory restrictions on transfers. Limitations upon the power of a stockholder to transfer his stock may be imposed by statute. The statutes may also authorize the corporation to place restrictions upon the power to transfer. The power to restrict the right of alienation, however, must be given to the corporation in express terms,[136] and such restrictions will be strictly construed.

Persons who become stockholders before passage of a statute restricting the transfer of stock are not bound by the restriction, for the power to transfer is an existing right that cannot be subsequently impaired.[137]

---

[128] Ibid.

[129] Benson Lumber Co. v Thornton, (1932) 185 Minn. 230, 240 NW 651.

[130] Milner v Brewer-Monaghan Mercantile Co. (Tex Civ App 1916) 188 SW 49.

[131] Gibbs v Long Island Bank, (1894) 83 Hun (NY 92) 31 NY Supp 406.

[132] Costello v Portsmouth Brewing Co., (1898) 69 NH 405, 43 A 640.

[133] Brinkerhoff-Farris Trust & Sav Co. v Home Lumber Co., (1893) 118 Mo. 447, 24 SSW 129.

[134] London, Paris, & American Bank v Aronstein, (1902) 117 F 601.

[135] In re Starbuck's Executrix, (1929) 251 NY 439, 167 NE 580.

[136] Howe v Roberts, (1923) 209 Ala. 80, 95 So 344. Manufacturers Trust Co. v Bank of Yorktown, (1935) 156 NY Misc 793, 282 NY Supp 507.

[137] In re W.W. Mills Co., (1908) 162 F 42, 54.

Methods of transferring stock. Any means by which one person is divested of ownership of stock and another person acquires such ownership is a transfer of the stock.[138] In the absence of a provision in the statute or charter to the contrary, such a change of ownership may be brought about in any of the various ways of transferring personal property.[139]

The Uniform Stock Transfer Act[140] was formerly the basic statute covering the transfer of stock certificates in the states in which it is in effect, though now it is largely superseded by the Uniform Commercial Code (see below). That act provides:

> Title to a certificate and to the shares represented thereby can be transferred only, (a) By delivery of the certificate indorsed either in blank or to a specified person by the person appearing by the certificate to be the owner of the shares represented thereby; or
>
> (b) By delivery of the certificate and a separate document containing a written assignment of the certificate or a power of attorney to sell, assign or transfer the same or the shares represented thereby, signed by the person appearing by the certificate to be the owner of the shares represented thereby. Such assignment or power of attorney may be either in blank or to a specified person.
>
> The provisions of this section shall be applicable although the charter or articles of incorporation or code of regulations or by-laws of the corporation issuing the certificate and the certificate itself provide that the shares represented thereby shall be transferable only on the books of the corporation or shall be registered by a registrar or transferred by a transfer agent.

After execution and delivery of the instruments, they are presented to the corporation with a request to transfer, the old certificate is surrendered and cancelled, a new certificate is issued to the transferee, and the stock is registered in his name.

Mere physical delivery of the custody of the certificates, without a written assignment or power transfer, does not constitute a valid transfer of the stock.[141] On the other hand, in the case of stock not subject to the Uniform Stock Transfer Act, physical delivery of the certificate is not necessary to transfer title to the shares.[142] Transfer on

---

[138] Wallach v Stein, (1927) 103 NJL 470, 136 A 209.

[139] Cliffs Corp v United States, (1939) 103 F2d 77; Crocker v Crocker, (1927) 84 Cal. App. 114, 257 P 611; Young v New Pedrara Onyx Co., (1920) 48 Cal. App. 1, 192 P 55.

[140] As noted, the Uniform Commercial Code is now in effect in all states except Louisiana.

[141] Zoller v State Bd of Tax Appeals, (1940) 124 NJL 376, 11 A2d 833.

[142] Simonton v Dwyer, (1941) 167 Ore. 50, 115 P2d 316; Copeland v Craig, (1940) 193 SC 484 8 SE2d 858. See also Helvering v Kaufman, (1943) 136 F2d 365; In re Penfield Distilling Co., (1942) 131 F2d 694; Robbins v Pacific Eastern Corp., (1937) 8 Cal. 2d 241, 65 P2d 42. Under the UCC, there is a duty to deliver: §8–314.

the books of the corporation, at the request of the record owner, takes from him all right, title, and interest in the stock thus transferred, and places it beyond his control. The corporation can no longer recognize his control of the stock.[143]

The transfer of stock is now mainly governed by the provisions of the Uniform Commercial Code.[144] That article amounts to a negotiable instruments law dealing with securities. It includes bearer bonds, registered bonds and stock certificates.[145]

Necessity for recording transfer of stock. Transfer on the books of a corporation is the most efficient and effective manner of transfer and is the final step in the process of changing title to the stock from one person to another.[146] Under the Uniform Stock Transfer Act a transfer on the corporate books is not a prerequisite to the transfer of stock.[147] Even when the statute, charter, or by-laws specifically provide that stock shall be transferable only on the corporate books, registration is not necessary to the validity of the transfer between the parties.[148]

In many states, however, the statutes specifically authorize corporations to make regulations concerning the transfer of stock. The by-laws of most corporations contain a provision requiring recording of transfers on the books of the corporation. These requirements for recording transfers are intended for the benefit and protection of the corporation,[149] so that it may know whom to recognize as a stockholder[150] in the payment of dividends,[151] holding of corporate

---

[143]Copeland v Craig, note 142 supra.

[144]Article 8, "Investing Securities."

[145]UCC Section 8–101, official comment.

[146]Copeland v Craig, (1940) 193 S C 484, 8 SE 2d 858.

[147]Upson v Otis, (1946) 155 F2d 606; Snyder Motor Co. v Universal Credit Co. (Tex Civ App 1947) 199 SW2d 792. However, the UCC does impose on the issuer an obligation to transfer when certain requirements are not met (see Section 8–401).

[148]Rule v Commissioner, (1942) 127 F2d 979; Townsend v Tatnall Bank, (1948) 76 Ga. App. 500, 46 SE2d 607. See also Drug v Hunt, (1933) 35 Del. 339, 168 A 87; Patterson v Fitzgerald McElroy Co., (1927) 247 Ill. App. 81; Dennistoun v Davis, (1930) 179 Minn. 373, 229 NW 353; Green v McKee, (1949) 361 Pa. 95, 63 A2d 3.

[149]Bank of Commerce v Bank of Newport, (1894) 63 F 898; In re Giant Portland Cement Co., (1941) 26 Del. Ch 32, 21 A2d 697; York's Ancillary Adm'r v Bromley, (1941) 286 Ky. 533, 151 SW2d 28; Mortgage Land Inv. Co. v. McMains, (1927) 172 Minn. 110, 215 NW 192; Chemical Nat'l Bank v Colwell, (1892) 132 NY 250, 30 NE 644; J.G. Wilson Corp. v Cahill (1929) 152 Va. 108, 146 SE 274; Lipscomb's Adm'r v Condon, (1904) 56 W Va. 416, 49 SE 392.

[150]In re Northeastern Water Co., (1944) 28 Del. Ch 139, 38 A2d 918; In re Giant Portland Cement Co., note 149 supra; Application of Friedman, (1945) 186 NY Misc 639; 54 NYS2d 45. See also Whitfield v Nonpareil Consol. Copper Co., (1912) 67 Wash. 286, 123 P 1078.

[151]Townsend v Tatnall Bank, (1948) 76 Ga. App. 500, 46 SE2d 607; Hale v West Porto Rico Sugar Co., (1922) 200 App. Div. 577, 193 NY Supp 555. But see Lindner v Utah Southern Oil Co., (1955) 3 Utah 2d 302, 283 P.2d 605.

meetings,[152] granting of voting rights,[153] and other matters relating to the internal affairs of the corporation.[154]

Although compliance with requirements of statute, charter, or by-law is necessary to make a transfer valid as against the corporation, a transfer may be valid as between the parties without such compliance.[155]

Effect as to corporation of failure to record transfer of stock. A transfer of stock is ineffective as against the corporation until actually made on the corporation's transfer books;[156] an unregistered transferee is not entitled to the rights and privileges of a stockholder in his relations with the corporation.[157] Thus, payment on final distribution of assets to the shareholder of record, although not the actual stockholder, has been upheld.[158] The corporation may, however, waive the benefit of the requirement and consider someone other than the recorded holder as the owner of the stock.[159] If an irregular transfer is accepted and acquiesced in by the corporation, the corporation is bound by it.[160] Failure of a transferee to register his stock does not bar his claim to it as against an irregular transfer,[161] nor does it prevent him from maintaining a stockholder's suit against the management for waste of corporate property.[162]

If the corporation refuses without justification to make a transfer on its books, it is deemed to have waived the requirement, and it must recognize the person entitled to the transfer as the owner of the

---

[152]Hale v West Porto Rico Sugar Co., Note 151 supra.

[153]See Morrill v Little Falls Mfg. Co., (1893) 53 Minn. 371, 55 NW 547.

[154]In re Canal Constr. Co., (1936) 21 Del. Ch 155, 182 A 545.

[155]J. G. Wilson Corp. v Cahill, (1929) 152 Va. 108, 146 S.E. 274.

[156]Salt Dome Oil Corp. v Schneck, (1945) 28 Del. Ch 433, 41 A2d 583; York's Ancillary Adm'r v Bromley, (1941) 286 Ky. 533, 151 SW2d 28; Double O Mining Co. v Simrak, (1942) 61 Nev 431, 132 P2d 605. Even if a transfer is recorded on the books, it may be shown that true ownership remains in the transferor. Swan v Swan's Ex'r, (1923) 136 Va. 496, 117 SE 858. See also Allen v Hill, (1860) 16 Cal. 113, in which it was held that a surviving partner could vote stock owned by the partnership even if the deceased partner appeared on the books as the record holder.

[157]Salt Dome Oil Corp. v Schneck, note 156 supra.

[158]Campbell v Perth Amboy Mut'l Loan, Homestead and Bldg. Ass'n, (1909) 76 NJ Eq 347, 74A 144.

[159]Johnson v Moore, (1926) 31 Ariz. 137, 250 P 995; Mortgage Land Inv. Co. v McMains, (1927) 172 Minn. 110 215 NW 192. Chemical Nat'l Bank v Colwell, (1892) 132 NY 250, 30 NE 644. American Nat'l Bank v Oriental Mills, (1891) 17 RI 551, 23 A 795; Stewart v Walla Walla Printing & Publishing Co., (1889) 1 Wash. 521, 20 P 605.

[160]Johnson v Moore, note 159 supra; Bassin v Enock-Pearl Co., (1947) 140 NJ Eq 428, 54 A2d 824; Stewart v Walla Walla Printing & Publishing Co., note 159 supra.

[161]Laden v Baader, (1943) 134 NJ Eq. 24, 34 A2d 82.

[162]Rosenthal v Burry Biscuit Co., (1948) 30 Del Ch 299, 60 A2d 106.

stock.[163] At the time of refusal to transfer stock on its books, the corporation must give its reasons for refusal, and any reasons not so given are waived.[164]

Effect between transferor and transferee of failure to record transfer of stock. As between a transferor and a transferee of shares of stock, the transfer is valid and effective without recording, even if recording is required.[165] An assignment duly executed on the back of a stock certificate, followed by delivery to the assignee, transfers the stock between the parties, even though stock is not transferred on the books of the corporation.[166] The fact that the assignor continues to receive dividends from the stock does not affect the validity of the transfer.[167] The corporation, however, is not compelled to recognize the possessor of the certificate as the legal owner, if the circumstances indicate that he may not be.[168]

An unrecorded transfer is valid against persons standing in the place of the transferor, such as administrators.[169] It may also be valid between a pledgor and pledgee,[170] or between a donor and a donee.[171]

Stock transfer books. The work involved in transferring stock and in keeping stock transfer books may be performed (1) by an officer of the corporation, generally the secretary or treasurer; (2) by a separate department of the corporation under the supervision of one of its officers, usually the secretary or treasurer; or (3) by an independent transfer agent appointed by the corporation. The method pursued depends upon the size of the corporation, the extent to which its shares are distributed, and the facilities of the corporation to handle the

---

[163] Bates v United Shoe Mach. Co., (1914) 216 F 140. See also Logan v Crissinger, (1923) 290 F 415.

[164] Hulse v Consolidated Quicksilver Mining Corp., (1944) 65 Idaho 768, 154 P.2d 149.

[165] United States v Rosebush, (1942) 45 F Supp 665; In re Giant Portland Cement Co., (1941) 26 Del. Ch 32, 21 A2d 697; In re Canal Constr. Co., (1936) 21 Del. Ch 155, 182 A 545; Bates v Peru Sav. Bank, (1934) 218 Iowa 1320, 256 N.W. 286; Dennistoun v Davis, (1930) 179 Minn. 373, 229 NW 353; State v Druggists Addressing Co. (Mo. App 1938) 113 SW2d 1061; Double O Mining Co. v Simrak, (1942) 61 Nev. 431, 132 P2d 605; Jones v Waldroup, (1940) 217 NC 178, 7 SE2d 366; A. M. Law & Co. v Cleveland, (1934) 172 SC 200, 173 S.E. 638. See also Bankers Mortgage Co. v Sohland, (1927) 33 Del. 331, 138 A 361; Hogg v Eckhardt, (1931) 343 Ill. 246, 175 NE 382; Nicollet Nat'l Bank v City Bank, (1887) 38 Minn. 85, 35 NW 577.

[166] Chatz v Midco Oil Co., (1946) 152 F 2d 153; Dunn v Wilson & Co., (1943) 51 F Supp 655; York's Ancillary Adm'r v Bromley, (1941) 286 Ky. 533, 151 SW2d 28.

[167] York's Ancillary Adm'r v Bromley, note 166 supra.

[168] Kund v Fort Bedford Inn Co., (1942) 46 D&C Pa. 394.

[169] Shires v Allen, (1910) 47 Col. 440, 107 P 1072.

[170] Bank of Steamboat Springs v Routt County Bank, (1927) 80 Col. 385, 252 P 355; Townsend v Tatnall Bank, (1948) 76 Ga. App. 500, 46 SE2d 607.

[171] Dulin v Commissioner, (1934) 79 F2d 828.

transfer work. In any case, the transfers are generally recorded in a transfer record and in a stock ledger. The transfer record lists the various shares transferred from day to day from one person to another. The stock ledger contains the running account of each individual stockholder.

A corporation need not keep a special stock ledger and transfer record unless the statute or its charter requires them. In the absence of such requirement, transfers may be recorded in any book or record. An account in the stock ledger has been held sufficient.[172] Entries inserted on a subscription list,[173] and a notation made in the stock certificate book,[174] have been held to constitute sufficient compliance with a statute requiring the corporation to keep a record of transfers. In some states, the statute indicates what items must be entered in the stock records. Compliance with these statutory requirements is essential.

If, as is often the case, the statute requires that stock books or records shall be kept at an office within the state,[175] the statute must be followed. A penalty is generally imposed upon the corporation and its officers for noncompliance.

Liability of corporation for unauthorized transfers of stock. A corporation must exercise ordinary care and reasonable diligence to prevent its stockholders from being injured by unauthorized transfers of stock.[176] It is liable for negligence in making transfers,[177] and hence may refuse to make a transfer if it acts in good faith and has reasonable grounds for refusing to do so.[178]

---

[172]Cecil Nat'l Bank v Watsontown Bank, (1882) 105 US 1039.

[173]Stewart v Walla Walla Printing & Publishing Co., (1889) 1 Wash. 521, 20 P 605.

[174]Bank of Commerce v Bank of Newport, (1894) 63 F 898.

[175]See, for example, Florida, GCL §608.39; Michigan GCL §450.36; New Jersey, GCL §14:5—1; New York SCL §10. These statutes will be found in Prentice-Hall's Corporation.

[176]Geyser-Marion Gold Mining Co. v Stark, (1901) 106 F 558. See also Seymour v Nat'l Biscuit Co., (1939) 107 F2d 58, cert denied, 309 US 665, 60 S Ct 590; Clark & Wilson Lumber Co. v McAllister, (1939) 101 F2d 70; Kentucky Util. Co. v Skaggs, (1943) 293 Ky. 622, 169 SW2d 808.

[177]Schneider v American Tel. & Tel. Co., (1939) 169 NY Misc 939, 9 NYS2d 564.

[178]Winans v Alpha Beta Food Markets, Inc., (1936) 11 Cal. App. 653, 54 P2d 48; Soltz v Exhibitors' Serv. Co., (1939) 334 Pa 211, 5A2d 899; Mundt v Commercial Nat'l Bank, (1919) 35 Utah 90, 99 P 454. See also Western Union Tel. Co. v Davenport, (1878) 97 US 369, in which the court said that, if the officers "upon presentation of a certificate for transfer . . . are at all doubtful of the identity of the party offering it with its owner, or if not satisfied of the genuineness of a power of attorney produced, they can require the identity of the party in the one case, and the genuineness of the document in the other, to be satisfactorily established before allowing the transfer to be made. In either case they must act upon their own responsibility. . . . Neither the absence of blame on the part of the officers of the company in allowing an unauthorized transfer of stock, nor the good faith of the purchaser of stolen property, will avail as an answer to the demand of the true owner."

As a general rule, a corporation is liable to the true owner for an unauthorized transfer of stock on its books. It is similarly liable to a transferee for refusal to record a legitimate transfer. As mentioned earlier, the Uniform Commercial Code specifically imposes that liability in Section 8–401. This section reads as follows:

DUTY OF ISSUER TO REGISTER TRANSFER

(1) Where a security in registered form is presented to the issuer with a request to register transfer, the issuer is under a duty to register the transfer as requested if
- (a) the security is indorsed by the appropriate person or persons (Section 8–308); and
- (b) reasonable assurance is given that those indorsements are genuine and effective (Section 8–402); and
- (c) the issuer has no duty to inquire into adverse claims or has discharged any such duty (Section 8–403); and
- (d) any applicable law relating to the collection of taxes has been complied with; and
- (e) the transfer is in fact rightful or is to a bona fide purchaser.

(2) Where an issuer is under a duty to register a transfer of a security the issuer is also liable to the person presenting it for registration or his principal for loss resulting from any unreasonable delay in registration or from failure or refusal to register the transfer.*

The officers charged with the responsibility of deciding whether or not the transfer should be made are not expected to decide legal technicalities.[179] Ordinarily, the corporation cannot decide the legality of the transfer, and base a refusal to record the transfer on that decision.[180] But a corporation is justified in refusing to transfer stock when there is a dispute as to the ownership,[181] or when a garnishment proceeding involving the stock is pending,[182] or when there is doubt as to the transferor's mental capacity.[183]

Before recording a transfer, the corporation should make sure that the signature on the assignment and the power of attorney are

---

*Copyright 1972 by The American Law Institute and the National Conference of Commissioners on Uniform State Laws. Reprinted with permission of the Permanent Editorial Board for the Uniform Commercial Code.

[179] United North & South Development Co. v Rayner, (1942) 124 F2d 512.

[180] Commonwealth v Camp, (1917) 258 Pa. 548, 102 A 205.

[181] United North & South Development Co. v Rayner, (1942), note 179 supra; Baxter v Boston-Pacific Oil Co., (1927) 81 Cal. App. 187, 253 P 185; Leff v N. Kaufman's, Inc., (1941) 342 Pa. 342, 20 A2d 786.

[182] United North & South Development Co. v Rayner, (1942) 124 F2d 512.

[183] Kentucky Util. Co. v Skaggs, (1943) 293 Ky. 622, 169 SW2d 808.

genuine, and that the person executing them had authority to do so.[184] The corporation is liable for conversion if it transfers stock upon the demand of an agent who, within the corporation's knowledge, has no authority to make such a demand.[185] Where the circumstances surrounding a transfer of stock are such as to put the corporation on inquiry, the corporation is deemed to have notice of all that an inquiry would reveal.[186]

A corporation cannot refuse to transfer and register a shareholder's newly acquired stock merely because a third party asserts a claim adverse to the shareholder's ownership.[187] Also, a corporation is liable to holders of stock warrants that required notice of dissolution, and so the corporation's failure to give such notice entitles holders to the amount they would have received upon distribution had they exercised their warrants.[188] A buyer of stock cannot compel an employee of the issuing corporation to issue stock certificates under a sales agreement that provided delivery of individual stock certificates would be made either (1) two weeks after a public stock offering or (2) after permission from the corporation's directors, since neither of these conditions occurred prior to the corporation's dissolution.[189]

Further, title to the shares did not pass to the attorney who was also the nephew of a decedent stockholder who had endorsed a share certificate in blank and given it to him, since evidence showed she had already overcompensated him for his services and her conduct showed she had not abandoned title to the shares.[190] Also a stock transfer agent was entitled to refuse to register the transfer of stock certificates, when it was shown that the purchaser knew that the certificates had been canceled before he accepted their delivery, that it was not a rightful transfer and that he was not a bona fide purchaser for value.[191] In another case, it was held that ownership of stock did not pass to a

---

[184] Aronson v Bank of America Nat'l Trust and Sav. Ass'n, (1937) 9 Cal. 2d 640, 72 P 2d 548; Baker v Atlantic Coast Line R.R., (1917) 173 NC 365, 92 SE 2d 170.

[185] Aronson v Bank of America Nat'l Trust and Sav. Ass'n, (1941) 42 Cal. App. 710, 109 P2d 1001.

[186] Baker v Atlantic Coast Line R.R., note 184 supra. See also West v American Tel. & Tel. Co., 108 F.2d 347, rev'd on other grounds, (1940) 301 US 223, 61 S Ct 179. But see Hiller v American Tel. & Tel. Co., (1949) 324 Mass. 24, 84 NE2d 548.

[187] Jacobsen v The Fine Ivy Corp. (NY S Ct 1973) NYLJ 2-8-73, p. 16.

[188] Tisch Family Foundation, Inc. v Texas Nat'l Petroleum Co. (DC D Del. 1971) 326 F Supp 1128.

[189] Molinaro v Frezza (NY App. Div. 1975) 49 AD2d 148.

[190] Feldheim v Plaguemine Oil and Development Company (La. App. 1972) 263 So2d 382, affirmed (La. S Ct 1973) 282 So2d 469.

[191] Folsom v Security Nat'l Bank (Col. Ct of App. 1973) 507 P2d 1114.

pledgee to whom it was transferred, when transfer was made to increase the value of the pledge by having dividends accrue to the pledgee.[192]

A sole stockholder of a holding company that owned stock of a second corporation did not make an effective assignment of corporation stock to his daughter, when he did not actually deliver the certificates and the holding company continued to vote the stock, collect dividends, and treated the stock as its own.[193] Finally, approval by a state's corporation commissioner may be necessary to validate a transfer of stock. Thus, it has been held that a stock transfer is void when it accompanies payment of a broker's commission, not approved by the state's commissioner of corporations.[194]

Transfer by life tenant; by trustee or executor. A corporation must frequently decide whether or not a requested transfer of stock is authorized when stock is willed to a life tenant and remaindermen. The stock should be registered on the corporation's books as "life tenant under will." Does the corporation have the right to transfer that stock upon demand from the life tenant? In deciding this question, the laws of the state of the testator and the laws of the corporation's domicile must be considered. However, the life tenant is not the owner of the shares and, therefore could not pass title under the Uniform Stock Transfer Act.[195] When a corporation has notice that a person is not entitled to a certificate indicating unlimited ownership, but only life tenancy, it is liable to the remaindermen if it transfers the stock upon demand from the life tenant.[196] It has been held that when a corporation, knowing that the transferor had only a life interest, nevertheless issued new certificates, and delivered them absolutely to the transferee, it was liable in an action for conversion, because it breached its duty to the remaindermen.[197] Even those statutes that make the corporation liable for transfer by a fiduciary only under

---

[192]Steiner v Zammit (La. App. 1973) 279 So2d 728.

[193]Hoffman v Wanson Concrete Co. (Wis. S Ct 1973) No. 298, 5-14-73.

[194]Southern Cal. First Nat'l Bank v Quincy Cass Associates, (1970) 91 Cal. Rptr. 605, 478 P2d 37.

[195]Seymour v Nat'l Biscuit Co., (1939) 107 F2d 58.

[196]West v American Tel. & Tel. Co., (1939) 108 F2d 347.

[197]Seymour v Nat'l Biscuit Co., note 195 supra. See 38 MICH L REV 726. But see Middendorf v Kansas Power & Light Co., (1949) 166 Kan. 610, 203 P2d 156, holding corporation will not be charged with knowledge of a will and executor's authority, and can permit a transfer by an executor-life tenant, where the proposed transfer is apparently in the ordinary course of business for the purpose of paying debts or legacies.

certain conditions do not authorize transfer of the whole title to the stock upon demand of one who has only a life interest in it.[198]

Ordinarily when a trustee is described as such on the face of a stock certificate, the corporation permits transfer of the stock at its own peril.[199] It is liable for a transfer on its books that deprives a trust of the stock. For example, the corporation knew that a trust provided that stock should be used for certain benevolent causes of a church. The church sold the stock and used the proceeds for a new church building. The corporation transferred the stock; it was, therefore, liable to the trustees of the benevolent causes.[200]

A corporation is not liable for transfer of stock by an executor in breach of fiduciary duty unless it had knowledge of the breach, or the transfer in bad faith.[201] The corporation is not bound to make inquiry, nor is the executor bound to give requested information. However, if the executor undertakes to supply requested information, he must state the facts fully and fairly. Otherwise, the corporation is justified in refusing to make the transfer.[202]

Appointment of transfer agent and registrar. Many large corporations with widely distributed stock follow the practice of employing transfer agents or registrars to assist them in the issuance and transfer of stock. The board of directors adopts a resolution of appointment, specifying the powers and duties of the transfer agent or registrar, and the class and number of shares for which the agency is created. Some trust companies that act as transfer agent and registrar issue a pamphlet indicating their documentary requirements and other regulations governing their relations with the corporation. The agency may be terminated at the will of the corporation or of the transfer agent or registrar. Usually, upon removal of the transfer agent by the corporation, the board of directors adopts a resolution terminating the agency, and designating an officer of the corporation to whom the transfer books and records are to be delivered.

Duties of registrar and transfer agent. The duty of the registrar is to see that the corporation does not issue its stock beyond the amount authorized. The registrar keeps a record of each share of stock issued

---

[198] Seymour v Nat'l Biscuit Co., (1939) 107 F2d 58.

[199] First Nat'l Bank v Pittsburgh, F.W. & C. Ry., (1930) 31 F Supp 381. See also Klein v Inman, (1944) 298 Ky. 122, 182 SW2d 34.

[200] King v Richardson, (1943) 136 F2d 849.

[201] Harris v General Motors Corp., (1942) 263 App. Div. 261, 32 NYS2d 556.

[202] Ibid.

and of each share of stock cancelled. It is not concerned with any of the details of transfer of stock. The transfer agent, on the other hand, not only attends to the actual transfer of the stock on the records of the corporation, and to the issuance of new certificates of stock, but it may also take care of stock subscriptions, preparation of stockholders' lists, payment of dividends, conversion or redemption of securities, and even mailing of notices to stockholders.

Liability of transfer agent and registrar. The transfer agent is the agent of the corporation employing it.[203] It owes no affirmative duty to the stockholders whose certificates of stock it issues and transfers, and incurs no personal liability in favor of such stockholders.[204] Thus it has been held that there is no direct liability of a transfer agent to the stockholder for wrongful nonfeasance in delaying or refusing to transfer stock.[205] The agent is answerable to the corporation for nonfeasance. The corporation is liable to the transferee. But the agent is not individually liable to the transferee.[206] The transfer agent is responsible to the corporation primarily for the following: (1) wrongful refusals to transfer stock;[207] (2) wrongful transfers of stock; and (3) failure to perform its duties as agent.[208] The statutes in some states impose a liability upon the transfer agent for failure to pay taxes due on transfers, or for allowing transfers to be made before required tax waivers have been obtained.

The registrar is liable both to the corporation and to an injured stockholder if it allows an overissue of stock. This liability is based on the principle that an officer or agent who issues unauthorized stock is liable to bona fide purchasers.

Issuance of new certificates of stock to transferees. Transferees of stock are entitled to new certificates upon surrender to the corporation of the old certificate.[209] A corporation, for its own protection, should refuse to issue a new certificate without the surrender of the old.[210] It cannot be compelled to issue a new one until the old one is surrendered

---

[203] Nicholson v Morgan, (1922) 119 NY Misc 309, 196 NY Supp 147.

[204] Palmer v O'Bannon Corp., (1925) 253 Mass. 8, 149 NE 112.

[205] Mears v Crocker First Nat'l Bank, (1950) 97 Cal. App. 2d 482, 218 P2d 91.

[206] Fowler v Nat'l City Bank, (1934) 49 Ga. App. 435, 176 SE 113.

[207] Age Publishing Co. v Becker, (1943) 110 Col. 319, 134 P2d 205; Young v Cockman, (1943) 182 Md 246, 34 A2d 428.

[208] Nicholson v Morgan, (1922) 119 NY Misc 309, 196 NY Supp 147.

[209] O'Neil v Wolcott Mining Co., (1909) 174 F 527; Handy v Miner, (1926) 258 Mass. 53, 154 NE 557. See also Morris v Hussong Dyeing Mach. Co., (1913) 81 NJ Eq 256, 86A. 1026.

[210] Holly Sugar Co. v Wilson, (1938) 101 Col. 511, 75 P2d 149; Suskin v Hodges, (1939) 216 NC 333, 4 SE2d 891.

to it, except where the original certificate is lost or destroyed.[211] A certificate of stock properly issued by a corporation having power to issue stock certificates is a declaration by the corporation to all who may innocently purchase the certificate that the person to whom it is issued is the owner of the number of shares of stock specified in the instrument.[212] The corporation must make sure that the person to whom it issues the certificate is the true owner.[213] A bona fide holder of the certificate, that is, one who has acquired the certificate in good faith, for value, properly indorsed, has a claim to recognition as a stockholder.[214] Obviously, if the corporation issues a new certificate of stock without demanding the surrender of the old one, it incurs the risk of having to recognize bona fide purchasers of both certificates as stockholders. Cancellation of an old certificate on the corporation books when issuing the new certificate, without demanding the surrender of the old certificate, will not protect the corporation from liability to a bona fide holder of the old certificate.[215] The position to be taken by the corporation in case surrender cannot be made because the certificate is lost is discussed on page 691 et seq.

It is not essential to the validity of a pledge that a new certificate be issued to the pledgee. However, the pledgee is entitled to a certificate and may demand it.[216] The corporation may required the pledgee to give satisfactory proof of his authority to demand the transfer and to receive the new certificate.[217] Reference to the pledge agreement should be made in the certificate. For example, the certificate should be issued to "John Smith, pledgee under agreement with Paul Jones, dated . . . ."

---

[211]Knight v Shutz, (1943) 141 Ohio St. 267, 47 NE 2d 886. See, however, Danbom v Danbom, (1937) 132 Neb. 858, 273 NW 502, in which it was held that a court could require a corporation to issue a new certificate to a purchaser at a sheriff's sale without surrender of the outstanding certificate.

[212]Manhattan Beach Co v Harned, (1886) 27 F 484.

[213]Greasy Brush Coal Co. v Hays, (1942) 292 Ky. 517, 166 SW2d 983.

[214]Rand v Hercules Powder Co., (1927) 129 NY Misc 891, 222 NY Supp 383. Stock may be transferred to an officer or director of a corporation in the same manner as to any individual, provided that the transaction is not fraudulent or in breach of any trust. Du Pont v Du Pont, (1919) 265 F 129.

[215]Nowy Swiat Publishing Co. v Misiewicz, (1927) 246 NY 58, 158 NE 19.

[216]Hurley v Pusey & Jones Co., (1921) 274 F 487; Lawrence v I.N. Parlier Estate Co., (1940) 15 Cal. 2d 220, 100 P2d 765. For the right of a pledgee to have a new certificate issued in his name, see Foto v Bussell, (1919) 45 Cal. App. 281, 187 P 432, and Banker's Trust Co. v Rood, (1930) 211 Iowa 289, 233 NW 794.

[217]Palmer v O'Bannon Corp., (1925) 253 Mass. 8, 149 NE 112.

Remedies of stockholder for failure of corporation to issue stock certificate. Upon refusal of the corporation to issue a certificate of stock when it is under obligation to do so, the person entitled to the stock certificate may pursue one of the following remedies against the corporation:

(1) Compel the corporation to issue the stock certificate by a bill in equity.[218]

(2) Compel the issuance of the stock certificate by mandamus proceedings.[219]

(3) Consider the refusal as a conversion of the stock, and recover the market value of the stock at the time of the conversion.[220]

(4) Treat the refusal as a breach of contract, and sue for damages.[221] However, a stockholder who disputes the price he is to be paid by the corporation for stock he sells in accordance with his stock transfer agreement, cannot demand access to the corporation's books and supporting documents, when the agreement fixed the purchase price as the proportionate value of assets as carried on the books, and attested to by the accountants' report. Another bookkeeping method might have produced a higher price, but the method used was agreed to by all the stockholders, and an audit would serve no purpose. Also, a corporation cannot subtract negative net earnings from base price per share to compute the price it must pay for stock under a restrictive stock agreement that employed the price formula of base price plus amount, if any, of accumulated net earnings per share.[222]

---

[218] First Nat'l Bank v Pittsburgh, F.W. & C. Ry., (1939) 31 F Supp 381; Young v Cockman, (1943) 182 Md 246, 34 A2d 428; H.M. Rowe Co. v Rowe, (1928) 154 Md 599, 141 A 334; Virginia Pub. Serv. Co. v Steindler, (1936) 166 Va. 686, 187 SE 353. This remedy is allowed only where the value of the stock cannot be readily ascertained with reasonable certainty, and where the recovery of damages would not give adequate relief. Falk v Dirigold Corp., (1928) 174 Minn. 219, 219 NW 72.

[219] The decisions as to whether or not mandamus is a proper proceeding to compel a transfer are conflicting. Some authorities have held that mandamus will not lie. Spangerburg v Western Heavy Hardware and Iron Co. (1913) 166 Cal 284, 135 P 1127; State ex rel Cooke v New York-Mexican Oil Co, (1923) 32 Del 244, 122 A 55; People ex rel Rottenberg v Utah Gold and Copper Mines Co., (1909) 135 App Div 418, 119 NY Supp 852. Other say that mandamus is an available remedy. In re Ballou, (1914) 215 F 810; Hanna v Chester Times, (1933) 310 Pa 583, 1 66 A 243. The general rule seems to be that mandamus will not lie when there is an adequate remedy at law (in damages), or in equity (by specific performance).

[220] Tobias v Wolverine Mining Co., (1932) 52 Ida 576, 17 P2d 338; Young v Cockman, note 207 supra; Prudential Petroleum Corp. v Rauscher, Pierce & Co., (Tex. Civ. App. 1955) 281 SW2d 457; Beaumont Hotel Co. v Caswell (Tex. Civ. App. 1929) 14 SW 2d 292. See also Seymour v Nat'l Biscuit Co., (1939) 107 F2d 58, cert denied 60 S Ct 590.

[221] In re Ballou, (1914) 215 F 810; DeLamar v Fidelity Loan & Inv. Co., (1924) 158 Ga 361, 123 SE 116.

[222] Baron v Royal Paper Corp., (NY App. Div. 1971) 36 AD2d 112.

(5) Consider the contract rescinded, and recover the money paid on the subscription.[223]

The court will not direct the issuance of stock if the certificates already outstanding represent the total amount that the corporation is authorized to issue.[224] The stockholder, in such cases, is relegated to his remedy of money damages.[225] In any case, before a stockholder may maintain any action for refusal to issue a certificate, he must make a demand for it.[226]

A stockholder may also have a right of action against a corporation for damages sustained because of delay in issuing a certificate,[227] but the officers of the corporation are not personally liable.[228]

Rules for transfer of stock. Corporations that handle their own transfers of securities, as well as transfer agents and registrars, often issue printed rules outlining their requirements for transfer of stock, as well as a set of rules to guide themselves in effecting the transfers. These rules generally outline: (1) the documents required for transfer of stock by individuals, corporations, fiduciaries, pledgees, bankrupts, and the like; (2) the manner in which the assignment of stock must be executed; and (3) the method of registration and issuance of new certificates of stock.

Actual delivery of the stock certificate may also be an important factor. Thus, for example, a purchaser was not held liable on promissory notes he gave in exchange for stock, when the corporate books merely contained unsigned stock certificates made out to the purchaser and no actual delivery was made, since without delivery there was no consideration for said notes. The purchaser's subsequent election as secretary-treasurer of the corporation, giving him the power to sign, did not fulfill the requirement that the seller complete the transfer.[229]

---

[223]Texla Oil Co. v Calhoun, (1927) 36 Ga. App. 536, SE 84; Beaumont Hotel Co. v Caswell, note 220 supra.

[224]Selwyn-Brown v Superno Co., (1918) App. Div. 420, 168 NY Supp. 18. See, however, McWilliams v Geddes & Moss Undertaking Co. (La. App. 1936) 169 So. 894, in which it was held that a corporation could cancel the shares of stock wrongfully issued.

[225]Dupoyster v First Nat'l Bank, (1906) 29 Ky. L Rep 1153, 96 SW 830.

[226]Swobe v Brictson Mfg. Co., (1922) 279 F 560; Teeple v Hawkeye Gold Dredging Co., (1908) 137 Iowa 206, 114 NW 906.

[227]Rock v Gustaveson Oil Co., (1922) 59 Utah 451, 204 P 96. The measure of damages for delay is the difference between the selling price at the time delivery was due and the selling price on the market when delivery was actually made.

[228]Radio Electronic Television Corp. v Bartniew Distributing Corp., (1940) 32 F Supp 431; Hulse v Consolidated Quicksilver Mining Corp., (1944) 65 Ida. 768, 154 P2d 149.

[229]Wolfe v Sachse (Wis. S Ct 1977) 248 NW 2d 407.

Lost, destroyed, or stolen certificates of stock. Since a stockholder is entitled to a duplicate certificate to replace one that has been lost, stolen or destroyed, most corporations make provision in their by-laws for replacing such certificates. The corporation will require evidence of the loss, usually in the form of an affidavit.

Where statutes regulate the issuance of duplicate certificates, they usually permit the corporation to require a bond to indemnify the corporation against any future claim if the old certificate should show up. The amount of the bond may be left to the discretion of the board, or a maximum or minimum may be set. In addition to supplying an affidavit and bond, the stockholder or the corporation itself may be required to advertise the loss.

If the statute permits, the board may be given complete discretion in regard to the issuance of a new certificate. To the clause regulating the issuance of duplicate certificates may be added a provision for the replacement of mutilated or partly-destroyed certificates. No affidavit or bond is necessary in this case since the old certificate can be surrendered. Additional provisions may deal with the keeping of records on the issuance of new certificates and with marking the certificate "duplicate."

Resolutions providing for issuance of new certificates. A resolution is usually required to authorize the issuance of a duplicate certificate. The resolution may be in pursuance of the appropriate by-law or, in the absence of a by-law provision, it must conform to statutory requirements. A blanket resolution is often used in the absence of a by-law.

When a stockholder has supplied the affidavit and bond required by the by-laws, the directors may adopt a resolution authorizing the transfer agent and registrar to issue a new certificate. If the directors are convinced that the old certificate has been destroyed—as in a fire—so that there is no danger of its reappearance, they may approve the issuance of a new certificate without requiring a bond. But in such a situation, the corporation's transfer agent and registrar may require a resolution of indemnity. Further, the corporation may also ask the stockholder to agree to indemnify the corporation.

Provisions of the Uniform Commercial Code. Every state except Louisiana has adopted the Uniform Commercial Code. The provision of the Code that applies to lost, destroyed, and stolen securities is Section 8–405. It reads as follows:

(1) Where a security has been lost, apparently destroyed or wrongfully taken and the owner fails to notify the issuer of that fact within a reasonable time after he has notice of it and the issuer registers a transfer of the security before receiving such a notification, the owner is precluded from asserting against the issuer any claim for registering the transfer or any claim to a new security under this section.

(2) Where the owner of a security claims that the security has been lost, destroyed, or wrongfully taken, the issuer must issue a new security in place of the original security if the owner

(a) so requests before the issuer has notice that the security has been acquired by a bona fide purchaser; and

(b) files with the issuer a sufficient indemnity bond; and

(c) satisfies any other reasonable requirements imposed by the issuer.

(3) If, after the issue of the new security, a bona fide purchaser of the original security presents it for registration of transfer, the issuer must register the transfer unless registration would result in overissue, in which event the issuer's liability is governed by Section 8–104. In addition to any rights on the indemnity bond, the issuer may recover the new security from the person to whom it was issued or any person taking under him except a bona fide purchaser.*

Note: "Overissue" here means the issue of securities in excess of those the issuer has the corporate power to issue (Sec. 8–104). Under that section, if registration would result in an overissue, the purchaser may recover from the corporation the price he or the last purchaser for value paid for the security, with interest.

Usual requirements for issuance of duplicate certificates. Following are the usual requirements for the issuance of duplicate certificates:

(1) An order from the stockholder, directing the corporation to stop any transfer of the lost certificate.

(2) An affidavit of the stockholder, setting forth the material facts surrounding the loss of the certificate.[230]

(3) An indemnity bond by the stockholder, approved by the board of directors of the corporation, to protect the corporation against loss

---

*Copyright 1972 by the American Law Institute and the National Conference of Commissioners on Uniform State Laws. Reprinted with permission of the Permanent Editorial Board for the Uniform Commercial Code.

[230] In re Trust Co. v Finsterwald, (1939) 188 Ga. 794, 4 SE2d 808, it was held that under the statute it was not necessary to state the "mode of loss." However, it is necessary to comply with the corporation's request for additional information, as long as its request is a reasonable one; if the alleged owner fails to provide that information, the corporation need not issue the new certificate: Glaser v Texon Energy Corp. (CA–5 1983) 702 F 2d 569.

that may result from issuance of the duplicate certificate. The bond is often set at double the amount of the market value of the stock for which the new certificate is being issued. Many corporations cover these transactions by a blanket bond.

(4) Usually the lapse of a specified period of time before issuance of the new certificate, to see if the old one will not turn up.

Rights of holders of lost certificates of stock. The rights of a bona fide holder of the old certificate of stock that allegedly has been lost, destroyed, or stolen are not affected by the issuance of the new certificate. The corporation must recognize him as a stockholder, as well as the bona fide holder of the new certificate.[231] To protect the corporation against any loss that it may later sustain if the old stock certificate should reappear, the court directing issuance of a new stock certificate will require the person requesting replacement to furnish a bond to indemnify the corporation.[232] The court may order issuance of a new certificate without requiring a bond if the facts show that no danger of reappearance of the old certificate exists.[233] A corporation that issues a new stock certificate without court order will require an indemnity bond as a condition of issuance. Note, however, that when a corporation honored a forged indorsement of the wife on an assignment to her husband of a jointly owned certificate, the certificate was not "lost" under the Uniform Commercial Code, so the wife did not have to post security.[234]

Replacement of lost certificates by transfer agent. Corporations that have a transfer agent and a registrar handling the issuance and transfer of shares sometimes authorize the transfer agent to replace lost certificates upon obtaining a satisfactory surety bond to such an amount as it provided by the by-laws. The board of directors is thus relieved of the necessity of handling each case of a lost certificate of stock. The authority may be given to the transfer agent by means of a separate resolution passed by the directors, or this duty of the transfer agent may be included in the general resolution covering the

---

[231] People's Bank v Lamar County Bank, (1915) 107 Miss. 852, 67 So 961.

[232] Davis v Lime Cola Bottling Works, (1922) 18 Ala. App. 562, 93 So 328; Will's Adm'r v George Wiedemann Brewing Co., (1916) 171 Ky. 681, 188 SW 788; State exrel McCay v New Orleans Cotton Exchange, (1905) 114 La. 324, 38 So 204.

[233] Ibid.

[234] Bile v Bile, (1983) 95 AD 2d 719, 464 NYS 2d 127.

appointment. The registrar, whose duty it is to see that there is no overissue of stock and who is required to countersign every certificate issued, may wish to be protected against any loss, damage, or liability that may arise from complying with the request of the corporation or its transfer agent to register and countersign certificates of stock issued in place of those that have been lost or destroyed. In such a case, the directors will authorize by resolution the execution of an agreement between the corporation and the registrar to indemnify the latter against such loss.

Chapter 22

FORMS RELATING TO
TRANSFER OF STOCK

Contents—Chapter 22

DIRECTORS' RESOLUTION AT FIRST MEETING ADOPTING STOCK BOOK AND TRANSFER BOOK

RESOLVED, That the stock book and the transfer book presented at this meeting are hereby adopted as the stock book and transfer book of the Company and that the same be kept at the registered office of the Company or otherwise as the Board of Directors shall by resolution determine from time to time.

DIRECTORS' RESOLUTION AUTHORIZING CORPORATION TO ACT AS ITS OWN TRANSFER AGENT, AND EMPOWERING PRESIDENT TO APPOINT AND REMOVE TRANSFER CLERKS

RESOLVED, That the Company shall act as its own transfer agent, and

RESOLVED FURTHER, That the President shall have the power from time to time to employ one or more transfer clerks, or to assign the duties of a transfer clerk to one or more officers or employees of the Company, and shall have the further power to discharge the transfer clerk or clerks, or to revoke the duties of transfer clerk granted to any officer or employee.

DIRECTORS' RESOLUTION APPOINTING TRANSFER AGENT AND REGISTRAR

RESOLVED, That the .... Trust Company of .... is hereby appointed Transfer Agent and Registrar of the Capital Stock of this Company.

RESOLVED FURTHER, That said Trust Company is hereby authorized to countersign as Transfer Agent and Registrar, when signed by the President or Vice president, and the Treasurer or one of the Assistant Treasurers of this Company, and sealed with its corporate seal, certificates for an original issue of the stock of this Company to the number of ..... (.....) shares of Common Capital Stock, each of the par value of ..... ($.....) Dollars, and to deliver the same, as may be specified in writing by the President or one of the Vice presidents of the Company, and to transfer and register such shares from time to time in books kept for that purpose, on the surrender for such transfer and registration of certificates for such stock, therefore countersigned and registered and delivered by it as such Transfer Agent and Registrar, and having thereon proper indorsements duly authorized, and to deliver in lieu of the certificates so surrendered new certificates that have been signed and sealed, countersigned, and registered in the manner prescribed above, and

RESOLVED FURTHER, That said Trust Company's authority shall also extend to the countersigning and registering of and delivery in the manner prescribed above, of any certificate or certificates of stock which may be issued by authority of this Company, evidenced by the written order of the President or the Vice president and one of the other aforementioned officers of this Company, in lieu of a lost or destroyed certificate or certificates of stock, and

RESOLVED FURTHER, That said Trust Company is authorized to open and keep such stock transfer and registration book or books of this Company as may be required by law or for its own convenience in the performance of its said agency, and

RESOLVED FURTHER, That when certificates of stock are presented to said Trust Company for transfer and registration, it is hereby authorized to refuse to transfer and register the same until it is satisfied that the indorsement on the certificate is valid and genuine, and that the requested transfer is legally authorized; and it shall incur no liability for the refusal, in good faith, to make transfers which it, in its judgment, deems improper or unauthorized. Where the indorsements on certificates presented for transfer are not known by the said Trust Company to be genuine, it is authorized to require the appearance before it of the registered holder of the certificate desiring to make the transfer, and the acknowledgment by him of his signature, or, in its discretion, it may accept in lieu thereof, as authority for making the transfer, the guaranty of the genuineness of the signature by some person or persons or corporation believed by it to be financially responsible. It may, in its discretion, decline to make transfers other than to one or more persons or corporations; and where stock is requested to be transferred into the name of a trustee, or other fiduciary, it may refuse to do so unless there is added a reference to the instrument defining the duties of such trustee or other fiduciary. The said Trust Company is charged with the duty of seeing that there shall be no certificates of stock of this Company issued and outstanding and registered by it in excess of the authorized issue above mentioned, and

RESOLVED FURTHER, That the Company lodge with said Trust Company, appropriately certified as such:

(1) Specimen signatures of the officers of the Company who are authorized by the foregoing resolutions to sign the certificates of stock of the Company,

(2) Specimens of all the certificates of stock of the Company,

(3) A copy of the Certificate of Incorporation of the Company, with all amendments,

(4) A copy of the By-laws of the Company, and

RESOLVED FURTHER, That, in acting in respect to certificates believed by said Trust Company to be certificates of stock of the Company, to be signed by the officers herein before authorized to sign the same, and to be sealed with the corporate seal of the Company, the Company will hold said Transfer Agent and Registrar harmless against all liability, and

RESOLVED FURTHER, That said Trust Company may use its own judgment in matters affecting its duties as such Transfer Agent and Registrar, and in its discretion may apply to and act upon instructions of its own counsel or of the counsel for this Company, in respect to any questions arising in connection with said agency, and in following such advice of counsel or its own judgment it shall be liable only for its own willful default or negligence, and

RESOLVED FURTHER, That the Secretary of the Company is hereby authorized to certify under its corporate seal a copy of these resolutions, and to lodge the same with said Trust Company as authority for all action to be taken by it as Transfer Agent and Registrar.

DIRECTORS' RESOLUTION AUTHORIZING APPOINTMENT OF TRANSFER AGENT/REGISTRAR, TO ACT IN ACCORDANCE WITH REGULATIONS SET FORTH IN PAMPHLET

(*Note:* This is a form furnished by a trust company acting as transfer agent and registrar.)

Appointment of $\begin{cases} \text{TRANSFER AGENT} \\ \text{REGISTRAR} \end{cases}$

. . . .
(NAME OF CORPORATION)

"*Resolved*, that . . . . Bank of the City of . . . .

is hereby appointed $\begin{cases} \text{sole} \\ \text{New York} \end{cases} \begin{cases} \text{Transfer Agent} \\ \text{Registrar} \end{cases}$ for

* all of the shares
. . . . . . shares   of the . . . . . Preferred stock, and

* all of the shares
. . . . . . shares   of the . . . . . Common stock

of this Company, to act in accordance with its general practice and with the regulations set forth in the pamphlet submitted to this meeting entitled 'Regulations of The . . . . Bank of the City of . . . . for the Transfer and Registration of Stock,' which pamphlet the Secretary is directed to mark for identification and file with the records of the Company."

I, the undersigned, Secretary of the above named Corporation, DO HEREBY CERTIFY that the foregoing is a true and correct copy of a resolution duly adopted by the Board of Directors of said Corporation at a meeting thereof duly called and held on . . . ., 19.., at which a quorum was present, and that said resolution has not been in any wise rescinded, annulled or revoked but the same is still in full force and effect.

---

* If the appointment is to cover less than the entire amount of authorized stock of a particular class, the words "all of the shares" should be stricken out and the number of shares to be covered by the appointment inserted on the line. If the appointment is to cover all of the stock of a particular class, now or hereafter authorized by the articles of incorporation, the line and the word "shares" should be stricken out.

AND I DO FURTHER CERTIFY to the following facts:

The authorized and outstnding stock of the Corporation is as follows:

CLASS	PAR VALUE	AUTHORIZED	OUTSTANDING**
. . . .	. . . .	. . . .	. . . .
. . . .	. . . .	. . . .	. . . .
. . . .	. . . .	. . . .	. . . .

The address of the Corporation to which notices may be sent is . . . .

The below named persons have been duly elected, have duly qualified, and this day are, officers of the Corporation, holding the respective offices below set opposite their names, and the signatures below set opposite their names are their genuine signatures.[†]

. . . . PRESIDENT . . . .
. . . . VICE PRESIDENT . . . .
. . . . TREASURER . . . .
. . . . ASSISTANT TREASURER . . . .
. . . . SECRETARY . . . .
. . . . ASSISTANT SECRETARY . . . .

The name and address of legal counsel for the Corporation is . . . .

The names and addresses of all of the Transfer Agents and Registrars of the stock of the Corporation are as follows:

CLASS OF STOCK	TRANSFER AGENT(S)	REGISTRAR(S)
. . . .	. . . .	. . . .
. . . .	. . . .	. . . .
. . . .	. . . .	. . . .
. . . .	. . . .	. . . .

WITNESS my hand and the seal of the Corporation this . . . . . day of . . . . , 19 . . .

. . . .
SECRETARY
(Corporate seal)

DIRECTORS' RESOLUTION APPOINTING SOLE TRANSFER AGENT

(*Note:* This is a form furnished by a trust company acting as transfer agent. The headings in boldface appear in the form as marginal notes.)

** Only stock outstanding prior to appointment should be shown. Do not include in this figure stock to be issued on or after appointment. If new company, the word "none" should be inserted. If new stock is to be issued in exchange for old outstanding stock, amount of old stock outstanding and terms of exchange should be shown.

† Only the names and signatures of the officers who will sign stock certificates or sign written instructions, requests, etc., to the Transfer Agent or Registrar need be included.

Appointment of
.... Company
As Transfer Agent of The Stock of
....
(Name)

....
(Business Address)

RESOLVED—

[Appointment]

FIRST: That the .... Company be, and it hereby is, appointed Transfer Agent of the shares of the stock of this Company, as hereinafter set forth, and that *all previous appointments in respect to the shares covered by these resolutions, and previous resolutions in connection therewith be, and the same hereby are, rescinded and revoked,* for which stock there has also been appointed as Registrar in New York City, ...

SECOND: That this Board of Directors hereby approved the Capital Stock Schedule, presented to and hereby ordered filed with the minutes of this meeting, and certifies that all of the shares of the Company's stock now outstanding, or which will be outstanding pursuant to this authorization, have been duly authorized to be issued, and are, or when issued will be, fully paid and nonassessable.

[Authorization to make transfers of stock]

THIRD: * That for the purpose of the original issue of certificates (that is, certificates *not* issued upon the transfer and cancellation of existing certificates now outstanding), the Transfer Agent is hereby directed:

(a) To record and countersign as Transfer Agent, when duly executed by the Company, certificates of stock of the class or classes set forth in the Capital Stock Schedule for not exceeding the number of shares of each class specified in Column 6 of said Schedule;

(b) To deliver such certificates to the Registrar of the Company or any successor Registrar appointed by the Company, for registration and counter-signature; and

(c) To deliver such certificates so countersigned, upon the receipt of the written order or orders of the Company signed by its .... and/or .... under its corporate seal, specifying: (1) the name or names and the number of shares in which such certificates shall be issued; and (2) the officer or other person or persons to whom or upon whose order such certificates shall be delivered.

---

* If all of the stock in respect to which Transfer Agent is being appointed has heretofore been issued, strike out this paragraph THIRD.

[Authorization to make transfer of stock]

FOURTH: That the Transfer Agent be, and it hereby is, authorized and directed, from time to time, when surrendered to it for such purpose, properly endorsed or accompanied by instruments of assignment, and duly stamped as may be required by the laws of *............, of New York and of the United States, and duly executed by the Company, to make transfers of:

(a) Certificates, if any, issued pursuant to the foregoing paragraph THIRD of these resolutions;

(b) Certificates, if any, heretofore issued and now outstanding, specified in Column 3 of the Capital Stock Schedule; and

(c) Certificates thus issued in transfer by it as Transfer Agent; and

to record and to countersign new certificates, when they shall have been duly executed by the Company, and to deliver such certificates to the Registrar for registration and countersignature, and, when so countersigned and returned by the Registrar, to deliver them in the usual course of business in lieu of and upon cancellation of the certificates so surrendered for transfer.

[Method of signing certificates*]

FIFTH: The Transfer agent is hereby authorized to recognize as duly executed by the Company any certificate which shall either (a) be manually signed by ** a President or a Vice president and a Treasurer or an Assistant Treasurer or a Secretary or an Assistant Secretary of the Company and on which the seal of the Company shall be impressed; or (b) bear the printed or engraved facsimile signatures of the said officers and a printed or engraved facsimile of the corporate seal of the Company.

When any officer of this Company shall no longer be vested with authority to sign for the Company written notice thereof shall immediately be given to the Transfer Agent, and, until receipt of such notice, the Transfer Agent shall be fully protected and held harmless in recognizing and acting upon certificates bearing the signature of such officer or a signature believed by it in good faith to be such genuine signature. In case any officer whose manual or facsimile signature appears on any unused stock certificates lodged with the Transfer Agent shall cease to be such officer, such certificates may nevertheless be issued and delivered (unless the Transfer Agent shall have been instructed in writing by an officer of the Company to the contrary), either in connection with any original issue or upon transfers, as though such officer had not ceased to be an officer. The Transfer Agent is authorized to recognize

---

* Here insert State of incorporation if stamps are required by the laws or rulings of that State.

** The officers authorized to sign must be in accordance with the provisions of the Certificate of Incorporation, the By-laws, and the laws of the State of Incorporation.

Strike out provision as to facsimile seals and signatures, except where same is authorized by statute and the by-laws and is desired by Company.

as duly executed and issued any outstanding certificate (a) which shall have been countersigned by any former transfer agent and/or registrar, without checking the signatures of the officers of the Company appearing on such certificate; or (b) the signatures on which (in case such signatures shall not have been lodged with the Transfer Agent pursuant to paragraph TWELFTH hereof) shall have been identified to the Transfer Agent by an officer of the Company, all officers being hereby authorized at any time to identify any such signature or signatures to the Transfer Agent on its request. The Transfer Agent shall be fully protected in conclusively relying upon any list of holders of shares, if any, now outstanding, furnished to it by any former Transfer Agent or by an officer of the Company.[†]

[Lost, stolen, or destroyed certificates]

SIXTH: That the Transfer Agent be, and it hereby is, authorized to issue a new or duplicate certificate in lieu of any alleged lost, stolen or destroyed certificate, upon being furnished with (a) an appropriate bond of indemnity in form and substance and with a surety company satisfactory to the Transfer Agent and in an amount at least equal to twice the market or par value of the stock represented by such lost, stolen, or destroyed certificate, naming the Transfer Agent as one of the obligees; and (b) a resolution of the Board of Directors, or the Executive Committee of the Board, specifically approving the indemnity bond as executed and the issuance of such new or duplicate certificate.

[Delay or refusal to effect transfers]

SEVENTH: That the Transfer Agent be, and it hereby is, authorized to refuse to transfer or delay in transferring (a) any certificate presented to it for transfer until it is satisfied, in its discretion, that the requested transfer is duly authorized, and in such connection may require such evidence of guaranty of the validity and genuineness of signatures, endorsements or assignments as is usual, or as it may in its discretion require, or until it is satisfied, in its discretion, as to whether any stamp, transfer, inheritance or other tax liability exists or has been paid in respect of any requested transfer or (b) any certificate reported lost, stolen or destroyed, or the ownership of which is in dispute, until satisfied in its discretion as to the ownership of such certificate; and shall be fully indemnified and saved harmless by the Company in connection with any such refusal or delay. That the Transfer Agent be, and it hereby is, authorized to act on the instructions of any officer of the Company in transferring or delaying or refusing to transfer any certificate, so reported lost, stolen or destroyed, or the ownership of which is in dispute, and if so instructed, may make any transfer notwithstanding any irregularity, and without further inquiry as to the validity or genuineness of any endorsement or assignment, and shall be fully protected in so doing.

[†] Certified list of stockholders as of the date that this appointment becomes effective must be furnished.

[Further instructions]

That when the Transfer Agent deems it expedient, it may apply to any officer of the Company or to . . . . of . . . . , counsel for the Company, or to its own counsel, for instructions and advice; and for any action taken in accordance with such instructions or advice, the Company will fully indemnify, protect and hold harmless the Transfer Agent from any and all liability.

[Stockholders' lists]

EIGHTH: That the Transfer Agent be, and it hereby is, authorized and directed to prepare and deliver lists of stockholders of the Company upon the order of the . . . . or . . . . of the Company.

[Supply of stock certificates]

NINTH: That the Company will at all times keep the Transfer Agent furnished with an adequate supply of certificates of each class of stock in respect to which it is appointed, duly executed by the Company. The Transfer Agent is hereby authorized, in its discretion, to retain any stock certificates cancelled in connection with transfers, together with all documents submitted therewith, and also to retain its books of original entry as Transfer Agent, on condition that the Transfer Agent, by accepting this appointment, agrees, in case of the termination of its appointment, or at any other time, when requested by the Company and on the payment of proper charges therefor, to furnish to the Company a certified list of stockholders and of certificates outstanding, and to permit the inspection, at reasonable times, of any such cancelled certificates, documents and original records.

[Compensation]

TENTH: That the Transfer Agent be, and it shall be, entitled to reasonable compensation for all services rendered by it in the execution of its duties, as well as all its reasonable expenses incurred or disbursed in the performance of such duties, including fees of its counsel for advice rendered in connection with such agency, and the proper officers of the Company are hereby authorized to pay all bills therefor when rendered.

[Indemnification]

ELEVENTH: That the Company shall indemnify, protect and hold harmless the Transfer Agent for any act, omission, delay or refusal made by it in reliance upon any stock certificate, signature, endorsement, assignment, order, certificate, document, or other instrument believed by it in good faith to be valid, genuine and sufficient, and in effecting any transfer believed by it in good faith to be duly authorized, and that the Transfer Agent shall not be liable for anything whatever in connection with this agency except its own willful misconduct. That the Transfer agent may employ agents or attorneys in fact, and shall not be answerable for the default or misconduct of any agent or attorney appointed by it in pursuance hereof, if such agent or attorney shall have been selected with reasonable care.

[Authority of officer of company to certify]

TWELFTH: That any officer of the Company be, and hereby is, authorized to lodge with the Transfer Agent (a) a certified copy of these resolutions, together with a copy of the Capital Stock Schedule referred to in paragraph SECOND of these resolutions; (b) specimens of certificates of each class of stock covered by these resolutions in the form adopted by the Company; (c) specimens or facsimiles of the signatures of (1) all officers of the Company duly authorized to sign or countersign any stock certificates hereafter issued, and (2) all other officers, if any, and if such signatures are readily available, heretofore authorized to sign or whose signatures appear upon stock certificates now outstanding, for the purpose of comparison with signatures appearing on certificates presented to it for issue or transfer; (d) a certified copy of the Certificate of Incorporation of the Company, including all of the amendments thereto; (e) a certified copy of the By-laws of the Company as at present in force; and (f) specimens or facsimiles of the signatures of any additional officers of the Company at any time hereafter duly authorized to sign stock certificates, and certified copies of any amendments that may, from time to time, be made to the Certificate of Incorporation or By-laws: and that the Transfer Agent be, and it hereby is, authorized to rely conclusively on any documents or signatures so lodged with it and be fully protected in so doing.

THIRTEENTH: This appointment shall be deemed to constitute an appointment of any banking corporation or trust company which by merger, consolidation, purchase of assets or otherwise, shall succeed to the banking and trust business of the bank of .... Company, and of the successor and successors of such banking corporation or trust company; and the term Transfer Agent (Registrar), wherever herein used, shall be deemed to include and apply to any such banking corporation or trust company, its successor and successors, whether organized under state or national law.

[on separate sheet]

The undersigned, ..., President, and ...., Secretary, of ...., a corporation duly organized and existing under the laws of the State of ...., DO HEREBY CERTIFY:

(1) That the foregoing is a true and complete copy of certain resolutions, and of the Capital Stock Schedule therein referred to, duly adopted at a meeting of the Board of Directors of said corporation, duly and regularly convened and held on ...., 19.., at which a quorum for the transaction of business was present and voting throughout;

(2) That accompanying this Certificate and *identified by the signature of the Secretary or an Assistant Secretary* are:

(a) Specimens of certificates of each class of stock of the Company covered by the foregoing resolutions in the form adopted by the Company, and in case facsimile signatures are authorized by said resolutions, specimen certificates bearing such facsimile signatures;

(b) A signature card bearing the names and specimens or facsimiles of the signatures of all the officers of the Company authorized to sign or countersign stock certificates hereafter issued, and also (where such signatures are available) of all the officers authorized to sign, or whose signatures appear upon, stock certificates, if any, heretofore issued;

(c) A true and complete copy of the By-laws of the Company, as at present in force; and

(d) A copy of the Certificate of Incorporation of the Company, with all amendments to date, duly certified by the state officer having custody of the original thereof.

IN WITNESS WHEREOF, we have hereunto set our hands and affixed the seal of the Company this ... day of ...., 19...

....
President

(Seal)

....
Secretary

DIRECTORS' RESOLUTION APPOINTING SOLE REGISTRAR

(*Note:* This is a form furnished by a trust company acting as registrar.)

Certified Copy of Resolutions
of the
Board of Directors
of
....
a .... corporation.

(1) RESOLVED, That, effective ...., 19.., ... TRUST COMPANY, a .... corporation, be and it hereby is appointed Registrar (hereinafter called the Registrar) for the registration of certificates for the shares of capital stock of this corporation Authorized For Issue as set forth on page 707.

(2) RESOLVED FURTHER, That the Registrar is hereby authorized and directed to register certificates for shares of said stock in accordance with these resolutions (whether upon transfer or upon original issue) only if such certificates (*a*) shall have been signed by or shall bear the facsimile signatures of the President or a Vice president of this corporation and of its Treasurer or Secretary or ...., at the time or previously in office (and shall have

CAPITAL STOCK SCHEDULE

Class	Par Value	1 Shares Now Authorized by Certificate of Incorporation	2 Total Shares Authorized To Be Issued by Previous Resolutions	3 Total Shares Now Issued and Outstanding	4* Balance Authorized To Be Issued Under Previous Resolutions and Not Yet Issued	5 Additional Shares Authorized by Present Resolution	6** Not Yet Total Shares Issued But Now Authorized Pursuant to This and Previous Resolutions	7† Total Shares Authorized To Be Issued

*Column **4** will be the difference between Column **2** and Column **3**.
Column **6 will be the sum of Column **4** and Column **5**.
†Column **7** will be the sum of Column **2** and Column **5**.

		NUMBER OF SHARES		
CLASS	PAR VALUE	AUTHORIZED BY CERTIFICATE OF INCORPORATION	AUTHORIZED FOR ISSUE	OUTSTANDING (INCLUDING SHARES IN TREASURY)

been sealed with the seal of this corporation or bear a facsimile thereof),* and (b) shall have been countersigned by ...., Transfer Agent, or by such other Transfer Agent as may hereafter be appointed in place thereof by resolution of the Board of Directors of this corporation, a certified copy of which shall have been duly lodged with the Registrar; and

(3) RESOLVED FURTHER, That the Registrar is hereby authorized and directed, upon surrender for cancellation of certificates for shares of said stock now outstanding or hereafter issued, to register as Registrar certificates (for the numbers of shares of stock represented by the certificates so cancelled) when such certificates shall have been countersigned and delivered to it for that purpose by the Transfer Agent, and to redeliver such certificates so registered to the Transfer Agent; provided, however, that the Registrar shall not be under any duty or responsibility with respect to the names in which such certificates are issued or the correctness of or authority for any transfer of certificates from one name to another; and

(4) RESOLVED FURTHER, That for Original Issues of said stock of the following classes and not exceeding in the aggregate the number of shares set forth below, viz.:

CLASS (*See Note***)   NUMBER OF SHARES (*See Note***)

certificates may be registered by the Registrar upon written orders of this corporation signed by its President or a Vice president and by its Treasurer or Secretary or ...., under the seal of this corporation; and that the Registrar is hereby authorized and directed, when such certificates shall have been countersigned and delivered to it for that purpose by the Transfer Agent, to register certificates for such number of shares as may be specified in any such written order and, when so registered, to redeliver the same to the Transfer Agent; and

(5) RESOLVED FURTHER, That this corporation immediately advise the Registrar in writing of all original issues of certificates, for shares of stock of the classes covered by this appointment, hereafter made or effected by this corporation or any transfer agent; and

(6) RESOLVED FURTHER, That the Registrar is hereby (a) authorized and directed to maintain records showing the serial numbers of the certificates registered by it and the numbers of shares represented thereby, together with such other records as the Registrar may deem necessary or advisable to discharge its duties as set forth in these resolutions, and (b) authorized to deliver from time to time to this corporation any such records, and any instruments or documents, made or accumulated in the performance of its

---

* *Note:* Strike out words in parentheses if seal is not required.

** *Note:* Insert here only the shares of which an *original issue* to be made hereafter has been authorized, i.e. shares shown in Resolution 1 as "Authorized for Issue" but not as "Outstanding." If no original issue to be made hereafter has been authorized, then this entire Resolution 4 should be stricken out.

duties as Registrar; and further that this corporation agrees to return such records, instruments or documents, or any thereof, when requested so to do to the Registrar; and

(7) RESOLVED FURTHER, That, in the event any certificate for shares of said stock shall be represented to have been lost, stolen, or destroyed (hereinafter called the old certificate), the Registrar, upon being furnished with (a) an indemnity bond (naming the Registrar as one of the obligees therein) in such form and amount and with such surety as shall be satisfactory to it and (b) a duly certified copy of a resolution of the Board of Directors of this corporation authorizing the issue of a new certificate or certificates in lieu of the old certificate and approving (or providing for the approval on behalf of this corporation of) such bond as to form, amount and surety, is hereby authorized, in lieu and without the surrender of the old certificate and without further proof of the ownership thereof, to register (when countersigned and delivered to it for that purpose by the Transfer Agent) a new certificate or certificates for the number of shares of stock represented by the old certificate and, when so registered, to redeliver such new certificate or certificates to the Transfer Agent; and

(8) RESOLVED FURTHER, That the Registrar may, but need not, rely conclusively and act without further investigation upon any list, instruction, certification, authorization, stock certificate or other instrument or paper believed by it in good faith to be genuine and unaltered, and to have been signed, countersigned, or executed by any duly authorized person or persons, or upon the instruction of any officer of this corporation or upon the advice of . . . ., No. . . . ., City of . . . ., State of . . . ., counsel for this corporation, or of counsel for the Registrar; and further that the Registrar may refuse to register any certificates for shares of said stock if in good faith the Registrar deems such refusal necessary in order to avoid any liability either to this corporation or to itself; and further that this corporation agrees to indemnify and hold harmless the Registrar from and against any and all losses, costs, claims, and liability that it may suffer or incur (a) by reason of so relying or acting or refusing to act, (b) by reason of any act or omission of this corporation or of any other registrar or of any transfer agent or of any other agent of this corporation, (c) by reason of the failure of this corporation or of any such person, firm, or corporation to do the acts by these resolutions contemplated to be done by this corporation or such person, firm, or corporation, and/or (d) by reason of any action or non-action taken by the Registrar in accordance with these resolutions; and

(9) RESOLVED FURTHER, That these resolutions shall remain in full force and effect except as altered or terminated by resolution of the Board of Directors of this corporation of which a duly certified copy shall have been filed with the Registrar, but no such alteration or termination shall affect or impair any rights or liabilities based on any action or non-action taken prior to such filing; and

(10) RESOLVED FURTHER, That the President or any Vice president and the Secretary or any Assistant Secretary of this corporation are hereby authorized and directed (*a*) to certify these resolutions under the seal of this corporation and to lodge the same with the Registrar together with the following documents (Nos. 1, 2, 3, 4, and 5 to be duly certified by the Secretary or an Assistant Secretary of this corporation):

1. copy of the by-laws of this corporation as now in effect;
2. specimens of certificates for shares of stock of each class covered by this appointment that the Registrar is authorized to register;
3. specimens of certificates for shares of stock now outstanding that differ in form from and are exchangeable for the certificates for shares of stock of classes covered by this appointment that the Registrar is authorized to register, together with a statement of the terms of such exchanges;
4. list of names and specimen signatures of all officers of this corporation whose signatures may appear on said stock certificates now outstanding or to be issued or who are authorized to give instructions to the Registrar as provided in these resolutions;
5. list of all stop transfer orders filed with this corporation or any transfer agent or registrar thereof;
6. list of names and specimen signatures of the officers of the Transfer Agent who are authorized to countersign said stock certificates, duly certified by the appropriate officer of the Transfer Agent;
7. copies of the Certificate of Incorporation of this corporation and of all amendments thereof, all duly certified by the Secretary of State, or other proper official, of the State of this corporation's incorporation;
8. opinion of counsel for this corporation covering the legality of the issue of said stock and the compliance thereof with the terms of the Securities Act of 1933, as amended; and
9. a certificate as to the number of shares of stock (of each of the classes above mentioned) outstanding immediately prior to the effective date of this appointment, signed by the registrar then acting as such or, if there be none, by the official custodian of the original transfer records of this corporation;

and (*b*) to notify the Registrar promptly of all changes that may from time to time be made with respect to said documents and to lodge with it duly certified copies of all documents that amend or supersede the same.

We, the undersigned, ..., ... President, and ...., ... Secretary, of ...., a .... corporation, hereby certify:

(1) That the foregoing are true and complete copies of resolutions duly adopted at a meeting of the Board of Directors of said corporation duly called and held at ...., in the City of ...., State of ...., on the .. day of ...., 19.., a quorum being

present, and that the same are now in full force and effect and are not inconsistent with the Certificate of Incorporation and By-laws of said corporation as now in effect.

(2) That accompanying this certificate are copies of all documents required to be furnished by the last of the foregoing resolutions, all duly certified, or originals, as therein provided.

WITNESS our hands and the seal of said corporation, this .. day of ...., 19...

(Seal)

....
President

....
Secretary

DIRECTORS' RESOLUTION APPOINTING SOLE REGISTRAR (ANOTHER FORM)

RESOLVED, That .... Trust Company is hereby appointed Registrar, to register certificates for the .... capital stock* of this Company, and

RESOLVED FURTHER, That the Registrar is hereby directed to record in its Register, and sign as Registrar, certificates for not exceeding ..... (.....) shares of ....** when executed by the President or a Vice president and the Treasurer or Secretary or .... and countersigned by .... Company, Transfer Agent, and thereupon to deliver said certificates to said Transfer Agent, and

RESOLVED FURTHER, That the Registrar is hereby authorized to register transfers of said certificates, and to sign and deliver new certificates accordingly when the same shall have been similarly executed and countersigned, and

RESOLVED FURTHER, That this Company lodge with the Registrar (a) specimen signatures of the officers of this Company and said Transfer Agent authorized to sign such certificates, and (b) specimens of certificates adopted by this Corporation for use by it for purposes of comparison and in such use and in relying upon certificates purporting to be such certificates and to bear

---

* If capital stock to be registered is not classified, no insertion is necessary; if capital stock to be registered is classified, the class to be registered should be indicated, e.g., "preferred," or "common," or "common and preferred," as the case may be.

** If capital stock to be registered is not classified, insert "such capital stock." If capital stock to be registered is classified, insert "such common capital stock," or "such preferred stock," or "such common capital stock and .... shares of such preferred capital stock," as the case may be (making proper insertion of amounts of shares).

signatures of such officers, this Company will protect the Registrar until written notice to it that any or all said officers respectively are no longer authorized so to sign, and

RESOLVED FURTHER, That, when the Registrar deems it expedient, it may apply to .... , City of .... , State of .... , Counsel for this Company, or to .... of .... , Counsel for said Registrar, for advice or instructions, and for its action in reliance thereon this Company shall fully protect and hold it harmless against all liability, and

RESOLVED FURTHER, That .... , President, and .... , Secretary, are hereby directed to certify these resolutions under the seal of this Company and to lodge same with the Registrar, together with certified copies of the Charter or Articles of Incorporation and of the By-laws of this Company.

DIRECTORS' RESOLUTION
APPOINTING CO-TRANSFER AGENTS

Certified Copy of Resolutions
of the
Board of Directors
of
....

RESOLVED:

FIRST: That the .... Trust Company of New York, New York, and .... , of .... , and .... , of .... , are each appointed Transfer Agent of certificates representing shares of stock of this Company hereinafter set forth.

Class	Par Value	Shares Authorized by Certificate of Incorporation	Shares Outstanding	Shares Authorized but Unissued
....	....	....	....	....
....	....	....	....	....
....	....	....	....	....
....	....	....	....	....

SECOND: That for the purpose of the original issue of certificates representing shares of stock authorized but unissued, each Transfer Agent is hereby directed:

(a) To record and countersign certificates signed by or bearing the facsimile signature of the officers of this Company authorized by its By-laws to sign stock certificates for not to exceed ..... shares as may be required for the following purpose(s) and upon the following terms and conditions:

. . . .

(Reserve for Conversions, etc.)

and to present such certificates to the Registrar of this Company in the same city as the Transfer Agent so countersigning, for registration and counter-signature, and when so countersigned, to deliver the certificates to or upon the written order of the person entitled thereto.

(b) To record and countersign certificates for shares authorized but unissued and not required for the purposes set forth in subdivision (a) hereof when signed by or bearing the facsimile signatures of the officers of this Company authorized by its By-laws to sign stock certificates in such names and in such amounts as this Company may direct in a writing signed by the . . . . or the . . . . of this Company, and to present such certificates to the Registrar of this Company in the same city as the Transfer Agent so countersigning, for registration and countersignature and when so countersigned, to deliver the certificates to, or upon the written order of, any officer of this Company.

THIRD: That each Transfer Agent is hereby authorized and directed to make transfers, from time to time, upon the books of the Company, of any outstanding certificates representing shares of such stock of this Company heretofore issued and of certificates representing shares of such stock of this Company that may hereafter be issued, and of certificates issued in exchange therefor, signed by or bearing the facsimile signatures of the officers of this Company authorized by its By-laws to sign stock certificates and counter-signed by any Transfer Agent and any Registrar, upon surrender thereof for transfer properly endorsed and duly stamped as may be required by the laws of the state of incorporation, of the State of New York, and of the United States, and upon cancellation of such certificates, to record and countersign new certificates, duly signed as aforesaid, for an equal number of shares of such stock and to present said certificates to the Registrar in the same city as the Transfer Agent so countersigning, viz.:

to . . . . in New York City,
to . . . . in . . . . ,
to . . . . in . . . . ,

for registration and countersignature, and when so countersigned to deliver said certificates to or upon the order of the person entitled thereto.

FOURTH: That said Transfer Agents are authorized and directed to maintain such records as the said Transfer Agents may deem necessary or advisable, provided, however, that . . . . as Transfer Agent in the

City of .... shall be the only Transfer Agent required to maintain stockholders' records showing the name, address, certificate numbers and number of shares represented by each certificate held by each holder of shares of such stock, and are authorized to deliver from time to time to this Company for safekeeping any such records, cancelled stock certificates, instruments and documents made or accumulated in the performance of their duties as Transfer Agents, and further that this Company agrees to return to said Transfer Agents such records, cancelled stock certificates, instruments or documents, or any thereof, when requested to do so, and agrees to indemnify and hold harmless said Transfer Agents from and against all losses, costs, claims and liabilites which they may suffer or incur by reason of the failure of this Company to so return the same.

FIFTH: That it is the intention and purpose of these resolutions that certificates representing stock of this Company shall be interchangeably transferable in the Cities of .... and New York, N.Y. The fact of the recording and countersignature of new certificates, whether by way of original issue or upon a transfer, shall be advised daily by mail by the Transfer Agent countersigning the same to the other Transfer Agents; and each Transfer Agent shall be fully protected and held harmless by this Company by reason of its failure or refusal to transfer any certificate countersigned by another Transfer Agent when it shall not have received notice of the issue or countersignature of such certificate. None of said Transfer Agents shall be in any manner liable for any act or omission of any other Transfer Agent.

SIXTH: That specimen signatures of the officers of this Company authorized to sign certificates of stock, as aforesaid, and of the officers of the respective Transfer Agents and Registrars authorized to sign for said respective Transfer Agents and Registrars, and specimen signatures of any additional officers who may be appointed by resolutions of the Board of Directors of this Company to sign such certificates and of any additional officers who may be appointed to sign on behalf of the respective Transfer Agents and Registrars, together with certified copies of the resolutions effecting such appointments, and specimen stock certificates, shall be lodged with each of the said Transfer Agents to be used by them for the purposes of comparison; and that said Transfer Agents and each of them shall be protected and held harmless in recognizing and acting upon any signature or certificate believed in good faith to be genuine. When any officer of this Company or of the respective Transfer Agents and Registrars shall no longer be vested with authority to sign for this Company or for the respective Transfer Agents or Registrars, as the case may be, written notice thereof shall immediately be given to each Transfer Agent, and until receipt of such notice each Transfer Agent shall be fully protected and held harmless in recognizing and acting upon certificates bearing the signature of such officer, or a signature believed in good faith to be such genuine signature.

SEVENTH: That in the event that any such certificate shall become lost or destroyed, no new certificate or certificates shall be issued in lieu thereof until an indemnity bond in such form as may be approved by the Board of Directors of this Company shall have been furnished. The bond shall be in form satisfactory to the Transfer Agent issuing the new certificate, and each Transfer Agent shall be named as an obligee therein.

EIGHTH: That when any of said Transfer Agents deems it expedient it may apply to the President, any Vice president, the Secretary, or the Treasurer of this Company or to ...., of ...., City of ...., State of ...., counsel for this Company, or to its own counsel, for instructions or advice and this Company shall fully protect and hold the Transfer Agent harmless from any and all liability for any action taken by the Transfer Agent in accordance with such instructions or advice.

NINTH: That ...., President, and ...., Secretary of this Company are hereby directed to certify a copy of these resolutions under the seal of this Company and to lodge the copy with each Transfer Agent, together with certified specimen certificates of the stock of this Company in the forms duly adopted by it, a copy of the Charter or Certificate of Incorporation and all amendments thereto properly certified by the Secretary of State, or other proper public official, and a certified copy of the By-laws of this Company, and from time to time to furnish to each Transfer Agent certified copies of any amendments that may be made to the Charter or Certificate of Incorporation or By-laws of this Company.

We, the undersigned, ..., President, and ...., Secretary of ...., a corporation duly organized and existing under the laws of the State of .... do hereby certify, pursuant to the foregoing Resolution, as follows:

(1) That the foregoing is a true and complete copy of Resolutions adopted at a meeting of the Board of Directors of said Company, duly called and held on ...., 19.., at which a quorum was present and acting throughout, and that said Resolutions have not been rescinded, revoked, or modified and are still in full force and effect.

(2) We further certify that said Company was duly organized under the laws of .... and that under the accompanying Charter or Certificate of Incorporation and all amendments thereto, said Company has an authorized capital stock of $....., divided into:
.... shares of the par value of .... each of .... stock,
.... shares of the par value of .... each of .... stock,
.... shares of the par value of .... each of .... stock,
.... shares of the par value of .... each of .... stock.

(3) That accompanying this certificate are:

(a) True and correct specimens of the certificates of each class of stock of said Company, mentioned in paragraph "FIRST" of the foregoing

Resolutions, which have been duly adopted by the Board of Directors of said Company.

(b) True and correct specimens of the certificates for capital stock or other securities which are convertible into or exchangeable for any shares of any class of stock mentioned in subdivision (a) of paragraph "SECOND" of the foregoing Resolutions.

(c) Signature list bearing the names and specimen signatures of the officers of said Company and of each Transfer Agent and Registrar of said Company authorized to sign such certificates or whose signatures may appear on such certificates for shares of stock now outstanding or to be issued and the names and specimen signatures of officers of said Company authorized to give instructions to the Transfer Agents.

(d) A true and complete copy of the By-laws of said Company, as amended to date, duly certified under seal to be still in full force and effect.

(e) A true and complete copy of the Charter or Certificate of Incorporation of said Company together with all amendments duly certified by the Secretary of State or other public official.

(f) An opinion of . . . ., counsel for this Corporation as to (i) the validity of this Corporation's organization, (ii) its authority to issue the shares of stock called for by the foregoing Resolutions and (iii) the registration or exemption from registration of the stock under the Federal Securities Act of 1933 as amended.

(g) Instructions of an officer of said Company with respect to the sending of advices of original issues and transfers of certificates for shares of said stock other than to co-transfer agents.

WITNESS our hands and the seal of this Company this . . . day of . . . ., 19. . .

. . . .
President
. . . .
Secretary

(CORPORATE SEAL)

DIRECTORS' RESOLUTION APPOINTING CO-REGISTRAR

Certified Copy of Resolutions of
Board of Directors
of
. . . .

RESOLVED, That this Board hereby certified that . . . . and
. . . . have been duly appointed, and are now authorized to act as,

Registrar and Transfer Agent, respectively, of this Corporation in ....
....., for certificates of its stock; and that .... (hereinafter referred
to as the "New York Transfer Agent") has been duly appointed, and is now
authorized to act as, Transfer Agent of this Corporation in the Borough of
Manhattan, City and State of New York, for certificates of its stock.

RESOLVED, That THE .... BANK OF NEW YORK (hereinafter
referred to as the "New York Registrar") be and hereby is appointed Registrar
of this Corporation in the Borough of Manhattan, City and State of New
York, for certificates of its stock, consisting of

Class of Stock:	Par Value Per Share:	Number of Shares Authorized:	Outstanding:
....	....	....	....
....	....	....	....
....	....	....	....

RESOLVED, That for the original issue of shares of said stock hitherto
unissued, the New York Registrar is hereby authorized to register and
countersign as Registrar certificates, signed by the President or a Vice
president and by the $\left\{ \begin{array}{c} \text{Secretary} \\ \text{Treasurer} \end{array} \right\}$ or by an Assistant $\left\{ \begin{array}{c} \text{Secretary} \\ \text{Treasurer} \end{array} \right\}$ of this
Corporation, and countersigned and delivered to it for that purpose by the
above named New York Transfer Agent for not exceeding in the aggregate:

.... Shares of the said .... Stock
.... Shares of the said .... Stock
.... Shares of the said .... Stock

and to redeliver such certificates, so registered, to said New York Transfer
Agent.

RESOLVED, That the New York Registrar is hereby authorized to
register transfers, from time to time, of certificates of said stock, whether now
outstanding or hereafter issued, when countersigned by a duly authorized
Transfer Agent or Co-Transfer Agent and a duly authorized Registrar or
Co-Registrar of this Corporation,* (or, as to certificates of said stock now
outstanding, when countersigned either by a duly authorized Transfer Agent
or Co-Transfer Agent or by a duly authorized Registrar or Co-Registrar of
this Corporation or when signed by the President or a Vice president and by
the $\left\{ \begin{array}{c} \text{Secretary} \\ \text{Treasurer} \end{array} \right\}$ or an Assistant $\left\{ \begin{array}{c} \text{Secretary} \\ \text{Treasurer} \end{array} \right\}$ of this Corporation), and
upon the cancellation of the old certificates, to register and countersign new
certificates for a corresponding aggregate number of shares of the same class
of stock when they shall have been signed by said officers of this Corporation
and countersigned and delivered to it for that purpose by the above named

---

* If the certificates now outstanding are countersigned both by a Transfer Agent and by a
Registrar strike out the matter in parentheses.

New York Transfer agent, and to redeliver said new certificates, when so registered and countersigned, to the said New York Transfer Agent; *provided,* that the New York Registrar shall be under no duty or responsibility in connection with the names in which certificates are issued or the correctness of any transfer from one name to another; or to examine into or approve the transfers of such shares, or the authority under which such transfers are made, or the payment of any taxes upon such transfers, but it shall be the sole duty of said Registrar to register the original issue, as above stated, and register additional certificates only upon cancellation of certificates of the same class and for a like number of shares, but it shall also register any certificate of stock which may be issued by authority of this corporation, in lieu of a lost or destroyed certificate of stock; and

RESOLVED FURTHER, That the New York Registrar's authority shall also extend to such additional issues of said stock as may be authorized by this Corporation; and

RESOLVED FURTHER, That the New York Registrar shall promptly advise all other Registrars of this Corporation of the registration by it of certificates of stock; and

RESOLVED FURTHER, That the New York Registrar shall not be liable to any extent or in any manner for any act or omission of any other Registrar of this Corporation, and shall be fully protected and held harmless by this Corporation for anything done or omitted by it in reliance upon advice received by it from any other registrar as to the registration or counter-signature, for original issue or for transfer, of certificates of stock by such other Registrar, and for its failure or refusal to register the transfer of any certificate registered or countersigned by any other Registrar of the registration or countersignature of which it shall not have been so advised.

RESOLVED FURTHER, That this Corporation indemnify and hold harmless the New York Registrar for any act done by it in good faith in reliance upon any instrument or stock certificate believed by it to be genuine and to be signed, countersigned, or executed by any person or persons authorized to sign, countersign or execute the same; and

RESOLVED FURTHER, That when any officer of this Corporation or of any other Registrar or of any Transfer Agent shall no longer be vested with authority to sign for this Corporation or for such other registrar or for such Transfer Agent, as the case may be, notice thereof shall be given to the New York Registrar; and, until receipt of such notice, the New York Registrar shall be indemnified and held harmless in recognizing and acting upon any certificate bearing the signature of such officer; and

RESOLVED FURTHER, That when the New York Registrar deems it expedient, it may apply to this Corporation, at ...., or to counsel for this Corporation, or to its own counsel, for instructions and advice; and for any action taken in accordance with such instructions or advice this Corporation will indemnify and hold harmless the New York Registrar from any and all liability; and

RESOLVED FURTHER, That in case of the alleged loss or destruction of any certificate of stock, no new certificate shall be issued in lieu thereof, unless there shall first be furnished an appropriate bond of indemnity in form, and issued by a surety company, satisfactory to the New York Registrar, in at least twice the then current market value of the stock represented by such lost or destroyed certificate, in which bond the New York Registrar shall be named as one of the obligees; and

RESOLVED FURTHER, That the New York Registrar may deliver from time to time, at its descretion, to this Corporation, for safekeeping or disposition by this Corporation in accordance with law, such records accumulated in the performance of its duties as it may deem expedient, and this corporation assumes all responsibility for any failure thereafter to produce any paper, record, or document so returned if, and when, required.

RESOLVED FURTHER, That this Corporation lodge with the New York Registrar: (1) specimen stock certificates in the form adopted by the Corporation; (2) specimen signatures of all officers of this Corporation authorized to sign or countersign stock certificates; (3) a copy of the Charter or Certificate of incorporation of this Corporation, with all amendments to date, duly certified by the state officer having custody of the original thereof; (4) a copy of the By-laws of this Corporation, as at present in force, duly certified by the Secretary or Clerk of this Corporation, under its corporate seal, and (5) a copy of these Resolutions, similarly certified.

Certificate of Secretary or Clerk

I, ... { Secretary / Clerk } of ....,

..........., a corporation duly organized and existing under the laws of the State of ....,
DO HEREBY CERTIFY:

I. That the foregoing is a true copy of certain Resolutions duly adopted at a meeting of the Board of Directors of the said Corporation, duly held on ...., 19.., and of the whole of the said Resolutions, and that the said Resolutions have not been rescinded or modified.

II. That accompanying this Certificate, and *authenticated by my autograph signature*, are:*

---

*These instruments MUST accompany this Certificate.

(1) Specimens of certificates of each class of stock of the said Corporation in the form adopted by the said Corporation;

(2) A signature card bearing the names and specimen signatures of all the officers of the said Corporation authorized to sign or countersign stock certificates;

(3) A copy of the Charter or Certificate of Incorporation of the said Corporation, with all amendments to date, duly certified by the state officer having custody of the original thereof, and

(4) A true and complete copy of the By-laws of the said Corporation, as at present in force.

III. That the total authorized stock of the said Corporation is:

. . . . Shares, divided into

. . . . . Shares of . . . . . Stock of . . . . . Par Value each;
. . . . . Shares of . . . . . Stock of . . . . . Par Value each;
. . . . . Shares of . . . . . Stock of . . . . . Par Value each.

That of the said authorized stock, there are now issued and/or about to be issued . . . . . Shares of the said . . . . . Stock, ... Shares of the said . . . . . Stock, ... Shares of the said . . . . . Stock, that such issue has been duly authorized, and that all of the said shares, when issued, will be full paid in the hands of the respective holders thereof.

IN WITNESS WHEREOF, I have hereunto set my hand, and affixed the seal of the said Corporation, this . . . . day of . . . ., 19. . .
(Affix corporate
   seal here)

. . . .
Secretary

. . . .
Clerk

DIRECTORS' RESOLUTION APPOINTING CO-REGISTRARS AND CO-TRANSFER AGENTS

WHEREAS, this Company has applied for the listing of its common stock upon the . . . . Stock Exchange, and, in connection therewith, the "A" Trust Company of . . . . (*City*), ... (*State*), has been appointed the Transfer Agent, and the "B" Bank of . . . . (*City*), ... (*State*), the Registrar for the transferring and registering of certificates of said common stock of this Company in that city, and

WHEREAS, the "C" Bank of ....(*City*), ...
(*State*), has previously been appointed Transfer Agent, and the "D" Trust Company has previously been appointed Registrar of said common stock of this Company issued in .... (*City*), ... (*State*), and

WHEREAS, the "D" Trust Company, Registrar in ....
(*City*), ... (*State*), has previously been directed and authorized to register and countersign, as Registrar, certificates of common stock of this company when executed by a duly qualified officer of this Company, and countersigned by the "C" Bank of .... (*City*), ... (*State*), the Transfer Agent of this Company in the City of ...., State of ...., and to redeliver said certificates to said Transfer Agent, be it

RESOLVED, That said Registrars are hereby authorized and directed to register the transfer, from time to time, of certificates of such common stock, upon the cancellation of certificates for a like amount of said stock, signed by the proper officers of this Company and countersigned by any Transfer Agent and any Registrar, and to register and countersign new certificates accordingly when they shall have been signed by the proper officers of this Company and countersigned by the Transfer Agent in the same city as the Registrar so countersigning; and to redeliver said certificates accordingly when they shall have been signed by the "D" Trust Company and the "B" Bank of the City of ...., State of ...., as Registrars, provided, however, that said Registrars shall be under no duty whatever in connection with the names in which certificates are issued or the correctness of any transfer from one name to another, and

RESOLVED FURTHER, That said Transfer Agents are hereby authorized and directed to make transfers from time to time of certificates of such common stock, upon the surrender and cancellation of certificates for a like amount of said stock, signed by the proper officers of this Company and countersigned by any Transfer Agent and any Registrar, and to issue new certificates accordingly, and deliver the same when they shall have been signed by the proper officers of this Company and registered by the Registrar in the same city as the Transfer Agent so signing and issuing, and

RESOLVED FURTHER, That it is the intention and purpose of these resolutions that the certificates of the common stock of this Company shall be interchangeably transferable in the Cities of .... and .... The fact of the registration and countersignatures of new certificates shall be advised immediately by mail by the Registrar registering and countersigning them to the other Registrar, and such advice shall be sufficient to warrant the Registrar's receiving the same in accepting said advice as conclusive evidence of the registration of the certificates therein set forth; and each Registrar shall be fully protected and held harmless by this Company by reason of its failure or refusal to register or countersign new certificates upon the transfer of any certificates countersigned by another Registrar, when it shall not have received such notice of the registry and countersignature of said certificates, and

RESOLVED FURTHER, That specimen signatures of the officers of this Company authorized to sign certificates of stock, as aforesaid, and of the officers of the respective Transfer Agents and Registrars authorized to sign for said Transfer Agents and Registrars, be lodged forthwith with each of said Registrars and Transfer Agents, to be used by them, and each of them, if desired, for the purposes of comparison with signatures appearing upon the certificates of stock of this Company presented to them or either of them, in their respective capacities, and that said Registrars, and each of them, be protected and held harmless in recognizing and acting upon any signature believed in good faith to be genuine, and

RESOLVED FURTHER, That when any officer of this Company or of any Transfer Agent or Registrar shall no longer be vested with authority to sign for this Company or for such Transfer Agent or Registrar, as the case may be, written notice thereof shall be given to each Registrar and Transfer Agent, and until receipt of such notice, said Registrar or Transfer Agent shall be fully protected and held harmless in recognizing and acting upon certificates bearing the signature of such officer, and

RESOLVED FURTHER, That when any Registrar or Transfer Agent deems it expedient, it may apply to this Company at . . . . (*Street*), ... (*City*), ... (*State*), or to its own counsel, for instructions or advice, and, for any action taken in accordance with such instructions or advice, this Company will fully protect and hold it harmless from any and all liability. None of said Registrars or Transfer Agents shall be in any manner liable for any acts or omissions of any other Registrar or Transfer Agent.

CERTIFIED COPY OF DIRECTORS' RESOLUTION APPOINTING TRANSFER AGENT, REGISTRAR, AND DIVIDEND PAYING AGENT

Resolution of

. . . .
(*Name of Corporation*)

Appointing

. . . . Trust Company

as

. . . .
Transfer Agent—Registrar—Dividend Paying Agent

"RESOLVED, That . . . . Trust Company (of New York) is hereby appointed . . . . for . . . .
(Transfer Agent or Registrar)

. . . .
(*Insert the number of shares and classes of stock included in this appointment*)

. . . .

. . . .

shares of the Capital Stock of this Company to act in accordance with its general practice and with the regulations set forth in the pamphlet submitted

to and approved by this meeting entitled "Regulations of the . . . .
Trust Company (of New York) for the Transfer and Registration of Stock,"
and the Secretary is hereby directed to mark said pamphlet for identification
and file the same with the records of the Corporation, and

RESOLVED FURTHER, That . . . . Trust Company (of New
York) is hereby appointed Agent for the disbursement of cash dividends,
which may from time to time, be declared and payable on the following shares
and classes of stock of this Corporation:
. . . .
. . . .
in accordance with the regulations set forth in the pamphlet herein above
referred to."

I, the undersigned, Secretary of the above Corporation, DO HEREBY
CERTIFY that the foregoing is a true and correct copy of a resolution duly
adopted by the Board of Directors of said Corporation at a meeting thereof
duly called and held on . . . ., 19. ., at which a quorum was present
and acting throughout, and that said resolution has not been in any wise
rescinded, annulled or revoked but the same is still in full force and effect.

AND I DO FURTHER CERTIFY to the following facts:

The authorized and outstanding stock of the Corporation is as follows:

CLASS	PAR VALUE	AUTHORIZED	OUTSTANDING
. . . .	. . . .	. . . .	. . . .
. . . .	. . . .	. . . .	. . . .
. . . .	. . . .	. . . .	. . . .

*(Only stock outstanding prior to appointment should be shown in
column "Outstanding." If new company, the work "none" should be inserted.
If new stock is to be issued in exchange for old outstanding stock, amount of
old stock outstanding and terms of exchange should be shown.)*

The address of the Corporation to which notices may be sent is
. . . .

The persons below named have been duly elected, have duly qualified,
and now are officers of the Corporation, holding the respective offices below
set opposite their names, and the signatures set opposite their names are their
genuine signatures.

NAME	OFFICE	SIGNATURE
. . . .	President	. . . .
. . . .	Vice president	. . . .
. . . .	Treasurer	. . . .
. . . .	Assistant Treasurer	. . . .
. . . .	Secretary	. . . .
. . . .	Assistant Secretary	. . . .

The name and address of legal counsel for the Corporation is
. . . .

The names and addresses of all of the Transfer Agents and Registrars of
the stock of the Corporation are as follows:

CLASS OF STOCK	TRANSFER AGENTS(S) AND ADDRESS(ES)	REGISTRAR(S) AND ADDRESS(ES)
. . . .	. . . .	. . . .
. . . .	. . . .	. . . .
. . . .	. . . .	. . . .
. . . .	. . . .	. . . .

WITNESS my hand and the seal of the Corporation this . . . . day of
. . . ., 19. . .

. . . .
Secretary
(CORPORATE SEAL)

CERTIFIED COPY OF DIRECTORS' RESOLUTION INCREASING AUTHORITY OF TRANSFER AGENT OR REGISTRAR

Increase of Authority of ⎰ TRANSFER AGENT
⎱ REGISTRAR

. . . .
(*Name of Corporation*)

RESOLVED, That the number of shares of the stock of this Company for
which THE . . . . BANK OF THE CITY OF NEW YORK is

authorized to act as ⎰ sole   Transfer Agent ⎱ is hereby increased by
⎱ New York   Registrar ⎰

. . . . shares of . . . . Preferred stock, and
. . . . shares of . . . . Common stock, and
. . . . shares of . . . . stock, and
. . . . shares of . . . . stock.

I, the undersigned, Secretary of the above named Corporation, DO
HEREBY CERTIFY that the foregoing is a true and correct copy of a resolution
duly adopted by the Board of Directors of said Corporation at a meeting
thereof duly called and held on . . . ., 19. ., at which a quorum was
present, and that said resolution has not been in anywise rescinded, annulled
or revoked but the same is still in full force and effect.

WITNESS my hand and seal of the Corporation this . . . . day of
. . . ., 19. . .

. . . .
Secretary

DIRECTORS' RESOLUTION TERMINATING AGENCY OF TRANSFER AGENT OR REGISTRAR

WHEREAS, pursuant to a resolution of the Board of Directors of this Corporation, adopted on ...., 19 .., the .... Company was duly appointed to act as transfer agent (or registrar) of the stock of this Corporation, and

WHEREAS, the said .... Company has acted as such transfer agent (or registrar) continuously since that date, and

WHEREAS, this Corporation desires to terminate the agency of the said .... Company as such transfer agent (or registrar), be it

RESOLVED, That the employment of the .... Company as transfer agent (or registrar) of the stock of this Corporation is hereby terminated, and the said .... Company is hereby authorized and directed to discontinue its services as transfer agent (or registrar) of the stock of this Corporation, and to turn over and deliver to the Secretary of this Corporation all books, documents, papers and records held by the said .... Company with respect to such agency.

DIRECTORS' RESOLUTION RESCINDING APPOINTMENT OF CO-TRANSFER AGENT AND CO-REGISTRAR IN A DESIGNATED CITY

RESOLVED, That the action taken by the Board of Directors at a meeting held on ...., 19 .., whereby the .... Bank was appointed a Co-Transfer Agent for the shares of the preferred stock of this Corporation, for the City of ...., State of ...., and whereby .... Trust Company was appointed Co-Registrar for the shares of preferred stock of this Corporation, for the city of ...., State of ...., is hereby rescinded.

DIRECTORS' RESOLUTION APPROVING BILL FOR SERVICES OF TRANSFER AGENT

RESOLVED, That the bill rendered by .... Bank for ..... ($.....) Dollars, to cover its services in acting as Transfer Agent for the Corporation during the year 19.., is hereby approved and ordered paid.

DIRECTORS' RESOLUTION AUTHORIZING TRANSFER AGENT TO CREMATE ALL UNUSED STOCK CERTIFICATES

RESOLVED, That the .... Bank, as Transfer Agent of this Corporation, is hereby authorized and directed to cremate all unused certificates of stock of the said Corporation now in its possession, and to furnish the Secretary of the said Corporation with a certificate of cremation of the said certificates of stock.

NOTICE TO STOCKHOLDERS OF APPOINTMENT
OF CO-TRANSFER AGENT

To the Stockholders of the .... Corporation:

For the convenience of its stockholders, ... Corporation has appointed the .... Trust Company, ... (*Street*), ... (*City*), ... (*State*), as Co-Transfer Agent. Further transfers of its stock may therefore be made either in .... (*City*) or in .... (*City*).

.... Corporation

Dated ...., 19..

By ....
Secretary

NOTICE TO TRANSFER AGENT AND REGISTRAR OF
REVOCATION OF APPOINTMENT WITH REQUEST TO TURN
RECORDS OVER TO NEW TRANSFER AGENT AND REGISTRAR

...., 19..

.... (*Company*)
.... (*Street*)
.... (*City*), ... (*State*)

Dear Sirs:

We enclosed a certified copy of a resolution adopted at a meeting of the Board of Directors of this Corporation held ...., 19.., revoking your appointment as Transfer Agent and Registrar of this Corporation, to take effect at the close of business on ...., 19... The .... Bank and Trust Company has been appointed Transfer Agent of this Corporation, and .... Trust Company has been appointed Registrar of this Corporation, to take effect on ...., 19... We will appreciate your arranging to deliver the stock transfer records of this Corporation to such Transfer Agent, and the stock register records to such Registrar as soon as possible after the close of business on ...., 19.., in order to enable such Transfer Agent and Registrar, respectively, to effect such transfers and registrations of stock on ...., 19.., as are presented to them.

We have greatly appreciated the cordial and efficient manner in which you have served this Corporation as Transfer Agent and Registrar.

Very truly yours,

.... Corporation

....

Treasurer

BLANKET DIRECTORS' RESOLUTION AUTHORIZING
ISSUANCE OF DUPLICATE CERTIFICATE

RESOLVED, That in the event of the loss, mutilation, theft, or destruction of any certificate of stock of the Corporation, a duplicate thereof may be issued, provided the owner makes a sufficient affidavit setting forth the loss, mutilation, theft, or destruction of the original certificate, and gives a surety bond to the Corporation to such amount as may be determined by the Treasurer.

DIRECTORS' RESOLUTION AUTHORIZING TRANSFER AGENT AND REGISTRAR TO ISSUE CERTIFICATE OF STOCK IN PLACE OF LOST CERTIFICATE

WHEREAS, ..., of .... (*City*), ... (*State*), has made affidavit that he is the owner of Certificate No. ......, issued in the name of .... for ..... (.....) shares of the ..... stock of this Company, and that said certificate has been (lost—stolen—destroyed), and

WHEREAS, the said .... has made application to the .... Trust Company, Transfer Agent, for the issuance of a new certificate for ..... (.....) shares of the said stock and has furnished bond of the .... (*insert name of bonding company*) to indemnify and save harmless the ...., the principal obligee, ... Trust Co., of .... (*City*), ... (*State*), Registrar, their successors and assigns, from and against any and all costs, actions, suits, damages, charges, or expenses attendant upon the issuance of the certificate in lieu of the lost certificate, be it

RESOLVED, That .... Trust Company is hereby authorized to issue, and .... Trust Co., of ...., is hereby authorized to register, a new stock certificate representing ..... (.....) shares of said stock in lieu of said (lost—stolen—destroyed) certificate in the name of the said ....

DIRECTORS' RESOLUTION INDEMNIFYING TRANSFER AGENT AND REGISTRAR UPON ISSUANCE OF NEW CERTIFICATE

RESOLVED, That this corporation at all times indemnify and save harmless ...., its Transfer Agent, and ...., its Registrar, from and against any and all claims, actions, and suits, whether groundless or otherwise, and from and against any and all liabilities, losses, damages, costs, charges, counsel fees, whether in connection with litigation or otherwise, and other expenses of every nature and character, arising from or by reason of the countersignature or registration of a certificate of stock to .... for ..... (.....) shares of the capital stock of this corporation, in place of Certificate No. ......, issued in the name of the said .... for the aforesaid shares, which certificate has been lost, destroyed, or stolen.

(*Note:* Where a corporation issues a new certificate without demanding a surety bond, the transfer agent and registrar will generally require a resolution of indemnity such as the above. The more usual procedure, however, upon issuance of a new certificate in place of one lost, destroyed, or stolen, is to require a bond of indemnity. The above form may be combined with the following form.)

LETTER TO STOCKHOLDER OUTLINING REQUIREMENTS FOR REPLACEMENT OF LOST CERTIFICATE

Stock Transfer Division

Subject: Requirements for Replacing Lost Stock Certificate

Dear Sir:

With reference to our recent correspondence regarding the . . . . Corporation common stock certificate which you reported as lost, mislaid, or stolen, we are enclosing herewith:

1. Affidavit of facts. This must be executed in triplicate before a notary. [If executed outside the state, the notary must attach county clerk's certificate showing his authority to act as a notary.]

2. Indemnity bond. You will find complete instructions as to the execution of this bond on the last page thereof. These instructions must be strictly followed, and any failure to do so will only result in delay in the issuance of the replacement certificate.

When these forms have been completed, kindly return them to the writer, who will submit same to our directors for approval and authority to issue new certificate.

Very truly yours,

. . . .
Transfer Agent

DIRECTORS' RESOLUTION AUTHORIZING ISSUE OF CERTIFICATE IN PLACE OF DESTROYED CERTIFICATE WITHOUT BOND

WHEREAS, ..., owner of record of . . . . shares of the Common Stock of this Corporation, evidenced by Certificate No. . . . ., notified this Corporation on . . . ., 19. ., that said certificate had been destroyed by fire on . . . ., 19. ., and has presented satisfactory proof of ownership and an affidavit setting forth the facts concerning the loss of said certificate, and

WHEREAS, this Board of Directors is convinced that the said certificate of stock was destroyed by fire and that there is no danger of its reappearance, be it

RESOLVED, That this Corporation issue a new certificate for . . . . . shares of the Common Stock of this Corporation, in place of Certificate No. . . . . ., to . . . . without requiring of him a surety bond, and the President and Secretary are hereby directed to execute such new certificate and to deliver the same to . . . .

DIRECTORS' RESOLUTION AUTHORIZING TRANSFER AGENT AND REGISTRAR TO ISSUE DUPLICATE CERTIFICATE

WHEREAS, ... , of . . . . (*City*), ... (*State*), has made affidavit that he is the owner of Certificate No. . . . . . . , issued in the name of . . . . . for . . . . . (. . . . .) shares of the . . . . . stock of this Company, and that said certificate has been (lost—stolen—destroyed); and

WHEREAS, the said . . . . has made application to the . . . . Trust Company, Transfer Agent, for the issuance of a new certificate for . . . . . (. . . . .) shares of the said stock and has furnished bond of the . . . . (*insert name of bonding company*) to indemnify and save, harmless the . . . . , the principal obligee, ... Trust Co., of . . . . (*City*), ... (*State*), Registrar, their successors and assigns, from and against any and all costs, actions, suits, damages, charges, or expenses attendant upon the issuance of the certificate in place of the lost certificate; be it

RESOLVED, That . . . . Trust Company is hereby authorized to issue, and . . . . Trust Co. is hereby authorized to register, a new stock certificate representing . . . . (. . . . .) shares of said stock in place of said (lost—stolen—destroyed) certificate in the name of the said . . . .

EXCERPT OF MINUTES SHOWING ACTION OF DIRECTORS DECLINING TO REPLACE LOST CERTIFICATE

The petition of "A" for the issuance of a certificate of stock in lieu of one heretofore issued, alleged to have been lost or mislaid, was read, and, after due consideration, was respectfully denied, for the reason that said certificate of stock, which is in its nature assignable by simple indorsement and delivery, might now be in the hands of an innocent purchaser for a valuable consideration.

NOTICE OF STOP TRANSFER TO BE SENT TO TRANSFER AGENT, REGISTRAR, AND STOCK EXCHANGES

Gentlemen:

Please be advised that the following stock certificates of the . . . . Corporation have been reported as (lost—stolen—destroyed):

Certificate No.	Class of Stock	Number of Shares	Name in Which Issued
. . . .	. . . .	. . . .	. . . .
. . . .	. . . .	. . . .	. . . .

Kindly record a stop order against these certificates.

Yours very truly,

. . . .
(*Signature*)

PUBLISHED NOTICE OF LOSS OF STOCK CERTIFICATE
AND OF INTENDED ISSUANCE OF NEW CERTIFICATE

NOTICE IS HEREBY GIVEN That Certificate No. ....., issued by .... Company, ... (*address*), for ..... shares of Capital stock of .... Dollars ($.....) par of said Company, to ...., on ...., 19.., has been lost, destroyed, or stolen, and that a new certificate is about to be issued in place thereof.

All persons are warned against purchasing or dealing in said lost certificate, as transfer thereof will be refused should it be presented. Any information with respect to said certificate should be communicated to .... at .... (*address*).

AFFIDAVIT OF FACTS FOR ISSUANCE
OF NEW CERTIFICATE

State of ....
$\left.\vphantom{\begin{array}{c}a\\b\end{array}}\right\}$ ss:

County of ....

.........., being duly sworn, deposes and says:

Deponent is the true and lawful, present and sole owner of the following certificate(s) of stock of the .... Corporation, which deponent believes have been (lost—stolen—destroyed):

Certificate	Class of Stock	Number of Shares	Name in Which Issued
....	....	....	....

Deponent believes that said certificates of stock have been (lost—stolen—destroyed) because:

....
....
....
....

Deponent further states that the certificates were not endorsed, that they have not been pledged, sold, delivered, transferred or assigned, and he does hereby agree that in the event of the recovery of any one or more of the certificates at any time, after the issuance of a new certificate in place thereof, deponent will cause the same to be returned to the Corporation for cancellation.

This affidavit is being made to induce the .... Corporation and the .... Trust Company, as Transfer Agent, to issue new or duplicate certificates to deponent in place of the certificates that have been (lost—stolen—destroyed).

Deponent states that the above statments are true to deponent's knowledge, information and belief.

....
(*Signature of deponent*)

Sworn to before me
...., 19..
[Seal of notary]

AGREEMENT OF STOCKHOLDER TO INDEMNIFY
CORPORATION UPON ISSUANCE OF NEW CERTIFICATE

I hereby agree to indemnify and hold free and harmless the .... Corporation from and against all manner of loss, damage, and liability arising from or by reason of the action of the Corporation in issuing to me Certificate No. ..... for ..... (.....) shares of the capital stock of the Corporation in place of Certificate No. ..... for the same number of shares issued in my name on ...., 19.., which Certificate No. ..... has been (lost—destroyed—stolen). Dated ...., 19...

....
(*Signature of stockholder*)

NOTICE OF STOP TRANSFER TO BE SENT TO TRANSFER AGENT,
REGISTRAR, AND STOCK EXCHANGES

Gentlemen:

Please be advised that the following stock certificates of the .... Corporation have been reported as (lost—stolen—destroyed):

Certificate No.	Class of Stock	Number of Shares	Name in Which Issued
....	....	....	....
....	....	....	....

Kindly record a stop order against these certificates.
Yours very truly,

....
(*Signature*)

FORM OF ASSIGNMENT REQUIRED BY THE
NEW YORK STOCK EXCHANGE

NOTICE: The signature to this assignment must correspond with the name as written upon the face of the certificate in every particular, without alteration or enlargement, or any change whatever.
For value received ....
hereby sell, assign, and transfer unto

Please insert social security or other identifying
number of assignee.
Please print or typewrite name and address
including zip code of assignee:

....

....

....

....

.... shares of the capital stock represented by the within Certificate,
and do hereby irrevocably constitute and appoint .... Attorney to
transfer the said stock on the books of the within named Corporation with full
power of substitution in the premises.

        Dated ...., 19...   ....

                                             (*Signature*)

FORM OF ASSIGNMENT IN CONFORMITY WITH UNIFORM STOCK TRANSFER ACT OR UNIFORM COMMERCIAL CODE

    For value received, ... hereby assign unto ....,
..... shares of the Common Stock represented by the within certificate.

        Dated ...., 19...   ....

                                    (*Signature of Registered Holder*)

ASSIGNMENT OF PART OF SHARES REPRESENTED BY ONE CERTIFICATE

    For value received, ... hereby sell, assign, and transfer unto
............, ... shares of the capital stock of the ....
Corporation, represented by this Certificate, and do hereby irrevocably
constitute and appoint .... Attorney to transfer the said stock on
the books of the .... Corporation, with full power of substitution in
the premises.

    The officers of the .... Corporation are hereby authorized
and directed to issue to .... a certificate for the number of shares
sold, assigned, and transferred to .... as indicated above, and to
issue to the undersigned a new certificate for the remaining ..... shares of the
stock represented by this certificate.

        Dated ...., 19...   ....

                                           (*Signature*)

Chapter 23

DIVIDENDS

Contents—Chapter 23

Definition of a dividend. A dividend is that portion of the profits and surplus funds of a corporation actually set aside by a valid act of the corporation for distribution among the stockholders of record on a stated date, in proportion to their holdings, to be paid on demand or at a fixed time.[1] However, a division of the assets of a corporation among its stockholders may be held to be a dividend, even though there is no formal declaration of a dividend.

For instance, a credit on the books of an informally conducted family corporation has been held a dividend sufficient to support a stockholder suit.[2] So too, when the owner of nearly all the stock withdrew corporate assets it was regarded as a dividend rather than the creation of a debt.[3] But the transfer of a portion of the corporation's earned surplus to its no par value capital stock account was held not to be a dividend declaration.[4] And a corporation's distribution of stock under divestiture isn't the payment of a dividend.[5]

Even though there was no formal dividend declaration and the distribution wasn't intended to be a dividend, it may have that effect.[6] So, for example, dividends may take the form of excessive salaries to stockholders.[7] Or the IRS may consider a corporation's payment of its sole stockholder's legal fees a dividend to him.[8] Similarly, it may treat a purported loan as a dividend.[9]

Classification of dividends. Dividends may be regular or extra and each of these may be divided into three classes—cash, stock, and property. An extra dividend is a dividend additional to the dividends regularly paid. If an extra dividend is paid regularly, it may lose its identity as an extra dividend and become a regular dividend. The

[1]See Mobile v Ohio Railroad v Tennessee, (1894) 153 US 486, 14 S Ct. 968; Sprouse v Com'r of Int. Rev, (CA-9 1941) 122 F2d 973; Intermountain B. & L. Ass'n v Gallegos (CA-9 1935) 78 F2d 972; State v Nebraska State Bank of O'Neill, (1932) 123 Neb. 289, 242 NW 613; Gable v S.C. Tax Com., (1939) 189 S.C. 346, 1 SE2d 244; Byerly v Camey, (1942) Tex. Civ. App. 161 SW2d 1105.

[2]Fidelity & Columbia Trust Co. v Louisville Ry. Co., (1936) 265 Ky. 820, 97 SW2d 825; Brown v Luce Mfg. Co., (1936) 231 Mo. App. 259, 96 SW2d 1098.

[3]Metropolitan Trust Co. v Becklenberg, (1939) 300 Ill. App. 453, 21 NE2d 152.

[4]Adams Elec. Light Co. v Graves, (1936) 272 N.Y. 77, 4 NE2d 941.
See also Black Motor Co. v Com. of Internal Revenue (CA-6 1942) 125 F2d 977; People v Glynn, (1909) 130 A.D. 332, 114 N.Y.S. 460 aff'd (1910) 198 N.Y. 605, 92 NE 1097; In re Reed, (1940) 173 Misc. 314, 17 N.Y.S. 2d 658; In re Price, (1942) 190 Okl. 261, 122 P2d 994; Cobb v Galloway, (1941) 167 Or. 604, 119 P2d 896.

[5]Fulweiler v Spruance, (1966) 43 Del. Ch. 196, 222 A2d 555.

[6]Oilwell Chemical & Materials Co. v Petroleum Supply Co., (1944) 64 Cal. App.2d 357, 148 P2d 720.

[7]Kohn v Kohn (Cal. Dist. Ct of App. 1950) 214 P2d 71.

[8]Jack's Maintenance Contractors, Inc. v C.I.R. (CA-5 1983) 703 F 2d 154.

[9]Williams v Comm. (CA-10 1980) 627 F 2d 1032.

payment of extra dividends and the labeling of dividends as regular and extra are purely matters of financial policy determined by the directors. Still another classification is that into "profits" and "liquidation" dividends. That distinction is mainly important in determining the income tax liability of the recipient; also, whether it's a distribution from earnings or profits or a stock dividend reflecting a dedication of earnings to capital is important in deciding whether the distribution is income to a beneficiary or part of the corpus of the estate.

There are also scrip dividends, but these now are of only historical interest.

Who may declare a dividend. The declaration of a dividend on preferred or common stock and the fixing of the amount, date and terms of payment rests generally in the discretion of the board of directors, acting in good faith.[10] This discretion doesn't extend to the elimination of dividends altogether.[11]

There are exceptions to the general rule giving directors discretion: (1) a statute may limit or control the action of the board. Or the control may be based on governmental administrative action, for example, to limit dividends. (2) The corporate charter, the by-laws, or a contract may obligate the directors to declare a dividend,[12] or may limit their power to do so.[13] (3) A court may in certain circumstances compel the declaration of a dividend when, for example, the directors act in bad faith.

Generally stockholders can't declare a dividend and enforce payment, even if they agree unanimously and take formal action at a legal meeting of stockholders, unless the directors approve.[14] Put another way, they can't preempt the authority of directors by agreeing among themselves to divide profits.[15] But an informal declaration of a dividend was valid when agreed to by all the stockholders and directors of a corporation at its annual stockholders meeting; the dividends were

---

[10]Schuckman v Rubenstein (CA–6 1947) (Ohio law) 164 F2d 952, cert den, (1948) 333 US 875, 68 S Ct 905; Long v Rike et al (CA–7, 1931) 50 F2d 124, cert den (1931) 284 US 657, 52 S Ct 35.

[11]OAG N.D., to Farmers Union Central Exchange, (12–7–39).

[12]Assoc. Grocers of Ala. Inc. v Willingham (ND Ala. 1948) 77 F Supp 990.

[13]Barclay v Wabash Ry. Co. (SD N.Y. 1928) 23 F2d 691, rev'd on other grounds (CA–2 1929) 30 F2d 260, rev'd on other grounds, Wabash Ry. Co. v Barclay, (1930) 280 US 197, 50 S Ct 50; Richards v Southwest Discount Corp., (1941) 44 Cal. App. 2d 551, 112 P2d 698.

[14]Milligan v G. D. Milligan Grocer Co., (1921) 207 Mo. App. 472, 233 SW 506.

[15]H.D.C. Holding Corp. v One Seventy One Realty Corp., (5–20–41) N.Y. S Ct, NYLJ, P 2265.

withdrawn by some, and sought to be enforced by those who didn't withdraw. *Reason:* The corporation was solvent and the action didn't impair capital.[16] Similarly, a dividend declared at an informal meeting of all the stockholders is valid when the directors are also stockholders and rights of third parties or creditors aren't prejudiced.[17] Also a dividend declared by a director who was virtual sole owner of a corporation was valid when the other directors had received two shares each merely to comply with state law requiring directors to be stockholders, and the sole owner performed all acts in behalf of the corporation.[18] A declaration of a dividend by the stockholders can be ratified by the board of directors.[19] Directors aren't disqualified from voting for a declaration of a dividend merely because they are stockholders.[20]

. A corporation can bind itself to pay dividends in the event they are earned.[21] The common way for this to be done is by contract with preferred stockholders. The directors can't make a contract binding themselves individually to vote for a dividend, since they owe a duty to stockholders to declare dividends only when, under the existing circumstances, a dividend will best serve the corporate interests.[22]

Necessity for formal declaration of dividends. The declaration of a dividend doesn't necessarily have to be made by formal resolution at a director's meeting, unless the statute, charter, or by-laws so provide.[23] Courts have held that dividends were in fact declared where no formal meeting of the board had been held and no record was made of the declaration of a dividend.[24] But the better practice is to take formal action in the declaration of dividends by adopting, at a meeting of the board of directors, a carefully drawn resolution, indicating: (1) the amount of the dividend; (2) the classes of stockholders to whom the dividend is payable; (3) the record date for determining who is entitled to the dividend; (4) the date when the dividend will be paid; and (5) the

---

[16]Spencer v Lowe (CA-8 1912) 198 F 961; N.Y. Pa. N.J. Utilities Co. v Public Service Com. (SD N.Y. 1938) 23 F Supp 313.

[17]Kearneysville Creamery Co. v American Creamery Co., (1927) 103 W. Va. 259, 137 SE 217.

[18]Metropolitan Trust Co. v Becklenberg, (1939) 300 Ill. App. 453, 21 NE2d 152.

[19]Quinn v Quinn Mfg. Co., (1918) 201 Mich. 664, 167 NW 898; Adams v Farmers Gin Co., (1938) Tex. Civ. App. 114 SW2d 583.

[20]Metropolitan Casualty Ins. Co. v First State Bank, (1932) Tex. Civ. App. 54 SW2d 358.

[21]Austin v Wright, (1930) 156 Wash. 24, 286 P 48.

[22]Lindgrove v Schulter & Co., (1931) 256 N.Y. 439, 176 NE 832.

[23]Groh's Sons v Groh, (1903) 80 A. D. 85, 80 N.Y.S. 438, rev'd on other grounds, 177 N.Y. 8, 68 NE 992.

[24]Atherton v Beaman (CA-1 1920) 264 F. 878.

medium of payment. Note that no special form of words is legally required.[25]

Advantages of formal declaration of dividends.
Declaration of a dividend by means of formal action has several distinct advantages. These are:

(1) It clearly defines rights of all persons to the dividend and thus minimizes the possibility of dispute between stockholders and their transferees and between the corporation and the stockholders.
(2) It gives directors an opportunity to look into the legality of the dividend.
(3) It allows those who oppose the declaration of the dividend to indicate their dissent at the meeting and to request their opposition to be entered in the minutes.
(4) It provides a record of what was done that can be *prima facie* evidence in suits between the corporation and the stockholders.[26]
(5) It minimizes the possibility of the dividend being declared invalid because no proof exists of formal declaration.[27]

Compelling or stopping declaration of dividend.
Stockholders have no legal claim or interest in the earnings of a corporation until a dividend has been declared.[28] And the declaration of a dividend rests in the discretion of the directors.

Stockholders may compel the declaration of a dividend under the following circumstances:

(1) The contract under which the stock is issued requires the directors to pay dividends to the stockholders in each year when there are sufficient earnings[29]; but not when the directors are left any discretion.[30]
(2) The directors have acted fraudulently, or in bad faith, or oppressively or unreasonably in refusing to declare a dividend[31]; and

---

[25] English & Mersick Co. v Eaton (D Conn. 1924) 299 F 646.
[26] Kelley-Koett Mfg. Co. v Goldenberg, (1924) 207 Ky. 695, 270 SW 15.
[27] American Wire Nail Co. v Gedge, (1895) 96 Ky. 513, 29 SW 353.
[28] Overland Sioux City Co. v Clemens, (1920) 189 Ia. 1293, 179 NW 954.
[29] New England Trust Co. v Penobscot Chemical Fibre Co. (Me 1947) 50 A2d 188; O'Neall Co. v O'Neall, (1940) 108 Ind. App. 116, 25 NE2d 656; Crocker v Waltham Watch Co., (1944) 315 Mass. 397, 53 NE2d 230.
[30] Malone v Armour Insulating Co., (1940) 191 Ga. 146, 12 SE2d 299.
[31] Knight v Alamo Mfg. Co., (1916) 190 Mich. 223, 157 NW 24; Jones v Van Husen Charles Co., (1930) 230 App. Div. 694, 246 N.Y.S. 204; Blair v Bishop's Restaurants, Inc., (1950) 202 Okl. 648, 217 P2d 161; Lydia E. Pinkham Medicine Co. v Gove, (1940) 305 Mass. 213, 25 NE2d 332; Patton v Nicholas (Tex. Civ. App. 1957) 302 SW2d 441.

(3) The corporation has a surplus which it can divide among stockholders without detriment to the business.[32]

The stockholder must allege that the corporation currently has a surplus.[33] That the corporation had a surplus 10 months before the suit doesn't imply that it still has.[34] But a court won't compel declaration of dividends just because a corporation has a large surplus.[35]

The courts won't interfere with the discretion of the directors if they have acted in good faith,[36] without fraud, without abuse of discretion and in a manner that is not unjust or oppressive to minority stockholders,[37] but they don't hesitate to set aside the discretion of the directors if it's found that the directors have acted in bad faith.[38] The complaining stockholders must show that the action of the directors is inimical to the interests of the corporation and all its stockholders.[39]

There is no precise definition of "bad faith". One court listed these as factors to be considered in establishing bad faith:

"There are no infallible distinguishing earmarks of bad faith. The following facts are relevant to the issue of bad faith and are admissible in evidence: intense hostility of the controlling faction against the minority; exclusion of the corporation; high salaries, or bonuses or corporate loans made to the officers in control; the fact that the majority

---

[32]Mitchell et al. v Des Moines & F. D. R. Co. (CA-2 1921) 270 F 465; In re Brantman (CA-2 1917) 244 F 101; Blanchard v Prudential Ins. Co., (1911) 78 N.J. Eq. 471, 79 Atl 533; Hennessey v Reeves-Ely Laboratories, Inc., (1948) 120 NYLJ 108. See also, US v Supplee-Biddle Hardware Co., (1924) 256 US 189, 44 S Ct 546; De Martini v Scavenger's Protective Ass'n, (1935) 3 Cal. App2d 691, 40 P2d 317; Jones v Motor Sales Co., (1936) 322 Pa. 492, 185 Atl 809.

[33]Gearhart v Lee-Clay Products Co., (1941); 287 Ky. 316, 152 SW2d 1003; Davidoff v Seidenberg, (1949) 121 NYLJ 1395.

[34]Steele v Locke Cotton Mills Co., (1950) 231 N.C. 636, 58 SW2d 620.

[35]Marks v Amer. Brewing Co., (1910) 126 La. 666, 52 So 983; Daniels v Briggs, (1932) 279 Mass. 87, 180 NE 717; Ochs v David Maydole Hammer Co., (1930) 138 Misc. 665, 246 N.Y.S. 539; Hopkins v Union Canvas Goods Co., (1932) 104 Pa. Super. 264, 158 Atl 301. See Raynolds v Diamond Mills Paper Co., (1905) 69 N.J. Eq. 299, 60 Atl 941 (court indicates there is a limit to the practice of putting profits back into the business while stockholders receive small dividends); Deough v St. Paul Milk Co., (1939) 205 Minn. 96, 285 NW 809.

[36]Morrison v State Bank of Wheatland, (1942) 58 Wyo. 138, 126 P2d 793; Zidell v Zidell, Inc., (1977) 560 P2d 1086 (giving higher pay and bonuses in family corporation was not proof of bad faith on part of board).

[37]Schuckman v Rubenstein (CA-6 1947) 164 F2d 952, cert den, (1948) 333 US 875, 68 S Ct 905; Schell v Alston Mfg. Co. (ND Ill. 1906) 149 F 439; Daniels v Briggs, (1932) 279 Mass. 87 180 NE 717; Liebman v Auto Strop Co., (1926) 241 N.Y. 427; 150 NE 505; Hopkins v Union Canvas Goods Co., (1932) 104 Pa. Super. 264, 158 Atl 301; Gottfried v Gottfried (S Ct 1947) 73 N.Y.S.2d 692. See Dodge v Ford Motor Co., (1919) 204 Mich. 459, 170 NW 668 (directors can refuse to declare dividend which would reduce surplus below what is needed to run the business).

[38]Spear v Rockland-Rockport Line Co., (1915) 113 Me. 285, 93 Atl 754; Hopkins v Union Canvas Goods Co., (Pa. 1932) 158 Atl 301.

[39]City Bank Farmers Trust Co. v Hewitt Realty Co., (1931) 257 N.Y. 62, 177 NE 309. See also Smith v Atlantic Properties, Inc. (Mass. App. 1981) 422 NE 2d 798.

group may be subject to high personal income taxes if substantial dividends are paid; the existence of a desire by the controlling directors to acquire the minority stock interests as cheaply as possible. But if they are not motivating causes they do not constitute "bad faith" as a matter of law. The essential test of bad faith is to determine whether the policy of the directors is dictated by their personal interests rather than the corporate welfare."[40]

It can be bad faith not to declare dividends during a period of high earnings.[41]

Compelling the declaration of a dividend may not always be a completely satisfactory remedy for a bad faith refusal to pay dividends. For one thing, bad faith can be a difficult case to prove—directors are granted broad discretion in the payment of dividends. Worse, once the dividend has been declared, there may be little to prevent the majority from repeating the offense. If convinced that repeated offenses are likely, courts will sometimes liquidate the corporation but they're extremely reluctant to do so because of the economic waste in forced liquidations, particularly if the corporation is solvent.

A Texas court proposed an unusual remedy for a minority stockholder in this situation. It decreed: (1) A mandatory injunction requiring the corporation and the controlling stockholder to pay a substantial dividend covering past years; (2) annual dividends thereafter; (3) retention of jurisdiction by the court for five years; (4) contempt liability and liquidation of the corporation for violation of the injunction. But the appointment of a liquidating receiver should be the extreme or ultimate remedy.[42]

The converse of an action to compel a declaration of a dividend is one to stop the payment of an excessive dividend or to compel its return to the corporation. If the dividend in question is not illegal it will be allowed to stand, since the court will not substitute its judgment for that of the directors. Thus, a parent corporation that dominated its subsidiary's board of directors was not liable to it in a derivative action for dividends paid by the subsidiary in excess of earnings when the dividends came from surplus profits, as permitted by the statutes of the state of incorporation, and there was no proof that (1) the dividend declaration resulted from fraud or overreaching by the parent, or (2) the parent benefited to the exclusion of the subsidiary's minority stockholders.[43]

---

[40]Gottfried v Gottfried (S Ct, 1947) 73 N.Y.S.2d 692.

[41]Miller v Magline, Inc., (1977)—Mich. App.—, 256 NW2d 761.

[42]Patton v Nicholas, (1955) 154 Tex. 385, 279 SW2d 848.

[43]Sinclair Oil Corp. v Levien (Del. 1971) 280 A2d 717, followed in Singer V Creole Petroleum Corp. (Del. 1973) 311 A2d 859.

Necessity for surplus or profits. The general rule is that a dividend in a going concern (there's a different rule for corporations in receivership or liquidation[44]) may be declared and paid out of profits or surplus only, and not out of capital of the corporation.[45] Most states have a statute expressing the rule. The statutes vary in language, but in substance they provide that the corporation can't declare a dividend that in substance amounts to paying back to the stockholders a part of the capital paid by them for their shares. Thus, some of the statutes provide that the "directors shall not make dividends except from surplus profits arising from the business"; that "no corporation shall pay any dividends except from its net profits or actual surplus"; that "no corporation shall declare or distribute any dividend except from the profits earned by the business"; that "no dividend shall be paid while the corporation is insolvent or that would render the corporation insolvent"; that "dividends may be paid from net earnings or from the surplus of assets over liabilities including capital". This last type of statute has been interpreted to mean that dividends may be paid out of current earnings despite a deficit in the capital account.[46]

Statutes in some states expressly permit the declaration of a dividend from the earnings or profits of the current or preceding fiscal year, even though the capital is impaired, that is, even though there is no surplus. Some statutes allow dividends from this source to be paid only to preferred shares. Such dividends may be barred if the value of the assets is less than the stated capital attributable to shares with a liquidation preference, or if the corporation is or would be rendered insolvent by the dividend. Insolvent here means unable to pay corporate debts as they become due.

The first problem of the directors in considering the declaration of a dividend is to determine whether there is surplus or net earnings legally available for dividends. If there is, the directors can then decide whether, from the standpoint of financial policy, it's expedient to use that surplus or earnings for dividends.[47]

---

[44]Zumpfe v Piccadilly Realty Co., (1938) 214 Ind. 282, 13 NE2d 715, 15 NE2d 362.

[45]Helvering v Northwest Steel Rolling Mills, Inc., (1940) 311 US 46, 61 S Ct 109; Mobile & O.R. Co. v Tennessee, (1894) 153 US 486; Davenport v Lines, (1899) 72 Conn. 118, 44 Atl 17; O'Neal v Automobile Piston & Parts Co., (1939) 188 Ga. 380, 4 SE2d 40; Young v Bradford County Telephone Co., (1941) 341 Pa. 394, 19 A2d 134; Welch v Land Development Co., (1944) 246 Wis. 124, 16 NW2d 402.

[46]Brooks Eqpt. and Mfg. Co. v US (Ct Cl. 1951) 95 F Supp 247; Dohme v Pacific Coast Co., (1949) 5 N.J. Super. 477, 68 A2d 490.

[47]General rule is that undistributed surplus retained for use in corporate business and invested in physical assets can be withdrawn and distributed as dividends. Bryan v Aiken, (1913) 10 Del. Ch. 446, 88 Atl 674.

When may a dividend legally be declared? Generally, a dividend may be declared when a corporation has a surplus. However, what the laws of one state may regard as a surplus, the laws of another may not. Not only do the provisions of the statutes vary, but various interpretations of similarly worded statutes have been made in different states. More recent statutes tend to give detailed descriptions of sources legally available for dividends.

Problems in determining whether legal surplus exists. The problems most likely to arise in determining whether surplus exists legally are:

(1) Must capital stock be taken at its par value, or may it be taken at the actual value received upon the sale of the par value stock?

(2) How shall the directors arrive at the amount of capital represented by stock without par value?

(3) What other items, if any, must be considered as capital liabilities in arriving at surplus or net profits?

Capital stock taken at par or actual value. Must capital stock be taken at its par value or the actual value received upon the sale of the par value stock in determining whether surplus is legally available for dividends? The answer depends upon the statutes and interpretative cases in each state.[48] Courts outside the state where the corporation is organized will look to that state's law.

In most states, capital stock having par value must be taken at its par value. By statute in a few states, par value stock may be issued at less than par in some circumstances, for example, when the directors determine that the stock isn't salable at par. In that case, the amount actually received becomes capital.

More recent statutes usually contain a definition of capital, labelling it "stated capital." The typical statute provides that stated capital equals the par value of par value stock plus the stated value of non-par shares, together with such additional amounts, if any, as from time to time are transferred by the board of directors to capital. If the directors fix the amount of capital of the corporation according to the statutory definition, they may, in most states, consider as surplus legally available for dividends, the net assets (that is, gross assets less liabilities and reserves) in excess of stated capital.[49]

---

[48] Goetz v Williams, (1932) 206 Wis. 561, 240 NW 181.

[49] US v Ogilvie Hardware Co. (CA–5 1946) 155 F2d 577 (all capital stock must be treated as liability in determining whether there is surplus of assets over liabilities out of which corporation (La.) may pay a cash dividend) aff'd, (1947) 67 S Ct 997; Randall v Bailey, (1942) 288 N.Y. 280, 43 NE2d 43.

Example: Upon the issuance of additional stock by a corporation that has an earned surplus, the price may be fixed at a figure that enables a ratable part of the consideration, equal to the amount of the earned surplus applicable to each share theretofore outstanding, to be regarded as paid-in surplus. This has the effect of keeping the surplus available for dividends proportionately the same after the additional shares are issued as it was before the increase. For example, suppose a corporation has capital stock of $100 a share and an earned surplus equivalent to $50 a share. Upon an increase in the stock, the price may be fixed at $150 a share, $100 to be regarded as capital and $50 as paid-in surplus.

Methods of determining legal existence of surplus or profits. The examples given below indicate various ways courts have determined whether surplus or net profits exist for the payment of dividends. As indicated in the preceding paragraph, the method to be used by a particular corporation will depend upon the local law.

Stock taken at par value: A legal surplus exists when there is an excess in the aggregate value of all assets of a corporation over the sum of its entire liabilities including capital stock at its par value. So dividends may be paid when the payment doesn't impair the capital stock of the corporation.[50]

> *Example:* If a corporation's balance sheet shows assets accurately valued at $100,000, capital stock outstanding having a par value of $50,000, and liabilities of $20,000, the corporation has a surplus of $30,000 which, in the discretion of the directors, may be distributed to the stockholders as dividends.

Stock taken at actual value received from sale: A legal surplus exists when there is an excess in the aggregate value of all assets of a corporation over the sum of its entire liabilities, including capital stock not at its par value, but at the actual value received from the sale of the stock.[51]

> *Example:* If a corporation has issued and outstanding par value stock in the face amount of $3,000,000 from the sale of which it has realized but $1,700,000, and its assets amount to $2,500,000 and its liabilities to $300,000, the corporation has a surplus of $500,000 available for dividends.

Under this method of determining surplus, a distinction is made between capital and capital stock. The capital of the corporation,

---

[50] Penington v Commonwealth Hotel Const. Co., (1931) 17 Del. Ch. 394, 155 Atl514; Goetz v Williams, (1932) 206 Wis. 561, 240 NW 181.

[51] Peters v United States Mtg. Co., (1921) 13 Del. Ch. 11, 114 Atl 598; citing Goodnow v American Writing Paper Co., (1907) 73 N.J. Eq. 692, 69 Atl 1014.

which is the amount received by it from the sale of its stock, will not be impaired by the distribution of $500,000 for, after the payment of the dividend, there will remain net assets equal to the amount realized upon the sale of the stock.

Capital stock not deemed indebtedness: The liability of a corporation on its capital stock has been held not to constitute an indebtedness that would be considered in determining whether it might lawfully pay dividends.[52] But that statute defining the source of dividends was a penal statute and thus to be strictly construed.

What is capital stock and surplus when stock is without par value? Generally, dividends can legally be declared only when the corporation has a surplus, that is, the corporation may not impair its capital by the payment of a dividend.

Here is the formula: Surplus = total assessts less the sum of liabilities, reserves, and an amount representing the stated capital.

In calculating the value of its stock, the corporation doesn't have to include the value of stock issued but not paid for.[53]

If the capital stock has par value, the amount of capital stock is readily determined; it's the number of shares outstanding multiplied by the par or actual value per share. What amount represents the capital stock of a corporation having stock without par value? If that amount is known, the surplus is easily ascertainable.

The portion not designated as stated capital is termed "capital-surplus," or "paid-in surplus," and may be available for dividends. The statutes permitting directors to allocate a portion of the consideration received for non-par stock to capital and the balance to capital surplus, usually also give them a limited right to turn back to the stockholders, in the form of dividends, a part of the price paid for the stock. The directors may be prohibited from paying dividends out of capital surplus in the following instances: (1) When not expressly authorized by the articles or the vote of, say, two-thirds of the outstanding stock; (2) when preferred dividends are in arrears, except to preferred stockholders; and (3) when the dividend would reduce net assets below the amount payable to preferred shares on involuntary liquidation.

Corporations having stock without par value must examine the statutes to determine the amount at which the no par shares must be

---

[52] Majestic Co. v Orpheum Circuit, Inc. (CA–8 1927) 21 F2d 720; Miller v Brodish (Iowa S Ct 1886) 28 NW 594.

[53] United Light & Power Co. v Grand Rapids Trust Co. (CA–6 1936) 85 F2d 331.

valued in arriving at surplus. To determine what is capital and what is surplus when no par shares are outstanding, you must check the statutes permitting no par shares and the statutes governing dividends.

Capital is the amount of consideration received for no par shares. To determine the surplus in such a case, you subtract the sum received for the no par stock from the assets.

> *Example:* If the corporation has assets of $500,000, par value stock outstanding of $200,000, non-par stock outstanding for which the corporation has received $110,000, and liabilities of $20,000, the corporate surplus is $170,000.

What determines the portion of consideration to be treated as stated capital and surplus. In most states, the articles of incorporation, the directors, or the stockholders fix the portion of consideration for non-par shares that shall be treated as capital and the portion that shall be treated as surplus. Some states fix a maximum percentage of the consideration that can be allocated to surplus.

The allocation to surplus must be made at or before or, within the time stated in the statute, after the stock is issued. A transfer of consideration from capital to surplus after the statutory period for allocation has expired is void.[54] So, if a portion of the consideration isn't allocated to surplus the entire consideration received is capital.

No provision in the statute for the determination of capital and no stated value required. Suppose the statute doesn't say how capital shall be determined and doesn't require that a stated value be given to each share of no par value stock in the articles of incorporation. In this case, unless some different arrangement was clearly stated to the buyers of no par stock when they bought it, the corporation should treat the full consideration received upon the sale of the no par shares as capital.

Payment of dividends while capital is impaired. Statutes in some states expressly permit payment of dividends from current earnings while capital is impaired. In other states, the statutes say dividends may be paid from "surplus or net earnings" or "net profits." These statutes raise this question: Do "net earnings" and "net profits" mean *accumulated* net earnings or net profits which is the same as earned surplus, or do they mean net earnings or profits *for the current year,* even though there may be no surplus of any kind and even though capital is impaired? In other words, must the corporation make up a

---

[54]Jones v First Nat'l Building Corp. (CA–10 1946) 155 F2d 815.

capital impairment before it pays a dividend, or can the corporation pay dividends from earnings for the current year, even though capital is impaired?

The majority view holds that net earnings or net profits means surplus and that a dividend may not be paid from current earnings if the capital is impaired.[55]

Advances by a director to his corporation to repair an impairment of capital can't thereafter be converted into corporate debts and if the advances do no more than repair the deficiency they can't be used for dividend purposes.[56] But undistributed profits or surplus in any form may be invested or employed in the business of the corporation without thereby becoming "capital," and until such profits are effectually and irrevocably dedicated to corporate purposes through, for example, a stock dividend, they don't pass beyond the control of the directors nor cease to be available for dividends.[57] Nor, unless there are special charter provisions to the contrary, does an accumulation of profits become capital by a mere lapse of time.[58]

Those statutes permitting dividends from current earnings while capital is impaired, usually fix a period beyond which the corporation can't go back in calculating its current net earnings, and add the condition that the corporation not be insolvent or rendered insolvent by the dividend (that is, unable to pay its debts as they become due), or that the assets after payment of the dividend exceed the liquidation preferences of the preferred stock. Some state statutes permit payment of dividends out of current earnings, while capital is impaired, to the preferred shares only.

"Nimble" dividends. Dividends paid out of current earnings while capital is impaired are called "nimble" dividends, meaning that the directors must be nimble in declaring the dividends before the earnings are closed to the surplus account and charged against the accumulated deficit.

Nimble dividends are really distributions out of capital. They can be avoided and dividends paid out of surplus if the capital is first

---

[55] Beneficial Corp. v Reading & Southwestern Street Railway Co. (CA–3, 1950) 185 F2d 238, aff'g (ED Pa., 1950) 91 F Supp 803; Nat. Newark & Essex Banking Co. v Durant Motor Co., (1939) 125 N.J. Eq. 435, 5 A2d 767. *Contra:* Weinberg v Baltimore Brick Co., (1955) 35 Del. Ch. 212, 114 A2d 812; US v Riely (CA–4 1948) 169 F2d 542 (Va. law later reversed by statute).

[56] West v Hotel Pennsylvania Inc., (1942) 148 Pa. Super. 373, 25 A2d 593.

[57] Smith v Dana, (1905) 77 Conn. 543, 60 Atl 117.

[58] Hemenway v Hemenway, (1902) 188 Mass. 406, 63 NE 919.

reduced and the amount by which it is reduced is applied to eliminate the deficit in the surplus account.

> *Example:* Corporation has $100,000 in assets, $80,000 stated capital, $30,000 in liabilities, and a surplus deficit of $10,000. Reducing stated capital to $60,000 will eliminate the deficit and create a capital surplus of $10,000 from which dividends can be paid. Note, however, that this procedure may (1) require consent of stockholders to the reduction of capital, (2) notice to stockholders of the source of the dividend, and (3) permit a dividend of only a certain kind or to only a certain class of stockholders.

Statutes in many states impose penalties on directors for payment of dividends out of capital. If the state statutes and cases don't clearly permit nimble dividends, the directors can avoid risk of liability by reducing capital to eliminate the deficit.

Depreciation of assets. By statute in a few states, the directors must make allowance for depreciation and losses when valuing the assets before declaring a dividend; in other words, the value of the assets must be reduced by the amount of unrealized depreciation.

Under statutes in other states, dividends are prohibited if unrealized depreciation reduces the value of the assets below the liquidation preferences of the preferred stock.

To prevent impairment of capital, an allowance for depreciation must be made for assets that depreciate.[59] In other words, assets, for dividend purposes, may not be counted at cost regardless of present worth, but should be computed with an allowance for depreciation.[60] The amount of that allowance is left to the discretion of the directors. In determining whether a corporation has impaired its capital in the distribution of a dividend a court may look behind the values of the tangible assets as they appear on the books of the corporation. Otherwise, directors could declare dividends out of capital by valuing the assets above their actual worth.[61]

Cases on impairment of capital and payment of dividends must be considered in connection with the kinds of assets involved. Thus, directors have been held personally liable for paying dividends when the current value of inventories plummeted far below cost, impairing

---

[59] People v Stevens, (1911) 203 N.Y. 7, 96 NE 114.

[60] Vogtman v Merchants Mortgage & Credit Co., (1935) 20 Del. Ch. 364, 178 Atl 99; Randall v Bailey, (1942) 288 N.Y. 280, 43 NE2d 43. See also E. L. Moore & Co. v Murchison, (CA-4, 1915) 226 F 679.

[61] Siegman v Electric Vehicle Co., (1907) 72 N.J. Eq. 403, 65 Atl 910.

capital.[62] A fall in the value of goodwill is a loss to be deducted in figuring whether capital is impaired.[63] And a radical, permanent decline in the value of marketable securities should be taken into account.[64]

Absent any legal authority, courts would probably follow accepted accounting practice and not require a company to mark down its securities for a mere fall in current market quotations. But they would require securities to be written down or written off when their fall in market value is attributable to the fact that their investment merit has been permanently impaired.

Impairment of capital in corporation with wasting assets. The rule that payment of dividends must not impair the capital of the corporation is modified when applied to corporations with wasting assets. These are corporations engaged in exploiting such natural resources as coal or iron mines, timber lands, oil or gas wells, or a corporation to hold property having a limited life—like a lease for a term of years—or patents. Such corporations may, in the absence of a contract to the contrary, declare dividends without making provision for restoring impairments of capital and without first providing for a depletion reserve.

A depletion reserve is a sum withheld from revenues equal to the value of the property exhausted in earning those revenues. Unless such a reserve is set up, dividends paid to stockholders are a return of their investment.

Such corporations may regard as profits for dividend purposes, all receipts less costs of production, costs of marketing, and overhead expenses without any charge or reserve for depletion of capital.[65] The corporation may not, however, on the basis of this doctrine, sell its capital assets, one of its mines, for example, and distribute the profits in the form of dividends.[66]

Following the Model Business Corporation Act, statutes in some states let a wasting assets corporation pay dividends out of its depletion reserves, if permitted to do so by its articles of incorporation and if the

---

[62]Branch v Kaiser, (1928) 291 Pa. 543, 140 Atl 498; Cornell v Seddinger, (1912) 237 Pa. 389; 85 Atl 446.

[63]Davenport v Lines, (1899) 72 Conn. 118, 44 Atl 17; Richardson v Buhl, (1899) 77 Mich. 632, 43 NW 1102.

[64]George E. Warren Co. v US (D Mass. 1948) 76 F Supp 587 (federal tax case deciding Maine Law).

[65]De Brabant v Commercial Trust Co., (1933) 113 N.J. Eq. 215, 166 Atl 533.

[66]Excelsior Water & Mining Co. v Pierce, (1891) 90 Cal. 131, 27 P 44.

source of the dividend and the amount paid from the depletion reserves are disclosed to the stockholders.

Wasting assets corporations, having two classes of stock, common stock and preferred stock which is preferred as to assets upon liquidation or dissolution of the corporation, may not, on the basis of the wasting assets doctrine, pay dividends on the class which is not preferred as to assets, if the capital is impaired to such an extent that there is not available for the preferred stockholders sufficient capital to pay them the par value of their shares in the event of dissolution or liquidation.[67] Before paying dividends on the common stock, provision must be made by means of a reserve, for paying off preferred stockholders.

Methods of eliminating a deficit. A corporation cannot declare a dividend if its balance sheet reveals a deficit. However, it may be able to use one of the following methods to eliminate the deficit:

(1) Revaluing assets that have been carried on the books at an undervaluation. An appraisal of all the property may be made and it may be found that some of the property has been carried on the books at less than its value, or the property may be revalued using a different basis. Any one of the following bases are available for the revaluation: (a) original cost less depreciation, (b) replacement cost, (c) value that may be realized at a forced sale, and (d) present market or present sales value.

(2) Converting unnecessary reserves into surplus. Reserves may prove to be too liberal and some of these may be converted into surplus, wiping out part of the deficit.

(3) Reducing capital stock.

Example: If the par value of a corporation's stock outstanding is $500,000, its assets $600,000 and its liabilities $200,000, the deficit of $100,000 can be wiped out and a surplus created by a reduction of the capital stock to $250,000, effected through a decrease in the par value per share or in the number of shares outstanding.

(4) Elimination of operating deficit by charging it against paid-in surplus.

The action of the board of directors in eliminating the deficit must be done under the following conditions in order for it to be legally effective:

(1) The directors must act honestly and in good faith; their action must be free from fraud.

---

[67]Wittenberg v Federal Mining & Smelting Co., (1927) 15 Del. Ch. 409, 138 Atl 347.

(2) The elimination of the deficit must not be effected in a way that is contrary to the provisions of the statute under which the corporation is organized or to the interpretation of the statutes as shown by court decisions.

(3) The action must be justified by the facts.

(4) Accounting Series Release No. 25 of the SEC calls for advance disclossure of all aspects of any quasi-reorganization to all stockholders entitled to vote on matters of corporate policy, and requires that appropriate stockholder consent be obtained. Although this does not have the force of a general law, it is wise to secure stockholder consent before making the action effective.

Since a quasi-reorganization is, in effect, a new start for the business, the books should be changed to reflect this fact. There should also be full disclosure of all the facts relating to the transaction including, particularly, the amount of the operating deficit that was eliminated.

Financial policy determining what part of the surplus shall be used for dividends. Having determined whether, from a legal standpoint, surplus or profits are available for the payment of dividends, the directors must decide whether it is advisable, as a matter of financial policy, to use part or all of that legal surplus or profits for dividends.

Surplus, as an accounting concept, is the amount shown on the corporate balance sheet as the difference between the value of the assets and the sum of the capital stock, liabilities, and reserves. It is immaterial whether the surplus assets are carried on the books of the company as surplus, segregated assets, or in a special fund account.[68] The directors know whether the value of the assets shown on the books of the corporation and in its balance sheet represents the actual value of the items listed. They know whether the property of the corporation has depreciated and whether proper allowance has been made. With a definite dividend policy in mind, and with an intimate knowledge of the affairs of the corporation, they can determine the extent to which reserves should be set up.

If the directors have decided on a definite dividend policy, they can determine what part of the surplus of the corporation should be plowed back into the business of the corporation, and what part they are willing to have the stockholders know is available for dividends. The part of the surplus that the corporation intends to keep in the business is generally termed "Earnings retained in the business" in

---

[68] Hyams v Old Dominion Mining & Smelting Co., (1913) 82 N.J. Eq. 507, 89 Atl 37.

the accounts of the corporation, and the part of the surplus that the corporation intends to use for dividend distributions is termed "Undivided profits." By an analysis of the balance sheet, the directors can determine whether the corporation has accumulated reserves beyond its requirements, and if so, whether the unnecessary reserves can be converted into a surplus to be distributed as dividends.

Dividends from surplus resulting from current earnings or an accumulation of past earnings. From the legal standpoint, as distinguished from the standpoint of financial expediency, the directors can disregard the profit and loss statement, that is, the statement showing earnings for the current year, and may study only the balance sheet to determine whether a surplus is available for dividends, in the absence of statutory, charter, or contract provision requiring or permitting dividends to be paid from current earnings. The balance sheet shows the accumulation of current and past earnings up to the time as of which the balance sheet is made up.

Dividends may be paid from surplus resulting from current earnings or from accumulated surplus.[69] For this reason dividends may be lawfully declared out of surplus accumulated from the profits of previous years, even though there is no profit for the period in which the dividend is paid.[70] A company that for a number of years accumulated profits that had been retained as working capital and as funds for creating greater security for the payment of dividends and for the protection of the company's credit, was held to be making a valid distribution of profits when it declared dividends on the common stock from the accumulation.[71] The company's charter provided that in case of liquidation or distribution of assets, the holders of the preferred stock of the corporation should be paid the par amount of their preferred stock before any amount should be paid to any of the holders of the common stock. The court took the position that the distributions in the form of dividends on the common stock were not a distribution of capital and that the charter provision must properly be interpreted as applying only to a case where the corporation was being dissolved or its entire assets were being liquidated by reason of a merger, consolidation, or other reorganization.

---

[69] Lynch v Hornby, (1918) 247 US 339, 38 S Ct 543; Moran v US Cast Iron Pipe & Foundry Co., (1924) 95 N.J. Eq. 309, 123 Atl 546. See also Nat'l Lock Co. v Hogland (CA–7 1939) 101 F2d 576.

[70] Murray v Beattie Mfg. Co., (1912) 79 N.J. Eq. 322, 82 Atl 1038.

[71] Peo. v Gt. Western Sugar Co. (CA–8 1929) 29 F2d 810.

Determining current profits. In determining profits for the current year, the net results of the year's operations will depend upon whether items of expenditure have been capitalized or charged to profit and loss.

> *Example:* If an expenditure of $5,000 upon a machine which is to last two years, is treated as an asset, the profit for the period will be $5,000 (less whatever is deducted for depreciation) more than it would be if the expenditure were charged as an expense.

Expenditures chargeable to earnings include the general expenses of keeping up the organization of the company and all expenses incurred in operating the business and in keeping its property in good repair. The manner of treating expenditures is left to the discretion of the directors. To determine current profits, there must be deducted from the revenues, the total of the operating expenses, fixed charges such as interest on bonded indebtedness, taxes, depreciation, and costs of maintenance and upkeep.[72]

Analysis of assets to determine if a surplus available for dividends really exists. Directors must ask themselves, "Does the value of the assets as they are carried on the books represent their present value?" They must examine the fixed assets to see that proper depreciation has been taken and that the items aren't carried at amounts representing estimated increases in the value of the physical property. They must examine the receivables to see if the figure at which they are carried represents the amount of collectible debts. They must scrutinize the working assets such as raw materials, goods in process, and finished products to see that the inventories don't include nonusable goods or unsalable goods. They must consider the outlook for prices of materials used by the corporation in judging the value of assets shown on the balance sheet. In times of falling prices, inventory values fall and surplus diminishes accordingly. Assets like patents, copyrights, and publishers' plates should not be carried at large values.

Because of the expense and time involved, the directors aren't bound to revalue assets before each dividend is declared to determine whether a surplus exists.[73]

By statute in at least one state, the directors can accept as a proper value of assets for dividend purposes, the value carried on the books in

---

[72]Corliss v US (CA–8 1925) 7 F2d 455; People v State Board of Tax Commissioners, (1908) 128 A.D. 13, 112 N.Y.S. 392, modified, 196 N.Y. 39, 89 NE 581.
[73]Randall v Bailey, (1942) 288 N.Y. 280, 43 NE2d 43.

accordance with generally accepted principles of sound accounting practice applicable to the kind of business conducted by the corporation, for example, original cost less depreciation for assets like plants and equipment.

"Appropriations of surplus," that is, surplus reserves. The account in the balance sheet, once commonly labelled "Earned surplus," represents the earnings accumulated over the years and retained in the business. Earned surplus is, of course, a legal source of dividends. Yet, the non-accountant and the uninformed stockholder have sometimes thought this account represented an amount *not needed to carry on the business* and so available for distribution as dividends. To avoid such misunderstanding, modern balance sheets give the Earned Surplus account a more descriptive title, such as "Earnings Retained in the Business" (although corporation statutes still refer to "earned surplus" and "reserves from surplus"). Then, to show the directors' intent in retaining rather than distributing this amount to stockholders, the Retained Earnings account is sometimes subdivided into various appropriations—for example, "Appropriated for retirement of preferred stock," "Appropriated for contingencies."

On the modern balance sheet, these appropriations are totalled, added to the capital stock, or stated capital, account and the grand total entered in an account titled "Stockholders' Investment (or Equity) in the Business." This serves further to emphasize the directors' business judgment that this sum should not be paid out in dividends.

The accounts labelled "Appropriations" and shown as portions of Retained Earnings were formerly, and are still by some corporations, labelled "Reserves" or "Surplus reserves" and entered on the balance sheet as accounts separate from earned surplus.

Statutes in many states expressly authorize the directors to create reserves out of earned surplus, or in modern accounting terms, to appropriate or segregate portions of retained earnings for a definite purpose. Some of these statutes say the earned surplus so reserved isn't available for dividends, but then go on to say that the reserves can be abolished in the directors' discretion. Abolishing the reserves would again make the amounts legally available for dividends.

Courts have also upheld the directors' discretion in creating and abolishing reserves. Thus, in an action to compel the payment of dividends to common stockholders in a real estate corporation, the court in denying relief approved the directors' action in creating and adding to reserves for contingencies, mortgage retirement and repairs,[74] and in a similar action against an oil company, another court approved setting up contingency reserves out of earnings when that was the general practice during the war years, although it was eventually determined to be better practice to set up the reserves out of surplus.[75]

Also, the action of the directors in paying dividends directly out of a permanent surplus fund they had created was upheld, although in creating the fund they had prohibited the payment of dividends from it, and although they had never formally abolished the fund.[76]

Secret reserves. Sometimes, through a desire to present the accounts of the company in the most conservative way, secret reserves are created. They may be built up in the following ways:

(1) Valuation of assets at less than their actual value;
(2) Writing off assets that exist and have value;
(3) Charging to expense items that may be charged to the capital account;
(4) Setting up liabilities at amounts in excess of their actual figure;
(5) Setting up potential liabilities that don't exist; and
(6) Setting up reserves for any purpose that are larger than the purpose demands.

Note: The harm done by creating hidden reserves is that stockholders may sell their shares for less than the shares are actually worth. Hidden reserves have the further disadvantage of making it appear they were created to evade taxes or to deceive stockholders.

Sources of surplus in general. The preceding paragraphs are a general discussion of the payment of dividends from surplus. In the succeeding paragraphs, the various sources of surplus will be indicated; also whether each source may be used to pay dividends legally, and whether it should be used as a matter of financial expediency.

Kinds of surplus available for dividends. There are at least four reasons for the restrictions placed upon dividend distributions by corporations:

(1) Since stockholders' liability to creditors is limited to their investment in the corporation, that investment should remain unimpaired to protect the creditors.

---

[74]City Bank Farmers Trust Co. v Hewitt Realty Co., (1931) 275 N.Y. 62, 177 NE 309.
[75]Koppel v Middle States Petroleum Corp., (1950) 197 Misc. 479, 96 N.Y.S.2d 38.
[76]National Lock Co. v Hogland (CA–7 1938) 101 F2d 576.

(2) Distributions to stockholders should be in fact distributions of profits from operation of the business and not a concealed return to them of a part of their original investment.

(3) Each class of stockholders has a right to expect that none of its investment is being distributed to another class.

(4) Prospective investors and creditors should be able to rely on the presumption that past distributions have been distributions of profits, not misleading distributions of the stockholders' investment.

The statutes of every state limit the sources from which dividends may be paid.

Usually, statutes permit dividends from surplus, or net profits, and prohibit dividends that would impair the corporation's capital and dividends paid when the corporation is insolvent or would be rendered insolvent by payment of the dividend. (Depending on state law, "insolvent" can mean that liabilities exceed assets, or that the corporation is unable to pay its debts as they become due, or both.)

Surplus is the excess of the aggregate value of all assets over the sum of all liabilities, including capital stock. Suppose a corporation has assets of $1,000,000, liabilities of $200,000 and capital stock outstanding with an aggregate par and stated value of $500,000. Its surplus is then $300,000.

Modern statutes divide surplus into two major classes: (1) Earned surplus and (2) All other kinds of surplus, collectively called capital surplus. Capital surplus in turn can be subdivided into five classes: (a) Paid-in surplus, (b) Reduction surplus, (c) Revaluation surplus, (d) Donated surplus, and (e) Surplus acquired on merger or consolidation.

Earned surplus. Broadly speaking, earned surplus is the total profits the company has accumulated and retained since it began business. The Model Business Corporation Act defines it as follows:

> "Earned surplus" means the portion of the surplus of a corporation equal to the balance of its net profits, income, gains and losses from the date of incorporation, or from the latest date when a deficit was eliminated by an application of its capital surplus or stated capital or otherwise, after deducting subsequent distributions to shareholders and transfers to stated capital and capital surplus to the extent such distributions and transfers are made out of earned surplus [MBCA, Sec.2(1)].

Earned surplus is the only surplus that results directly from profitable conduct of the business.[77] It's the natural source of dividend

---

[77] See Conine v Leikam (Okla. S Ct 1977) 570 P2d 1156.

payments and is a legal source in all states, by statute or court decision. By statute in some states, dividends may be paid from earned surplus only and, in some states with more restrictive statutes, from unreserved or unrestricted and unreserved earned surplus only.

In many states, earned surplus is an alternative source of dividends with, for example, current earnings, and capital surplus. The various classes of capital surplus are discussed in succeeding paragraphs.

Paid-in surplus. Paid-in surplus is part of the consideration received for the issue of the corporation's shares. In the case of par value shares, it's the consideration received in excess of par value. In the case of non-par shares, it's the amount of the consideration which the directors designate as paid-in surplus before or at the time the shares are issued.

Many states impose no restrictions on the use of capital surplus, including paid-in surplus, for the payment of cash dividends. Thus, when a corporation retired one $175 bond for one $100 par common share, it could pay a dividend on the common out of the $75 difference. This was held not to be capital under a statute barring dividends from capital.[78] Other courts hold dividends can't be paid from paid-in surplus.[79]

Some states have statutory restrictions on the use of paid-in surplus for cash dividends. Two principal reasons for the restrictions are:

(1) To avoid giving a false impression of prosperity. For example, if a corporation has both paid-in and earned surplus, by paying dividends out of paid-in surplus it could leave the earned surplus figure unchanged.

(2) To preserve the backing for preferred shares. For example, unless the practice were restricted, dividends could be paid on common shares out of paid-in surplus created on the sale of preferred shares.

Statutes may permit cash dividends from paid-in surplus only if there are no dividend arrearages on the preferred, or only if earned surplus and current earnings aren't available, and then may permit such dividends only to preferred shareholders on notice to them of the source of the dividend. Further, a dividend out of paid-in surplus to

---

[78] Equitable Life Assurance Soc. of the United States v Union Pac. R.R., (1914) 212 N.Y. 360, 106 NE 92. However, gain from repurchase of bond at discount is not surplus. Dohme v Pacific Coast Co., (1949) 5 N.J. Super. 477, 68 A2d 490.

[79] For example, Merchants' and Insurers' Reporting Co. v Schroeder, (1918) 39 Cal. App. 226, 178 P 540.

common shareholders may be considered a liquidating dividend under some statutes. Payment of a liquidating dividend is even more restricted. For example, the consent of *all* classes of stock may be needed for the dividend, or the dividend may not be payable if, after payment, assets are less than twice liabilities.

In some states, paid-in surplus can be applied to reduce or eliminate a deficit in the earned surplus account, but the consent of the preferred stock may have to be obtained.

Stock dividends can be distributed from paid-in surplus in most states. Yet, a few states require that notice of the source be given to stockholders.

Reduction surplus. The stated capital, or capital stock, of a corporation consists of the par value of all issued par value shares, plus the stated value of all issued non-par shares, plus amounts that may have been transferred to stated capital from time to time. (The stated value of non-par shares is fixed by the directors, or in the articles of incorporation, or by the shareholders, depending on state statute and the articles of incorporation.)

In states where the source of the dividend isn't limited to net earnings or profits, capital stock may usually be reduced to create surplus or to increase surplus in one of the four following ways:

(1) Request each stockholder in a close corporation to surrender a percentage of his shares for cancellation.
(2) Reduce the par value of each share of stock.
(3) Change par value stock to no par value and prescribe a smaller stated value for the latter than the par value of the former.
(4) Reduce the stated value of stock without par value.

Methods 2, 3 and 4 can usually be accomplished under statutory provisions.

When stated capital is reduced, the amount by which it's reduced becomes "reduction surplus." Stockholder consent may be needed for the reduction of capital.

In those states permitting dividends out of surplus without qualifying or defining surplus, dividends can be paid from reduction surplus without limitations.[80]

Dividends can be paid on common out of reduction surplus without first paying passed non-cumulative preferred dividends when, during the years in which dividends were passed, there was no legal

---

[80]Dominques Land Corp. v Daugherty, (1925) 196 Cal. 453, 238 P 697; Graham v Louisville Transit Co. (Ky. Ct of App. 1951) 243 SW2d 1019.

source from which they could have been paid.[81] In *Lich* the court said that the New Jersey "dividend credit" rule that says dividends accumulate on non-cumulative preferred stock during the years in which they could have been paid but weren't did not apply.

But, on liquidation of the corporation, preferred stockholders aren't entitled to have accumulated dividends paid out of reduction surplus; such surplus, after payment of full par value of preferred stock, belongs to common stockholders.[82]

Revaluation surplus. Whether an increase in surplus arising from an increase in the value of the assets owned by the corporation is available for dividends is highly controversial.

Surplus is the excess of the aggregate value of all assets of a corporation over the sum of all its liabilities, including its capital stock. So in order to arrive at the amount of surplus from which dividends may be paid you must determine the value of the assets.

Under conventional accounting practice, fixed assets are valued on the corporation's books at acquisition cost less depreciation; current assets at lower of cost or market value. But suppose the value of the assets has appreciated, although this appreciation hasn't been realized through a sale of the asset. Can the directors enter the appreciated value on the corporate books and thus create "revaluation surplus" from which dividends may be paid? The answer depends on (1) state law, (2) the kind of assets revalued, whether fixed or current, and (3) the kind of dividends paid, whether cash or stock dividends, and whether on preferred or common.

The first step toward an answer is to check the state statutes. Statutes in some states expressly prohibit the payment of cash or property dividends from unrealized appreciation in any kind of assets—others only from unrealized appreciation in fixed assets. Statutes in other states expressly or impliedly permit the payment of *stock* dividends from unrealized appreciation, but may require that stockholders be notified of the source of the dividend.

Court decisions are confusing. Many concern impairing capital by overcapitalization or fictitious writeup of assets, not actual appreciation in a general rise in prices.[83] But generally courts have accepted the common law rule that unrealized appreciation in the value of fixed assets is not available for dividends.[84]

---

[81]Lich v US Rubber Co. (CA–3 1941) 123 F2d 145 (N.J. law).
[82]Hull v Pfister & Vogel Leather Co., (1940) 235 Wis. 653, 290 NW 18.
[83]Southern California Home Builders v Young, (1920) 45 Cal. App. 679, 188 P 586; Coleman v Booth, (1916) 268 Mo. 64, 186 SW 1021.
[84]Berks Broadcasting Co. v Craumer, (1947) 356 Pa. 620, 5 A2d 571.

An increase in the market price of the corporation's inventories would not be a proper source of dividends.[85]

Profits realized from the sale of capital assets—unless the company is in liquidation—enter into earnings or surplus accounts and are a proper source of dividends.[86] Cash or property dividends can also be paid from unrealized appreciation in the value of fixed assets;[87] stock dividends can be paid from revaluation surplus.[88]

Donated surplus. This results from a contribution to the corporation of money or property. An example is the contribution by a city of cash or a plant site to induce a corporation to locate there.

Sometimes these contributions are called "capital contributions". By statute in at least one state, they constitute capital surplus. In either event, the contribution increases assets without a corresponding increase in liabilities and, therefore, increases the surplus account. But, since this surplus was not derived from the operation of the business, it is capital surplus rather than earned surplus. If dividends are paid from donated surplus, the payment is subject to the same limitations as any from capital surplus.

Surplus on merger or consolidation. By statute in many states, surplus available for dividends in each of the constituent corporations just before a merger or consolidation stays available for payments by the surviving or new corporation, to the extent it isn't transferred to stated capital.

By statute in many states, surplus available for dividends in each of the constituent corporations immediately prior to the merger or consolidation, continues to be available for payments by the surviving or new corporation, to the extent it isn't transferred to stated capital.

General accounting practice treats surplus differently depending on whether the merger or consolidation was a "pooling of interests" or a "purchase." Some factors in a pooling of interest are these: The equity interests in the predecessor corporation continue as such in the surviving corporation and in substantially the same proportions. So do voting rights. The influence of the management of a predecessor corporation also remains significant in the surviving corporation.

---

[85]Sexton v C. L. Percival Co., (1920) 189 Iowa 586, 177 NW 83; Hill v International Products Co., (1925) 129 Misc. 25, 220 N.Y.S. 711.

[86]National Newark & Essex Banking Co. v Durant Motor Co., (1939) 125 N.J. Eq. 435; 5 A2d 767.

[87]Randall v Bailey, (1942) 288 N.Y. 280; 43 NE2d 43.

[88]State v Bray, (1929) 323 Mo. 562, 20 SW2d 56; Northern Bank & Trust Co. v Day, (1951) 83 Wash. 296, 145 P 182; *Contra,* Cole v Adams (Tex. Civ. App. 1898) 49 SW 1052.

As a basic principle, in a pooling of interests the combined earned surpluses and deficits of the constituent corporations can be carried forward to the surviving company. But it would be inappropriate to eliminate the deficit of one constituent against its capital surplus and to carry forward the earned surplus of another constituent. Also, if the stated capital of the new or surviving corporation is less than the total stated capitals of the constituent corporations, the difference is capital surplus of the new corporation.

If the transaction is a purchase, the assets purchased are entered on the books of the acquiring corporation at acquisition cost so there would be no surplus of the constituent corporation that could be carried forward.

Miscellaneous items of surplus as sources of dividends. *Interest:* A corporation may not consider as available for dividends, interest that has matured upon a loan by the corporation, but that hasn't been paid, regardless of how certain the corporation is to collect the amount.[89]

Under a statute that allows corporations to pay dividends from "net earnings," a corporation must deduct interest charges from earnings to arrive at net earnings.[90]

Estimated profits: A corporation can't regard profits estimated to accrue ultimately from partially executed contracts as available for dividends.[91]

> *Example:* Under both the N.Y. and N.J. corporation laws, anticipated profits couldn't be deemed surplus for dividend purposes.[92]

On the other hand, there would seem to be no reason why profits, actually earned but not yet appearing on the corporate books, shouldn't be taken into consideration in determining the existence of a surplus legally available for dividends. It is not necessary to wait until the close of the fiscal year to write up actually earned profits so as to have them available as surplus for dividends. Such profits may be calculated on a monthly, quarterly, or other basis, the surplus written up accordingly and a balance sheet prepared that shows such surplus available for dividends.

---

[89]Southern Cal. Home Builders v Young, (1920) 45 Cal. App. 679, 188 P 586; Hill v International Products Co., (1925) 129 Misc. 25, 220 N.Y.S. 711.

[90]Coast Cities Coaches v Whyte (Fla. Dist. Ct of App. 1958) 102 S2d 848.

[91]Southern Cal. Home Builders v Young, (1920) Cal. App. 679, 188 P 586.

[92]Hutchinson v Curtiss, (1904) 45 Misc. 484, 92 N.Y.S. 70.

Interests in and profits upon sale of stock of other corporations: Such a profit is available for dividends.[93] However, the undistributed earnings of a wholly owned subsidiary weren't part of its parent's net income available under formula for declaring dividends on its preferred stock when the subsidiary kept its own records and the I.C.C. had barred its merger with the parent.[94]

Whether directors should pay dividends as a matter of financial expediency. Once the directors decide they can legally declare and pay a dividend, they are faced with the question whether as a business matter they should. Here are some factors they must consider:

Dividends from capital surplus: Even though directors legally can pay dividends from capital surplus, before doing so they should check the effect of such a dividend on the corporation's financial reputation and credit standing. Creditors may expect that the corporation retain its stockholders' investment unimpaired, whether that investment be labeled Stated Capital, Capital Surplus, or whatever.

Maintaining cash and working capital position: Whatever the source of the dividend—earned surplus or capital surplus—a cash dividend must be paid from money in the bank. So the corporation must have enough cash after the dividend to maintain its cash and working capital position.

It's possible for a corporation to borrow money to pay a dividend. (Actually, it would borrow the money for operating purposes and then use regular cash receipts for the dividend.) But because the need to borrow would itself be evidence of a possibly dangerous cash shortage and because the interest on the loan would add a further burden on the corporation's finances, this procedure would be unusual.

Retaining earnings for expansion: When a corporation is young and growing, retained earnings may be the only feasible source of funds for expansion. Needed capital may be obtainable from outside sources only at very high cost, and additional common stock may be salable only at a price lower than the stock's worth to present common stockholders.

Market price per share: Directors who encourage a "growth company" reputation tend to set dividend payouts at low levels. The appeal of growth to an investor is in the expectation that compounding

---

[93] Equitable Life Assur. Society v Union Pac. R. Co., (1914) 212 N.Y. 360, 106 NE 92, aff'g 162 A.D. 81, 147 N.Y.S. 382.

[94] Kern v Chi. & E. Ill. R. Co., (1972) 6 Ill. App. 3d 247, 285 NE2d 501. To same effect, Cintas v Amer. Car & Foundry Co., (1942) 132 N.J. Eq. 460, 28 A2d 531.

the return on retained earnings at a high rate will increase his investment per share. Market price of the stock reflects this expectation. The price of growth stocks is usually volatile and over the long term it is expected to increase more than enough to offset the loss of current dividend income.

Effect of federal tax law: Under the federal tax law, retention of earnings beyond the reasonable needs of the business will mean the imposition of an almost confiscatory penalty tax on the earnings. Purpose is to discourage stockholders, especially in close corporations, from leaving the earnings in the business so they can avoid paying a personal income tax on dividend payments to them. See P-H *Federal Taxes.*

Regular dividend policy: A policy of regular payment of dividends can have these effects: (1) It may make it easier for the corporation to issue additional stock in the future. Prospective investors may place more confidence in a corporation with a record of regular dividend payments than in one with an erratic dividend record; (2) It may improve the company's cash standing and stabilize or increase the market price of the stock; and (3) It can strengthen the present stockholders' confidence in management.

Multiple classes of stock. When a corporation has more than one class of stock, the declaration and payment of dividends calls for particularly careful analysis of the corporate financial position.

Right of preferred stock to dividends. The rights and preferences of the holders of one class of stock over another in respect to dividends depend upon the terms of the contract between the holders of the different classes of stock. The terms of the contract between the corporation and the stockholders and between the stockholders of one class and stockholders of another class may be found in the statute, the articles of incorporation, by-laws, the certificate of stock, and, in some cases, in resolutions passed by the directors when the statute or charter gives them the power to fix the preferences of stock by resolution.[95]

Stock described merely as preferred "means only a stock that differs from other stock in having a preference of some sort attached to it, without expressing the special nature of the preference."[96] If no description of preferences is indicated, the designation of stock as

---

[95] O'Neal v Automobile Piston & Parts Co., (1939) 180 Ga. 380, 4 SE2d 40; Whitney v Puro Filter Corp., (1933) 63 F2d 811; Harr v Pioneer Mechanical Corp. (CA–2 1933) 65 F2d 332.
[96] Scott v Baltimore & O. R. Co., (1902) 93 Md. 475, 49 Atl 327.

"preferred" is ineffectual, and the shares are treated the same as common stock.[97]

If a fixed dividend is guaranteed it's a preferred dividend, though not so expressed.[98] Holders of stock designated as "preferred" entitled "to the payment of $6 per share semi-annually" are preferred over other stockholders; it's not essential to the creation of a preference that there be an express provision that the preferred dividend shall be paid before any dividend is paid on other classes of stock.[99]

Elimination of dividend arrearages on preferred stock. Sometimes accrued but undeclared dividends on preferred stock accumulate to a point that the corporation considers unduly burdensome or restrictive of corporate financial policy. The question then becomes, can the corporation eliminate or cancel the arrearages without paying them?

Statutes in several states expressly permit the corporation to eliminate the arrearages by amendment of its articles. The amendment might take the form, for example, of converting the preferred with arrearages into a new class of preferred, or into common, or into a combination of securities.

But when there is no express statutory authority, courts differ as to whether the arrearages can be eliminated by amendment of the articles. Some states hold the right to accrued dividends is a vested right that can't be divested.[100]

Others say that a provision in the statute or articles giving the stockholders the power to change the rights and preferences of the preferred includes the power to eliminate accrued undeclared dividends by amendment of the articles,[101] *except* when the preferred stock was issued before the enactment of the statute authorizing the elimination of arrearages.[102]

---

[97]Rice & Hutchins, Inc. v Triplex, (1929) 16 Del. Ch. 298, 147 Atl 317.

[98]Boardman v Lake Shore Ry. Co., (1881) 84 N.Y. 157.

[99]Bates v Androscoggin R.R. Co., (1860) 49 Me. 491. Holders of shares with limited priority until dividends amounting to a fixed figure per share have been received cannot, after receiving the amount determined, object to equality of treatment in respect of further dividends. Whitney v Puro Filter Corp. (CA–2 1933) 63 F2d 811.

[100]Consolidated Film Ind. v Johnson, (1937) 22 Del. 407, 197 Atl 489; Patterson v Durham Hosiery Mills, (1939) 214 N.C. 806, 200 SE 906.

[101]McQuillen v Nat'l Cash Register Co. (CA–4 1940) 112 F2d 877, cert den, 311 US 695, 61 S Ct 140; O'Brien v Socony Mobil Oil Company, (1967) 207 Va. 707, 152 SE2d 278.

[102]Wheatley v A. I. Root Co., (1946) 147 Ohio St. 127, 69 NE2d 187; Wessel v Guantanamo Sugar Co., (1944) 135 N.J. Eq. 506, 39 A2d 431; Schaad v Hotel Easton Co., (1952) 369 Pa. 486, 87 A2d 227.

In states prohibiting elimination of dividend arrearages by amendment of the articles, the same result can be effected by a merger with a wholly-owned subsidiary,[103] even a subsidiary created for that very purpose,[104] providing there is no fraud or unfairness so great as to amount to fraud.[105]

> **Note:** Eliminating dividend arrearages by merger means in many states that dissenting preferred stockholders must be paid the appraised value of their shares; this is not so in the case of a charter amendment. However, in some states dissenting stockholders needn't be paid for their shares when the merger is between a parent and its wholly- or 95 percent-owned subsidiary.

Holders of preferred stock with dividend arrearages can sometimes be persuaded to voluntarily surrender their claims. This is done by creating an issue of prior preferred to be offered in exchange for the old preferred and its arrearages. Those who elect not to make the exchange retain their rights to the arrears, but the likelihood of payment of those arrears has been reduced. Courts have upheld plans of this type.[106]

Again a corporation can change preferred into common stock; but it can't use that as a device to extinguish preferred stockholders' right to be paid cumulative dividends in arrears.[107]

Holders of preferred stock may waive their right to accrued dividends by contract[108] or by participation in recapitalization plan.[109]

A court will enjoin a plan for elimination of dividend arrearages by charter amendment that is unfair to the preferred stockholders, even though it is legal in all respects.[110] But such a plan isn't absolutely

---

[103] Federal United Corp. v Havender, (1940) 24 Del. Ch. 318, 11 A2d 331.

[104] Hottenstein v York Ice Machine Corp. (CA–3 1943) 136 F2d 944.

[105] MacCrone v American Capital Corp. (D Del. 1943) 51 F Supp 462; Zobel v American Locomotive Co., (1943) 182 Misc. 323, 44 N.Y.S.2d 33; Anderson v Cleveland-Cliffs Iron Co. (Ohio Com. Pl. 1948) 87 NE2d 384.

[106] Shanik v White Sewing Machine Corp., (1940) 25 Del. Ch. 371, 19 A2d 831; Johnson v Fuller (CA–3 1941) 121 F2d 618, cert den, (1941) 314 US 681, 62 S Ct 184; Francke v Axton-Fisher Tobacco Co., (1942) 289 Ky. 687, 160 SW2d 23. See also In re Community Power & Light Co. (SD, N.Y. 1940) 33 F Supp 901. *Contra,* Patterson v Durham Hosiery Mills, (1939) 214 N.C. 806, 200 S.E. 906.

[107] Wessel v Guantanamo Sugar Co., (1944) 134 N.J. Eq. 271, 35 A2d 215, aff'd, (1934) 135 N.J. Eq. 506, 39 A2d 431.

[108] Philip Morris & Co., Ltd. v Stephano Bros., (1938) 331 Pa. 278, 200 A2d 605.

[109] Gidwitz v Armour & Co. (Ill. App. 1939) 20 NE2d 175.

[110] Kamena v Janssen Dairy Corp., (1943) 133 N.J. Eq. 214, 31 A2d 200, aff'd, (1944) 134 N.J. Eq. 359, 35 A2d 894.

void and a stockholder may be barred from equitable relief by acquiescence and delay.[111]

Must directors pay preferred dividends? The rule that dividends must be paid only when there are surplus profits or net earnings applies to preferred as well as to common stock.[112] Thus, an express agreement to pay preferential dividends whether or not profits sufficient for the purpose have been earned, is *ultra vires;* dividends paid when the corporation has no earnings would be a return of capital.[113] The preferred dividend isn't a guaranteed debt; it's merely a right to a dividend from the earnings and income of the corporation. The obligation and right to declare it doesn't arise until there is a fund from which it can properly be made.[114]

Similarly the rule that the declaration of a dividend rests in the discretion of the board of directors applies to preferred as well as to common stock.[115] The fact that the corporation has guaranteed dividends on preferred stock under a statute permitting the guaranty of cumulative dividends payable out of net profits, doesn't require the directors to declare a dividend out of net profits when in their judgment the corporation's business and financial condition doesn't warrant it.[116] Nor does the fact that profits sufficient to pay a preferential dividend have been earned, if in the directors' honest judgment, such a declaration wouldn't be for the best interest of all concerned. A provision that the preferential dividends shall be dependent on the profits of each particular year doesn't obligate the directors to declare dividends.[117] Similarly a provision in the articles of incorporation that the preferred stock shall be entitled to dividends out of the net profits of the company as determined by the directors doesn't mean that if there are net profits they must be distributed in any event without regard to the condition of the company.[118]

---

[111] Romer v Porcelain Products, Inc., (1938) 23 Del. Ch. 52, 2 A2d 75; Bay Newfoundland Co. v Wilson & Co., (1939) 24 Del. Ch. 30, 4 A2d 668. To same effect, Langfelder v Universal Laboratories, Inc. (Del. law) (CA-3 1947) 163 F2d 804.

[112] N. Y. L. E. & W. R. R. Co. v Nickals, (1886) 119 US 296, 7 S Ct 209; Hazel Atlas Glass Co. v Van Dyk & Reeves, Inc. (CA-2 1925) F2d 716.

[113] Lockhart v Van Alstyne, (1875) 31 Mich. 76; Castorland Milk & Cheese Co. v Shantz (S Ct 1919) 179 N.Y.S. 131; Guaranty Mtge. Co. v Flint, (1925) 66 Utah 128, 240 P 175.

[114] Peoples-Pittsburgh Trust Co. v US (WD Pa. 1944) 54 F Supp 742.

[115] Morse v Boston & M. R. R., (1928) 263 Mass. 308, 160 NE 894; Bassett v United States Cast Iron Pipe & Foundry Co., (1909) 75 N.J. Eq. 539, 73 Atl 514.

[116] Collins v Portland Electric Co. (CA-9 1926) 12 F2d 671.

[117] Hasset v S. F. Iszard Co. (S Ct 1945) 61 N.Y.S.2d 451.

[118] Fernald v Frank Ridlon Co., (1923) 246 Mass. 64, 140 NE 421.

A certificate may be so drawn as to entitle preferred stockholders to the payment of dividends whenever the corporation makes a profit.[119] Here are several instances where the corporation was compelled to pay dividends in years when there were net profits:

(1) A provision in the certificate of preferred stock and in the certificate of incorporation that the holders of preferred stock are "entitled to dividends, not to exceed 6 percent, payable semi-annually, not cumulative, whenever in any year the net earnings after payment of all interest charges, suffice for the payment thereof," gives the preferred stockholders the right to dividends if the earnings of the corporation in each year exceed the expenses, and this right doesn't depend upon a declaration of the dividend by the board of directors.[120]

(2) Where a by-law provided that the preferred carried a 6 percent per annum noncumulative dividend, payable semi-annually on January 1 and July 1 of each year out of the net profits of the preceding year, and a lesser dividend if the profits were less, the directors had to pay a dividend on the preferred stock whenever in any year there were net profits available.[121]

(3) An agreement that the "preferred stock shall be paid (if earned) 10 percent dividends payable annually, 2 and one-half percent quarterly," means that the holders of the preferred stock should be paid the stipulated return whenever earned, or, if not earned, then out of assets at dissolution.[122]

(4) Corporate by-law provided "Second preferred stock * * * shall be entitled to dividends of 7 percent per annum and no more, payable quarterly * * *. Such dividends shall be cumulative * * *." Held, directors' discretion to declare or withhold dividends was controlled by this preferred stock contract which entitled stockholders to dividends, if earned, as a matter of right.[123]

Right of preferred stock to participate in surplus. Preferred stock can be "participating." This means that after it receives its agreed dividend in any given year, it shares with the common in further distributions of profits for that year.

Cumulative and non-cumulative preferred stock. Dividends upon preferred stock can be either cumulative or non-cumulative. If the dividends are cumulative, either expressly or impliedly, it means that if the specified rate upon preferred isn't paid in one year, an arrearage

[119]Hastings v International Paper Co., (1919) 187 App. Div. 404, 175 N.Y.S. 815.
[120]Wood v Lary, (1888) 47 Hun 550, appeal dismissed, 124 N.Y. 83, 26 NE 338.
[121]Burk v Ottawa Gas & Electric Co., (1912) 87 Kan. 6, 123 P 857.
[122]Langben v Goodman, (1925) Tex. Civ. App. 275 SW 843.
[123]New England Trust Co. v Penobscot Chemical Fibre Co., (1947) 142 Me. 286, 50 A2d 188.

arises that must be made up in subsequent years before any dividends can be declared on the common stock.[124] If the contract with the preferred stockholders says nothing as to whether dividends shall be cumulative or non-cumulative, but entitles the preferred stockholders to a certain annual dividend and doesn't make the dividends payable in each year dependent upon the profits of that year, the dividends are cumulative.[125]

If the preferred stock is non-cumulative and dividends haven't been declared upon the stock, the dividends omitted in any year don't accumulate and need not be made up, even though earned for the year in which the dividend has been omitted. The United States Supreme Court has said:

> We believe that it has been the common understanding of lawyers and business men that in the case of non-cumulative stock entitled only to a dividend if declared out of annual profits, if those profits are justifiably applied by the directors to capital improvements and no dividend is declared within the year, the claim for that year is gone and cannot be asserted at a later date.[126]

The declaration of dividends earned on non-cumulative preferred stock is within the directors' discretion and courts won't interfere as long as the directors don't abuse their discretion.[127]

But dividends on non-cumulative participating preferred stock payable out of annual net earnings, earned but not declared and paid in a particular year, may be distributed in a subsequent year.[128] And payment of balance of dividends on non-cumulative preferred stock is legal when funds for payment in full were available in prior years and dividends were partially paid in that year.[129]

"Dividend credit" rule: This rule states that when dividends on non-cumulative preferred stock are passed (not declared) in a year in which corporate earnings were sufficient to have paid them, the

---

[124]Cintas v American Car & Foundry Co., (1942) 131 N.J.Eq. 419, 25 A2d 418, aff'd, (1942) 132 N.J.Eq. 460, 28 A2d 531.

[125]Hazel Atlas Glass Co. v Van Dyk & Reeves, Inc. (CA–2 1925) 8 F2d 716; In re Louisville Gas & Electric Co. (D Del. 1948) 77 F Supp 176; Cotting v N. Y. & N. E. R. Co., (1886) 54 Conn. 156, 5 Atl 851.

[126]Wabash Ry. Co. v Barclay, (1930) 280 US 17, 50 S Ct 106; Collins v Portland Electric Power Co. (CA–9 1926) 12 F2d 671; Norwich Water Co. v Southern Ry. Co., Joslin v Boston & Maine R. Co., (1931) 274 Mass. 551, 175 NE 156.

[127]Guttman v Illinois Cent. R. Co. (E.D., N.Y. 1950) 91 F Supp 285.

[128]Gallagher v New York Dock Co., (1940) 19 N.Y.S.2d 789, aff'd, (1942) 263 A.D. 878, leave to appeal denied, 263 A.D. 957.

[129]Diamond v Davis, Jr., (1942) 38 N.Y.S.2d 103, aff'd, (1942) 265 A.D. 919, 39 N.Y.S.2d 412, aff'd, (1944) 292 N.Y. 552, 54 NE2d 683.

dividends nevertheless accumulate. The rule has been established by court decision[130] or statute in few states. However, since preferences on stock are a matter of contract, express provision for dividend credit can be granted or denied in the articles.[131]

Corporations in liquidation or dissolution: Most states hold that on dissolution or liquidation of a corporation, the cumulative preferred stock must be paid accrued undeclared dividends for years in which there were no earnings before any distribution can be made to the common, or other junior shares.[132] However, the preferred stock contract may expressly grant[133] or impliedly deny[134] the right to accrued, undeclared dividends on liquidation.

Provisions for dividends on partly paid shares. In the absence of some provision in the statute, charter, by-laws, or contract under which the subscription to shares is made as to the payment of dividends upon partly paid shares, a mere subscriber to shares who hasn't paid for his shares in full isn't entitled to participate with the shareholders whose shares have been entirely paid for.[135] But where certificates have been actually issued for partly paid shares the shares stand on an equality, irrespective of the fact that a larger amount has been paid on some of them than upon others, and dividends must be divided among the shareholders in proportion to the nominal amounts of their shares and not in proportion to the amounts respectively paid up on the shares.[136] In some states, statutes provide that the directors may declare and pay dividends upon the basis of the amount actually "paid in" upon shares. In many states, a certificate may not be issued until the share is fully paid. Most states, though, have no provision covering dividends on partly paid shares.

A corporation with a surplus has the power, as between itself and the stockholders, to agree that the dividend declared from such surplus shall be applied to the payment of subscriptions. A corporation

---

[130] Agnew v American Ice Co., (1949) 2 N.J. 291, 66 A2d 330.

[131] Leeds & Lippincott Co. v Nevius, (1959) 30 N.J. 281, 153 A2d 45.

[132] Wilson v Laconia Car Co., (1931) 275 Mass. 435, 176 NE 182; Warburton v John Wanamaker, Philadelphia, (1938) 320 Pa. 5, 196 Atl 506; Pennington v Commonwealth Hotel Const. Corp., (1931) 17 Del. Ch. 394, 155 Atl 514; Hay v Hay, (1951) 38 Wash. 2d 513, 230 P2d 791 *Contra.* Hull v Pfister & Vogel Leather Co., (1940) 235 Wis. 653, 294 NW 18; Wouk v Merin (1st Dept. 1954) 283 A.D. 522, 128 N.Y.S.2d 727.

[133] Waldner v Equitable Loan Soc. (D Del 1945) 60 F Supp 372.

[134] Powell v Craddock-Terry Co., (1940) 175 Va. 146, 7 SE2d 143.

[135] Baltimore City Pass. Railway Co. v Hambleton, (1893) 77 Md. 341, 26 Atl 279.

[136] Oakbank Oil Co. v Crau, 8 A.C. 65. Compare Gellerman v Atlas Foundry Co., (1906) 45 Wash. 92, 87 P 1059.

agreeing to treat stock as fully paid in consideration of the surrender by the stockholders of accumulated profits, cannot afterwards in its own behalf or in behalf of subsequent creditors with notice, disturb the arrangement.[137]

Upon the sale of stock on the installment plan, an arrangement may be made for the payment of interest on the amount received, or for the payment of dividends and the charging of interest.

In what medium may dividends be paid? The board of directors may declare dividends payable in (1) cash, (2) property, (3) bonds, (4) stock, or (5) stock or cash, at the option of the stockholder.

What medium to use is left to the discretion of the directors, since they're the ones most familiar with the financial situation of the corporation. Once the directors have determined the medium in which the dividends are to be paid, an officer of the corporation has no power to change it; hence the execution of a promissory note by the officer in behalf of the corporation, given in substitution of an outstanding dividend check, is not within the implied powers of the officer (president). But the corporation may be bound on the note by express or implied ratification.[138]

The amount of cash the corporation has on hand and in the bank is no indication of the corporation's ability to declare and pay a dividend, although it may have a strong influence on the medium in which a dividend is paid.

Borrowing to pay cash dividends. A corporation having a surplus and cash available, generally will pay dividends in cash. The usual practice is to pay cash dividends by check. Payment by currency is unusual.[139]

If a corporation has no ready funds to pay a cash dividend, it may borrow a sum not exceeding the amount of the corporate surplus for the purpose of paying a dividend.[140] The fact that the money is borrowed to pay dividends doesn't make the declaration and payment illegal if it appears that the corporation had used surplus profits equal to the amount of the dividend paid, for the purpose of improving the corporate property.[141] If the profits have been invested in corporate

---

[137] Kenton Furnace R. & Mfg. Co. v McAlpin (SD Ohio 1880) 5 F 737.

[138] Hannigan v Italo Petroleum Corp. of America, (1945) 43 Del. 333, 47 A2d 169.

[139] Vertex Inv. Co. v Schwabacher, (1943) 57 Cal. App. (2d) 406, 134 P2d 891.

[140] Alabama Consol. Coal & Iron Co. v Baltimore Trust Co. (D Md 1912), 197 F 347; Cox v Leahy, (1924) 209 App. Div. 313, 204 N.Y.S. 741.

[141] Excelsior Water & Mining Co. v Pierce, (1891) 90 Cal. 131, 27 P 44.

property so that money must be borrowed to pay dividends, this constitutes a borrowing of money to carry on the corporate business and the payment of the dividend with the borrowed money isn't illegal.[142]

When a corporation has to pay dividends on its preferred, but doesn't have enough cash, there's no reason it can't borrow the necessary funds, if it has enough credit.[143]

Property dividends. The surplus of a corporation, as represented by the excess of assets over debts and capital may be represented in any of the corporation's assets. In the absence of a charter or statutory provision to the contrary, if the surplus is in the form of distributable property, a property dividend may be declared.[144]

> *Example:* If among the assets of a corporation having a surplus there is real estate that's no longer necessary for the corporate purposes, or if the corporation that has a surplus holds stock in another corporation, that real estate or stock is legally distributed to the extent of the surplus, precisely the same as if it were cash.[145]

A company doesn't necessarily warrant the title to property that it distributes as a property dividend.[146]

A stockholder of the corporation can't be compelled to take property on account of the dividend in a form he hadn't bargained for. So a nonassenting holder of cumulative preferred stock could not be compelled to accept long-term income notes of wholly-owned subsidiaries in discharge of dividend arrearages.[147]

Also, if the corporation were distributing stock of another corporation to its shareholders, the shareholder might not wish to have imposed upon him the liability as a stockholder of the corporation whose stock is being distributed. For example, the stockholder may not want to incur liability for unpaid corporate debts. A stockholder who receives assets of an insolvent corporation in the form of property

---

[142]Gilbert Paper Co. v Prankard, (1923) 204 App. Div. 83, 198 N.Y.S. 25.

[143]New England Trust Co. v Penobscot Chemical Fibre Co., (1946) 142 Me. 286, 50 A2d 188.

[144]Williams v Western U. Tel. Co., (1883) 93 N.Y. 162; Bank of Morgan v Reid, (1921) 27 Ga. App. 123, 107 SE 555; Grants Pass Hardware Co. v Calvert, (1914) 71 Ore. 103, 142 P 569; Sunseri v Sunseri, (1947) 358 Pa. 1, 55 A2d 370.

[145]Liebmann v Auto Strop Co., (1926) 241 N.Y. 427, 150 NE 505; Fraser v Great Western Sugar Co., (1935) N.J. Eq., 185 Atl 60, aff'd, (1936) 120 N.J. Eq. 288, 185 Atl 64.

[146]Olsen v Homestead Land & Improvement Co., (1894) 87 Tex. 368, 28 SW 944.

[147]Strout v Cross, Austin & Ireland Lumber Co., (1940) 283 N.Y. 406, 28 NE2d 890, motion to amend remittitur granted, (1940) 284 N.Y. 27, 29 NE2d 669.

dividends is liable, to the extent of the property received, for taxes due from the corporation.[148]

If the stockholder refuses to take the property dividend, the corporation may retain it in trust for him, or possibly sell it for his benefit.[149] The courts haven't decided how the refusal of the stockholder will be handled, but one has said, "In case of his refusal, the corporation will find some way to deal with the stock which the law will sanction." The stockholder has no option to receive an equivalent amount of cash in lieu of a property dividend.[150]

Scrip dividends. Scrip is a written certificate, a form of promissory note, declaring that the stockholder is entitled to a certain percent of the amount of capital stock held by him, or to a certain number of dollars per share, or to stock, bonds, land or other property, at some future date. The payment date doesn't have to be absolutely fixed. The offer of means whereby holders of scrip may convert their scrip into cash may be revoked by the corporation at any time.[151] The scrip may be issued convertible into stock or bonds of the company. Scrip dividends are legal but are rarely used any more.[152]

Bonds as dividends. Though the practice is rare, bonds may be distributed as dividends by a corporation having a surplus, absent statutory provision to the contrary, and the bonds may be secured by a mortgage upon the corporation's property.[153]

What is a stock dividend? A stock dividend is a distribution of additional shares of stock to existing stockholders on a pro rata basis—that is, so many shares of new stock for each share of stock held. When a stock dividend is declared, the corporate earnings are "capitalized." This is a bookkeeping procedure in which the amount of the stock dividend is transferred from the corporation's earnings account—usually called earned surplus—to its capital stock account.

> *Example:* Able Corporation has $1 million in capital stock and an earnings (surplus) account of $150,000. It pays a dividend of $50,000 in stock. It then has $1,050,000 in capital stock and $100,000 in surplus.

---

[148] Scott v Commissioner of Internal Revenue (CA–8 1941) 117 F2d 36.

[149] Williams v Western U. Tel. Co., (1883) 93 N.Y. 162.

[150] State v B. & O. R. R. Co., (1847) 6 Gill (Md.) 363.

[151] Hupp Motor Car Corp. v Guaranty Trust Co. of N.Y., (1939) 171 Misc. 21, 11 N.Y.S.2d 855.

[152] Bankers' Trust Co. v R. E. Dietz Co., (1913) 157 A.D. 594, 142 N.Y.S. 847.

[153] Butler v Glencove Starch Co., (1879) 18 Hun. 47. Wood v Lary, (1888) 47 Hun N.Y. 550, appeal dismissed, 124 N.Y. 83, 26 NE 338.

"A stock dividend really takes nothing from the property of the corporation and adds nothing to the interests of the stockholders. Its property is not diminished and their interests are not increased . . . the proportional interest of each shareholder remains the same. The only change is in the evidence which represents that interest, the new shares and the original shares together representing the same proportional interests that the original shares represented before the issue of the new ones."[154]

If the statute or charter requires dividends be paid in cash, the corporation cannot declare a stock dividend and compel the stockholders to accept stock instead of cash.[155] A dividend payable in cash or stock at the option of the stockholder isn't a stock dividend.[156]

The corporation can't distribute a stock dividend to a particular class of stockholders if the effect of such action would be to deprive stockholders of another class of their rights.

Example: Suppose Corporation A has $100,000 of 7 percent preferred stock and $100,000 of common stock, the only difference between the two classes being that the preferred has a preference as to dividends. The corporation proposes to capitalize its surplus of $50,000 and to declare a stock dividend on the common stock alone. The corporation may not do so, for the issuance of a stock dividend to the common stock to the exclusion of the preferred stockholders would constitute an impairment of the rights of the preferred stockholders; they would be entitled to relief in equity if the stock has not been delivered, or to damages for breach of contract obligation if it were delivered.[157] However, it has been held that when the certificate of incorporation provides that the preferred stock would "receive interest or dividends of 8 percent per annum and be preferred as to capital as well as to dividends," a stock dividend to the common stockholders alone was valid.[158]

Corporations sometimes distribute stock they own in another corporation to their own stockholders. That is a property dividend, not a stock dividend.

Stock dividend versus stock split: There is a distinct difference between a stock dividend and a stock split. It's explained below, starting on page 778.

---

[154] Eisner v Macomber, (1920) 252 US 189, 40 S Ct 189.

[155] Hardin County v Louisville & N. R. Co., (1891) 92 Ky. 412, 17 SW 860.

[156] Kellogg v Kellogg, (1938) 166 Misc. 791, 4 N.Y.S.2d 219.

[157] Riverside & Dan River Cotton Mills v Thomas Branch & Co., (1927) 147 Va. 509, 137 SE 620.

[158] Niles v Ludlow Valve Mfg. Co. (CA–2 1913) 141; Tennant v Epstein, (1934) 356 Ill. 26, 189 NE 864.

Why do corporations pay stock dividends? (1) *To conserve cash:* Corporations contemplating an expansion program may be reluctant to increase their regular cash dividend, or pay an extra cash dividend when they have had a very profitable year, since they will need the cash to carry out their plans. On the other hand, they want to give their stockholders some tangible evidence of the improved profits.

A stock dividend offers a solution to companies in this situation. It requires no cash outlay by the corporation and at the same time the stockholders are given tangible evidence, in the form of additional stock, that the earnings on their stock are being reinvested in the business.

> **Note:** If they want to, stockholders can convert the stock dividend into cash by selling the stock received on the market, though of course they thereby reduce their relative interest in the corporation.

(2) *To increase the marketability of their stock:* When the price of a share of stock rises beyond a certain level, investors are reluctant to buy it. It has been shown, for example, that an investor will more readily buy 100 shares of a $20 stock than 20 shares of a stock selling at $100. When a corporation feels the price of its stock is too high, it can reduce the price by paying a substantial stock dividend and thereby increase the marketability of the stock. (A stock split will have the same effect.)

> **Note:** The total value of a corporation's stock will often rise concomitant with the declaration of a large stock dividend.

Many investors find periodic small stock dividends, in addition to the regular cash dividend, are a strong inducement to investment particularly where the company is in an expanding industry. *Reason:* They are more interested in the long-term market appreciation of their stock interest than in immediate, larger dividend payments.

> **Warning:** If a corporation has been paying $2 on each share and then pays a 100 percent stock dividend, it should be prepared to pay, soon thereafter, somewhat over $1 per share on the shares that will then be outstanding. In other words, a higher cash pay out is expected.
>
> In the case of periodic small stock dividends it goes without saying that the corporation should pay at least the old dividend rate on the larger number of shares outstanding after the payment of each stock dividend.
>
> Marketability may be adversely affected if small stock dividends are paid instead of no cash dividend at all. This should be done only when the need for cash for expansion of the corporation's business is compelling and, even then, only if the corporation's shares are held, for

the most part, by stockholders who are less interested in current cash income, subject to high individual income tax rates, than in capital appreciation.

(3) *To maintain a long-established dividend rate rather than increase the rate:* Some corporations prefer to pay periodic stock dividends instead of raising a long-established dividend rate on their stock. Certain investors favor corporations with a record of stable cash dividend payments.

How to declare a stock dividend. Every state gives directors the power to declare dividends. Therefore the declaration of a stock dividend is within the discretion of the board of directors. The directors can declare a stock dividend by an appropriate resolution; they don't need the consent of the stockholders.

But if the corporation must increase its authorized capital stock to make enough shares available for the stock dividend, the stockholders must approve the increase in authorized capital stock. (State statutes require stockholder consent for a change in capitalization.) In this situation, the directors must pass a resolution (1) proposing an increase of capital stock for the purpose of making stock available for the payment of a stock dividend, and (2) calling a meeting of stockholders to vote on the proposal. Then the stockholders must pass a resolution approving the increase of capital stock. It's only then that directors can pass a resolution declaring the stock dividend.

> **Note:** Check your state statutes governing the proportion of stockholder vote needed to increase or decrease capital stock. Also, be prepared to pay any filing fees or franchise taxes imposed on the increased capitalization.

How are stock dividends treated tax-wise? As a general rule, stockholders don't have to pay any federal income tax on stock they receive on payment of a stock dividend.

Stock in another corporation distributed as a dividend is a property dividend and is taxable as such. There are special rules for taxing such distributions in certain situations. See P-H *Federal Taxes.*

But after the receipt of a stock dividend, the cost basis of the stock to the stockholder changes. A stockholder has to know the cost basis of the stock he holds because his profit or loss on any subsequent sale of the stock is computed by subtracting the cost basis from the price realized on the sale.

When a stockholder receives a non-taxable stock dividend, he figures out the cost basis of his stock by dividing the amount he originally paid for his stock by the number of shares he has after receiving the stock dividend.

> *Example:* Doe bought 100 shares of Able Corporation common stock in 1975 for $12,000 ($120 a share). In 1979 Able paid a nontaxable 50 percent stock dividend. Doe then had 150 shares. The cost basis of each share became $80 or $12,000 divided by 150. If Able sells any stock at more than $80 a share, he will realize a gain. If he gets less than $80 a share, he sustains a loss.

To determine whether any gain or loss on the sale of stock is a long-term or a short-term gain or loss, a stockholder has to know the date basis of the stock.

When a stock dividend is paid, the date basis of both the original stock and the stock received as a dividend is the same as the date basis of the original stock. In the example shown here, Doe's date basis for all the 150 shares he has after receiving the stock dividend is 1975.

When stock is transferred to a new owner by will or inheritance, the same tax treatment applies to stock received as a dividend as to stock bought by a decedent during his lifetime. For further information, see P-H *Federal Taxes.*

State taxes: State income tax laws generally treat stock dividends in the same manner as the federal income tax law. For the taxability of a stock dividend in a particular state, see P-H *State & Local Taxes.*

Documentary stamp taxes: In some states corporations have to pay a state documentary stamp tax when they pay a stock dividend. That's because the capital is increased by the payment of the stock dividend.

What accounting steps should be taken upon the payment of a stock dividend? The American Institute of Certified Public Accountants recommended that a corporation paying a stock dividend should consider taking the following accounting steps:

Small stock dividends: Many stockholders consider small stock dividends as distributions of corporate earnings in an amount equal to the value of the shares received. This view is natural because small stock dividends usually don't have any long range effect upon the market price of the stock on which they are paid.

Therefore, the AICPA said that a corporation paying a small stock dividend should transfer from its earned surplus account to its capital surplus accounts an amount equal to the "fair" value of the stock issued as a dividend. This will often require the capitalization of more earned surplus than the law requires. (State laws generally require corporations to capitalize only the par value or stated value of shares issued as a dividend.) Unless this is done, the amount of earnings (above par or stated value) will be left in earned surplus subject to possible further similar stock issuances or cash distributions.

Substantial stock dividends: The AICPA also said that a stock dividend, large enough to materially affect the market price of the stock on which it is paid, is like a stock split and thus there is no need to capitalize any larger amount of earned surplus than the law requires. Where do you draw the line between small and substantial stock dividends? No exact standard can be applied. The dividing line, if any, might be between 20 percent and 25 percent.

> **Note:** Originally these principles were issued in Accounting Research Bulletin of the AICPA in 1941, revised 1952. FASB has now taken over the function of promulgating accounting principles; these rules are now in FASB's Financial Accounting Standards [see No. 43, Ch. 7B].

What are the New York Stock Exchange's standards for listing stock issued as a stock dividend? The New York Stock Exchange recognizes that many listed companies prefer, at times, to pay stock dividends instead of or in addition to cash dividends. The Exchange has no objection to this practice. It is concerned, however, about guarding against possible misconceptions by stockholders in such companies of the effect of the stock dividend upon their equity in the company and the dividend's relation to current earnings. To this end, it requires companies paying stock dividends to disclose certain information about them and to adopt specified accounting methods for them if they want to have the dividend stock listed. Here's what the NYSE requires:

If the corporation pays a stock dividend of less than 25 percent it must capitalize as much earned surplus as the fair value of the stock distributed as a dividend. Fair value in this connection means the approximate market price of the stock distributed as a dividend.

> *Example:* Able Corporation's stock sells at about $40 a share. It has 100,000 shares outstanding. It proposes to pay a 10 percent stock dividend or 10,000 shares. Immediately after the stock dividend, Able's stock would sell at about $36. If Able wants to have the 10,000 shares listed, it should be prepared to transfer about $360,000 from earned surplus to capital.

Stock dividends of 100 percent or more don't come within this rule. Those between 25 percent and 100 percent may require compliance. As to these, the NYSE's opinion should be obtained.

The NYSE also requires that a notice be sent to stockholders with the stock dividend advising them of the amount capitalized per share, the aggregate amount capitalized, the relation of this aggregate amount to current undistributed earnings and the accounts to which this amount has been charged and credited. The stockholders must also be told the reason for the payment of the stock dividend and that if the stock received as a dividend is sold, the stockholder's proportionate equity in the company will be reduced.

Should a corporation pay periodic stock dividends? Why do companies pay stock dividends regularly? Two reasons are usually given:

(1) A nontaxable stock dividend provides a desirable tax shelter.

(2) The capital growth potential of the stock of a company paying stock dividends is superior to that of a similar company paying the same amount in cash.

Both of these reasons have some objective validity—*when you compare a regular stock dividend payer with a roughly equivalent cash dividend payer.* But they have no such objective validity *when you are comparing a regular stock and cash dividend payer with a similar company earning about the same amount per share and paying the same cash dividend only.*

In other words—*assuming equivalent earnings*—a regular stock dividend payer is superior to a generous cash dividend payer, but not to a stingy cash dividend payer that doesn't pay stock dividends.

Or—from the company's point of view—a corporation can create a net after-tax gain for its stockholders by paying stock instead of cash dividends. But, objectively, it would do equally well for its stockholders by holding down its cash dividend and plowing back additional earnings into the company—without declaring any stock dividends.

> *Example:* Assume three companies A, B, and C, each earning 8 percent per year after taxes on its current price. That means a price-earnings ratio of 12.5 to 1. (Or take one company, ABC, with these earnings.) A pays 6 percent in cash, B 2 percent in cash and 4 percent in stock, and C 2 percent in cash only. (Or company ABC can elect one of these same three options, A, B, or C.)

Which is the better tax shelter? It is clear that both B and C are better tax shelters than A; but B is not intrinsically superior to C. Stockholders under B can sell their stock dividends at capital gain tax rates; but stockholders under C can achieve the same result by selling off a small part (presumably somewhat less than 4 percent) of their undiluted stock.

What about price appreciation? Whether a stockholder's total assets will increase faster under B or under C depends, in part, on whether investors generally prefer a stock dividend payer to a stingy cash dividend payer.

In many cases, at least in the short run, they seem to prefer stock dividend payers—as witness the price excitement when stock dividends are expected or announced. In other words, most stockholders act as if they like dividends—in stock if not in cash—and especially where the old cash dividend rate is maintained on the larger number of shares.

Over the longer run, the final choice between B and C probably can't be decided statistically—if only because you just can't know what would happen if a company had chosen C rather than B—that is, neither declared a stock dividend nor raised the cash dividend.

In short, a stock dividend can be realistically viewed as essentially a public relations device designed to bring the growth potential of a company to the attention of investors.

> **Suggestion:** Proceed warily on regular stock dividends. If the company is really growing, the stock dividend often provides an extra price lift, at least for a while. But if growth is absent or only occasional, the stock dilution resulting from stock dividends or stock splits will also bring price weakness—eventually, if not at once.

Here's an easy two-step test of whether a stock dividend is excessive in terms of a company's current earning power and price:

(1) Get the current earnings yield on the current price. Use anticipated earnings per share for the current fiscal year, rather than reported earnings for the last year. For example, if the expected earnings for the current year are $3 per share and the current price is $24, the earnings yield is 12 and one-half percent (3 ÷ 24).

(2) Add the percent stock dividend declared for the current fiscal year to the annual cash dividend yield—for example, 2 percent stock + 6 percent cash = 8 percent.

If the total dividend yield (stock plus cash exceeds the earnings yield, the shareholder faces stock dilution and probable price weakness—unless the future rise in earnings promises to be very rapid indeed.

What is a stock split? There are two kinds of stock splits: (1) Split-ups, where one share is split into a greater number of shares; and (2) reverse splits or split-downs where a number of shares are combined into a smaller number of shares. In both cases the amount in the capital account remains unchanged. They must be distinguished from a stock dividend which often looks to be very much the same. Thus, a 2-for-1 stock split is similar to a 100 percent stock dividend since in both cases the stockholders are left with the same total equity but with twice as many shares as before. But, in a split-up, the total amounts of capital stock and surplus in the balance sheet are not changed, whereas, in the case of a stock dividend, surplus must be transferred to the capital stock account for the additional shares issued. Another important practical distinction is that, in the case of a stock dividend, no action by the stockholders is needed if the necessary treasury or authorized stock is available for distribution, since the declaration of dividends is a power of the board of directors. In the case of stock splits, on the other hand, stockholder approval is usually required to amend the corporate charter, authorize new stock and change the par value of outstanding stock.

Both in a stock split and a stock dividend, the stockholder has the same proportionate interest in the corporation after the event as he had before, but he holds a greater number of shares. It's as though the stockholder had exchanged a $5 bill for five singles. So, in the case of the stockholder who transferred his shares reserving the right to rebuy at a stated price, he could still rebuy the entire block at that price after the shares had been split 4 for 1.[159]

Why corporations split stock. Though there are numerous reasons why stock may be split, the one most frequently given by corporate management is the desire to increase the marketability and broaden the distribution of the company's common stock and by increasing the supply of the stock to make it less subject to extreme price fluctuations. Another reason frequently cited is the split symbolizes an increase in the value of the company.

Experience has shown that new stockholders can be attracted to a good stock within a short time after a stock split. That's because of the psychological effect on many purchasers of the price of common stock. It has been shown that investors would rather buy 100 shares at $25 than 10 shares at $250 although their equity in the company would be exactly the same. As the price of a stock goes up, because of general market conditions or because of the performance of the specific company, trading may slow down. The most popular price range among investors is around $20 to $40.

Many companies don't think it desirable for their stock to be held in large blocks by institutional investors. That may be the result if the price is too high to attract small investors. A stock split helps prevent

[159]McCormick v Frisch, (1952) 199 Md. 181, 85 A2d 793.

such concentration. A larger number of stockholders makes future stock financing more likely to succeed and may make the company better known.

If a new issue of common stock is contemplated, it's desirable to have a broad market available. If outstanding shares are selling at a rather high price, a stock split may be a good idea so that all outstanding stock can be brought down to the desired range. It's advisable to analyze the probable future price range for the stock in average as well as in boom and recession times so as to be able to make the stock split with the long range price fluctuation in mind.

Following this reasoning, that it's best to sell the company's stock at the "popular" price level, it would be logical to do a reverse split for low-selling stocks; i.e., to reduce the number of shares outstanding by getting the shareholders to take one share for each two or more they hold, and thus force the price up. However, management usually hesitates to do this as investors might consider it an admission of loss of value of the stock.

> **Caution:** Stock shouldn't be split only to profit from the rise in market value that will supposedly automatically result from the split. The reason why two new shares often sell for more than one old is that companies that split their stock are usually growing. There is no guarantee that a split of a stable or declining stock will result in more than a temporary rise in total market value.

Companies sometimes split their stock because they want to maintain a constant cash dividend per share even though their earnings justify an increase in their total dividend distributions.

Tax consequences of a stock split. (1) *Federal.* Income taxes: A stock split resulting in no change in capitalization is tax free.

Though the declaration and distribution of the stock split have no federal tax consequences for the corporation, stockholders realize gain or loss when the stock they acquired in a stock split is sold. The method of issuing the additional stock determines how the capital gain or loss will be taxed. The example below demonstrates the various ways by which additional stock can be distributed to the stockholders.

> *Example:* Jones acquired stock in the Smith Co. by a series of purchases. In 1968, he bought 100 shares at $90; in 1973, 80 shares at $70; and in 1978, 50 shares at $100. The company now declares a 2-for-1 split and issues to Jones a certificate for an additional 230 shares. If Jones attempted to sell a number of shares represented by a part of his *new* certificate, the Treasury and the courts would no doubt apply a first-in-first-out rule so that Jones' loss or gain would be measured for

tax purposes as if he had sold his 1968 shares first [Kraus v Commissioner, 88 F 2 616]. If the stock is now selling at $60 per new share (remember each share has as its basis half the price paid for each when bought), Jones might prefer to be taxed as if he were selling the shares he bought in 1973. (This could be so for a variety of reasons, such as that his income this year is going to be less than usual, and he wants to pay the tax on the largest possible gain now.) The first-in-first-out rule would probably also apply if the company took back Jones' old certificates and issued him one new certificate for 460 shares or 4 certificates for 100 shares each plus a certificate for 60 shares.

In order for Jones to get the tax treatment he desires, the new certificates must be issued in such a way that each new certificate can be identified with a definite purchase time (i.e., 1968, 1973, or 1978). This can be done in either of 2 ways: (1) the company could issue additional certificates, one for 100 shares to match the 1968 shares, another for 80 shares to match the 1973 purchase, and a certificate for 50 shares to match the 1978 purchase; or (2) Jones could be required to surrender his old certificates and then be given new certificates, one for 200 shares that would have the 1968 price for its basis, one for 160 shares having the 1973 price for its basis, and one certificate for 100 shares having the 1978 price for its basis. In both cases it would be wise to number the new certificates in such a way that the lowest numbered one going to an individual (like Jones here) would match his earliest purchase (1968 in this case).

Remember that in (1) in the example above, when a new certificate can be matched against the old purchase for which it was issued, each new share will have a basis of one-half the original purchase price per share, but the old certificate itself will have only one-half the price paid for it as the basis for capital gain or loss treatment. In (2) above, each new *certificate* would have the same basis as the old one it replaced.

Another reason why it is important to the stockholder to be able to identify the new certificates with specific old certificates is the question of short versus long-term capital gain or loss treatment.

Example: Brown bought 50 shares of Black Co. stock at $100 in 1975, and another 50 shares at $100 on October 1, 1977. The stock was split 2-for-1 on December 1, 1977. On March 1, 1978 the stock is selling at $40 per new share and Brown decides to sell 100 of the 200 shares he now owns. Since all the shares were bought at $100 each, they now have a basis of $50 each as a result of the split. The loss on 100 shares would therefore be $1,000. Whether this loss is to be short-term or long-term may be important to Brown under the following circumstances: As a result of other transactions in the same year Brown has a long-term gain of $1,500 and also a short-term gain of $1,500. A long-term loss of $1,000 would reduce his net long-term gain (taxed at favorable capital gain rates) to $500 and leave his short-term gain (fully taxable as income) at $1,500. A short-term loss of $1,000, on the other hand, will offset the short-term gain, so that only $500 will be taxed fully while the $1,500 long-term gain will be taxed at capital gain rates. If the Black Co. had issued only one certificate for the additional 100 shares to which Brown was entitled at the time of the split, Brown could sell the 50 shares represented by the October 1977, certificate, but then would have to sell 50 shares represented by part of his December 1977, certificate which, on a first-in-first-out basis, would result in a long-term loss based on his 1975 purchase. But if Brown received separate identifiable certificates, he can now sell 100 shares with an October 1977 basis and get the desired short-term loss.

The date of the purchase of the old stock, and not the date of the stock split, determines whether you will receive long- or short-term capital gain or loss treatment. Thus the fact that you got new certificates only three months ago does not make a sale now a short-term transaction if you bought the stock that was split several years ago.

(2) *State.* Excise taxes based on issuing capital stock have been held not to apply in the case of a stock split: "A mere change in the number of units or shares outstanding, without any increase in the total capital stock does not involve the issuance of any capital stock. A stock split up is simply a further division of the existing units of capital stock."[160]

Dividends payable in stock or cash—reinvestment plans. In recent years automatic dividend reinvestment plans have been developed, especially among some of the larger utility and industrial corporations, of declaring dividends and authorizing the application of the dividend to the purchase of stock, unless payment in cash is requested within a certain number of days. In some cases provision is made that all dividends are paid in cash, unless notice to the contrary is received; in others, all dividends are applied to the purchase of shares unless notice is received by the corporation that the stockholder elects to receive his dividend in cash. Such a dividend differs distinctly from a stock dividend in that under a stock dividend, while the stockholder may refuse to accept the shares offered as a stock dividend, he can't demand cash in lieu of them while in the declaration of a dividend payable in cash or in stock the stockholder has the right to elect to take cash or apply his dividend to the purchase of additional shares. Where a dividend was declared out of earned surplus for the past year, payable

---

[160]Lake Superior District Power Co. v Public Service Comm., (1947) 250 Wis. 39, 26 NW2d 278.

quarterly during the ensuing year, stockholders who elected to purchase stock with their dividends might get credit for all their dividends to apply toward the purchase of more stock when the first quarterly payment was made, without waiting to take their credits quarterly in the same manner as those stockholders who elected to take their dividends in cash.[161]

Who are entitled to dividends—in general. Unless the statutes or articles provide otherwise, each share of stock is entitled to share equally with all other shares in the profits or dividends, in proportion to the fractional interests in the capital represented by the respective shares.[162] The rights of the stockholders and the corporation are fixed at the date of the declaration of the dividend.[163]

In the absence of an agreement to the contrary, the owner and holder of the legal title to stock in a corporation is entitled to the earnings of the company by way of dividends.[164] But a power to collect dividends on corporate stock may be lodged in one person while title to the stock is in another.[165] But a gift of dividends for an unlimited time amounts to a gift of the shares on which the dividends are declared.[166]

All the stockholders of a particular class upon which a dividend has been declared must be given their pro rata share of the dividend according to their stockholdings, without discrimination, and regardless of the time when the stock was acquired;[167] the moment a transferee becomes a shareholder, all the incidents of ownership attach and he's entitled to participate in any subsequent dividend.[168] There can be no discrimination such as declaring the dividend payable to certain stockholders of the class only and not others,[169] or giving certain stockholders of the class larger dividends than others,[170] or paying the same dividend at different times to different stockholders of the same class.[171] The following proposed amendment to the bylaws

---

[161] OAG Fla. 1932.

[162] McGahan v United Engineering Corp., (1935) 118 N.J. Eq. 410, 180 Atl 195.

[163] In re Nirdlinger's Estate, (1937) 327 Pa. 160, 193 Atl 33.

[164] Richards v Southwest Discount Corp., (1941) 44 Cal. App. 2d 551, 112 P2d 698.

[165] Estate of Brenner, (1938) 169 Misc. 412, 7 N.Y.S.2d 932; Albert M. Greenfield & Co. v Philadelphia Workingmen's Saving Loan & Bldg. Ass'n, (1948) 162 Pa. Super. 350, 57 A2d 435.

[166] Syfer v Fidelity Trust Co., (1945) 184 Md. 391, 41 A2d 293.

[167] State v Neb. State Bank of O'Neill, (1932) 123 Neb. 289, 242 NW 613.

[168] Jones v Terre Haute R. R. Co., (1874) 57 N.Y. 196.

[169] Segerstrom v Holland Piano Mfg. Co., (1924) 160 Minn. 95, 199 NW 897. A corporation cannot deprive stockholders of dividends by making distributions of funds available therefor under the guise of wages to employees-stockholders. De Martini v Scavenger's Protective Ass'n, (1935) 3 Cal. App. 2d 691, 40 P2d 317.

[170] Erdman v Yolles, (1975) 62 Mich. App. 594 (favored stockholders had got bonuses and pay raises).

[171] Tichenor v Dr. G. H. Tichenor Co., Ltd., (La. App. 1935) 164 So 275.

was held to be an improper attempt to discriminate among stockholders:

> "As soon as reasonably may be after the end of the calendar year 1931, and of each calendar year of the Company's existence, thereafter, and under and in accordance with all the terms of this Article, the Treasurer of the Company shall ascertain the net profits of the Company for such year, and shall pay and distribute an amount of such net profits equal in the aggregate to five percent (5%) thereof to and among those officers and employees of the Company who have both been in the employ and own Common Stock of the Company as hereinafter stated as an extra dividend upon and in the proportion among such officers and employees of such shares of Common Stock thus owned by them respectively."[172]

A dividend payable in preferred stock to preferred stockholders and in common stock to common stockholders isn't discriminatory.[173] The corporation can't declare a dividend on corporate stock held in the treasury.[174] If all the stockholders entitled to participate in a dividend authorize, ratify or acquiesce in a distribution of the surplus among themselves other than on a pro rata basis, the dividend may be distributed on the agreed upon basis. Thus, dividends in form of price rebates could be proportionate to amount of business stockholders did with corporation.[175]

Note that a prospective employee who bought the corporation's stock under a buy-back agreement in contemplation of a definite employment contract could keep all the dividends (cash and additional stock) when the employment contract never eventuated and the corporation bought back the stock.[176]

Right to dividends as between different classes of stockholders. Unless otherwise specified, all shares of stock of a corporation stand upon the same footing and participate equally in the organization, control, and distribution of funds of the corporation, regardless of whether they are earnings or assets. There may be a classification of stock, such as preferred stock, common stock, Class A stock, and Class B stock, which gives to members of one class rights and privileges not enjoyed by other classes, for example, that the rate of dividends on one

---

[172]Scott v P. Lorillard Co., (1931) 108 N.J. Eq. 153, 154 Atl 515, aff'd 109 N.J. Eq. 417, 157 Atl 388.

[173]Howell v Chicago & N. W. R. Co., (1868) 51 Barb. (N.Y.) 378.

[174]Gearhart v Standard Steel Car Co., (1909) 223 Pa. 385, 72 Atl 699.

[175]Allied Supermarkets, Inc. v Grocers Dairy Co., (1974) 391 Mich. 729, 219 NW2d 55.

[176]Anacomp, Inc. v Wright (Ind. App. 1983) 449 NE 2d 610.

class of stock shall be one and one-half times the dividends on the other class.[177] Or that gives shareholders a right to vote but not to receive dividends.[178] So a preferred stockholder whose rights haven't been affected and who has suffered no damage by charter amendment creating new class of preferred stock cannot enjoin payment of dividends on the new shares.[179]

In order for shares of stock of one class to have preference over shares of stock of another class, it's necessary that such preferences be stated either in the statute under which the corporation is organized, the certificate of incorporation, the by-laws, or some other form of contract binding on the corporation and the holders of such stock, and such documents constitute evidence of the contract between the different classes of stockholders, as well as between the corporation and the stockholders of such classes.[180] Therefore, it has been held that stock described merely as preferred means only a stock that differs from other stock in having some sort of a preference attached to it, without expressing the special nature of the preference.[181]

To whom are dividends payable? In the absence of any agreement to the contrary, only those who are the record stockholders on the day the dividend is declared are entitled to participate in the dividend;[182] the payment must be made to the person in whose name the stock stands registered upon the books at the time the dividend is declared.[183] By the terms of the resolution declaring the dividend, the dividend may be vested in the stockholders of record on a date later than that on which the resolution was passed. And the dividend vests in those stockholders even though it's payable at a still later date.[184] But when the stock has been sold, the seller-record owner may have to account to the buyer for the dividends.[185]

---

[177]McGahan v United Engineering Corp., (1935) 118 N.J. Eq. 410, 180 Atl 195.

[178]Stroh v Blackhawk Holding Corp., (1971) 48 Ill. 2d 471, 272 NE2d.

[179]Ainsworth v Southwestern Drug Corp. (CA–5 1938) 95 F2d 172.

[180]Lyman v Southern Ry. Co., (1928) 149 Va. 274, 141 SE 240. See also Tennant v Epstein, (1934) 356 Ill. 26, 189 NE 864, rev'g 271 Ill. App. 204; James E. Powers Foundry Co. v Miller, (1934) 166 Md. 590, 171 Atl 842.

[181]Scott v Baltimore & O. Ry. Co., (1901) 93 Md. 475, 49 Atl 327.

[182]Richards v Southwest Discount Corp., (1941) 44 Cal. App. (2d 551, 112 P2d) 698; Nutter v Andrews, (1923) 246 Mass. 224, 140 NE 744.

[183]New England Merchants v Old Colony Trust Co. (Mass. S Ct 1982) 429 NE 2d 1143; Villere v Com'r of Int. Rev. (CA–5 1943) 133 F2d 905; Hansen v Bear Film Co., (1945) Cal App. 158 P2d 779.

[184]Smith v Taecker, (1933) 133 Cal. App. 351, 24 P2d 182; Hill v Newischawanick Co., (1876) 8 Hun N.Y. 459, affirmed, 71 N.Y. 593; J.G. Wilson Corp. v Cahill, (1929) 152 Va. 108, 146 SE 274.

[185]Lunt v Genesee Valley Trust Co., (1937) 162 Misc. 859, 297 N.Y.S. 27. See also Baar v Fidelity Columbia Trust Co., (1946) Ky., 193 SW2d 1011.

A declared dividend is no part of the assets of the corporation but is the property solely of the person to whom it's declared payable.[186] The corporation need not look beyond its books to determine who is entitled to dividends.[187] But the corporation may require proof of ownership of the stock before it pays a dividend, although there are no conflicting claims.[188] Corporation can't refuse to pay dividends to the record owner where the only other person who had ever claimed any right to the stock had relinquished his right by formal assignment.[189] Yet if the corporation's books are erroneous through its own fault, it will be compelled to pay the dividend to the rightful owner.[190] So when a corporation transferred shares on the basis of forged endorsement, it remained liable to the stockholder even though he didn't investigate why he hadn't received any dividends.[191] Furthermore, in the absence of a binding statute or by-law, the corporation will not be protected in the payment of a dividend to a registered holder if it has notice of the transfer from the registered holder to another.[192] The corporation in that case remains liable to the transferee, even if the latter fails to have the transfer registered. But notice of loss or theft is not notice that the securities were transferred wrongfully to an innocent purchaser for value. So until the corporation received notice that an innocent purchaser obtained good title against the original owner, and that such purchaser claimed from the corporation the right to dividends, the corporation can continue to recognize the exclusive right of the person registered on its books as the owner of shares to receive dividends.[193]

Knowledge by the proper officers independently of the corporation's books may constitute notice to the company.[194] But if the corporate officer has obtained the knowledge while acting for his individual benefit, and not in behalf of the corporation, the corporation doesn't have knowledge.[195]

---

[186]Commercial Life Ins. Co. v Wright, (1946) 64 Ariz. 129, 166 P2d 943.

[187]Brisbane v D. L. & W. R. R. Co., (1883) 94 N.Y. 204.

[188]Barbato v Breeze Corp., (1942) 128 N.J. Law 309, 26 A2d 53.

[189]Greasy Brush Coal Co. v Hays, (1942) 292 Ky. 517, 166 SW2d 983.

[190]Ashton v Zeila Mining Co., (1901) 134 Cal. 408, 66 P 494; Blooming-Grove Cotton Oil Co. v First Nat. Bank, (1900) Tex. Civ. App. 56 SW 552.

[191]Schneider v Union Oil Company, (1970) 6 Cal. App. 3d 987, 86 Cal. Rptr. 315.

[192]Guarantee Co. of North America v East Rome Town Co., (1895) 96 Ga. 511, 23 SE 503; Robinson v Nat'l Bank of New Berne, (1884) 95 N.Y. 637; Homestake Oil Co. v Rigler, (CA–9 1930) 39 F2d 40.

[193]Turnbull v Longacre Bank, (1928) 249 N.Y. 159, 163 NE 135, modifying 224 N.Y.S. 928, 222 A.D. 655; Brisbane v D.L.&W. R. Co., (1883) 94 N.Y. 204.

[194]Guarantee Co. of North America v East Rome Town Co., (1895) 96 Ga. 511, 23 SE 503.

[195]Fourth Nat'l Bank v Manchester Real Estate & Mfg. Co., (1915) 77 N.H. 481, 93 Atl, 661.

Many large corporations appoint an agent, usually a trust company, to take care of the details involved in the payment of dividends. The appointment is usually made by a resolution of the board of directors.

Dividend rights of purchaser and seller. Before a dividend is declared, the intangible right to share in the earnings of the corporation is a mere incident to the stock and passes with it at a sale. But when the dividend is declared it constitutes a property interest separate from the stock and doesn't pass on a sale of the stock.[196] So in the absence of a provision in the contract of sale to the contrary, a purchaser of stock isn't entitled to dividends already declared, even though the dividends aren't payable until a date after the sale has taken place.[197] If, as a matter of custom or usage on a stock exchange, the rule prevails that dividends already declared and not paid pass with the stock, and the seller has actual knowledge of this custom, or knowledge that may be implied from his awareness of the fact that his agent would trade through the exchange, the seller will be bound by the rules.[198]

Any dividend declared subsequent to an executed sale of stock belongs to the purchaser.[199] A purchaser in default under an installment contract for the sale of stock isn't a stockholder entitled to dividends.[200] Where there is a binding agreement to sell stock and a dividend is declared between the time the agreement to sell is made and the delivery of the certificates, the dividend belongs in equity to the purchaser and not to the seller.[201] In the absence of an agreement to the contrary, even though the shares aren't transferred upon the books of the company before they are closed, owing to the neglect of the seller to make prompt delivery of the securities, the seller is bound to turn over to the purchaser of stock,[202] the dividend received by him from the corporation, or an equivalent amount. This rule applies also in cases

---

[196] Wheeler v Northwestern Sleigh Co. (ED Wis. 1889) 39 F. 347.

[197] Nutter v Andrews, (1923) 246 Mass. 224, 140 NE 744; Hopper v Sage, (1889) 112 N.Y. 530, 20 NE 350.

[198] Ford v Snook, (1923) 205 App. Div. 194, 199 N.Y.S. 630, aff'd, 240 N.Y. 624, 148 NE 732, Pacific Coast Music Jobbers Inc. v CIR(UST Ct 1971) 55 TC No. 87.

[199] Sautbine v Stroud (CA-8 1925) 5 F2d 809; Brower v Fenner & Beane, (1939) 237 Ala. 632, 188 So. 240; Martindell v Fiduciary Counsel, Inc., (1942) 131 N.J. Eq. 523, 36 A2d 171, aff'd, (1943) 133 N.J. Eq. 408, 30 A2d 281.

[200] Schwartz v Manufacturers' Casualty Ins. Co., (1939) 335 Pa. 130, 6 A2d 299.

[201] Thompson v Exchange Bld'g, (1928) 157 Tenn. 275, 8 SW2d 489. Seller who keeps dividend after sale converts it though he stays record owner Herzfeld & Stern v Freidus, (1971) 69 Misc.2d 578, 330 N.Y.S. 2d 479.

[202] Brower v Fenner & Beane, (1939) 237 Ala. 632, 188 So 240; Stuart v Sargent, (1933) 283 Mass. 536, 186 NE 649.

where the purchaser isn't obligated to pay for the stock immediately. Thus, where shares of stock are sold on August 1, to be paid for on August 29, and a dividend is declared between the day of the sale and the day set for payment, the dividend belongs to the purchaser of the shares, in the absence of an agreement to the contrary.[203] But under an executory contract for the sale of stock the buyer isn't entitled to dividends on it until legal title actually passes, unless there's an agreement to the contrary.[204] Likewise, when a contract for the future sale of stock says nothing about who should get dividends declared between the date of the contract and the payment of the price and the delivery of the certificates those dividends belong to the seller.[205]

Where stock is sold at a fixed price plus accrued dividends, the stipulated price per share of the stock is increased by a sum equivalent to the dividend rate from the date of the last dividend to the date when the sale takes place. Such a contract imposes on the buyer the obligation to pay such dividend rate to the time of the sale, in addition to the price specified.[206]

Stock sales "ex dividend": Special rules apply when stock is sold through brokers on an exchange or over the counter. The exchange rules, or, in the case of over the counter stocks the rules of the National Association of Securities Dealers, govern when the stock sells "ex dividend." Excepted are transactions made specifically for cash in which delivery has to be made on the transaction date. Ex dividend means without the right to the dividend. To get the dividend then, the buyer must buy the stock before the date when the stock goes ex dividend. When a stock sells ex dividend, the price is usually reduced from that of the previous day by the amount of the dividend.

Dividend rights of life tenant and remainderman. When stock stands in the name of a trustee on the books of the corporation the dividends declared on the stock are payable to the trustee, just as in the case of any other stockholder of record.

Where the trustee is to pay the income from the stock to a person during his life, the stock itself to go to others upon the death of that person, problems may arise as to the apportionment between the beneficiaries of dividends declared during the life of the life tenant. But

---

[203] Black v Homersham, (1879) L.R. 4 Exch. Div. 24. See, also, La Fountain & Woolson Co. v Brown, (1917) 91 Vt. 340, 101 Atl 36; Hubbard v George, (1918) 81 W. Va. 538, 94 SE 974.
[204] Richards v Southwest Discount Corp., (1941) 44 Cal. App2d 551, 112 P2d 698.
[205] Deering Milliken, Inc. v The Clark Estates, (1978) 473 N.Y.2d 545, 373 NE2d 1212.
[206] Kennedy Bros. v Bird, (1934) 287 Mass. 477, 192 NE 73. See McJannet v Strehlow Supply Co., (1946) Wash., 171 P2d 173.

the question of the division of the proceeds of a dividend between owners of successive interests in stock is one that ordinarily is of interest to the owners themselves and the trustees who represent them, and not of direct interest to the corporation's directors.

Closing transfer books for payment of dividends. A corporation may close its transfer books temporarily for a reasonable time before payment of a dividend to determine who gets the dividend. This is rarely done any more, especially by publicly held corporations. Instead a record date is set.

Fixing a record date that determines stockholders entitled to dividend. Most statutes provide that, unless otherwise stated in the article or by-laws, the directors may fix a time not over a certain number of days before the date fixed for the payment of any dividend, as a record date for the determination of the stockholders entitled to get the dividend; and in such case the stockholders of record on the date so fixed can get that dividend despite any transfer of any shares on the books of the corporation after any record date fixed by the directors.

> **Suggestion:** The resolution declaring a dividend should state distinctly that the dividend is payable on a certain day to stockholders of record at the close of business on a set earlier day.

Where dividends are payable without closing the stock transfer books, a list of stockholders as of the record date is prepared from the stock record and is certified. This list governs the distribution of the dividends. Reference is made to the stock books in case any question arises.

By fixing the record date as of which those entitled to dividends are determined, the corporation fixes the date when the debt created by the declaration of the dividend accrues.[207] The debt exists from the time of the declaration of the dividend, although payment is postponed for the convenience of the company.[208] The corporation can't fix as the record date for determining who shall be entitled to dividends, a date before the date of the resolution. Should it do so, the stockholders of record the day the resolution is passed will be deemed entitled to the dividend.[209]

---

[207] Geo. Feick & Sons Co. v Blair (D.C. Cir. 1928) 26 F2d 540.
[208] Wheeler v Northwestern Sleigh Co. (ED Wis. 1889) 39 F 347.
[209] Jones v Terre Haute, etc. R.R. Co., (1874) 57 N.Y. 196.

Notice of dividends declared and dividends passed. Companies having stock listed on the New York Stock Exchange must give immediate publicity to the public press of *any* action on dividends. This includes declaring, postponing, reducing, or omitting a dividend. Otherwise, there are no formal requirements in this area.

Effect of pledge of stock. Upon the pledge of stock as collateral security for a debt, the pledgee gets as an incident to his special ownership the right to receive dividends and he must apply those dividends to the debt for which the stock is pledged, or hold them in trust for the pledgor.[210]

This is the rule in the absence of some agreement between the pledgee and the pledgor that the right to collect dividends remains with the pledgor.[211] The rule applies to stock dividends also.[212] The corporation must pay the dividends to the pledgee if the transfer has been registered on the books of the corporation, or if it has notice of the pledge; otherwise it will become liable to the pledgee for any dividends paid to the pledgor.[213] The pledgee obtains no right to dividends declared prior to the contract.[214]

When a corporation voluntarily liquidated and paid to the record holder of stock both normal dividends and liquidating dividends, without notice that the stock had been pledged, the pledgee could recover against the corporation for the liquidating dividends but not for the normal dividends.[215]

Also, a pledgee can recover liquidating dividends from an officer of a dissolved corporation who paid the dividends to the pledgor without requiring surrender of the stock certificates.[216]

In the absence of a statute or agreement to the contrary, the pledgee of a stock continues entitled to dividends after the death of the pledgor, but can't continue to hold the stock indefinitely when the obligation that the stock secures is due and the estate of the pledgor is being administered. The pledgee must either sell the stock, apply to the

---

[210] Railroad Credit Corp. v Hawkins (CA–4 1936) 80 F2d 818.

[211] Guarantee Co. of North America v East Rome Town Co., (1895) 96 Ga. 511, 23 SE 503.

[212] In re Brewer's Estate 141 Misc. 563, 253 N.Y.S. 213. See also, Commercial Nat'l Bank v Nat'l Surety Co., (1932) 259 N.Y. 181, NE 92.

[213] Guarantee Co. of North America v East Rome Town Co., (1895) 96 Ga. 511, 23 SE 503; Mandel v North Hudson Investment Co., (1933) 112 N.J. Eq. 144, 164 Atl 455; Powell v Md. Trust Co. (CA–4 1942) 125 F2d 260, cert den, (1942) 316 US 671, 62 S Ct 1041; Garvy v Blatchford Cal. Meal Co. (CA–7 1941) 119 F2d 973; McGhie v First & Am. Nat'l Bank of Duluth, (1944) Minn., 14 NW2d 436.

[214] Fairbanks v Merchants' Nat'l Bank, (1889) 132 Ill. 120, 22 NE 524.

[215] Bay City Bank v St. Louis Motor Sales Co., (1931) 255 Mich. 261, 238 NW 241.

[216] Bogardus v Kentucky State Bank (Ky. Ct of App. 1955) 281 SW2d 904.

proceeds against the amount due and account to the estate for any excess, or release the stock to the estate for sale, retaining a lien against the proceeds of the sale.[217]

Dividends on pledged stock, which belong to the pledgee, can't be attached at the suit of the pledgor's creditors.[218]

A seller of pledged stock at a public sale has no right to dividends not declared before the sale.[219]

Right of corporation to set off dividend against debt due corporation. After a dividend is declared, a corporation owes its stockholders the amount of the dividend.[220] If a stockholder owes the corporation money, the corporation may keep any dividends due to the stockholder and apply them in satisfaction of the debt.[221] Where, however, the dividend isn't declared till after the death of a stockholder, the corporation can't apply the dividend against the deceased stockholder's debt to it. It is an asset of the decedent's estate, payable to his personal representative.[222] If the stock is transferred before the declaration of the dividend, the corporation can't set off a dividend against the transferee of the stockholder who is indebted to the corporation, if the corporation knows the stock has been transferred even though the transfer hasn't been recorded on the books.[223]

Compelling payment after dividend has been declared. A stockholder can sue his corporation to collect a dividend it declared[224] unless the dividend was illegal.[225] A credit on the corporate books is a declaration of a dividend, for which a stockholder can sue.[226]

---

[217] Rosel v Hill, (1941) 21 Ohio Ops. 415.

[218] Womack v De Witt, (1939) 40 Del. 304, 10 A2d 504.

[219] Kimmer v New Gin, Inc., (1940) 199 Ark. 1187, 137 SW2d 749.

[220] Peoples-Pittsburgh Trust Co. v US (WD Pa. 1944) 54 F Supp 742; Smith v Taecker, (1933) 133 Cal. App. 351, 24 P2d 182; In re Central N.J. Land & Improv. Co., (1933) 113 N.J. Eq. 332, 116 Atl 705.

[221] J. G. Wilson Corp. v Cahill, (1929) 152 Va. 108, 146 SE 274.

[222] Corporation, depositor in closed bank, has no right of set-off, by reason of such deposit, in suit by receiver of closed bank to recover dividends declared by corporate depositor, after bank closed on cumulative preferred stock of corporation owned by bank when it closed and retained by it thereafter. Harr v Bankers Securities Corp., (1938) 129 Pa. Super. 547, 196 Atl 522.

[223] Grafton v North American Transp. & Trading Co., (1919) 216 Ill. App. 262; Gemmell v Davis, (1892) 75 Md. 546, 23 Atl 1032.

[224] In re Sutherland (CA-2 1928) 23 F2d 595, modifying decree in (WD N.Y. 1927) 21 F2d 667; Geo. Feick & Sons. Co. v Blair (CA 1929) 26 F2d 540.

[225] Adams v Farmers Gin Co., (1938) Tex. Civ. App. 114 SW2d 583.

[226] Fidelity & Columbia Trust Co. v Louisville Ry. Co., (1936) 265 Ky. 820, 97 SW2d 825; Brown v Luce Mfg. Co., (1936) 231 Mo. App. 259, 96 SW2d 1098. See also Sharp v Commissioner (CA-3 1937) 91 F2d 802; Wis. Gas & Elec. Co. v US (CA-7 1943) 138 F2d 597.

Stockholders are general creditors of the corporation after the declaration of a dividend and in the event of bankruptcy of the corporation share pro rata with general creditors.[227] A dividend declared payable at a future date can't be sued for until the payment date arrives.[228] If, however, the corporation has set aside a fund upon the declaration of a dividend out of which the dividend is to be paid, the action creates a trust fund in the hands of the corporation for payment to the stockholders[229] and in the event of bankruptcy, general creditors can't reach the fund.[230] As a general rule a stockholder can't recover interest on a dividend after it has been declared,[231] though he may be allowed interest after a demand and refusal.[232] A stockholder who leaves his dividend with the corporation is not in default since he is under no obligation to draw or to demand his dividend within any prescribed period.

Liability of stockholders to return dividends improperly distributed. Illegal dividends paid to stockholders are generally recoverable by the corporation.[233] Dividends paid in impairment of the capital of a corporation are illegal and must be returned by stockholders.[234] *Exception:* When the corporation is solvent and the stockholders took the dividends in good faith.[235] And a promoter to whom stock is issued so as to make him a stockholder can't be compelled to return dividends received only because the validity of the stock issuance is questioned.[236]

If restitution isn't enforced by the corporation, a stockholder may compel repayment.[237] So can creditors of the corporation.[238] A receiver of a corporation[239] and a trustee in bankruptcy[240] may take steps to

---

[227] In re Central N.J. Land & Imp. Co., (1933) 113 N.J. Eq. 332, 166 Atl 705.

[228] Berkowitz v Palm Springs La Quinta Development Co., (1940) 37 Cal. App. 2d 249, 99 P2d 372.

[229] In re Associated Gas & Electric Co. (CA-2 1943) 137 F2d 607; Cassidy Southwestern Commission Co. v Guaranty Trust Co. of N. Y., (1943) Tex. Civ. App. 174 SW2d 494.

[230] In re Interborough Consol. Corp. (CA-2 1923) 288 F 334.

[231] Klein v Compania Azucarera Vertientes—Camaguey de Cuba, (1967) 28 A.D. 142, 283 N.Y.S.2d 478.

[232] J. G. Wilson Corp. v Cahill, (1929) 152 Va. 108, 146 SE 274.

[233] Sparling v General Discount & Mortgage Co., (1934) 178 Wash. 663, 35 P2d 60.

[234] Oilwell Chemical & Materials Co. v Petroleum Supply Co., (1944) 64 Cal. App. 2d 357, 148 P2d 720.

[235] Bates v Brooks, (1937) 222 Iowa 1128, 270 NW 867.

[236] McAllister v Eclipse Oil Co., (1936) 128 Tex. 449 98 SW2d 171.

[237] Gager v Paul, (1901) 111 Wis. 638, 37 SW 263.

[238] American Steel & Wire Co. v Eddy, (1904) 138 Mich. 403, 101 NW 578; Chisnell v Ozier Co., (1942) 140 Ohio St., 355, 44 NE2d 464.

[239] Hayden v Williams (CA-2 1899) 96 F 279; Klages v Cohen (CA-2 1945) 146 F2d 641.

[240] Cottrell v Albany Card & Paper Mfg. Co., (1911) 142 App. Div. 148, 126 N.Y.S. 1070; Ulness v Dunnell, (1931) 61 N.D. 95, 237 NW 208.

recover illegally paid dividends, as may an assignee for the benefit of creditors where the right is included in the assignment.[241]

This liability of stockholders to return dividends illegally paid isn't usually affected by the fact that the stockholders got the dividends in good faith and without knowledge that they had been illegally declared.[242] But a trustee in bankruptcy of a national bank could not recover from a stockholder a dividend paid out of capital while the corporation wasn't insolvent and was a going concern at the time of the payment, if the stockholder got the dividend in good faith and in the full belief that the corporation was solvent and prosperous.[243] Where a bank was insolvent at the time of the declaration of the dividend, the court held that the receiver could recover the illegal dividends from a stockholder who had received them in good faith.[244] A stockholder who has received, in good faith, dividends declared without negligence by the directors while the corporation was solvent, can't be compelled to return such dividends merely because, due to later disasters, the corporation becomes insolvent.[245]

The liability on the part of stockholders to make restitution of illegally declared dividends isn't discharged by a transfer of the shares after payment of the dividend, even though the statute provides that every person becoming a stockholder by transfer "shall, in proportion to his shares, succeed to all the rights and be subject to all the liabilities of prior shareholders."[246] Nor is the stockholder who received the illegal dividend exonerated from repayment for the benefit of creditors by a provision in the statute making the directors liable personally for repayment of unlawful dividends.[247]

By statute in many states, stockholders who accept a dividend knowing it to be illegal, must turn over the illegal dividend to directors, when the latter are liable to the corporation for declaring it.

Rights of creditors who become such after payment of illegal dividends. A corporate creditor whose claim arose after an illegal distribution of dividends may recover from the stockholders[248]; but not

---

[241] Grant v Ross, (1896) 100 Ky. 44, 37 SW 263.

[242] Detroit Trust Co. v Goodrich, (1913) 175 Mich. 168, 141 NW 882.

[243] McDonald v Williams, (1898) 174 US 397; Ratcliff v Clendenin (CA-8 1916) 232 F 61. See also Guaranty Trust Co. v Grand Rapids, G. H. & M. Ry. Co. (D Mich 1931) 7 F Supp 511.

[244] Hayden v Williams (CA-2 1899) 96 F 279.

[245] 160 Atl 440, 161 Atl 509; Bartlett v Smith, (1932) 162 Md. 478; Quintel v Adler, (1933) 146 Misc. 300, 262 N.Y.S. 126; Bates v Brooks, (1937) 222 Iowa 1128, 270 NW 867. See also, Burton v Roos (D Tex 1937) 20 F Supp 75.

[246] Hurburt v Tayler, (1885) 62 Wis. 607, 22 NW 855.

[247] Derbes v Till, (1930) 13 La. App. 495, 128 So. 196; Powers v Heggie, (1929) 268 Mass. 233, 167 NE 314.

[248] Cottrell v Albany Card & Paper Co., (1911) 142 App. Div. 148, 126 N.Y.S. 1070.

if the corporation was solvent when the dividend was declared.[249] If the dividend was declared while the corporation was insolvent, recovery may be had by creditors regardless of whether the creditor became such before or after the illegal dividend was declared.[250]

Liability of directors for unlawful dividends. In most states some provision is found placing a personal liability upon directors to the corporation and to creditors for the declaration and payment of unlawful dividends. In some states, they are also subject to fine and imprisonment. Though criminal liability of directors for improperly declared dividends can't be enforced in the courts of a state other than that of the corporation's domicile, criminal liability can be.[251]

In recent years, many states have enacted statutes that describe in considerable detail the extent of directors' liability for illegal declaration of dividends, and the circumstances in which the liability is imposed. The statutes vary widely in detail but broadly provide as follows:

(1) Directors who vote for or assent to the illegal declaration of a dividend are jointly and severally liable to the corporation for the amount of the dividend which is in excess of what could legally have been paid.

(2) A director who was present at the meeting is presumed to have assented to the dividend unless his dissent is entered in the minutes or unless he files his dissent with the secretary of the meeting before adjournment or by mail immediately after adjournment.

(3) In some states, absent directors also are liable unless, on learning of the illegal payment, they have their dissent entered in the minutes or file their dissent with the corporation.

(4) A statute imposing personal liability on directors for illegal dividends, but excepting absent directors, is penal and to be strictly construed; thus, an absent director was not liable for declaring a dividend out of capital although he had notice that the dividend was to be declared and accepted his shares.[252]

Directors who vote for an illegal dividend are relieved of liability if they relied in good faith on financial statements presented by a responsible officer or an independent accountant.

The injury to the corporation caused by an illegal or improvident

---

[249] Ratcliff v Clendenin (CA–8 1916) 232 F 61.
[250] Finn v Brown, (1891) 142 US 56, 12 S Ct 136; In re Bay Ridge Inn, Inc. (CA–2 1938) 98 F2d 85.
[251] Stratton v Bertlies, (1933) 238 A.D. 87, 263 N.Y.S. 466.
[252] Watkinson v Adams, (1939) 187 Okla. 432, 103 P2d 498.

declaration of dividends may be redressed in an action by the corporation directly against the directors responsible.[253]

Unless a statute provides otherwise, the directors are liable to the corporation[254] and to creditors if they unlawfully pay dividends out of capital.[255]

If the directors in good faith and without negligence declare a dividend that later turns out to have impaired capital, they can't be held personally liable.[256] But they are liable if they act without any report of the company's earnings and without any investigation of the company's affairs.[257]

The liability of directors to repay to the corporation dividends improperly declared may be enforced in a stockholder's derivative action.[258]

The liability of directors for unlawful dividends can't be enforced by a trustee in bankruptcy of the corporation;[259] however it survives the director's death.[260]

It has generally been held that the statute of limitations, outlawing claims because of delay in bringing an action to enforce directors' statutory liability, begins to run from the time the dividends were declared and not from the time the illegality was discovered.[261] Good faith and ratification are not defenses for directors sued under statutes imposing liability for illegal declaration of dividends.[262]

---

[253]Southern California Home Builders v Young, (1920) 45 Cal. App. 679, 188 P 586; Siegman v Electric Vehicle Co., (1907) 72 N.J. Eq. 403, 65 Atl 910; Appleton v American Malting Co., (1903) 65 N.J. Eq. 375, 54 Atl 454.

[254]National Lock Co. v Hogland (CA-7 1939) 101 F2d 576.

[255]Klages v Cohen (CA-2 1945) 146 F2d 641; Aiken v Insull (CA-7 1941) 122 F2d 746; De Met's, Inc. v Insull (CA-7 1941) 122 F2d 755, cert den, (1942) 315 US 806, 62 S Ct 638, 639; Boyd v Schneider (CA-7 1904) 131 F 223; Irving Trust Co. v Gunder, (1934) 152 Misc. 83, 271 N.Y.S. 795; Cochran v Shelter, (1926) 286 Pa. 226, 133 Atl 232. Cf Berman v LeBeau InterAmerica, Inc. (DC SD NY 1981) 509 F Supp 156.

[256]Williams v Spensley (CA-7 1917) 251 F 58; Stratton v Anderson, (1936) 278 Mich. 499, 270 NW 764; Diamond v Davis, Jr., (1942) 38 N.Y.S.2d 103, aff'd, (1942) 265 App. Div. 919, 39 N.Y.S.2d 412, aff'd, (1944) 292 N.Y. 552, 54 NE2d 683.

[257]Kahle v Mount Vernon Trust Co., (1940) 22 N.Y.S.2d 454; Fell v Pitts, (1919) 263 Pa. 314, 106 Atl 574.

[258]Weinberger v Semenenko, (1942) 36 N.Y.S.2d 396; Scullin v Mutual Drug Co., (1941) 138 Ohio St. 132, 33 NE2d 992.

[259]Morris v Sampsel, (1937) 224 Wis. 560, 272 NW 53; Smalley v Bernstein, (1927) 165 La. 1, 115 So. 347, cert den, 277 US 599, 48 S Ct 561; Fitzgerald v Marshall (D Colo. 1958) 161 F Supp 470. *Contra:* Stratton v Bertles, (1933) 238 A.D. 87, 263 N.Y.S. 466; Ulness v Dunnell, (1931) 61 ND 95, 237 NW 208; Claypoole v McIntosh, (1921) 182 N.C. 109, 108 SE 433.

[260]Aiken v Peabody (CA-7 1947) 168 F2d 615 (Ill. law).

[261]Pourroy v Gardner, (1932) 122 Cal. App. 521, 10 P2d 815; McGill's Adm'x v Phillips, (1932) 243 Ky. 768, 49 SW2d 1025.

[262]Cowin v Jonas, (1943) 43 N.Y.S. 2d 468, aff'd 267 A.D. 947, 48 N.Y.S. 2d 460, (1944) 293 N.Y. 838, 59 NE2d 436.

Absent and dissenting directors. Provision is made in many of the statutes that directors who dissent from the declaration of a dividend, or are absent at the time the dividend is declared, shall not be personally liable for dividends unlawfully paid. The statute of the particular state should be studied carefully to see what, if anything, must be done by a director who was absent or who dissented from the payment of a dividend in order to escape personal liability.

In the absence of statutory provision on the subject, the general rule as to liability of a director for acts of his co-directors may be applied in determining the liability of absent directors. An absent director will not be held liable for acts of his associates, if he hasn't connived at or participated in the acts, or was not negligent in not acting.[263] A director isn't required to attend every meeting of the board and therefore may ordinarily not be held liable for acts in which he hasn't concurred.[264]

> **Suggestion:** Upon learning of an illegally declared dividend, the absent director should inform the board of directors of his dissent from the act if he wishes to escape liability for the acts of his co-directors. This follows from the general rule that a director is held equally responsible with his associates where wrongful acts of the board have come to his knowledge and he acquiesces and takes no steps to avert the injurious consequences of the acts when by due diligence he might have prevented the wrongful act from being done.[265]

Revocation of dividends. A corporation generally can't revoke the declaration of a dividend without the consent of the stockholders.[266] Also, if the corporation has become not only a debtor but a trustee by the deposit of funds out of which the dividend is to be paid, the directors can't end the trust relation by a resolution rescinding its action in declaring the dividend and in setting aside the fund established for its payment.[267] Under the following circumstances, however, a dividend is revocable:

(1) If it impaired the capital of the corporation.[268]
(2) If the declaration of the dividend hasn't been made public, and no fund has been set aside for the payment of the dividend.[269]

---

[263] Schout v Conkey Ave. Saving Aid & Loan Assn., (1895) 11 Misc. 454, 32 N.Y.S. 713.
[264] Murphy v Penniman, (1907) 105 Me. 452, 66 Atl 282.
[265] Schout v Conkey Ave Saving Aid & Loan Assn., note 263, supra.
[266] Com'r of Internal Revenue v Cohen (CA-5 1941) 121 F2d 348; Grant v Ross, (1896) 100 Ky. 44, 37 SW 263; Hope Lumber Co. v Stewart, (1922) Mo. App. 241 SW 675. See also, Meyers v El Tejon Oil & Ref. Co., (1946) 29 Cal. 2d 184, 174 P2d 1.
[267] Staats v Biograph Co. (CA-2 1916) 236 F. 454; Van Dyk v McQuade, (1881) 86 N.Y. 38.
[268] Benas v Title Guaranty Trust Co., (1924) 216 Mo. App. 53, 267 SW 28; Sunseri v Sunseri, (1947) 358 Pa. 1, 55 A2d 370.
[269] Ford v Easthamption Rubber Thread Co., (1893) 158 Mass. 84, 32 NE 1036. *Contra:* McLaran v Crescent Planing Mill Co., (1906) 117 Mo. App. 40, 93 SW 819.

(3) If before a fund has been created for the payment of the dividend, the corporation experiences some major loss that makes it inadvisable to pay it.

Example: After a fire, the funds that would have gone to pay the dividends were needed for the rehabilitation of the company.[270]

The directors of a corporation that had declared a scrip dividend about the time that World War I broke out, were permitted to revoke the dividend when it appeared that the war had seriously affected the business of the corporation.[271]

Revocation of stock dividends. A distinction is made between cash dividends and stock dividends so far as the right to revoke a dividend is concerned. Directors may revoke the stock dividend at any time prior to the actual issuance of the stock when the stock dividend simply "capitalizes surplus."[272] If however, the stock dividend is payable in shares that the corporation acquired by purchase, the dividend won't be revocable, since this is a distribution of corporate earnings.[273]

Unclaimed dividends. Shareholders don't always cash each dividend check. Often the envelope is returned to the corporation as undeliverable; the shareholder moved and failed to inform the corporation of his whereabouts. Or the dividend check is received but then it's lost or destroyed by the shareholder and because the amount is small, he doesn't ask for a replacement check. These unclaimed dividends represent a real nuisance to a corporation. It tries to contact the shareholder to pay him and clear its records. But it is a recurring problem and in most states a shareholder can ask for payment years after the intended date. The State of Ohio prohibits this; it outlaws claims after six years from the date of mailing of the dividend check.[274]

Nearly all states have escheat or abandoned property laws that provide: (1) dividends remaining unclaimed for a specified number of years escheat to the state, (2) the corporation is freed from liability to the stockholder when it turns over the unclaimed dividends to the state, and (3) the real owner's interest is cut off after a specified number of years.

---

[270] *See* Dock v Schlichter Jute Cordage Co., (1895) 167 Pa. 370, 31 Atl 656.

[271] Staats v Biograph Co. (CA-2 1916) 236 F. 454.

[272] Terry v Eagle Lock Co., (1879) 47 Conn. 141; McLaran v Crescent Planing Mill Co., (1906) 117 Mo. App. 40, 93 SW 819.

[273] Dock v Schlichter Jute Cordage Co., (1895) 167 Pa. 370, 31 Atl 656.

[274] Ohio G.C.L. §1701.34.

Chapter 24

FORMS RELATING TO DIVIDENDS

Contents—Chapter 24

DIRECTORS' RESOLUTION DECLARING REGULAR DIVIDEND

RESOLVED, That a regular ("annual," "quarterly," or "semi-annual") dividend is hereby declared out of the undivided profits of this Corporation, payable on . . . ., 19. ., to the holders of record at the close of business on . . . ., 19. ., as follows: A dividend of . . . . . percent (. . . . .%) on the outstanding Preferred Stock, and a dividend of . . . . . Dollars ($. . . . .) per share on the outstanding Common Stock without par value.

DIRECTORS' RESOLUTION DECLARING CASH
DIVIDEND ON PREFERRED STOCK

RESOLVED, That the semi-annual dividend of . . . . . percent upon the outstanding preferred stock of this company is hereby declared, the same to be payable from the surplus profits of this company to the stockholders of preferred stock of record on . . . ., 19. .; said dividend to be paid on . . . ., 19. ., and

RESOLVED FURTHER, That the treasurer is hereby instructed and directed to give due notice of such dividend and to pay the same on the date aforesaid.

DIRECTORS' RESOLUTION DECLARING CASH
DIVIDEND ON PREFERRED AND COMMON STOCK

RESOLVED, That there is hereby declared from the surplus profits of the Corporation, a dividend of one dollar and fifty cents ($1.50) per share on both the preferred and the common stock of the Corporation, payable on . . . ., 19. ., to holders of record of said stock at the close of business on . . . ., 19. ., and the Treasurer is directed and authorized to cause the same to be paid on the date specified.

DIRECTORS' RESOLUTION DECLARING DIVIDEND ON
PREFERRED AND COMMON STOCK, TO BE PAID BY
TRANSFER AGENT

RESOLVED, That the regular quarterly dividend of . . . . . (. . . . .¢) Cents per share on the participating convertible stock of this Corporation is hereby declared payable on . . . ., 19. ., to stockholders of record of said stock at the close of business on . . . ., 19. ., and

RESOLVED FURTHER, That a dividend of . . . . . (. . . . .¢) Cents per share on the common stock of this Corporation is hereby declared, payable on . . . ., 19. ., to stockholders of record of said stock at the close of business on . . . ., 19. ., and

RESOLVED FURTHER, That the Secretary is hereby directed and authorized to certify these resolutions and to affix the seal of this Corporation hereto; and the Treasurer is directed and authorized to lodge the same with the Transfer Agents of the several classes of stock, and to take such other steps and perform any and all such further acts as may be necessary and proper to carry out the intents and purposes of the foregoing resolutions.

MINUTES OF DECLARATION OF CASH DIVIDEND ON PREFERRED AND COMMON STOCK

WHEREAS, it appears from the report of the Treasurer that the net profits of this Corporation for the three-months' period ending ...., 19.., after interest charges and reserves have been deducted, amount to the sum of ..... ($.....) Dollars, and

WHEREAS, it appears from the report of the Treasurer that the surplus (exclusive of Special Surplus account) available for dividends on ...., 19.., is ..... ($.....) Dollars, and the Treasurer has reported that the same has not diminished since that date, be it

RESOLVED, That for the purpose of paying the regular quarterly dividend of one and three-quarters (1¾%) percent on ..... ($.....) Dollars preferred stock of the .... Corporation, there is hereby set apart, out of the surplus net profits arising from the business, the sum of ..... ($.....) Dollars, and from such sum so set apart the Treasurer is hereby authorized and directed to pay, or cause to be paid, the said regular quarterly dividend of one and three-quarters (1¾%) percent on ...., 19.., to the preferred stockholders of record at the close of business on ...., 19..

The Treasurer further reported that the present condition of the Special Surplus account complied in all respects with the conditions required by the Certificate of Incorporation to exist for the payment of dividends on the common stock, and that the surplus available for dividends on the common stock on ...., 19.., after the sum of ..... ($.....) Dollars, heretofore at this meeting set apart for the payment of the quarterly dividend on the preferred stock, has been deducted, is ..... ($.....) Dollars.

Upon motion duly made and seconded, it was unanimously

RESOLVED, That for the purpose of paying a quarterly dividend of one ($1) dollar per share on ..... (.....) shares of the common stock of the .... Corporation now outstanding, there is hereby set apart, out of the surplus net profits arising from the business of the Corporation, the sum of ..... ($.....) Dollars and from such sum so set apart the Treasurer is authorized and directed to pay, or cause to be paid, the said quarterly dividend of one ($1) Dollar per share on ...., 19.., to the common stockholders of record at the close of business on ...., 19..

DIRECTORS' RESOLUTION DECLARING AN
EXTRA DIVIDEND

WHEREAS, the surplus net earnings of this Corporation are sufficient in amount to warrant the declaration of a larger dividend than the usual quarterly dividend of ..... Dollars ($.....), be it

RESOLVED, That an extra dividend of ..... Dollars ($.....) is hereby declared upon the Common Stock of this Corporation, payable on ...., 19.., to stockholders of record at the close of business on ...., 19..

DIRECTORS' RESOLUTION DECLARING REGULAR
AND EXTRA DIVIDEND

WHEREAS, the surplus net earnings of this Corporation are sufficient in amount to warrant the declaration of a larger dividend than the regular quarterly dividend of ..... Dollars ($.....) upon the Common Stock of this Corporation, and

WHEREAS, it is the opinion of this Board of Directors that it is not advisable at this time to place the Common Stock definitely on a dividend basis higher than ..... Dollars ($.....) per annum, but that it is advisable to declare the regular quarterly dividend of ..... Dollars ($.....) and an extra dividend of ..... Dollars ($.....) upon the Common Stock of this Corporation, be it

RESOLVED, That the regular quarterly dividend of ..... Dollars ($.....) and an extra dividend of ..... Dollars ($.....) are hereby declared upon the Common stock of this Corporation, payable on the .. day of ...., 19.., to stockholders of record at the close of business on ...., 19..

DIRECTORS' RESOLUTION TURNING EXTRA DIVIDEND
INTO REGULAR DIVIDEND AND DECLARING
DIVIDEND AT NEW RATE

WHEREAS, this Corporation has paid a regular dividend of ..... Dollars ($.....) per annum and an extra dividend of ..... Dollars ($.....) per annum and an extra dividend of ..... Dollars ($.....) per annum upon its Common Stock without par value for the past ..... years, and

WHEREAS, this Board of Directors now deems it advisable to place the Common Stock without par value on a regular dividend basis of ..... Dollars ($.....) per annum, be it

RESOLVED, That it is the policy of this Corporation to place the Common Stock on a regular dividend basis of ..... Dollars ($.....) per annum, payable quarterly, on the first days of February, May, August, and November of each year; and

RESOLVED FURTHER, That a regular dividend of . . . . . Dollars ($. . . . .) per share for the quarterly period ending . . . ., 19 . ., hereby declared upon all the Common Stock without par value issued and outstanding, said dividend to be payable on . . . ., 19. ., to stockholders of record at the close of business on . . . ., 19. .

DIRECTORS' RESOLUTION AUTHORIZING OFFICERS TO NEGOTIATE A LOAN FOR PURPOSE OF PAYING DIVIDEND

WHEREAS, the Corporation has accumulated a surplus which would be more than sufficient to pay the declared dividend of . . . . . Dollars ($. . . . .) on the preferred stock and . . . . . (. . . . . %) percent on the common stock payable on . . . ., 19. ., to stockholders of record at the close of business on . . . ., 19. . and

WHEREAS, the cash surplus has temporarily been used for the expansion of the business, be it

RESOLVED, That the President is hereby authorized to negotiate a loan from . . . . Bank for the amount of the dividend declared, and

RESOLVED FURTHER, That, upon obtaining the said loan, the Treasurer is hereby directed and authorized to pay out from the fund so borrowed the declared dividend on the date specified.

DIRECTORS' RESOLUTION DECLARING DIVIDEND PAYABLE IN STOCK OR IN CASH

RESOLVED, That there is hereby declared out of the surplus profits or net earnings of the Corporation, a regular quarterly dividend of sixty (60¢) cents per share on the outstanding Common Stock of the Corporation without par value, payable . . . ., 19. ., to the holders of record of said stock at the close of business on . . . ., 19. .; and

RESOLVED FURTHER, That the holders of said Common Stock without par value of this Corporation can apply such dividend to the purchase of shares of Common Stock without par value of this Corporation, at the rate of one fiftieth (1/50) of a share for each share held by them; and

RESOLVED FURTHER, That there be issued to each holder of Common Stock without par value of this Corporation, who elects to receive the dividend hereby declared in additional shares, certificates for Common Stock, fully paid and nonassessable, of this Corporation, at the rate of one fiftieth (1/50) of a share for each share held; and

RESOLVED FURTHER, That, in any and all cases where any amount of stock issuable for such stock dividend shall be less than one share, fractional shares shall not be issued, but an equivalent payment shall be made in cash, the basis of the value of one whole share being ..... ($.....) Dollars; and

RESOLVED FURTHER, That for each share of Common Stock issued for the quarterly dividend, there shall be charged to the net earnings or surplus of the Corporation the amount of thirty dollars ($30) exactly as though the dividend had been paid in cash.

DIRECTORS' RESOLUTION DECLARING DIVIDENDS PAYABLE ON PARTLY PAID STOCK ON BASIS OF AMOUNT PAID IN

RESOLVED, That the holders of partly paid stock of this Corporation shall be entitled to receive dividends, when and as declared by the Board of Directors, out of the surplus earnings or net profits of the Corporation, in proportion to the amounts respectively paid up on the shares.

DIRECTORS' RESOLUTION DECLARING REGULAR DIVIDEND AND AUTHORIZING DEPOSIT OF FUNDS FOR PAYMENT

RESOLVED, That a regular (annual, quarterly, or semiannual) dividend is hereby declared out of the undivided profits of this Corporation, payable on ...., 19.., to the holders of record at the close of business on ...., 19.., as follows: A dividend of ..... (.....%) percent on the outstanding preferred stock, and a dividend of ..... ($.....) Dollars per share on the outstanding common stock without par value, and

RESOLVED FURTHER, That the sum of ..... ($.....) Dollars is hereby appropriated from the funds of this Corporation, to be deposited in the .... Bank for the payment of said dividend, and

RESOLVED FURTHER, That the Treasurer is hereby authorized and directed to send notice of the above dividend to all stockholders entitled thereto, and to publish notice thereof immediately in the (*insert name of newspaper*).

RESOLUTION OF EXECUTIVE COMMITTEE RECOMMENDING DECLARATION OF DIVIDEND

RESOLVED, That the Executive Committee hereby recommends to the Board of Directors that there be declared from the surplus profits of this Corporation, a dividend of ..... ($.....) Dollars per share on both the preferred and the common stock of this Corporation, payable on ...., 19.., to holders of record of said stock at the close of business on ...., 19..

DIRECTORS' RESOLUTION RATIFYING ACTION OF EXECUTIVE COMMITTEE IN DECLARING DIVIDEND

RESOLVED, That the action taken by the Executive Committee of this Corporation at its meeting on ...., 19.., in declaring a dividend of ..... ($.....) Dollars per share, payable on ...., 19.., to holders of record of both preferred and common stock of this Corporation at the close of business on ...., 19.., is hereby in all respects ratified, approved, confirmed, and adopted as the act of the Board of Directors.

DIRECTORS' RESOLUTION AUTHORIZING ISSUANCE OF COMMON STOCK IN SETTLEMENT OF CUMULATIVE DIVIDENDS ON PREFERRED STOCK

WHEREAS, this Corporation has outstanding certain shares of its preferred stock entitled to cumulative preferential dividends at the rate of seven (7%) percent per annum, and

WHEREAS, this Corporation is in arrears in the payment of dividends on its outstanding shares of preferred stock, to and including ...., 19.., in the amount of ..... ($.....) Dollars, and

WHEREAS, the holders of a large number of the shares of the preferred stock of the Corporation have indicated their willingness to liquidate and discharge their claims for accrued dividends on such shares of preferred stock in the manner hereinafter provided, and

WHEREAS, it is deemed desirable and advisable by the Board of Directors of this Corporation that the liquidation of such dividends be effected in the manner and on the terms hereinafter stated, be it

RESOLVED, That this Corporation, when its authorized common stock shall have been increased as provided in the amendment to the amended Certificate of Incorporation of the Corporation proposed by resolutions this day adopted by the Board of Directors of the Corporation, shall offer to deliver to the holder of each share of preferred stock of the Corporation (in respect of which the Corporation shall be in arrears in the payment of dividends), shares of common stock of the Corporation without any nominal or par value, at the rate of ..... ($.....) Dollars per share of such common stock, and to pay in cash any fractional amount of such accrued and unpaid dividends remaining after the delivery of said shares of common stock at the rate aforesaid. Such shares of common stock and cash, when accepted, shall be in lieu and full satisfaction of the accumulated and unpaid preferred dividends, up to and including ...., 19.., due to such holders of shares of the preferred stock of the Corporation. The proper officers of this Corporation are hereby authorized to cause to be executed and delivered certificates for such shares of common stock of the Corporation, and to be paid such amounts in cash as may be required as aforesaid. The delivery of such dividend payments in common stock and cash shall be made on . . . ., 19. ., to stockholders of record at the close of business on . . . ., 19. ., and

RESOLVED FURTHER, That concurrently with the issuance of shares of the common stock of the Corporation as aforesaid, the capital of the Corporation shall be increased by the transfer from the capital surplus to the capital account of the Corporation of the sum of . . . . . ($. . . . .) Dollars per share for each share of common stock so issued, and that all such shares of common stock of the Corporation, when issued as aforesaid, shall be declared to be fully paid and nonassessable.

DIRECTORS' RESOLUTION DECLARING ACCUMULATED DIVIDEND PAYABLE

RESOLVED, That all dividends accumulated and unpaid upon the preferred stock of the . . . . Company since . . . ., 19. ., namely, ... (. . . . .%) percent, are hereby declared payable on . . . ., 19. ., from surplus, to holders of such preferred stock, according to the Company's books and records of transfer and registration at the close of business on . . . ., 19. .

DIRECTORS' RESOLUTION DECLARING DIVIDEND AND AUTHORIZING APPLICATION OF DIVIDEND TO PURCHASE OF STOCK, UNLESS PAYMENT IN CASH IS REQUIRED

RESOLVED, That there is hereby declared out of the surplus profits or net earnings of the Corporation, a regular quarterly dividend of sixty (60¢) Cents per share on the outstanding Class A Common Stock of the Corporation without nominal or par value, payable on . . . ., 19. ., to the holders of record of said stock at the close of business on . . . ., 19. ., and

RESOLVED FURTHER, That the holders of said Class A Common Stock without nominal or par value of this Corporation can apply such dividend to the purchase of shares of Class A Common stock without nominal or par value of this Corporation, at the rate of one fiftieth (1/50) of a share for each share held by them, and

RESOLVED FURTHER, That there be issued to each holder of Class A Common Stock without nominal or par value of this Corporation, as of the close of business on . . . ., 19. ., certificates for Class A Common Stock, fully paid and nonassessable, of this Corporation, and/or nondividend-bearing scrip certificates therefor, at the rate of one fiftieth (1/50) of a share for each share held, unless on or before the close of business on . . . ., 19. ., such stockholders shall advise . . . . Bank, ... (*Street*), ... (*City*), ... (*State*), as hereinafter provided, that they do not elect to exercise the right to apply the said dividend to the purchase of additional shares of such Class A Common Stock of the Corporation, and request that said dividend be paid in cash, and

RESOLVED FURTHER, That said .... Bank, as Transfer Agent of the Class A Common Stock of the Corporation and of the said scrip certificates, is hereby authorized to record in its transfer records and countersign as Transfer Agent, certificates for Class A Common Stock, fully paid and nonassessable, and/or scrip certificates, at the rate prescribed above for the shares of the Class A Common Stock of the Corporation, of record as at the close of business on ...., 19.., and, as Dividend Disbursing Agent, to send such certificates for full shares of such stock, when countersigned by .... Company of ...., as Registrar, by first class mail, and to send such scrip certificates by first-class mail on or after ...., 19.., to all stockholders of such Class A Common Stock as shall not, on or before ...., 19.., have advised said .... Bank that they do not elect to apply the said dividend to the purchase of additional shares of such Class A Common Stock and as shall not, on or before ...., 19.., have advised said .... Bank that they do not elect to apply the said dividend to the purchase of additional shares of such Class A Common Stock and as shall not have requested that such dividend be paid in cash, and

RESOLVED FURTHER, That .... Company of ....., as Registrar, is hereby directed to register and countersign upon the original issuance thereof, such certificates for Class A Common Stock as .... Bank shall from time to time present to it for such purpose, with advice that the same are to be issued pursuant to these resolutions, the shares of Class A Common Stock to be issued pursuant to these resolutions not to exceed in the aggregate, however, one fiftieth (1/50) of the total shares, plus one (1) issued and outstanding at the close of business on ...., 19.., and

RESOLVED FURTHER, That all certificates of Class A Common Stock issued pursuant to these resolutions shall be transferable in the City of New York, New York, or Chicago, Illinois, in like manner as the certificates for Class A Common Stock now outstanding, and the authority of .... Bank of the City of ...., and .... Bank of ...., Chicago, Illinois, as Transfer Agents, and of .... Company of New York, and .... Company, Chicago, Illinois, as Registrars, is hereby expressly extended so as to authorize the transfer, from time to time, of certificates for Class A Common Stock issued pursuant to these resolutions, in like manner as the certificates for Class A Common Stock now outstanding, and

RESOLVED FURTHER, That the President or a Vice president, or the Treasurer or an Assistant Treasurer, or the Secretary or an Assistant Secretary of this Corporation are hereby authorized and directed to certify these resolutions, to have the seal of this Corporation affixed thereto, and to lodge the same with the Transfer Agents and Registrars of the Class A Common Stock, and to take any and all such other steps and perform any and all such further acts as may be necessary and proper to carry out the intents and purposes of the foregoing resolutions, and

RESOLVED FURTHER, That for each one fiftieth (1/50) share of Class A Common Stock issued for the quarterly dividend, there shall be charged to the net earnings or surplus of the Corporation the amount of sixty (60¢) Cents, exactly as though the dividend had been paid in cash.

RESOLUTION DECLARING DIVIDEND AND MAKING PROVISION FOR DIVIDENDS ON UNEXCHANGED STOCK

RESOLVED, That out of the surplus or net profits of the Corporation, a dividend of $.... on each share of .....% Cumulative Preferred Stock of this Corporation is hereby declared, payable on ...., 19.., to stockholders of record at the close of business on ...., 19.., and

RESOLVED, That this Corporation set aside and reserve out of its surplus or net profits, a fund equal to the dividends which would be payable as aforesaid on all shares of its .....% Cumulative Preferred Stock issuable in exchange for the Preferred Stock of .... Company outstanding and unexchanged on ...., 19.., if all of said shares had been exchanged for shares of Preferred Stock of this Corporation, pursuant to the agreement of merger of said Company into this Corporation; and that on or subsequent to ...., 19.., upon surrender of any certificates for shares of said Preferred Stock in exchange for certificates for shares of Preferred Stock of this Corporation, an amount without interest, equal to the dividend so reserved with respect to the shares of .....% Cumulative Preferred Stock of this Corporation so issued, be paid to the person or persons to whom such shares shall be issued.

DIRECTORS' RESOLUTION DECLARING DIVIDEND PAYABLE IN PROPERTY

WHEREAS, undivided profits of this Corporation, amounting to approximately ..... ($.....) Dollars, are invested in certain pieces of real estate as follows (*insert description*), and

WHEREAS, said pieces of real estate are not directly used for the purposes for which this Corporation is organized, and

WHEREAS, such undivided profits are not now necessary for the business of this Corporation, and should be divided proportionately among the stockholders by way of dividend, and

WHEREAS, the stockholders of this Corporation have expressed a willingness to accept their proportionate shares of the said real estate in a joint conveyance from the Corporation to the stockholders, instead of having the same reduced to money and divided, be it

RESOLVED, That the President and the Secretary of this Corporation are hereby authorized, empowered, and directed to convey the real estate hereinbefore described, of the approximate value of ..... ($.....) Dollars, to the following-named stockholders of this Corporation, being all the stockholders thereof, in the proportions set opposite their respective names, as tenants in common.

....	.....%
....	.....%
....	.....%
....	.....%
....	.....%

RESOLUTION OF BOARD OF DIRECTORS DECLARING EXTRA DIVIDEND PAYABLE IN STOCK OF ANOTHER CORPORATION

WHEREAS, this Company is the owner and registered holder of six hundred thousand (600,000) shares of the fully paid nonassessable preferred capital stock of .... Corporation (A corporation organized under the laws of the State of ....), of the par value of one ($1) Dollar for each share, which it acquired by purchase out of its accumulated surplus profits, and

WHEREAS, the Board of Directors of this Company deems it wise to distribute such shares to the shareholders of this Company at their cost value to this Company—viz., one ($1) Dollar per share, be it

RESOLVED, That an extra dividend of one ($1) Dollar per share is hereby declared payable on ...., 19.., to shareholders of this Company of record at the close of business on ...., 19.., by the distribution of six hundred thousand (600,000) shares of the fully paid nonassessable preferred capital stock of .... Corporation, a .... corporation, of the par value of one ($1) Dollar for each share, now forming part of the accumulated surplus profits of this Company, in the proportion of one share of the preferred stock of said .... Corporation to each share of the present outstanding six hundred thousand (600,000) shares of the stock of this Company, such dividend to be represented by a duly executed stock certificate of .... Corporation for the number of full shares of such preferred stock to which each shareholder of the .... Company is entitled under this resolution, and that to that end the shares of such preferred stock now held and owned by this Company be indorsed and transferred by this Company to the respective shareholders of this Company, as they may be severally entitled thereto, and

RESOLVED FURTHER, That the President and Secretary of this Company are hereby authorized and directed to take such other steps and perform any and all further acts as may be necessary and proper to carry out the intents and purposes of the foregoing resolution.

DIRECTORS' RESOLUTION DECLARING A DIVIDEND PAYABLE IN SECURITIES HELD BY CORPORATION

WHEREAS, this Company has accumulated profits that are not necessary for the conduct of the business for which this company was chartered and organized and in which it is engaged, which profits are invested in low interest-bearing securities—to wit, United States Government bonds, and United States Treasury certificates—in the sum of ..... ($.....) Dollars, be it

RESOLVED, That a dividend is hereby declared upon the outstanding capital stock of this Company in the sum of ..... (.....%) percent, and that said dividend be paid on ...., 19.., to stockholders of record at the close of business on ...., 19.., by delivering and transferring to such stockholders the investments held by this Company in government bonds and treasury certificates, in such amounts as the stockholders shall be entitled to under this resolution.

RESOLUTION AUTHORIZING DIVIDEND PAYABLE IN STOCK OF ANOTHER CORPORATION, WITH CASH ADJUSTMENT FOR FRACTIONAL SHARES

RESOLVED, That a dividend payable in common stock of the .... Company, now owned by this Corporation, is hereby declared on the common stock of this Corporation, payable on .... , 19.., to holders of the common stock of this Corporation of record as of the close of business on .... , 19.., such dividend to be at the rate of one twentieth of one share of the common stock of the .... Company for each share of the common stock of this Corporation, provided that in no case shall fractional shares of common stock of the .... Company be distributed; but in lieu of such fractional shares, the officers of this Corporation are hereby authorized to make such cash adjustments as they may deem appropriate with the common stockholders who would otherwise be entitled to receive fractional shares of such stock.

DIRECTORS' RESOLUTION DECLARING, SUBJECT TO APPROVAL OF SECURITIES AND EXCHANGE COMMISSION, A DIVIDEND BASED ON PROMISSORY NOTE TO BE RECEIVED AS DIVIDEND FROM ANOTHER CORPORATION

WHEREAS, this Company is to be the recipient of a dividend on the common stock declared and paid by the .... Corporation, a .... corporation, to its common stockholders of record as of the close of business on .... , 19.., said dividend to be payable on or before .. .., 19.., and

WHEREAS, said dividend is to be received by this Company in the form of a promissory note executed by the .... Corporation as payor, to this Company as payee, said note to be drawn for the principal amount of ..... ($.....) Dollars, dated .... , 19.., due and payable on or before ...., 19.., to bear interest until paid at the rate of ..... (.....%) percent per annum, payable semi-annually, and

WHEREAS, the Board of Directors of this Company is agreed that such dividend note to be received from the .... Corporation, as set out above, should be received by this Company at face value, and

WHEREAS, the Board of Directors of this Company is of the opinion that the receipt of such note from the . . . . Corporation will place this Company in such a position that it would be to the best interests of the Company and of its stockholders that a dividend be declared out of the earnings of this Company in the amount of . . . . . ($. . . . .) Dollars per share, be it

RESOLVED, That there be declared, subject to the approval and consideration of the Securities and Exchange Commission under the Public Utility Holding Company Act of 1935, a dividend in the amount of . . . . . ($. . . . .) Dollars per share on all of the outstanding common stock of this Company, payable on or before . . . ., 19. ., to the common stockholders of record at the close of business on . . . ., 19. ., and

RESOLVED FURTHER, That said dividend shall be paid by assigning a . . . . . ($. . . . .) Dollar interest in and to the said . . . . Corporation note to the . . . . Bank of . . . . (*Street*), ... (*City*), ... (*State*), to be held by it in trust for the sole benefit of the stockholders of this Company as of record at the close of business on . . . ., 19. .; the said trustee shall issue beneficial certificates to the various stockholders entitled to participate in this dividend on the basis of . . . . . ($. . . . .) Dollars per share of the common stock held in this Company by such stockholders, and shall receive all payments made or to be made on said note by the . . . . Corporation, its successors or assigns, for the benefit of the said certificate holders, and shall distribute such receipts to each of the stockholders in such amount as their proportionate interest may appear, and

RESOLVED FURTHER, That the officers of this Company are hereby authorized and empowered to enter into a trust indenture with the said . . . . Bank of . . . . (*Street*), ... (*City*), ... (*State*), for the purpose set out above and to assign, without recourse, such interest in the . . . . Corporation note to such trustee as shall be necessary to pay and fully discharge this dividend obligation; and further, that the officers of this Company are hereby authorized and empowered to take all such steps as are proper and necessary to carry out the payment of the above specified dividend, and to execute such papers, reports, applications, and other documents as are necessary to obtain the approval of the Securities and Exchange Commission for this dividend declaration.

DIRECTORS' RESOLUTION AUTHORIZING SCRIP DIVIDEND AND MAKING SCRIP CERTIFICATES REDEEMABLE IN CASH OR CONVERTIBLE INTO STOCK

WHEREAS, this Corporation has hitherto expended, of its earnings, money equal in amount to . . . . . (. . . . .%) percent of the capital stock of the Corporation, in the purchase of real estate and other properties, with the object of increasing its profits, and

WHEREAS, this Corporation has not been paying dividends for the past three years, be it

RESOLVED, That a certificate, signed by the President and Treasurer of the Corporation, be issued to each of its stockholders, such certificate to represent a dividend in the amount of . . . . . (. . . . .%) percent of the amount of the capital stock held by each stockholder and to bear dividends at the same rate and at the same times as dividends shall be paid on shares of the capital stock of the Corporation; and

RESOLVED FURTHER, That the Corporation may, at its option, redeem such certificate in cash out of future earnings, or make such certificate convertible into stock of the Corporation, whenever the Corporation shall be authorized to increase its capital stock to an amount sufficient for such conversion.

DIRECTORS' RESOLUTION AUTHORIZING REDEMPTION OF SCRIP

RESOLVED, That the scrip heretofore issued by this Corporation in lieu of cash dividends be called for redemption on . . . ., 19..; and

RESOLVED FURTHER, That the respective officers of this Corporation are hereby authorized and directed to take any and all steps that may be necessary or proper for the redemption of such scrip.

DIRECTORS' RESOLUTION AUTHORIZING PAYMENT OF EXTRA STOCK DIVIDEND (WHERE CORPORATION HAS SUFFICIENT UNISSUED STOCK TO COVER THE DIVIDEND)

WHEREAS, a dividend of 2 percent upon the first preferred capital stock and 2 percent upon the common capital stock has this day been declared, and

WHEREAS, the surplus net earnings of the . . . . Company are, after the declaration of the said dividend, sufficient in amount to warrant the declaration and payment of an extra dividend of 12 and one-half percent upon said common capital stock, and

WHEREAS, the Board of Directors deems it advisable to conserve the cash resources of the Company by declaring such dividend in shares of fully paid common stock, rather than in cash, be it

RESOLVED, That, as an extra dividend upon the outstanding common capital stock of the Company, this Company issue to the holders of such stock, of record at . . . .M. on . . . ., 19.., common stock of the Company, of a par value equal to 12 and one-half percent of the par value of the common stock on said date standing in the name of such holders, severally and respectively, and the Board of Directors hereby declares such dividend, and

RESOLVED FURTHER, That the President and the Secretary are hereby authorized to issue, as of . . . ., 19.., such additional amount of authorized common stock as shall be necessary for such dividend—namely, ... ($.....) Dollars par value—and to execute and deliver certificates of such stock on and after ...., 19.., without closing the transfer books, and

RESOLVED FURTHER, That, in any and all cases where any amount of stock issuable for such dividend shall be less than one share, the Company shall deliver scrip for such fractions, in a form to be approved by counsel of the Company. Such scrip certificates, when surrendered to the Company in amounts aggregating one full share of stock or multiples thereof, shall be exchangeable for certificates of common stock of the Company with any accumulated dividends on such stock, but, until so exchanged, scrip certificates shall not be entitled to receive any dividends, or to have any voting rights, stock subscription rights, or other rights appertaining to such common stock.

DIRECTORS' RESOLUTION DECLARING STOCK DIVIDEND FROM UNISSUED STOCK

WHEREAS, there has been expended for permanent improvements and betterments during the years 19.., 19.., and 19.., the sum of ..... ($.....) Dollars, all of which sum has been furnished from the net earnings of the Corporation, and fairly belongs to the stockholders of the Corporation, be it

RESOLVED, That the President and the Secretary are hereby authorized to issue ..... (.....) shares of the authorized and unissued capital stock of the Corporation, payable on ...., 19.., to holders of record of said stock at the close of business on ...., 19.., in proportion to their holdings.

DIRECTORS' RESOLUTION DECLARING STOCK DIVIDEND FROM SHARES HELD IN THE TREASURY OF A CLOSE CORPORATION

WHEREAS, there is now in the treasury of the Company .... shares of its capital stock, representing undivided profits invested in said security, and

WHEREAS, it is deemed advisable to divide said stock as a dividend among the present stockholders, be it

RESOLVED, That the President and the Secretary be and they hereby are authorized and directed to distribute the ..... shares of the capital stock of this Company now held in the treasury of the Company to the present stockholders, in proportion to their present holdings, as follows:

To ....;	.... shares
To ....;	.... shares
To ....;	.... shares

DIRECTORS' RESOLUTION RECOMMENDING INCREASE OF STOCK FOR PURPOSE OF DECLARING STOCK DIVIDEND AND CALLING STOCKHOLDERS' MEETING TO VOTE THEREON

WHEREAS, this Corporation now has capital stock for $100,000 issued and outstanding, and a surplus in excess of $50,000, and

WHEREAS, it is desirable that said surplus, to the extent of at least $50,000, should be retained by the Corporation as working capital, and to that end that its capital stock should be increased to $150,000 and a stock dividend of $50,000 (50%) declared out of such increase, be it

RESOLVED, That it is advisable to increase the capital stock of this Corporation to $150,000, and

RESOLVED FURTHER, That it is advisable to declare and pay to the stockholders of the Corporation, a stock dividend of $50,000 out of such increase of stock, and

RESOLVED FURTHER, That the Board does hereby call a special meeting of the stockholders, to be held at the Corporation's office at ....
(*address*), on ...., 19.., at .. ...M., to take action upon the above resolutions and decide whether or not such increase of stock shall be made.

STOCKHOLDERS' RESOLUTION AUTHORIZING INCREASE OF CAPITAL STOCK FOR PURPOSE OF DECLARING A STOCK DIVIDEND

WHEREAS, the Articles of Incorporation of this Corporation provide that the capital stock thereof shall be $100,000, with power to increase or decrease the same at any time to such amount as a majority of the stockholders deem advisable, and

WHEREAS, the Board of Directors at a meeting held at the office of the Corporation at .... (*address*), on ...., 19.., passed a resolution declaring that it is advisable to increase the capital stock of this Corporation to $150,000, and that it is also advisable to declare and pay to the stockholders thereof a stock dividend of $50,000 out of such increase of stock, be it

RESOLVED, That the stock of this Corporation is hereby increased to the sum of $150,000, and

RESOLVED FURTHER, That the officers of the Corporation are hereby empowered and instructed to file a proper certificate of such increase in the office of the Secretary of State of the State of .... within 30 days from this date; and

RESOLVED FURTHER, That the directors are hereby authorized and empowered to declare, at such time as they may determine, a stock dividend of $50,000, or 50%, on the present issued capital stock of this Corporation.

DIRECTORS' RESOLUTION AUTHORIZING STOCK DIVIDEND AFTER INCREASE OF CAPITAL STOCK

WHEREAS, the resolution passed by the Board of Directors on . . . ., 19. ., advising the increase of the capital stock of the Corporation to $150,000 and a declaration of a stock dividend of $50,000 out of such increase of stock was approved at a meeting of the stockholders on . . . ., 19. ., and a certificate of such increase was thereupon duly filed in the office of the Secretary of State of the State of . . . ., be it

RESOLVED, That the directors declare a stock dividend of $50,000, or 50%, on the present issued capital stock of this Corporation, payable on . . . ., 19. ., to the stockholders of record of this Corporation at the close of business on . . . ., 19. ., out of such increase of stock, and

RESOLVED FURTHER, That the President and Treasurer are hereby authorized and directed to issue on . . . ., 19. ., to the several stockholders of record at the close of business on . . . ., 19. ., in payment of said stock dividend, stock certificates for as many whole shares of fully paid and nonassessable stock of this Corporation as said stockholders shall severally be entitled to under this resolution, and

RESOLVED FURTHER, That in any and all cases where any amount of stock issuable for such dividend shall be less than one share, the Corporation shall pay cash at the rate of . . . . . ($. . . . .) Dollars per share in lieu of such amount of stock to the stockholders entitled to receive the same.

(*Note:* In the event scrip is issued to handle fractions of shares the following may be substituted for the last paragraph.)

"RESOLVED FURTHER, That in any and all cases, where any amount of stock issuable for such dividend shall be less than one share, the Corporation shall deliver scrip for such fractions of shares in form to be approved by counsel for the Corporation. Such scrip certificates when surrendered to the Corporation in amount aggregating one full share of stock or multiples thereof, shall be exchangeable for certificates of common stock of the Corporation, with any accumulated dividends on such stock, but until so exchanged, scrip certificates shall not be entitled to receive any dividend or to have any voting rights or stock subscription rights or other rights appertaining to such common stock."

RESOLUTION AUTHORIZING COMMON STOCK DIVIDEND AND SCRIP CERTIFICATES FOR FRACTIONAL SHARES, AND AUTHORIZING TRANSFER AGENT AND REGISTRAR TO ISSUE AND RECORD STOCK

WHEREAS, at a special stockholders' meeting held on . . . ., 19. ., the increase of the common stock of this Corporation from sixteen million ($16,000,000) Dollars to twenty million ($20,000,000) Dollars was authorized, and such increase has become effective, and

WHEREAS, the Capital Issue Committee has approved the issue of one million six hundred thousand ($1,600,000) Dollars of common stock of this Corporation, in payment of a dividend of ten (10%) percent on the common stock of this Corporation, in accordance with the resolution of this Board of Directors adopted . . . ., 19. ., be it

RESOLVED, That the officers of this Corporation are hereby authorized and directed to issue an aggregate of one million six hundred thousand ($1,600,000) Dollars par value of common stock of this Corporation, in payment of a special dividend of ten (10%) percent on the common stock of this Corporation, such dividend to be payable in such common stock on . . . ., 19. ., to the holders of record of the outstanding common stock of this Corporation at the close of business on . . . ., 19. ., and

RESOLVED FURTHER, That the officers of this Corporation are hereby authorized and directed to issue scrip certificates representing fractions of shares to which stockholders will be entitled on the payment of such dividend, such scrip certificates, when surrendered with other like certificates in sums aggregating one hundred ($100) Dollars or multiples thereof, to be exchangeable for a certificate of common stock of the Corporation to an amount equal at par value to the aggregate amount at par value of the scrip certificates so surrendered, and to provide that the holders thereof shall have no right to vote in respect to such scrip certificates and shall not be entitled to the payment of dividends thereon, and

RESOLVED FURTHER, That the . . . . Company, Transfer Agent, is hereby authorized and directed to issue and record on its transfer books, stock certificates and scrip certificates representing such additional sixteen thousand (16,000) shares of common stock, and the . . . . Company, Registrar, is hereby authorized and directed to register stock certificates and scrip certificates representing such additional sixteen thousand (16,000) shares of common stock, making the total number of common shares that said Transfer Agent is to issue and record in its books and which said Registrar is to register, one hundred seventy-six thousand (176,000) shares of common stock.

DIRECTORS' RESOLUTION DECLARING STOCK DIVIDEND UPON STOCK WITHOUT PAR VALUE, AND DECLARING CASH DIVIDEND UPON ALL STOCK WITHOUT PAR VALUE AFTER INCREASE

WHEREAS, this Corporation now has an authorized capital stock of ..... (.....) shares of stock without nominal or par value, of which ..... (.....) shares are issued and outstanding, and

WHEREAS, this Corporation has undivided profits amounting to ..... ($.....) Dollars, and

WHEREAS, the market value of said stock is now too high to permit widespread distribution and ready marketability, and further declarations of dividends would have the effect of further increasing the market value, and

WHEREAS, in the opinion of this Board of Directors, it is advisable to reduce the market value of each share of stock without nominal or par value of this Corporation by declaring a stock dividend of one hundred (100%) percent upon the capital stock without nominal or par value issued and outstanding, and to maintain the dividend rate of ..... (.....%) percent per annum upon the increased shares of stock without nominal or par value that will be issued and outstanding upon the payment of such stock dividend, be it

RESOLVED, That a dividend of one hundred (100%) percent upon the common stock without nominal or par value of this Corporation is hereby declared, payable in shares of common stock without nominal or par value of this Corporation, on ...., 19.., to stockholders of record at the close of business on ...., 19.., and that all stockholders of record at the close of business on ...., 19.., shall be deemed to be holders of said increased capital stock at said time, and the President and Secretary are hereby authorized and directed to issue such additional amount of authorized common stock without nominal or par value as shall be necessary for such dividend, and to execute and deliver certificates of such stock on ...., 19.., without closing the transfer books, and

RESOLVED FURTHER, That a dividend of ..... (.....%) percent upon all the capital stock without nominal or par value issued and outstanding on ...., 19.., is hereby declared payable in cash on ...., 19.., to stockholders of record at the close of business on ...., 19.., and the Treasurer is hereby authorized and directed to cause the same to be paid on the date specified.

DIRECTORS' RESOLUTION AUTHORIZING CORPORATION TO PAY CASH FOR FRACTIONAL SHARES UPON DECLARATION OF STOCK DIVIDEND

(*Note*. The resolution may be substituted for a provision permitting the issuance of scrip for fractional shares.)

RESOLVED, That, in any and all cases where any amount of stock issuable for such stock dividend shall be less than one share, fractional shares shall not be issued, but an equivalent payment shall be made in cash, the basis of the value of a share being the par value thereof. [If stock is without par value, insert the words "the basis of value of one whole share being . . . . . ($. . . . .) Dollars."]

DIRECTORS' RESOLUTION AUTHORIZING DIVIDENDS TO BE PAID ONLY UPON FULLY PAID STOCK

RESOLVED, That no dividend shall be paid upon any share of preferred stock until said stock has been fully paid for, and that dividends shall be computed only from the time when such stock is paid for in full.

DIRECTORS' RESOLUTION DECLARING DIVIDEND AND PROVIDING THAT DIVIDEND SHALL BE SET OFF AGAINST INDEBTEDNESS

RESOLVED, That a regular dividend of . . . . . cents per share be paid on . . . ., 19. ., to all stockholders of record at the close of business on . . . ., 19. ., without closing the transfer books, and

RESOLVED FURTHER, That the dividend this day declared shall not be paid to any stockholder who may be indebted to the Corporation or who has not paid in full for his stock, but the amount of the dividend due to such shareholders under this resolution shall be entered as a credit against the indebtedness or the unpaid amount on the stock.

DIRECTORS' RESOLUTION MAKING DIVIDENDS PAYABLE SEMI-ANNUALLY RATHER THAN QUARTERLY

WHEREAS, dividends on the . . . . stock of this Corporation have heretofore been payable quarterly, one the . . day of . . . ., ..., ..., and . . . ., and

WHEREAS, the Board of Directors now deems it advisable to have dividends payable semiannually, rather than quarterly, be it

RESOLVED, That dividends shall be payable semi-annually on the . . day of . . . . . and . . . ., when and as declared by the Board of Directors.

DIRECTORS' RESOLUTION STATING CORPORATION'S
DIVIDEND POLICY

RESOLVED, That it is the dividend policy of the Company to place the capital stock of the Company on a dividend basis of $..... per annum, payable in equal quarterly installments on the first days of ...., ..., ..., and ...., should the earnings of the Company warrant the same, subject to the declaration of the said dividends from time to time by the Board of Directors.

RESOLUTION OF STOCKHOLDERS REQUESTING DIRECTORS
TO DECLARE A DIVIDEND

WHEREAS, it appears from the yearly reports of the .... Railroad Company that dividends on the preferred issues have been earned for several years past, be it

RESOLVED, That the directors be requested to declare, within thirty (30) days from this date, dividends on both preferred issues in such proportions as are warranted, provided that the same shall have been earned.

DIRECTORS' RESOLUTION "PASSING" A DIVIDEND

WHEREAS, it is the desire of the directors to improve the financial condition of the Company, be it

RESOLVED, That no dividends be declared on the stock of the Company for the year 19.., and that the earnings of the Company for the year 19.. be credited to the Surplus Account.

DIRECTORS' RESOLUTION "PASSING" A DIVIDEND
AND INDICATING BUSINESS REASONS FOR THE ACTION

WHEREAS, it is the belief of the Board of Directors of this Corporation, based on the results of a comprehensive survey, a copy of which is included in the minutes of the meeting of this Board, dated ...., 19.., that the Corporation's competitive position will be strengthened by an expansion of facilities for the production of our leading products, and

WHEREAS, inquiries into the cost of financing such expansion from outside sources show that the cost would be prohibitive, and

WHEREAS, the directors of this Corporation believe that the best interests of the Corporation require that an expansion plan be started as soon as possible, be it

RESOLVED, That the above expansion be financed, insofar as possible, by funds of the Corporation which are in the form of undistributed profits, and

RESOLVED FURTHER, That no dividends be declared on the stock of the Corporation for the present year, and that earnings of the Corporation for the year be used in the above expansion plan.

DIRECTORS' RESOLUTION "PASSING" A DIVIDEND WITHOUT GIVING REASONS FOR THE ACTION

RESOLVED, That the quarterly dividend of ..... (.....¢) cents per share on the Common Stock of the .... Corporation be not, at present, declared.

LETTER TO STOCKHOLDERS EXPLAINING "PASSING" OF DIVIDEND

To the Stockholders of .... Corporation

The directors of your Corporation have decided not to declare a dividend at the present time on the stock of the Corporation and to use the funds thus conserved to strengthen the Corporation's competitive position by expanding its production facilities.

A survey prepared for your directors indicated that the cost of financing such needed expansion from outside sources would be prohibitive. Since the best interests of the corporation require that the expansion plan be started as soon as possible, and since as just indicated, outside financing of the plan would be prohibitively expensive, the directors of your Corporation believe that the best interests of the Corporation will be served by not paying a dividend at this time.

....
President

DIRECTORS' RESOLUTION AUTHORIZING CLOSING OF TRANSFER BOOKS FOR PAYMENT OF DIVIDENDS

RESOLVED, That, for the purpose of paying dividends this day declared, the stock transfer books of the Company be closed from ...., 19.., at ....M., until ...., 19.., at ..... M.

DIRECTORS' RESOLUTION REVOKING DIVIDEND

WHEREAS, a dividend equal to ..... (.....¢) Cents a share on each share of the capital stock of this Corporation was declared by the Board of Directors at a meeting held on ...., 19.., payable on ...., 19.., to stockholders of record on ...., 19.., and

WHEREAS, the stockholders of this Corporation have not been notified of the declaration of said dividend, and notice of said dividend has not been made public, and

WHEREAS, no fund has been set aside for payment of said dividend, and

WHEREAS, since the declaration of said dividend, the Corporation has been notified that it must vacate the premises at . . . . (*address*), now occupied by this Corporation, and the removal of the Corporation will involve expenses not heretofore contemplated, and

WHEREAS, it is the opinion of this Board of Directors that the payment of the said dividend may jeopardize the financial condition of the Corporation and make it unable to meet its debts and obligations and that the best interests of the Corporation require the revocation of said dividend, be it

RESOLVED, That the dividend equal to . . . . . cents a share on each share of the capital stock of this Corporation, declared by the Board of Directors on . . . ., 19. ., to be paid on . . . ., 19. ., to stockholders of record at the close of business on . . . ., 19. ., is hereby rescinded, revoked, and canceled.

DIRECTORS' RESOLUTION REVOKING STOCK DIVIDEND ON RECOMMENDATION OF EXECUTIVE COMMITTEE

RESOLVED, That, upon the recommendation of the Executive Committee, the stock dividend equal to . . . . . (. . . . .%) percent of the capital stock of this Corporation, declared by the Board of Directors on . . . ., 19. ., to be paid on . . . ., 19. ., to stockholders of record at the close of business on . . . ., 19. ., is hereby rescinded, revoked, and canceled.

DIRECTORS' RESOLUTION REDUCING THE DIVIDEND PAYMENT

RESOLVED, that a quarterly dividend of . . . . . (. . . . .¢) Cents per share, which represents a reduction from the last quarterly dividend, be and hereby is declared upon all the common stock without par value issued and outstanding, said dividend to be payable on . . . ., 19. ., to stockholders of record at the close of business on . . . ., 19. . .

DIRECTORS' RESOLUTION REDUCING THE REGULAR DIVIDEND RATE AND PAYMENT

WHEREAS, the directors of this corporation believe that the best interests of the corporation require that the regular dividend on the common stock without par value be reduced, be it

RESOLVED, that the regular quarterly dividend of . . . . . (. . . . .¢) Cents per share on the outstanding common stock without par value, be reduced, and

RESOLVED FURTHER, that a dividend of . . . . . (. . . . .¢) Cents per share for the quarterly period ending . . . ., 19. ., is hereby declared upon all the common stock without par value issued and outstanding, said dividend to be payable on . . . ., 19. ., to stockholders of record at the close of business on . . . ., 19. . .

RESOLUTION RESCINDING SCRIP DIVIDEND

RESOLVED, That the action taken at the meeting of the Board of Directors held on . . . ., 19. ., declaring a scrip dividend of fifty (50%) percent, is hereby rescinded.

DIRECTORS' RESOLUTION APPROPRIATING EMERGENCY FUND TO ADJUST INEQUITIES IN DIVIDENDS RESULTING FROM REFUNDING

WHEREAS, under the plan for refunding outstanding 6% Preferred Stock of this Corporation and funding the accumulated dividends thereon, by the issue of 7% Preferred Stock to the extent of one and three-tenths shares of such new 7% Preferred Stock for each share of old 6% Preferred Stock, as set forth in a resolution adopted by this Board of Directors at its meeting held on . . . ., 19. ., the 6% Preferred Stockholders surrendering their 6% Preferred Stock for exchange prior to . . . ., 19. ., received in exchange therefor, on and after . . . ., 19. ., 7% Preferred Stock drawing 7% dividends from . . . ., 19. ., and

WHEREAS, the time for exercising the privilege of exchange has been extended from time to time, and

WHEREAS, stockholders who surrendered their 6% Preferred Stock subsequent to . . . ., 19. ., became entitled to receive 7% Preferred Stock on the quarterly dividend date next succeeding the date of the surrender of the 6% Preferred Stock, and

WHEREAS, several 6% stockholders, through no default or negligence of their own, were unable to make the exchange prior to . . . ., 19. ., and

WHEREAS, this Board is of the opinion that the resulting inequalities should be rectified insofar as is practicable and deserved, be it

RESOLVED, That an emergency fund of an amount not to exceed . . . . ($. . . . .) Dollars be set aside and put at the disposal of the executive officers of this Corporation, to be used, in their discretion, for the purpose of adjusting any inequities or inequalities which, in their opinion, may have occurred in connection with the exchange of the 6% Preferred Stock for the 7% Preferred Stock of this Corporation.

RESOLUTION AUTHORIZING SPECIAL FUND FOR DIVIDEND AND INTEREST PAYMENTS

The President stated that in order to facilitate the disbursement of dividends and note and bond interest payments, it was desired to create special deposit accounts by the withdrawal from the general fund, from time to time, of sums sufficient to meet the different interest and dividend requirements, each such withdrawal to be accomplished by a check drawn and signed in accordance with the by-laws, and to comprise a separate and distinct deposit to cover the exact amount of one full interest payment, and that he had, subject to the approval of the Board, appointed .... as Deputy Treasurer, with full power, in conjunction with ...., Coupon or Dividend Clerk, to sign checks against this special deposit account, for the purpose of making the payment in question; whereupon

Upon motion duly seconded, it was

RESOLVED, That the appointment of .... as Deputy Treasurer of this Company with power, in conjunction with ...., to disburse special funds set apart for the payment of dividends and notes and bond interest, is hereby ratified, approved, and confirmed.

DIRECTORS' RESOLUTION APPOINTING DIVIDEND DISBURSING AGENT

RESOLVED, That the .... Trust Company, Transfer Agent of this Corporation, is hereby appointed Dividend Disbursing Agent for the Capital Stock of this Corporation, and it hereby is authorized and directed to pay such dividends as may be declared by the Board of Directors of this Corporation, after the Corporation has lodged with said .... Trust Company, certified copies of the resolution of the Board of Directors declaring such dividends, and deposited with said .... Trust Company an amount sufficient for the payment of such dividends at least two days before each dividend date.

DIRECTORS' RESOLUTION AUTHORIZING TRANSFER OF PROFITS TO UNDIVIDED PROFITS ACCOUNT AND SURPLUS ACCOUNT

RESOLVED, That ..... ($.....) Dollars of the profits for the year 19.. be transferred to the Undivided Profits account, and ..... ($.....) Dollars be transferred to the Surplus account.

DIRECTORS' RESOLUTION AUTHORIZING REAPPRAISAL OF FIXED ASSETS

WHEREAS, it is the opinion of this Board of Directors that the real estate, plants, equipment, and other fixed assets owned by this Corporation are carried on the books of the Corporation at a value considered below their true market value, and

WHEREAS, it is the desire of this Board of Directors to have the value of said assets appraised, and to increase the Surplus account by the difference between the aggregate value of the fixed assets, as they at present appear on the books of the Corporation, and the aggregate value determined after an appraisal has been made by a disinterested and reputable firm of engineers, be it

RESOLVED, That the President is hereby authorized and directed to obtain the services of a reputable firm of engineers to appraise the value of the real estate, plants, equipment, and other fixed assets owned by this Corporation, and to cause the proper entries to be made on the books of the Corporation to reflect the present value of the real estate, plant, equipment, and other fixed assets of the Corporation as appraised.

DIRECTORS' RESOLUTION AUTHORIZING ADJUSTMENT IN SURPLUS AFTER REAPPRAISAL OF ASSETS

WHEREAS, the report submitted by .... Company on ...., 19.., indicates that the real estate, plants, equipment, and other fixed assets owned by this Corporation have an aggregate true market value of ..... ($.....) Dollars, and

WHEREAS, the said assets, more particularly described in the report hereinbefore mentioned, are carried on the books of the Corporation at an aggregate value of ..... ($.....) Dollars, and

WHEREAS, it is the desire of this Board of Directors to have the fixed assets owned by this Corporation carried on the books of the Corporation at their present true market values, and to increase the surplus account by the difference between the aggregate value of the fixed assets, as shown by the report of the .... Company, and the aggregate value of said assets, as it at present appears upon the books of the Corporation, be it

RESOLVED, That the values indicated in the report of the .... Company as the true market values of the real estate, plants, equipment, and other assets owned by this Corporation, and more particularly described in the report of said .... Company as appended hereto, are hereby accepted as the values at which said assets shall be carried upon the books of the Corporation; and

RESOLVED FURTHER, That .... and ...., auditors of the books of this Corporation, are hereby authorized to make the necessary entries to show that the values of the fixed assets owned by this Corporation are those indicated in the report of the .... Company, and to increase the Surplus account by the sum of ..... ($.....) Dollars, which amount is the difference between the aggregate value of the real estate, plants, equipment, and other fixed assets, as they are at present valued on the books of the Corporation, and the aggregate reappraised value of said assets, as shown by the report of said .... Company.

[*Insert appraisers' report.*]

DIRECTORS' RESOLUTION FIXING RESERVES

RESOLVED, That the following sums be reserved for depreciation of the following fixed assets:

Furniture and Fixtures..	$.....
Investments	.....

EXCERPT OF MINUTES OF DIRECTORS' MEETING AUTHORIZING WRITING OFF OF BAD DEBTS

A list of the bad accounts of the Company, resulting during the period from ...., 19.., to ...., 19.., was submitted to the directors by the Treasurer, who reported that the usual methods of collection pursued by the Company had been useless in the collection of the accounts and that he had consulted with .... , attorneys for this Company, as to the possibilities of collection by suit and had been informed by them that collection by legal action was inadvisable. After due consideration it was concluded that the following accounts must be regarded as completely worthless:

(Here insert list of accounts.)

Thereupon, the following resolution was unanimously adopted:

WHEREAS, the accounts listed above are deemed by the directors to be worthless, be it

RESOLVED, That the accounts above listed, totaling ..... ($.....) Dollars, be charged to the Profit and Loss account.

DIRECTORS' RESOLUTION AUTHORIZING WRITING OFF OF GOODWILL

WHEREAS, the intangible asset goodwill is carried on the books of this Corporation at a value of ..... ($.....) Dollars, and

WHEREAS, it has been the policy of this Corporation to write off from year to year a part of said intangible asset, with a view to eliminating said account from the books of the Corporation, and

WHEREAS, the surplus of the Corporation, as shown by the books of account at the close of the fiscal year ending ...., 19.., is sufficiently large to warrant writing off the entire asset goodwill at this time, be it

RESOLVED, That the asset goodwill be written off the books of the Corporation by debiting the Surplus account with the sum of ..... ($.....) Dollars, and crediting the Goodwill account with the same amount, and that the asset goodwill be carried upon the books of this Corporation at the value of one ($1) Dollar.

DIRECTORS' RESOLUTION AUTHORIZING CONVERSION OF UNNECESSARY RESERVES TO SURPLUS

WHEREAS, in each of the years 19.. to 19.., inclusive, there was charged to the Depreciation of Buildings account, and credited to the Reserve for Depreciation of Buildings account, ... ($....) Dollars, or ..... (.....%) percent of the book value of the buildings owned by this Corporation, and there is now credited to the Reserve for Depreciation of Buildings account the sum of ..... ($....) Dollars, and

WHEREAS, the value of said buildings on ...., 19.., was conservatively estimated by .... (*insert name of appraiser*) to be ..... ($.....) Dollars, and, in view of said valuation, said reserve for depreciation of buildings appears to be excessive to the extent of ..... ($....) Dollars, and

WHEREAS, It is the opinion of this Board of Directors that it is to the best interests of this Corporation and its stockholders that said unnecessary reserve in the amount of ..... ($.....) Dollars be converted to surplus and made available for distribution to stockholders in the form of dividends, at such time or times as the Board of Directors may declare dividends, be it

RESOLVED, That the auditors of this Corporation are hereby authorized and directed to transfer ..... ($.....) Dollars from the Reserve for Buildings account to the Surplus account.

DIRECTORS' RESOLUTION AUTHORIZING INCREASE IN SURPLUS BY WRITING UP ASSET GOODWILL AND DECLARING DIVIDEND OUT OF SURPLUS

WHEREAS, in the year 19.., this Corporation operated at a deficit, owing to drastic declines in the market value of commodities sold by this Corporation, and at the close of the fiscal year ending ...., 19.., the balance sheet of this Corporation showed a deficit of ..... ($.....) Dollars, and

WHEREAS, in each of the ..... (.....) years following said year 19.., this Corporation earned net profits aggregating ..... ($.....) Dollars, which profits have been sufficient to wipe out the deficit and leave a surplus of ..... ($.....) Dollars, and

WHEREAS, it is the opinion of this Board of Directors that the stockholders of this Corporation are entitled to a distribution of profits as a return upon their capital investment, and

WHEREAS, the goodwill of this Corporation has been carried on the books of this Corporation at a nominal value of one ($1) Dollar, and

WHEREAS, it is the opinion of this Board of Directors that it is now advisable to carry the intangible asset goodwill at a higher value, in order that the surplus may be increased to an amount sufficient to permit the payment of a dividend of ..... (.....%) percent upon the capital stock of this Corporation, be it

RESOLVED, That the goodwill of this Corporation is hereby valued at ..... ($.....) Dollars, and

RESOLVED FURTHER, That the auditors of this Corporation are hereby authorized and directed to make the necessary entries upon the books of the Corporation to include goodwill, in the amount of ..... ($.....) Dollars, among the assets of this Corporation, and to credit the Surplus account with the sum of ..... ($.....) Dollars, and

RESOLVED FURTHER, That there is declared, out of the surplus of the Corporation, a dividend of ..... (.....%) percent upon all the capital stock issued and outstanding, payable on ...., 19.., to stockholders of record at the close of business on ...., 19.., and the Treasurer is hereby authorized and directed to cause the same to be paid on the date specified.

(*Note:* Generally, goodwill is carried in the accounts only when it is purchased. It is not good accounting practice to write up its value for purposes of paying dividends.)

DISSENT OF DIRECTOR TO DECLARATION OF DIVIDEND, ENTERED UPON MINUTES OF MEETING

.............., director of this Corporation, opposed the motion made at this meeting to declare a dividend of ..... percent (or $..... per share, if stock is without par value) upon all the outstanding capital stock of this Corporation, on the ground that said dividend would impair the capital stock of this Corporation and was therefore in violation of the laws of the State of ...., and, upon passage of the motion and declaration of the dividend without his vote, demanded that his dissent from the declaration of said dividend be entered upon the minutes of this meeting of the Board of Directors. This entry is made to satisfy the demands of ....

PROTEST OF DIRECTOR AGAINST DECLARATION OF DIVIDEND

WHEREAS, a motion was made at this meeting of the Board of Directors to declare a dividend of ..... percent (or $..... per share, if stock is without par value,) upon all the outstanding common stock of this Corporation, and

WHEREAS, I opposed said motion on the ground that said dividend would impair the capital stock of this Corporation and would therefore violate the laws of the State of .... , and

WHEREAS, said motion was seconded and passed, and said dividend was declared without my vote, be it

ADVISED, That I dissent from the declaration of said dividend and demand that my dissent be entered upon the minutes of the meeting of the Board of Directors, held on ...., 19..

NOTICE OF DIVIDEND ON COMMON STOCK
HAVING PAR VALUE

The .... Company
.... Street
..... City, ...
..... Consecutive Common Dividend

A dividend of 4 percent ($2 a share) has been declared upon the common stock of the par value of $50 a share of .... Company, payable in cash on ...., 19.., to stockholders of record at the close of business on ...., 19.. Checks will be mailed.

....
Treasurer

Dated ...., 19..

NOTICE OF DIVIDEND UPON PREFERRED AND
COMMON STOCK

...., 19..

The .... Company
Office of the Secretary
.... City, ... State

The Board of Directors this day declared, for the three (3) months ending ...., 19.., from the net profits of the company, a dividend of ..... cents per share on the preferred stock of the Company.

The Board also declared, from the surplus profits of the Company, a dividend of ..... cents per share on the common stock of the Company.

Both dividends are payable ...., 19.., to stockholders of record at the close of business on ...., 19..

The transfer books will not be closed.

....
Secretary

NOTICE OF REGULAR AND EXTRA DIVIDEND
UPON COMMON STOCK

Dividend Notice
.... Corporation

At a meeting of the Board of Directors of the ....
Corporation, held this day, it was resolved that this Corporation declare and
pay to the holders of its Common Stock of record at the close of business on
...., 19.., a dividend of one Dollar and sixty-five ($1.65) Cents
per share, being the regular quarterly dividend on said Stock, and also an
extra dividend of fifteen (15¢) Cents per share, payable ...., 19..

....
President

Dated ...., 19..

NOTICE ACCOMPANYING STOCK DIVIDEND SHOWING EFFECT
ON STATED CAPITAL, CAPITAL SURPLUS, AND EARNED
SURPLUS ACCOUNTS

The Board of Directors of .... Corp. declared a 2 percent
common stock dividend on ...., 19.., payable ....,
19.., to stockholders of record on ...., 19... The stock dividend
aggregating..... shares will be shown as a charge to earned surplus of $.....
representing $..... for each share, said value having been determined by the
Board of Directors, a credit to stated capital of $..... representing the par
value of the shares issued; and a credit to capital surplus of the balance.

Comment: If the amounts to be charged the accounts discussed aren't determinable, follow
the form of the notice on page 844, stating that fact and show the estimated effect.

NOTICE OF STOCK DIVIDEND

The Board of Directors has today declared a dividend of two (2%)
percent, payable in Common Stock, upon the Common Stock of ....
Corporation, payable ...., 19.., to holders of Common Stock of
record at the close of business on ...., 19... Stock certificates will
be mailed.

....
Treasurer

NOTICE OF DIVIDEND, INCLUDING NOTICE TO STOCKHOLDERS
WHO HAVE NOT EXCHANGED STOCK

.... Company
Preferred Stock Dividend No. .....
Common Stock Dividend No. .....

There have been this day declared a dividend of ..... on the preferred
stock and a dividend of one and one-half ($1.50) Dollars per share on the

common stock without par value, of this Company, payable Thursday, ..., 19.., to stockholders of record at the close of business Tuesday, ..., 19...

Those stockholders who have not exchanged, as of said record date, their certificates representing the former common stock of the par value of $100 per share, shall be deemed the owners of two shares without par value for each share of the par value of $100, for the purpose of the dividend on the common stock.

Checks will be mailed to stockholders by the .... Trust Company of ....

....
Vice President

....
Secretary

Dated ...., 19..

NOTICE OF CASH DIVIDEND AND WITHHOLDING UPON UNEXCHANGED STOCK

The Board of Directors of the .... Corporation has this day declared a quarterly dividend ..... Cents a share on the outstanding stock of the Corporation of the issue of 160,000 shares, provided by an amendment to the Certificate of Incorporation of ...., 19.., payable on ...., 19.., to the stockholders of record at the close of business on ...., 19..

The officers of the Corporation are authorized to withhold payment of this dividend upon stock of the issue of 800,000 shares until such stock has been exchanged for the new stock. Stockholders who have not exchanged their certificates should do so at once at the .... Company, ... (*Street*), ... (*City*), ... (*State*).

....
Treasurer

.... (*Street*), ... (*City*), ... (*State*) ...., 19..

NOTICE OF DIVIDEND PAYABLE IN CASH OR IN RIGHT TO SUBSCRIBE TO STOCK

To the Holders of
$6 Dividend Series Preferred Stock
of .... Company:

The Board of Directors has declared the quarterly dividend on the $6 Dividend Series Preferred Stock of $1.50 per share or 4 one hundredths of one share of Class A Stock for each share held, payable on ...., 19.., to stockholders of record at the close of business on ...., 19..

This dividend may be applied to the purchase of Class A Stock at the price of about $37.50 per share, whereas the present market price is $40.50 per share. The stock dividend is equivalent to a rate of about 6 and one-half percent per annum, yielding $6.48 per share per annum as compared with the cash dividend of $6.

A postcard, upon which you may indicate how you wish your dividend to be applied, is enclosed. It also contains a provision by which you may make your directions permanent. It is suggested that you avail yourself of this convenience if you wish to be saved the trouble incident to these quarterly advices. This permanent dividend order can, of course, be changed at any time, if requested in writing.

If there is anything which you do not understand about this arrangement or the Class A Stock, please write us, and we will be pleased to furnish you with further information.

If you wish cash in payment of your dividend, you may disregard this notice and destroy the enclosed postcard.

Very truly yours,

. . . .
Secretary

NOTICE OF DECLARATION OF CUMULATIVE DIVIDENDS

. . . . Corporation
. . . . Street
. . . . . City, ...

The Board of Directors, at its meeting held . . . ., 19.., declared on the 5 Percent Cumulative First Preferred Stock of the Company, a dividend of $3.75 per share, payable . . . ., 19.., to stockholders of record at the close of business on . . . ., 19...

In declaring the above dividend, the directors had in mind the cumulative dividend covering payments due on:

. . . ., 19.., of $1.25 per share
. . . ., 19.., of $1.25 per share
. . . ., 19.., of $1.25 per share

The transfer books will not be closed. Checks will be mailed.

. . . .
Treasurer

NOTICE OF DIVIDEND PAYABLE IN CASH OR IN
RIGHT TO SUBSCRIBE TO STOCK—FRACTIONAL SHARES
PAYABLE IN CASH

New York, ..., 19. .

To the Holders of Common Stock:

At a meeting of the Board of Directors, held on ...., 19. ., a dividend of thirty-seven and one-half (37½¢) Cents per share was declared on the Common Stock, for the quarter ending ...., 19. ., payable ...., 19. ., to holders of record at the close of business on ...., 19. .

By proper action of the Board, the holders of Common Stock are given the right to subscribe to additional shares of Common Stock, at the price of twenty-five ($25) Dollars per share to the extent of the dividends receivable on ...., 19. ..

The Board of Directors has determined that it is impracticable to issue scrip certificates with reference to the dividend payable on ...., 19. ., on fractional shares, and that such dividend will be paid in cash. In cases where the holders of fractional shares are entitled to a payment of less than ten (10¢) cents, no payment will be made on account of the fractional certificates.

Certificates for full shares of Common Stock will be issued for each twenty-five ($25) Dollars of Dividends receivable.

The .... Trust Company of .... (*address*), Transfer Agent, has been instructed to issue and forward stock certificates for Common Stock to the stockholders, unless advised, on or before the close of business on ...., 19. ., that the stockholder does not elect to exercise the right to subscribe for additional Common Stock, and requests that the dividend, at the rate of thirty-seven and one-half (37½¢) Cents per share, be paid in cash. A form requesting payment of the dividend in cash is enclosed.

REQUEST FOR PAYMENT OF DIVIDEND IN CASH

[*Attention:* This form, if used, should be returned to the .... Trust Company, ... Street, ..., and not to .... Corporation.]
The .... Trust Company
....
.............., ...

Gentlemen:
The undersigned holder of Common Stock of .... Corporation, does not elect to exercise the right to subscribe for additional

Common Stock and requests that the dividend payable on ....,
19.., be paid in cash.

....
(Name)
....
(Address)

(This form and the preceding form are used together.)

REQUEST FOR PAYMENT OF DIVIDEND IN CASH
(SENT WITH THE NOTICE OF DIVIDEND)

(Note: This form, if used, should be returned to the .... Trust Company of
New York, ... Street, New York City, and not to ....
Corporation.)

The .... Trust Company of New York
.... Street
New York City

Gentlemen:

The undersigned holder of Common Stock, Class A, of ....
Corporation, does not elect to exercise the right to subscribe for additional
Common Stock, Class A, and requests that the dividend payable on
...., 19.., be paid in cash.

....
(Name)
....
(Address)

NOTICE OF ELECTION TO SUBSCRIBE TO SHARES TO EXTENT
OF DIVIDENDS PAYABLE (SENT WITH NOTICE OF DIVIDEND)

Date ...., 19..

The .... Trust Company of New York
.... Street
New York City, New York

Attention of Stock Transfer Department

Gentlemen:

Until otherwise directed in writing, the undersigned holder of Common
Stock, Class A, of .... Corporation, hereby elects to subscribe
to additional shares of Common Stock, Class A, to the extent of dividends
receivable thereon, and hereby authorizes and requests you to apply all such
dividends to the purchase of additional shares of said stock at the price of $25

per share, and to issue nondividend-bearing scrip certificates for any fractional shares to which the undersigned may be entitled.

· ·
(Signature)

This order must be signed by the party in whose name the stock stands, exactly as the name appears on the face of the stock. If it is signed by someone other than the stockholder, documentary evidence is required.

NOTICE OF EXTRA CASH DIVIDEND WITH RIGHT OF ELECTION, IN LIEU OF CASH DIVIDEND, TO PURCHASE STOCK IN CORPORATION TO BE ORGANIZED

· · · · · · · · · · · ·, 19· ·

Notice to Stockholders

The Board of Directors of the "A" Company has declared an extra dividend of $10 per share on each of the shares of the common stock, payable out of the surplus of the Company on · · · · · · · · · · · ·, 19· ·, to stockholders of record at the close of business on · · · · · · · · · ·, 19· ·

The Board of Directors has authorized the payment of this dividend either:

(1) In cash, or (2) in rights to subscribe for shares of the capital stock of the "B" Company, now being organized under the laws of the State of · · · · · · · · · · · · · ·, at $87.50 per share, but not in amounts exceeding 10 percent of the holdings of record at the close of business on · · · · · · · · · ·, 19· ·, and for which capital stock the Board of Directors has subscribed in the name of the "A" Company.

The "B" Company now being formed will have a capital stock issue of 50,000 shares of common stock, par value of $100 per share, of which 30,000 shares will be presently outstanding, the remainder being reserved for future requirements. The Company is being organized: (1) to take over options which have already been secured in its behalf for the lease under long-term leases or the purchase outright of property situate along the · · · · · · · · · · · · · · River at · · · · · · · · · · · · · · City, · · · · · · · · · · · · · · ; (2) to assume the permits already obtained from the Federal Government granting the right to construct a dam across the · · · · · · · · · · · · · · River at · · · · · · · · · · · · · · City, · · · · · · · · · · · · · ·, and to erect and operate a power plant thereat; and (3) to take over the development of the coal mines underlying the property under option, the coal from which will be used for the generation of electric power. The sale of the output of the "B" Company is assured through the action of the Board of Directors of the "A" Company taken on · · · · · · · · · ·, 19· ·, whereby the said "A" Company agreed to enter into a contract with the "B"

Company when its organization had been completed, subject to the confirmation of its Board of Directors at that time, for the purchase of its entire output for ten (10) years from the date it begins operation, upon equitable terms and conditions.

Stockholders electing to take advantage of their rights hereunder to purchase shares of capital stock of the "B" Company must exercise said rights before 12:00 o'clock noon on ...., 19.., by delivering power of attorney, similar to the attached form, to the Secretary of the "A" Company, and granting to the said Secretary power to: (1) receive the cash dividend; (2) exercise the right to subscribe for shares of capital stock of the "B" Company; and (3) apply said cash dividend as a payment of said stock subscription. Delivery of the power of attorney will automatically result in the conversion of the dividend into a payment on the subscription of shares of the "B" Company, the balance due on said subscription, if any, being payable any time prior to ...., 19... Failure to deliver the power of attorney or otherwise subscribe for shares of stock will operate as a waiver of said right, which right expires that time and on that date, and will be construed as an election to receive the cash dividend. Checks for the amount of the cash dividend to shareholders who do not exercise their rights hereunder will be mailed immediately after ...., 19...

....
President

POWER OF ATTORNEY TO RECEIVE EXTRA DIVIDEND AND APPLY IT TO SUBSCRIPTION FOR SHARES OF COMPANY TO BE ORGANIZED (SENT WITH PRECEDING FORM)

KNOW ALL MEN BY THESE PRESENTS, That I, ..., stockholder of ..... (.....) shares of the common stock of the "A" Company, do hereby appoint ...., Secretary of the "A" Company, as my attorney and agent, for me and in my name and behalf: to receive the extra cash dividend to which I am entitled under notice given me by the said "A" Company as of the .... day of ...., 19.., and to give a receipt therefor; (2) to exercise my right under said notice to subscribe for shares of the Capital Stock of the "B" Company, a company now being organized; and (3) to apply said dividend so received by him on the subscription of shares of stock of the said "B" Company.

Witness my hand and seal this ... day of ...., 19...
Witnesses:

....

....
(Signature of stockholder)

....

....
(Address of stockholder)

NOTICE OF DECLARATION OF REGULAR DIVIDEND AND EXTRA DIVIDEND PAYABLE IN CASH OR PREFERRED STOCK; FRACTIONAL SHARE WARRANTS TO BE ISSUED; INITIAL DIVIDEND DECLARED ON PREFERRED STOCK; NOTICE OF ELECTION TO TAKE DIVIDENDS IN PREFERRED STOCK

To the Shareholders of .... Co.:

Your Board of Directors, on ...., 19.., declared a cash dividend upon the common shares of your Company at the rate of fifty (50¢) Cents per share, payable on or before ...., 19.., to shareholders of record at the close of business on ...., 19...

In addition to this cash dividend, the directors declared an extra dividend payable in the alternative of (1) cash at the rate of fifty (50¢) Cents per share, or (2) preferred shares at the rate of one two-hundredth of a share per each share of present common stock outstanding, payable on or before ...., 19.., to shareholders of record on ...., 19... The shareholders may elect to receive this dividend either in cash or preferred shares, or part in cash and part in preferred shares. For example, if a shareholder owned two hundred and ten (210) shares of common stock, he would be entitled to receive one full share of preferred stock and a Fractional Share Warrant representing ten two-hundredths of a share of preferred stock, or one full share of preferred stock and five ($5) Dollars in cash. The shareholder must indicate his election as between these alternatives on or before the close of business on ...., 19... A form is enclosed herewith upon which this election should be indicated. In the absence of such election by the shareholder, he will be deemed to have elected to receive cash. Consequently, shareholders desiring to receive cash need make no response of any kind.

If election is so made by any shareholder as to involve the issuance of a fractional share of preferred stock, the Company will not issue a certificate representing such fractional share, but in lieu thereof will issue a Fractional Share Warrant representing such fraction. The Fractional Share Warrant will entitle the bearer thereof upon surrender of the same, together with other Fractional Share Warrants (acquired on the market or otherwise), making a total in the aggregate of one or more full shares of preferred stock, to receive one or more full shares of such stock. No dividends or interest will be paid on or in respect to such Fractional Share Warrant, and the holder thereof, as such, will not be entitled to any voting or other rights with respect thereto, but any share of stock issued upon the exercise thereof will participate in dividends thereafter paid on the same basis as the preferred shares then outstanding.

A shareholder desiring to receive this extra dividend in preferred shares must, on or before ...., 19.., deliver to the .... Bank, at its office .... (*Street*), ... (*City*), ... (*State*), the enclosed blank properly filled out and signed by him.

In the space left for the numbers of shares, he must insert the number of shares of common stock as to which he desires his dividend in preferred shares. As to all other shares, his dividend will be paid to him in cash.

An initial dividend will be paid upon these preferred shares to holders of record . . . ., 19. ., payable on or before. . . . ., 19. . . This dividend will be payable only upon outstanding full shares of stock and will not be paid upon Fractional Share Warrants. It, therefore, behooves all shareholders to divest themselves of Fractional Share Warrants by sale thereof (which can be accomplished in the market or otherwise), or purchase other Fractional Share Warrants sufficient to aggregate a share of preferred stock, and acquire the same on or before . . . ., 19. . .

. . . . Co.

By . . . .

Secretary

Dated . . . ., 19. .

ELECTION TO TAKE DIVIDEND IN PREFERRED SHARES
(sent with preceding form)

. . . ., 19. .,

To . . . . Co.:

I desire to receive the extra dividend declared by your Company on . . . ., 19. ., to shareholders of record on . . . ., 19. .:

(1)   *All in preferred shares at the rate of one two-hundredth share of such preferred stock for each share of common stock standing in my name

(2)   **In full shares of preferred stock representing dividend on . . . . . shares of common stock standing in my name and the balance in cash

(Signature must agree with name on stock certificate)

Notice. Shareholders electing to receive this dividend wholly in cash need not return this form.

Shareholders electing to receive the dividend wholly or partly in preferred shares must return this form, properly signed and filled out, to the office of The . . . . Bank, ... (*Street*), ... (*City*), ... (*State*), on or before . . . ., 19. . .

*Shareholders electing to receive the entire dividend in preferred shares should place an "X" in the space left after item "(1)."

**Shareholders electing to receive the dividend partly in preferred shares and partly in cash should place an "X" in the space left after item "(2)," being careful to fill in the blank in item "(2)."

NOTICE OF INCREASE IN ANNUAL RATE OF DIVIDENDS ON COMMON STOCK, OF DECLARATION OF ADDITIONAL DIVIDEND, PAYABLE IN CASH OR COMMON STOCK PURSUANT TO SUCH INCREASE, AND RIGHT TO SUBSCRIBE FOR ADDITIONAL COMMON STOCK

To the Holders of Common Stock:

NOTICE IS HEREBY GIVEN That, the Board of Directors of the Corporation, at a meeting held on . . . ., 19. ., adopted a resolution declaring the policy of the Corporation to place the common stock on a dividend basis of ten ($10) Dollars per share per annum, payable two ($2) Dollars quarterly in cash, and the remaining two ($2) Dollars payable, at such times, quarterly, semi-annually, or annually, as the Board of Directors may from time to time determine, in cash or, at the option of the Corporation and subject to the approval by the stockholders of the Corporation of an increase in the authorized number of shares of common stock of the Corporation at a special meeting of stockholders to be held on . . . ., 19. ., in shares of common stock of the Corporation without par value taken at such valuation per share as the Board of Directors shall determine at the time each such dividend is declared.

NOTICE IS ALSO HEREBY GIVEN That, pursuant to such policy and to resolutions adopted by the Board of Directors and Finance Committee of the Corporation, at meetings held on . . . ., 19. ., the Corporation declared the additional dividend of two ($2) Dollars per share on the common stock of the Corporation in respect of the current fiscal year, to stockholders of record on . . . ., 19. ., payable on . . . ., 19. ., subject to approval by the stockholders of the Corporation of such increase in the authorized number of shares of common stock of the Corporation, in shares of such common stock without par value taken at a valuation of one hundred ($100) Dollars per share, or, in the event of the failure of the stockholders to approve such increase, in cash.

NOTICE IS ALSO HEREBY GIVEN That, at the same meeting, the Board also declared the regular quarterly cash dividend upon the common stock for the quarterly period commencing . . . ., 19. ., payable on . . . ., 19. ., to stockholders of record on . . . ., 19. . .

NOTICE IS ALSO HEREBY GIVEN That, pursuant to resolutions adopted by the Board of Directors and Finance Committee of the Corporation at the meetings above mentioned, and subject to the approval by the stockholders of the Corporation of such increase in the authorized number of shares of the common stock of the Corporation without par value above referred to, your Corporation offers to holders of record of its Common Stock at the close of business on . . . ., 19. ., the right to subscribe, on or before . . . ., 19. ., for one share of said common stock for each two shares held by such common stockholders (including in the number of shares held the number of shares to which such common stockholder is entitled upon payment of the additional dividend above mentioned), at the price of one hundred and seven Dollars and forty-nine Cents ($107.49) per share (which price includes the accrued regular quarterly cash dividend for the period from ...., 19.., to ...., 19..). Payment of the full subscription price for said stock may be made at the time of subscription, or, at the option of the subscriber, may be made in two installments, the first to accompany the subscription and the second to be made on ...., 19...

The stock subscribed and paid for in full on or before ...., 19.., will be dated as of ...., 19.., and will be entitled to share in all dividends on the common stock of the Corporation declared to holders of record after that date. The stock subscribed and paid for in installments will be issued on or as of ...., 19.., and will be entitled to share in all dividends on the common stock of the Corporation declared to holders of record after that date.

Subscribers electing to pay the subscription price in installments will be entitled to deduct one dollar and twenty-four cents ($1.24) per share from the amount of the second installment, such deduction being an adjustment in respect of the regular cash dividend accruing on one share of common stock for the quarterly period commencing ...., 19...

Subject to the approval by the stockholders of the Corporation of such increase in the authorized number of shares of common stock of the Corporation, there will be mailed on ...., 19.., or on the earliest practicable date thereafter, to each holder of common stock of the Corporation of record at the close of business on ...., 19.., one or more subscription warrants specifying the number of shares of common stock to which the stockholder is entitled to subscribe. Subscription warrants will be issued only for full shares, but where a stockholder is entitled to subscribe for a fraction of a share, a fractional warrant will be issued. No subscription may be made on a fractional warrant, but such fractional warrants with other fractional warrants aggregating in amount one or more full shares will be exchangeable for a subscription warrant or warrants for the aggregate number of full shares represented thereby. Fractional warrants desired by stockholders to complete full shares, or fractional warrants which stockholders desire to dispose of, must be bought or sold in the market, as the Corporation will not sell or purchase such fractional warrants.

Subscription warrants must be returned to the principal office of .... Trust Company, ... (*Street*), ... (*City*), ... (*State*), on or before ...., 19.., by the respective stockholders or their assignees, accompanied by payment of the first installment of the subscription price, amounting to fifty-three Dollars and seventy-five Cents ($53.75) per share, or, if full payment is made, then by payment of one hundred and seven Dollars and forty-nine Cents ($107.49) per share, in New York funds. In case payment of the subscription price is made in installments, the second installment, amounting to fifty-two Dollars and fifty

Cents ($52.50) per share [being one-half of the full subscription price less a deduction of one Dollar and twenty-four Cents ($1.24)], the amount of the adjustment in respect of the regular cash dividend accruing on one share of common stock for the quarterly period commencing ...., 19.., must be paid at said office of said Trust Company on or before ...., 19... All checks must be certified and made payable to the order of .... Corporation. On the back of the subscription warrant will be found two forms, one to be signed to exercise the subscription right, and the other a form of assignment. Holders of subscription warrants authorizing subscription for two or more shares may exchange such warrants for other subscription warrants for lesser amounts but for the same aggregate number of shares. No subscription or assignment of subscription privilege will be recognized unless made on the forms furnished by the Corporation.

Subscription receipts evidencing payment of the first installment of the subscription price will be issued upon payment of such installment. When the second installment is paid, the subscription receipts for the first installment must be surrendered for cancellation, and stock certificates, or full-paid subscription receipts exchangeable for stock certificates on or after ...., 19.., will then be issued. In case the full subscription price is paid at the time of subscription, stock certificates, or full-paid subscription receipts exchangeable for stock certificates on or after ...., 19.., will be issued at the time of payment.

NOTICE ACCOMPANYING DIVIDEND

...., 19..

The .... Company

.... Street

..... City, ...

Enclosed herewith please find a check in payment of the quarterly dividend of six (6%) percent ($1.50 per share) on the shares of the capital stock of our Company, standing in your name.

Yours respectfully,

....

Secretary

No acknowledgment is necessary. Please notify us promptly of any change in your post office address.

NOTICE ACCOMPANYING STOCK DIVIDEND AND CASH PAYMENT FOR FRACTIONAL SHARES

To the Class A Shareholders
.... Corporation:

Re: Fractional Shares.

In addition to the enclosed certificate for shares issued as a stock dividend, you are entitled to a fractional share. There is/ herby tendered the attached check as payment in full of your rights to a fractional share. Your officers consider this method of settlement of fractions more convenient to the shareholders, as well as more economical to your Corporation, than other methods. The amount of the check represents the current market value of the fraction due you. A corresponding fractional share, together with other fractional shares, will be sold as full shares by the Corporation on the .... Stock Exchange.

....
President

NOTICE TO STOCKHOLDERS OF DIVIDEND POLICY, REDUCTION IN DIVIDEND RATE, AND OFFER OF LARGE STOCKHOLDERS TO PURCHASE SHARES OF DISSATISFIED STOCKHOLDERS

To the Stockholders of .... Company:

A dividend of one (1%) percent has been declared payable to stockholders of record as of ...., 19... A check for your dividend is enclosed.

The assets of the Company consist exclusively of cash and readily marketable securities. The Company has a small surplus and the market value of the securities owned is in excess of their cost value.

The directors, however, feel that it is advisable to build up a surplus to act as a cushion for any possible decrease in market value of securities, and to take care of any unforeseen contingencies. They have, therefore, decided to discontinue the practice of paying dividends of 1 percent every other month, or at the rate of 6 percent a year, and to pay semiannual dividends of 2 percent on the 15th of April and the 15th of October, or a total of 4 percent annually. Inasmuch as dividends of 3 percent have already been paid this year, the directors have decided that the only remaining dividend to be paid this year under this policy would be a 1 percent dividend on October 15, if declared, making a total of 4 percent this year.

In adopting this policy, the directors have consulted with the larger stockholders, who have said that if any stockholders prefer to invest their money where it will bring a larger current return than four (4%) percent, they will purchase any of the .... Company stock from such stockholders at its par value. Stockholders desiring to sell their stock may send an offer to the Company, at the address of its principal office, ... (*Street*), ... (*City*), ... (*State*). The offer will then be transmitted to the larger stockholders.

LETTER TO STOCKHOLDERS EXPLAINING PASSING OF DIVIDEND

To the Stockholders of ...., Inc.:

Your Company has about completed the first six months' operations of its fiscal year ending ...., 19... Business conditions have presented the greatest difficulties for operations that have, in our experience, ever existed. There has been a continuous decline in the price of commodities in the past fifteen (15) months, and with the product that your Company manufactures and sells, this factor affects the operating profits very seriously.

Numerous economies and improvements in organization have been effected in the last six (6) months, which should materially reduce expenses.

Inventories have been priced at current replacement values, and with the first sign of steadying prices and improved market conditions, your Company will be in a favorable position to benefit therefrom.

The financial position of your Company is strong, and it has no funded debt or incumbrances of any kind, but in view of general conditions, and to maintain its current cash position, your directors have deemed it wise to follow the more conservative policy and have, therefore, decided to defer paying any dividend at this time. We are now entering into the second half of the fiscal year, which in our business is always the most profitable period— and there is every reason to believe that this period should prove more profitable to your Company, and your directors feel that by the end of the fiscal year they will be able to make a favorable report on the operating results.

For the directors,

. . . .

Chairman of the Board

. . . .

President

. . . . City, ...
. . . ., 19. .

NOTICE ACCOMPANYING CASH OR PROPERTY DIVIDEND FROM SOURCES OTHER THAN EARNED SURPLUS WHEN EFFECT ON STATED CAPITAL, CAPITAL SURPLUS, AND EARNED SURPLUS IS NOT DETERMINABLE

Enclosed check represents dividend of $. . . . . on each share of common stock as declared on . . . ., 19. . . The aggregate dividend paid amounted to $. . . . . which was in excess of the earned surplus as of . . . ., 19. ., the last date for which surplus information is available. The amount of this dividend will be charged, to the extent available, to earned surplus as of . . . ., 19. ., (*insert date when next quarterly accounting period will end*); the balance will be charged to capital surplus. The amounts of such charges are not now determinable but management estimates that the capital surplus charge will be substantial (use estimate in dollars if available). Stated capital will not be affected (if it is affected, estimate the extent).

(If the charges to the named accounts are available the notice will be substantially the same as above, but with the exact figures.)

DIRECTORS' RESOLUTION APPOINTING
DIVIDEND DISBURSING AGENT

RESOLVED, That the .... Trust Company Transfer Agent of this Corporation, is hereby appointed Dividend Disbursing Agent for the Capital Stock of this Corporation, and it hereby is authorized and directed to pay such dividends as may be declared by the Board of Directors of this Corporation, after the Corporation has lodged with said .... Trust Company, certified copies of the resolution of the Board of Directors declaring such dividends, and deposited with said .... Trust Company an amount sufficient for the payment of such dividends at least two days before each dividend date.

LETTER ACCOMPANYING ORDER FORM FOR PURCHASE
OR SALE OF FRACTIONAL SHARES

.... Corporation

.... Street

New York, N.Y.

.............., 19..

To the Stockholders of
.... Corporation:

The two percent (2%) stock dividend on ...., 19.., is payable today to stockholders of record at the close of business on ...., 19... This stock dividend has been declared to capitalize a portion of the earnings that the Board of Directors deems desirable to retain in the business.

If your holdings of $10 par value Common Stock on the record date amounted to an even multiple of fifty shares, only a stock certificate is enclosed. If you held forty-nine shares or less, only a fractional interest Order Form is enclosed. Otherwise, both a stock certificate and an Order Form are enclosed.

If you have received an Order Form, the information set forth below should be read carefully. The Order Form represents an interest in your stock dividend and has a definite value.

Very truly yours,

.... Secretary

Order Forms

The enclosed Order form is not transferable, but entitles you, on or before ...., 19.., to instruct .... Trust Company of New York, Agent either:

(1) to purchase for your account the additional fractional interest required to make up one full share, bill you for its cost, consolidate the fractions and deliver to you a certificate for a full share, or

(2) to sell your fractional interest and send a check for the proceeds to you.

For example, if you held fifteen shares of $10 par value Common Stock on the record date, you are entitled to fifteen fiftieths of a share as a stock dividend. You have the option of instructing the Agent to purchase an additional thirty-five fiftieths of a share for you, which would then entitle you to one additional full share; or you can instruct the Agent to sell your fifteen fiftieths of a share and send you a check for the proceeds.

To exercise either such right, you should mark an "X" in the appropriate box on the Order Form, sign it, and return it in the enclosed envelope to .... Trust Company of New York.

.... Trust Company of New York, as Agent, will execute such Orders as soon as practicable, for the account of the individual stockholders, at a price determined by the Agent in its discretion which will be based on the currently prevailing market price for .... Company shares on the New York Stock Exchange. The value of the fractional interest will, of course, vary depending upon the market price of the stock at the time your Order is executed .... Trust Company of New York as Agent, may match and offset purchase and sale Orders. No charge will be made to stockholders for performing these services. The Corporation has agreed to reimburse the Agent for these costs.

All shares held to cover fractional interests with respect to which .... Trust Company of New York, Agent, does not receive completed Order Forms from the holders thereof before the close of business on ...., 19.. will be sold in due course for the account of such holders, and the proceeds distributed to them. The order form will therefore become valueless after ...., 19 ...

INDEMNITY LETTER SENT UPON NOTICE OF LOST DIVIDEND CHECK

To .... Company,
Dividend Disbursing Agent,

Dear Sirs:

I hereby request that you issue to me a duplicate of the original dividend check of .... Corporation, dated ...., 19.., No. ....., for $....., being dividend No. ....., to which I am entitled as owner of ..... shares of the ..... stock of .... Corporation; in consideration therefor, I agree, for myself, my heirs, executor, and assigns, to indemnify and save you harmless at any and all times thereafter from actions, proceedings, claims, and demands that may be made or brought against you in respect of such original check, upon the issuance by you of such duplicate check. I agree to deliver or cause to be delivered to you such original check now lost or destroyed for cancellation and destruction if the same shall be found, and to reimburse you for all expenses incurred by you by reason of the issuance of such duplicate check.

Very truly yours,

. . . .
(Signature)

State of . . . .
County of . . . . } ss.

. . . . , being duly sworn, deposes and says that affiant was, on the . . . . . day of . . . . , 19. . , the owner of . . . . . shares of the . . . . . stock of . . . . Corporation, and as such was entitled to the dividend accruing on such stock on that date.

Affiant further says that any dividend check issued to affiant by . . . . Corporation, as agent for said Corporation, for the above-mentioned dividend, is to affiant's best knowledge and belief, lost or destroyed, and that affiant has not at any time indorsed, transferred, or otherwise negotiated any such check, but affiant believes that if the same was sent by the Corporation, it has been lost or destroyed. This affidavit is made to induce . . . . Corporation to issue a duplicate check in lieu of said check so lost.

. . . .
(Signature)

Subscribed and sworn to before me this . . . . . day of . . . . , 19. . .

. . . .

(*Note:* The stockholder's signature to this request must be acknowledged by a notary public.)

FORM LETTER INQUIRING AS TO STOCKHOLDER'S LATEST ADDRESS

Dear Sir:

We are trying to locate . . . . (*name of stockholder*) whose last known address in . . . . (*name of city, town*) on . . . . , 19. . , was at . . . . (*address*).

It would be to the advantage of this person, or, if deceased, to his or her estate, if we could locate him, or a relative [see notes on page 848].

Accordingly, we would appreciate it if you would advise us of anything in your records which might be helpful in this search. We enclosed a form on which you may note any information, or any helpful suggestion you may have. A stamped return envelope is also enclosed for your convenience.

With many thanks for your attention to this inquiry.

Sincerely yours,

. . . .
Secretary

[In writing to a bank, the following sentence can be substituted for the second sentence in the form letter: "A dividend check mailed to this person on . . . ., 19. ., was deposited in your bank to this person's account on . . . ., 19. ."

In writing to a broker, the following sentence can be substituted for the second sentence in the form letter: "Our records show that a certificate for . . . . . shares of . . . . . stock of this Corporation, bearing number . . . . . was presented for transfer on . . . ., 19. ."]

FORM OF REPLY TO BE ENCLOSED WITH FORM LETTER INQUIRING STOCKHOLDER'S LATEST ADDRESS

. . . .
(Name of person sought)
We believe the above-named person may be found at . . . .
Street . . . . City and Zone . . . ., State . . . .
Try: Our records show:

. . . .
. . . .
. . . .
No information □
                                          Signed . . . .
Date: . . . .   Position . . . .

DIRECTORS' RESOLUTION CREATING A DIVIDEND POLICY COMMITTEE

RESOLVED, That there be, and hereby is, established a committee to be known as the "Dividend Policy Committee" which shall have the following powers and duties:

(1) To conduct periodic studies of matters relating to the payment of cash dividends on this Corporation's Common Stock.

(2) To make recommendations to the Board of Directors of this Corporation concerning the amounts of such dividends.

(3) Such other powers and duties as from time to time may be specified by this Board.

RESOLVED FURTHER, That the Dividend Policy Committee shall consist of 4 members of this Board, 3 of whom shall not be employees of this Corporation and who shall be appointed, and shall be subject to removal with or without cause at any time, by this Board.

Chapter 25

AMENDMENT OF CHARTER AND BY-LAWS

Contents—Chapter 25

Amendment of articles in general. The state usually reserves the right to amend the articles of incorporation by constitutional or charter provision.[1] The general corporation law and the articles or certificate of incorporation, taken together, constitute the charter.[2] It follows that any change or amendment of either the general corporation law or the articles or certificate of incorporation is a change or amendment of the charter.

Amendments by the state. A change in the corporation's charter, although usually made by the corporation pursuant to statutory authority granted to it by the state, is sometimes brought about indirectly by the acts of the state itself by amendment of its corporation laws. A corporation cannot refuse to accept a lawful amendment of the corporation laws and continue in business; if it continues after the change has been effected, it will be deemed to have accepted the amendment.[3] Thus a corporation that originally had been incorporated under the state's 1901 Corporate Code but surrendered its charter and reincorporated after new 1954 Code was subject to the provisions of the latter, not the earlier Code.[4]

Though the state has reserved power to amend corporate charters by changing the corporation laws, it cannot destroy property rights.[5] But it can amend to protect the public, stockholders, or creditors and to promote due administration of corporate affairs.[6]

Amendments by the corporation. Statutes in all states permit a corporation to amend its charter. Some of these statutes contain merely a broad general power; others specify in what respect the articles may be amended; and still others make elaborate provision for the method of amendment.

In some states, a general provision permits such other amendments, alterations, or changes of the corporate charter as may be desired. In many cases the articles may be amended in any respect, provided that, as amended, they could lawfully have been included in the original certificate. States differ on whether a private business

---

[1]Greenwood v Union Freight R. Co., (1882) 105 US 13.
[2]Keller v Wilson & Co., (1935) 21 Del. Ch. 13, 180 Atl 584, rev'd on other grounds, (1936) 21 Del. 391, 90 Atl 115. Kreicker v Naylor Pipe Co., (1940) 374 Ill. 364, 29 NE2d 502 aff'd, (1941) 312 US 659, 61 S Ct 735; In re Collins-Doan Co., (1949) 4 N.J. Super. 385, 67 A2d 353.
[3]Bank of Blytheville v State, (1921) 148 Ark. 504, 230 SW 550.
[4]Reiner v Washington Plate Glass Co., Inc. (CA–DC 1983) 711 F 2d 414.
[5]Piqua Branch of State Bank of Ohio v Knoep, (1853) 16 How. (US) 369. See also, Phillips Petroleum Co. v Jenkins, (1936) 297 US 629, 56 S Ct 611.
[6]Phillips Petroleum Co. v Jenkins, (1936) 297 US 629, 56 S Ct 611.

corporation for profit can, by amending its articles of incorporation, become a cooperative,[7] or a non-profit corporation.[8] However, as to the latter it has been held the change can be made with the unanimous consent of stockholders.[9] Non-fundamental changes may be made by the ordinary procedure of amendment.[10] An amendment to require unanimity in transacting corporate business at all directors' and stockholders' meeting didn't eliminate a charter provision for cumulative voting for directors.[11]

Generally the articles are amended by the corporation to effect the following:

(1) change of name;
(2) change of location of business;
(3) change of powers and purposes;
(4) change in number of directors;
(5) renewal or extension of corporate existence;
(6) increase, decrease, or reclassification of capital stock.

Some of these changes can affect fundamental rights. A stock reclassification can adversely affect interests of the dissenting minority. A change in the number of directors can shift the balance of power. In such case the dissenting minority can argue that the contract between the stockholders is being arbitrarily altered. Whether the change can be freely made depends upon the statute and decisional law of the state and the scope of the amendment.

> *Examples:* A court of one state held that a corporation can't, by vote of two-thirds of its stockholders, change fully paid nonassessable stock to assessable stock.[12]
>
> The court of another state held that an amendment creating a new class of preferred stock superior to an existing preferred class was valid and dissenters need not be paid for their shares.[13]
>
> A corporation can amend its articles to shorten the period of its existence and so achieve a dissolution; however it remains in existence for winding up purposes.[14]

---

[7]OAG Okl. 2-26-37, Heuttle v Farmers Elevator, (1944) 145 Neb. 424, 16 NW2d 855; OAG Iowa No. 74-12-12, 12-17-75.

[8]OAG Mont. 293, (1936) aff'd, (1938); OAG N.D., 2-3-72. *Contra:* OAG Tenn. No. 218, 5-8-79.

[9]OAG Utah, 7-7-38.

[10]Martin Orchard Co. v Fruit Growers' Canning Co., (1930) 203 Wis. 97, 233 NW 603.

[11]Slavin v A. & G. Mfrs. Inc., (1973) 40 App. Div. 2d 373, 340 N.Y.S.2d 486.

[12]A.C. Frost & Co. v Coeur D'Alene Mines Corp., (1939) 60 Ida. 491, 92 P2d 1057. See also Levin v MGM, Inc. (Del. Ch. 1966) 221 A2d 499.

[13]In re Kinney, (1939) 279 N.Y. 423, 18 NE 645.

[14]OAG Ohio No. 77-089, 12-12-77.

A corporation doesn't violate the statute when it amends its articles to provide for mergers to require 80 percent stockholder approval if the directors disapprove the merger, but only a majority if the merger is one the directors do approve.[15]

When the statute authorizing the amendment affecting property rights predates the beginning of corporate existence, the corporation has a better chance of amending than when the statute post dates corporate existence,[16] though even in the latter case amendments have been upheld.

Sometimes what may not be done by amendment may be done by some other method, like merger.[17]

A corporation may amend its charter for the purpose of incorporating into it provisions authorized by subsequent legislative enactments.[18]

> *Example:* Corporations organized under earlier statutes that didn't let them deny preemptive rights can now amend their articles to do so.[19]

When an amendment is tendered to the secretary of state or other officer for filing he must see that it contains all the information prescribed by statute. If it appears from the face of the amendment that required statements of fact and information are not included, or if the amendment provides for the exercise of powers contrary to express or implied provisions of law, the secretary of state must refuse to file the amendment.[20] But the secretary of state cannot inquire whether the amendment was legally adopted.[21]

The corporation commissioner of a state in which a foreign corporation is qualified and does a substantial part of its business can bar an amendment to the foreign corporation's charter when the amendment, though in conformity with its home state law, is contrary to qualifying state law and unfair to resident stockholders.[22]

A court lacks the power to amend the articles to create a new class of nonvoting stock, even though it finds each of the two close corporation stockholders breached his duty to deal fairly with the

---

[15]Seibert v Gulton Industries (Del. Ch. 1979) Civ. Act. No. 5631, 6–21–79.
[16]"Alteration of Shareholders Rights," 69 Harv. LR 538, (1956).
[17]Langfelder v Universal Laboratories, Inc. (CA–3 1947) 163 F2d 804.
[18]OAG N.Y. to Sec. of State, 2–10–42.
[19]Mobile Press Register, Inc. v McGowin, (1960) 271 Ala. 414, 124 S2d 812.
[20]Kansas Milling Co. v Ryan, (1940) 152 Kan. 137, 102 P2d 970.
[21]OAG N.Y. to Sec. of State, 1–22–58.
[22]Western Air Lines, Inc. v Sobieski, (1961) 191 Cal. App2d 399, 12 Cal. Rpts. 719; OAG Okl., No. 68–380, 12–23–68.

other in the issuance of further shares, and wants to issue the new class to enable it to correct that breach.[23]

Methods of amendment. The procedure to be followed in amending the articles necessarily is different for different states.[24] Only the particular state law will show what a corporation may do by amending its articles and how it must do it. A corporation cannot by amending its by-law amend its charter.[25]

A corporation, having only a statutory existence, can exercise its powers only in the manner prescribed by the law under which it was organized.[26] If there is a provision in the charter or statute indicating the manner of amendment, this provision must be complied with, and an amendment in a different manner may be ineffective.[27]

> *Examples:* Amending under one provision of law when another is applicable is fatal.[28]
>
> In a case where the statute prescribed the requisites for an amendment to increase stock, failure to carry out the details rendered the stock absolutely void.[29]
>
> Under a statute that prohibited an increase of capital stock of the corporation if the consent of the persons holding the larger amount in value of the stock was not obtained at a meeting called for that purpose upon sixty days' public notice, the court held that, although all the holders of stock were present at the meeting and signed a written consent to the proposed increase, the increase was invalid because the public notice specified had not been given.[30]

The importance of complying strictly with the statutory provisions cannot be too strongly emphasized.

Restating articles of incorporation. In the course of time, a corporation's original articles of incorporation may be amended many times. When this happens, it can be a serious inconvenience to have to go through the whole series in trying to determine how the articles presently read. These multiple amendments can also add considerably to the expense of filing or publishing the articles.

---

[23]Cressy v Shannon Continental Corp. (Ind. App. 1978) 78 NE2d 941.
[24]Comstock v Wood, (1927) 204 Ia. 1027, 216 NW 640.
[25]Steiner v Steiner Land & Lumber Co., (1898) 120 Ala. 128, 26 So. 494.
[26]McNulta v Corn Belt Bank, (1897) 164 Ill. 427, 45 NE 954.
[27]United Hosiery Mills Corp. v Stevens, (1921) 146 Tenn. 531, 243 SW 656.
[28]In re Horace Keane Aeroplanes, Inc., (1920) 194 A.D. 873, 185 N.Y.S. 163.
[29]Farmers' & Traders' Bank v Nat'l Laundry & Linen Supply Co., (1917) 30 Ida. 788, 160 P 670.
[30]Navajo Min. & Dev. Co. v Curry, (1905) 147 Cal. 581, 82 P 247.

To eliminate this inconvenience and expense, many states allow the filing of "Restated Articles" or a "Composite Certificate." This is one document that incorporates all the amendments into the original articles, so that the articles read as they would if all the amendments had been there from the inception.

> **Note:** Most states won't allow *new* amendments to be made as part of the filing of the restated articles.[31] Nor can a non-profit corporation amend and restate its charter to become a corporation for profit.[32] They do permit such changes as listing as directors those who hold that office at the time of filing, rather than the original directors, and leaving out the names of the original incorporators, even if those were required by the original certificate.

Some states also let foreign corporations file these restated articles.

Amendment procedure. Scarcely two states prescribe exactly the same methods of amending the articles of incorporation. However, the procedures outlined generally include the following requirements: (1) consent of stockholders,[33] and (2) filing of certificate of amendment with designated state and county authorities. Note that failure to file is not fatal; it's merely a ministerial act.[34]

If no definite method is outlined by statute, the most common procedure, and the one dictated by good practice, is the following:

(1) The directors, at a meeting duly called, adopt a resolution (a) recommending the proposed amendment of the certificate of incorporation and (b) calling a meeting of the stockholders to consider the proposed amendment.

(2) A meeting of the stockholders is duly called upon notice, with a copy of the directors' resolution attached, and a resolution approving the amendment is adopted by the stockholders at their meeting. Under some states' statutes the charter can require a greater number to amend than the statute requires, but not a lesser number.[35] Under other state statutes, the charter can provide for a lesser number to amend than that required by statute.[36]

---

[31]OAG Ky. 77–485, 8–17–77.

[32]OAG Tenn. No. 79, 11–28–73.

[33]Sellers v Joseph Bancroft & Sons Co., (1938) 23 Del Ch. 13, 2 A2d 108 final hearing (Del. Ch. 1941) 17 A2d 831; OAG Mich. No. 2596, 6–25–56; Honikman v Ruedd, Inc. (CA–5 1966) 363 F2d 839; Dunham v Dunham (La. App. 1976) 336 S2d 337 (stockholder consent to amendment makes it valid though it's not filed); Ski Roundtop, Inc. v Hall (Mont. S Ct 1983) 658 P 2d 1071 (minority cannot object to amendment authorizing new class of stock on ground of failure to give statutory notice when it accepted benefits of changes made).

[34]Dunham v Dunham (La. App. 1976) 336 S2d 337.

[35]See cases cited in note 33, supra

[36]John P. King Mfg. Co. v Clay, (1962) 218 Ga. 382, 128 SE2d 68.

(3) The officers of the corporation file the certificate of amendment and any other papers required by statute to effect the amendment. Express authority to do so is usually granted by the stockholders' resolution.
(4) Sometimes a copy of the amendment is published.

The written assent of a proportion of the stockholders may make it possible, under some statutes, to dispense with a meeting to pass upon the proposed amendment. In some states, the amendment may be affected without any action on the part of the directors. The stockholders pass a resolution at a duly convened meeting, authorizing the amendment and directing the officers to file the necessary certificate. In some instances, the action of the stockholders in resolving to amend the articles of incorporation must be approved by the board of directors. In other states, the stockholders must authorize the directors to apply to the Secretary of State for an amendment to the charter; or the statute may require application for amendment to be directed to the court.

Change of name. A corporation has no power, unless authorized by law, to change its name.[37] Statutes in most states fix the manner in which corporations may change their names and the procedure to be followed. In many states, the change is accomplished by amending the articles of incorporation. Be careful to strictly follow the prescribed procedure, so as not to omit an essential element.[38] While complete compliance is required, it has been held that, where the corporation failed to file a certificate changing its name as required by the statute, it could not take advantage of its own wrong to avoid contracts made either under the old or the assumed name.[39]

Amendment procedure. To change the corporate name, you'll have to get the stockholders' consent and file a certificate of amendment with the proper state authorities. Check your state statute for details as to proportion of vote required for stockholder approval, time element, filing requirements, etc.

The next step will generally be the passage by the board of directors of a resolution recommending that the articles of incorporation be amended to change the corporation's name and calling a special stockholders' meeting.

---

[37] Am. Elementary Elec. Co. v Normandy, (1917) 46 App. Cas. (D.C.) 329.
[38] Maxwell v Eureka Mut. Ben. Corp., (1931) 262 Ill. App. 342.
[39] Pilsen Brewing Co. v Wallace, (1919) 291 Ill. 59, 125 NE 714.

> **Note:** You don't have to call a special meeting to have the stockholders approve the new name. It can be done at the regular annual meeting if so desired for reasons of economy.

In your call of the meeting be sure your notice specifically says that the resolution will be considered and voted on at the meeting. If your corporation solicits proxies, you should also include in your proxy statement the reasons for the change in name and the text of the amendment.

After the stockholders have voted in favor of changing the name of the company, the officers of the company must file the certificate of amendment with the proper authorities. Be sure to check state law for variations in requirements for this certificate.

In states in which you have qualified as a foreign corporation, you may have to apply for an amended certificate of authority.

> **Note:** When the corporation law is silent as to what to do with the outstanding certificates, the general, and safer practice, is to call in the certificates and imprint the new name with a rubber stamp, and then return the certificates to the stockholders. No tax problem is involved.

Effect of change of name. The courts have repeatedly decided that the mere change of name does not alter the character or identity of the corporation,[40] and that in fact it has no more effect on its identity than a change in the name of a natural person.[41] The change in name does not create a new corporation, nor does it affect any rights or avoid any liabilities that accrued before modification.[42] The corporation continues as before, responsible in its new name for liabilities previously contracted or incurred, and possessing the right to sue on contracts made before the alteration.[43] In order to create a new corporation, there must be more than a mere change of name—there must also be a substantial change in the scope, rights, and powers of the corporation.[44]

Checklist of changes resulting from change of name. When the corporate name has been officially changed, it is usually necessary for the directors to authorize the proper officers to perfect all other changes made necessary by the adoption of a new name. The following

---

[40] Paulk v Calvert Mortg. Co., (1925) 160 Ga. 7, 127 SE 134.

[41] Stewart v Preston, (1920) 80 Fla. 473, 86 So 348.

[42] J. M. Huber Petroleum Co. v Quillin (Tex. App. 1933) 60 SW2d 261; Hare v United Airlines Corp. (ND Ga. 1968) 295 F Supp 860; Lindenborg v M & L Builders & Brokers, Inc., (1973) 158 Ind. App. 311, 302 NE2d 816.

[43] Stewart v Preston, (1920) 80 Fla. 473, 86 So 348.

[44] Com. v Belknap Hardware & Mfg. Co., (1918) 182 Ky. 155, 206 SW 277.

checklist may help remind officers of the more important matters to be attended to.

Items to be considered when company name is changed.

(1) Change bank accounts.
(2) Change bank records as regards loan authorizations.
(3) Change corporate seal.
(4) Change contracts:
    a. Advertising.
    b. Freight or traffic consultants.
    c. Insurance consultants.
    d. Haulers.
    e. Rodent or insect control.
    f. Roof or building maintenance and service.
(5) Change leases.
(6) Change deeds to real property.
(7) Change insurance policies and indemnity bonds.
(8) Change property registration at tax offices:
    a. Local.
    b. County.
    c. Special school or road district.
(9) Change checks:
    a. Pay roll.
    b. Petty cash.
    c. General fund.
    d. Work fund.
    e. Bond account.
(10) Change check protector.
(11) Change postage meter.
(12) Change trade-mark, copyright, and patent or patent application registry in Patent Office.
(13) Change shipping cases, cartons, and labels. Also embossing dies and stamps used on product.
(14) Change window and door lettering.
(15) Change stationery:
    a. Letterheads.
    b. Inter-office memorandum forms.
    c. Envelopes.
    d. Credit memoranda.
    e. Invoices.
    f. Statements.
    g. Bills of lading.
    h. Receiving reports.
    i. Shipping memoranda.
    j. Purchase order forms.
    k. Salesmen's order forms.
    l. Production and cost control forms.

  m. Master forms for any of the above when duplicating machines
      are used.
(16) Change Social Security account number listing.
(17) Change State Unemployment Compensation account number
      listing.
(18) Change rubber stamps for check endorsement, mail receiving
      daters, and other rubber stamps wherever they may be found, in
      office or plant.
(19) Notify all customers and suppliers.
(20) Change telephone book listings.
(21) Notify credit agencies.
(22) Notify District Director of Internal Revenue.
(23) Notify proper state agency for state income tax, and all other state
      agencies with which you are required to register.
(24) Notify U.S. Department of Commerce, Bureau of Census.
(25) Notify post office departments.
(26) Notify trade agencies, and publishers of trade directories in which
      you may be listed.
(27) Write stockholders to send in stock certificates.

Gummed stickers bearing the new name and correct post office
address are of considerable help in making name changes on envelopes
and certain forms, minimizing waste and obsolescence.

Change of place of business. The general corporation laws of
most of the states require the certificate or articles of incorporation to
state the principal office or place of business of the corporation. Some
statutes require that, in addition to stating the location of the principal
office or place of business of the corporation, the articles of
incorporation must say where the operations of the company are to be
carried on. Compliance with these statutory provisions is mandatory.

> *Example:* When the general corporation law required the name of
> the town as well as the county where the principal office or place of
> business was to be located to appear in the articles of incorporation and
> an amendment was presented containing only the name of the county,
> the attorney general ruled it invalid.[45]

In some states, in order to effect a change in the location of the
principal place of business, the articles of incorporation must be
amended. The provisions of the statute must, in this case, as in the
amendment to effect a change in name, be strictly observed.[46] The
usual procedure for the amendment of the charter is as follows:

The directors pass a resolution that they think it advisable to

---

[45] OAG Mont., (1936).
[46] Hawk & Buck Co. v Cassidy (Tex. App. 1942) 164 SW2d 245.

amend the articles so as to change the principal place of business of the corporation. They then call a meeting of the stockholders, upon notice, to consider the question. The stockholders then adopt a resolution authorizing the amendment and directing the officers to do all acts required by statute in order legally to effect the change. In some cases, the written consent of a proportion of the stockholders will make a stockholders' meeting unnecessary.

A change in location may sometimes be effected simply by (1) a resolution of the board of directors and the filing of a certificate with some designated authority or (2) a resolution adopted at a duly convened meeting of stockholders, and the filing of a certificate of change with the secretary of state, signed by the chairman and the secretary of the stockholders' meeting and a majority of the board of directors.

Change of purpose. It is a familiar and fundamental rule that a corporation possesses only such powers as are expressly or impliedly granted by its charter, or such as are necessary to carry into effect the powers expressly granted. If the corporation wants to expand these powers, an amendment of the articles of incorporation is necessary. Under the common law a single stockholder could prevent a radical change of purpose; today non-fundamental changes may be made by the ordinary procedure of amendment.[47]

The old English rule, which has been followed in this country, said that corporate powers cannot be extended to authorized enterprises or operations different in their nature and kind from those comprehended within the terms of the original charter.[48]

For example, a corporation organized for a private business cannot by amendment turn itself into a corporation organized for a public purpose.[49] However, this doctrine does not apply if, say, articles are amended to include corporate purposes that could have been, but were not, authorized in the original charter—that kind of change imposes no injury on minority stockholders.[50]

Change in number of directors. Statutes often provide that the number of directors must be stated in the articles, and sometimes they even set the maximum number. On the other hand statutes may allow

---

[47] Martin Orchard Co. v Fruit Growers' Canning Co., (1930) 203 Wis. 97, 233 NW 603.
[48] Fower v Provo Bench Canal & Irr. Co., (1940) 99 Utah 267, 101 P2d 375, cert den (1941) 313 US 564, 61 S Ct 841.
[49] West Duluth Land Co. v Northwestern Textile Co., (1929) 176 Minn. 588, 224 NW 245; State v Sec'y St., (1942) 140 Ohio St. 541, 45 NE2d 598.
[50] Detroit & Canada Tunnel Corp. v Martin (S Ct Mich. 1951) 91 NW2d 525.

the number to be fixed by by-laws. If the number is determined by the articles of incorporation, an increase or decrease can be affected only by an amendment to those articles, unless some other method is prescribed by statute. The statutes of many states make specific provision for a change in the number of directors by an amendment to the articles of incorporation.[51] The statute must be strictly followed, or the change may be held not legally effective.

> *Examples:* (1) If the articles of incorporation must definitely state the number of directors, an amendment stating that the number shall not be less than three nor more than seven is invalid.[52]
> (2) If the statute calls for three directors, an amendment can't reduce the number to two, even in a close corporation.[53]

Apart from the number of directors, an amendment may be made as to their method of election, cumulative or straight.

If the number is fixed by by-law the stockholders who are competent to enact the by-laws may also amend them to increase or to reduce the number of directors. In some states, a change in the number of directors is allowed specifically by an amendment to the by-laws. The certificate of incorporation, if authorized by statute, may stipulate some other manner of changing the number of directors.[54]

Note that a corporation may not be bound by the number of directors set in its articles when it failed to adopt a by-law fixing a number that's consistent with the statute and the articles; that can be so, even if the articles don't specifically state that by-laws will be adopted.[55]

If the statute providing for a change in the number of directors states that a transcript of the proceedings shall be filed in the office where the certificate of incorporation is filed, the change in number does not take effect until such record is filed,[56] but where the statute requires that the change be made by amending the by-laws and that the amendment be filed, specifying no time limit for filing, it has been held that failure to file such amendment for several years does not invalidate the change in number, nor make illegal the election of directors held in compliance with the change.[57]

---

[51] A change in the method of electing directors is also sometimes effected by an amendment of the charter. See Prickett v American Steel and Pump Corp. (Del. Ch. 1969) 251 A2d 576.

[52] OAG Mont., (1934)

[53] Somers v AAA Temporary Services, Inc., (1972) 5 Ill. App. 3d 931, 284 NE2d 462.

[54] Model, Roland & Co. v Industrial Acoustics Co., Inc. (N.Y. Ct of App. 1965) 261 N.Y.S.2d 897, 16 N.Y.2d 703, 209 NE2d 553.

[55] OAG N.D. No. 81–12 12-9-81.

[56] Lewis v Matthews, (1914) 161 A.D. 107, 146 N.Y. Supp. 424.

[57] Willis v Lauridson, (1911) 161 Cal. 106, 118 P 530.

If a reduction in number is authorized, but the manner of effecting the decrease is not prescribed, the reduction cannot be accomplished until the terms of the existing directors, or the terms of enough of them to meet the change, have expired, or until such directors voluntarily resign.[58]

Renewal or extension of corporate existence. The duration of the corporation's existence is now generally determined by its charter or by the general law in force in the state in which it is incorporated. Most states permit perpetual existence. But some statutes require that a definite period of existence be stated in the articles of incorporation.

The charter of a corporation can be extended beyond the period of which it was created only by legislative authority.[59] The general laws under which corporations are organized sometimes contain provisions for the extension of the corporate existence for an additional period by compliance with certain prescribed preliminaries, or the charter itself may authorize a renewal.[60] In some states, the extension of corporate existence is effected by amending the articles of incorporation.[61] In others, the renewal is accomplished by filing a certificate with designated authorities, signed by the officers of the corporation upon the authorization of a fixed proportion of the stockholders obtained at a stockholder's meeting.[62] Some states provide that dissenting stockholders must be paid the real value of their stock.[63] The consent of the stockholders may, in some instances, be procured in writing without a meeting. Statutory requirements must be complied with strictly.

Note that a change in the statute giving a majority, rather than two-thirds, the right to extend corporate existence, did not impair the minority's constitutional rights, since the belief that the corporation will cease to exist is not a vested contractual right.[64]

The amendment must be made before the expiration of the life of the corporation. A corporation that does not renew its charter ceases to exist at the end of its term.[65] Renewal must be done according to

---

[58] In re Manoca Temple Ass'n, (1908) 128 A.D. 796, 113 N.Y.S. 172.
[59] OAG Okl. (11–26–43).
[60] McKemie v Eady-Baker, (1917) 146 Ga. 753, 92 SE 282; Drew v Beckwith, Quinn & Co., (1941) 57 Wyo. 140, 144 P2d 98, reh'g den, (1941) 57 Wyo. 140, 115 P2d 651.
[61] OAG Iowa No. 78-2-76, 2-24-78.
[62] State v Leader Co., (1934) 97 Mont. 586, 37 P2d 561; Loeffler v Federal Supply Co., (1940) 187 Okl. 373, 102 P 862.
[63] Robbins v Beatty, (1954) 67 NW2d 12.
[64] Miller v Magline, Inc., (1981) 105 Mich. App. 413, 306 NW 2d 533.
[65] OAG Col. 9–12–43; OAG Ark. to C. G. Hall 9-24-59.

statute. If the statutory fee is not paid, renewal will be denied.[66] If the corporate entity becomes legally extinct, it cannot be revived by a subsequent law without the consent of the stockholders.[67] Extending corporate existence does not create a new or different corporation. The corporation's affairs are not terminated, and there is no break in its continued existence;[68] the life of the old corporation is merely continued.[69] A stockholder doesn't waive option rights to repurchase stock by voting for renewal of corporate charter if he does not demand the preservation of those rights.[70] But a stockholder cannot inspect the list of the dissenting shareholders to urge renewal of corporate charter after the majority has voted to reorganize; the charter cannot be revived once its existence has been so terminated.[71]

It is well established that the mere act of succession does not have the effect of cancelling the continuing obligation of the corporation.[72] Nor can persons who have dealt with a corporation as a legal entity and who have received something of value from it deny the legality of its existence.[73]

A corporation can amend its charter to shorten its life and thus terminate its existence without dissolution proceedings.[74]

Reclassification. Modification of a corporation's capital structure may be necessary because of changing business conditions, or the desire of management to keep control, or conditions in the securities market when financing is to be arranged.

A reclassification of stock, or a recapitalization as it is sometimes called, may be brought about: (1) by issuing of one or more additional classes of stock;[75] or (2) by changing existing classes as to their number, par value, preferences, or relative, participating, optional, or other special rights including the right to vote.[76]

Some kinds of reclassification leave the relative rights of shareholders unchanged. Such reclassifications include a stock split, a

---

[66]OAG Okl. to Sec'y of State. 1-31-40.

[67]Lyon-Gray Lumber Co. v Gibraltar Life Ins. Co., (1923) Tex. Civ. App. 247 SW 652.

[68]Ohio Valley Tire Co. v Burner, (1912) 148 Ky. 358, 146 SW 749.

[69]Ozan Lumber Co. v Davis Sewing Mach. Co., (1922) 284 F 161, aff'd, 292 F 135. See also Hanks v Borelli, (1966) Ariz. App. 589, 411 P2d 27.

[70]Northern Lumber Co. v White, (1959) 250 Iowa 801, 96 NW2d 463.

[71]Willard v Harrworth (Del. 1970) 267 A2d 577.

[72]First Presbyterian Church v Nat'l State Bank, (1894) 57 N.J. Law 27, 29 Atl 320.

[73]Consolidated Textile Corp. v Exposition Cotton Mills, (1924) 158 Ga. 747, 124 SE 707.

[74]OAG W. Va. 10-30-56.

[75]Ainsworth v Southwestern Drug Corp. (CA-5 1938) 95 F2d 172; In re Kinney, (1939) 279 N.Y. 423, 18 NE2d 645.

[76]Brown v McLanahan (D Md. 1944) 58 F Supp 345; Goldman v Postal Telegraph, Inc. (D Del. 1943) 52 F Supp 763.

stock dividend, or an increase of stock allowing for preemptive rights. Other reclassifications aim to change relative rights of stockholders and may either leave the stockholder with a final option to accept the change or may impose the change on him without getting his consent.

Under the optional reclassification, one class of shareholders is offered attractive terms to exchange their shares for a junior security or for common stock. The aim is to simplify the capital structure, perhaps with a view to further financing. Some optional plans have been found coercive and have been set aside.[77] Others, though unfavorable to the minority, have not been found unfair and were upheld.[78]

> *Note:* The *Clark* and *Teschner* cases [see fntes. 77 and 78 respectively] both dealt with reverse stock splits aimed at eliminating minority stockholders. (By causing the smaller stockholders to wind up with fractional shares, the corporation would be able to retire such fractional shares by buying them from their holders.) In *Teschner,* the corporation said it wanted to reduce the expense of having small stockholdings, and the court found that a proper purpose. In *Clark,* however, where the aim was to buy out ex-employees, the court found no legitimate business purpose and enjoined the plan.

When reclassification imposes a change in relative rights more than an act of the board of directors is needed to accomplish it. The statutes in some states authorize such reclassification upon the vote or consent of a specified proportion of the stockholders, including the class of stock affected.[79] In many instances an amendment of the article is required, since the articles fix the various classes into which the capital stock is divided. Courts have interpreted some of these statutes to permit creation of a new preferred, superior to the old.[80] Alterations in stockholders' relative rights are usually made by an amendment to the charter proposed by resolution of the board of directors and submitted to the stockholders for approval. After approval, the amendment is filed in the appropriate state office.

Whether or not the amendment is binding depends on many factors, including the date of enactment of the enabling statute, its

---

[77] Berger v Amana Society, (1959) 250 Iowa 1060, 95 N.Y. 2d 909; Bowman v Armour & Co., (1959) 17 Ill. 2d 43, 160 NE2d 753; Clark v Pattern Analysis & Recognition Corp., (1976) 87 Misc. 2d 385, 384 N.Y.S. 2d 660 (1 for 4,000 reverse split found unfair).

[78] Johnson v Fuller (CA-3 1941) 121 F2d 618, cert den 314 US 681; 62 S Ct 184; Kriecker v Naylor Pipe Co., (1940) 374 Ill. 364, 29 NE2d 502, aff'd 312 US 659, 61 S Ct 735; Johnson v Lamprecht, (1938) 133 Ohio St. 567, 15 NE2d 127; Teschner v Chi. Title & Trust Co., (1974) 59 Ill. 2d 452, 322 NE2d 54, app dism, (1975) 422 US 1002, 95 S Ct 262.

[79] Johnson v Bradley Knitting Co., (1938) 228 Wis. 566, 280 NW 688.

[80] Haar v Pioneer Mechanical Corp. (CA-2 1933) 65 F2d 332, modf'g (SD N.Y. 1932) 2 F Supp 517, cert den, (1933) 290 US 673, 54 S Ct 92.

scope, prior decisional law and the underlying contract of stockholders as embodied in the statutes, charter and by-laws. If the statute under which the amendment was made pre-dates the corporate contract with the shareholder, its chances of being valid are better than if the statute post-dates the contract.[81]

In some states changes are binding only on stockholders who have agreed to the recapitalization.[82] In others dissenters may have redress through the statutory rights of appraisal proceedings[83] or through court actions for impairment of contract. Although courts are reluctant to intrude into the corporations' business affairs and necessities to set aside reclassification[84] they have done so, under their equitable powers, for the following reasons:

(1) Fraud or marked unfairness of the plan[85]
(2) Breach of fiduciary duty owed by majority stockholders to minority.[86]
(3) Breach of director's fiduciary duty to stockholders.[87]

Preferred shareholders are the ones usually affected by reclassification. To attract further capital, management may try to (1) eliminate arrearages of preferred dividends, (2) reduce the dividend rate, or (3) eliminate provisions in the preferred stock contract burdensome to the corporation. Some states will not permit a readjustment that eliminates dividend arrearages.[88] Others will, with the consent of stockholders.[89]

---

[81] Janes v The Washburn Co., (1950) 326 Mass. 356. See also Wheatley v A. L. Root Co., (1946) 147 Ohio St. 127, 69 NE2d 187; Fed. United Corp. v Havender, (1940) 24 Del. Ch. 318, 11 A2d 331.

[82] Frank v Wilson & Co., (1943) 27 Del. Ch. 292, 32 A2d 277; Trounstine v Remington Rand, Inc., (1937) 22 Del. Ch. 122, 194 Atl 95.

[83] Matter of Kinney, (1939) 279 N.Y. 423, 18 NE2d 645.

[84] Bailey v Tubize Rayon Corp. (D Del. 1944) 56 F Supp 418.

[85] Kamena v Janssen Dairy Corp., (1943) 133 N.J. Eq. 214, 31 A2d 200, aff'd, (1944) 134 N.J. Eq. 359, 35 A2d 894. See also Speed v Transamerica Corp. (CA–3 1956) 235 F2d 369; Gottlieb v Heyden Chemical Corp., (1962) 33 Del. Ch. 82, 90 A2d 660; Theis v Durr, (1905) 125 Wis. 651, 104 NW 985.

[86] Mount v Seagrave Corp. (SD Ohio 1953) 112 F Supp 330, aff'd (CA–6 1954) 212 F2d 389; Zahn v Transamerica Corp. (CA–3 1947) 162 F2d 36; Hay v Big Bend Land Co., (1949) 32 Wash. 2d 887, 204 P2d 488.

[87] Brown v Eastern States Corp. (CA–4 1950) 181 F2d 26, cert den, (1950) 340 US 864, 71 S Ct 88; Liebschutz v Schaffer Stores Co., (1949) 276 A.D. 1, 93 N.Y.S.2d 125.

[88] Keller v Wilson & Co., (1936) 21 Del. 391, 190 Atl 115, See also Consolidated Film Industries, Inc. v Johnson, (1938) 22 Del. Ch. 407, 197 Atl 489; Wessel v Guantanamo, (1944) 134 N.J. Eq. 271, 35 A2d 215, aff'd, (1944) 135 N.J. Eq. 506, 39 A2d 431; Patterson v Henrietta Mills, (1941) 219 N.C. 7, 12 SE2d 686.

[89] McQuillen v Nat'l Cash Register Co. (D Md. 1939) 27 F Supp 639, aff'd (CA–4 1940) 112 F2d 877, cert den, (1940) 311 US 695, 61 S Ct 140.

Some courts have placed the burden of proving fairness of the plan on the dissenters,[90] others on the corporation.[91]

Sometimes what cannot be done by amending the certificate of incorporation can be done by the mere technical merger into the parent corporation of its wholly owned subsidiary, thereby effecting a reclassification of the stock and destroying the preferred stockholders' rights to past dividend preferences that had accrued.[92]

But the merger plan must not be so unfair as to be constructively fraudulent. If it is, consummation of it may be enjoined; otherwise dissenting stockholders will be remitted to their statutory remedy of appraisal and payment for their stock.[93]

More often than not changes in the capital stock structure are effected through the sale of the assets of the corporation to be affected to a new corporation that has the desired capital structure and stocks of the two companies are exchanged, whereupon, the desired result having been obtained, the old company is usually dissolved.[94]

Increase of stock. A change in the capital stock structure of the corporation may be made by increasing the capital stock.[95] The amount of capital stock that the corporation is authorized to issue is fixed by its charter.

If a company finds it desirable to raise additional capital and all of its authorized capital stock has been issued, it cannot issue more stock. If it does the certificates are void, even in the hands of a bona fide purchaser,[96] at least to the extent the certificates exceed authorized shares.[97] The corporation's only remedy is to increase its authorized capital stock.

---

[90] Bailey v Tubize Rayon Corp. (D Del. 1944) 56 F Supp 418; Davis v Louisville Gas & Elec. Co., (1928) 16 Del. Ch. 157, 142 Atl 654, Warren v Fitzgerald, (1948) 189 Md. 476, 56 A2d 827.

[91] Hueftle v The Farmers Elevator, (1944) 145 Neb. 424, 16 NW2d 855; cf. Starr v Engineering Contracting Co., (1948) 149 Neb. 390, 31 NW2d 213. See also Kamena v Janssen Dairy Corp., (1943) 133 N.J. Eq. 214, 31 A2d 200, aff'd, (1944) 134 N.J. Eq. 359, 35 A2d 894.

[92] Langfelder v Universal Laboratories, Inc. (CA-3 1947) 163 F2d 804; MacCrone v American Capital Corp. (D Del. 1943) 51 F Supp 462; Porges v Vadsco Sales Corp., (1943) Del. Ch., 32 A2d 148; Zobel v Am. Locomotive Co., (1943) 182 Misc. 323, 44 N.Y.S.2d 33.

[93] Porges v Vadsco Sales Corp., (1943) 27 Del. Ch. 127, 32 A2d 148; Zobel v Am. Locomotive Co., (1943) 182 Misc. 323, 44 N.Y.S.2d 33.

[94] Topkis v Delaware Hardware Co., (1938) 23 Del. Ch. 125, 2 A2d 114.

[95] First Ave. Land Co. v Parker, (1901) 111 Wis. 1, 86 NW 604.

[96] In re R. Rombach & Co. (CA-3 1926) 9 F2d 359; Garnett v State, (1933) 162 Okl. 195, 19 P2d 375.

[97] Scovill v Thayer, (1881) 105 US 968; Randell v Mickle, (1931) 103 Fla. 1229, 138 So 14, 141 So 317; Larkin v Maclellan, (1922) 140 Md. 570, 118 Atl 181; Einstein v Rochester Gas & Elect. Co., (1895) 146 N.Y. 46, 40 NE 631.

Certain corporate acts that might appear to effect an increase of the authorized capital stock have been held not to do so.

Example: A change of par value shares into an equal number of no par shares is not an increase of the capital stock. Likewise, it has been held that no increase takes place where 50,000 shares of par value stock are changed into 100,000 shares of no par value stock, the capital remaining the same.[98] However, increasing the number of no par value shares of capital stock effects an increase.[99] Classifying capital stock without changing the number of shares does not effect an increase in the capital stock.[100]

Source of right to increase the authorized capital stock. Every state has statutory provisions conferring on corporations organized under its laws the right to increase their authorized capital stock.[101] The right to make the increase may be conferred by the statute directly or indirectly by authorizing provisions for increasing the stock in the certificate or articles of incorporation. The authority to increase the authorized capital stock must be express or it does not exist. In some states, the extent to which capital stock may be increased is limited. The power to authorize an increase in the capital stock of a corporation ordinarily rests with the stockholders. A change so organic and fundamental as that of enlarging the capital stock of the corporation beyond the limit fixed by the charter cannot be made by the directors alone, unless the power is expressly conferred upon them.[102] If the charter of the corporation fails to state by whom the power to increase its capital stock is to be exercised, its directors have not, merely by virtue of their position as directors, the power to do so.[103] In the absence of statutory provisions to the contrary, authority to increase the stock may be conferred on the board of directors by the charter or by charter amendments.

Method of increasing capital stock. The statutes that confer upon the corporation the right to increase its authorized capital stock usually provide the method to be utilized in effecting the increase. This method must be followed or the increase may be without effect.[104]

---

[98] Hood Rubber Co. v Com., (1921) 238 Mass. 369, 131 NE 201.

[99] Olympia Theatres v Com., (1921) 238 Mass. 374, 131 NE 204.

[100] Calif. Telephone & Light Co. v Jordan, (1912) 19 Cal. App. 536, 126 P 598.

[101] Heller Inv. Co. v So. Title & Trust Co., (1936) 17 Cal. App2d 202, 61 P2d 807.

[102] Railway Co. v Allerton, (1873) 85 US 902; Eidman v Bowman, (1871) 58 Ill. 444, 11 Am. Rep. 90. See also Scovill v Thayer, (1881) 105 US 968.

[103] McNulta v Corn Belt Bank, (1897) 164 Ill. 427, 45 NE 954.

[104] Farmers & Traders Bank v Nat'l Laundry & Linen Supply Co., (1917) 30 Idaho 788, 168 P 670. See also Hartford Accident & Indemnity Co. v W. S. Dickey Clay Mfg. Co., (1941) 26 Del. Ch. 16, 21 A2d 178, aff'd, (1942) 26 Del. Ch. 411, 24 A2d 315.

Where the method of increasing the capital stock is by an amendment of the articles or certificate of incorporation, as it is in most states, the procedure generally followed by the corporate management is the passage, by the board of directors at a duly called meeting, of a resolution recommending the increase and calling a meeting of the stockholders to take action on the amendment of the charter. The notice of the meeting must state the nature of the business to be acted upon by the stockholders. Failure to give notice to the stockholders will invalidate the increase.[105]

If essential statutory steps are omitted (and creditors' rights aren't involved), subscribers to the increased stock can void their subscriptions.[106] Indeed, it may be held that such stock has no existence.[107] But there is a difference between the situation where the company had no power to issue the stock and that where it had the power but failed to exercise it properly.[108] In the latter case, the stock is not defective if there has been substantial compliance. In other words, an overissue of stock is void—an irregular issue merely voidable.[109] Only the state can raise the issue of irregularity, so that a purchaser of such stock cannot resist paying for it if the corporation had the power to issue it.[110] Thus increases were not invalidated as to stockholders when there was a failure to publish a statute-mandated notice[111] or a failure to file a certificate.[112] A stockholder especially has no cause to complain if he has received benefits such as dividends or has otherwise asserted or enjoyed stockholders' rights.[113] But if the corporation had no power to increase stock, the purported issue is void even if the complaining stockholder participated in the meeting where the resolution increasing the stock was passed.[114] Even the corporation cannot be bound by a void increase.[115]

---

[105]Danzig v Lacks, (1932) 235 A.D. 189, 256 N.Y.S. 769.

[106]In re Rombach & Co. (CA–3 1926) 9 F2d 359; Taylor v Lounsbury-Soule Co., (1927) 106 Conn. 41, 137 Atl 159; Larkin v Maclellan, (1922) 140 Md. 570, 118 Atl 181; Danzig v Lacks, (1932) 235 A.D. 189, 256 N.Y.S. 769.

[107]Farmers' & Traders' Bank v Nat'l Laundry & Linen Supply Co., (1917) 30 Idaho 788, 168 P 670.

[108]Scovill v Thayer, (1881) 105 US 143; Garnett v State, (1932) 162 Okl. 195, 19 P2d 375.

[109]Garnett v State, (1932) 162 Okl. 195, 19 P2d 375.

[110]In re R. Rombach & Co. (CA–3 1926) 9 F2d 359, aff'g (D D.C. 1924) 3 F2d 46; Upton v Tribilcock, (1875) 91 US 45.

[111]Handley v Stutz, (1890) 139 US 417.

[112]In Jackson v Pittsburgh, F. W. & C. Ry. Co., (1921) Ind., 132 NE 710.

[113]Mitchell v Mitchell Woodbury Co., (1928) 263 Mass. 160 160 NE 539.

[114]Randle v Walker, (1919) 17 Ala. App. 211, 84 So 551; Tschumi v Hill, (1897) 6 Kan. App. 549, 51 P 619.

[115]Scovill v Thayer, (1881) 105 US 143.

The stockholders usually authorize an increase of capital.[116] Unless the statute bars that, the charter, or a charter amendment, may confer on the board of directors the power to increase the authorized capital stock. By statute in some states directors can increase the capital stock to take care of the conversion rights incident to an issue of bonds convertible into stock where there is not enough stock with which to make the change.

An increase in shares, of course, can mean that the state will exact an additional fee. Note though, that a corporation that amended its articles to (1) increase the number of shares and (2) change them from par to no par, but covered each aspect by a separate certificate of amendment was obligated to pay only tax of $10, not the $318,050 demanded by the state on the second filing, since that neither increased the total number of shares nor increased the total authorized capital stock.[117]

Overissue of the authorized capital stock. When the charter limit is reached, the corporation's agreement to issue additional stock is void[118] and stock issued pursuant to such an agreement is void.[119] A certificate for such stock is likewise void.[120] A reissue of surrendered, purchased or forfeited shares of its own capital stock by a corporation is not an overissue, nor is there an overissue by the issuance of new certificates of stock for lost or destroyed ones.[121] If the first issue of the entire amount of the authorized capital stock is not a real issue, then a later issue is not an overissue.[122] If the corporation overissues its capital stock, it may be liable in damages to bona fide holders of the certificates.[123] The corporation, or a stockholder for himself and other stockholders, if the company refuses to act, may sue for the cancellation of certificates of an overissue of stock,[124] unless barred by delay or compromising conduct.[125]

---

[116]Orloff v Stott, (1927) 239 Mich. 536, 215 NW 1.

[117]Chrysler Corp. v Delaware (Del. S Ct 1983) 457 A 2d 345.

[118]Anthony v Household Sewing Machine Co., (1889) 16 R.I. 571, 18 Atl 176.

[119]New York & E. Tel. & Tel. Co., (1908) 74 N.J. Eq. 221, 69 Atl. 528, aff'd, (1909) 75 N.J. Eq. 297, 72 Atl 1119.

[120]Smith v Worcester & S. St. R. Co., (1916) 224 Mass. 564, 113 NE 462.

[121]Kinnan v Forty-Second St. M. & St. N. Ave. Ry. Co., (1893) 1 Misc. 457, 21 N.Y.S. 789, aff'd, (1893) 140 N.Y. 183, 35 NE 498.

[122]Gordon v Cummings, (1914) 78 Wash. 515, 139 P 489.

[123]National Bank of Webb City v Newell Morse Royalty Co., (1914) 259 Mo. 637, 168 SW 699; Hobson v Marsh, (1912) 62 Wash. 326, 124 P 912.

[124]US Light & Heat Corp. v Walker, (1916) 94 Misc. 687, 158 N.Y.S. 664, aff'd, (1916) 175 A.D. 929, 161 N.Y.S. 1148.

[125]Jutte v Hutchinson, (1899) 189 Pa. St. 218, 42 Atl 123.

Reduction of stock. The authorized capital stock, being a security upon which creditors and stockholders have a right to rely for the protection of their respective interests, cannot be reduced or decreased without authority and without full compliance with all the relevant laws and regulations.[126] The corporation can't reduce stock if that would prejudice creditors' rights.[127] When the capital stock is reduced it is proper to carry the amount by which it is reduced to the surplus capital account.[128] It represents a surplus of capital.[129] It may be distributed as dividends if thereafter there is actual capital available for the payment of corporate debts exceeding the amount to which the capital stock was reduced. Stock reduction may be used to withdraw capital from the business at a time of retrenchment without dissolution. Many of the rules discussed in connection with an increase of the authorized capital stock apply, in many respects, to a reduction.

Following a valid reduction of the authorized capital stock of a corporation, the shares cease to exist for any purpose. A reduction is effected only when the amount of the authorized and fixed capital stock is diminished. Where the corporation simply reduces the number of par value shares without diminishing its stated capital there is no real reduction.[130]

> *Example:* If a corporation having a capital stock of $10,000, divided into 100 shares of the par value of $100 each, reduces the number of shares to 50, and changes the par value of each share to $200, no real reduction has been made. The capital stock is still $10,000.

The mere act of reclassifying capital stock without changing the number of shares is not a reduction, any more than it's an increase.[131] Nor does a corporation reduce its stock by purchasing shares, where it does not retire them but sells or transfers them to others, or holds them ready for such sale or transfer.[132]

Ways of reducing capital stock. Here are some ways of reducing capital stock:

---

[126] Botz v Helvering (8 Cir. 1943) 134 F2d 538 (Mo. law); Williams v Davis, (1944) 297 Kan. 626, 180 S W 2d 874; State v Stewart Bros. Cotton Co., Inc., (1939) 193 La. 16, 190 So 317; State v La. Navigation & Fisheries Co., (1942) La. App., 8 S2d 796.

[127] Sherrard St. Bank v Vernon, (1928) 243 Ill. App. 122.

[128] Dominguez Land Corp. v Daugherty, (1925) 196 Cal. 468, 238 P 703.

[129] Roberts v Roberts-Wicks Co., (1906) 184 N.Y. 257, 77 N.E. 13.

[130] State v Benson, (1924) 32 Del. 576, 128 Atl 107. See also Ryan v American Nat'l Invest. Co., (1957) 7 Utah 2d 95, 318 P2d 1105.

[131] Cal. Tel. & Light Co. v Jordan, (1912) 19 Cal. App. 536, 126 P 598.

[132] Ruffner v Sophie Mae Candy Corp., (1926) 35 Ga. App. 114, 132 SE 396. See also Barrett v W. A. Webster Lumber Co., (1931) 275 Mass. 302, 175 NE 765.

(1) Purchasing shares and cancelling or retiring them.

(2) Cancelling shares owned by the corporation.

(3) Exchanging shares for a decreased number of shares of the same or a different class.

(4) Exchanging stock having a par value for stock having no par value.

Example: Assume that a corporation has capital stock of $400,000, represented by 4,000 shares of the par value of $100 each. It wants to reduce its capital stock to $200,000. It can do this by exchanging the 4,000 par value shares for: (1) 4,000 no par shares, an equal number; (2) 2,000 no par shares, a smaller number; or (3) 8,000 no par shares, a larger number. In the first case, each no par share will be worth $50; in the second, $100; and in the third $25.

(5) Reducing the par value of stock.[133]

(6) Reducing the amount of capital represented by shares having no par value.

How stock decreases are authorized. Each state has statutory provisions authorizing corporations to decrease their authorized capital stock. And most of these statutes also provide a method for doing so. This can be by charter amendment, or by resolution of the board that is then approved after by the stockholders. Such approval must generally be given at a duly called meeting though, if the assent is in writing the meeting may be waived.

The purchase and resale by the corporation of its own shares is not a stock reduction.[134] But the corporation may effect a reduction by just buying its own stock.[135] And a corporation's actual capital, as distinct from its authorized capital, was validly reduced when its preferred stockholders delivered their stock for cancellation, so that a later charter amendment wasn't necessary to effect the reduction.[136]

Rights of stockholders upon a decrease of authorized capital stock. Unless a statute permits otherwise, after a decrease the stockholder must have the same proportionate interest in the corporation that he had before the reduction.[137]

In some states there are statutes providing a method of stock reduction resulting in a change in the stockholder's interest in the

[133] Chisnell v Ozier Co., (1942) 140 Ohio St. 355, 44 NE2d 464; Hay v Big Ben Land Co., (1949) 32 Wash. 2d 887, 204 P2d 488.

[134] In re Culbertson's (CA–9 1932) 54 F2d 753; Ruffner v Sophie Mae Candy Corp., (1926) 35 Ga. App. 114, 132 SE 396; Shafer v Home Trading Co., (1932) Mo. App., 52 SW2d 462.

[135] Security Nat'l Bank v Crystal Ice & Fuel Co., (1937) 145 Kan. 899, 67 P2d 527. *Contra:* Botz v Helvering (CA–8 1943) 134 F2d 538 (Mo. law).

[136] Jack Cole-Dixie Highway Cr. v Red Ball Motor Freight, Inc. (Miss. 1971) 254 S2d 734.

[137] Page v American & British Mfg. Co., (1908) 129 App. Div. 346, 113 N.Y.S. 734; Hildreth v Western Realty Co., (1932) 62 N.D. 233, 242 NW 679.

company. The results produced by compliance with the provisions of these statutes are not within the scope of the general rules here discussed.[138]

If the corporation effects the reduction by buying the stock for retirement, it should be acquired ratably from each stockholder desiring to sell.[139] This does not mean, however, that a corporation cannot buy its own stock in the open market.[140]

If the reduction is valid, stockholders can be compelled to accept stock certificates for fractional parts of the shares originally held by them.[141]

Generally, if there is no contrary statutory provision, common and preferred stock must be reduced in the proportion that the issue of each bears to the other.[142] Of course, by unanimous consent, stockholders may agree to a reduction in an unequal proportion. In some states, the statutes specifically provide that any class of stock may be reduced. The vote of each class of stockholders is sometimes required to effect a reduction.

Rights of creditors upon a decrease of authorized capital stock. Even with statutory authority, the corporation cannot reduce its authorized capital stock to the prejudice of existing creditors. In many states it is provided, expressly or impliedly, in the statutes authorizing a reduction of the authorized capital stock, that the reduction cannot be made if it will impair the corporation's ability to meet its obligations.[143]

Subsequent creditors have no standing to complain of a prior reduction.[144] Nor can they hold liable stockholders to whom full paid stock has been issued.[145]

After a reduction of the authorized capital there must remain available assets equal to the issued capital stock plus the amount necessary to cover all liabilities. After a valid reduction, any excess of funds over and above the amount required indicated, it may be distributed by the corporation as surplus.[146]

---

[138] Jay Ronald Co. v Marshall Mortgage Corp., (1943) 291 N.Y. 227, 52 NE2d 108.

[139] Ocean City Title & Trust Co. v Strand Properties, Inc., (1930) 106 N.J. Eq. 25, 149 Atl 817, aff'd, 107 N.J. Eq. 594, 153 Atl 906.

[140] Downs v Jersey Central Power & Light Co., (1934) 115 N.J. Eq. 448, 171 Atl 306.

[141] Perry v Bank of Commerce, (1919) 118 Miss. 852, 80 So 332.

[142] Page v Amer. & British Mfg. Co., (1908) 129 App. Div. 346, 113 N.Y.S. 734.

[143] Chisnell v Ozier Co., (1942) 140 Ohio St. 355, 44 NE2d 464.

[144] Rice v Thomas, (1919) 184 Ky. 168, 211 SW 428.

[145] In re State Ins. Co. (ND Ill. 1882) 14 F 28.

[146] Benas v Title Guaranty & Trust Co., (1924) 216 Mo. App. 53, 267 S.W. 28; Jay Ronald Co., Inc. v Marshall Mortgage Corp., (1943) 291 N.Y. 227, 52 NE2d 108; Strong v the Brooklyn Cross-Town Railroad Company, (1883) 93 N.Y. 426; Page v Amer. & British Mfg. Co., (1908) 129 App. Div. 346, 113 N.Y.S. 734.

By-laws defined and distinguished from resolutions. By-laws are the rules and regulations made by a corporation to regulate its affairs, to define and determine the rights and duties of its stockholders in their relation to it and among themselves and the rights, power and duties of the directors and officers. In other words, they may be thought of as statutes adopted by the corporation for its own government and that of its stockholders, directors and officers. By-laws are permanent and continuing except as they may be amended.

By-laws must be distinguished from resolutions. While a by-law or set of by-laws may be adopted by a resolution, a resolution is not necessarily a by-law. A resolution may authorize a single corporate act or transaction whereas a by-law is a permanent and continuing rule. A resolution may be passed at any meeting of the directors or stockholders, providing the meeting has been properly called by notice (if notice is required). A resolution can change a previous resolution as long as vested rights are not disturbed.

If a resolution of the board of directors is inconsistent with a by-law, the by-law must prevail.[147]

Authority for making and changing by-laws. Most statutes specifically empower corporations to make by-laws and prescribe the methods of making and changing them and the subject matter they may cover.

A corporation doesn't need statutory authority, though, to make or change by-laws. At common law the power to do so was an incident to every corporation.[148]

In fact, a by-law of a close corporation was upheld as such even though it was never formally adopted, when it was recognized in practice as being adopted and effective.[149]

To be valid and enforceable, a by-law must be consistent both with the charter and with the governing statute as of the time of the by-law's adoption,[150] and also with later enacted mandatory statutes[151]

---

[147]Rosenfeld v Inland Iron Works, Inc., (1932) 267 Ill. App. 254.

[148]Nat'l Surety Co. v Williams, (1917) 74 Fla. 446, 77 S 212; Thomson v Thomson, (1920) 293 Ill. 584, 127 NE 882; Miller v Farmers' Milling & Elevator Co., (1907) 78 Neb. 441, 110 NW 995.

[149]Taylor's Adm'r v Taylor (Ky. App. 1957) 301 SW2d 579.

[150]San Francisco Real Estate Investors v Real Estate Investment Trust (CA–1 1983) 701 F 2d 1000; Quinn v Stuart Lakes Club, Inc. (Ct of App. 1982) 57 N Y 2d 1003, 457 NYS 2d 471, 443 NE 2d 945; in re Warns (S Ct 1941) NYLJ, 11–10–41, p. 1448; Comm. v Green, (1945) 351 Pa. 170, 40 A2d 492; Security Sav. & Trust Co. v Coos Bay Lumber & Coal Co., (1935) 219 Wis. 647, 263 NW 187.

[151]St. John of Vizzini v Cavallo, (1929) 134 Misc. 152, 234 N.Y.S. 683.

and with later charter amendments. Thus, a charter amendment permitting cumulative voting supersedes a by-law providing for removal of directors without cause.[152] Also, in general, an amendment to the by-laws must be made in substantial compliance with the statute as to amendment of by-laws.[153] However, a by-law may be amended by a course of conduct inconsistent therewith,[154] may be abrogated by non-usage,[155] or waived by the corporation[156] or by a stockholder.[157]

> *Example:* A by-law reserving to the board of directors the right to fix the salaries of officers was waived by the board's acquiescence in the fixing of those salaries by the president and general manager.[158]

Of course, an amended by-law, like a newly adopted one, must be consistent with law and with the corporate charter.[159] It must also be reasonable and capable of being complied with.[160] Absent clear and strong intent, it isn't retroactive.[161] Finally it must not be violative of a vested or contract right[162] like the right to vote[163] or to vote cumulatively.[164]

A close corporation's by-law providing for corporate action by majority vote was negated, when one of the stockholders was induced to buy his stock by a representation that no action would be taken without 90 percent stockholder consent.[165] Similarly, a by-law

---

[152]Matter of Rogers Imports, Inc. (S Ct 1952) 128 NYLJ 583.

[153]Noble v Cal. etc., Ass'n, (1929) 98 Cal. App. 230, 276 P. 237; Klein v Scranton Life Ins. Co., (1940) 139 Pa. Super 369, 11 A2d 770; Benintendi v Kenton Hotel, Inc., (1943) 181 Misc. 897, 45 N.Y.S.2d 705, aff'd, 268 A.D. 857, 50 N.Y.S.2d 843, aff'd in part and rev'd in part, (1945) 294 N.Y. 112, 60 NE2d 829.

[154]Belle Isle Corp. v Mac Bean (Del. Ch. 1946) 49 A2d 5. See, also, Dixies Glass Co., Inc. v Pollak (Tex. App. 1960) 341 SW2d 530; Conlee Construction Co. v Cay Construction Co. (Fla. App. 1969) 221 S2d 792.

[155]Elliot v Lindquist (Com. Pls. 1946) 94 Pitts L.J. 295; Pomeroy v Westaway, (1947) 189 Misc. 307, 70 N.Y.S.2d 449, aff'd 273 A.D. 760, 75 N.Y.S.2d 654.

[156]Ledebuhr v Wis. Trust Co., (1902) 112 Wis. 657, 88 NW 607.

[157]Grand Valley Irr. Co. v Fruita Improvement Co., (1906) 37 Col. 483, 86 P 324.

[158]Bay City Lumber Co. v Anderson, Jr., (1941) 8 Wash. 2d 191, 111 P2d 771.

[159]Rowland v Rowland, (1981) 102 Idaho, 534, 633 P 2d 599: Brooks v State, (1911) 26 Del. 1, 79 A. 790; Mutual Fire Ins. Co. v Farquhar, (1898) 86 MD. 668, 39 A. 527; Nicholson v Franklin Brewing Co., (1910) 82 Ohio St. 94, 91 NE 991; Tempel v Dodge, (1895) 89 Tex. 69, 33 SW 222, 32 SW 514; Matter of Hellenic Cultural Circle, Inc. v Kotsilimbas, (1973) 79 Misc. 2d 675, 361 N.Y.S.2d 797.

[160]State v Jessup & Moore Paper Co., (1910) 24 Del. 379, 77 A. 16; Saltman v Nesson, (1909) 201 Mass. 534, 88 NE 3.

[161]Novo Corp. v Air Express Int'l Corp. (SD N.Y. 1977) 13 Civ. 819, 5-4-77.

[162]Born v Beasley, (1921) 145 Tenn. 64, 235 SW 62.

[163]In re Crown Heights Hospital, Inc., (1944) 183 Misc. 563, 49 N.Y.S.2d 658.

[164]Comm. v Garrett Water Co., (1941) 41 Pa. D. & C. 357.

[165]Katcher v Ohsman, (1953) 26 N.J. Super 28, 97 A2d 180. *Contra:* Kear v Levinson (Com. Pls. 1950) 71 Pa. D. & C. 475.

restricting sale of stock couldn't be repealed by the majority stockholder against the wishes of nearly all the minority.[166]

The power to adopt and amend by-laws may be exercised only by the stockholders and not by the directors or the officers,[167] unless the stockholders delegate that power to the directors,[168] or unless the charter or a statute vests the power in the directors.[169]

When the directors can amend the by-laws and they make a contract inconsistent with existing by-laws, they are deemed to have amended the by-laws to the extent of the inconsistency.[170] Director-adopted by-laws are always subject to change or repeal by the stockholders.[171] The stockholders can, by by-law, prohibit the directors from removing the chairman of the board without cause.[172] When a shareholders' agreement was made part of the by-laws, amendments to it didn't require the unanimous consent of all the stockholders; they could be made by a majority of the directors the same way any by-law could be amended.[173]

> **Suggestion:** When drafting by-laws, it's advisable to include all matters suggested by the statute as proper subjects for by-laws. Thus, in a state with a statute that provides that certificates of stock shall be signed by officers designated in the by-laws, the by-laws should designate such officers. Also by-laws should avoid needless rigidity in minor details. For example, it's better to let the board of directors set the date of its regular meeting by resolution instead of fixing that date in the by-laws.

Persons bound by by-laws—constructive notice. Certain persons are chargeable with constructive notice of corporate by-laws and so are bound by them. (A person is said to have constructive notice of something, if knowledge of it may be imputed to him although he has no actual knowledge of it.) Other persons aren't bound by by-law provisions, unless they have actual notice of them.

There's a conclusive presumption that stockholders, directors, and officers of a corporation are acquainted with all its legally adopted

---

[166]Bechtold v Coleman Realty Co., (1951) 367 Pa. 208, 79 A2d 661.

[167]SEC v Transamerica Corp. (D. Del. 1946) 67 F Supp 326; Darrin v Hoff, (1904) 99 Md. 491, 58 Atl 196; Borgards v Farmers' Mut. Ins. Co., (1890) 79 Mich. 440, 44 NW 856.

[168]Hingston v Montgomery, (1906) 121 Mo. App. 451, 97 SW 202.

[169]Avant v Sandersville Production Credit Ass'n, (1979) 243 Ga. 173, 253 SE2d 176; Templeman v Grant, (1924) 75 Colo. 519, 200 P 555.

[170]Hill v American Cotton Co-operative Ass'n, (1940) 195 La. 590, 197 So 241; Hernandez v Banco DeLas Americas (Ariz. 1977) 570 P2d 494.

[171]Boericke v Weise, (1945) 68 Cal. App. 2d 407, 156 P2d 781.

[172]In re Buckley, Jr., (1944) 183 Misc. 189, 50 N.Y.S.2d 54; State v Kreutzer, (1919) 100 Ohio St. 246, 126 NE 54.

[173]Blount v Taft, (1978) N.C. 246, SE2d 763.

by-laws.[174] They can't plead ignorance of them any more than they can plead ignorance of the law of the state.[175] Thus a contract employing a general manager for a year was subject to a by-law providing for removal of an officer or employee, of which the general manager had actual or presumptive knowledge, and recovery couldn't be had for salary for balance of year.[176] Similarly, a 50 percent stockholder can't set aside an election of directors on the ground he didn't know, when he voted to adopt the by-laws, that they barred him from gaining control of one-half of the board.[177]

Third persons dealing with the corporation ordinarily are not charged with constructive notice of by-laws, unless the by-law is expressly authorized by the statutes.[178] Consequently, they are not bound by by-law provisions unless they have actual notice, or knowledge, of them. If they have such knowledge, of course, they are bound.[179]

Construction of by-laws. In construing by-laws a reasonable construction should be placed upon them.[180] It is desirable, if possible, to sustain their validity[181] and to render their operation equitable.[182] Unless the contrary intention appears, by-laws should be construed with an eye to future instead of in the light of past developments.[183] By-laws imposing penalties or forfeitures, where these are legal, should

---

[174]State v Shaw, (1921) 103 Ohio St. 660, 134 NE 643; Wilson v Union Mut. Fire Ins. Co., (1904) 77 Vt. 28, 58 Atl 799; Model Land & Irr. Co. v Madsen, (1930) 87 Colo. 166, 285 P 1100.

[175]Ginter v Heco Envelope Co., (1925) 316 Ill. 183, 147 NE 42; Miller v Hillsborough Fire Assn, (1887) 42 N.J. Eq. 459, 7 Atl 895; Am. Nat'l Bank v Wheeler-Adams Auto Co., (1913) 31 SD 524, 141 NW 396.

[176]Cohen v Camden Refrigerating & Terminals Co., (1943) 129 N.J.L. 519, 30 A2d 428.

[177]Gwin v Thunderbird Motor Hotels, Inc., (1961) 216 Ga. 652, 119 SE2d 14.

[178]Brent v Bank, (1836) 10 Pet. (US) 596, 9 L Ed 547; In re Millward-Cliff Crasler Co.'s Estate, (1894) 161 Pa. St. 157, 28 Atl 1072; Yarnell Ware & Tr., Inc. v Three Ivory Bros. Mov. Co. (Fla. Ct of App. 1969) 226 So2d 887; Chemtronix Laboratories, Inc. v Solocast Co., (1968) 5 Conn. Cir. 533, 258 A2d 110; Long v Nat'l Bank & Trust Co. of Central Pennsylvania (Pa. Orph. Ct. 1968) 89 Dauph. 238.

[179]E. Van Norden & Co. v US (CC, D. Mass. 1934) 8 F Supp 279; Newton v Johnston Organ & Piano Mfg. Co., (1919) 180 Cal. 185, 180 P 7; Arapahoe Cattle & Land Co. v Stevens, (1889) 13 Col. 534, 22 P 823; Ashley Wire Co. v Ill. Steel Co., (1896) 164 Ill. 149, 45 NE 410; Baer v Waseca Milling Co., (1919) 143 Minn. 483, 173 NW 401; Lutz v Webster, (1915) 249 Pa. 226, 94 Atl 834; Uline Loan Co. v Standard Oil Co., (1921) 45 SD 81, 185 NW 1012; Washington & Devonshire Realty Co. v Lewis Diamond Co., (1928) 263 Mas. 554, 161 NE 883.

[180]Mancini v Patrizi, (1928) 87 Cal. App. 435, 262 P 375; Carney v N. Y. Life Ins. Co., (1900) 162 N.Y. 453, 57 NE 78.

[181]Morton v Talmadge, (1928) 166 Ga. 620, 144 SE 111; Hibernia etc. Co. v Comm., (1880) 93 Pa. St. 264.

[182]First Mtg. etc. Ass'n v Baker, (1929) 157 Md. 309, 145 Atl 876; Thibeault v Ass'n, (1899) 21 R.I. 157, 42 Atl 518; Denton Milling Co. v Blewett, (1923) 254 SW 236, 114 Tex. 582, 278 SW 1114.

[183]Kaemmerer v Kaemmerer, (1907) 231 Ill. 154, 83 NE 133.

be strictly construed.[184] In determining stockholders' rights under by-laws, all by-laws having a material bearing on the right or rights concerned must be construed together.[185] The cardinal rule of construction is to ascertain the design and intent of the framers of the by-laws and follow such design and intent.[186] Ordinarily the practical construction, if it will sustain the validity of the by-law, will prevail.[187]

> *Example:* When the by-laws clearly authorize the president to execute all contracts and deeds in the name of the corporation, he is thereby given the general management and supervision of the affairs of the company, including the authority to act for it in executing a contract of sale of its real estate.[188]

By-law prohibiting any stockholder from owning over 9.8 percent of stock is valid when it would prevent loss of entity's tax status as REIT.[189]

How to avoid unnecessary amendments of by-laws. It may often be wiser and far more expedient for a corporation to couch the wording of its by-laws in such general terms that an amendment will not be necessary each time some minor change is desired. Many detailed matters may be safely left to the discretion of the directors to be determined by the adoption of a resolution at the time the particular action is taken. To give one typical illustration of many that may be offered: the by-laws may allow the board to determine by resolution when its regular meetings shall be held instead of definitely fixing a particular meeting date. Should the directors from time to time desire to change the day of meeting an amendment of the by-laws will not be necessary. Of course, the interests of the members of the corporation should be properly safeguarded. In the particular instance mentioned, for example, proper provision should be made in the by-laws for giving all the directors notice of any resolution to be considered thereunder.

---

[184]Egg Harbor B. & L. Ass'n, (1907) 72 N.J. L. 603, 65 Atl 864.
[185]Penhall v Ass'n, (1914) 126 Minn. 323, 148 NW 472.
[186]Baltimore etc. Ass'n v Powhatan etc. Co., (1898) 87 Md. 59, 39 Atl 274.
[187]Frances v Brigham-Hopkins Co., (1908) 108 Md. 233, 70 Atl 95.
[188]Krueger v W. K. Ewing Co., Inc., Tex. Civ. App., (1940) 139 SW2d 836.
[189]Pacific Realty Trust v APC Investments, Inc. (CA–9 1982) 685 F 2d 1083.

Chapter 26

RESOLUTIONS RELATING TO AMENDMENT OF CHARTER AND BY-LAWS

Contents—Chapter 26

DIRECTORS' RESOLUTION RECOMMENDING AMENDMENT OF CHARTER AND CALLING STOCKHOLDERS' MEETING TO CONSIDER AMENDMENT, SETTING FORTH AMENDED CERTIFICATE OF INCORPORATION

RESOLVED, That the Board of Directors of . . . . Corporation does hereby declare it advisable that the Certificate of Incorporation of said Corporation be amended so that, as amended, it shall read as follows:

(Here insert amended certificate of incorporation.)

RESOLVED FURTHER, That a meeting of the stockholders of the Corporation entitled to vote on such amendment is hereby called to be held at the office of the Corporation, ... *(Street)*, in the City of . . . . , State of . . . . , on . . . . , 19.., at . . . . . M.; and

RESOLVED FURTHER, That if and when the persons or bodies corporate holding the majority of each class of stock of the Corporation have voted in favor of such amendment, the President or a Vice president, and the Secretary or an Assistant Secretary, of the Corporation are hereby authorized and directed to make, under the seal of the corporation, a certificate setting forth such amendment, and certifying that such amendment has been duly adopted in accordance with the provisions of Section . . . . . of . . . . . Code of the State of . . . . as amended, and to file such certificate in the office of the Secretary of State of the State of . . . . , and to have a copy thereof certified by said Secretary of State recorded in the office of the Recorder of the County in which the original Certificate of Incorporation of the Corporation is recorded.

RESOLUTION OF STOCKHOLDERS APPROVING CHARTER AMENDMENT RECOMMENDED BY BOARD OF DIRECTORS, AND AUTHORIZING OFFICERS TO FILE CERTIFICATE, SETTING FORTH NEW PROVISION IN FULL

WHEREAS, the Board of Directors of the . . . . Corporation has declared it advisable that Article . . . . . , Section . . . . . , of the charter of the Corporation be changed, amended, and altered, as hereinafter set forth, and

WHEREAS, the stockholders of the . . . . Corporation do hereby approve of the said proposed amendment,

RESOLVED, That Article . . . . . , Section . . . . . , of the charter of the said Corporation be amended, changed, and altered so as to read as follows:

(Here insert new provision.)

RESOLVED FURTHER, That the Chairman and Secretary of this meeting are hereby authorized and directed to make, execute, and acknowledge a certificate under the corporate seal of this Corporation, embracing the foregoing resolution, and to cause such certificate to be filed and recorded in the manner required by law, and

RESOLVED FURTHER, That upon completion of the proceedings required to effect the amendment hereinabove set forth, a duplicate of the certificate of amendment be set forth in full on the minutes of this meeting.

RESOLUTION OF STOCKHOLDERS AUTHORIZING AMENDMENT OF CERTIFICATE OF INCORPORATION, SETTING FORTH OLD AND NEW PROVISIONS OF CERTIFICATE OF INCORPORATION

RESOLVED, That article First of the Certificate of Incorporation of this Corporation be amended so that said Article, now reading as follows: "First: The name of the Corporation is . . . ., Inc." will, as amended, read as follows: "First: The name of the Corporation is . . . ., Inc.," and

RESOLVED FURTHER, That the initial paragraph of Article Fourth of the Certificate of Incorporation of this Corporation be amended so that said paragraph, now reading as follows:

Fourth: The total number of shares of all classes of stock which the Corporation shall have authority to issue is eight hundred seventy-five thousand (875,000), consisting of twenty-five thousand (25,000) shares of 6 percent Cumulative Convertible Preferred Stock (hereinafter called "Preferred Stock"), of the par value of one hundred ($100) Dollars per share, and eight hundred fifty thousand (850,000) shares of Common Stock, of the par value of ten ($10) Dollars per share.

will, as amended, read as follows:

Fourth: The total number of shares of all classes of stock that the corporation shall have authority to issue is eight hundred sixty-two thousand three hundred one (862,301), consisting of twelve thousand three hundred one (12,301) shares of 6 percent Cumulative Convertible Preferred Stock (hereinafter called "Preferred Stock"), of the par value of one hundred ($100) Dollars per share, and eight hundred fifty thousand (850,000) shares of Common Stock, of the par value of ten ($10) Dollars per share, and

RESOLVED FURTHER, That a certificate setting forth the amendment, certifying that such amendment has been duly adopted in accordance with the provisions of Section . . . . . of the Corporation Law of the State of . . . ., and containing such other statements as may be necessary or advisable, be made under the seal of the Corporation and signed by its President and its Secretary and acknowledged by its said President, and that the said certificate, so executed and acknowledged, be filed in the office of the Secretary of State, and a copy thereof certified by said Secretary of State, be recorded in the office of the Recorder of the County of . . . ., in which County the original Certificate of Incorporation is recorded, and

RESOLVED FURTHER, That the officers of this Corporation are hereby authorized, empowered, and directed to take any and all further acts or proceedings that they may deem necessary or proper to effectuate the said amendment.

DIRECTORS' RESOLUTION RECOMMENDING AMENDMENT OF ARTICLES, CALLING MEETING OF STOCKHOLDERS TO CONSIDER AMENDMENT, AND DIRECTING SECRETARY OF CORPORATION TO SERVE AND PUBLISH NOTICE OF MEETING, SETTING FORTH SUBSTANCE OF AMENDMENT

RESOLVED, That it is deemed advisable to amend the Articles of Incorporation of this Corporation in the following respects:

(1) Reducing the number of its directors from ..... to ....., and to that end striking out paragraph ..... of said Articles and inserting in lieu thereof "That the number of its directors is ...."

(2) Confirming the change of its principal place of business from .... (*State*), to .... (*State*), and to that end striking out in paragraph ..... of said Articles the words .... and inserting in lieu thereof ....

(3) Changing its authorized common stock from ..... shares of the par value of $..... each, to ..... shares of common stock without par value; and authorizing the issue of ..... shares of such stock without par value for each share of the existing common stock of the par value of $..... outstanding.

RESOLVED FURTHER, That a special meeting of the stockholders of this Corporation be called to convene on ...., 19.., at ..... M., in the office of the Corporation in .... (*County*), State of ....., for the purpose of considering the amendment of the Articles of Incorporation in the manner and form hereinabove set forth, and that* the Secretary of this Corporation is hereby directed to serve written notice upon each and every stockholder, stating the time, place, and purpose of said stockholders' meeting, and specifically stating that an amendment of the Articles of Incorporation in the manner and form aforesaid has been proposed, and to publish the said notice at least once a week in a newspaper published in the county where the principal business of this Corporation is located, for at least ..... days prior to the aforesaid meeting.

---

*The following clause may be used instead of the clause given above: "due notice of said meeting to be given by the Secretary of this Corporation as required by law."

RESOLUTION OF STOCKHOLDERS AMENDING ARTICLES OF INCORPORATION AND PROVIDING FOR PUBLICATION OF AMENDMENT, SETTING FORTH SUBSTANCE OF AMENDMENT

RESOLVED, That the Articles of Incorporation of the .... Corporation be so amended as to *(insert purpose of amendment here as, for example, to increase or diminish capital stock, increase or decrease the number of directors, change name or location, modify or enlarge business or purposes, or provide anything that might have been provided in the original articles)*, and

RESOLVED FURTHER, That the President and the Secretary file and record in the time, manner, and place required for filing and recording the original articles, duplicate copies of the aforesaid amendment, with a certificate affixed thereto, signed by the President and the Secretary and sealed with the corporate seal, setting forth the facts required by law, and that they do all other things and acts necessary fully to effect the amendment hereinabove set forth, and

RESOLVED FURTHER, That the Secretary of this Corporation is hereby authorized and directed to publish a notice of the aforesaid amendment for the period and in the manner provided by law.

RESOLUTION OF STOCKHOLDERS AUTHORIZING BOARD OF DIRECTORS TO APPLY FOR AMENDMENT TO CHARTER

WHEREAS, the Board of Directors has duly called a meeting of the stockholders upon .... days' written notice mailed to each stockholder, to consider the advisability of amending the charter of this Corporation, and

WHEREAS, the stockholders believe that it is to the best interests of the Corporation to amend the charter as hereinafter set forth, be it

RESOLVED, That the charter of the Corporation be amended so as to change Article ..... thereof to read as follows:

(Here insert new article.)

RESOLVED FURTHER, That the Board of Directors is hereby authorized, empowered, and directed to make proper application to the Secretary of State of the State of ...., for an amendment of the charter in the respects hereinabove mentioned, and to execute, present, and file the applications, petitions, and other documents required by the laws of the State of .... to effect the aforesaid amendment.

DIRECTORS' RESOLUTION RATIFYING ACTION OF STOCKHOLDERS IN AMENDING ARTICLES OF INCORPORATION

WHEREAS, at a special meeting of the stockholders of the . . . . Corporation, duly called and held in the City of . . . . State of . . . ., on . . . ., 19. ., at . . . . . M., at which meeting . . . . shares out of a total of . . . . . shares of the capital stock of the said Corporation issued and outstanding were represented in person or by proxy, the following resolution was adopted by votes representing . . . . .% of the said issued and outstanding stock. Be it

RESOLVED, That Article . . . . . of the Certificate of Incorporation of the . . . . Corporation is hereby amended to read as follows:

(Here insert new provision.)

RESOLVED FURTHER, That the President and Secretary of this Corporation are hereby authorized and directed to make, execute, and acknowledge a certificate under the corporate seal of this Corporation, embracing the foregoing resolution, and to cause such certificate to be filed, recorded, and published in the manner required by law, and

WHEREAS, the Board of Directors believes it to be to the best interests of this Corporation that the Articles of Incorporation be amended as recommended by the stockholders, be it

RESOLVED, That the resolution of the stockholders hereinabove set forth and said Articles of Incorporation so amended are hereby duly adopted, ratified, and confirmed.

RESOLUTION OF INCORPORATORS TO AMEND CERTIFICATE OF INCORPORATION BEFORE PAYMENT OF CAPITAL

WHEREAS, the original Certificate of Incorporation of this Company was filed in the office of the Secretary of State of the State of . . . ., on . . . ., 19. ., and

WHEREAS, a certified copy thereof was duly recorded in the office of the . . . . of the State of . . . ., in and for the County of . . . . on . . . ., 19. ., and

WHEREAS, no part of the capital of the Company has been paid, it is

RESOLVED, That the said Certificate of Incorporation be modified, changed, and altered so as to read as follows:

(Here insert complete certificate with new provisions.)

RESOLVED FURTHER, That the Chairman of this meeting is hereby authorized and directed to file with the Secretary of State an amended certificate duly signed and acknowledged by the incorporators named in the original Certificate of Incorporation, and to do all other things required by law to effect the aforesaid amendment of the Certificate of Incorporation.

DIRECTORS' RESOLUTION CALLING SPECIAL MEETING OF STOCKHOLDERS TO PASS UPON AMENDMENT OF CERTIFICATE OF INCORPORATION TO CHANGE CORPORATE NAME

RESOLVED, That, in the judgment of the Board of Directors of the .... Corporation, it is deemed advisable to amend the Certificate of Incorporation so as to change the name of the Corporation from ...., its present name, to ...., and that to that end Article ..... be changed to read as follows:

(Here insert new article.)

RESOLVED FURTHER, That a special meeting of the stockholders of this Corporation is hereby called, to be held at the principal office of the Corporation at .... (*Street*), ... (*City*), ... (*State*), on ...., 19.., at ..... M., to take action upon the said resolution, and that ..... days' written notice of the said meeting be given personally or by mail to the stockholders by the Secretary of the Corporation.

DIRECTORS' RESOLUTION TO INSTITUTE COURT PROCEEDINGS FOR CHANGE OF NAME

WHEREAS, in the judgment of this Board of Directors, it is to the best interests of this Corporation that its name be changed from ...., its present name, to ...., be it

RESOLVED, That the corporate name be accordingly changed to ...., and that the officers of this Corporation are hereby authorized and directed to take any and all legal steps necessary to institute and complete proceedings as provided by law to accomplish the aforesaid change, and to sign and execute all papers and documents relative and necessary thereto, and

RESOLVED FURTHER, That the President of the Corporation is hereby authorized and directed to employ ...., of .... (*Street*), ... (*City*), ... (*State*), as attorneys of the Corporation for that purpose, and to pay the necessary expenses thereof and disbursements therefor.

RESOLUTION OF STOCKHOLDERS CHANGING
NAME OF CORPORATION

WHEREAS, by Section ..... of the Act of Assembly incorporating this Company, approved ...., 19.., it is provided that "the stockholders of the Company, by and with the consent of the holders of not less than two thirds of the stock, are hereby authorized to change the name and title of the said Company," and

WHEREAS, it is now deemed expedient to change the name and title of the Company, be it

RESOLVED, That the name and title of this Company be changed from .... to ...., and that the officers of the Company are hereby empowered and directed to file in the office of the .... (*designate official and state*) the requisite certificate setting forth the change of name hereby authorized and effected.

DIRECTORS' RESOLUTION AMENDING ARTICLES OF
INCORPORATION TO CHANGE NAME, AND ADOPTING
SUPPLEMENTAL ARTICLES

RESOLVED, That the Articles of Incorporation of this Corporation, dated ...., 19.., and filed in the office of the Secretary of State of the State of ...., on ...., 19.., and in the office of the Clerk of .... on ...., 19.., be amended so as to change the name of the said Corporation from .... to ....; that supplemental Articles of Incorporation embodying the said amendment be hereby duly adopted; and that the President and the Secretary of the Corporation are hereby authorized and directed to file, as required by law, the said supplemental Articles of Incorporation and such other notices and documents as are required to effect the aforesaid change of name.

RESOLUTION OF STOCKHOLDERS AUTHORIZING
AMENDMENT OF CERTIFICATE OF INCORPORATION TO
CHANGE PRINCIPAL PLACE OF BUSINESS

RESOLVED, That the Certificate of Incorporation of the .... Corporation be amended to change the location of the principal place of business of the Corporation from .... (*Street*), in the County of ...., to .... (*Street*), in the County of ....., and that the President and the Secretary of the said Corporation are hereby authorized and directed to file all certificates, documents, and papers necessary and to do all the acts required by law to effect the aforesaid amendment.

DIRECTORS' RESOLUTION CHANGING PRINCIPAL PLACE OF BUSINESS ON WRITTEN CONSENT OF STOCKHOLDERS, AND PROVIDING FOR PUBLICATION OF NOTICE OF CHANGE

WHEREAS, the holders of more than two thirds (or such other proportion as may be required by statute) of the issued capital stock of this Corporation—to wit, the holders of . . . . . shares of the issued capital stock— have consented in writing and authorized and empowered the Board of Directors and officers of this Corporation to change the principal place of business from its present location at . . . . (*Street*), in the County of . . . . , State of . . . . , to . . . . (*Street*), in the County of . . . . , State of . . . . , which consent is now on file in the office of this Corporation, be it

RESOLVED, That the principal place of business of this Corporation is hereby changed from . . . . (*Street*), in the County of . . . . , State of . . . . , to . . . . (*Street*), in the County of . . . . , State of . . . . , and

RESOLVED FURTHER, That the Secretary of the Corporation is hereby authorized and directed to cause a notice of the aforesaid change to be published at least once a week for three successive weeks *(or such other time as is required by statute)* in the . . . . , a newspaper of general circulation, published in the County of . . . . , State of . . . . where the present principal place of business is located, and

RESOLVED FURTHER, That the Secretary of the Corporation is hereby authorized and directed to file in each office where the original Articles of Incorporation are, or where any copy thereof is required to be filed, a copy of this resolution, together with a copy of an affidavit showing the above publication, duly certified by the President and the Secretary of the Corporation under the corporate seal, and

RESOLVED FURTHER, That the officers of the Corporation are hereby authorized and directed to do any and all other acts necessary in their judgment and required by law to effect the change of the principal place of business of this Corporation.

DIRECTORS' RESOLUTION CHANGING LOCATION OF PRINCIPAL PLACE OF BUSINESS

RESOLVED, That, for the more convenient transaction of its business, the location of the principal office of this Corporation within the state is hereby changed from . . . . (*Street*), in the County of . . . . , to . . . . (*Street*), in the County of . . . . ; that the name of the agent therein and in charge thereof, upon whom process against this Corporation may be served, is . . . . ; and that the officers of the Corporation are hereby authorized and directed to file a copy of this resolution, signed by the

President and the Secretary of the Corporation, and sealed with the corporate seal, in the office of the Secretary of State (or of any other official designated by statute).

RESOLUTION OF STOCKHOLDERS AUTHORIZING CHANGE OF PRINCIPAL PLACE OF BUSINESS

RESOLVED, That the place where the principal business of the Corporation is to be transacted be changed from . . . . (*Street*), in the County of . . . ., to . . . . (*Street*), in the County of . . . ., and that the Chairman and the Secretary of this meeting and the directors of the Corporation are hereby authorized and directed to file the necessary certificate of change of corporate headquarters in the office of the Secretary of State, and to do all other acts necessary to effect the aforesaid change.

DIRECTORS' RESOLUTION CALLING MEETING OF STOCKHOLDERS TO AMEND CERTIFICATE OF INCORPORATION TO PERMIT BUSINESS TO BE DONE OUTSIDE THE UNITED STATES

RESOLVED, That it is advisable to amend the charter of the . . . . Corporation as follows:

To amend Article . . . . . of said charter so as to authorize the Corporation to conduct in any locality outside the United States of America, as well as in the localities now specified in said charter, the carrying on of the business of a telephone, telegraph, cable, and wireless company, and business incidental to such business, as set forth in Subdivision . . . . . and Subdivision . . . . . of said Article . . . . . of said charter, and accordingly to amend said Article so as to read as follows:

To carry on the business of a telephone, telegraph, cable, and wireless company in all localities within the United States of America and all other localities outside of the United States of America; to construct, maintain, and operate telegraph, telephone, and cable lines located or to be located in any and all of said localities; to purchase, acquire, lease, sell, and convey real property and easements, rights of way, or other interests, and to construct, maintain, and operate building and plants used for or incidental to such purposes, located or to be located in any and all of said localities. Nothing specified above shall be construed to limit the activities permitted by law to a corporation engaging in the telephone, telegraph, cable, and wireless business.

That a meeting of the stockholders of the Corporation to take action upon the amendment advised as aforesaid is hereby called to convene at the principal office of the Corporation at . . . . (*Street*), City of . . . ., State of . . . ., on . . . ., 19. ., at . . . . . M., and that notice of the said meeting be given as provided by the By-laws.

DIRECTORS' RESOLUTION AMENDING ARTICLES OF INCORPORATION TO CHANGE PURPOSES

RESOLVED, That Section ..... of the Articles of Incorporation be amended so as to extend the business of the Corporation, and to enlarge and change the objects for which it was formed to include the following:

(Here insert purposes in full.)

RESOLVED FURTHER, That a special meeting of the stockholders of the Corporation to take action upon the amendment aforesaid is hereby called, to be held at the principal office of the Corporation at .... (*Street*), on ...., 19.., at ..... M., and that the Secretary of the Corporation is hereby directed to serve the stockholders with notice of the said meeting in the manner provided by the By-laws.

DIRECTORS' RESOLUTION REQUESTING STOCKHOLDERS TO APPROVE AMENDMENT OF CHARTER CHANGING NUMBER AND MANNER OF ELECTING DIRECTORS

WHEREAS, Article ....., Section ...., of the Articles of Incorporation provide that the number of directors and, within certain limitations, the manner of electing directors, shall be as provided in the By-laws, and

WHEREAS, the By-laws presently provide in Article ...., Section ...., for a Board of 18 members, divided into three classes of 6 each, and

WHEREAS, it is deemed advisable to make the board of directors more immediately responsive of the stockholders' interests, be it

RESOLVED, That Article ...., Section ...., of the By-laws be amended to read as follows:

Section .... The Board of Directors of the Corporation shall be such number of Directors, within the minimum of 12 and maximum of 18 specified in the Articles of Incorporation, as shall be stated from time to time by resolution of the Board of Directors. In the event of any increase in the number of directors within such limits by such resolution, the vacancy or vacancies so resulting shall be filled by a vote of the Directors then in office. The Directors elected at each annual meeting of the stockholders, commencing with the meeting in 19.., shall be elected to hold office until the next annual meeting and until their successors are elected and qualified. Directors whose terms expire in 19.. and 19.. shall continue to hold office for the respective terms for which they were elected. After the election of directors at the annual meeting in 19.., the Directors shall no longer be divided into classes. Except as is otherwise provided for filling vacancies, all Directors shall be chosen by ballot by a plurality of the votes cast at such election.

RESOLVED FUTHER, That the officers are authorized and requested to call a meeting of the stockholders, to be held at the principal office of the Company, on ...., 19.., at ..... M., to take action upon the foregoing resolution.

RESOLUTION OF STOCKHOLDERS AUTHORIZING INCREASE IN NUMBER OF DIRECTORS AND FILING BY CLERK OF CERTIFICATE OF CHANGE

WHEREAS, it appears that the number of directors of this Corporation is inconvenient for the transaction of its business, be it

RESOLVED, That the number of directors of . . . Corporation is hereby increased from 5 to 12, and

RESOLVED FURTHER, That the clerk of said Corporation is hereby authorized and directed to file the required certificate of such change in the number of directors with the Secretary of State of the State of ....

RESOLUTION OF STOCKHOLDERS TO AMEND CERTIFICATE OF INCORPORATION TO INCREASE OR DECREASE NUMBER OF DIRECTORS

RESOLVED, That the Certificate of Incorporation of the .... Corporation be amended so as to change the number of directors from ..... to .....; and that the President (or the Secretary) of the Corporation is hereby authorized to file with the Secretary of State (or with other officials designated by statute) an affidavit of change in the number of directors.

RESOLUTION OF STOCKHOLDERS EXTENDING TERM OF INCORPORATION AND AUTHORIZING OFFICERS TO FILE NECESSARY PAPERS

WHEREAS, this Corporation was incorporated on ...., 19.., and

WHEREAS, the term of incorporation, according to its Articles of Incorporation, will expire on ...., 19.., be it

RESOLVED, That the corporate existence of this Corporation be extended for a period of twenty (20) years from and after the date of the expiration of its corporate life, and

RESOLVED FURTHER, That the President and the Secretary are hereby authorized and directed to certify this resolution under the corporate seal of the Corporation, to send such certificate to the Secretary of State of the State of ...., to file duplicate certificates under the seal of the Corporation in the office of the Recorder of Deeds of the County of ...., State of

........., and to do all acts and things necessary and proper to carry into effect the foregoing resolution.

DIRECTORS' RESOLUTION TO SUBMIT TO STOCKHOLDERS PROPOSITION EXTENDING TERM OF CORPORATE EXISTENCE, AND TO OBTAIN STOCKHOLDERS' WRITTEN ASSENT TO EXTENSION

RESOLVED, That it is deemed to be in the best interests of this Corporation to extend the term of its existence for a period of ..... years from ...., 19.., the date of its expiration, and that the proposition so extending the term of the corporate existence be submitted to the stockholders for their written assent.

FURTHER RESOLVED, That, upon obtaining the written assent of stockholders representing two thirds of the capital stock of this Corporation, the President and the Secretary and the Directors of this Corporation are hereby authorized and directed to do all acts necessary and proper to carry out the foregoing resolution.

RESOLUTION OF STOCKHOLDERS AMENDING CERTIFICATE OF INCORPORATION TO EXTEND CORPORATE EXISTENCE

RESOLVED, as deemed and declared advisable by the Board of Directors of The .... Company, a corporation of the State of ...., at its meeting duly convened and held on ...., 19.., that the corporate existence of the Company be extended for a period of ..... years from ...., 19.., to ...., 19.., and to that end that Article ..... of the Certificate of Incorporation of the Company be amended so as to read as follows:

"*Fifth.* The period at which the Company shall commence is ...., 19.., and the period at which it shall terminate is ...., 19.."

RESOLUTION OF STOCKHOLDERS TO AMEND CERTIFICATE OF INCORPORATION TO PROVIDE FOR WITHHOLDING FROM STOCKHOLDERS OF THEIR PREEMPTIVE RIGHT

RESOLVED, That the Certificate of Incorporation of the .... Corporation be amended by adding the following article:

No holder of any of the shares of the capital stock of the Corporation shall be entitled as of right to purchase or to subscribe for any unissued stock of any class, or any additional shares of any class, to be issued by reason of any increase of the authorized capital stock of the Corporation of any class, or bonds, certificates of indebtedness, debentures, or other securities convertible into stock of the Corporation or carrying any right to purchase stock of any class, but any such unissued stock, or such additional authorized issue of any stock, or of other securities convertible into stock or carrying any right to purchase stock, may be issued and disposed of, pursuant to resolutions of the Board of Directors, to such persons, firms, corporations, or associations and upon such terms as may be deemed advisable by the Board of Directors in the exercise of its discretion.

RESOLVED FURTHER, That the officers of this Corporation are hereby authorized, empowered, and directed to do all acts necessary and proper to carry out the foregoing resolution.

DIRECTORS' RESOLUTION CALLING SPECIAL MEETING OF STOCKHOLDERS TO TAKE ACTION ON AMENDMENT OF CERTIFICATE OF INCORPORATION TO INCREASE CAPITAL STOCK

RESOLVED, That, in the judgment of the Board of Directors of .... Corporation, it is deemed advisable to amend the Certificate of Incorporation so as to increase the capital stock of said Corporation, and for that purpose to change Article ..... thereof to read as follows:

ARTICLE ..... The total amount of capital stock of this Corporation is eight thousand (8,000) shares, divided into three thousand (3,000) shares of 7 Percent Cumulative Preferred Stock of the par value of one hundred ($100) Dollars a share (total par value three hundred thousand ($300,000) Dollars), and five thousand (5,000) shares of common stock without par value.

RESOLVED FURTHER, That a special meeting of the stockholders of this Corporation is hereby called, to be held at .... *(Street),* .... *(City),* .... *(State),* on ...., 19.., at .....M., to take action upon said resolution, and that the Secretary is hereby instructed to notify said stockholders accordingly as required by law.

DIRECTORS' RESOLUTION RECOMMENDING CHANGE IN PAR VALUE OF STOCK AND INCREASE IN AUTHORIZED CAPITAL STOCK, ADDITIONAL SHARES TO BE USED FOR ACQUISITION OF PROPERTY

RESOLVED, That, in the judgment of this Board of Directors, it is advisable that the par value of the present authorized common stock of this Company be changed from ..... ($.....) Dollars per share to ..... ($.....) Dollars per share, the number of shares into which the same is divided being changed from ..... (.....) shares to ..... (.....) shares, two and one-half shares to be issued for each share of common stock now outstanding, and

RESOLVED FURTHER, That, in the judgment of this Board, it is advisable that the authorized capital stock of this Company be increased by ..... ($.....) Dollars, such increase to consist of ..... (.....) shares of common stock of the par value of ..... ($.....) Dollars each, so that the total amount of authorized capital stock of the Company will be . . . . . ($. . . . .) Dollars, divided into . . . . . (. . . . .) shares, of which . . . . . (. . . . .) shares of the par value of . . . . . ($. . . . .) Dollars each are preferred stock, and . . . . . (. . . . .) shares of the par value of . . . . . ($. . . . .) Dollars each are common stock; that said additional common shares shall be issued by the Board from time to time for the acquisition of properties for the development and expansion of the Company's business; and that when such shares are so issued, no shareholders shall have subscription rights, and

RESOLVED FURTHER, That, in the judgment of this Board, it is advisable, provided that the necessary consent of the stockholders to the change of the par value of the common stock and to the increase in the amount of authorized capital as aforesaid be obtained, that the Certificate of Incorporation be further amended so as to provide that, upon the dissolution of the Company and the distribution of its net assets, the holders of the preferred stock shall be paid in full the par value of the shares held by them, plus any accumulated dividends unpaid thereon, before any amount shall be distributed among the holders of the common shares, and after such payment to the holders of the preferred shares, the remaining net assets, if any, shall be distributed among the holders of the common stock, and

RESOLVED FURTHER, That, in the judgment of this Board, it is advisable to the ends aforesaid that the first paragraph of Article . . . . . of the Certificate of Incorporation of this Company be amended so that said paragraph as amended shall read as follows:

(Here insert new capital stock clause in full.)

RESOLVED FURTHER, That the aforesaid changes and amendments be submitted to the annual meeting of the stockholders of this Company to be held on . . . ., 19. ., at the principal office of the Company, ... (*Street*), ... (*City*), ... (*State*), at . . . . . M., and that the Secretary be instructed to give notice of such meeting to all stockholders in the manner provided in the By-laws, and

RESOLVED FURTHER, That the Secretary be instructed to cause to be made, at least . . . . . (. . . . .) days before such meeting, a full, true, and complete list in alphabetical order of all the stockholders entitled to vote at said meeting, such list to be kept at the principal office of the Company, and to be open to the examination of any stockholder at said office at all times during the usual hours of business.

RESOLUTION OF STOCKHOLDERS AUTHORIZING AMENDMENT OR ARTICLES OF INCORPORATION TO INCREASE CAPITAL STOCK, AND DIRECTING OFFICERS TO FILE PAPERS

RESOLVED, That the authorized preferred capital stock of this Corporation be increased from the present amount, namely . . . . . ($. . . . .) Dollars, consisting of . . . . . (. . . . .) shares of the par value of . . . . . ($. . . . .)

Dollars each, to . . . . . ($ . . . . .) Dollars, consisting of . . . . . (. . . . .) shares of the par value of . . . . . ($ . . . . .) Dollars each.

RESOLVED FURTHER, That Articles . . . . . and . . . . . of the Certificate of Incorporation of this Corporation be amended to read as follows:

(Here insert new articles, showing total capital stock and division into shares.)

RESOLVED FURTHER, That the President and the Secretary of this Corporation are hereby authorized and directed to make, sign, verify, and acknowledge the certificates of proceedings required by statute, and to cause one of such certificates to be filed in the office of the Secretary of State, and a duplicate original thereof in the office of the Clerk of the County of . . . ., and to do all acts and things that may be necessary or proper to carry into effect the foregoing resolution in compliance with the laws of the State of . . . .

DIRECTORS' RESOLUTION AMENDING ARTICLES OF INCORPORATION ON WRITTEN CONSENT OF STOCKHOLDERS TO INCREASE THE CAPITAL STOCK BY INCREASING THE NUMBER OF NO PAR SHARES, AND FIXING PRICE AT WHICH INCREASED STOCK SHALL BE OFFERED FOR SALE

WHEREAS, the holders of all the issued capital stock of this Corporation have duly consented in writing, and have authorized and empowered this Board of Directors and the officers of this Corporation to increase the capital stock from . . . . . (. . . . .) shares to . . . . . (. . . . .) shares, which consent is now on file in the minute book of this Corporation, be it

RESOLVED, That the Articles of Incorporation be amended so as to change the amount of the capital stock from . . . . . (. . . . .) shares to . . . . . (. . . . .) shares, and that Article . . . . . of the Articles of Incorporation of this Corporation be amended to read as follows:

ARTICLE . . . . . The capital stock of this Corporation shall consist of . . . . . (. . . . .) shares of no par value stock, which stock may be issued by the Corporation from time to time for such consideration in labor, services, money, or property as may be fixed by the Board of Directors. The Corporation will begin to carry on business upon a capital of . . . . . ($ . . . . .) Dollars.

RESOLVED FURTHER, That the officers of this Corporation are hereby authorized, empowered, and directed to take all proper and necessary steps for the consummation of the said amendment to the Articles of Incorporation, and

RESOLVED FURTHER, That, upon said amendment becoming effective, the said . . . . . (. . . . .) shares of increased capital stock shall be offered for sale to the present stockholders at not less than . . . . . ($ . . . . .) Dollars per share net to the Corporation, in proportion to their present holdings; and that the officers of the corporation are hereby authorized to effect such sale.

RESOLUTION OF STOCKHOLDERS AUTHORIZING DIRECTORS TO APPLY FOR AN AMENDMENT OF THE CHARTER TO INCREASE CAPITAL STOCK

RESOLVED, That the Board of Directors of this Corporation be hereby authorized, empowered, and directed to apply to the State of . . . . ., under the general laws of the land, for an amendment to the charter of this Corporation, for the purpose of investing the said Corporation with power to increase its capital stock from . . . . . ($. . . . .) Dollars to . . . . . ($. . . . .) Dollars, and to do all other and further acts necessary to effect the aforesaid increase of the capital stock of this Corporation.

RESOLUTION OF STOCKHOLDERS INCREASING CAPITAL STOCK BY TRANSFER FROM SURPLUS TO CAPITAL ACCOUNT

RESOLVED, That the capital stock of this Corporation be increased from . . . . . ($. . . . .) Dollars to . . . . . ($. . . . .) Dollars, to be divided into . . . . . (. . . . .) shares of the par value of . . . . . ($. . . . .) Dollars each, and that such increase be paid up by transferring . . . . . ($. . . . .) Dollars from the Surplus account of said Corporation to the Capital account of said Corporation, and

RESOLVED FURTHER, That said increased stock be distributed and taken by the present stockholders in proportion to their present holdings, and

RESOLVED FURTHER, That the directors and officers of this Corporation are hereby authorized, empowered, and directed to do all things and acts necessary and proper to effect the aforesaid increase of the capital stock of the corporation in the manner herein above provided.

RESOLUTION OF STOCKHOLDERS SPLITTING COMMON STOCK AND CREATING A NEW CLASS OF PREFERRED

RESOLVED, That the capital stock of this Corporation be increased and changed and converted from 1,915,000 shares, consisting of 515,000 shares of $7 cumulative Preferred Stock, 300,000 shares of $6 cumulative Preferred Stock, and 1,100,000 shares of Common Stock, all without nominal or par value, to 3,515,000 shares, consisting of 515,000 shares of $7 cumulative Preferred Stock, 300,000 cumulative shares of $6 Preferred Stock, 500,000 shares of $5 cumulative Preferred stock, and 2,200,000 shares of Common Stock, all without nominal or par value, and that there be issued two (2) shares of said Common Stock without nominal or par value in exchange and conversion for each of the shares of Common Stock of this Corporation now issued and outstanding.

The designations, rights, privileges, limitations, preferences, voting powers, prohibitions, restrictions, or qualifications of the voting and other rights and powers, and the terms as to redemption of the shares of said $5 cumulative Preferred Stock, are as follows:

(1) The shares of $5 cumulative Preferred Stock shall be entitled, equally with cumulative shares of $7 Preferred Stock and with the shares of $6 cumulative Preferred Stock, in preference to the shares of Common Stock, to cumulative dividends at the rate of $5 per share per annum, payable as the Board of Directors may determine. The shares of $5 cumulative Preferred Stock, equally with shares of $7 cumulative Preferred Stock and with the shares of $6 cumulative Preferred Stock, shall also have a preference over the shares of Common Stock, in any distribution of assets other than profits, until the amount of $100 on each share and the further amount of $5 per share per annum from the date of issue thereof shall have been paid by dividends or distributions. The shares of $5 cumulative Preferred Stock shall not receive any dividends from profits in excess of $5 a share per annum, nor any share in the distribution of assets in excess of $100 a share and the amount of such accrued and unpaid dividends.

(2) The Corporation, by vote of the holders of a majority in number of all its outstanding shares of capital stock entitled to vote, may, at any general or special meeting, redeem all, but not less than all, of the shares of $5 cumulative Preferred Stock then outstanding, for $110 a share, plus accrued and unpaid dividends, after such notice to the holders of shares of the $5 cumulative Preferred Stock as is now provided in the By-laws with respect to the redemption of $7 Preferred Stock.

(3) Dividends may be paid on the Common Stock only when dividends have been paid or funds have been set apart for the payment of dividends on shares of $7 cumulative Preferred Stock, on the shares of $6 cumulative Preferred Stock, and on the shares of $5 cumulative Preferred Stock, from the date after which dividends thereon became cumulative to the beginning of the period then current with respect to which such dividends are usually declared, but whenever there shall have been paid, or whenever funds shall have been set apart for the payment of all such dividends upon shares of $7 cumulative Preferred Stock, upon the shares of $6 cumulative preferred Stock, and upon the shares of $5 cumulative Preferred Stock as aforesaid, then dividends upon the Common Stock may be declared payable then or thereafter out of any surplus or net profits then remaining.

Subject to the rights of the holders of shares of $7 cumulative Preferred Stock, the shares of $6 cumulative Preferred Stock, and the shares of $5 cumulative Preferred Stock, and in subordination thereto, and subject to the rights of any class of stock hereafter authorized, the Common Stock alone shall receive all further dividends and shares in distribution.

(4) Each of said shares of $5 cumulative Preferred Stock, shares of $6 cumulative Preferred Stock, shares of $7 cumulative Preferred Stock, and

shares of Common Stock shall be equal one to the other in voting power and shall entitle the holder thereof to one vote upon any question presented to any stockholders' meeting.

RESOLUTION OF STOCKHOLDERS AUTHORIZING ISSUANCE OF NEW CLASS OF PRIOR PREFERRED STOCK WITH PROVISION FOR PRIOR OFFER FOR VOLUNTARY EXCHANGE OF OLD CLASS OF PREFERRED CUMULATIVE STOCK UPON WAIVER OF ACCRUED DIVIDENDS

WHEREAS, the total number of shares which the Corporation is authorized to issue is 15,000 shares, classified as follows:

10,000 shares of common stock without par value, and

5,000 shares of cumulative preferred stock of the par value of $100.00 each, and

WHEREAS, it is deemed desirable and for the best interest of the Corporation that the authorized capital stock of the Corporation be increased by the issuance of a new class of preferred stock hereinafter called Class A preferred and it is deemed desirable and for the best interest of the corporation and all its stockholders to first offer the Class A preferred to owners of cumulative preferred stock by voluntary exchange of one share of cumulative preferred for one share of Class A preferred provided that each exchange shall constitute a waiver of any claim to accumulated dividends associated with the cumulative stock which is exchanged, and further provided that an owner of preferred cumulative stock may retain his stock and any claim to cumulative dividends rather than participate in the voluntary exchange, be it

RESOLVED, That the Articles of Incorporation are hereby amended so that Article . . . . . which now reads as follows:

(Here insert old provision as to authorized capital stock.)

is amended to read as follows:

Article . . . . . The total number of shares that may be issued by the Corporation shall be 20,000 shares, classified as follows:

10,000 shares of common stock without par value,
5,000 shares of cumulative preferred stock of the par value of $100.00 each, and
5,000 shares of Class A preferred stock of the par value of $100.00 each

RESOLVED FURTHER, That the officers of this Corporation are hereby authorized and directed to execute and file all documents and to do all things necessary to effect the foregoing amendment.

RESOLVED FURTHER, That the designations, rights, privileges, limitations, preferences, voting powers, prohibitions, restrictions, or qualifications of the voting and other rights and powers and terms as to redemption of the Class A preferred are as follows:

(Here insert capital stock clauses.)*

RESOLVED FURTHER, That the officers are hereby authorized, empowered, and directed to issue Class A preferred by voluntary exchange of one (1) share of Class A preferred for each share of cumulative preferred, provided that each exchange shall constitute a waiver of any claim to accrued cumulative dividends associated with the cumulative preferred stock so exchanged, and provided further that the Class A preferred stock certificate shall contain a clause in bold face type on its face that expresses this waiver. Any owner of cumulative preferred stock may refuse to participate in the exchange and retain his cumulative preferred stock and any claim to accrued cumulative dividends. All cumulative preferred stock acquired by the Corporation shall be retired.

RESOLVED FURTHER, That the right of cumulative preferred stockholders to participate in the exchange of cumulative preferred for Class A preferred shall expire at . . . . .M., on . . . ., 19. ., and that after that date, the directors and officers of the Corporation are hereby authorized to sell and dispose of said stock as they see fit, and that failure of stockholders to subscribe within the time set herein shall be deemed a waiver by said stockholders of any right they may have in the new issued.

RESOLUTION OF STOCKHOLDERS INCREASING CAPITAL STOCK, CONVERTING SHARES, DIVIDING STOCK INTO NEW CLASSES, AND PROVIDING FOR REDEMPTION AND PRIVILEGES OF PREFERRED STOCK

RESOLVED, That the capital stock of this Corporation be increased and changed and converted from 1,915,000 shares, consisting of 515,000 cumulative shares of $7 Preferred Stock, 300,000 cumulative shares of $6 Preferred Stock, and 1,100,000 shares of Common Stock, all without nominal or par value, to 3,515,000 shares, consisting of 515,000 cumulative shares of $7 Preferred Stock, 300,000 cumulative shares of $6 Preferred Stock, 500,000 cumulative shares of $5 Preferred Stock, and 2,200,000 shares of Common Stock, all without nominal or par value, and that there be issued 2 shares of said Common Stock without nominal or par value in exchange and conversion of each of the shares of Common Stock of this Corporation now issued and outstanding.

---

*The new stock is usually given priority as to dividends and priority as to dissolution rights, and other priorities in order to induce cumulative preferred stockholders to voluntarily exchange their stock and waive accrued dividend claims.

The designations, rights, privileges, limitations, preferences, voting powers, prohibitions, restrictions, or qualifications of the voting and other rights and powers and the terms as to redemption of the cumulative shares of said $5 Preferred Stock are as follows:

(Here insert capital stock clauses.)

RESOLUTION OF STOCKHOLDERS INCREASING CAPITAL STOCK, WHICH CONSISTS OF PREFERRED STOCK WITH PAR VALUE AND COMMON STOCK WITHOUT PAR VALUE, AND FIXING CONSIDERATION FOR STOCK WITHOUT PAR VALUE

RESOLVED, That the capital stock of this Corporation be increased from the present authorized amount—namely, 100,000 shares of preferred stock having a par value of $100 each, amounting in the aggregate to $10,000,000, and 100,000 shares of common stock without par value—to 200,000 shares of preferred stock having a par value of $100 each, amounting in the aggregate to $20,000,000, and 200,000 shares of common stock without par value, and that Article . . . . . of the Certificate of Incorporation, relating to capital stock be amended to read as follows:

(Here insert new article.)

RESOLVED FURTHER, That the price at which such increase of common stock without par value shall be subscribed and paid for by the stockholders be fixed at . . . . . ($. . . . .) Dollars, and that the time and manner of subscription and payment for such increased preferred stock and common stock shall be as follows:

(Here insert time and manner of payment for stock.)

RESOLVED FURTHER, That the directors of this Corporation are hereby authorized to sell, at not less than the price so fixed, any part of such increase not subscribed for by the stockholders, after they have had a reasonable opportunity to make subscription for their proportionate shares thereof.

RESOLVED FURTHER, That the President and the Secretary are hereby authorized and directed to do any and all things necessary or proper to cause said amendment of the Certificate of Incorporation to take effect.

DIRECTORS' RESOLUTION INCREASING CAPITAL STOCK AND AUTHORIZING ISSUANCE OF STOCK FOR CASH OR IN EXCHANGE FOR ALL OR MAJORITY CONTROL OF STOCK OF ANOTHER COMPANY

RESOLVED, that it is advisable that the capital stock of this Company be increased from one million ($1,000,000) Dollars, divided into fifty thousand (50,000) shares of the par value of twenty ($20) Dollars each, to two million

($2,000,000) Dollars, divided into four hundred thousand (400,000) shares of the par value of five ($5) Dollars each, and that the Charter or Certificate of Incorporation of this Company be amended so that Paragraph Fifth shall read as follows:

> Fifth. The amount of capital stock of said Company is two million ($2,000,000) Dollars, divided into four hundred thousand (400,000) shares of the par value of five ($5) Dollars each.

RESOLVED FURTHER, That the Board of Directors of this Company shall have the authority to issue the capital stock of this Company, as increased by the amendment of its charter, in such amounts, at such times, and for such prices as shall seem proper to the Board, and that said stock may be issued by the said Board of Directors either for cash or in exchange for all or a majority in control of the stock of any company or companies that the Board of Directors shall deem for the best interests of the Company to purchase or acquire, provided said stock shall not be issued for less than its par value.

RESOLVED FURTHER, That a meeting of the stockholders shall be called to be held at the Company's office, in the City of . . . . , on . . . ., 19. ., at . . . . . .M., to take action on the above resolutions.

DIRECTORS' RESOLUTION RECOMMENDING AMENDMENT OF ARTICLES OF INCORPORATION TO INCREASE NUMBER OF SHARES OF STOCK WITH PAR VALUE, AND CALLING STOCKHOLDERS' MEETING TO ACT THEREON

RESOLVED, That the Board of Directors of . . . . Corporation desires to amend, and recommends to the stockholders that they do amend, the Articles of Incorporation in the following manner:

That the capital stock of . . . . Corporation be increased from $15,000,000, consisting of 1,500,000 shares of common stock of a par value of $10 each, to $30,500,000, consisting of 2,000,000 shares of common stock of a par value of $10 each, and 350,000 shares of convertible preferred stock of a par value of $30 each.

That all of the designations, and the powers, preferences, and rights, and the qualifications, limitations, or restrictions thereof with respect to the common stock and preferred stock be as follows:

(Here follow designations in full.)

RESOLVED FURTHER, That a special meeting of the stockholders be held at the principal office of the Corporation, ... Street, City of . . . . , State of . . . . . , on . . . ., 19. ., at . . . . . .M., Eastern Standard Time, for the purpose of considering the question of adopting said recommendation, and that the proposed amendment to the Articles of Incorporation be submitted to a vote at said meeting, and

RESOLVED FURTHER, That notice of said meeting be given to each stockholder of record entitled to vote at said meeting in accordance with the By-laws of this corporation and the laws of the State of . . . . ., and

RESOLVED FURTHER, That the Board of Directors does hereby fix . . . ., 19.., as the record date for the determination of stockholders entitled to notice of or to vote at said special meeting of stockholders.

RESOLUTION OF BOARD OF DIRECTORS TO INCREASE NUMBER OF SHARES OF COMMON STOCK WITHOUT PAR VALUE TO MEET CONVERSION OF BONDS

WHEREAS, the . . . . Corporation, pursuant to authority of its Board of Directors, and with the consent of its stockholders, has issued . . . . (*insert description of bonds*) bonds of the Corporation in the aggregate amount of . . . . . ($. . . . .) Dollars, all of which are now outstanding and convertible at the option of the holders into common shares without par value of the Corporation, provided that the holders of such bonds shall have given due notice to the Corporation of their election to convert the said bonds on or before . . . ., 19.., and

WHEREAS, the holders of such bonds in the total amount of . . . . . ($. . . . .) Dollars have duly served such notice of their election so to convert the bonds held by them, and

WHEREAS, the Corporation has no common shares without par value available to carry into effect the aforesaid conversion, be it

RESOLVED, That the number of shares of the common stock of the Corporation is hereby increased from . . . . . (. . . . .) shares without par value to . . . . . (. . . . .) shares without par value, and

RESOLVED FURTHER, That the additional . . . . . (. . . . .) shares of common stock without par value hereby authorized shall be issued to the aforesaid bondholders who have given notice of their election to convert, in exchange for . . . . . ($. . . . .) Dollars per value of the outstanding bonds of said Corporation, and that the officers of the Corporation are hereby authorized, empowered, and directed to do all the acts necessary and proper to carry this resolution into effect.

RESOLUTION OF STOCKHOLDERS INCREASING NUMBER OF SHARES, FIXING SUBSCRIPTION PRICE OF ADDITIONAL SHARES, AND LIMITING SUBSCRIPTION RIGHTS

RESOLVED, That the capital of . . . . Company be increased from the present amount of $. . . . . to $. . . . ., and that the number of shares of stock be increased from . . . . . to . . . . ., and

RESOLVED FURTHER, That newly authorized additional . . . . . shares of stock be sold and offered for subscription to stockholders at the rate of $ . . . . . per share, each stockholder of record on . . . ., 19. ., to have the right to subscribe to one share of newly authorized stock for every two shares of stock held as of that date, and

RESOLVED FURTHER, That the right of stockholders to subscribe for such newly authorized stock of . . . . Company shall expire at . . P.M., on . . . ., 19. ., and that after that date, the directors and officers of said Company are hereby authorized to sell and dispose of said stock as they see fit, and that failure of stockholders to subscribe within the time set herein shall be deemed a waiver by said stockholders of said right to subscribe.

RESOLUTION OF STOCKHOLDERS AMENDING CERTIFICATE OF INCORPORATION TO INCREASE NUMBER OF SHARES AND REDUCE PAR VALUE, WITHOUT CHANGING AUTHORIZED CAPITAL STOCK

RESOLVED, That the capital stock of this Corporation be changed from 1,000 shares of common stock of the par value of $100 each to 2,000 shares of common stock of the par value of $50 each, the authorized capital stock of the Corporation remaining at $100,000 as heretofore, and that the Certificate of Incorporation be amended and altered accordingly so that Article . . . . . thereof shall read as follows:

Article . . . . . The amount of the total authorized capital stock of this Corporation is one hundred thousand ($100,000) Dollars, divided into two thousand (2,000) shares of fifty ($50) Dollars each.

RESOLVED FURTHER, That the officers of this Corporation are hereby authorized and directed to execute and file all documents and to do all things necessary to effect the foregoing amendment.

RESOLVED FURTHER, That, within . . . . . months after the date of this meeting, every stockholder of this Corporation shall surrender the shares of stock owned and held by him, and that the officers of this Corporation are hereby authorized and directed to issue to the said stockholder two shares of stock of the par value of $50 each for every share of common stock of $100 surrendered by him.

RESOLUTION OF STOCKHOLDERS INCREASING NUMBER OF SHARES WITHOUT PAR VALUE, AND AMENDING CERTIFICATE OF ORGANIZATION ACCORDINGLY

RESOLVED, That the authorized number of shares of this Corporation without a par or face value be increased from 3,600,000 shares without a par or face value to 4,850,000 shares without a par or face value, and that the Certificate of Organization of this Corporation be amended to state, in lieu of the statements now in the Certificate as to the amount of the Corporation's capital stock and the number and par value of the shares into which the same is to be divided, that the number of shares with a par or face value that may be issued by the Corporation is none, and that the number of shares without a par or face value that may be issued by the Corporation is 4,850,000, and that the classes into which said shares are divided are 100,000 shares of $7 preferred stock, 100,000 shares of $6 preferred stock, 650,000 shares of participating preferred stock, and 4,000,000 shares of common stock, the designations, preferences, voting powers, restrictions, and qualifications thereof being and to be as fixed and determined in the By-laws, and

RESOLVED FURTHER, That the clerk of this Corporation is hereby authorized and directed forthwith to file with the Secretary of State of the State of .... a certificate of the action taken by the adoption of the foregoing resolution, and to pay the necessary fees required to be paid in connection with the filing of such certificate.

DIRECTORS' RESOLUTION TO AMEND CHARTER OF CORPORATION TO REDUCE AMOUNT OF CAPITAL STOCK BY PURCHASING, CALLING IN, AND CANCELLING PREFERRED AND COMMON STOCK

RESOLVED, That it is advisable to amend the charter of the Corporation so as to reduce the amount of capital stock now issued and outstanding by purchasing, calling in, and cancelling all the preferred stock of said Corporation now outstanding, and nine hundred and fifty (950) shares of the common stock with a par value of one hundred ($100) Dollars per share, having an aggregate par value of ninety-five thousand ($95,000) Dollars, to the end that the entire authorized and outstanding capital stock of said Corporation shall hereafter consist of fifty (50) shares of common stock with a par value of one hundred ($100) Dollars per share, having an aggregate par value of five thousand ($5,000) Dollars, and

RESOLVED FURTHER, That a meeting of the stockholders of the Corporation to take action upon the purchase of stock and upon the amendment advised as aforesaid is hereby called to convene at the principal office of the Corporation in the City of ...., on ...., 19.., at .. ...M.

RESOLUTION OF STOCKHOLDERS AUTHORIZING AMENDMENT OF CERTIFICATE OF INCORPORATION TO REDUCE CAPITAL STOCK BY RETIREMENT AND CANCELLATION OF PREFERRED STOCK PREVIOUSLY PURCHASED

RESOLVED, That the Certificate of Incorporation of this Corporation be amended and altered so that Articles Third and Fourth thereof will read as follows:

Third. The number of shares of capital stock that may be issued by said Corporation is five hundred thousand (500,000) shares, which shall have no nominal or par value.

Fourth. The right is hereby reserved to create new or additional stock, either preferred or common, at any time, upon proper authorization by the stockholders of the Corporation, pursuant to the provisions of law applicable thereto.

Any new or additional stock, preferred or common, may be issued and sold in such amounts and proportions as shall be determined by the Board of Directors; provided, however, that ownership of preferred stock shall not entitle the holder thereof to subscribe for a pro rata share or any portion of any such new or additional issue of stock, preferred or common, or of any issue of bonds convertible into stock.

RESOLVED FURTHER, That the number of shares which said Corporation may issue be reduced from eight hundred thousand (800,000) shares to five hundred thousand (500,000) shares, all of which shall be shares without any nominal or par value, by the retirement and cancellation of three hundred thousand (300,000) shares of preferred stock of the par value of one hundred ($100) Dollars each, all of which preferred stock has been purchased by the Corporation in the exercise of the right reserved in its Certificate of Incorporation.

RESOLVED FURTHER, That the President and the Secretary of this Corporation are hereby authorized and directed to make, sign, verify, and acknowledge the certificates of proceedings required by statute, to cause one of such certificates to be filed in the office of the Secretary of State, and a duplicate original thereof in the office of the Clerk of the County of ...., and to do all acts and things that may be necessary or proper to carry into effect the foregoing resolution in compliance with the laws of the State of ....

RESOLUTION OF STOCKHOLDERS DECREASING
CAPITAL STOCK BY CANCELLING
UNISSUED CAPITAL STOCK

RESOLVED, That the capital stock authorized to be issued by the .... Corporation be reduced from $100,000 to $75,000, and that the officers of this Corporation are hereby authorized and directed to give notice to the Secretary of State of the action of this meeting, and

RESOLVED FURTHER, That the aforesaid decrease be effected by cancelling the unissued capital stock of this corporation to the extent of $25,000.

RESOLUTION OF STOCKHOLDERS AUTHORIZING REDUCTION OF CAPITAL STOCK BY RETIREMENT AND CANCELLATION OF TREASURY STOCK

RESOLVED, That the Agreement of Association and Articles of Organization of The . . . . Company, as previously amended, are hereby further amended by reducing the authorized capital stock of the Company, now consisting of 221,943 shares without par value, divided into 21,943 shares of preferred stock and 200,000 shares of common stock all without par value, to 221,271 shares without par value, divided into 21,271 shares of preferred stock and 200,000 shares of common stock, all without par value, such reduction to consist of 672 shares of preferred stock without par value, and to be accomplished by the retirement and cancellation of 672 shares of the preferred stock of the Company now held in its treasury.

RESOLVED FURTHER, That the President or Vice president and the Treasurer or an Assistant Treasurer and a majority of the directors of The . . . . Company are hereby authorized and directed to file with the proper authorities for the State of . . . . such amendment to the Agreement of Association and Articles of Organization, as amended, of The . . . . Company as will carry out and effectuate the amendment authorized by the stockholders this day, reducing the authorized capital stock of the Company by the retirement and cancellation of 672 shares of the preferred stock, without par value, of the Company now held in its treasury.

RESOLUTION OF STOCKHOLDERS AMENDING ARTICLES OF INCORPORATION TO DECREASE CAPITAL STOCK BY REDUCING THE NUMBER AND PAR VALUE OF OUTSTANDING SHARES

RESOLVED, That the capital stock of the . . . . Corporation be decreased by reducing the par value of the shares of the capital stock of the said Corporation from $100 to $50, and reducing the number of shares of the capital stock of the said Corporation from 10,000 to 5,000 shares, and

RESOLVED FURTHER, That the Articles of Incorporation be amended to read as follows:

(Here insert new article as to amount of capital stock and classification.)

RESOLVED FURTHER, That the directors and officers of the Corporation are hereby authorized and directed to execute all the affidavits, statements, certificates, and other documents necessary to effectuate the said reduction, and to file them as required.

RESOLUTION OF STOCKHOLDERS DECREASING CAPITAL STOCK BY REDUCING THE NUMBER AND PAR VALUE OF SHARES, AND DIRECTING SURRENDER OF SHARES AND ISSUANCE OF PROPORTIONATELY DECREASED NUMBER

RESOLVED, That the capital stock of the .... Corporation, consisting of 1,000 shares of the par value of $100 each, be reduced from $100,000 to $25,000, to consist of 500 shares of the par value of $50 each; and that the officers of this Corporation execute and file all documents and do all things necessary and proper to carry out the said reduction of capital stock, and

RESOLVED FURTHER, That, within three months after the date of this meeting, every stockholder of this Corporation shall surrender the shares of stock owned and held by him, and that the officers of the Corporation are hereby authorized and directed to issue to the said stockholders, in lieu thereof, a proportionately decreased number of shares, so that thereafter each stockholder shall have the same proportion of the whole capital stock as he had before the decrease herein provided for.

DIRECTORS' RESOLUTION AUTHORIZING REDUCTION OF CAPITAL STOCK BY REDUCING PAR VALUE OF SHARES

WHEREAS, the authorized capital stock of this Corporation is $100,000, divided into 1,000 shares of the par value of $100 each, and

WHEREAS, in the opinion of this Board of Directors, it will be to the best interests of this Corporation and its stockholders to reduce the capital stock of the Corporation to $50,000, to be divided into 1,000 shares of the par value of $50 each, and

WHEREAS, this Corporation has no outstanding indebtedness other than its capital stock liability, be it

RESOLVED, That the capital stock of this Corporation is hereby reduced from $100,000, divided into 1,000 shares of the par value of $100 each, to $50,000, to be divided into 1,000 shares of the par value of $50 each, and

RESOLVED FURTHER, That the officers of this Corporation are hereby authorized and permitted to submit this resolution to the stockholders of the Corporation, for their consideration, and that, upon obtaining the approval of the proportion of stockholders required by law, the said officers are hereby authorized and directed to execute and file all instruments and to do all acts and things necessary to effect the aforesaid reduction of the capital stock.

RESOLUTION OF STOCKHOLDERS APPROVING AND RATIFYING ACTION OF BOARD OF DIRECTORS IN REDUCING CAPITAL STOCK

WHEREAS, the Board of Directors of this Corporation, at a meeting duly called and held on ......, 19.., at .. ...M., adopted a resolution reducing the capital stock of the Corporation as hereinafter set forth, and submitted the said resolution to the stockholders of this Corporation for their consideration, and

WHEREAS, the stockholders believe that it is to the best interests of the Corporation so to reduce the capital stock of this Corporation, be it

RESOLVED, That the stockholders of this Corporation do hereby approve, ratify, and assent to the action of the Board of Directors in adopting the following resolution:

(Here insert preceding resolution of directors.)

RESOLVED FURTHER, That the proper officers of this Corporation are hereby authorized, empowered, and directed to execute and file all documents, certificates, and papers, and to do all things necessary to effect the reduction of the capital stock hereinabove set forth.

DIRECTORS' RESOLUTION AUTHORIZING REDUCTION OF CAPITAL STOCK AND TRANSFER OF SURPLUS ASSETS TO RESERVE ACCOUNT FOR DISTRIBUTION TO STOCKHOLDERS

WHEREAS, this Corporation has on hand available assets in excess of the amount required to cover all its liabilities, and beyond the amount required for working capital, be it

RESOLVED, That the capital stock of this Corporation is hereby reduced from $500,000, divided into 5,000 shares of the par value of $100 each, to $250,000, divided into 2,500 shares of the par value of $100 each, and

RESOLVED FURTHER, That all capital and surplus assets, however, derived, in excess of the aggregate of the said sum of $250,000, plus the amount necessary to cover all liabilities and the amount required for working capital, are hereby transferred to a reserve account, subject to distribution to the stockholders of this Corporation by this Board of Directors, in the manner and by the proceedings authorized by law and the By-laws of this Corporation, and

RESOLVED FURTHER, That the officers of this Corporation are hereby authorized and directed to submit this resolution to the stockholders for their approval, and that, upon obtaining the approval of the proportion of stockholders required by law, the said officers are hereby authorized and directed to execute and file all instruments and to do all things necessary to carry out the aforesaid reduction to the capital stock.

DIRECTORS' RESOLUTION RECOMMENDING AMENDMENT OF CERTIFICATE OF INCORPORATION CHANGING SHARES OF PAR VALUE TO SHARES WITHOUT PAR, DECREASING AMOUNT OF CAPITAL, INCREASING NUMBER OF SHARES OF STOCK WITHOUT PAR AS CHANGED, AND GIVING DIRECTORS POWER TO ISSUE BONDS CONVERTIBLE INTO STOCK

RESOLVED, That the Board of Directors of . . . . Corporation, a corporation of the State of . . . ., deems it advisable and hereby declares it to be advisable:

That the authorized common stock of said Corporation, consisting of 12,500,000 shares of the par value of $100 each, be changed into 12,500,000 shares without par value;

That the capital of the Corporation be decreased from $1,230,606,300 to $1,013,025,000;

That such change of common stock with par value into common stock without par value shall be effected by changing each share of the presently authorized common stock with par value (including the shares presently issued and outstanding) into one share of common stock without par value;

That such decrease of capital of the corporation shall be effected by reducing the capital represented by each share of issued and outstanding common stock so changed as aforesaid to $75;

That certificates for shares of such common stock without par value shall be issued in exchange for certificates for the presently issued and outstanding shares of common stock with par value, share for share;

That the authorized common stock of the Corporation, as so changed, be increased from 12,500,000 shares without par value to 15,000,000 shares without par value, thus making the total authorized capital stock of the Corporation, after such change and increase in the common stock shall have been effected, 4,000,000 shares of preferred stock of the par value of $100 each and 15,000,000 shares of common stock without par value;

That the shares of common stock without par value, other than the shares into which the presently issued and outstanding shares of common stock with par value shall be changed as aforesaid, may be issued and may be sold by the Corporation from time to time in such manner and for such consideration as from time to time may be fixed by its Board of Directors;

That, in order to give effect to the foregoing change and increase in the authorized capital stock of the Corporation and decrease in its capital, the Certificate of Incorporation of the Corporation, filed in the office of the Secretary of State of the State of ..... on ...., 19.., as heretofore amended, be further amended so that the first paragraph of Article IV thereof shall read as follows:

IV. The amount of the total authorized capital stock of the Corporation is 19,000,000 shares, 4,000,000 of which are to be preferred stock of the par value of $100 each, and the remaining 15,000,000 shares are to be common stock without par value. The capital represented by the 8,703,252 shares of common stock without par value into which the previously issued and outstanding 8,703,252 shares of common stock of the par value of $100 each have been changed is $75 per share, thus decreasing the capital of the Corporation in the amount of $217,581,300. Such capital is subject to increase from time to time by transfers of surplus or portions thereof to capital account as now or hereafter provided by law. Any or all of said shares of common stock without par value (other than the 8,703,252 shares into which the previously issued and outstanding shares of common stock with par value have been changed) may be issued and may be sold by the Corporation from time to time in such manner and for such consideration as from time to time may be fixed by its Board of Directors.

RESOLVED FURTHER, That the Board of Directors of said .... Corporation deems it advisable and hereby declares it to be advisable that the Certificate of Incorporation of the Corporation filed in the office of the Secretary of State of the State of ...., on ...., 19.., as heretofore amended, be further amended by adding thereto a new article, which shall read as follows:

VIII. The Board of Directors shall have power to issue bonds, debentures, or other obligations convertible into the Corporation's common stock upon such terms, in such manner, and under such conditions as may be fixed by resolution of the Board of Directors prior to the issue of such bonds, debentures, or other obligations; subject, however, to the provisions of the fifth paragraph of Article VII hereof with respect to any such bonds, debentures, or other obligations to be secured by any mortgage on or pledge of any of the real property of this Corporation or any shares of capital stock of any other corporation.

RESOLVED FURTHER, That, in the event of the adoption of the proposed amendments, the Certificate of Incorporation of the Corporation shall read as set forth in the copy thereof submitted to the Board of Directors at this meeting and appended to these minutes, marked Exhibit "A" (identical with the present Certificate of Incorporation, except for the above-stated amendments, which are incorporated in Exhibit "A"), and that, in the event that only one of such amendments shall be adopted, the Certificate of Incorporation shall read as said Exhibit "A," except that the first paragraph of Article IV, if that shall not be amended, shall read as at present and except that Article VIII, if that shall not be adopted, shall not be included therein, and

RESOLVED FURTHER, That the foregoing matters shall be submitted to the stockholders for action thereon at their annual meeting for the election of directors to be held at the principal office of the Corporation, ... *(Street)*, in the City of . . . . , County of . . . . , State of . . . . , on . . . . , 19. . . , at . . . . .M., or at any adjournment thereof; that the proposed change and increase in the authorized common stock of the Corporation and decrease in its capital and the proposed amendment of the Certificate of Incorporation of the Corporation, as heretofore amended, to effect such change, increase, and decrease by amending Article IV of such Certificate shall be submitted to the stockholders for action thereon separately from the proposed amendment to the Certificate of Incorporation to effect the addition thereto of Article VIII as aforesaid, and that the notice of such meeting shall clearly state that action will be taken upon the foregoing matters.

RESOLUTION OF STOCKHOLDERS CHANGING STOCK WITH PAR VALUE TO STOCK WITHOUT PAR VALUE

RESOLVED, That the authorized number of shares—to wit: . . . . . (. . . . .) shares having a par value of . . . . . ($. . . . .) Dollars each, aggregating . . . . . ($. . . . .) Dollars—be changed to an authorized number of . . . . . (. . . . .) shares without par value, and that the Articles of Incorporation of this Corporation be amended for that purpose so that Article . . . . . shall be in the following form:

(Here insert new capital stock clause in full.)

RESOLUTION OF STOCKHOLDERS AUTHORIZING RECLASSIFICATION OF STOCK BY EXCHANGING COMMON AND PREFERRED STOCK WITH PAR VALUE FOR COMMON STOCK WITHOUT PAR VALUE

RESOLVED, That the authorized capital stock of the . . . . Corporation, in the amount of $1,000,000, consisting of 10,000 shares, 5,000 of which are preferred stock of the par value of $100 each, and 5,000 of which are common stock of the par value of $100 each, be reclassified, and that Article . . . . . of the Certificate of Incorporation of this Corporation be amended, changed, and altered to read as follows:

Article . . . . . The total number of shares that may be issued by the Corporation is 10,000, all of which shall be of one class, without any nominal or par value, and shall be known as common stock. The capital of the Corporation shall be at least equal to the aggregate par value of all issued shares having par value, plus the aggregate amount of consideration received by the Corporation for the issuance of said shares without par value, and plus such amounts as may from time to time, by resolution of the Board of Directors, be transferred thereto.

RESOLVED FURTHER, That the said 10,000 shares of stock without any nominal or par value shall be substituted for and take the place of the 5,000 outstanding shares of preferred stock, and the 5,000 outstanding shares of common stock with a par value, and the holders of the said outstanding shares of stock with a par value, shall surrender the certificates for the same to the Corporation for cancellation, and shall receive and accept in place of each certificate thereof a certificate of share of stock without any nominal or par value.

RESOLVED FURTHER, That the President and the Secretary of this Corporation are hereby authorized and directed to make, sign, verify, and acknowledge the certificate of proceedings required by statute, to cause one of such certificates to be filed in the office of the Secretary of State, and a duplicate original thereof in the office of the Clerk of the County of . . . . . and to do all acts and things that may be necessary and proper to carry into effect the foregoing resolution in compliance with the laws of the State of . . . .

RESOLUTION OF STOCKHOLDERS AUTHORIZING CHANGE OF SHARES WITHOUT PAR VALUE INTO A LARGE NUMBER OF SHARES OF THE SAME CLASS WITHOUT PAR VALUE

WHEREAS, the total number of shares of stock that the Corporation is now authorized to issue is 15,000,000 shares of stock, classified as follows:

10,000,000 shares of preferred stock of the par value of $ . . . . . each, and
5,000,000 shares of common stock without par value, and

WHEREAS, the number of shares of each class issued and outstanding is as follows:

9,000,000 shares of preferred stock, and
4,500,000 shares of common stock, and

WHEREAS, 500,000 shares of common stock have not been issued, and

WHEREAS, it is deemed desirable and for the best interest of the Corporation and its stockholders that all the 5,000,000 authorized shares of common stock without par value of the Corporation be changed into 20,000,000 shares of common stock without par value; be it

RESOLVED, That all the 5,000,000 authorized shares of common stock without par value of the Corporation be changed into 20,000,000 shares of common stock without par value, and

RESOLVED FURTHER, That the previously authorized 4,500,000 shares of common stock without par value which have been issued and are now outstanding shall be changed into 18,000,000 shares of common stock without par value, on the basis that each such previously authorized share of common stock without par value now issued and outstanding shall be changed into 4 shares of common stock without par value, and that the previously authorized 500,000 shares of common stock without par value which have not been issued shall be changed into 2,000,000 shares of common stock without par value, and

RESOLVED FURTHER, That the Corporation may issue and sell the authorized shares without par value which have not been issued, for such consideration as may from time to time be fixed by the Board of Directors, and

RESOLVED FURTHER, That the designations, preferences, privileges, voting powers, restrictions, and qualifications of each class of shares shall be the same as heretofore, and

RESOLVED FURTHER, That the statement respecting capital, contained in the Certificate of Incorporation of this Corporation, remain unchanged, and

RESOLVED FURTHER, That the officers of the Corporation are hereby authorized and directed to execute and file in the proper offices a certificate of change of all previously authorized shares of common stock without par value into a different number of shares of the same class without par value, indicating the terms upon which such change is to be made, and stating that the capital is to remain unchanged, and to do all things that may be essential to effectuate such change, all as set forth in the foregoing resolutions.

RESOLUTION OF STOCKHOLDERS AMENDING CERTIFICATE OF INCORPORATION TO CHANGE THE NUMBER AND PAR VALUE OF SHARES WITHOUT CHANGING CAPITAL STOCK

RESOLVED, That the number of shares of capital stock of .... Corporation, and the par value thereof, be changed from 10,000 shares of the par value of $100 each to 20,000 shares of the par value of $50 each, the authorized capital stock of the Corporation to remain at $100,000 as heretofore, and

RESOLVED FURTHER, That Article ..... of the Certificate of Incorporation of .... Corporation be amended, changed, and altered to read as follows:

(Here insert new article.)

RESOLVED FURTHER, That the officers of this Corporation are hereby authorized and directed to execute and to file all documents and to do all things necessary to effect the aforesaid amendment, and

RESOLVED FURTHER, That within . . . . . months after the date of this meeting, each stockholder of this Corporation shall surrender the shares of stock owned and held by him, and the officers of this Corporation are hereby authorized and directed to issue to such stockholder two shares of stock of the par value of $50 each for every share of stock of $100 par value surrendered by him.

RESOLUTION OF STOCKHOLDERS AMENDING CERTIFICATE OF INCORPORATION TO AUTHORIZE DIRECTORS TO ISSUE STOCK IN SERIES AND TO FIX TERMS BY RESOLUTION

WHEREAS, the Certificate of Incorporation of this Corporation authorizes the issuance of . . . . . (. . . . .) shares of preferred stock, each share having a par value of . . . . . ($ . . . . .) Dollars, of which . . . . . (. . . . .) shares are still unissued, and

WHEREAS, the stockholders deem it advisable to authorize the Board of Directors to issue such unissued shares of preferred stock in series, with such designations, preferences, and relative participating, optional, or other rights, qualifications, limitations, or restrictions thereof as shall be stated and expressed in a resolution of the Board of Directors, and

WHEREAS, under the provisions of the Certificate of Incorporation of this Corporation, no power is granted to the Board of Directors to issue the said remaining unissued preferred stock in series and to fix the terms of such series by resolution, be it

RESOLVED, That the Certificate of Incorporation be amended so that Article . . . . . shall read as follows:

The amount of the total authorized capital stock of this Corporation is . . . . . (. . . . .) shares of preferred stock of the par value of . . . . . ($ . . . . .) Dollars per share, amounting in the aggregate of . . . . . ($ . . . . .) Dollars, and . . . . . (. . . . .) shares of common stock without nominal or par value, which shares without nominal or par value may be issued from time to time without action by the stockholders, for such consideration as may be fixed from time to time by the Board of Directors, and shares so issued, the full consideration for which has been paid or delivered, shall be deemed fully paid stock, and the holders of such shares shall not be liable for any further payment thereon.

The preferred stock may be issued in series from time to time with such designations, preferences, and relative participating, optional, or other rights, qualifications, limitations, or restrictions thereof as shall be stated and expressed in the resolution or resolutions providing for the issue of such class, classes, or series adopted by the Board of Directors, pursuant to the authority hereby given as provided by statute. Each class or series may be made subject to redemption at such time and at such price or prices as such resolution or resolutions providing for the issue of such stock shall state and express. The holders of the preferred stock of any class or series shall be entitled to receive dividends at such rates, on such conditions, and at such times, and shall be entitled to such rights upon the dissolution of, or upon any distribution of, the assets of the Corporation, and the preferred stock of any class or series may be convertible into or exchangeable for shares of any other class, classes, or series of capital stock of the Corporation, at such price or prices, or at such rates of exchange, and with such adjustments, as shall be stated and expressed in the resolution or resolutions of the Board of Directors providing for the issuance thereof, and

RESOLVED FURTHER, That the officers of this Corporation are hereby authorized and directed to file all certificates, documents, and papers, and to do all acts required by law to effect the aforesaid amendment.

RESOLUTION OF STOCKHOLDERS AMENDING CERTIFICATE OF INCORPORATION TO INCLUDE PROVISION FOR MAKING AND ALTERING BY-LAWS; RESTRICTION ON POWER OF DIRECTORS TO ALTER BY-LAW WITH RESPECT TO STOCK DEALINGS

RESOLVED, as deemed and declared advisable by the Board of Directors of The . . . . Company, a corporation of the State of . . . ., at its meeting duly convened and held on . . . ., 19. ., that the Certificate of Incorporation of the Company be amended by adding a new Article Seventh, which shall read as follows:

"*Seventh.* The directors of the Company shall have power to make and alter the Company's By-laws from time to time. A report respecting By-laws so made or altered by the directors shall be made to the stockholders at their annual meeting held next thereafter. By-laws so made or altered by the directors may be altered or repealed by the stockholders at any time, but if not so altered or repealed shall remain in effect without ratification by the stockholders. Notwithstanding the foregoing provisions of this article, the directors shall not have power to alter the provisions of Article . . . . . of the By-laws, restricting dealings by the Company and its constituent companies in the stock of the Company and of its constituent companies, which provisions shall continue to be unalterable save by the vote of the holders of a majority of each and every class of stock of the Company, voting thereon, at a meeting called as provided for in the By-laws."

DIRECTORS' RESOLUTION APPROVING AMENDMENT OF BY-LAWS AND CALLING SPECIAL MEETING OF STOCKHOLDERS TO PASS UPON PROPOSED AMENDMENT

RESOLVED, That, in the judgment of the Board of Directors of the . . . . Corporation, it is deemed advisable to amend the By-laws of the said Corporation so as to provide (*insert substance of amendments*), and to that end to change Sections ..... and ..... of Article ..... of the said By-laws to read as follows:

(Here insert new by-law in full.)

RESOLVED FURTHER, That a special meeting of the stockholders of this Corporation is hereby called to be held at the office of the Corporation at .... (*Street*), ... (*City*), ... (*State*), on ...., 19.., at .. ...M., to consider and take action upon the foregoing resolution, and that the Secretary of the Corporation is hereby authorized and directed to give due notice of the said meeting to stockholders of the Corporation.

DIRECTORS' RESOLUTION AMENDING A BY-LAW PROVISION UPON SPECIFIC AUTHORIZATION OF STOCKHOLDERS

WHEREAS, the holders of more than two-thirds of the subscribed capital stock of the corporation have, by a resolution adopted at a meeting duly called upon notice, authorized and directed the Board of Directors of this corporation to amend Section ..... of Article ..... of the By-laws, be it

RESOLVED, That the aforesaid Section ..... of Article ..... of the By-laws be amended in accordance with the said resolution of the stockholders, to read as follows:

(Here insert new by-law.)

RESOLVED FURTHER, That the Secretary of the corporation is hereby authorized and directed to copy the said Section ..... of Article ..... of the By-laws, as amended, in the book of By-laws of the corporation, and properly to certify the same.

RESOLUTION OF STOCKHOLDERS ANNULLING ALL BY-LAWS PASSED BY CORPORATION AND ADOPTING NEW BY-LAWS

RESOLVED, That the By-laws adopted on ...., 19.., including all By-laws heretofore adopted, are hereby vacated, abrogated, and repealed, and that there be this day adopted as the By-laws of the company the By-laws presented and read to this meeting, and that a copy thereof be spread upon the face of the minutes.

RESOLUTION OF STOCKHOLDERS GIVING BOARD OF DIRECTORS UNLIMITED POWER TO AMEND BY-LAWS

RESOLVED, That the Board of Directors of the .... Corporation is hereby authorized and empowered to amend, alter, change, add to, repeal, or rescind any and all By-laws of said corporation from time to time as in its judgment shall be deemed fitting and proper, without action or consent on the part of the stockholders, and

RESOLVED FURTHER, That the stockholders reserve the right to revoke the above grant of power to the Directors by resolution duly passed at any subsequent stockholder meeting, but until such revocation, the stockholders shall not exercise their power to amend, alter, change, add to, repeal or rescind the By-laws of the Corporation presently contained in Article . . . . . of said By-laws.

RESOLUTION OF STOCKHOLDERS REVOKING POWER GIVEN TO DIRECTORS TO MAKE AND AMEND BY-LAWS

RESOLVED, That the power to repeal and amend the By-laws of this corporation and to adopt new By-laws, delegated to the Board of Directors by resolution adopted at a special meeting of stockholders held on . . . . . ., 19.., is hereby revoked.

RESOLUTION OF STOCKHOLDERS AMENDING BY-LAWS BY ADDING A NEW PROVISION

RESOLVED, That the By-laws of the corporation are hereby amended, by adding to Article . . . . . thereof a new section numbered . . . . ., and reading as follows:

(Here insert new by-law in full.)

(*Note:* Where directors have power to amend by-laws without action of stockholders, this resolution may be used by directors without any change in wording.)

RESOLUTION OF STOCKHOLDERS AMENDING BY-LAWS BY SUBSTITUTING ONE SECTION FOR ANOTHER

RESOLVED, That the By-laws of the corporation are hereby amended by striking out Article . . . . ., Section . . . . ., reading as follows:

(Here insert old by-law.)

and substituting therefor the following:

(Here insert new by-law in full.)

DIRECTORS' RESOLUTION CHANGING BY-LAWS TO ALLOW FLEXIBILITY IN DATE FOR ANNUAL STOCKHOLDERS' MEETING

WHEREAS, The second . . . . . (*day*) in . . . . . (*month*), the date presently set for the annual meeting of the stockholders by Article . . . . ., Section . . . . ., of the By-laws of this Corporation has been designated by the Governors of several states as a legal holiday, and

WHEREAS, a large proportion of the stockholders of this Corporation reside in such states and would find it inconvenient to attend a stockholders' meeting upon such date, be it

RESOLVED, That Article . . . . ., Section . . . . ., of the By-laws of this Corporation shall be amended to read:

Section . . . . . The annual meeting of the stockholders of the . . . . Corporation shall be held at the principal office of the Corporation in the City of . . . ., State of . . . ., or at such other place in the City as the Board of Directors shall designate in the notice of the meeting, on the third . . . . of . . . . of each year, at . . . . .M.

Chapter 27

BORROWING AND LENDING

Contents—Chapter 27

Power of a corporation to borrow money. A corporation has power to borrow money to pay its debts, and give the usual security for the loan.[1] It can issue bonds,[2] with or without a mortgage on its property as security.[3] This power is inherent—it need not be expressly granted in the corporate charter.[4] It is not limited to corporations organized for a particular purpose, but applies to practically all corporations whose business requires raising money.[5] Often the power to borrow is expressly conferred by statute; it includes the corporation's assumption of others' debts.[6]

There is practically no statutory limit anywhere on the amount a corporation can borrow.[7]

Who has general authority to borrow. The board of directors, entrusted with control and management of the corporate affairs, can borrow money for the furtherance of the corporate business as an incident to this general power.[8] It can do so without stockholder approval.[9] But this authority doesn't, except as indicated below, extend to an officer solely by virtue of his office[10] although it may be delegated to the managing officer of the corporation or to any other agent or officer by express resolution of the board of directors.[11] The power of an officer to borrow may also be inherent in the duties of his office. Thus, a vice president in charge of real estate may have implied

---

[1] Sheffield Chamber of Commerce, Inc. v Hatch, (1930) 220 Ala. 601, 127 So 173; J. K. Siphon Ventilator Co. v Hutton, (1951) 116 Ark. 545, 175 SW 30; Hinchliffe v Nat'l Dyeing & Printing Co., (1939) 126 N.J. Eq. 386, 8 A2d 710; Jacobs v Monabon Realty Investment Corp., (1914) 212 N.Y. 48, 105 NE 968; Weinberger v Quinn, (1942) 264 App. Div. 405, 35 N.Y.S.2d 567; Humphreys & Son, Inc. v Broughton, (1928) 149 Va. 789, 141 SE 764.

[2] Intermountain B. & L. Ass'n v Gallegos (CA–9 1935) 78 F2d 972; North Hudson Mut. B. & L. Ass'n v First Nat'l Bank of Hudson, (1890) 79 Wis. 31, 47 NW 300.

[3] Howeth v Coulbourne Bros. Co., (1911) 115 Md. 107, 80 Atl 916.

[4] Provident Stores' Receiver v Tanner, (1928) 226 Ky. 364, 10 SW2d 1077; Taylor Feed Pen Co. v Taylor Nat'l Bank, (1915) Tex. Civ. App. 181 SW 534.

[5] Alton Mfg. Co. v Garrett Biblical Institute, (1910) 243 Ill. 298, 90 NE 704.

[6] Religious Films, Inc. v Potts, (1946) Tex. Civ. App. 197 SW2d 592.

[7] Corporation Commissioner cannot question proposed corporate debt ceiling increase approved by three-fourths shareholder's vote and authorized under articles and by-laws. OAG Ariz. No. 74–6 (R–12) 2-25-74.

[8] Ala. Nat'l Bank v O'Neill, (1900) 128 Ala. 192, 29 So 688; H. B. Rice & Co. v Miners' Elkhorn Coal Co., (1930) 234 Ky. 580, 28 SW2d 783; Humphreys & Son, Inc. v Broughton, (1928) 149 Va. 789, 141 SE 764.

[9] H. Watson Devil. Co. v Bank & Trust Co., (1978) 58 Ill. App.3d 423.

[10] American Business Credit Corp., Inc. v First State Bank of Lantana (Fla. App. 1980) 385 S 2d 1081; Smoltz v North Waterloo Meat Co., (1929) Iowa, 224 NW 536.

[11] Watson v Proximity Mfg. Co., (1908) 147 N.C. 469, 478, 61 SE 273. See National Surety Co. v Wingate, (1932) 153 Okla. 132, 5 P2d 376.

authority to borrow money to pay realty taxes.[12] But the board should not divest itself of entire control of the finances of the corporation.[13]

Even though an officer has neither express nor implied authority to borrow, he may be clothed with apparent authority by acquiescence of the corporation in his unauthorized acts.[14] Although an officer or an agent may have no authority to borrow money for the payment of corporate debts, a corporation cannot disown the unauthorized act of borrowing if it retains the benefits of the loan.[15] Corporation must repay loan made by check payable to its president, when the check was deposited in its bank account and the proceeds used by it.[16] It follows that the estate of a deceased guarantor of the corporation's notes is liable to the lender when the corporation defaults, even if the loans were unauthorized, when the corporation got and used the funds and the decedent assumed liability "irrespective of the validity, regularity, or enforceability" of the instrument evidencing the debt.[17] It has even been held that a close corporation is liable to a bank when it was co-maker with its president of a note, though the loan was for the president's personal use and the bank knew that, when all the stockholders acquiesced in the loan and it was obtained from the bank in the same way as previous transactions.[18]

Rate of interest that can be charged corporations. In most states, corporations can be charged any rate of interest—statutes in those states say a corporation cannot plead the defense of usury when sued on a debt.

This has led some lenders to require individual borrowers to form a corporation to take the loan when the loan would be usurious if made

---

[12]St. James Co. v Security Trust & Life Ins. Co., (1903) 82 App Div 242, 81 N.Y.S. 739; Warren v Littleton Orange Crush Bottling Co., (1933) 204 N.C. 288, 168 SE 226; Madill Oil, etc. Co. v City Nat'l Bank, (1918) Okla. 193 P 873; A. F. Anderson Est., Inc. v Puget Sav. & Loan Ass'n, (1933) 171 Wash. 378, 18 P2d 5.

[13]Smith v California Thorn Cordage, Inc., (1933) 129 Cal. App. 93, 18 P2d 393.

[14]Farmers State Bank of Victor v Johnson (S Ct Mont. 1980) 610 P 2d 1172; Cunningham v German (CA–9 1900) 101 F 977; Alton Mfg. Co. v Garrett Biblical Institute, (1910) 243 Ill. 298, 90 NE 704; Beers v Phoenix Glass Co., (1852) 14 Barb. (N.Y.) 358; Humphreys & Son, Inc. v Broughton, (1928) 149 Va. 789, 141 SE 764; Hartley v Ault Woodenware Co., (1918) 83 W. Va. 780, 97 SE 137; Guaranty Bank etc. Co. v Beaumont (Tex. Civ. App. 1920) 218 SW 638.

[15]Hartley v Ault Woodenware Co., (1918) 82 W. Va. 780, 97 SE 137.

[16]Empire Diesel, Inc. v Brown, (1961) 146 Col. 477, 361 P2d 964.

[17]Bank of N. Amer. v Shapiro, (1969) 31 A.D. 2d 465, 298 N.Y.S.2d 399.

[18]H. M. Popp Truck Line, Inc. v First Nat'l Bk. (Col. App., 1971) 485 P2d 141.

to an individual. This technique has been upheld in some cases.[19] Other courts say the loan is usurious if made *in fact* to the individual though *in form* to a corporation[20] or for the benefit of a corporation.[21]

When a corporation is barred from defending on the ground of usury, a guarantor[22] and an accommodation endorser[23] of a corporate note are also barred. Neither can a second lienor attack the first lien as usurious if the borrower is a corporation.[24] However, when a corporation and an individual sign as co-makers of a note, the note can be usurious as to the individual even though it is not usurious as to the corporation.[25] The individual needn't join the corporation as a necessary party in a suit to recover a penalty for usury.[26]

When a statute denies a corporation the defense of usury, the corporation can't sue to recover allegedly usurious interest it has already paid.[27]

---

[19] R.J. Carter Enterprises, Inc. v Greenway Bank & Trust (Tex. App. 1981) 615 SW 2d 826; Holland v Gross (Fla. S Ct, 1956) 89 S2d 255; Bradley v Selengut, (1945) 269 A.D. 209, 54 N.Y.S.2d 547; Gangadean v Flori Investment Co., (1970) 106 Ariz. 245, 474 P2d 1006 (formalities followed); Leader v Dinkler Management Corp., (1967) 20 N.Y.2d 393, 283 N.S.2d 281. Compare, Monmouth Capital Corp. v Holmdel Village Shops, Inc., (1966) 92 N.J. Super. 480, 224 A2d 35; Hoffman v Lee Nashem Motors, (1967) 20 N.Y.2d 513, 285 NYS2d 68; Stein v Astro Properties, (1968) 31 A.D.2d 553, 295 N.Y.S.2d 390.

[20] First Mutual Corp. v Grammercy & Maine, Inc., (1980) 176 NJ Super. 428, 423 A 2d 680; Gilbert v Doris R. Corp. (Fla. Dist. Ct of App. 1959) 111 S2d 682; Lesser v Strubbe, (1959) 56 N.J. Super 274, 152 A2d 409; Matter of Bank of N.Y. & 5th Ave. Bank, (1953) 305 N.Y. 764, 113 NE2d 154 aff'g 280 A.D. 947 which reversed, (1951) 126 NYLJ 1478; Jenkins v Moyse, (1930) 254 N.Y. 319, 172 NE 521.

[21] National Equipment Rental, Ltd. v Hendrix (CA–2 1977) NYLJ 11–30–77, p. 1 (equipment lease treated as loan); Ranhand v Sinowitz, (1970) 26 N.Y.2d 232, 257 NE2d 887 (no showing of any corporate obligation).

[22] Reynolds v Service Loan & Finance Co., (1967) 116 Ga. App. 740, 158 SE2d 309; Merchants Mortgage Co. v Bogan (CA–D.C. 1970) 434 F2d 400; Soparge v Rosenblatt, (1971) 36 A.D. 2d 174, 319 N.Y.S.2d 466; E'Town Shopping Center, Inc. v Lexington Finance Co. (Ky. 1969) 436 SW2d 267; A.J. Armstrong, Inc. v Lincoln Finance & Thrift, Inc. (DC, E.D. Tenn. 1968) 291 F Supp 1008; Dahmes v Industrial Credit Co., (1961) 261 Minn. 26, 110 NW2d 484; Gen. Phoenix Corp. v Cabot, (1949) 300 N.Y. 87, 89 NE2d 238; Sundseth v Roadmaster Body Corp., (1976) 74 Wis. 2d 61, 245 NW2d 919; Charmoll Fashions, Inc. v Otto (Minn. 1976) 248 NW2d 717; cf OAG Ky. 71492, 11–15–71.

[23] Raby v Commercial Banking Corp., (1966) 208 Pa. Super. 52, 220 A2d 659; Nationwide, Inc. v Scullin (DC, D. N.J. 1966) 256 F Supp 929; A. J. Armstrong, Inc. v Janburt Embroidery Corp., (1967) 97 N.J. Super. 246, 234 A2d 737; Pardee v Fetter, (1956) 345 Mich. 548, 77 NW2d 124; Metz v Taglieri, (1961) 29 Misc. 2d 841, 215 N.Y.S.2d 263; Waterman v Howard Paper Co., (1971) 124 Ga. App. 511, 184 SE2d 226.

[24] Bud v Morris (Tex. Civ. App. 1973) 492 SW2d 335.

[25] Country Motors, Inc. v Friendly Finance Corp., (1961) 13 Wis.2d 475, 109 NW2d 137. Compare Artistic Greetings v Sholom Greeting Card Co., Inc., (1971) 36 A.D.2d 68, 318 N.Y.S.2d 623; Arrow S. & L. Ass'n. v Wilmikwil Corp., (1971) 35 A.D.2d 840, 317 N.Y.S.2d 232; Sundseth v Roadmaster Body Corp., (1976) 74 Wis. 2d 61, 245 NW2d 919.

[26] Grove v Chicago Title and Trust Co., (1960) 25 Ill. App. 2d 402, 166 NE2d 630; Boyer Enterprises, Inc. v Evans Grocery & Delicatessen, Inc., (1950) 124 NYLJ 99; Astra Pictures, Inc. v Schapiro, (1944) 182 Misc. 19, 48 N.Y.S.2d 858.

[27] Gen. Investment Funds v Gildenhorn, (1970) 260 Md. 170, 271 A2d 650.

A loan to a corporation was held not usurious though the lender got a bonus in stock, because the stock had belonged to the promoters and was not a corporate asset even though it had been set aside for uses that the promoters deemed beneficial to the corporation.[28] And an alleged loan made to the sole stockholders personally was not usurious when the transaction took the form of a purchase by the "lender" of certain assets from the stockholders and a resale of the assets to the stockholders' corporation at a price about 50 percent higher.[29]

Courts in one state with a statute denying corporations the defense of usury have held the statute covers only "such obligations as bonds, mortgages, and the like." They have permitted a corporation to plead usury when sued on checks it issued in payment of a loan and on which checks it had stopped payment,[30] and barred the defense of usury when the total interest and discount was within the statutory maximum and when the corporation was sued on promissory notes containing an acceleration clause, provision for attorney's collection fees and, in part at least, secured by a chattel mortgage.[31]

A loan to a partnership with two corporate partners was not a loan to a corporation on which there was a higher maximum interest rate.[32]

An individual borrower can waive the defense of usury even though proceeds of loan went to his construction business.[33]

A loan can be usurious even though made to a corporation, when the actual purpose of the loan was to enable the corporation to make a loan to an employee.[34]

The D.C. statute barring corporations from pleading usury applies to both domestic and qualified corporations. The latter can't avoid obligations to pay usurious rates by filing certificate of withdrawal. However, they may recover excess interest if it is shown lenders weren't properly licensed under lending law.[35]

Borrowing from stockholders, directors and officers. A corporation may borrow from its stockholders, directors, or officers and pay

[28] Greenberg v Manganese Products, Inc., (1951) 139 Wash. 735, 238 P2d 1194.
[29] Michaelson v Rosenthal & Rosenthal, Inc., (1955) 133 NYLJ.
[30] Pick v Brand, (1947) 135 N.J. Law 526, 53 A2d 304.
[31] Reisman v Wm. Hartman & Son, Inc., (1966) 51 Misc. 2d 393, 273 N.Y.S.2d 295. Compare, Shaheen Natural Resources Co., Inc. v Mobil Oil Corp., NYLJ, 12–8–66, p. 16; Cohen v Buckeye Corp., NYLJ 11–18–66, p. 16; Berlin v Sun Rock Enterprises, Inc., NYLJ, 1–29–68, p. 20. Eine v H. Klein, Inc. (1950) 10 N.J. Super 295, 77 A2d 295.
[32] OAG Tex. No. H–589, 4–23–75.
[33] National Equipment Rental, Ltd. v Hendrix (CA–2 1977).
[34] CBS Real Estate of Cedar Rapids, Inc. v Harper (Iowa S Ct 1982) 316 NW 2d 170.
[35] Indian Lake Estates, Inc. v Ten Individual Defendants (CA–D.C. 1965) 350 F2d 435.

them interest unless forbidden to do so by its charter or a statute or by-law.[36]

Because of the fiduciary relation existing between a corporation and its officers and directors, any transactions between them will be subject to the rigid scrutiny of the courts,[37] but will be upheld if the parties acted in good faith and the transaction is fair to the corporation.[38]

Stockholders, directors and officers can become the creditors of the corporation either by lending it money directly, or by lending their credit,[39] that is, by indorsing its notes or other evidences of its indebtedness. However, a director or officer cannot lend to a corporation at interest if the corporation is not in need of funds.[40]

As a general rule, a stockholder, director, or officer can take security for his debt in the same manner as third persons.[41] And this is true as to directors even though the loan could not have been approved by the board without their votes when the entire transaction was fair, the corporation needed the money to carry on business, and the money was actually used in the business.[42] So, also, when the president of a corporation, in good faith, loaned money to his company and took back mortgages to secure its repayment, the mortgages were held to be valid as against a stockholder-creditor who, together with other stockholders and directors, ratified the transaction.[43]

And another court refused to treat a stockholder's loan to his corporation as an investment of capital when there was no fraud or

---

[36] Twin-Lick Oil Co. v Marbury, (1875) 91 US 328; In re Knox Automobile Co. (D Mass. 1915) 229 F 241; White v Staehly, (1939) 7 Conn. Supp 71, 60; Welliver v Coate, (1917) 65 Ind. App. 195, 114 NE 775; H. B. Rice & Co. v Miners' Elkhorn Coal Co., (1930) 234 Ky. 580, 28 SW2d 783; Gilman v Bailey Carriage Co., Inc., (1928) 127 Me. 91, 141 Atl 321; Wall v Rothrock, (1916) 171 N.C. 388, 88 SE 633; Hartford Sterling Co., (1944) 330 Pa. 277, 38 A2d 229.

[37] Geisenberger & Friedler v Robert York & Co. (CA-5 1919) 262 F 739, Wabash R. Co. v Iowa & S.W.R. Co., (1925) 200 Iowa 384, 202 NW 595; N.Y. Stock Exchange v Pickard & Co. Inc. (Del. Ch. 1972) 296 A2d 143 (subordinated lenders couldn't get priority over claims of directors who made arm's length loans to shore up staggering corporations).

[38] Schnittger v Old Home Consol. Min. Co., (1904) 144 Cal. 603, 78 P 9.

[39] Corey v Hamilton Nat. Bank et al. (CA-6 1929) 31 F2d 379; aff'g In re Federal Coal Co. (ED Ky. 1927) 31 F2d 375; Gilman v Bailey Carriage Co., Inc., (1928) 127 Me. 91, 141 Atl 321. But see Weyerhaeuser Co. v Clark's Material Supply Co., (1966) 90 Ida. 455, 413 P2d 180; Womack v Ballard Sales Co. (Tex. Civ. App. 1967) 411 SW2d 956.

[40] Consumers' Ice & Coal Co. v Security Bank & Trust Co., (1926) 170 Ark. 530, 280 SW 677.

[41] In re Paul De Laney Co., Inc. (CA-2 1928) 26 F2d 961; Cornelius v C. C. Pictures, Inc. (CA-2 1925) 7 F2d 308; McClean v Bradley (CA-6 1924) 299 F 379; Mary E. Scully v Colonial Trust Company, (1929) 105 N.J. Eq. 309, 147 Atl 776.

[42] Foster v Arata, (1958) 74 Nev. 143, 325 P2d 759.

[43] Schmitz v Wisconsin Soap Mfg. Co., (1931) 204 Wis. 149, 235 NW 409. See also Fischer v Streeter Milling Co., (1931) 60 N.D. 362, 234 NW 392.

misrepresentation and the corporation was adequately capitalized; the stockholder was permitted to share as a general creditor in distribution of corporate assets on dissolution.[44]

A solvent corporation, in the absence of fraud or intent to delay other creditors, may give security for a pre-existing or subsequent debt, even though in the end it thereby effectuates a preference.[45] However, if a corporation is insolvent, a stockholder, director, or officer may not obtain a preference for his debt to the disadvantage of the other creditors.[46] An officer stands in a fiduciary relation to the creditors as well as to the corporation when insolvency occurs, and he will not be permitted to use his official position to the detriment of other creditors.[47] However, in some cases, even an insolvent corporation may borrow from a stockholder, director, or other officer in order to extricate itself from financial embarrassment, and may secure the loan by a lien on its property or a transfer of its assets, as long as the transaction is made in good faith and not for the purpose of obtaining an undue advantage over general creditors.[48]

> *Example:* A mortgage, executed by a corporation to its president as security for a loan, has been declared valid even though the corporation was actually insolvent at the time the mortgage was executed, so long as the transaction was made in good faith and there was no fraud or intent to delay the general creditors of the corporation.[49]

A stockholder, director, or officer who has made a valid loan to a corporation, may like any other creditor, enforce the collection of the debt in a judicial proceeding against the corporation.[50]

When a stockholders' agreement guaranteeing their corporation's debt makes them jointly and severally liable, each is liable in the ratio of the shares each owns, in the absence of other agreement among themselves.[51]

---

[44] Obre v Alban Tractor Co., (1962) 228 Md. 291 179 A2d 861.

[45] Cory v Hamilton Nat'l Bank et al. (CA–6 1929) 31 F2d 379, aff'g. In re Federal Coal Co. (D. Ky. 1927) 31 F2d 375; Cheney v San Francisco Mines, Inc., (1942) 101 Utah 524, 125 P2d 424. To same effect, Advance Dry Wall Co. v Regency Homes, Inc., (1969) 20 Mich. App. 80, 173 NW2d 827.

[46] Synder Electric Co. v Fleming (Minn. S Ct 1981) 305 NW 2d 863; Stuart v Larson (CA–8 1924) 298 F 223; White v Staehly, (1939) 7 Conn. Supp. 71; Gordon v Hartford Sterling Co., (1944) 330 Pa. 277, 38 A2d 229.

[47] Lytle v Andrews (CA–8 1929) 34 F2d 252, aff'g (ND Iowa 1928) 27 F2d 898; In re Salvator Brewing Co. (SD N.Y. 1910) 183 F 910; Tauber v Noble (DC App. 1961) 172 A2d 552.

[48] In re Lake Chelan Land Co. (CA–9 1919) 257 F 497.

[49] Chattanooga Coffin & Casket Co. v Whitley, (1929) 168 Ga. 153, 147 SE 392. See also Jacobs v Colcord, (1929) 136 Okla. 158, 275 P 649.

[50] Western Inn Corp. v Heyl (Tex. Civ. App. 1970) 452 SW2d 752.

[51] Brown v Goldsmith (Supp Ct Okla. 1968) 437 P2d 247.

A creditor can't set aside a corporation's conveyance of its real estate to its president's son, when he doesn't show (1) the corporation was insolvent at the time of the conveyance, or (2) the consideration was unreasonable; later use of that consideration by the corporation to repay its debt to the president isn't an unlawful preference.[52]

The mere fact that a loan from incorporators was not reflected in the minutes does not make it uncollectable, especially when other records showed that an interest-free loan had been made.[53] Nor does the fact that a loan from an officer had been designated a capital contribution make it that, when it was shown that it was given as a loan to enable the corporation to buy needed inventory.[54]

Methods of borrowing. A corporation may either borrow money on its general credit or may give security to ensure repayment of its debt. This is a matter generally decided between the corporation and the lender, and such factors as the financial standing of the corporation, the past dealings of the parties, and the amount to be loaned are considered.

Corporations often raise money on their general credit by issuance of short-term notes or by long-term issues. Collateral security is often given in both instances. Bond issues may be made in the form of debentures, that is, unsecured bonds, but are often secured by a mortgage or a pledge of corporate property. Examples of methods of procuring money on secured credit are the mortgage of specific real or personal property of the corporation, by the pledge of personal property, and by general or blanket mortgages on the presently-owned and after-acquired property.

Raising capital: short-term versus long-term borrowing. Raising funds through the issuance of bonds is known as long-term borrowing; when it is done by issuing notes and other short-term securities it is known as short-term borrowing. Short-term includes financing of merchandise purchased for resale by drafts or bills of exchange drawn by the seller of the goods against credit established at a bank in favor of the buyer. The long-term form of borrowing is peculiar to corporations; the short-term form of borrowing can be used by corporations or by individuals.

Generally it is easier to negotiate short-term loans, chiefly because the lender then has the opportunity at frequent periods to test

[52] Land Red-E-Mixed Concrete Co. v Cash Whitman, Inc. (Mo. S Ct 1968) 425 SW2d 919.
[53] Scott v Potter Plumbing & Heating, Inc. (Mo. App. 1980) 596 SW 2d 492.
[54] Parquette v Arceneaux Music Center, Inc. (La. App. 1982) 425 S 2d 362.

the strength of the corporation and its ability to liquidate the loan. Sometimes, however, the proceeds of the loan are to go into capital assets, such as buildings or machinery, and then the usual form of short-term borrowing through the bank will not be available. Moreover, even where the loan is to go into inventory that is to be turned over, the loan should, as a matter of good finance, be for a long period, if, as inventory is liquidated, new inventory requiring more borrowing will be acquired. In other words, if a loan or series of loans is constantly to appear as a liability it will be cheaper to "fund" the loan, since the interest on a "funded" or bond loan is generally lower than that on a bank loan. On the other hand, interest is payable for use every day of the year and unless the funds are used every day of the year they will be costly for the time used since they will demand interest even when not being used.

Suggestion: If a corporation has use for variable amounts of capital, the excess of the peak demand over the minimum demand should be raised by short-term loans and the minimum demands should be raised by some form of capital financing—either stock or bonds.

Raising capital: issuing stock or bonds. Before determining whether to raise capital by issuing stock or bonds the following considerations should be taken into account:

(1) What is the nature of the corporate business? Usually if there are no salable assets to protect the bond—even though it be a debenture or unsecured bond—a bond issue will not be advisable.
(2) Are the company's earnings sufficiently large and stable to guarantee regular payment of bond interest and thereby avoid the litigation or reorganization that is likely to follow default in interest payment?
(3) Can bonds be sold at a low enough rate of return to make the risk worth while?
(4) Since bonds mature and must be paid off (this is the usual rule but it is not universal, for bonds may be made perpetual or for so long a period that they may be regarded as perpetual), will the company want and be able to meet that obligation in the future?
(5) What will the bankers who will offer the securities be able to market best—stocks or bonds—giving due regard to the desires of their customers?
(6) In the current business cycle, are people taking bonds or stocks? Bonds are more attractive when it is expected that interest rates will fall.
(7) Tax consequences are important: payments of interest on bonds are deductible by the corporation; payments of dividends on stock aren't.

Note: There is another factor, though not specifically a financial one: bondholders ordinarily are not given a voice in management—stockholders are.

Definition of a mortgage. A mortgage is a conveyance of real or personal property to a creditor as security for the repayment of a loan. The mortgagor has the right to redeem the property by payment of the debt within the time specified in the conveyance. Under the law of some states, title to the property does not pass to the mortgagee—the mortgage merely creates a lien on the property that may be foreclosed if the mortgagor defaults in his payment.

The right of the mortgagor to redeem his property may be denied upon his failure to fulfill the terms of the mortgage, either through court procedure or pursuant to statutory authority. Most states will not permit a strict foreclosure by the mortgagee immediately following default by the mortgagor, but allow a certain period for redemption. When foreclosure proceedings are instituted in a court, the court will either decree a sale of the mortgaged property, or set a certain period within which the mortgagor must pay his debt; if he fails to pay within that time he forfeits his right to redeem the property. When foreclosure is had without court proceedings pursuant to statutory authority, the mortgage usually contains a power of sale; the terms under which the sale may be made and the requisite amount of notice that must be given are generally set forth in the statute or incorporated in the mortgage contract.

A mortgage of corporate property may also be given to secure loans to be made in the future, in which event the mortgage does not become operative until the loan is actually made. Property mortgaged to secure future advances is subject to the claims of general creditors until the lien accrues.[55]

A corporation cannot disclaim the validity of a mortgage it put on its property on the ground that it was for the benefit only of a third party, its sole stockholder, and even though it was to secure a pre-existing debt.[56] And a contractor could properly assert the validity of his mechanic's lien over a mortgage placed by a bank on the corporation's property even though he owned two sevenths of the corporation's stock, since the stockholders are separate from their corporation.[57]

---

[55] Brown v Gunthrie, (1888) 110 N.Y. 435, 18 NE 254.
[56] Continental Bank of Pennsylvania v Barclay Riding Academy, (1983) 95 N J 153, 459 A 2d 1163.
[57] Northwestern Nat'l Bank of Sioux City v Metro Center, Inc. (Iowa S Ct 1981) 303 N W 2d 395.

Authorization of a mortgage. The power to incure a debt carries with it the authority to give security for its repayment and a corporation has the implied authority to mortgage any part or all of its property to secure a loan which is necessary to the furtherance of corporate purposes.[58]

The authority to mortgage corporate property is vested in the board of directors unless it is placed elsewhere by charter, statute, or by-law provision.[59]

A mortgage, executed without previous authority of the directors, is valid against later judgment creditors and against a mechanic's lienor who filed his lien after the mortgage was authorized.[60]

Where directors alone have power to authorize a mortgage, a resolution of the stockholders directing officers to execute a mortgage is not a sufficient authorization.[61] Corporate officers have no power to mortgage corporate property merely by virtue of their official position.[62] However, the corporation can give the officer authority bind the corporation either by express resolution of the board of directors; or it may be implied from the apparent power which the corporation holds the officer out as possessing. A corporation cannot deny the validity of a mortgage on the ground that the officers executing it were not authorized to do so by a resolution, when the corporation has accepted the benefits of the mortgage.[63]

A chattel mortgage signed by the president and secretary, who constituted a majority of the board, was held valid.[64] When the board

---

[58] Bell & Coggeshall Co. v Kentucky Glass Works, (1899) 106 Ky. 7, 50 SW 2, 1092, dis. op., 51 SW 180; City of Williston v Ludowese, (1926) 53 N.D. 797, 208 NW 82.

[59] First Nat. Bank v Casselton, (1919) 44 N.D. 353, 175 NW 720; Peyton v Sturgis, (1918), Tex. Civ. App. 202 SW 205. Bordy v Goodman-Buckley Trust Co., (1936) 131 Neb. 347, 268 NW 286.

[60] Attleboro Braiding Co. v Delhi Braiding Co., (1930) 137 Misc. 615, 245 N.Y.S. 92.

[61] Blood v La Serena Land & Water Co., (1896) 113 Cal. 221, 226, 45 P 252.

[62] Flint v Farwell, (1922) 192 Ind. 439, 134 NE 664; Grafeman Dairy Co. v Northwestern Bank, (1921) 290 Mo. 311, 235 SW 435; Lycette v Green River Gorge, Inc., (1944) 21 Wash. 2d 859, 153 P2d 873; First Nat'l Bank v Tri-State Repair & Equipment Co., (1930) 108 W. Va. 686, 152 SE 635; In re National Consumers Exchange (CA–4 1922) 284 F 764; In re Joseph (WD, N.Y. 1931) 46 F2d 324; Fisher v Peter Milling Co., (1931) 60 N.D. 362, 234 NW 392, (1956) 334 Mass. 100, Kagan v Levenson (Mass. S. 134 NE2d 415.

[63] Dowdle v Central Brick Co., (1934) 206 Ind. 242, 189 NE 145; Trifield v Winchester Dev. Co. et al, (1928) 105 N.J. Eq. 50, 146 Atl 873; Ekstrom v D. Dierssen, Inc., (1935) 180 Wash. 493, 40 P2d 138; Fed. Min. & Engineering Co. v Pollak, (1939) 59 Nev. 145, 85 P2d 1008. A mortgagee who took title to property when a real estate investment trust defaulted on a loan was not guilty of fraud though the transfer of that property by the corporation that owned it to the trust had been fraudulent as to the corporation's creditors, when the mortgagee had no actual knowledge of the fraudulent plan, and a title search revealed nothing; the court refused to attribute the mortgagee's attorneys' knowledge to the mortgagee. Bastianelli v Toco International, Inc. (N.H. S Ct 1977) 375 A2d 595.

[64] First Nat'l Bank v Frazier, (1933) 133 Ore. 662, 22 P2d 325. Compare In re J.A.M.A. Realty Corp. v Goess (CA–2 1937) 92 F2d 3; Wilcox v Goess (CA–2 1937) 92 F2d 8.

of directors authorizes the execution of a mortgage, the resolution should clearly designate the officer who is to execute it.

Some states still require the consent of the stockholders to a valid execution of a mortgage on corporate property, at least if the corporation's bonded debt rises.

Those statutes that require the consent of the stockholders before execution of a mortgage should be distinguished from statutes that don't limit the powers of the board of directors in mortgaging the corporate property, but that are intended to give the requisite number of stockholders power, if they so elect, to compel the directors to make a sale of, or to mortgage, all of the corporate property.[65] Where the statute provides that the consent to a mortgage shall be evidenced by a vote appearing on the corporate records, or by written consents filed with the corporation, and no provision is made in the statute for the withdrawal of consent, a withdrawal, in order to be effective, must be by vote at a proper meeting or must be in writing, filed with the corporation.[66] Such statutes must, of course, be complied with.[67] A mortgage authorized only by directors was valid when the directors owned the amount of stock required by statute to authorize the mortgage.[68]

A mortgagee can't take advantage of its agent's error when, upon his advice, a borrowing corporation executed a mortgage by consent of the directors rather than of the stockholders as required by statute.[69]

But an existing mortgage upon property purchased by the corporation may be assumed as part of the payment price upon authorization of the directors alone, without the consent of the stockholders,[70] even if stockholders have a right to determine whether a mortgage shall be placed upon corporate property.

Effect of failure to comply with statutory requirements in executing mortgage. The burden of proving that a mortgage was

---

[65] Godfrey L. Cabot, Inc. v Gas Products Co., (1933) 93 Mont. 497, 19 P2d 878.

[66] Stott v Stott Realty Co., (1929) 246 Mich. 261, 224 NW 621.

[67] In re Astell Eng. & Iron Works (CA-2 1922) 284 F 967; Mettaloid Co. v Luboil Refining Co., (1929) 85 Col. 146, 274 P 826; Leffert v Jackman, (1919) 227 N.Y. 310, 125 NE 446; Maryland Casualty Co. v Schaefer, (1930) 141 Misc. 629, 253 N.Y.S. 709.

[68] Royal Con. Min. Co. v Royal Con. Mines, (1910) 157 Cal. 737, 110 P 123; Timmer v Crimmins, (1933) 262 Mich. 314, 247 NW 191. See also Matter of Endicott Laundry Co., Inc., (1926) 128 Misc. 413, 219 N.Y.S. 632.

[69] Atlas Finance Corp. v Trocchi, (1939) 302 Mass. 477, 19 NE2d 722.

[70] In re Beaver Knitting Mills (CA-2 1907) 154 F 320.

executed without the required consent of the stockholders, or by officers without proper authorization, falls upon the persons attacking the validity of the mortgage. There is a presumption, in the absence of proof to the contrary, that the mortgage has been authorized in accordance with the requirements.[71] Failure to comply with the formal requirements of a statute as to obtaining stockholder consent to a mortgage of corporate property may be questioned only by the stockholders.[72] General creditors of the corporation cannot avail themselves of that failure to set aside the conveyance so as to subject the mortgaged property to the payment of their debts,[73] nor can a trustee in bankruptcy.[74]

Even stockholders may be barred by delay from attacking the mortgage.[75] Although general creditors can't set aside the mortgage for want of due execution, trust receipt holders can.[76] But when the certificate of stockholder consent, prescribed by statute, was filed after a mechanic's lien had attached, the mortgage was subordinated.[77]

Where consent of the stockholders is required by statute, the corporation must, of course, comply with the provision,[78] but a mortgage will not be declared invalid merely because certain specified procedures were not followed.[79] A mortgage of all the corporate property without stockholder consent is voidable, but it can be ratified by the stockholders.[80] However, a mortgage executed in the name of a proposed corporation is invalid and can't be ratified.[81] Also, stockholders' general acquiescence in anything a dominating officer might do is not sufficient approval of a chattel mortgage executed by him when there is no showing that the corporation benefited in any way.[82]

---

[71] Austin v Dermott Canning Co., (1931) 182 Ark. 1128, 34 SW2d 773; Denike v N.Y. and R. Lime, etc. Co., (1880) 80 N.Y. 599.

[72] Metalloid Co. v Luboil Refining Co. et al, (1929) 85 Colo. 146, 274 P 826; Day v Jade Contracting Co., (1920) App. Term 181 N.Y.S. 740.

[73] In re Constantine Tobacco Co. (CA–2 1923) 290 F 128.

[74] U.S. v Jones (CA–10 1956) 229 F2d 84.

[75] Gallup v Pring, (1941) 108 Colo. 277, 116 P2d 202.

[76] In re James, Inc. (CA–2 1929) 30 F2d 555.

[77] Cohn v Gersh Realty Corp., (1930) 137 Misc. 245, 242 N.Y.S. 671. See also, In re Victoria Fusilli Co. (CA–2 1935) 79 F2d 611; Timmer v Crimmins, (1933) 262 Mich. 314, 247 NW 191.

[78] In re James, Inc. (CA–2 1929) 30 F2d 555; In re Astell Eng. & Iron Works (CA–2 1922) 284 F 967; Leffert v Jackman, (1919) 227 N.Y. 310, 125 NE 446; Cohn v Gersh Realty Corp., (1930) 137 Misc. 245, 242 N.Y.S. 671.

[79] McCarty v Nostrand Lumber Co., (1931) 232 A.D. 63, 248 N.Y.S. 606.

[80] Greene v R.F.C. (CA–1 1938) 100 F2d 34.

[81] In re Jeandros Dye & Print Works, Inc. (D Mass 1938) 22 F Supp 26.

[82] In re J. A. M. A. Realty Corp. v Goess (CA–2 1937) 92 F2d 3.

Examples: If the stockholders do not actually vote on the mortgage as required by statute, but acquiesce in its validity by permitting the corporation to receive the benefits thereof, the mortgage is valid.[83] A failure of the stockholders to vote upon the execution of a mortgage has been held to be cured by a subsequent resolution ratifying the acts of the board of directors in authorizing the mortgage.[84] Failure to make a written authorization required by the statute, can be cured by the personal participation of a majority of the stockholders in the act of executing the mortgage.[85] General creditors are precluded from impeaching the validity of a mortgage on the ground of informality in the proceedings in which consent was given, if all the stockholders were present at the meeting and voted in favor of the execution of the mortgage.[86] Nor will the corporation be permitted to set up technical objections to the validity of a mortgage it has allowed to stand for a long period of time.[87]

Statutory requirements regarding the recording of mortgages are designed for the protection of the mortgagor's creditors and for subsequent purchasers of and holders of liens on the corporate property and should be complied with. In some states, an affidavit of consideration must accompany and be recorded with the mortgage.[88] A failure to record a mortgage will not invalidate it as between the mortgagor and the mortgagee.[89]

An attorney who failed to file certain chattel mortgages was held liable to his client for the negligent discharge of his duties.[90]

Mortgaging after-acquired property. A corporation can mortgage property that it expects to acquire, the mortgage being enforced as an agreement to give a lien upon the property as between the mortgagor and the mortgagee.[91] The mortgage must specifically state that the lien

---

[83] In re Paul De Laney Co., Inc. (CA–2 1928) 26 F2d 961; see also In re Paul De Laney Co., Inc. (WD N.Y. 1929) 33 F2d 945.

[84] Stott v Stott Realty Co., (1929) 246 Mich. 261, 224 NW 621.

[85] Liverpool & London & Globe Ins. Co. Ltd. v Aleman Planting & Mfg. Co., (1928) 166 La. 457, 117 So 554; Sun Coal Corp. v New Upper Lehigh Coal Co., (1941) 340 Pa. 547, 17 A2d 885.

[86] Wm. Firth Co. v S. Carolina Loan & Trust Co. (CA–4 1903) 122 F 569.

[87] New Blue Point Mining Co. v Weissbein, (1926) 198 Cal. 261, 244 P 325; Ponsiglione v Gee Jay Ess Realty Holding Corp., (1949) 121 NYLJ 2137; Sun Coal Corp. v New Upper Lehigh Coal Co., (1941) 340 Pa. 547, 17 A2d 885.

[88] Mitschele-Baer, Inc. v Livingston Sand & Gravel Sales Co., (1931) 108 N.J. Eq. 286, 154 Atl 752.

[89] Martin v Bankers Trust Co., (1916) 18 Ariz. 55, 156 P 87; Karasik v People's Trust Co. (E.D. N.Y. 1917) 252 F 324; Grand Victory Theatre Co. v Solomon, (1923) 224 Mich. 451, 195 NW 132.

[90] Degen v Steinbrink, (1922) 202 App. Div. 477, 195 N.Y.S. 810, aff'd 236 N.Y. 669, 142 NE 328.

[91] Monmouth County Elec. Co. v McKenna, (1905) 68 N.J. Eq. 160, 60 Atl 32.

is to cover property yet to be acquired, or the language used must clearly show that this was the intention of the parties.[92] Some statutes expressly grant the power to mortgage after-acquired property.[93]

After-acquired property may consist of either real property, chattels or personal property,[94] or future income.[95]

An after-acquired property clause in a corporate mortgage may have an effect upon acquisitions made by virtue of corporate powers existing at the date of the mortgage different from the effect upon acquisitions acquired under later charter amendments.[96]

Rights of the parties under a mortgage of after-acquired real property. The mortgagee's lien usually attaches to after-acquired real property as soon as the property comes into the possession of the mortgagor.[97] However the mortgagee's lien is subject to the priority of other liens that may have attached to the property before it came into the hands of the mortgagor.[98]

> *Example:* If a mortgagor of after-acquired property buys property that is encumbered with a mechanic's lien, and the seller of the property has a lien on it for its purchase prices, both liens are superior to the mortgagee's lien.[99]

Rights of parties under mortgage of after-acquired personal property. As a general rule there must be an intervening act by the mortgagee before he can establish his rights under a mortgage of after-acquired personal property, to the exclusion of claims of the general creditors of the corporation, as for example, where the mortgagee takes possession of the property.[100]

In some states, by express statutory provision, a lien is created when the mortgagor comes into possession, and no further act is necessary. Under a mortgage covering all the property held by a corporation doing a mechanical business, and any improvements

---

[92] Merchants & Farmers Bank v Pearson, (1923) 186 N.C. 609, 120 SE 210.

[93] Cummings v Consolidated Mineral Water Co., (1905) 27 R.I. 195, 61 Atl 353.

[94] Pierce v Bound Brook Engine & Mfg. Co. (D N.J. 1921) 274 F 221; Commercial Trust Co. v L. Wertheim Coal & Coke Co., (1917) 88 N.J. Eq. 143, 102 Atl 448 (covering book accounts).

[95] Atlantic Trust Co. v Dana (CA-8 1903) 128 F 209.

[96] Bear Lake & River Water Works & Irrigation Co. v Garland, (1896) 164 US 1, 17 S Ct 7; Union Trust Co. v Southern Sawmills & Lumber Co. (CA-4 1908) 166 F 193 (1935).

[97] In re Adamant Plaster Co. (ND N.Y. 1905) 137 F 251.

[98] Shooters Island Shipyard Co. v Standard Shipbuilding Corp. (CA-3 1923) 293 F 706; U.S. Iron Pipe & Foundry Co. v Henry Vogt Mach. Co., (1918) 182 Ky. 473, 206 SW 806.

[99] Cummings v Cons. Mineral Water Co., (1905) 27 R.I. 195, 61 Atl 353.

[100] Roebling's Sons Co. v Neb. Elec. Co., (1921) 106 Neb. 255, 183 NW 546.

made thereafter, the mortgagee's lien attaches immediately upon the acquisition of the new property by the corporation.[101] As usual, statutory provisions are all-important in determining how the lien is created.

Mortgage of future income. Unless a statute says otherwise, a mortgage of after-acquired property may include future earnings of the corporation, if the mortgage so says. However, the mortgagee's lien does not attach to future earnings as long as the mortgagor is in possession of its property and has control over the receipt and disposition of its income.

No rights accrue to the mortgagee until default by the mortgagor. General creditors of the mortgagor have a prior right to the corporate earnings up to the time the mortgagee asserts his claim by taking possession of the corporate property. The lien then attaches to any income earned after the mortgagee takes possession but not to income earned after default in payment of the mortgage debt but before the taking of possession.[102] Judgment creditors of the mortgagor have the right to have their claims paid out of the corporate income, but the mortgagee may defeat this right by foreclosing his mortgage immediately upon default of the mortgagor to pay the mortgage debt, and applying the corporate earnings to the satisfaction of his debt.[103]

Power to mortgage corporate franchise. Some corporations, most commonly railroads and public utilities, are given rights or franchises, like the power to condemn property for rights of way, utility lines and the like. That kind of right is a property of the corporation—like other corporate rights, it can be mortgaged.[104]

Partial release of mortgaged property. A corporation cannot sell mortgaged property without the mortgagee's consent. So a clause providing for the release of part of the property, subject of course, to certain enumerated conditions, is incorporated in most corporate mortgages. Under such a clause the board of directors generally passes a resolution authorizing the application to the mortgagee for a release. The mortgagee then executes an instrument releasing his right, title and interest in the property to be sold. This release must be filed and recorded in the same manner as the original mortgage. The proceeds of

---

[101] Valdosta & W. R. R. Co. v Atlantic Coast Line R. R. Co., (1918) 148 Ga. 842, 98 SE 465; Roebling's Sons Co. v Neb. Elec. Co., (1921) 106 Neb. 255, 183 NW 546.

[102] Zartman v First Nat'l Bank, (1907) 189 N.Y. 267, 82 NE 806.

[103] Atlantic Trust Co. v Dana (CA–8 1903) 128 F 209.

[104] First Union Trust & Sav. Bank v Miss. Power Co., (1933) 167 Miss. 876, 150 So 381.

the sale of the property are then deposited with the mortgagee or for his benefit. However, it is often provided that the mortgagor may substitute other property of equal value to replace property released under a mortgage lien, in lieu of placing the proceeds of the sale in trust for the mortgagee.

> **Note:** Releases of property subject to a mortgagee's lien are often desired when the mortgagor no longer needs the property.

Real estate mortgages. A mortgage on specific real property of the corporation is called a special mortgage, as distinguished from a general mortgage, which the corporation may place upon all its property, present and future. As a general rule, the duration of the special mortgage is comparatively short. The borrower executes: (1) a mortgage, which creates the security interest in the lender, and (2) a bond or a note, which is the evidence of the debt.[105] The real estate mortgage is executed in the same manner as a deed of real property, and in most states must be recorded in the place where the property is situated.

Personal property mortgages. In the absence of statutory restriction, any personal property of the corporation may be mortgaged. The rules for mortgages of corporate personal property are usually found in the Uniform Commercial Code.

Only such property as is mentioned in the mortgage is covered by the lien. Like the mortgage of real estate, the mortgage of personal property is a special mortgage.

> **Suggestion:** A description of the property, so specific as to admit of no dispute as to its identity, should be incorporated in the resolution authorizing the execution of the mortgage, and in the mortgage itself.

Chattel mortgages. Before the widespread adoption of the Uniform Commercial Code chattel mortgages were often used by corporate borrowers. When the mortgage did not actually secure any debt of the corporation, but was in reality an illegal dividend to stockholders, it was invalid as to creditors.[106] An affidavit of good faith, to the effect that the chattel mortgage was made without any design to hinder, delay, or defraud creditors, or an affidavit of consideration,[107] sometimes had to be executed. A corporation could

---

[105] Martin v Bankers Trust Co., (1916) 18 Ariz. 55, 156 P 87.
[106] In re Bay Ridge Inn, Inc. (CA-2 1938) 98 F2d 85.
[107] In re Central Stamping & Mfg. Co. (ED Mich. 1948) 77 F Supp 331.

get credit by giving and renewing its promissory note and it could secure the payment of the note by giving a chattel mortgage.[108]

Distinction between chattel mortgage and conditional sale. Before the widespread adoption of the Uniform Commercial Code it was sometimes important to distinguish chattel mortgages from conditional sales. While the attributes of a conditional sale varied according to the statutes and decisions of each state, the feature that differentiated it from a chattel mortgage was this: In the chattel mortgage, title passed to the buyer upon the execution of the instrument, while in the conditional sale, title was expressly reserved by the seller,[109] until the performance of some condition, like payment of the purchase price.[110]

Distinction between chattel mortgage and pledge of property. The chief difference between a pledge and a mortgage is that a pledge requires delivery of the property given to secure the indebtedness.[111] The pledge, as a rule, need not be in writing.[112] A mortgage may be valid without delivery of the property, and is generally formally executed, like a conveyance of property. The pledge never passes title to the pledgee, but merely creates a lien on the property. The property that is deposited as security is taken back upon payment of a certain sum. While a chattel mortgage may also create only a lien, in some states it conveys title to the property to the mortgagee, with a right in the mortgagor to redeem upon payment of a certain sum. The intention of the parties determines whether the transaction is a mortgage or a pledge of property. If there is doubt as to whether it is one or the other, the law favors the conclusion that it is a pledge.[113] Accounts receivable may be pledged,[114] as well as bonds,[115] and stocks. Pledges are now covered by the Uniform Commercial Code.

Note that statutory requirements must be strictly observed: A verbal notice of intention to reclaim stock will not suffice when a written notice is required.[116]

The Uniform Commercial Code. The Uniform Commercial Code completely rewrote and changed previous laws on many subjects, for

---

[108] Schwartz v Maguire, (1941) 130 N.J. Eq. 152, 21 A2d 670, modified and aff'd, (1942) 131 N.J. Eq. 578, 25 A2d 920.

[109] Bice v Harold L. Arnold, Inc., (1925) 75 Cal. App. 629, 243 P 468.

[110] McDaniel v Chiaramonte, (1921) 61 Or. 403, 122 P 33.

[111] People's Bank of Harrisville v Continental Supply Co., (1926) 213 Ky. 44 280 SW 458.

[112] Oden v Vaughn, (1920) 204 Ala. 445, 85 So 779.

[113] Martin v Bankers Trust Co., (1916) 18 Ariz. 55, 156 P 87.

[114] Houston v Gregg, (1918) Tex., 282 SW 805.

[115] Worth v Marshall Field & Co., (CA-4 1917) 240 F 395.

[116] Szelaga v Farega Realty Corp. (NY App. Div. 1983) No 45483, 469 NYS 2d 271.

example, sales, negotiable instruments and secured transactions in personal property. The code has been adopted by all the states except Louisiana.

Security transactions in personal property, including sales of accounts and contract rights are covered in Article 9 of the Code. The Article repeals and supersedes the Conditional Sales Act, Chattel Mortgage Act, and Trust Receipts Act. It governs secured transactions.

Article 9 abolishes all distinctions, *as to their effect,* among the traditional forms of security agreements. For example, although the *forms* of conditional sale, bailment lease, chattel mortgage, and trust receipt may still be used, the choice of one rather than the other will not affect the applicability of Article 9—whichever form is used, the provisions of Article 9 as to filing, and the rights and remedies of the parties, for instance, must still be complied with.

As to matters not covered by Article 9, the parties may make any agreement they choose. For example, it is immaterial under Article 9 whether title to the property is in the buyer or the seller. If the parties for tax or other reasons want title to remain in the seller they may use the pertinent form of agreement for their state—a conditional sale, for example. The distinction made by Article 9 are on the type of property that form the collateral—inventory, equipment, consumer goods, farm products. In practice, the traditional forms of security agreement—conditional sale, for example—remain in common use in Code states.

Power to pledge personal property—unissued stock or bonds. A corporation may pledge its personal property unless restricted by charter, statutory, or by-law provision. By statute in some states, stockholder consent must be obtained. A pledge of personal property unlike a mortgage need not be in writing,[117] but the property must be delivered to the pledgee.[118] Title, however, does not pass upon delivery but remains in the pledgor.[119]

As a general rule, a corporation may pledge its unissued stock to secure the repayment of a loan, unless prohibitory provisions are found in the charter or statute. If the face value of the stock exceeds the amount of the loan to be secured, it may be pledged to the debtor though a statute bars the issuance of stock except for labor done,

---

[117] Oden v Vaughn, (1920) 204 Ala. 445, 85 So 779.

[118] People's Bank v Continental Supply Co., (1926) 213 Ky. 44, 280 SW 458; MacQueen v Dollar Sav. Bank Co., (1938) 133 Ohio St. 579, 15 NE2d 529.

[119] Ownership of stock didn't pass to pledgee to whom it was transferred, when the transfer was made to increase the value of the pledge by having dividends accrue to the pledgee. Steiner v Zammut (La. App. 1973) 279 S2d 728. (*Ed. note:* Louisiana is the only non-code state.)

services performed, or money or property actually received.[120] There is a conflict of authority as to whether, under such a statutory provision, unissued stock may be pledged for an antecedent debt. The better authority seems to be that such a statutory prohibition bars the corporation from pledging its unissued stock as collateral security for the payment of an antecedent debt.[121]

A corporation may pledge its bonds, subject, of course, to any regulations that the state may have imposed upon it.[122] Bonds pledged by a corporation have the status of bonds issued, and are subject to the rules governing the issuance of bonds. Bonds, pledged as collateral security for a loan made to a corporation owning all the pledgor-corporation's stock are enforceable even though no consideration passes to the pledgor, when there are no creditors of the pledgor, nor any stockholders to complain.[123]

Bona fide holders of pledged bonds can demand payment of coupons falling due before maturity of the debts which the bonds were given to secure.[8] Though a note for which collateral security has been pledged is outlawed by the statute of limitations, the borrower can't recover the security unless he repays the note.[124]

Procedure upon default in contract of pledge. The pledgee does not acquire an absolute title to the pledged property by the failure of the pledgor to pay the debt on time. Upon default, the pledgee may either sell the property without judicial process, on reasonable notice to the pledgor, or maintain an action in equity in the nature of a foreclosure and get a decree for the judicial sale of the property. When the claim of the pledgee is satisfied, the surplus, if any, is transferred to the pledgor.

In the absence of any statutory requirement, the pledgee must give public notice of the sale of the pledged property. Mailing notice of an intended sale to the pledgor alone is insufficient.[125] And the pledgee of stock in an unlisted, little known corporation, who is given the power upon the pledgor's default to sell the stock at public sale without notice, must nevertheless give sufficient notice to "alert investors and invite competition." Publication in newspapers of the number of

---

[120]Granite Brick Co. v Titus (CA–4 1915) 226 F 557; Turner v Tjosevig—Kennecott Copper Co., (1921) 116 Wash. 223, 199 P 312.
[121]Central Lumber Co. v Fall, (1924) Tex. Civ. App. 264 SW 513.
[122]Central Trust Co. v Southern Oil Corp. (CA–8 1925) 8 F2d 338.
[123]Harvey v Guaranty Trust Co., (1929) 134 Misc. 417, 236 N.Y.S. 37.
[124]Cloverdale Cotton Mills v Ala. Nat'l Bank, (1929) 219 Ala. 50, 121 So 54.
[125]See Richardson v Foster, (1918) 100 Wash. 57, 170 P 321.

shares to be sold, the corporate name and the state of incorporation is not enough.[126] If the contract fixes no time within which the property must be redeemed and the statute does not otherwise provide, the pledgor has a right to redeem until the property is sold. This right remains with him during his lifetime, unless the pledgee calls upon him to redeem and upon failure to do so, sells the property; if the pledgor dies before such call and sale, the right of redemption descends to his representatives.[127] The right of the pledgor cannot be cut off by a simple notice that, if he fails to pay within a specified time, the pledgee will claim the property as his own.[128] Nor can a pledgee transfer pledged stock to himself on the pledgor's default (even though the pledge agreement permits it) if (1) the stock is worth more than the debt, and (2) the pledgee doesn't really want his money back but is seeking a large position in the stock.[129]

Bond issues in general. A corporate bond, whether or not secured, is a long-term promissory note, distinguished from the ordinary promissory note only by its length and complexity. When bonds are sold to the public, the bonds themselves usually contain only a summary of the terms and conditions of the debt while the underlying contract—the "trust indenture"—is made with a trustee for the bond-holders. The bond is the evidence of the contract between the corporation and the bondholder. Its terms cannot be changed by the corporation without the holder's consent.[130]

When a bond is issued under a trust deed, the bond generally refers to the trust deed for a statement of the rights of the bondholders. While these terms and conditions generally must be complied with, the corporation may be barred from denying the validity of the bonds on the ground that some condition was not met. For example, where the trust deed required that a certificate be attached to each bond, executed by the trustee, to the effect that it was one issued under the trust deed, and no certificate was attached, the corporation could not deny the validity of the bonds when it had sold the bonds and kept the proceeds; the provision was waived.[131]

---

[126] In re Kiamie's Estate, (1955) 309 N.Y. 325, 130 NE2d 745.
[127] White River Savings Bank v Capital Savings Bank, (1904) 77 Vt. 123, 59 Atl 197.
[128] Groeltz v Cole, (1905) 128 Iowa 340, 103 NW 977.
[129] Elmer v Elmer (La. Ct of App. 1967) 203 S2d 391.
[130] Heider v Hermann Sons Hall Ass'n, (1932) 186 Minn. 494, 243 NW 699.
[131] Easton v Butterfield Live Stock Co. et al, (1929) 48 Idaho 153, 279 P 716. See, to the same effect, Hicks v Fruen Cereal Co., (1930) 182 Minn. 93, 233 NW 828.

A bondholder is not ordinarily bound by limitations on his right to sue, contained only in the trust deed.[132] An instrument is not necessarily a bond because it is so labeled.[133]

> *Example:* A "bond" entitling the holder to a share of the profits of the corporation is held to be a certificate of stock, not a bond.

On the other hand an instrument labeled something else, as, for example, a certificate of stock, may be a bond and so treated.[134] The test usually applied is this: Generally, the special feature of the debtor-creditor relation is the presence of a fixed maturity date at which time the holder can demand payment whether or not there are net earnings. If the instrument has this feature, it's a bond or debenture and not stock.[135]

A bond needn't be in any particular form.[136] However, if bonds are to be listed on a securities exchange they must be prepared in accordance with the requirements of the exchange.

Since a bond is a contract, to sue on it a bondholders' committee must either own some bonds or have received an assignment to sue from the bondholders.[137] Directors who induce the corporation to break a contract with its bondholders by pledging assets in violation of a covenant in the bond, may be held personally liable for damages resulting to bondholders. However, if the directors acted jointly with others a release given to the others discharges them.[138]

The validity of a contract generally is determined by the law of the place where made. If valid there, it is valid everywhere.[139] For an obligation evidenced by an instrument, such as a bond, the place where it is "made" is the place of its delivery.[140]

Bonds, if not in default, usually don't give the holders any voice in the management of the corporation and usually provide for the

---

[132] Betts v Mass. Cities Realty Co., (1939) 304 Mass. 117, 23 NE2d 152; Guardian Depositors Corp. v David Stott Flour Mills, Inc., (1939) 291 Mich. 180, 289 NW 122; Perry v Darlington Fireproofing Co., (1945) 76 Ohio App. 101, 63 NE2d 222. But see Mitchell v Madison Avenue Offices, Inc., (1933) 147 Misc. 149, 263 N.Y.S. 442.

[133] Heider v Hermann Sons Hall Ass'n, (1932) 186 Minn. 494, 243 NW 699.

[134] First Nat. Bank v Baltimore (D. Md. 1939) 27 F Supp 444.

[135] Com'r v H. P. Hood & Sons (CA-1 1944) 141 F2d 467.

[136] Cass v Realty Securities Co., (1912) 148 App. Div. 96, 132 N.Y.S. 1074, aff'd in 206 N.Y. 649, 99 NE 1105.

[137] Meyer v Lowry & Co., Inc., (1939) 257 A.D. 81, 12 N.Y.S.2d 177.

[138] Aiken v Insull (CA-7 1941) 122 F2d 746, and De Met's, Inc. v Insull (CA-7 1941) 122 F2d 755, cert den, (1942) 315 US 806, 62 S Ct 638, 639.

[139] Mutual Life Ins. Co. v Liebing, (1922) 259 US 209, 42 S Ct 467.

[140] In re Motor Products Mfg. Corp. (CA-9 1936) 85 F2d 381. See also Central Hanover Bank & Trust Co. v Siemens & Halske Aktiengesellschaft (SD N.Y. 1936) 15 F Supp 927, aff'd (CA-2 1936) 84 F2d 993.

payment of a definite principal amount on a certain date with specified interest in the meantime payable regularly. But sometimes "hybrid" securities are issued trying to combine the features of both bonds and stock.[141]

Tax factors in issuing bonds. While corporate earnings may be paid out in dividends or accumulated for future distribution to the owners, dividends are taxable income to the shareholders so that a second tax is imposed on the same money. To lessen the tax bite, corporations generally strive for a proper balance between bonds and stock in light of the corporation's overall capital structure, including the availability of deductions for interest, salaries, depreciation, and the like.

> *Example:* Individuals want to form a corporation with $200,000 in capital. If they issue $200,000 in stock, they'll get no interest deduction. On the other hand, by issuing $50,000 of stock, and $150,000 in bonds or notes, the following advantages are available:
>
> (1) The redemption of bonds, if used, permits a tax-free recovery of cost without reference to the corporation's earned surplus, while a redemption of stock with earned surplus might be taxed as a dividend.[142]
> (2) If notes are used, their payment would be a return of capital without tax consequences as long as the indebtedness was genuine.[143]
> (3) Interest paid or accrued on either bonds or notes is deductible by the corporation.
> (4) On liquidation, the shareholder—debtor would share with other creditors of the same class.

In most cases, the tax advantages increase as the ratio of debt (bonds or notes) increases, i.e., the equity is *thinned*. But this can be overdone. If the corporation is found to be undercapitalized, the so-called debt would represent equity investment—so, without a bona fide debt, the interest payments would be taxable to the recipients as dividends and wouldn't be deductible to the corporation.

> **Caution:** Repayments of the principal could also result in taxable dividend income to the extent of the corporation's earnings and profits.[144]

---

[141] In re Fechheimer Fishel Co. (CA–2 1914) 212 F 357; Kettenhofen v Sterling Oil Co., (1937) 226 Wis. 178, 275 NW 425.
[142] Silver v US (D. Mont. 1963) 215 F Supp 477.
[143] Haley v US (D. Ore. 1959) 5 AFTR2d 365.
[144] Himmel v Com'r (CA–2 1964) 338 F2d 815.

How thin the corporation may be made without fear of the above treatment depends on more than the mere debt-equity ratio, however. Other related considerations are the availability of credit to the corporation and whether the debt is in proportion to stock ownership.

Note: The Internal Revenue Service may disallow interest deductions even though the purported debt is held by a non-shareholder, if the money loaned to the corporation is, in reality, risk capital.[145]

The Trust Indenture Act of 1939. The Trust Indenture Act of 1939 regulates trust indentures covering bonds, debentures, notes and like securities that are publicly offered by the means and instrumentalities of transportation or communication in interstate commerce. The purposes of the Act are: (1) to provide full and fair disclosure of the essential provisions of the indenture at original issue and throughout the life of the securities issued under the indenture; (2) to provide machinery for such continuing disclosure and to enable security holders to unite for the protection of their own interests; (3) to assure security holders that they will have the services of a disinterested trustee, who will conform to the high standards of conduct observed by the more conscientious trust institutions; and (4) to provide minimum standards of qualifications of corporate trustees and of terms of indentures. The standards prescribed affect those provisions of the indenture that relate to the protection and enforcement of the rights of the investors.

These purposes are sought to be accomplished by requiring that indentures subject to the Act shall be "qualified" as conforming to specific statutory requirements expressed in the Act. Securities exempted from the provisions of the Securities Act of 1933, with a few exceptions, are exempt from the Trust Indenture Act. Certain small issues are also exempt. Indentures covering securities required to be registered under the Securities Act of 1933 do not require formal qualification; the registration requirements are sufficient to assure a trust indenture that conforms with the Trust Indenture Act. To qualify a trust indenture covering securities not required to be registered under the Securities Act, the issuer must file an application with the Securities and Exchange Commission (SEC). The processing of this application is a check-up on the provisions of the trust indenture to see that they conform with the law.

The SEC is entrusted with the duty of seeing that the terms of each indenture conform to the Act. It has no power to enforce the provisions

---

[145]The Motel Co. v Com'r (CA–2 1965) 340 F2d 445.

of the indenture. Civil and criminal liabilities imposed for violation of the Trust Indenture Act are much like those in the Securities Act of 1933.

To conform with the Act, the indenture must contain certain prescribed provisions, the most important of which are the following:

(1) It must name a financially responsible corporate trustee with a combined capital and surplus of not less than $150,000, whose interests do not conflict with those of the indenture security holders. It may also name individual co-trustees.

(2) It must provide that where certain defined conflicting interests arise, the trustee must either resign, remove the conflicting interest, or notify security holders, and that the latter possess certain powers of removal.

(3) It must require the corporation to furnish the trustee with names and addresses of security holders at stated intervals.

(4) It must require the corporate trustee either to make such lists of security holders available to security holders, or to mail communications from security holders to other security holders, or apply to the Commission to be excused from doing so.

(5) It must provide for annual reports and certain interim reports to security holders by the trustee.

(6) It must require the corporation to file annual reports with the trustee and to furnish the trustee with (a) evidence of recording of the indenture, (b) evidence of compliance with conditions precedent relating to issuance of additional securities and to other matters of interest to security holders, and (c) certificates of independent engineers, appraisers, or other experts, or opinions of officers of the corporation, as to the fair value of property or securities released from the lien of the indenture, and of securities or property deposited with the trustee as the basis of issuance of securities, the withdrawal of cash, or the release of property or other securities subject to the lien of the indenture.

(7) It must require the trustee to give security holders notice of all defaults known to the trustee within 90 days after they occur. However, the indenture may provide that the trustee may withhold notice of all defaults except defaults in the payment of principal or interest or any sinking or purchase fund installment, if the trustee determines that course to be in the interest of security holders.

(8) It must provide that in case of default the trustee shall exercise the rights and powers vested in it with the care and skill that a prudent person would exercise under the circumstances in the conduct of her own affairs.

For complete information about the Trust Indenture Act, see P-H *Securities Regulation.*

Coupon and registered bonds. Bonds may be either coupon bonds or registered bonds. Coupon bonds have interest coupons attached to them, each of which is, in effect, a written contract for the payment of a definite sum of money on a certain date. If the bond provides that both its principal and interest on it shall be payable to bearer, the instrument is negotiable in the same manner as any other negotiable commercial paper.[146] The holder of the bond may present the interest coupon for payment at a named bank or at the office of the company on the date the interest falls due. Upon maturity of the bond presentment for payment may be made in the same way. If the bond is not paid at maturity, the holder is entitled to interest until the date of payment at the legal rate prescribed by local law at the place where the bonds were payable.[147] The interest coupons are detachable from the bond and may be negotiated[148] and sued upon without proof of ownership or production of the bond.[149] Coupons attached to the bond are part of the bond and have all the rights conferred by the bond itself.[150]

The holder of overdue bond coupons may recover interest from the due dates unless the debtor corporation shows that at maturity it had on deposit sufficient funds to pay the coupons; in the absence of such a showing, presentation, and demand at the place of payment are unnecessary for recovery of interest.[151]

When a negotiable bond is lost or stolen, the owner loses title to it as soon as it passes into the hands of an innocent purchaser.[152] However, requesting the bond can be a protection against this loss.

A registered bond is one which is recorded on a register in the transfer officer in the name of the bondholder. It may be registered both as to principal and interest. Sometimes the principal of a coupon bond is registered. When the bond is registered, a check is mailed to the bondholder, as recorded on the register, whenever the principal, or an interest payment falls due. When a registered bond is sold the seller must indorse the instrument and send it to the transfer office so that the name of the purchaser may be recorded.

Registered bonds may be grouped into the three classes shown below.

---

[146]Stuart Court Realty Corp. v Gillespie, (1928) 150 Va. 515, 143 SE 741.

[147]Sears v Greater New York Development Co. (CA–1 1931) 51 F2d 46.

[148]Sears v Greater New York Development Co. (CA–1 1931) 51 F2d 46; Mississippi Power & Light Co. v A. E. Kusterer & Co., (1930) 156 Miss. 22, 125 So 429.

[149]Aurora City v West, (1868) 74 US 82.

[150]Weinstein v Siemens & Halske A.G. (ED N.Y. 1939) 26 F Supp 410.

[151]American Surety Co. v Sterling Hotel Co. (Pa. Com. Pls., Luzerne Co. 1949) 40 Luz. Leg. Reg. Rep. 432.

[152]Continental Casualty Co. v Aetna Casualty & Surety Co., (1937) 251 App. Div. 467, 296 N.Y.S. 833.

Fully registered bonds. The bond is issued without coupons attached. The name of the payee is entered on the books of the corporation as the registered owner. On the day when, by the terms of the bond, the interest falls due, the interest is paid directly by check to the registered owner. An assignee of fully registered non-negotiable bonds, who fails to give prompt notice of the assignment, is subject to intervening equities arising in favor of the issuer and cannot compel a transfer or registration of the bonds when the issuer is prejudiced.[153]

Coupon or bearer bonds with registration privilege. The coupon bonds may, at the option of the holder, be converted into registered bonds. Upon presentation of the bond to the company, or its registrar, the coupons are clipped, the name of the owner is entered on the books of the company, and a proper indorsement is made on the bond itself, showing its registration, thus reducing it as nearly as possible to the form and shape of an original registered bond. In old indentures, the provision was frequently made that, after a coupon bond had been changed into a registered bond, the bond could not again be converted into a coupon bond. The bond, in other words, was exchangeable, but not interchangeable. Under modern indentures, bonds are interchangeable and may be changed from coupon bonds to registered bonds and later back to coupon bonds. Ordinarily though a bond that has once been converted from a coupon bond into a registered bond cannot again be converted into a coupon bond unless a new bond is issued. The holder of a coupon bond that entitles him to have it converted at his option into a registered bond may enforce such contract by an action for specific performance.[154]

Registered coupon bonds. The bond is registered as to principal and not as to interest. The coupons remain attached to the bond and are collectible precisely as if the principal had never been registered. They are payable to any person presenting them for payment, and no questions are asked as to whether or not the person presenting them is the registered owner of the bond. Such a bond may be reconverted into a bearer coupon bond by an assignment on the back of the bond, payable to the bearer, and an entry upon the registration books to the effect that the bond is again a bearer coupon bond.

Because of the diversified nature of bonds it would be difficult to make a detailed classification covering every type of bond. However, in

---

[153]First Nat'l Bank of Binghamton, N.Y. v Mayor & City Council of Baltimore (D Md. 1939) 27 F Supp 444.
[154]Benwell v Mayor, etc. of City of Newark, (1897) 55 N.J. Eq. 260, 36 Atl 668.

the main bonds may be said to fall within two main groups, secured bonds and unsecured bonds.

Secured bonds. When borrower pledges certain of its property or assets to insure repayment to the bondholder you have a secured bond. Bonds of this type are generally mortgage bonds, collateral trust bonds, or equipment bonds.

Mortgage bonds. A mortgage bond is the evidence of a promise by the corporation to pay a stated sum with interest, secured by a mortgage on specified real property of the corporation. The mortgage is often called interchangeably a "trust deed" or "trust indenture"; it differs, of course, from the trust indenture underlying unsecured bonds. The evident purpose of the provision for a trustee is to insure that there shall be at all times a bondholders' representative authorized to act for a numerous, changing and widely scattered class of principals.[155]

The original trustee is designated in the trust indenture. Provision is sometimes made for the appointment of a successor trustee, upon the resignation of the first trustee, by the holders of a stated proportion of the outstanding bonds. If a successor meeting the qualifications in the indenture (usually a bank or trust company having its principal office in a specified place and with a specified minimum surplus) and willing to accept the trust upon customary terms cannot be found, a bondholder, in a representative action in equity, may ask a court to appoint a successor trustee. It may appoint an individual where no qualified financial institution will act, though it is a deviation from the terms of the trust instrument.[156] The mortgage given to secure a bond issue may be a mortgage on the real property held by the corporation, on its personal property, or on the corporate franchise restricted only in accordance with the general rules on mortgages. The most common form of mortgage bond, however, covers all the property of the corporation, including after-acquired property. The trust deed or indenture is a contract setting forth the terms and conditions under which the bonds are issued, and the rights of the various parties in them, including the steps to be taken to foreclose upon default.

> **Note:** The corporate trust deed permits corporations to deposit security conveniently with a single trust for the benefit of all bondholders.

---

[155] Manufacturers Trust Co. v Roanoke Water Works Co., (1929) 172 Va. 242, 1 SE2d 318.
[156] Purdy v Westchester Service Corp. (N.Y. S Ct 1946) NYLJ, 7–17–46m p. 104. See also, Baumer v Johnstown Trust Co., (1942) 345 Pa. 51, 25 A2d 723.

Construction of trust indenture: The terms and conditions in the trust deed must be read together with the bond to arrive at the intent of the parties.[157] Bondholders are charged with knowledge of the contents of the trust indenture because the bonds refer to the trust indenture. As a general policy, the courts will sustain provisions in the trust indenture that tend to protect the security for benefit of the bondholders. So, too, when such provisions are inserted in the mortgage and the provisions of the mortgage are referred to in the bonds in plain and unambiguous terms, courts universally give them effect as a proper means of protecting the security for the benefit of the entire series of bonds.

In construing the trust indenture, the ordinary meaning of language will be applied to the words of the contract, in the absence of anything to show that they were used in a different sense. The writing must be construed as a whole, and all its provisions read together. If possible, the court will give effect to all parts of the instrument; a construction that gives reasonable meaning to all its provisions will be preferred to one that leaves a portion of the writing useless or inexplicable.[158] But if the language of the trust deed is plain and unambiguous, no room is left for construction.[159]

The general rule is that a promise to pay a negotiable bond will not be subject to any restriction or limitation by provisions of the mortgage securing the bond, unless language on the face of the bond gives bondholders reasonable notice of such restriction or limitation. For example, bonds secured by mortgage provided that after six months' default in payment of interest they should be subject to conditions of the mortgage. The mortgage subjected the action of the trustee in enforcing the mortgage lien to control of majority bondholders and latter were given power to agree to reorganization. The court held that the general rule stated above would not give non-assenting minority bondholders the right to payment of interest contrary to the reorganization plan agreed on by majority bondholders. However, the bonds were bought after default and with knowledge of it.[160]

When there is an inconsistency, the provisions of the bond prevail over those in the trust deed, because the bond is the instrument on which the holder relies primarily when he is making his purchase. This

---

[157] Watson v Chicago, R.I. & P.R. Co., (1915) 169 A.D. 663, 155 N.Y.S. 808; Lubin v Pressed Steel Car Co., (1933) 146 Misc. 462, 263 N.Y.S. 433.

[158] Rothschild v Jefferson Hotel Co. (E.D. Mo. 1944) 56 F Supp 315.

[159] In re Allied Properties Co. (CA–6 1941) 118 F2d 773.

[160] Gilmor v Indianapolis Gas Co. (CA–7 1943) 136 F 2d 925.

is particularly true as to restrictions upon the right of a bondholder to sue for payment. Certain restrictions must appear upon the face of the bond; a general reference on the face of the bond to the present mortgage and the terms and conditions on which the bonds were issued and secured is not enough.[161] A typical "no action" clause in an indenture or in a mortgage bars a bondholder from bringing suit for a default unless the holders of a specified percentage of the outstanding bonds have first given the trustee notice of the claimed default and asked the trustee to sue. A no-action clause in the mortgage does not bar bondholders from suing on the bond, whether or not the bonds incorporated the no-action clause of the mortgage by recital or reference.[162] However, the bondholders are bound by a statement in the bond clearly indicating that their remedy upon default was controlled by the terms of the trust deed.[163]

A no-action clause does not preclude a non-complying bond-holder from suing to recover on his matured, interest-bearing bond,[164] particularly when the bondholders do not have the protection of an intervening trustee.[165] Nor does it bar a suit by a bondholder to void an agreement between the corporation and the trustee extending the maturity date of the bonds.[166] But a suit to have the extension of the maturity date declared illegal was dismissed when the procedure fixed in the trust deed for extending the maturity date was followed, the bondholders knew the date had been changed and accepted interest after the change, and the no-action clause had not been complied with.[167] Similarly, a utility company's use of a special fund to redeem its bonds did not contravene its contract with the bondholders, nor did its redemption of the bonds ahead of schedule, since that was in accord with industry practice and was not forbidden in the trust indenture.[168]

If the bond specifically refers to the resolution pursuant to which the instrument was issued, and indicates that the bond is issued and accepted subject to the terms, conditions, restrictions, rights, and

---

[161] Guardian Depositors Corp. v David Stott Flour Mills, Inc., (1939) 291 Mich. 180, 289 NW 122; Lubin v Pressed Steel Car Co., (1933) 146 Misc. 462, 263 N.Y.S. 433; Putnam v Pittsburgh Rys Co., (1938) 330 Pa. 210, 199 Atl 211.

[162] Dunham v Omaha & C.B. St. Ry. Co. (SD, N.Y. 1938) 28 F Supp 287. See also Union Guardian Trust Co. v Building Securities Corp., (1937) 280 Mich. 717, 276 NW 697.

[163] Mitchell v Madison Ave. Offices, Inc., (1933) 147 Misc. 149, 263 N.Y.S. 442; Gordon v Conlon Corp., (1944) 323 Ill. App. 380, 55 NE2d 821.

[164] Miller v Corvallis Gen. Hosp. Ass'n, (1947) 182 Ore. 18, 185 P2d 549.

[165] Hershfield v Astoria Associates, Inc. (S Ct 1955) 139 N.Y. Supp. 2d 519.

[166] Borg v New York Majestic Corporation (S Ct 1954) 139 N.Y. Supp. 2d 72.

[167] Aladdin Hotel Corp. v Bloom (CA–8 1953) 200 F2d 627.

[168] John Hancock Mutual Life Insurance Co. v Caroline Power and Light Co. (CA–2 1983) 717 F 2d 664.

privileges set forth in the resolution, the bond, its coupons, and the resolution must be construed together. If there is any inconsistency between the bonds, the coupons, and the provisions of the resolution, the provisions of the bonds and coupons prevail, as these have terms that the bondholder can readily see.[169]

Foreclosure upon default in payment. You must carefully follow the foreclosure procedure stipulated in the trust deed.[170] But you don't have to go through useless steps.[171] Restrictions on the method of bringing foreclosure proceedings do not limit the inherent right of bondholders to protect their interests.[172] Generally, bondholders instituting proceedings to enforce their rights under the trust deed act for all bondholders in a similar position.[173]

Effect of foreclosure. When all the property of a corporation is sold on foreclosure of the mortgage, the purpose of the mortgage has been satisfied. The lien ceases to exist; the fund raised by sale takes its place and only bondholders who had a lien on the property by virtue of the mortgage may share in fund. Bonds unissued at the time of foreclosure may not participate in the proceeds of the sale.[174]

Power of trustee to buy at foreclosure sale. If the trust deed has a provision authorizing the trustee to buy at the sale, most courts uphold it.[175] In the absence of a provision in the trust deed, there are two rules:

(1) The trustee cannot bid or buy without express authorization.[176]
(2) The trustee may, if a majority of the bondholders approve, and if the action is necessary to protect the bondholders' interests, bid and buy

---

[169]Goodjon v United Bond & Bldg. Corp., (1929) 226 AD 137, 234 N.Y.S. 522.

[170]See Rodman v Richfield Oil Co. (CA–9 1933) 66 F2d 244; Munch v Central West P. S. Co., (1935) 128 Neb. 645, 259 NW 736; Bullowa v Thermoid Co., (1934) 12 N.J. Misc. 608, 173 Atl 925; Moore v Tumwater Paper Mills Co., (1935) 181 Wash. 45, 42 P2d 29. For contra decision, see Townsend v Milaca Motor Co., (1935) 194 Minn. 423, 260 NW 525.

[171]Cloverdale Cotton Mills v Ala. Nat'l Bank, (1929) 219 Ala. 50, 121 So 54.

[172]Hoyt v E. I. DuPont De Nemours Powder Co., (1913) 88 N.J. Eq. 169, 102 Atl 666. See, to the same effect, Tachna v Pressed Steel Car Co., (1933) N.J. Eq. 174, 163 Atl 806.

[173]See New Orleans Pac. Ry. Co. v Parker, (1891) 143 US 42, 12 S Ct 364; Betts Mass. Cities Realty Co., (1939) 304 Mass. 117, 23 NE 152; Guardian Depositors Corp. v David Stott Flour Mills, Inc., (1939) 291 Mich. 180, 289 NW 122; Seibert v Minneapolis & St. L. Ry. Co., (1893) 52 Minn. 148, 53 NW 1134; Perry v Darlington Fireproofing Co., (1945) 76 Ohio App. 101, 63 NE2d 222.

[174]Miners Nat'l Bank of Pottsville v Frackville Sewerage Co., (1945) 157 Pa. Super. 167, 42 A2d 177.

[175]Sage v Central R. R., (1878) 99 US 334, 25 L Ed 394; Kitchen Bros. Hotel Co. v Omaha Safe Deposit Co., (1934) 126 Neb. 744, 254 NW 507; James v Cowing, (1880) 82 N.Y. 449.

[176]Equitable Trust Co. v United States Oil & Refining Co. (D. Wyo. 1928) 35 F2d 508, rev'd, on other grounds, Werner, Harris & Buck v Equitable Trust Co. (CA–10 1929) 35 F2d 513; Cosmopolitan Hotel v Colorado Nat'l Bank, (1934) 96 Col. 62, 40 P2d 245; Chicago Title & Trust Co. v Robin, (1935) 361 Ill. 261, 198 NE 4; Christ v Collins, (1937) 211 Ind. 474, 6 NE2d 698; Detroit Trust Co. v Stormfeltz-Lovely Co., (1932) 257 Mich. 655, 242 NW 227

at a price not exceeding the principal and interest due on the mortgage.[177]

The trustee, after having bought the mortgaged property at the foreclosure sale, has implied power to mortgage it again.[178]

Collateral trust bonds. A collateral trust bond is one in which the promise of the borrower is secured by a pledge of securities of other companies, such as stocks or bonds. It is distinct from a mortgage bond, which is secured by physical property. As a general rule the securities are deposited with the trustee for the benefit of the bondholders.

A corporation which has contracted to keep collateral security at a fixed ratio to the amount of the bonds can be compelled to specifically perform its agreement and barred from so disposing of its assets as to render itself incapable of fulfilling its promise.[179]

Equipment bonds. An equipment bond is one issued to finance purchases of railroad equipment. Ordinarily a railroad corporation that has several outstanding bond issues secured by mortgages with clauses covering after-acquired property, would be unable to purchase additional equipment, pledging such equipment as security for the purchase price, without the payment of a heavy premium, since the holders of the prior mortgages would have liens superior to that of the new pledgee under the after-acquired property clauses. For this reason the corporation does not buy the equipment outright and pledge it to secure the purchase price, but issues what are called equipment bonds. There are two plans of procedure followed in the issuance of such a bond: The Philadelphia plan and the New York plan.

Under the *Philadelphia plan* the vendor transfers the equipment to a trustee who delivers possession of the equipment to the railroad company under a lease for a cash consideration that is actually part of the purchase price, and that is applied thereto. The trustee then issues equipment trust notes, or bonds secured by the equipment purchased, to secure payment of the remainder of the purchase price. These notes or bonds are sold to the public and the proceeds are turned over to the vendor of the equipment. These bonds are, on their face, the obligation

---

[177] Hoffman v First Bond & Mortgage Co., (1933) 116 Conn. 320, 164 Atl 656; Silver v Wickfield Farms, (1929) 209 Iowa 850, 227 NW 97; First Nat'l Bank v Neil, (1933) 137 Kan. 436, 20 P2d 528, Sneve v First Nat'l Bank & Trust Co., (1934) 192 Minn. 355, 256 NW 730; N.J. Nat'l Bank & Trust Co. v Lincoln Mortgage & Title Guaranty Co., (1930) 105 N.J. Eq. 557, 148 Atl 713.

[178] Smith v Mass. Mut. Life Ins. Co., (1934) 116 Fla. 390, 156 So 498.

[179] Marine Midland Trust Co. v Allegheny Corp. (SD N.Y. 1939) 28 F Supp 680.

of the trustee, but are guaranteed by the railroad company both as to principal and interest. They are usually issued in series so that only a portion of them will mature each year. The railroad company, holding the equipment under the trustee's lease, makes regular rental payments to the trustee that are applied to the redemption of the bonds. After maturity and payment of all the bonds, and after fulfillment of all the conditions of the lease by the corporation, the trustee executes a bill of sale covering the equipment to the railroad company.

Under the *New York plan* the vendor transfers the equipment to a trustee, who executes a conditional bill of sale to the railroad company, thus giving possession to the railroad, but retaining legal title. The trustee then issues bonds that are secured by a mortgage on the equipment and sold to the public. The proceeds of the sale of the bonds are applied to the purchase price of the equipment. Retirement of the bonds is provided for by the railroad company issuing time notes to the trustee who applies the periodic installment payments to the redemption of the bonds as they mature. When full payment of the purchase price has been made to the trustee, title to the equipment, which under a conditional bill of sale remains in the seller (the trustee here) vests in the railroad company.

Oil companies, tank car companies, and tank line companies, as well as other organizations that require large amounts of capital to be invested in movable and salable equipment, may make use of equipment trust obligations to finance the purchase of equipment.

Unsecured bonds (debentures) An unsecured bond is a bond issued without security and entirely upon the general credit of the corporation. Such a bond is commonly referred to as a debenture.[180] (In England "debenture" is used to designate all bonds.) Under a debenture bond the corporation promises to pay the bondholder a certain sum of money at a stipulated time and place with interest as provided for in the bond. A debenture on its face is an acknowledgement of a debt. The debenture evidences a debt with a fixed maturity date on which the holder can demand payment whether or not there are corporate earnings. This is the test usually applied in solving the problem of whether an instrument is a debenture or a preferred stock certificate.[181]

---

[180] Mueller v Howard Aircraft Corp., (1946) 329 Ill. App. 570, 70 NE2d 203; Mercantile Properties, Inc. v State Tax Commission, (1938) 278 N.Y. 325, 16 NE2d 352.
[181] Com'r v H. P. Hood & Sons, Inc. (CA–1 1944) 141 F2d 467.

The issuance of unsecured bonds is generally accompanied by the execution of a so-called trust deed to a trustee containing promises or obligations running to the trustee but for the benefit of the bondholders. The trust deed embodies the borrowing corporation's promises as to the manner in which it will conduct its business as a sort of assurance to the bondholders of the integrity of the corporation. The execution of the trust deed in conjunction with the issuance of the bond is a feature which distinguishes a debenture from an ordinary note of the corporation. One of these promises or obligations in the trust deed may be to refrain from mortgaging or pledging corporate property adversely to the existing debentures, known as a "negative pledge" clause. Some courts construe the negative pledge clause as applicable only to long term funded loans and permit the obligor to encumber assets for short term loans.[182] Other courts have held short term loans to be within the negative pledge clause.[183] A non-consenting debenture bondholder may pursue the assets of a corporation, all of which were transferred without consideration under an informal reorganization plan, though the bonds have not yet matured.[184] On the other hand, a clause in a close corporation's debentures that 85 percent of holders must join before a suit can be begun for nonpayment of principal or interest is binding on later buyers.[185]

Other forms of unsecured bond issues. (1) An income bond, issued during the financial reorganization of a corporation in exchange for creditor's claims, the payment of interest on which is made, contingent upon the corporation having earnings; (2) a receiver's certificate, issued to raise funds for the continuance of the current corporate business after the corporation has passed into the hands of a receiver.

Consideration for issuance of bonds. Statutes and constitutional provisions in some states prohibit the issuance of bonds except for cash, property actually received or services or labor done.

Corporate bonds issued without consideration are not enforceable in hands of holders, whether or not they are for value, with notice. To recover, a holder must show that he acquired the bonds for value and without notice.[186]

---

[182] Kelly v Central Hanover Bank & Trust Co. (SD N.Y. 1935) 11 F Supp 497.
[183] In Chase Nat. Bank v Sweezy, (1931) 281 N.Y. Supp 487, aff'd, (1932) 236 App Div 835, 259 N.Y.S. 1010, aff'd, (1933) 261 N.Y. 710, 185 NE 803 and Kaplan v Chase Nat'l Bank, (1934) 156 Misc. 471, 281 N.Y.S. 825.
[184] Berwich v Asso. G. & E. Co., (1934) 20 Del. Ch. 265, 174 Atl 122.
[185] Sass v New Yorker Towers Ltd, (1965) 23 A.D. 2d 105, 258 NYS 2d 765.
[186] Nelson v Dailey, (1940) 239 Ala 87, 194 So 177.

While corporation cannot issue stocks and bonds for property not actually received, it can, if it has a *bona fide* surplus, issue these securities out of surplus as a dividend.[187] However, dividends paid in bonds are rare. It has been held that bonds may be issued also for the purpose of being pledged as collateral security for a pre-existing indebtedness.[188]

Even in the absence of any statutory provision, the issuance of bonds for no consideration at all would ordinarily be *ultra vires*. However, bonds may be issued at less than par, that is, at a discount, and still be enforced at their par or face value.

Substitution of bonds for stock. Generally, even in states whose statutes limit the consideration for which bonds may be issued to cash, property actually received, or services and that prohibit all fictitious increases of indebtedness, the issued and outstanding shares of the capital stock of the corporation may be returned or surrendered to the company in consideration for the issuance to the holders of the bonds of the corporation. This is certainly true where no statute prescribes what consideration the corporation must receive for the issuance of its bonds. Even where a statute does make such requirement, it is generally considered that the shares of stock are property within the meaning of the statute and hence consideration for the issuance of bonds. However, a corporation can't compel its preferred stockholders, without their unanimous consent, to take debentures for their stock.[189]

Rights, powers, duties and liabilities of trustee. A trustee (usually a trust company) under a deed covering secured or unsecured bonds occupies a fiduciary position the same as any other trustee.[190] Its primary duty is to protect the interest of the bondholders,[191] and it is held to the greatest good faith.[192] The trustee, independently of the provisions of the trust deed, has power, and it is its duty, whenever the necessity arises, to invoke the aid of a court of equity to preserve the trust

---

[187]Young v Bradford County Telephone Co., (1941) 341 Pa. 394, 19 A2d 134.

[188]In re Mifflinburg Body Co. (CA–3 1942) 127 F2d 59.

[189]Bowman v Armour & Co. (Ill. S Ct 1959) 17 Ill. 2d 43, 160 NE2d 753.

[190]President and Directors of Manhattan Co. v Kelby (CA–2 1945) 147 F2d 465; York v Guaranty Trust Co. of N.Y. (CA–2 1944) 143 F2d 503, rev'd, on other grounds, Guaranty Trust Co. of N.Y. v York, (1945) 326 US 99, 65 S Ct 1464, rehearing den., (1945) 326 US 806, 66 S St 7; Citizens Banking Co. v Monticello State Bank (CA–8 1944) 143 F2d 261; Koplar v Rosset, (1946) 355 Mo. 496, 196 SW2d 800.

[191]Bancroft v Allen, (1939) 138 Fla. 841, 190 So 885; Himmel v Straus, (1937) 288 Ill. App. 566, 6 NE2d 494; Green v Title Guarantee & Trust Co., (1928) 223 App. Div. 12, 227 N.Y.S. 252; Harvey v Guaranty Tr. Co., (1929) 134 Misc. 417, 236 N.Y.S. 37.

[192]Continental & C. Trust & Savings Bank v New Orleans Drainage Co. (ED La. 1922) 278 F 811.

estate and this power cannot be abrogated or restricted, even by agreement of the parties.[193]

The ministerial duties of the trustee are usually incorporated in the body of the trust deed which gives it its position and authority. Besides these duties, the broad general duties of the trustee include overseeing the manner in which the corporation is handling the property covered by the mortgage to preserve it for the benefit of the bondholders.

> *Example:* The trustee should see that the corporation pays all taxes due on the property and that it fully insures the property.

The corporation is accountable to the trustee for any delay or neglect in its management of the property. However, the corporation is not responsible to the bondholders individually or collectively, and the bondholders may not sue the corporation for its failure to protect their property unless there is an express provision so authorizing them in the trust deed.[194] It is the right and duty of the trustee to sue the corporation, and if it neglects its duty the bondholders may by direct proceeding in court, have the trustee removed and a new one appointed in its place.

The trust deed generally provides for removal of the trustee by bondholders. Where the unrestricted power to remove the trustees and to appoint other trustees was vested in a majority of the bondholders, the power to determine whether there was cause to remove them was necessarily in them also, subject only to the restraining power of a court of equity against its abuse.[195] However, the court will not interfere with the trustee's discretion in instituting a foreclosure proceeding against the wishes of the majority of the bondholders but in accordance with the deed of trust.[196]

At common law, holders of corporate indenture notes can sue the corporation to enforce payment of the notes after maturity unless the indenture provisions expressly or by necessary implication bar that right.[197] The holder of mortgage bonds issued by a corporation can, in

---

[193] Seelig v First Nat'l Bank of Chicago (ND Ill. 1936) 20 F Supp 61; New York Trust Co. v Michigan Traction Co. (WD Mich. 1912) 193 F 175.

[194] McPherson v Commercial Bldg. & Securities Co. et al., (1928) 206 Iowa 562, 218 NW 306.

[195] March v Romare (CA-5 1902) 116 F 355.

[196] Chic. Title & Trust Co. v Chief Wash Co., (1938) 368 Ill. 146, 13 NE2d 153.

[197] Japha v Del. Valley Utilities Co., (1940) 40 Del. 599, 15 A2d 432; Halle v Van Sweringen Corp., (1936) (37 Del.) 491, 185 Atl 236; Friedman v Am. Nat'l Co., (1939) 172 Misc. 1044, 16 N.Y.S.2d 887; Miller v Corvallis Gen. Hosp. Ass'n, (1947) 182 Ore. 18, 185 P2d 549; Collier v E. C. Miller Cedar Lumber Co., (1942) 13 Wash.2d 201, 124 P2d 555.

his own behalf and in behalf of all other bondholders similarly situated, sue to foreclose the mortgage if the trustee fails or refuses to act, or if for any reason the trustee has made itself incompetent to act.[198]

The mortgage or trust deed sometimes gives a certain minimum percentage of bondholders power to act when the trustee refuses or fails to act. Bond indenture provisions authorizing minority bond-holders to institute foreclosure proceedings must be strictly followed. All the conditions precedent to the bringing of the action must be met.[199] A demand on the trustee to bring the action and an offer of indemnity must be shown.[200] It would seem that such provisions are binding upon dissenting bondholders.[201]

A successor trustee can sue the former trustee for an accounting of the trust assets.[202]

The trustee of a corporate bond issue can sue to enforce the liability of a guarantor further securing payment of principal and interest of the bonds. However, individual bondholders cannot sue unless, after due demand, the trustee fails to act.[203]

The trustee is not a guarantor of the bonds nor of the sufficiency of the security nor the regularity of the conduct of the obligor.[204] His signing of a certificate that the bonds were those of the designated corporation described in the indenture does not make him a guarantor of the bonds.[205] However, a trustee is liable to the bondholders for breach of his trust,[206] and bondholders who have been misled by the

---

[198] Central Hanover Bank & Trust Co. v Siemens & Halske Aktiengesellschaft (SD N.Y. 1936) 15 F Supp 927, aff'd (CA-2 1936) 84 F2d 993; Woman's Athletic Club of San Francisco v Anglo-California Nat'l Bank of San Francisco, (1950) Cal. App2d 772, 222 P2d 675; Townsend v Milaca Motor Co., (1935) 194 Minn. 423, 260 NW 525; Meyer v Lawry & Co. (S Ct, 1940) 19 N.Y.S.2d 835; Ryan v Carnegie Metals Co., (1941) 43 Pa. D. & C. 188.

[199] Lauinger v Carrillo Bldg. Co., (1940) 41 Cal. App2d 660, 107 P2d 287.

[200] Rodman v Ridgefield Oil Co. (CA-9 1933) 66 F2d 244; Dietzel v Anger, (1937) 8 Cal.2d 373, 65 P2d 803; Oswianza v Wengler & Mandell, Inc., (1934) 358 Ill. 302, 193 NE 123; Munch v Central West P. S. Co., (1935) 138 Neb. 645, 259 NW 736; McQuistion v Third Ave, Transit Corp., (1949) 121 NYLJ 1177; Moore v Tumwater Paper Mills Co., (1935) 181 Wash. 45, 42 P.(2d) 29, cert den, (1935) 296 US 597, 56 S Ct 113.

[201] Allan v Moline Plow Co. (CA-8 1926) 14 F2d 912. Compare Gellert v Baldwin Locomotive Works (ED Pa. 1933) 3 F Supp 812.

[202] Newmark v National Bank & Trust Co. of Norwich (N.Y. S. Ct 1955) 147 N. Y. S.2d 565.

[203] First Trust Co. v Maxcy, (1938) 229 Wis. 284, 282 NW 81. Contra, Security-First Nat'l Bank v Lloyd-Smith, (1940) 259 A.D. 220, 18 N.Y.S.2d 584. See, also, First Nat'l Bank & Trust Co. of Ann Arbor, v Dolph, (1938) 287 Mich. 219, 283 NW 35.

[204] Thayer v South Side Foundary & Machine Works, (1932) 112 W. Va. 134, 163 SE 821.

[205] Bell v Title Trust & Guarantee Co., (1928) 292 Pa. 228, 140 A. 900.

[206] President and Directors of Manhattan Co. v Kelby (CA-2 1945) 147 F2d 465; York v Guaranty Trust Co. of N. Y. (CA-2 1944) 143 F2d 503, rev'd, on other grounds, (1945) 326 US 99, 65 S Ct. 1464 rehearing den., (1945) 326 US 806, 66 S Ct 7; Citizens Banking Co. v Monticello State Bank (CA-8 1944) 143 F2d 261; First Trust Co. v Carlsen, (1935) 129 Neb. 118, 261 NW 333; In re Union Real Estate Inv. Co., (1938) 331 Pa. 569, 1 A2d 662.

false representations of a trustee as to the kind and nature of the securities held in trust for their benefit may have a new trustee appointed.[207] A trustee who fails to ascertain that securities deposited are not of the kind required by the indenture is guilty of negligence.[208] A trustee who permits a substitution by the trustor of less valuable securities for those originally given to secure the bond issue is liable in damages to the bondholders.[209] But he is not liable to unsecured creditors and stockholders. A corporate receiver can't sue for unsecured creditors and stockholders for the trustee's wrong in releasing property covered by the lien. It is the bondholders who have that right of action.[210]

Bondholders have the right to rely on the particular security that was given unless substitution was provided for in the trust deed, and any tampering with the securities on the part of the trustee destroys the safety and security of the bond issue and amounts to a breach of its trust duty. A trustee who releases the property held in trust upon the mortgagor's assertion that all bonds and coupons had been paid is liable in damages to the holder of bonds and coupons which have not been paid.[211] The trust indenture may make the trustee liable for "bad faith." However, irrespective of such provision the trustee is, by law, made liable for "gross negligence."[212]

Power of corporation to issue bonds. The power to issue bonds falls within the scope of the right of the corporation to borrow money for the payment of its debts; it is inherent in every corporation as an incident to its power to contract a debt, unless expressly prohibited by a statute or by the articles of incorporation.[213]

Who has authority to issue bonds. In the absence of provision to the contrary the power to authorize the issuance of bonds is vested in the board of directors as an incident to its power to borrow money, and the consent of the stockholders is not necessary.[214] After the

---

[207] Sullivan et al. v Ark. Valley Bank, (1928) 176 Ark 278, 2 SW2d 1096.

[208] Doyle v Chatham & Phoenix Nat'l Bank of the City of N.Y., (1930) 253 N.Y. 369, 171 NE574.

[209] President and Directors of Manhattan Co. v Kelby (CA-2 1945) 147 F2d 465; Bancroft v Allen, (1939) 138 Fla. 841, 190 S 885; Richardson v Union Mortgage Co., (1939) 210 Iowa 346, 228 NW103.

[210] Jackson v Bowie (Tex. App. 1838) 114 SW 2d 342.

[211] Harvey v Guaranty Trust Co., (1929) 134 Misc. 417, 236 N.Y.S. 37.

[212] National Bondholders Corp. v Seaboard Citizens Nat'l Bank (CA-4 1940) 110 F2d 138; Savings Bank of New London v N.Y. Trust Co., NYLJ, 4-15-41, p. 1671.

[213] Orme v Salt River Valley Water Users' Assn., (1923) 25 Ariz. 324, 217 P 935; Pratt v Higginson, (1918) 230 Mass. 256, 119 NE 661.

[214] Citrus Growers' Dev. Assn. v Salt River Valley Water Users' Assn., (1928) 34 Ariz. 105, 268 P 773.

bonded indebtedness has been authorized by the board of directors, the president may bind the corporation to pay an attorney he hired to do preliminary legal work.[215]

If the corporation has sold the bonds and kept the proceeds, it cannot deny the validity of its bonds on the ground that no certificate was attached to each bond as required in the trust deed. The provision will be deemed waived.[216] Nor can a corporation that got the benefit of payment for its note, question the legality of the directors' authorization of the issuance of bonds as collateral security to secure the original indorsers of the note.[217]

Consideration for bonds—antecedent debt. Statutes or constitutional provisions commonly say that no corporation shall issue bonds, except for money or property actually received or for labor done, and that all fictitious increases of indebtedness shall be void. The word "issue," in this connection, has been interpreted as including the pledge of bonds.[218] Such statutes are passed for the protection of the public, as well as the corporate stockholders, against the issuance of worthless securities.

These statutes usually do not permit the issuance of bonds, either by way of a mortgage or a pledge, to secure the payment of an antecedent debt.[219] However, the borrowing and the issuing of the bonds need not be simultaneous.[220] Thus, where the borrowing corporation promises the lender, before the loan is actually made, that it will issue and deliver the bonds as collateral security after the loan is made, the bonds are deemed to have been issued for a present consideration when the corporation fulfills its promise and issues the bonds.[221] So, too, where a loan was made to a corporation within four months after execution of the security, it was held that this was sufficient to satisfy the statutory requirement that bonds be issued only for money paid.[222] An extension of time for the repayment of a loan will not be deemed sufficient consideration for the issuance of bonds

---

[215] Argue v Monte Regio Corp., (1931) 115 Cal. App. 575, 2 P2d 54.

[216] Easton v Butterfield Live Stock Co. et al., (1929) 48 Idaho 153, 279 P 716. See to the same effect Hicks v Freun Cereal Co., (1930) 182 Minn. 93, 233 NW 828.

[217] Dennis v Co-Operative Pub. Co. et al., (1928) 46 Idaho 534, 269 P 82.

[218] In re Valecia Condensed Milk (CA-7 1917) 240 F 338, rev'g 233 F 173. See also: In re Metalcraft Corporation (ED Mo. 1940) 31 F Supp 194; Hinkley Co. v Pelton, (1929) 200 Wis. 48, 227 NW 308.

[219] Davis v Seneca Falls Mfg. Co., (1925) 8 F2d 546, aff'd and mod., on another ground, in (CA-2 1927) 17 F2d 546; Hess Warming & Ventilating Co. v Burlington Grain & Elevator Co., (1919) 280 Mo. 163, 217 SW 493.

[220] Westinghouse Electric & Mf'g Co. v Brooklyn R. T. Co. (SD N.Y. 1923) 288 F 221.

[221] Rahway Nat. Bank v Thompson (CA-3 1925) 7 F2d 419.

[222] In re Metalcraft Corporation (ED Mo. 1940) 31 F Supp 194.

under the requirements of the statutes mentioned above.[223] But the release of a mortgage given as collateral to secure a debt is present consideration for the issuance of bonds in substitution of the mortgage. It is immaterial whether the property mortgaged is equal in value to the market value of the bonds, property of any value being sufficient if it is really intended as consideration for the bonds and not merely as a cover to obtain security for a pre-existing debt.[224]

Issuance of bonds at less than par. A corporation may sell its bonds on the open market for the best price it can secure and in the absence of charter or statutory provision to the contrary it may issue its bonds at a discount.[225] Corporate bonds may be sold or pledged at less than par[226] if the transaction is not made with intent to defraud the general creditors of the corporation.[227] As a general rule the board of directors has the power to exercise its best judgment in the disposition of corporate bonds; honesty and fair dealing are all that is required of them.[228]

Bonds issued without consideration are invalid but are good in the hands of innocent holders for value.[229] Bonds issued for the good will of the business bought, valued by capitalizing the seller's earnings, are valid.[230]

Suppose a statute bars a corporation from issuing bonds except for money paid, labor done, or property actually received and declares fictitious increases of debt to be void. Does that bar the corporation from selling its bonds at a discount?[231] The usual answer is that it can issue bonds at less than par but it must get a just and reasonable consideration that at least approximates the amount of the debt.[232] A corporation can reacquire and pledge its bonds at less than par without violating constitutional and statutory provisions about consideration for issuance of bonds and fictitious increases of debt.[233]

---

[223] In re Progressive Wall Paper Corp. (CA-2 1916) 229 F 489.

[224] In re Paul Delaney Co. (WD, N.Y., 1928) 23 F2d 737, rev'd (CA-2 1928) 26 F2d 961; rehearing, 33 F2d 945.

[225] In re Radio-Keith-Orpheum Corp. (CA-2 1939) 106 F2d 22; Mercer v Steil, (1922) 97 Conn. 583, 117 Atl 689; OAG No. 317, 9–29–70.

[226] Westinghouse Electric & Mfg. Co. v Brooklyn R. T. Co. (SD N.Y. 1923) 288 F 221.

[227] Pueblo Foundry & Machine Co. v Lannon, (1920) 68 Col. 131, 187 P 1031.

[228] Central Trust Co. v Southern Oil Corp. (CA–1925) 8 F2d 338.

[229] Clark v Freeling, (1938) 196 Ark. 907, 120 SW2d 375.

[230] Estate Planning Corp. v C.I.R., (CA–2 1939) 101 F2d 15.

[231] McKee v Title Insurance & Trust Co., (1911) 159 Cal. 206, 113 P 140.

[232] In re Wyoming Valley Ice Co. (D Pa. 1907) 153 F 787; Nelson v Hubbard, (1892) 96 Ala. 238, 11 So 428; Pollitz v Wabash R. Co., (1915) 167 App. Div. 669, 152 N.Y.S. 803; Northside Ry. Co. v Worthington, (1895) 88 Tex. 562.

[233] Slupsky v Westinghouse Elec. & Mfg. Co. (CA–8 1935) 78 F2d 13.

Some states still permit a corporation to set up usury as a defense to its obligation to repay a debt. But when a corporation in good faith pledges its bonds at less than their face value as collateral to secure its debt no usury exists. The primary duty of the corporation is to pay its debt and to release the collateral security that it has put up. The loan is not usurious merely because collateral in excess of the debt may be sacrificed after a default occurs, because there was no intent to violate the statutes against usury at the inception of the loan.[234] In those states where the corporation may not plead usury as a defense the corporation may issue its bonds at any price under par unless a statute expressly bars this right.

Obligation to pay interest and principal. A corporation that can prove that it stood in readiness to pay interest coupons when due, will not be liable for interest upon past-due coupons.[235] It need not set aside, specifically for the benefit of coupon holders, funds that will be entirely beyond its control.[236] Continued readiness to pay is enough. However, the corporation must pay interest on coupons after their maturity if the coupons are presented for payment and payment is denied.[237] The corporation may even become liable for interest on matured coupons where no demand or presentation for payment is made, if it shows no readiness to pay the interest at the place designated for its payment.[238] Negotiable coupons, whether or not detached, bear interest after maturity at the legal rate of interest.[239]

A bondholder who got a judgment for interest can't execute it against property covered by the mortgage. The mortgage remains as security for the other bondholders. Nor can he bar payment of dividends until the interest is paid, when he can instead enforce the judgment against other property of the corporation, namely rentals for equipment it leased.[240]

If the principal of bonds is not paid upon the due date, the bonds continue to draw interest thereafter, unless the corporation can show

---

[234] Rudisill Soil Pipe Co. v Eastham Soil Pipe & Foundry Co., (1923) 210 Ala. 145, 97 So 219.

[235] H. Abraham & Son v New Orleans Brewing Ass'n, (1903) 110 La. 1012, 35 So 268.

[236] Fox v Hartford & West Hartford Horse R. Co., (1897) 70 Conn. 138 Atl 871.

[237] Aurora City v West, (1868) 74 US 42; Rea v Pennsylvania Canal Co., (1915) 249 Pa. 239, 94 Atl 833.

[238] Walnut v Wade, (1880) 103 US 526.

[239] Sears v Greater New York Dev. Co. (CA-1 1931) 51 F2d 46.

[240] Schmitt v Wyoming Valley Public Service Co., (1938) 33 Pa. D. & C. 317.

that it had, and continued to keep, at the time and place of payment, moneys ready to meet the obligation.[241]

The deposit of funds with a bank, trustee, or other agent to meet the payment of bonds at maturity or to redeem bonds before maturity does not discharge the obligation of the issuing corporation, and upon insolvency of the agent, the corporation continues to be responsible to the bondholder even if the agent becomes insolvent.[242] The funds are held by the bank as agent of the corporation, and not as agent of the bondholder; hence the corporation's liability.[243] Similarly, a deposit of funds with a bank or paying agent, for the purpose of meeting interest, does not relieve the corporation from liability to the coupon holder in the event that the bank fails and certain coupons remain unpaid.[244] The funds deposited with a paying agent for the payment of interest do not become a trust fund for the benefit of coupon holders, if the bonds and interest coupons contain nothing more than the corporation's promise to pay the interest at its office or agency.[245] Thus, the receiver of a corporation can recover money the corporation deposited in a bank to pay bond interest from time to time.[246] On the other hand, when the deposit was made with the intention of creating a trust, not a debtor-creditor relationship, the corporation's trustee in bankruptcy could not recover money deposited with the depositary trustee to meet coupon interest.[247] Also, when the intention is to have the deposit create a trust, the depositary is not the agent of the corporation, and upon insolvency of the depositary, the corporation is not liable.[248]

> *Example:* If the provisions of the bond and mortgage indicate that payment of the bonds and interests is to be made through a trustee, and that the deposits are to be held in trust for the bond and coupon holders, the deposit with the trustee of funds for the payment of principal and interest, as required by the trust agreement, relieves the corporation from any further liability on the indebtedness, and any loss due to the financial failure of the trustee falls upon the holder of the bond. The

[241] Ohio v Frank, (1881) 103 US 531; Cromwell v Sac County, (1887) 96 US 681; Brewster v Wakefield, (1859) 22 How. 118; First Nat. Bank v Jersey Central Power & Light Co., (1934) 115 N.J. Eq. 242, 170 Atl 209; Whaley v Coronal Institute, (1932) Tex. Civ. App 48 SW2d 687.
[242] First Nat. Bank v Jersey Central Power & Light Co., (1934) 115 N.J. Eq. 242, 170 Atl 209.
[243] Cheney v Libbey, (1890) 134 US 68, 10 S Ct 498.
[244] Williamsport Gas Company v Pinkerton, (1880) 95 Pa. St., 62.
[245] In re Interborough Consolidated Corporation (CA–2 1923) 288 F 334.
[246] Noyes v First Nat'l Bank of N. Y., (1917) 180 App. Div. 162, 167 N.Y.S. 288; Guidise v Island Refining Corp. (SD N.Y. 1923) 291 F 922.
[247] In re National Public Service Corp. (SD N.Y. 1933) 3 F Supp 262.
[248] Rogers Locomotive Works v Kelly, (1882) 88 N.Y. 235.

trustee, in this instance, receives the money as agent of the bondholder, and not as agent of the corporation.[249]

When the trustee makes the loan to the corporation, receives its bond and mortgage, retains them and issues trust certificates, he becomes an agent of the certificate holders. Thus as between the corporation, which makes principal payments to the trustee, and the certificate holders, the certificate holders bear the loss caused by the trustee's bankruptcy.[250]

Extinction of bonded indebtedness. A corporation may extinguish its bonded indebtedness in any one of the following three ways: (1) by redemption either before or at maturity; (2) by conversion; or (3) by refunding.

Redemption. "Redemption" means the exchange of bonds for cash. The exchange may take place: (1) at maturity; (2) before maturity at the opinion of the corporation; or (3) before maturity, pursuant to an agreement between the corporation and the bondholders. When the corporation determines whether the bonds should be retired, the right to make the election generally rests with the directors. This right in the directors may be abrogated by a provision in the bond itself, or by an express requirement in the articles of incorporation or in a state statute to the effect that a vote of stockholders is essential to the validity of a retirement of all outstanding corporate bonds.

Redemption before maturity. A corporation's right to redeem its bonds is usually stated in the indenture; it may also be stated in an agreement with individual bondholders.

Redemption is at the option of the corporation. The corporation must generally give notice to the bondholders of its intention to redeem the bonds, and to specify a date on which the bonds will be called in. However, debenture purchases could not bar a corporation from redeeming its debentures without notifying them that it intended to use funds derived from issuing common stock, when the indenture did not require such notification.[251] Usually the corporation must pay a premium if it redeems its bonds before maturity, like one year's interest.

Often, the premium decreases as the date of redemption approaches the date of maturity. The bondholder cannot require

---

[249] Morley v University of Detroit, (1933) 263 Mich. 126, 248 NW 57u.

[250] First Trust Co. v Maryott, (1939) 135 Neb. 679, 283 NW 518.

[251] Morgan Stanley & Co. v Archer Daniels Midland Co. (SD NY 1983) 570 F Supp 1529.

redemption; that is solely at the corporation's option. And only upon exercise of the option must the corporation pay a premium. However, when the continued existence of the corporation is made impossible by law, or the corporation is involuntarily compelled to redeem, redemption can be made without paying the premium.[252]

If the agreement to redeem is in the terms of the bond issue, the corporation may either buy the bonds in the open market, or use a broker to do its buying, or it may negotiate directly with the individual bondholder. A corporation can redeem its bonds before maturity under an agreement with an individual bondholder, unless it has given up this right by a prior contract.[253]

The General Corporation Act itself may expressly empower a corporation to acquire, usually by purchase, its own bonds. However, express statutory grant is uncommon. Usually the statutes simply provide that a corporation shall have the power to purchase, hold and convey real and personal property for corporate objects. This grant of general power has been construed to include the specific power of a corporation to acquire its own bonds.[254]

When a corporation no longer needed the proceeds of a bond issue, it could use a surplus it later accumulated to buy the bonds in the open market.[255]

A corporation may buy its own bonds and reissue them before maturity. A purchase of bonds and reissuance is distinguishable from an extinction of bonded indebtedness by redemption. When issued and outstanding bonds are purchased by the obligor corporation, they are not necessarily redeemed or retired.[256] They may be held by the corporation for resale. Such bonds generally are called treasury securities.

Securities issued to an officer to hold pending delivery to those entitled to them are not treasury bonds.[257]

---

[252]New York Trust Co. v SEC (CA-2 1942) 134 F2d 274; City Nat'l Bank & Trust Co. v SEC (CA-7 1943) 134 F2d 65.

[253]Fleming v Montana Coal & Iron Co. (CA-9 1923) 289 F 793. See also Mueller v Howard Aircraft Corp., (1946) 329 Ill. App. 570, 70 NE2d 203; John Hancock Mutual Life Insurance Co. v Carolina Power & Light Co. (CA-2 1983) 717 F 2d 664. *Contra:* Miners Nat'l Bank of Pottsville, Pa. v Frackville Sewerage Co., (1945) 157 Pa. Super. 167, 42 A 2d 177.

[254]Fleming v Montana Coal & Iron Co. (CA-9 1923) 289 F 793.

[255]In re Hitchcock, (1912) 149 App. Div. 824, 134 N.Y.S. 174.

[256]Clafin v S.C.R.R. Co. (D SC 1880) 8 F 118; Broomall v North American Steel Co., (1912) 70 W.Va. 591, 74 SE 863. *Contra:* Continental Bank & Trust Co. v W.A.R. Realty Corp., (1943) 265 A.D. 729, 40 N.Y.S.2d 854 holding obligor corporation's acquisition of bonds at or before maturity extinguished them.

[257]Miners Nat'l Bank of Pottsville, Pa. v Frackville Sewerage Co., (1945) 157 Pa. Super. 167, 42 A2d 177.

Bonds reacquired by the issuer, and presumably kept alive for subsequent reissuance, when held by a trustee in reorganization are subordinate to the outstanding publicly held bonds.[258]

Payment at maturity from sinking fund. The corporation has to pay its debt at maturity. To be sure it has enough money to redeem its bonds at their maturity, the corporation, either of its own volition or under the terms upon which the bonds were issued, may set up a "sinking fund." The corporation sets aside a certain amount of cash out of each year's earnings to build up a fund for the specific purpose of retiring the bonds. This trust fund belongs to the bondholders and cannot be attached by creditors of the corporation.[259] The fund may be administered by the corporation, the trustee, or a sinking fund agent for the benefit of bondholders. It may be built up by depositing in the fund fixed or variable installments of money, or by buying bonds for the fund at certain intervals. A corporation can't meet sinking fund requirements with unissued debentures.[260]

When the trust deed specifies how the fund is to be paid, it controls. If, for example, bonds are to be paid as drawn by lot, and the corporation goes bankrupt on the day of the drawing, the trustee must redeem the drawn bonds. The other bondholders bought with notice of this provision in the trust deed so they can't complain.[261]

Bondholders can waive sinking fund payments to themselves.[262]

The trustee is bound to follow the terms of the trust and, if in doubt, to apply to the court for directions.[263]

Very often the bond issue is divided into series with varying maturity dates.

Example: The bonds are distinguished by a designating letter such as A, B, C, and so on. Series A is made payable in five years; Series B, in six years; Series C, in seven years. The series that matures each year is paid out of the sinking fund.

Note: Corporations, like public utilities, that tend to need increasing amounts of borrowed capital will generally rely more on refunding and new borrowing for funds to retire maturity debt.

---

[258] In re Third Avenue Transit Corp. (CA–2 1955) 222 F2d 466.
[259] Brown v J. P. Morgan & Co. Inc., (1943) 265 App. Div. 631, 40 N.Y.S.2d 229, aff'd, (1946) 295 N.Y. 867, 67 NE2d 263, First Nat'l Bank of Portland v Stretcher, (1942) 169 Ore. 532, 129 P2d 830.
[260] Birn v Childs Co., (1942) 37 N.Y.S.2d 689.
[261] Truby v M. & T. Trust Co., (1931) 141 Misc. 507, 253 N.Y.S. 108.
[262] Williamsport Nat. Bank v First Nat'l Bank, (1939) 334 Pa. 130, 5 A2d 228.
[263] Appeal of Colonial Trust Co., (1913) 241 Pa. 554, 88 Atl 798.

Conversion. Extinction of a corporation's bonded debt by conversion is effected by substituting some other form of security, usually common or preferred stock, for the bonds. This may be done at the option of the bondholders, and the conditions under which the exchange may be made are generally fixed by the terms of the bond. A corporation cannot issue convertible bonds without express statute or charter authorization. Issuance of convertible bonds was illegal when it denied stockholders' preemptive rights.[264] A corporation that can increase its capital stock can issue convertible bonds.[265]

A corporation that refuses to convert bonds, in accordance with a provision for that, is guilty of breach of contract, for which a bondholder may recover damages. The bondholder need not resort to the trustee as intermediary, but may sue in his own name, since his right is personal and is not for the interest of the bondholders as a class. Redemption of a redeemable, convertible bond issue ends its convertibility. A bondholder who, after refusal of the corporation to recognize her conversion right, accepts the redemption money can't later litigate the right.[266]

A corporation isn't liable to convertible bondholder of another corporation when, as an inevitable result of its acquiring nearly all the latter's stock, it eliminated the public market for that stock and so lessened the value of that bondholder's right to convert his bonds.[267] Similarly, when acquisition by another corporation resulted in removal of stock from exchange listing.[268] And an indenture agreement was fair and did not breach any fiduciary duty when it provided that, upon merger, convertible debenture holders convert only into the same kind and amount of property that they would have received had the conversion occurred immediately prior to the merger.[269]

Bonds, however, are often issued with the provision that after notice of redemption is given, the holder shall have a short period in which to exercise his right to convert.

Refunding. Refunding means that a corporation exchanges bonds that have a later maturity date for bonds coming due. The outstanding debt of the corporation is not affected, the new bonds

---

[264]Wall v Urah Copper Co., (1905) 70 N.J. Eq. 17, 62 Atl 533.

[265]Van Allen v Illinois Central R. R. Co., (1861) 7 Bos. (N.Y.) 515.

[266]Brooks & Co., Inc. v N. C. Public Service Co., 32 F2d aff'd (CA–4 1930) 37 F2d 220. See also Mueller v Howard Aircraft Corp., (1946) 329 Ill. App. 570, 70 NE2d 203.

[267]Levine v C. & O. Ry. Co., (1977) 60 AD2d 246, 400 N.Y.S.2d 76.

[268]Kessler v General Cable Corp., (1979) 92 Cal. App3d 531, 155 Cal Rep 94.

[269]Broad v Rockwell International Corp. (CA–5 1981) 642 F 2d 929.

taking the place of the old ones. If the proceeds of an issue of refunding bonds are to go to the trustee to discharge the original debt, the procedure will raise the corporate debt in violation of a charter provision limiting the amount of debt that a corporation may incur, since the new bonds extinguish the old debt and the aggregate outstanding debt is the same at all times.[270]

Since a bondholder has the right to demand payment of his bond upon maturity,[271] the refunding of bonds may generally be effected only if the bondholder consents, unless the terms of the bond provide otherwise.

> **Observation:** Corporations sometimes offer a cash premium or a higher rate of interest as an inducement to the bondholder to refund his bond. Or, instead of offering the new refunding obligations to the holders of the maturing securities, the corporation may offer the new securities to the public and apply the proceeds to the payment of the maturing obligations. If the new securities consist of bonds convertible into stock, they are generally offered first to the stockholders and then to holders of the maturing securities.

The issuance of the new obligations must, of course, be duly authorized by resolution of the board of directors, and in proper cases must be registered with the Securities and Exchange Commission. Indentures covering securities issued in exchange for other securities of the same issue may have to be qualified under the Trust Indenture Act of 1939.

Issuance of notes. A corporation able to borrow money may issue notes as evidences of its obligations as an incident to its general authority.[272] Notes issued to stockholders by a solvent corporation for property of less value than the face value of the notes are not a "fictitious indebtedness" within constitutional bars when all the stockholders approve the notes and third parties are not injured. A transferee of the note cannot complain of the inadequacy of consideration.[273] Having issued the notes the corporation becomes liable on them. A corporation may not borrow money on its notes, and then

---

[270] Citrus Growers Dev. Assn. v Salt River Valley Water Users' Assn., (1928) 34 Ariz. 105, 268 P 773; George Backer, Inc. v Textile Realty Corp., (1948) 90 N.Y.S.2d 223, aff'd in part and rev'd in part, (1949) 275 App. Div. 369, 89 N.Y.S.2d 569.

[271] Dunham v Omaha & Council Bluffs Street Ry. Co. (CA-8 1939) 106 F2d 1; Fleming v Fairmont & M. R. Co., (1913) 72 W. Va. 835, 79 SE 826.

[272] Western Nat'l Bank v Wittman, (1916) 31 Cal. App. 615, 161 P 137; Curtis v Leavitt, (1857) 15 N.Y. 66.

[273] Pacific Am. Gasoline Co. v Miller (Tex. Civ. App. 1934) 76 SW2d 833.

repudiate the loan because its directors and officers used the proceeds in making an improvident investment.[274]

Trust notes, secured by collateral, need not be issued for a cash loan but may be given in payment for legal services rendered to the corporation, and the transaction is not void because the notes were given to secure an antecedent debt.[275]

At common law the holder of corporate indenture notes has the right to sue the corporation to enforce payment of the notes after maturity unless indenture provisions expressly or by necessary implication preclude such right.[276] However, the holder of a corporate note, issued under and referring to a trust agreement providing that no action can be taken by any single noteholder against the corporation until a majority in amount of the noteholders have requested the trustee in writing to declare a default, cannot proceed without the acquiescence of the other noteholders as required by the trust agreement.[277]

Who has authority to issue notes. The general power to issue notes falls within the scope of the power of the board of directors to authorize the borrowing of money. The board usually delegates this authority to a particular officer of the corporation either by resolution or through the by-laws. A third party was held unable to enforce a note executed by other than those designated in a resolution.[278] Delegation of authority need not be express however. If the board of directors permits the treasurer to act as the financial agent of the corporation, the authority to execute a note may be implied.[279] Also third parties may presume the treasurer has power to execute notes from past dealings of the corporation.[280] Sometimes the corporate charter or by-laws will designate the officer in whom sole authority to execute the notes of the corporation is to be placed. But such a by-law provision cannot be pleaded by a corporation to deny its liability on a note executed by another appropriate officer if the provision was not known to the plaintiff.[281]

Officers have no authority to bind the corporation by the

---

[274] Brown v Ins. Equities Corp., (1936) 21 Del. Ch. 273, 187 Atl 18.
[275] Ex parte Parsons, Clausson & McIlvaine (CA-2 1929) 32 F2d 691.
[276] Halle v Van Sweringen Corp., (1936) 37 Del. 491, 185 Atl 236.
[277] McAdoo v Oregon City Mfg. Co. (CA-9 1934) 71 F2d 879.
[278] Padgham v Inyo Marble Co., (1931) 116 Cal. App. 328, 2 P2d 531.
[279] Gilman v Bailey Carriage Co., Inc., (1928) 127 Me. 91, 141 Atl 321.
[280] Humphreys & Son, Inc. v Broughton, (1928) 149 Va. 789, 141 SE 764.
[281] La Grange Lumber & Supply Co. v Farmers'& Traders'Bank, (1927) 37 Ga. App. 409, 140 SE 766.

execution of notes merely because they hold office.[282] But it has been held the making and indorsing of negotiable paper is presumed to be within the power of the treasurer of a manufacturing and trading corporation whenever from the nature of its ordinary business as usually conducted the corporation is naturally to be expected to use its credit in carrying on commercial transactions.[283] But an officer, having the power to borrow money on behalf of the corporation, whether express or implied, may execute a note as evidence of a loan made under the exercise of this power.[284] Corporations have been held liable on notes executed by officers who were entrusted with the management of the corporation,[285] or who were otherwise clothed with apparent authority.[286] Similarly, a corporation can't recover from its bank the amount of a check signed by one of its officers though a directors' resolution authorized the bank to pay only on the signature of two officers, when the bank had repeatedly honored checks with one signature with no objection from the corporation.[287] And a corporation is bound by a note its president-general manager gave to pay the premium on a pension insurance policy when the payee did not have actual knowledge that the directors had not authorized the pension plan and when the directors did not protest the purchase of the policy until some months after they must have known about it.[288] Relief from debt on the part of the corporation can be valid consideration for a promissory note that is signed by shareholders who have a vital interest in the corporation.[289] On the other hand, a corporation has been held not liable on a promissory deed of trust note, when the president of the corporation signs it "individually and as trustee," since that designation after his signature does not make the corporation a maker or a guarantor of the note.[290]

---

[282]St. Vincent College v Hallett (CA–7 1912) 201 F 471; Clebourne County Bank v Butler Gin Co., (1931) 184 Ark. 503, 42 SW2d 769; Wallace v Mouton, (1930) 170 La. 47, 127 So 360; First Nat'l Bank v Tristate Equipment & Repair Co., (1930) 108 W.Va. 686, 152 SE 635.

[283]Merchants' Nat'l Bank v Citizens' Gaslight Co., (1893) 159 Mass. 505, 34 NE 1083.

[284]McCormick v Stockton & T. C. R. R. Co., (1900) 130 Cal. 100, 62 P 267; Citizens Bank v Public Drug Co., (1921) 190 Iowa 983, 181 NW 274; Charleston Nat. Bank v Lemkuhl-Shepherd Co., (1924) 97 W.Va. 284, 125 SE 241.

[285]Harris v H. C. Talton Wholesale Grocery Co., (1929) 11 La. App. 331, 123 So 480; Aronofsky v Humes, (1929) R.I., 147 Atl 749; Eastern Public Service Corp. et al. v Funkhouser, (1929) 153 Va. 128, 149 SE 503.

[286]Clebourne County Bank v Butler Gin Co., (1931) 184 Ark. 503, 42 SW2d 769; Platt v Montclair Feed & Fuel Co., (1931) 9 N.J. Misc. 1319, 157 Atl 553.

[287]Berdane Furs, Inc. v First Pa. Banking and Trust Co., (1959) 190 Pa. Super. 639, 155 A2d 465.

[288]Blair v J. R. Andres, Inc. (WD Pa. 1956) 141 F Supp 51.

[289]Parrish v Terre Haute Savings Bank (Ind. App. 1982) 431 NE 2d 132.

[290]Vector Corp v First State Bank & Trust Co. of Port Lavaca (Tex. Civ. App. 1968) 430 SW 2d 536.

A corporation must pay the personal note of its general manager who gave it as security for a corporate debt.[291]

A creditor can't attack the validity of a corporate trust deed given to secure a loan to a corporation when he got the benefit of the loan, nor can stockholders consenting to the transaction attack it though net assets were reduced below stated capital and corporate assets were used to secure a director's personal debt.[292]

Suppose the president makes a note for his corporation and also personally endorses it. Is he discharged from personal liability just because he later, as president, but not personally, agrees to extend the corporation's time to pay the note? The answer seems to be, yes.[293]

Trust receipts. All states except Louisiana have adopted the Uniform Commercial Code. The Code repeals and supersedes the Uniform Trust Receipts Act. The Code makes no distinction between trust receipts and other security instruments as to filing and the rights and remedies of the parties.

Power of corporation to lend its funds. Ordinarily a corporation may not lend money unless it is authorized so to do by charter or statutory provision. The rule is important since lending money is strictly a banking function. It is not necessary, however, that the statutory grant of power be set forth in express terms; it may be inferred from the authority to make such contracts as are reasonably necessary to the transaction of the business for which the corporation was organized.[294]

> *Example:* The power to lend money to its customers and to receive notes as evidence of business transactions is incidental to the authority of a corporation to engage in a general merchandise and commercial business.[295]

Mercantile or manufacturing corporations may not engage in the business of money lending.[296] They can make a temporary loan though, which is reasonably necessary to the carrying on of the corporate

---

[291] In re Eton Furniture Co. (CA-3 1961) 286 F2d 93.

[292] Hawkins v Mall, Inc. (Mo. S Ct 1969) 444 SW2d 369.

[293] London Leasing Corp. v Interfina, Inc., (1967) 53 Misc. 2d 657, 279 N.Y.S.2d 209.

[294] Dench & Hardy Co. v John J. Hanson, Inc., (1936) 247 App. Div. 355, 287 N.Y.S. 435.

[295] Holt v Farmers Loose Leaf Tobacco Warehouse Co., (1923) 201 Ky. 184, 256 SW 6; Seymour & Co. v Castell, (1926) 160 La. 371, 107 So 143; Opinion of Attorney General of Maine, 5-28-63.

[296] National Trust & Credit Co. v Orcutt & Sons Co. (CA-7 1919) 259 F 830; American Credit & T. Co. v New Era Chandelier Co., (1917) 208 Ill. App. 181; Garrison Canning Co. v Stanley, (1907) 133 Iowa 57, 110 NW 171.

business.[297] Also, a corporation, which has a large surplus of funds, can lend the money temporarily on safe security.[298] But it can't engage in a program of extensive speculation with corporate funds.[299] Nor may a parent corporation borrow money to lend to its subsidiary if the loan benefits only the subsidiary and not the parent.[300]

Loans to stockholders, directors, or officers. Statutes in most states prohibit a corporation from making loans to directors, officers, or stockholders. The statutes vary considerably. For example, some prohibit loans to officers, directors, and stockholders, others to officers and directors, and others to shareholders alone; and some of these permit loans under certain circumstances, for example when approved by the stockholders. Usually, the statutes make the directors who approve an illegal loan personally liable to the corporation for the amount of the loan.[301]

The corporation cannot legally do indirectly what it is prohibited from doing directly. It cannot, for example, borrow money for its officers, mortgage its property to secure their debts, or guarantee repayment of loans made to them. The officers may be held personally liable for waste of corporate assets resulting from such transactions at the derivative suit of a minority stockholder.[302] When a corporation accommodates its officer by issuing its note and pledging its assets for payment of his debt and later pays the note without hurting its creditors or its stockholders (particularly if the latter know all about it and are estopped), it cannot recover moneys paid pursuant to the completed transaction.[303]

Statutes in a few states expressly permit corporate loans to officers and directors.

If there is no statutory prohibition, a corporation may lend its funds to its directors, officers, or stockholders in the way it can lend to outsiders.[304] The general rules governing transactions between the

---

[297]Murray v Smith, (1915) 166 N.Y. App. Div. 528, 152 N.Y. Supp. 102 modified, on another point, 224 N.Y. 40, 120 NE 60.

[298]Bank of Berwick v George Vinson Shingle & Mfg. Co., (1913) 132 La. 861, 61 So 850.

[299]Felsenheld v Bloch Bros. Tobacco Co., (1937) 119 W.Va. 167, 192 SE 545.

[300]Silverman v Lehrman, (1960) 25 Misc. 2d 339, 203 N.Y.S.2d 171. See also A. Gay Jenson Farms Co. v Cargill, Inc. (Minn. S Ct 1981) 309 NW 2d 285.

[301]Clarkson Co., Ltd. v Shaheen (CA-2 1981) 660 F 2d 506.

[302]First Mercantile Nat'l Bank & Trust Co. v Murdock Realty Co., (1942) 111 Ind. App. 226, 39 NE2d 507. See Crowley v First Merchants' Nat. Bk. of Lafayette, (1942) 112 Ind. App. 80, 41 NE2d 669; Fardy v Mayerstein (Ind. App. 1942) 41 NE2d 851; Brinson v Mills Supply Co., (1941) 219 N.C. 498, 14 SE2d 505.

[303]Futurity Realty Corp. v Passaic Nat'l Bank & Trust Co., (1948) 22 N.J. Super. 175, 62 A2d 706. Compare Ladd Estate Co. v Wheatley, (1967) 246 Ore. 627, 426 P2d 878.

[304]The Garrison Canning Co. v Stanley, (1907) 133 Iowa 57, 110 NW 171.

corporation and its officers or directors are applicable when such loans are made; the main requirements are that the borrower act in good faith, and that the terms of the transaction are fair to the corporation. Of course, even if there is no statutory prohibition, an inside loan may be forbidden by the corporation's own charter.

Loans by a corporation of its surplus funds to officers or directors are legal in the absence of fraud, participation in the authorization of the loans by interested directors, or disregard of the interests of the company in making the loans.[305] Courts will enforce the statutes of another state that make the officers and directors of corporations incorporated there individually liable for corporate debts when they lend corporate funds to officers and directors.[306]

A director is personally liable to a creditor for an illegal loan to a stockholder even though the creditor became such after the director's resignation.[307] However, officers and directors weren't liable for breach of duty though they took an illegal loan from their corporation when they repaid the loan with interest.[308]

An illegal loan to a director must be repaid at 6 percent though it was made at a lower rate.[309]

Stockholder's sale of notes to a corporation is not void, though the corporation paid for them by cancelling an outstanding loan it had made to the stockholder in violation of statute.[310]

The corporate attorney or executive called upon to deal with this question should remember that besides express statutory authorization or bar, there may be an implied one. He should note, where pertinent, the conditions laid down by the statute—like stockholder consent, or posting security—and that in some states a qualified foreign corporation, or an unqualified foreign corporation doing business there, must follow the statutes of that state, and not of its home state, for loans consummated there.

Best procedure when a loan may properly be made is to have the board of directors authorize it by appropriate resolution. A loan made without such authority may, of course, be ratified later.

---

[305] Felsenheld v Bloch Bros. Tobacco Co., (1937) 119 W.Va. 167, 192 SE 545.
[306] Houk v Martin, (1980) 82 Ill. App. 3d 205, 402 NE 2d 421; Pullum Window Corp. v Feldstein, (1959) 357 Mich. 82, 97 NW2d 762.
[307] National Refractories Co. Inc. v Bay State Builders Supply Co. Inc., (1956) 334 Mass. 541, 137 NE2d 221.
[308] Campbell v Vose (CA–10, 1975) 515 F2d 256 (Okl. law).
[309] Maclary v Pleasant Hills, Inc., (1954) 35 Del. Ch. 39, 109 A2d 830.
[310] Holt v Queen City Loan & Investment Inc. (Mo. 1964) 377 SW2d 393.

Power of corporation to lend its credit as a guarantor. By statute in most states corporations are expressly granted the power to guarantee the contracts or obligations of others. However, the statutes vary considerably as to

(1) What kinds of obligations can be guaranteed—for example, contracts, bonds, or dividends;
(2) Under what conditions—for example, provided the power is granted in the articles, or provided the guarantee is in furtherance of the corporate purposes;
(3) For what class of persons—for example, other corporations, or customers or suppliers, or anyone.

As a general rule a corporation may not lend its credit as a guarantor unless it is expressly authorized to do so by its charter[311] or by a statutory provision.[312] However, under some circumstances, the right of a corporation to guarantee the debt of another may be implied from the express powers granted to it, under the principle that a corporation may do whatever is reasonable and necessary to enable it to conduct its business successfully and to accomplish the ends for which the corporation was formed.[313]

A corporation has implied power to guarantee the obligation of another where such act "directly" tends to promote the purposes for which the corporation was organized. A guaranty contract that will only indirectly benefit the corporation's business is beyond its powers.[314] Thus, a corporation cannot guarantee a mortgage when it has no interest in the mortgagor nor in the mortgaged land.[315] And even though the charter of a business corporation authorizes it to guarantee the obligations of other persons or companies when advantageous to itself, the corporation can't pledge bonds held in its treasury to secure previously incurred indebtedness of its treasurer. The advantage referred to in the articles could not be dissociated from its business objectives.[316]

---

[311] L. G. Balfour Co. v Gossett, (1938) 131 Tex. 348, 115 SW2d 694.

[312] Commercial Cas. Ins. Co. v Daniel Russell Boiler Works, Inc., (1927) 258 Mass. 453, 155 NE 422.

[313] Dench & Hardy Co. v John J. Hanson, Inc., (1936) 247 App. Div. 355, 287 N.Y.S. 435; North Star Co. v Howard (Ky. Ct of App 1960) 341 SW2d 251.

[314] W. Md. R.R. Co. v Blue Ridge Hotel Co., (1905) 102 Md. 307, 62 Atl 351; Norfolk Mattress Co. v Royal Mfg. Co., (1933) 160 Va. 623, 169 SE 586; Hall v Pauser, (1942) 128 N.J. L 211, 24 A2d 575 (oil company could guarantee rent of service station operator who sold its oil). *Contra:* Thomas v E. G. Curtis Sons Co. (ED Mich. 1934) 7 F Supp 114.

[315] Crowley v First Merchants' Nat'l Bank of Lafayette, (1942) 112 Ind. App. 80, 41 NE2d 669. See also Fardy v Mayerstein (Ind. App. 1942) 41 NE2d 851.

[316] Fidelity Nat'l Bank & Trust Co. v Southern United Ice Co. (CA–8 1935) 78 F2d 438.

However, a number of courts have upheld corporate acts otherwise outside the corporation's powers, including guaranty contracts of an accommodation nature, where (1) all the stockholders have assented (or merely "acquiesced," according to some), (2) the rights of creditors are not involved, and (3) the state does not object.[317] Formal action by the directors of a close corporation is not necessary to authorize a guarantee when they are the only stockholders,[318] and officers can bind their corporation to assume a third party's guarantee of his business' debts even without prior authorization or subsequent ratification, when the assumption agreement is made in connection with the corporation's continuing program of buying other businesses.[319]

As stated above, under some circumstances a corporation has implied power to guarantee the obligation of another to promote the purposes for which the corporation was formed. In fact it is more and more likely that a court will uphold a corporate guaranty if the guarantor's directors thought the corporation would benefit by giving it.

> *Example:* An auto sales company can guarantee a loan to one of its salesmen who had several "live" prospects in order to dissuade him from quitting employment.

A corporation's implied power to make a loan to an officer may let it guarantee a loan by a third party to the officer.[320] But note that corporate loans to officers are prohibited by statute in most states.

A corporation authorized to buy and develop town sites and improve them, had implied power to borrow money to finance its undertaking. This it could do either by giving a direct mortgage to secure a loan or by letting a contract to another corporation to do the work, and indorsing the bonds of that corporation and guaranteeing their payment. Whenever a corporation can take and dispose of securities of another corporation of whatever kind, it may, for the

---

[317] Santos v Nat'l Bank, (1927) 130 Misc. 348, 223 N.Y.S. 817; Cooper Petroleum Co. v LaGloria Oil & Gas Co. (Tex. Civ. App. 1967) 423 SW2d 645. Norfolk Mattress Co. v Royal Mfg. Co., (1933) 160 Va. 623, 169 SE 586. See also, Osborn v Montelac Park, (1895) 89 Hun, 167, 35 N.Y.S. 610, aff'd, (1897) 153 N.Y. 672, 48 NE 1106, for a fact situation closely in point with Fidelity.
[318] B.F Building Corp. v Coleman (CA-6 1960) 284 F2d 679. But see Matter of Spinner & Graulich, Inc. (S Ct 1967) NYLJ 8-11-67, P. 9.
[319] Harvard Industries, Inc. v Wendel, (1962) 40 Del. Ch. 219, 178 A2d 486.
[320] M. Burg & Sons v Twin City Four Wheel Drive Co., (1918) 140 Minn. 101, 167 NW 300. Compare Warren Creamery Co. v Farmers' State Bank, (1924) 81 Ind. App. 453, 143 NE 635.

purpose of giving them a marketable quality, guarantee their payment.[321]

Security agreement given by subsidiary to avert its parent's bankruptcy was for a valid corporate purpose; stockholder ratification isn't required.[322]

A corporation has implied authority to guaranty a construction bond for a contractor it sold equipment to though its board never specifically authorized or ratified it.[323]

Other courts refuse to recognize an implied power to guarantee loans.[324] The cases on this point are conflicting, and it would be impossible to set forth a definite rule, each case being decided on its own merits.[325]

> *Examples:* A corporate indorsement on the note of another was declared to be a guaranty and was upheld where it was found to be to the advantage of the guarantor-corporation to have the debt of the other corporation paid.[326] But it was held that a trading corporation could not act as surety on the appeal of another corporation even though a benefit would be enjoyed by the surety-corporation.[327]
>
> A corporation, sued on a lease which it guaranteed and which was signed by the individuals who conducted the corporate business, cannot plead that the guaranty was beyond its powers when it appears that the corporation received the primary benefits of the lease and had paid the rent.[328]
>
> A bankrupt furniture corporation's guaranties of trade debts of its corporate suppliers of trade items was enforceable; they weren't deemed securities requiring consideration.[329]
>
> A corporation with broad general powers could guaranty notes of its debtor to improve its chances of collecting the debt.[330]
>
> A corporation's guarantee of the second corporation's debt and mortgage it gave as security aren't necessarily invalid, though the guarantee and mortgage (1) weren't authorized at a stockholder's meeting, and (2) served no corporate purpose, when it may be shown

---

[321] State v Long-Bell Lumber Co., (1928) 321 Mo. 461, 12 SW2d 64.

[322] Matter of Ollag Const. Equipment Corp. (CA-2 1978) 578 F2d 904.

[323] American Casualty Co. v Dak. Tractor & Equipment Co. (D ND 1964) 234 F Supp 606.

[324] Germania Safety-Vault & Trust Co. v Boynton (CA-6 1896) 71 F. 797; Park Hotel Co. v Fourth Nat'l Bank (CA-8 1898) 86 F. 742; Heidler v Werner & Co., (1925) 97 N.J. Eq. 505, 128 Atl 237.

[325] Wm. Filene's Sons Co. v Gilchrist Co. (CA-1 1922) 284 F. 664, cert den, (1922) 260 US 750, 43 S Ct 250; Robert Gair Co. v Columbia Rice Packing Co., (1909) 124 La. 193, 50 So 8.

[326] In re New York Car Wheel Works (WD N.Y. 1905) 141 F. 430.

[327] Best Brewing Co. v Klassen, (1900) 185 Ill. 37, 57 NE 20.

[328] Ostrow v Koch, (1928) 131 Misc. Rep. 697, 227 N.Y.S. 292.

[329] H. J. Cohn Furniture (No. 2) Co. v Tex. Western Fin. Corp. (CA-5 1977) 544 F2d 886.

[330] Fremont Nat. Bank v Furguson & Co., (1934) 127 Neb. 307, 255 NW 39.

that the third of three equal stockholders had acquiesced in and ratified the "informal consent" the other two gave earlier.[331]

As a general rule a corporation cannot indorse negotiable paper for the accommodation of another unless expressly authorized to do so, and is not liable to the holder of such paper who has knowledge of the fact that the indorsement was for accommodation only.[332] However, a bona fide holder for value without notice that the indorsement was made without consideration and for accommodation only may enforce the paper.[333] The reason for this rule is that a bona fide holder may presume that the paper was issued for value and for a lawful purpose.[334] Some jurisdictions have taken the view that a private corporation, if not expressly forbidden, may, with the consent of all the directors and stockholders, become an accommodation indorser provided no harm is done to creditors.[335] In this instance the corporation would be liable even to holders with knowledge that the indorsement was for accommodation only. This rule does not, however, apply to railroad or other public utility companies.

Power of a corporation to lend its credit as a guarantor to its subsidiary companies. A corporation does not have implied power to control another corporation, but must get its authority by express statute or charter provision.[336] But a corporation has implied authority to own stock in another corporation unless barred by statute, when the purpose is to facilitate the legitimate business of the parent company.[337] A parent corporation is liable on guarantee of its wholly owned subsidiary's debt, signed by the parent's officers, in furtherance of the parent's business interests.[338] Some states specifically let a holding company guarantee the debts of its subsidiaries. They place upon this right such limitations as that (1) the subsidiary company be engaged in the same general line of business as the parent company; (2)

---

[331]Commercial Trading Co. Inc. v Jane Corp., (1966) 27 A.D.2d 533, 275 N.Y.S. 2d 621. Compare Rosa & Co. v Syndicate First Corp., (1956) 7 Misc. 2d 198, 155 N.Y.S. 2d 368; Burlington Industries, Inc. v. Foil, (1974) 284 N.C. 740, 202 SE2d 591. Cf. Keystone Leasing Corp. v Peoples Protective Life Insurance Co. (ED NY 1981) 514 F Supp 841.

[332]N. H. Nat'l Bank v Garage & Factory Equipment Co., (1929) 267 Mass. 483, 166 NE 840.

[333]Johnson v Johnson Bros., (1911) 108 Me. 272, 80 Atl 741; Food Products Co., Inc. v Pierce, (1930) 154 Va. 74, 152 SE 562.

[334]Tod et al. v Kentucky Union Land Co. et al. (D. Ky. 1893) 57 F 47.

[335]Murphy et al. v Arkansas & L. Land & Imp. Co., Ltd., et al. (WD Ark. 1899) 97 F 723; Sargent v Palace Cafe Co., (1917) 175 Cal. 737, 167 P 146.

[336]Dunbar v American Tel. & Tel. Co., (1906) 224 Ill. 9, 79 NE 423.

[337]State v Long-Bell Lumber Co., (1928) 321 Mo. 461, 12 SW2d 64.

[338]Cellulose Sales Co., Inc. v Hygrade Packaging Corp. (S Ct 1968) NYLJ, 6–27–68, p. 12.

the holding company must own a certain amount of the stock of the subsidiary company; (3) a vote of a certain number of stockholders of the parent company is essential to the validity of the loan.

> *Examples:* A parent corporation had to pay its former subsidiary's debt guaranteed by the parent's president acting under authority of the board of directors before the subsidiary was sold.[339]
>
> A parent corporation was liable on a loan to its subsidiary for which its chairman, with apparent authority, gave the parent's guarantee.[340]

---

[339]Sperti Products, Inc. v Container Corp. of Amer. (Ky. 1972) 481 SW2d 43.
[340]City Nat'l Bank of Detroit v Basic Food Industries, Inc. (CA–5 1975) 520 F2d 336.

Chapter 28

RESOLUTIONS RELATING TO BORROWING AND LENDING

Contents—Chapter 28

Execution of Indentures

Guaranty of Obligations

Payment of Interest

Redemption of Bonds

Conversion of Bonds

Refunding—Extension of Maturity

Loans by Corporation

AUTHORITY TO BORROW

DIRECTORS' RESOLUTION AUTHORIZING OFFICERS TO BORROW MONEY

RESOLVED, That the officers of this Corporation are hereby authorized and directed to borrow, in behalf of this Corporation, from such banks or trust companies as they may in their judgment determine, an amount not to exceed ..... ($.....) Dollars, for such period of time and upon such terms and rate of interest as may to them in their discretion seem advisable, and to execute notes in respect thereto in the name of the Corporation for the payment of the amount so borrowed.

RESOLUTION OF EXECUTIVE COMMITTEE AUTHORIZING OFFICERS TO BORROW MONEY AND REPORT ON LOANS

RESOLVED, That the Treasurer, with the approval of the President, be authorized, for and in the name of this Corporation, to borrow from time to time from any bank or trust company such amounts of money as may be deemed necessary for the current needs of this Corporation in the transaction of its business, and to give as evidence thereof a note or notes of this Corporation, which shall be signed by the Treasurer and countersigned by the President.

RESOLVED FURTHER, That any loans made by banks or trust companies pursuant to the above resolution shall be reported by the Treasurer to the Board of Directors (*or* the Executive Committee) at its next meeting after the date of such loans.

DIRECTORS' RESOLUTION AUTHORIZING NEGOTIATION OF LOAN TO MEET PAYROLL AND CURRENT OBLIGATIONS

RESOLVED, That the directors do hereby empower *(insert name and office or descriptive title, such as President of the Corporation, or General Manager, etc.)* to negotiate a loan to meet the present payroll, and to pay the current obligations of the Corporation, upon such terms and in such manner as may be deemed best for the interests of the Corporation.

DIRECTORS' RESOLUTION RATIFYING ACTION OF OFFICERS IN ARRANGING ADVANCE FROM BANK

(One form)

RESOLVED, That the action of the officers of this Company in arranging with the .... Trust Company for an advance of $...., as of ...., 19.., payable on ......, 19.., bearing interest at the rate of .. percent, under an agreement dated ...., 19.., and, in executing said agreement, is hereby ratified, approved, and adopted as the act of this Company.

(Another form)

RESOLVED, That the action of the Treasurer in negotiating loans for the benefit of the Corporation to the amount of . . . . . ($. . . . .) Dollars and the issuance of the notes of the Corporation for the same amount is hereby ratified and approved.

DIRECTORS' RESOLUTION AUTHORIZING OFFICERS TO PROCURE LOANS SECURED BY PLEDGE OF MERCHANDISE

RESOLVED, That the officers of this Company are hereby authorized to procure a loan or loans for the purposes of this Company, not exceeding in the aggregate . . . . . ($. . . . .) Dollars, for such time and upon such terms as they may deem proper, and to pledge as security for the payment thereof the ore and pig iron now on hand or hereafter received by the Company, and for this purpose to make and enter into such agreements of lease and other contracts as they may deem necessary and proper in carrying out the authority hereby granted.

DIRECTORS' RESOLUTION AUTHORIZING OFFICERS TO BORROW FROM A NAMED BANK UPON A NOTE

RESOLVED, That the officers of this Company are hereby authorized, empowered, and directed to borrow the sum of . . . . . ($. . . . .) Dollars from the . . . . Trust Company at . . . . . (. . . . .%) percent, payable . . months after date, and to execute a note therefor, to be signed in behalf of the Company by the President and the Treasurer, who are duly authorized to execute such documents according to the By-laws of this Company.

DIRECTORS' RESOLUTION AUTHORIZING OFFICERS TO PROCURE A LOAN TO FINANCE PURCHASE OF STOCK OF ANOTHER CORPORATION

WHEREAS, in order temporarily to finance the purchase of . . . . . shares of cumulative 7 Percent Preferred Stock of . . . . Co., it is necessary to procure a loan for an amount of . . . . . ($. . . . .) Dollars, being the amount of the purchase price of said stock plus the dividends accrued thereon, be it

RESOLVED, That the President or Vice president and the Treasurer or the Secretary are hereby authorized to borrow not more than . . . . . ($. . . . .) Dollars from the . . . . Bank of New York, or the . . . . Trust Co., or any other bank or trust company, for such period and on such terms as may be agreed upon by the officer effecting such loan, and

RESOLVED FURTHER, That there be pledged as security for the repayment of any such loan or loans the said shares of cumulative 7 Percent Preferred Stock of . . . . Co., or any part thereof, or such other collateral as may be available for the purpose, and

RESOLVED FURTHER, That the President or Vice president and the Secretary or the Treasurer are authorized to execute, in behalf of this

Corporation, such note or loan agreement or other papers or documents as may be necessary or advisable in order to effect such loan or loans.

DIRECTORS' RESOLUTION AUTHORIZING CORPORATION TO BORROW FROM OFFICER AND TO EXECUTE NOTE AS EVIDENCE OF OBLIGATION

WHEREAS, the Board of Directors deems it advisable and necessary for the Corporation to borrow the sum of . . . . . ($. . . . .) Dollars to meet current obligations, and

WHEREAS, in view of the present market conditions, the Corporation finds itself unable to raise the said sum except upon the payment of an exorbitant premium, and

WHEREAS, ..., President of this Corporation, has indicated his willingness and ability to lend the said sum of . . . . . ($. . . . .) Dollars to the Corporation for a period of . . . . . (. . . . .) years, at a low rate of interest, be it

RESOLVED, That this Corporation borrow the said sum of . . . . . ($. . . . .) Dollars from . . . ., its President, and that the Treasurer of this Corporation is hereby authorized and directed to execute and deliver to the said . . . ., President of this Corporation, a note to the amount of . . . . . ($. . . . .) Dollars, payable in . . . . . (. . . . .) years with interest at the rate of . . . . . (. . . . .%) percent per annum.

RESOLUTION OF STOCKHOLDERS GIVING BOARD OF DIRECTORS GENERAL AUTHORITY TO BORROW ON NOTES AND TO PLEDGE ACCOUNTS RECEIVABLE AND OTHER AVAILABLE ASSETS AS SECURITY

WHEREAS, this Corporation desires to borrow money for its corporate purposes, be it

RESOLVED, That the Board of Directors of this Corporation is hereby authorized to borrow, from time to time, such sums of money as it may deem advisable, upon the notes of this Corporation, and for that purpose to pledge and assign any or all bills and accounts receivable or any other available assets of the Corporation to secure such notes.

RESOLUTION OF STOCKHOLDERS GIVING DIRECTORS GENERAL POWER TO MORTGAGE AND PLEDGE PROPERTY, PRIVILEGES, AND FRANCHISES TO SECURE BOND OBLIGATION OF CORPORATION AND SUBSIDIARY UP TO FIXED AMOUNT

RESOLVED, That the stockholders of . . . . Corporation do hereby consent that said Corporation mortgage and pledge the property, rights, privileges, and franchises now owned by it or which it may hereafter acquire, such part thereof as its Board of Directors may determine and as shall be described and specified in the mortgage or mortgages or deed or deeds of trust or instrument or instruments of pledge by which said mortgage and pledge shall be created, or as shall be subjected thereto in accordance with provisions therein contained, for any or all of the following purposes as said Board of Directors may, in its discretion, determine:

(1) To secure the payment of the principal and interest of bonds or other obligations of said Corporation, issued in payment for property purchased, or in connection with any operations of the Corporation;

(2) To secure the payment of bonds or other obligations of subsidiary companies now outstanding or hereafter issued, and for the payment of which said Corporation is now or may hereafter become liable; and

(3) To secure the guaranty by said Corporation of the principal and interest, or both, of bonds or other obligations of any subsidiary company or companies; provided, however, that the aggregate principal amount of bonds or other obligations, the payment of which, or the guaranty of the payment of which, shall be secured by said mortgage and pledge including bonds and other obligations issued or reserved for issue to pay off or retire existing bonds or other obligations of the Corporation or of subsidiary companies shall not exceed at any one time . . . . . ($. . . . .) Dollars, or an amount equal to twice the aggregate amount of the capital stock of said Corporation of all classes at the time outstanding, whichever shall be the larger amount; and provided further, that said aggregate principal amount of bonds or obligations, to be secured as aforesaid, shall not exceed in any event at any one time, ... ($. . . . .) Dollars, without the consent of the holders of two thirds of the capital stock of said Corporation of each class having voting powers represented and voted upon in person or by proxy at a meeting specially called for the purpose of procuring such consent, or, if such purpose be specified in the notice thereof, then at any annual meeting.

DIRECTORS' RESOLUTION AUTHORIZING ASSIGNMENT OF ACCOUNTS RECEIVABLE TO SECURE A NOTE

WHEREAS, this Corporation has borrowed from . . . . the sum of . . . . . ($. . . . .) Dollars, for which the Corporation has issued to him its demand note in that amount, dated . . . ., 19. ., and

WHEREAS, this Corporation desires to secure the said . . . . for the amount loaned by him to the Corporation as aforesaid, be it

RESOLVED, That the Treasurer of this Corporation is hereby authorized and instructed to transfer and assign, from time to time, to said . . . ., as security for the payment to him of the said note executed as above mentioned, bills and accounts receivable belonging to this Corporation, to be selected by the said . . . ., the face value of which bills and accounts receivable shall be, at all times, ... (. . . . . %) percent greater than the aggregate amount of the above-mentioned note, and

RESOLVED FURTHER, That the Treasurer is hereby authorized and instructed to render a report to the said . . . ., on the first day of each and every month, and at such other reasonable times as the said . . . . may desire, of all moneys that have been received by or in behalf of this Corporation, on account of any bills and accounts receivable so transferred and assigned, and

RESOLVED FURTHER, That, on the first day of each month, the Treasurer of this Corporation shall pay to the said . . . . any and all amounts collected on account of the bills or accounts receivable aforesaid, to be applied to the reduction of the amount due from the Corporation to the said . . . ., unless the said . . . . elects to accept, in lieu of such payment, other bills and accounts receivable due this Corporation, it being understood that, upon full payment of the note executed by this Corporation as hereinbefore mentioned, the said . . . . shall return to the Treasurer of this Corporation any and all bills and accounts receivable then remaining in his possession or under his control.

DIRECTORS' RESOLUTION GIVING OFFICERS GENERAL AUTHORITY TO ISSUE NOTES IN SERIES, SECURED BY ASSIGNMENT OF ACCOUNTS RECEIVABLE TO TRUSTEE

RESOLVED, That this Company, by virtue of authority given by resolution of its stockholders on . . . ., 19. ., borrow, from time to time, such amounts of money as may be necessary for the business requirements and purposes of the Company, upon the promissory notes of the Company, to be designated as Series "A," and numbered from one (1) to one thousand (1,000), inclusive, to be issued at such time or times, in such amounts, and payable at such dates, respectively, as may be determined by the President and the Treasurer of the Company, and to be collaterally secured by the assignment and delivery, in pledge, of bills and accounts receivable and other available assets to a trustee for the holders of such notes pro rata, the value of which shall be at least . . . . . (. . . . . %) percent greater than the aggregate amount of said notes, and the President and the Treasurer are hereby authorized and directed to execute the notes as aforesaid, and any notes that may be given in renewal thereof, and to deliver the same, and

RESOLVED FURTHER, That the President and the Treasurer are hereby authorized and directed to execute assignments to such trustee, of any and all such bills and accounts receivable and other available assets to the amount aforesaid, and the Treasurer is hereby authorized and directed to pay over to said trustee, to be applied to the retirement of the amounts due by this Company on such notes or renewals thereof, any moneys that shall be collected on such pledged bills and accounts receivable and assets, and the Treasurer is also hereby authorized and directed to render an account to said trustee, as often as may be required by the latter, of all moneys that have been received by the Company on account of any bills and accounts receivable and assets that shall have been so assigned and delivered in pledge, and

RESOLVED FURTHER, That, upon the payment of said notes of the Company, the trustee shall return to the Treasurer of the Company all accounts and bills receivable and assets belonging to the Company and then remaining in said trustee's hands, and

RESOLVED FURTHER, That .... is hereby appointed to act as trustee in accordance with the terms and requirements specifically set forth in the foregoing resolution.

DIRECTORS' RESOLUTION AUTHORIZING BORROWING ON EXECUTION OF PROMISSORY NOTE AND PROVIDING FOR RENEWAL OF NOTE

WHEREAS, this Company desires to borrow money for its corporate purposes, be it

RESOLVED, That the proper officers of this Company are hereby authorized and empowered to borrow from the .... Bank, for and in behalf of this Company, a sum not to exceed ..... ($.....) Dollars, on its promissory note maturing ..... (.....) days from the date hereof, to be signed by the proper officers of this Company, and to bear interest at the rate of ..... (.....%) percent per annum, with the privilege, however, of renewing said loan at the maturity thereof for a further period of .....(.....) days, upon payment of ..... ($.....) Dollars on account of the principal amount thereof, and with the additional privilege of renewing the balance of said loan at the maturity of said further period of ..... (.....) days, for another period of ..... (.....) days, upon payment of ..... ($.....) Dollars on account of said balance, thereby reducing said loan to ..... ($.....) Dollars; and the proper officers of this Company are hereby authorized and directed to sign any new or renewal note or notes required by said .... Bank to carry out the provisions of this resolution, which new note or notes shall bear such rate of interest as shall be agreed upon between this Company and the said .... Bank at the time of such renewal or renewals, and

RESOLVED FURTHER, That ...., Vice president of this Company, is hereby authorized and empowered, for and in behalf of this Company, to countersign the aforesaid promissory note, or any new or renewal note or notes above mentioned.

DIRECTORS' RESOLUTION RATIFYING ACTION OF OFFICERS IN EXECUTING NOTE GIVEN AS EVIDENCE OF LOAN TO CORPORATION

WHEREAS, the President and the Treasurer of this Corporation have executed and delivered to the .... Company three (3) notes of this

Corporation, each for . . . . . ($. . . . .) Dollars, each note dated . . . .,
19. ., and payable to bearer with interest at the rate of . . . . . (. . . . .%) percent
per annum, on . . . . ., in 19. ., 19. ., and 19. ., respectively, at . . . ., as
evidence of the loan to this Corporation by the . . . . Company of . . . . .
($. . . . .) Dollars, be it

RESOLVED, That the said action of the President and the Treasurer in
executing and delivering to the . . . . Company the three notes of this
Corporation as aforesaid is hereby in all respects ratified, confirmed, and
approved.

RESOLUTION OF STOCKHOLDERS PLEDGING UNISSUED STOCK AS COLLATERAL SECURITY, AND GIVING PLEDGEE RIGHT TO VOTE STOCK PLEDGED

RESOLVED, That the Board of Directors is hereby authorized to deliver
to the . . . . Company . . . . . (. . . . .) shares of the unissued common
stock of this Corporation, of the par value of . . . . . ($. . . . .) Dollars each, to
be held by the said . . . . Company as collateral security for the advance
by the said . . . . Company to this Corporation, of the sum of . . . . .
($. . . . .) Dollars, the said stock to be delivered to the . . . . Company
immediately upon receipt of the said sum as aforesaid, and

RESOLVED FURTHER, That the said . . . . . Company shall have the right
and power to vote the said stock during the time it is held by said company as
security for the indebtedness aforesaid.

DIRECTORS' RESOLUTION AUTHORIZING ISSUANCE OF NOTE SECURED BY PLEDGE OF BONDS

WHEREAS, ..., the Treasurer of this Corporation, has been able
to arrange a loan from the . . . . Bank to meet current need for funds, be
it

RESOLVED, That this Corporation borrow from the . . . . Bank the
sum of . . . . . ($. . . . .) Dollars, to be repaid within . . . . . years, with interest
at the rate of six (6%) percent per annum, and

RESOLVED FURTHER, That . . . ., the President of this Corporation, and . . . ., its Treasurer, are hereby authorized, empowered, and
directed jointly to execute and deliver a promissory note to the said bank in
the amount aforementioned, in the name and under the seal of this
Corporation, payable in . . . . . years, with interest as aforesaid, to evidence
the aforementioned loan, and to secure the payment of the said promissory
note by delivering to . . . . ., President of the said bank, in pledge, ...
(. . . . .) first mortgage bonds of the . . . . Railway Company, of the face
value of one thousand ($1,000) Dollars each, belonging to and now in the
possession of this Corporation, and to do any and all other acts necessary to
carry this resolution into effect.

DIRECTORS' RESOLUTION AUTHORIZING OFFICERS TO BORROW AND TO EXECUTE A MORTGAGE ON REAL PROPERTY AS SECURITY

RESOLVED, That the officers of this Company are hereby authorized, empowered, and directed to borrow the sum of . . . . . ($. . . . .) Dollars from the . . . . Bank at . . . . . (. . . . .%) percent interest, for a period of . . . . . years, and to execute as security for said loan a first mortgage on the real property of the Company, situated *(insert description of the property to be mortgaged),* and to do such other things and to execute such other documents as may be necessary and proper to effect the foregoing.

DIRECTORS' RESOLUTION AUTHORIZING BORROWING ON DEBENTURES, FIXING AMOUNT, LIMITING DURATION OF LOAN AND RATE OF INTEREST, AND CALLING STOCKHOLDERS' MEETING FOR APPROVAL

RESOLVED, That this Company borrow, for its corporate purposes, the sum of . . . . . ($. . . . .) Dollars, for a period not exceeding . . . . . (. . . . .) years, with interest at a rate not exceeding . . . . . (. . . . .%) percent per annum, payable semi-annually; that such indebtedness be evidenced by coupon notes or debentures of the Company, issued independently under and in pursuance of a trust agreement between the Company and a trustee, in such form, and containing such terms and conditions in conformity with the foregoing, as the Board of Directors may determine; and

RESOLVED FURTHER, That a special meeting of the stockholders of this Company be called to convene at its general office, ... *(Street),* . . . . *(City),* . . . . at . . . . . M., on . . . ., 19. ., to take action for or against the above resolution, and

RESOLVED FURTHER, That the Secretary is hereby directed to give notice of such meeting as required by law.

RESOLUTION OF PREFERRED STOCKHOLDERS CONSENTING TO CREATION OF INDEBTEDNESS BY BORROWING

RESOLVED, That the holders of the preferred stock of this Corporation do hereby consent to the creation of indebtedness by the Corporation in an amount not exceeding $. . . . ., by loan or loans from one or more banks or other institutions, such loan or loans to bear interest at such rate or rates, be payable on such date or dates, be upon such other terms and conditions and be evidenced by such notes or other evidences of indebtedness as the Board of Directors of the Corporation shall approve; provided, however, that the amount of any such indebtedness, together with the Corporation's presently outstanding bank loan of $. . . . ., if such loan shall not be paid off, shall in no event exceed $. . . . .

DIRECTORS' RESOLUTION PROPOSING INCREASE OF INDEBTEDNESS AND CALLING MEETING OF STOCKHOLDERS FOR APPROVAL

RESOLVED, That it is the purpose of this Company to increase its indebtedness from ..... ($.....) Dollars to ..... ($.....) Dollars, and that a meeting of the stockholders be called to convene at the general office of the Company on ...., 19..., at ..... M., to take action on the approval or disapproval of the proposed increase of indebtedness of the Company, the notice by publication required to be given by the Constitution and laws of this state having been waived by the unanimous consent of the stockholders.

RESOLUTION OF STOCKHOLDERS RATIFYING INDEBTEDNESS PREVIOUSLY INCURRED, AND INCREASING INDEBTEDNESS OF CORPORATION

WHEREAS, the stockholders have heretofore authorized an increase in the indebtedness of this Company to three million ($3,000,000) Dollars, and there has been issued its bond in the aggregate principal amount of two million ($2,000,000) Dollars, part of which has been redeemed in accordance with the terms of the issuance thereof, and there has been issued its note in the principal amount of one million ($1,000,000) Dollars, and

WHEREAS, it is the desire of this Company to increase its indebtedness from three million ($3,000,000) Dollars to a total of five million ($5,000,000) Dollars by the creation of additional indebtedness or by, from time to time, recreating indebtedness not to exceed five million ($5,000,000) Dollars at any one time, be it

RESOLVED, That the indebtedness heretofore incurred and created pursuant to previous authorization of an increase of indebtedness to three million ($3,000,000) Dollars be ratified, approved, and confirmed and consent given thereto, and

RESOLVED FURTHER, That the indebtedness of this Company be increased from three million ($3,000,000) Dollars to five million ($5,000,000) Dollars, and

RESOLVED FURTHER, That upon adoption of the foregoing resolution the Company will be authorized to incur or create any such indebtedness up to a total of five million ($5,000,000) Dollars on terms determined by the Board of Directors.

DIRECTORS' RESOLUTION AUTHORIZING APPLICATION FOR PERMIT TO CREATE BONDED INDEBTEDNESS IN EXCESS OF SUBSCRIBED CAPITAL STOCK

WHEREAS, the subscribed capital stock of this Corporation is ..... ($.....) Dollars, and

WHEREAS, this Corporation desires to create an indebtedness in excess of its subscribed capital stock, be it

RESOLVED, That . . . ., the President of this Corporation, and . . . ., its Secretary, are hereby authorized and directed to sign and verify an application to the *(insert official name of the commission)* of the State of . . . ., for a permit to create a bonded indebtedness aggregating . . . . . ($. . . . .) Dollars in excess of its subscribed capital stock.

DIRECTORS' RESOLUTION AUTHORIZING PLEDGE OF SECURITIES TO SECURE COLLATERAL TRUST BONDS AND AUTHORIZING OFFICERS TO EXECUTE CONTRACT OF PLEDGE

RESOLVED, That, to secure the payment of the proposed issue of bonds of this Corporation, to the amount of . . . . . ($. . . . .) Dollars, there be deposited with the . . . . Company of . . . . ., under a contract of pledge, ... (. . . . .) shares of the capital stock of this Corporation, and

RESOLVED FURTHER, That the President of this Corporation is hereby authorized to execute, under the corporate seal, and the Secretary is authorized duly to attest, a contract of pledge, in the form now presented to and approved by this Board of Directors.

DIRECTORS' RESOLUTION AUTHORIZING FILING OF REGISTRATION STATEMENT AND PROSPECTUS AND ISSUANCE OF DEBENTURES

RESOLVED, That the requisite forms of registration statement and prospectus be prepared and filed as speedily as practicable under the Securities Act of 1933, as amended, and that as soon as the same shall have become fully effective, the Company proceed with respect to the issuance and sale of the 10-year 6% Convertible Debentures as then called for by its agreement with its underwriters.

DIRECTORS' RESOLUTION APPROVING FORM OF REGISTRATION STATEMENT AND PROSPECTUS RELATING TO ISSUE OF BONDS

RESOLVED, That the forms of Registration Statement and Prospectus relating to the Company's issue of $. . . . . First Mortgage Bonds, Series A, Sinking Fund 5's due 19. ., submitted to the meeting, are approved for initial filing, and that only such changes shall be made therein as shall be approved by the Chairman of the Board of Directors of the Company and by counsel for the Company.

DIRECTORS' RESOLUTION AUTHORIZING APPLICATION TO PUBLIC SERVICE COMMISSION FOR PERMISSION TO ISSUE AND SELL AN AMOUNT OF BONDS PREVIOUSLY AUTHORIZED BY COMMISSION AT A LOWER PRICE

WHEREAS, the Public Service Commission, State of . . . ., has heretofore issued an order dated . . . ., 19. ., Case No. . . . . . ., and an order dated . . . ., 19. ., Case No. . . . . . ., authorizing this Corporation to issue . . . . . ($. . . . .) Dollars and . . . . . ($. . . . .) Dollars of bonds, and to sell the same at a price of eighty-nine (89%) percent and eighty-eight (88%) percent of par, respectively, and

WHEREAS, owing to market conditions, it has been impossible to dispose of bonds at the figures hereinabove set forth, and

WHEREAS, the President of this Corporation has recommended that he be authorized to make application to the Public Service Commission for permission to sell bonds heretofore authorized to be issued by said Commission at a price not less than eight-five (85%) percent of par, be it

RESOLVED, That, in accordance with the foregoing, the President is hereby authorized to make application to the Public Service Commission, State of . . . ., for permission to sell bonds heretofore authorized to be issued by said Commission at eight-five (85%) percent of par.

DIRECTORS' RESOLUTION AUTHORIZING DELIVERY OF BONDS TO BROKER FOR SALE AT LESS THAN PAR

WHEREAS, this Board of Directors heretofore and on . . . ., 19. ., did issue . . . . . (. . . . .) bonds of this Company, of the face value of . . . . . ($. . . . .) Dollars each, bearing interest at the rate of five (5%) percent per annum, payable semi-annually, upon the consent of the stockholders of this Company, given at a meeting duly held for that purpose, and

WHEREAS, the said stockholders did authorize and empower this Board of Directors to fix the price at which the said bonds might be sold, be it

RESOLVED, That the firm of . . . ., brokers, is hereby authorized and empowered to sell the said bonds of this Company at a price not less than seventy-five (75%) percent of the face value thereof, the said firm of . . . . to receive a commission of . . . . . (. . . . . %) percent of the sales made by it, the same to be deducted from the proceeds of the sale of said bonds, and

RESOLVED FURTHER, That the Treasurer of this Company is hereby authorized and directed to deliver said bonds, properly indorsed, to the said firm of . . . ., and to obtain the proper receipt therefor.

DIRECTORS' RESOLUTION AUTHORIZING EMPLOYMENT OF FINANCE COMPANY TO SELL BONDS ISSUED UNDER MORTGAGE, AND MAKING PROVISION FOR COMPENSATION

RESOLVED, That the Vice president of this Corporation is hereby authorized to employ the . . . . Trust Company to sell, for the account of this Corporation, at not less than par and accrued interest, each and all of the bonds authorized to be issued under the mortgage to be executed by this Corporation, to the . . . . Trust Company and . . . ., as Trustees, and to pay to said . . . . Trust Company, as compensation for its services in selling said bonds, an amount equal to . . . . . (. . . . .%) percent of the principal amount of the bonds so sold.

EXCERPT OF MINUTES OF DIRECTORS' MEETING AUTHORIZING EXECUTION OF AGREEMENTS TO SELL ISSUE OF SECURED NOTES TO BANKERS

The President presented to the meeting a letter dated . . . ., 19. ., sent by this Corporation to . . . . & Co., containing an option to the latter Company to purchase, upon the basis named therein, $1,000,000 in aggregate principal amount of this Corporation's 5% Secured Notes, due . . . ., 19. .

The President also presented to the meeting a letter dated . . . ., 19. ., sent by . . . . & Co. to this Corporation, stating in effect that the terms of the option were in accordance with the understanding of the option by . . . . & Co. Said letters are as follows *(insert letters)*.

Upon motion, duly made, the following resolutions were adopted:

RESOLVED, That the arrangement between . . . . & Co. and this Corporation, evidenced by the letters above set forth under date of . . . ., 19. ., is hereby ratified, approved, confirmed, and adopted as the action of this Corporation, and

RESOLVED FURTHER, That the officers of the Corporation are hereby authorized to execute all or any part of $1,000,000 in aggregate principal amount of its 5% Secured Notes, dated . . . ., 19. ., and maturing . . . ., 19. ., and that said notes shall be authenticated from time to time by the Trustee, upon written orders of the Corporation, signed by its President or a Vice president, under its corporate seal, and attested by its Secretary or an Assistant Secretary, and

RESOLVED FURTHER, That the officers of the Corporation are hereby authorized, in accordance with the terms and conditions of the agreement dated . . . ., 19. ., between this Corporation and the . . . . Trust Co. of . . . ., Trustee, under which agreement the notes are issued, to pledge, under said agreement, as notes shall be ordered authenticated from time to time, First and Refunding Mortgage Thirty-Year 5% Bonds of the . . . .

Co., for a principal amount equal to . . . . . percent of the principal amount of such notes. In pledging bonds as aforesaid, there must be taken into consideration $. . . . . in aggregated principal amount of such bonds already deposited with the Trustee in excess of the amount previously required.

DIRECTORS' RESOLUTION AUTHORIZING OFFICERS TO TAKE NECESSARY STEPS TO SELL BONDS TO DESIGNATED PURCHASER

RESOLVED, That the officers of this Company be and they hereby are authorized to take all necessary steps to sell, to the . . . . Engineering Corporation, all the Refunding and Improvement Bonds that have been authorized to be issued by the Public Service Commission for capital expenditures for the new . . . . railroad line, at prices authorized in orders issued by the Public Service Commission.

DIRECTORS' RESOLUTION AUTHORIZING OFFICERS TO APPLY FOR PERMISSION TO ISSUE BONDS, AND PROVIDING FOR SALE TO DESIGNATED PURCHASER ON RECEIPT OF PERMIT

RESOLVED, That . . . ., the President of this Corporation, and . . . ., its Secretary, are hereby authorized and directed to sign and verify an application to the *(insert official name of Commission)* of the State of . . . . ., in the name and in behalf of this Corporation, requesting permission for the issuance, by this Corporation, of . . . . . ($. . . . .) Dollars of its bonds, and the sale and delivery of said bonds for a consideration in cash of not less than . . . . . (. . . . .%) percent of the aggregate principal amount of said bonds, together with accrued interest from the date of said bonds to the date of their delivery to the purchaser thereof, and

RESOLVED FURTHER, That, upon receipt of the permission from the . . . . Commission as aforesaid, to sell and deliver the bonds as aforesaid, the officers of this Corporation are hereby authorized and directed forthwith to sell and deliver, or cause to be sold and delivered, in behalf of this Corporation, all or any part of said bonds, to or upon the order of the . . . . Company, upon payment of the purchase price therefor—to wit, ... (. . . . .%) percent of the principal amount of said bonds—together with accrued interest thereon from the date thereof to the date of such payment, the amount of said payment to be deposited with the . . . . Trust Company, as Trustee, pursuant to the provisions of the mortgage or deed of trust under which the said bonds are issued.

DIRECTORS' RESOLUTION AUTHORIZING ISSUE OF REGISTERED DEBENTURE BONDS TO PROVIDE FUNDS FOR CONSTRUCTION EXPENDITURE

RESOLVED, That, for the purpose of providing for the construction expenditures on the various roads of this Company, and for other purposes,

the Board of Directors, in pursuance of lawful authority, hereby authorizes
the President and the Secretary to execute and issue, under the corporate seal
of the Company, ... ($.....) Dollars of registered debenture bonds, in
sums of one thousand ($1,000) Dollars each, to be dated ...., 19.., due in
..... (.....) years, with interest at ..... (.....%) percent per annum,
payable semi-annually, which bonds shall be in the following form (*insert
form of bond*).

DIRECTORS' RESOLUTION AUTHORIZING ISSUANCE
OF BONDS IN PAYMENT OF DEBT

WHEREAS, the .... Company has rendered an itemized statement
of account against this Corporation for the cost of grading the right of way of
a portion of this Corporation's line of railroad, in the sum of ..... ($.....)
Dollars, and

WHEREAS, said .... Company is willing to accept the First
Mortgage 5 Percent Thirty-Year Bonds of this Corporation in the total
aggregate sum of ..... ($.....) Dollars, in full satisfaction and discharge of
all claims and demands whatsoever that it now has or claims to have growing
out of any matter or thing whatsoever against this Corporation, be it

RESOLVED, That the Treasurer of this Corporation is hereby authorized
to deliver to the .... Company, the First Mortgage 5 Percent Thirty-
Year Bonds of this Corporation in the aggregate amount of ..... ($.....)
Dollars, after the .... Company has executed and delivered to this
Corporation a receipt in full of all claims or demands whatsoever that it now
has or claims to have for or on account of any matter or thing whatsoever.

RESOLUTION OF BOARD OF DIRECTORS AUTHORIZING ISSUE
OF NEGOTIABLE PROMISSORY NOTES SECURED BY BONDS,
TO PAY EXISTING DEBT AND TO COVER FUTURE ADVANCES

WHEREAS, the stockholders of the .... Railroad Corporation, a
corporation of the State of .., on ...., 19.., did authorize the issue of
bonds in the aggregate of ..... ($.....) Dollars, to be issued and disposed of
on the terms and conditions set forth in a certain mortgage or deed of trust,
dated ...., 19.., and

WHEREAS, said mortgage or deed of trust authorized the said bonds to
be used by the .... Railroad Corporation to build, finish, improve, or
operate its railroad, and to pay the indebtedness incurred in building,
improving, or operating its railroad, and

WHEREAS, this Corporation desires to borrow an additional amount of
money from the .... Company, for the purpose of extending,
completing, equipping, and operating its line of railroad, and desires to secure
the amount which it now owes, or the amount that may hereafter be advanced

by the said .... Company, or loaned to it by the said ....
Company, as hereinafter stated, be it

RESOLVED, That this Corporation issue its negotiable promissory notes, payable in two, three, and four years, respectively, from ...., 19.., with interest at the rate of six (6%) percent per annum, in such denominations as the .... Company may desire, in the aggregate sum of ..... ($.....) Dollars, payable either to the .... Company or to order, as security for the amount due or owing to the said .... Company, and as security for such further amounts as may hereafter be advanced by or from the said .... Company, and

RESOLVED FURTHER, That this Corporation delivered to the said .... Company, ... (.....) of its First Mortgage 5% Thirty-Year Bonds, of the par value of one thousand ($1,000) Dollars each, as collateral security for the payment of said note or notes.

RESOLUTION OF STOCKHOLDERS AUTHORIZING ISSUE OF CONVERTIBLE NOTES

RESOLVED, That authority and consent are hereby given to the issuance of this Corporation's Six (6%) Percent Registered Debenture Notes, in the aggregate face amount not exceeding ..... ($.....) Dollars, to bear date as of ...., 19.., to be callable at par and interest on any interest day after ...., 19.., to mature not later than ..... years from date, and to be convertible into common stock of this Corporation on and after ...., 19.., the exchange and conversion to be made on the basis of one share of such common stock without par value for each ..... ($.....) Dollars in face value of such notes so converted.

BLANKET RESOLUTION OF DIRECTORS AUTHORIZING OFFICERS TO ISSUE DUPLICATE BONDS TO REPLACE BONDS LOST, DESTROYED, OR STOLEN

WHEREAS, this Corporation did, on ...., 19.., duly issue ..... (.....) First Mortgage 5% Bonds of the face value of ..... ($.....) Dollars each, under a certain trust deed dated ...., 19.., and

WHEREAS, under the terms of the said trust deed, it is provided that this Corporation shall issue, and the .... Trust Company, Trustee under the said trust deed, shall certify, duplicate bonds to replace any bonds lost, destroyed, or stolen, upon the furnishing by the owner and holder thereof of satisfactory evidence of ownership and loss, destruction, or theft, and upon his furnishing of an undertaking in twice the amount of the bond so lost, destroyed, or stolen, plus interest thereon until maturity, to indemnify this Corporation and the said .... Trust Company against any loss, damage, or liability suffered or incurred by reason of the issuance of any duplicate bonds as aforesaid, be it

RESOLVED, That the proper officers of this Corporation are hereby authorized and empowered to execute, and the . . . . Trust Company is hereby authorized to certify and deliver, duplicate bonds to replace any bonds lost, destroyed, or stolen, provided that the alleged owner and holder thereof furnishes satisfactory evidence of his ownership and of the loss, destruction, or theft, and provided that the said owner and holder thereof furnishes an undertaking in twice the face amount of the bonds so lost, destroyed, or stolen, plus interest thereon until maturity, indemnifying this Corporation and saving it harmless from and against any and all losses, damages, or liabilities whatsoever that this Corporation or the said . . . . Trust Company may incur through the issuance of the said duplicate bond, and

RESOLVED FURTHER, That no duplicate bond shall be issued as aforesaid until the expiration of 6 months from the date of receipt by this Corporation of notice of the said loss, destruction, or theft.

DIRECTORS' RESOLUTION AUTHORIZING OFFICERS AND TRUSTEE TO ISSUE DUPLICATE BOND TO REPLACE ONE LOST, DESTROYED, OR STOLEN

WHEREAS, ..., of . . . ., claims to be the owner of a First Mortgage 5% Bond of this Company numbered . . . . . ., in the face amount of . . . . . ($. . . . .) Dollars, issued under the provisions of a certain trust deed dated . . . ., 19. ., and claims that the said bond has been lost (destroyed or stolen) and cannot be found, and

WHEREAS, more than 6 months have elapsed since the said . . . . notified this Company of the loss (destruction or theft) aforesaid, and the said . . . . has furnished this Company with satisfactory evidence of ownership and loss (destruction or theft), be it

RESOLVED, That the officers of this Company are hereby authorized and directed to execute, and the . . . . Trust Company, Trustee under the aforesaid trust deed, is hereby requested to certify and deliver to . . . ., a duplicate bond of the face value of . . . . . ($. . . . .) Dollars, with the proper notations thereon, to replace the bond lost (destroyed or stolen) as aforesaid, upon receiving from the said . . . . an undertaking in the sum of . . . . . ($. . . . .) Dollars, indemnifying this Company and the said . . . . Trust Company against any damages, losses, or liabilities whatsoever that they or either of them may suffer or incur through the issuance of the aforesaid duplicate bond.

DIRECTORS' RESOLUTION AUTHORIZING OFFICER TO SELL CERTAIN LAND, AND REQUESTING TRUSTEE TO RELEASE SAID LAND FROM LIEN OF MORTGAGE

RESOLVED, by the Board of Directors of the . . . . Company, that the following-described real estate owned by said Company is no longer necessary for use in connection with its railway—namely, a parcel of land consisting of ...., and more particularly described as follows (*insert description*).

RESOLVED FURTHER, That the President of said Company is hereby authorized and empowered to dispose of the same on such terms as his judgment shall dictate, and to execute a deed therefor on behalf of the Company and

RESOLVED FURTHER, That the .... Company, Trustee under the mortgage made by the .... Company, under date of ...., 19.., is hereby authorized and requested to release from the lien of said mortgage said above-described property, at the request of the President of the .... Company.

DIRECTORS' RESOLUTION REQUESTING TRUSTEE TO RELEASE CERTAIN PROPERTIES FROM LIEN OF MORTGAGE, AND AUTHORIZING DEPOSIT WITH TRUSTEE OF CASH RECEIVED UPON SALE OF PROPERTY

RESOLVED, That .... Trust Co., as Trustee under the mortgage made by this Company to .... Trust Co., as Trustee, dated ...., 19.., and the indentures supplemental thereto, is hereby requested to execute and deliver to this Company a release from the lien of said mortgage and supplemental indentures, of the following-described properties, which are no longer required or useful for or in connection with the business of this Company conducted upon the property covered by said mortgage, or for the conduct and operation thereof, and that this Company has sold for an amount in cash at least equal to the value of the property so sold—to wit, $..... (For description of lands, see deed of .... Co. to ...., dated ...., 19.., and recorded in the office of the registrar of deeds of .... County, ..., on ...., 19.., in Book ..... of deeds, p .....)

RESOLVED FURTHER, That the officers of this Company are hereby authorized and directed to take all steps necessary or convenient to obtain the release of the above-described properties by .... Trust Co. from the lien of the mortgage made by this Company to .... Trust Co., as Trustee, dated ...., 19.., and the indentures supplemental thereto, including the execution and delivery to the Trustee, under said mortgage, of any certificates that may be required by said mortgage, or any certificates that may be required by said Trustee, pursuant to such mortgage, of the purchase price for said property, execution, and delivery to ...., of proper conveyances covering the above-described properties, and the delivery to said ...., of the release of said properties from the lien of this Company's first mortgage and the indentures supplemental thereto.

DIRECTORS' RESOLUTION AUTHORIZING EXCHANGE OF SECURITY UNDER COLLATERAL TRUST AGREEMENT

RESOLVED, That .... Trust Company, as Trustee under the collateral trust agreement made by this Company to .... Trust Company, as Trustee, dated ...., 19.., is hereby requested to deliver to ...., Treasurer of the Company, or ...., Assistant Treasurer of the Company, ... (.....) shares of the aggregate par value of ..... ($.....) Dollars of .... Corporation common stock, upon delivery to the Trustee of ..... (.....) shares of no par value common stock, which was issued in exchange for all of the issued and outstanding common stock of the par value of $100 each of .... Corporation.

EXECUTION OF INDENTURES

RESOLUTION OF STOCKHOLDERS AUTHORIZING EXECUTION OF MORTGAGE ON FIXTURES AND STOCK OF MERCHANDISE AND OTHER PERSONAL PROPERTY, PRESENTLY OWNED AND AFTER-ACQUIRED

RESOLVED, That ...., the President, and ...., the Secretary of this Corporation, are hereby authorized and directed to borrow the sum of ..... ($.....) Dollars from .... for a period of ..... (.....) years, and to make and execute, in evidence of said indebtedness, a promissory note in the aforesaid amount, bearing interest at the rate of ..... (.....%) percent per annum, payable to said .... on ...., 19.., together with a mortgage to secure the payment of the said note, covering all the furniture and fixtures and the entire stock of merchandise, an inventory of which is listed below, and all other goods, chattels, and personal property of any kind or character which this Corporation now has or which it may hereafter acquire, all of which property is now located at .. .. (*Street*), in the City of ...., State of ....., and

RESOLVED FURTHER, That ...., the President, and ...., the Secretary of this Corporation, are hereby authorized and directed to cause the required notices to be given to the creditors of this Corporation, and to do and perform all other things and acts necessary and proper to carry out the provisions of this resolution.

(Here insert inventory list of fixtures and stock of merchandise.)

RESOLUTION OF STOCKHOLDERS AUTHORIZING MORTGAGE WITH SINKING FUND

RESOLVED, That the President and Secretary are hereby authorized and directed to make and execute, under the corporate seal of said company, an indenture of mortgage covering all the personal property of the company, consisting of .... (*give full description of property*), together also with the privileges, franchises, and appurtenances of and belonging to this company, wheresoever situate, or that may be hereafter acquired by or conferred upon this company, including the franchise to be a corporation, and

RESOLVED FURTHER, That for the better securing of the money due to the purchasers of the bonds secured by said mortgage, a sinking fund be created for the purchase and cancellation of the bonds to be issued by this company, and to that end the income from the business to be conducted by this company, after first paying all salaries and other expenses of any kind or character, and before paying any dividend to the holders of shares of capital stock of this company, the balance in the hands of the Treasurer at the end of each fiscal year shall be credited to the sinking fund account for the purpose aforesaid.

DIRECTORS' RESOLUTION AUTHORIZING PRESIDENT TO EXECUTE AND DELIVER TRUST DEED COVERING ALL PERSONAL PROPERTY FOR ANTECEDENT DEBT AND FUTURE ADVANCES

WHEREAS, this Corporation is indebted to the firm of . . . . , in the amount of . . . . . ($. . . . .) Dollars, for money advanced for the payment of timber lands and operating expenses, and for the construction of a saw mill, a stave mill, and a dimension mill, and

WHEREAS, the said firm has agreed to advance an additional sum of . . . . . ($. . . . .) Dollars to this Corporation, to enable it to meet its note to . . . . , due . . . ., 19. ., be it

RESOLVED, That, in order to secure the present and future indebtedness of this Corporation to the said firm of . . . . ., as aforesaid, ..., President of this Corporation, is hereby authorized and instructed to execute and deliver to the said firm of . . . . a trust deed covering all the personal property of this Corporation, consisting of (*give full description of personal property*), and a second mortgage upon its timber lands situated in the . . . ., and described as follows (*incorporate complete description of real property*).

EXCERPT OF MINUTES OF DIRECTORS' MEETING PROPOSING ISSUANCE OF MORTGAGE BONDS TO LIQUIDATE UNFUNDED DEBT, AND AUTHORIZING APPLICATION FOR CONSENT OF PUBLIC SERVICE COMMISSION, PREPARATION AND FILING OF A REGISTRATION STATEMENT, AND COMPLIANCE WITH TRUST INDENTURE ACT OF 1939

The Chairman further reported that negotiations were again in progress for the issuance and sale of bonds of this Company for the purpose of liquidating the unfunded debt of this Company, particularly its open-account indebtedness to . . . . Company of . . . ., Inc., which aggregates $25,000,000 as of . . . ., 19. .

It was pointed out that the negotiations contemplate that, with a guaranty by .... Company of .... Inc., of payment of principal and interest of said bonds, the bonds can probably be sold to a responsible investment house or group of investment houses to net not less than 98% of the face amount, or $24,500,000.

On motion duly made and seconded, it was

RESOLVED, That the proposed issuance and sale of $25,000,000 aggregate principal amount of this Company's bonds (to be known as its "Consolidating Mortgage Bonds," or such other designation as may be determined upon), dated as of ...., 19.., bearing interest at the rate of not more than ..... (.....%) percent per annum, maturing ......, 19.., and to be issued under and secured by a new mortgage of the property and franchises of this Company (subject to existing mortgages) to be executed and delivered to .... Trust Company, as Trustee, or such other Trustee as may be determined upon, and the sale of the same to a responsible investment house or group of investment houses at not less than 98% of the face amount thereof to yield proceeds of approximately $24,500,000, are hereby approved, and

RESOLVED FURTHER, That the proper officers of this Company are hereby authorized and directed to take all such action as may be necessary and proper to effectuate the issuance and sale of the aforesaid bonds, including making of application to the Public Service Commission for its consent and authority for the issuance and sale of said bonds, the preparation, execution, and filing of a Registration Statement with the Securities and Exchange Commission pursuant to the provisions of the Securities Act of 1933, as amended, and the preparation of a Mortgage or Trust Indenture pursuant to which such bonds are to be issued, which shall comply with the requirements of the Trust Indenture Act of 1939.

RESOLUTION OF STOCKHOLDERS AUTHORIZING INCREASE OF INDEBTEDNESS AND EMPOWERING DIRECTORS TO EXECUTE BONDS SECURED BY GENERAL MORTGAGE COVERING ALL PROPERTY OF CORPORATION, INCLUDING FRANCHISE AND AFTER-ACQUIRED PROPERTY

RESOLVED:

First, that the stockholders of this Company, duly assembled in pursuance of the resolution of the Board of Directors of the Company, do hereby consent to and authorize an increase of the indebtedness of the Company from ..... (.....) Dollars to ..... ($.....) Dollars.

Second, that the Board of Directors of this Company is hereby authorized and directed to have prepared and executed, in the name of this Company, bonds in the sum of ..... ($.....) Dollars each, dated ......, 19.., and payable as follows: ..... ($.....) Dollars thereof on the first day of ......, and ..... ($.....) Dollars thereof on the first day of . . . . in each and every year thereafter until and including the first day of . . . . . , 19. ., at the rate of . . . . . (. . . . .%) percent per annum, payable semi-annually, both principal and interest being payable in lawful money of the United States of America, which bonds shall be secured by a mortgage upon all the property and assets, real, personal, and mixed, and the franchise of the Company now owned or hereafter acquired, said bonds and mortgage aforesaid to be in terms and form satisfactory to the officers of this Company and to be submitted to the stockholders of this Company for their approval.

Third, that the Board of Directors of this Company is hereby authorized to execute and deliver the mortgage hereinbefore referred to, to a trustee to be designated by it, and that it shall also designate the time and place at which the principal and interest of the said bonds shall be payable.

Fourth, that the Board of Directors of this Company is hereby authorized and directed to use the entire issue of said bonds for the purpose of carrying out the terms of the proposition made by the . . . . Company to this Company, and this day accepted by the stockholders of this Company.

EXCERPT OF MINUTES OF DIRECTORS' MEETING AUTHORIZING MORTGAGE OF PROPERTIES TO SECURE BOND ISSUE

The Secretary read to the meeting certain resolutions adopted at the special meeting of stockholders of the Company, held on . . . ., 19. ., authorizing a mortgage on the properties of the railroad, lands, buildings, terminals, equipment, rolling stock, franchises, and concessions of the Company, in order to guarantee bonds not to exceed, in the aggregate amount, ... ($. . . . .) Dollars, and authorizing the present issuance thereunder, and as part of the said mortgage debt, of . . . . . ($. . . . .) Dollars, aggregate principal amount, First Mortgage Bonds, Series A.

The Secretary also exhibited to the meeting a draft of the mortgage called "First Mortgage," which draft had been prepared by the officers in accordance with the resolutions of the stockholders, and which contains the proposed text of the said $. . . . . principal amount of bonds which will be called "First Mortgage Bonds, Series A," and the trustee's certificate that will appear on the back thereof.

RESOLVED, That the draft of the mortgage now exhibited to this meeting and the text of the bonds and of the trustee's certificate that appear therein be approved, and that the said draft be considered an integral part of the minutes of this meeting and be inserted in the minute book, and

RESOLVED FURTHER, That the President, or any one of the Vice presidents of this Company, is hereby authorized and instructed to execute, under the seal of this Company, affixed by its Secretary, or by any one of its Assistant Secretaries, any one of whom is hereby authorized to affix the said seal and to sign and execute in favor of the .... Bank of ...., as Trustee, a mortgage in substantially the form now approved by this meeting, and

RESOLVED FURTHER, That, upon the execution and signing of the said mortgage, the President, or any one of the Vice presidents of this Company, is hereby authorized and instructed to execute, under the seal of this Company, affixed by its Secretary or by any one of its Assistant Secretaries, any one of whom is hereby authorized to affix the same, one or more bonds under and secured by the said mortgage, which shall be designated as "First Mortgage Bonds, Series A," of this Company, in substantially the form that shall be set forth in the said mortgage, and for an aggregate principal amount of ..... ($.....) Dollars, and

RESOLVED FURTHER, That the proper officers of this Company are hereby authorized and instructed to deliver the bond or bonds thus executed to the said .... Bank of ...., as Trustee, under the said mortgage, and that the said Trustee is authorized and requested to authenticate the said bonds upon receipt thereof, and to deliver the said bond or bonds to or upon the written order of this Company, signed by its President, or by any one of its Vice presidents, and by its Secretary, or any one of its Assistant Secretaries, and

RESOLVED FURTHER, That full power and authority is hereby granted to the President and to each of the Vice presidents, and to the Secretary and each of the Assistant Secretaries of this Company, in their discretion, to agree to and approve, and to make and cause to be made, any modification or addition in respect to the said form of bond and in respect to the provisions which are to be inserted in the said mortgage, and to approve and execute any form of mortgage that contains the provisions which they, or any one of them, considers proper, and that the signatures of the officers who may authorize any bond and the execution of the said mortgage shall be considered for all purposes as full proof of the approval thereof and of all the terms, stipulations, and conditions contained in the said bond and mortgage. Any and all acts which the said officers may do or perform in conformity with the powers conferred upon them by these resolutions are hereby expressly authorized, approved, ratified, and confirmed, and

RESOLVED FURTHER, That the President, or any one of the Vice presidents of the Company, is hereby authorized and requested to sell and deliver to the .... Company, represented by its President, or by any other competent officer, the bond or bonds of the present issue called "First Mortgage Bonds, Series A," to the aggregate principal amount of ..... ($.....) Dollars, represented by one or more temporary or definitive certificates, for the sum of ..... ($.....) Dollars, United States currency; to receive and give receipt for the said amount; and to sign and execute any documents, public or private, that may be necessary or proper in connection therewith.

RESOLUTION OF STOCKHOLDERS AUTHORIZING CREATION AND ISSUANCE OF MORTGAGE BONDS, AND EMPOWERING OFFICERS TO TAKE ACTION NECESSARY TO COMPLY WITH SECURITIES ACT OF 1933

RESOLVED, That this Corporation, for the purpose of borrowing money for its corporate purposes, create and issue its bonds, to be issued in one or more series, under and secured by a mortgage and deed of trust of all the property of the Corporation, now owned or hereafter acquired; that such bonds be designated as "the general mortgage bonds" of this Corporation and, subject to such limitations as may be imposed by law, be unlimited in aggregate principal amount; that the bonds of each series be originally issuable as either coupon bonds registerable as to principal, with interest coupons attached, having the facsimile signature of the present or any future Treasurer of the Corporation impressed thereon, and/or as fully registered bonds, without coupons, issuable as may be provided in said mortgage and deed of trust, in lieu of or in exchange for such coupon bonds; such bonds, subject at such terms and provisions as may be stated in said mortgage and deed of trust, to bear such dates, to be issued in such series and amounts, at such rate or rates of interest, at such dates of maturity, in such denominations, with such provisions for redemption and/or purchase funds, sinking funds, or analogous provisions, if any, with such terms and conditions of exchange-ability and/or convertibility, if any, in regard to payment of taxes, and otherwise to be issued upon such terms and conditions, and to be in such form, as may be determined and authorized, from time to time, by the Board of Directors of this Corporation, subject to the provisions of such mortgage and deed of trust, and

RESOLVED FURTHER, That the initial issue of said general mortgage bonds, being bonds of Series A, shall be designated as "the General Mortgage Bonds, 9 Percent, Series A," of this Corporation, and be of the aggregate principal amount of $500,000,000; that such Series A bonds be dated . . . . . , 19. ., and mature . . . . . , 19. ., bear interest at the rate of 9 percent per annum, payable semi-annually, be coupon bonds registerable as to principal, and be issued otherwise in such form, and upon such terms and conditions, as may be provided in said mortgage and deed of trust and in the indenture of . . . ., 19. ., supplemental thereto, hereafter referred to in these resolutions, and

RESOLVED FURTHER, That a mortgage and deed of trust be made by this Corporation, as security for all such bonds, in such form, and containing such terms and provisions, and mortgaging and pledging such property of this Corporation, as may be determined or authorized by the Board of Directors of this Corporation, and that contemporaneously with the making of such mortgage and deed of trust, an indenture supplemental thereto be made by this Corporation with particular reference to the bonds of Series A, in such form, and containing such terms and provisions, as may be determined or authorized by the Board of Directors of this Corporation; that said mortgage and deed of trust and said supplemental indenture be dated . . . ., 19. ., and be made to such trustee or trustees as may be approved by the Board of Directors of this Corporation, and

RESOLVED FURTHER, That the proper officers of this Corporation are hereby authorized and directed to take all such action as may be necessary and proper to effectuate the issuance and sale of the aforesaid bonds, including the preparation, execution, and filing of a registration statement with the Securities and Exchange Commission pursuant to the provisions of the Securities Act of 1933, as amended.

DIRECTORS' RESOLUTION AUTHORIZING ISSUE OF MORTGAGE BONDS

RESOLVED, That this Corporation, for its corporate purposes, issue its first and refunding mortgage bonds for such principal amount or amounts as the Board of Directors may from time to time determine, subject, however, to the restrictions as to the issue of said bonds contained in the mortgage and deed of trust presented at this meeting, said bonds to be issued in one or more series, maturing at such dates, and bearing interest at such rates, and containing such other terms and provisions respectively, as the Board of Directors of this Corporation, prior to the issue thereof, may, in accordance with the provisions of said mortgage and deed of trust, determine, and that to secure said bonds, the Corporation execute and deliver to .... Trust Co., as Trustee, a mortgage and deed of trust, substantially in the form presented to this meeting, mortgaging and pledging all of the property and franchises of this Corporation now owned or hereafter acquired, except cash, shares of stock, obligations, bonds, and securities not specifically required by the terms of said mortgage and deed of trust to be now or hereafter pledged thereunder, and

RESOLVED FURTHER, That, in accordance with the provisions of the mortgage and deed of trust from this Corporation to .... Trust Co., as Trustee, authorized at this meeting, the provisions and the form, designation, and title of a series of bonds and appurtenant coupons to be issued under said mortgage and deed of trust, to be known as "First and Refunding Mortgage Bonds, 9 Percent, Series of 19..," and to be coupon bonds in denominations of $1,000 and $500, and, at the option of this Corporation, in denominations of $100, registerable as principal, and registered bonds without coupons in denominations of $5,000 and $1,000, and, at the option of this Corporation, in any other multiple or multiples of $1,000, are hereby established as follows (*insert form of bond*).

(*Note:* If all or substantially all of the assets of the corporation are mortgaged or pledged, a vote of stockholders authorizing the transaction is required by statute in most states. The act of the directors is insufficient to accomplish this purpose. See page 1008 for the type of resolution that should be employed.)

DIRECTORS' RESOLUTION PROVIDING FOR ISSUANCE OF CALLABLE BONDS UPON STOCKHOLDERS' APPROVAL OF INCREASE OF BONDED INDEBTEDNESS, AND EXECUTION OF MORTGAGE INDENTURE

WHEREAS, at a special meeting held on . . . ., 19. ., the stockholders of this Corporation duly consented (*if upon written assent of stockholders, say:* "Whereas, the stockholders of this Corporation signified their assent in writing on . . . ., 19. ."), to an increase in the bonded indebtedness of this Corporation, from . . . . . ($. . . . .) Dollars to . . . . . ($. . . . .) Dollars, and the proper documents and certificates relating to the creation of such increase of bonded indebtedness have been properly filed with the Secretary of State of the State of . . . . and the County Clerk of . . . . County, be it

RESOLVED, That . . . . . (. . . . .) First Mortgage Five (5%) Percent Sinking Fund Bonds of the denomination of . . . . . ($. . . . .) Dollars each, dated . . . ., 19. ., all due and payable on . . . ., 19. ., shall be executed and issued by this Corporation in the manner set forth in Article . . . . . of the trust indenture hereinafter set forth, and

RESOLVED FURTHER, That this Corporation shall have the right to call in and retire all or any of said bonds on any interest payment date before the maturity of same, upon and by the payment of the principal thereof and all accrued interest thereon, together with a premium of five (5%) percent of the principal thereof, such redemption to be effected in the manner required by said trust indenture, and

RESOLVED FURTHER, That each of said bonds shall bear interest at the rate of . . . . . (. . . . .%) percent per annum from the date thereof, payable semi-annually on the first days of April and October in each year, said interest to be evidenced by proper coupons attached to said bonds, and

RESOLVED FURTHER, That, to secure the payment of said bonds and the interest thereon, ..., the President of this Corporation, and . . . . ., its Secretary, are hereby authorized, empowered, and directed to make, execute, and deliver a trust indenture in the following form, conveying, and mortgaging the property of the Corporation to . . . . . Trust Company, which is hereby designated and appointed Trustee under the said trust indenture (*insert trust indenture*).

DIRECTORS' RESOLUTION AUTHORIZING ANOTHER SERIES OF BONDS UNDER AN EXISTING MORTGAGE

RESOLVED, That the . . . . . series of bonds to be issued under the mortgage of this Corporation, dated as of . . . ., 19. ., to . . . . Trust Company of . . . . (to which the Bank has succeeded by merger), as Trustee, is hereby by these resolutions created, and the same shall be distinguished from the bonds of all other series issuable under said mortgage, by the title "First Mortgage . . . . . % Bonds due 19. . " The bonds of said series shall be dated as of . . . ., 19. ., shall mature on . . . ., 19. ., and shall bear interest at the rate of . . . . . (. . . . . %) percent per annum, payable semi-annually on the first day of . . . . and . . . . in each year, until the payment of the principal thereof. The principal and interest of the bonds of said series shall be payable at the office or agency of this Corporation in the City of . . . ., ..., in lawful money of the United States of America. The aggregate principal amount of bonds of the said . . . . . series which may at any one time be issued and outstanding under said mortgage, shall be limited to . . . . . ($. . . . .) Dollars, and

RESOLVED FURTHER, That the bonds of said series, the coupons to be attached to the coupon bonds of said series, and the certificate of the Trustee to be indorsed thereon, shall be substantially in the following forms, respectively, the denominations and numbers thereof to be appropriately inserted (*insert forms of bond and interest coupon and trustee's certificate in full*), and

RESOLVED FURTHER, That the bonds of said series may, at the option of this Corporation, be redeemed at the principal office of the Trustee, in the Borough of . . . ., City of . . . ., at any time prior to maturity, as a whole, or in part, from time to time, in the manner, upon the terms, and with the effect provided in Article . . . . . of said mortgage, as amended, and hereinafter in these resolutions in respect thereof, and upon payment of the principal thereof and interest thereon accrued to the date of redemption, but without any premium on said principal, and

RESOLVED FURTHER, That the notice of redemption required by the provisions of Article . . . . . of said mortgage, as amended, shall be published in one daily newspaper printed in the English language, of general circulation in the City of . . . ., at least once a week (on any day in the week) for at least three (3) successive calendar weeks, the first publication to be made at least . . . . . (. . . . .) days before the date fixed for redemption; and such notice shall also be sent by this Corporation through the mails, postage prepaid, at least . . . . . (. . . . .) days prior to such date of redemption, to the registered holders of all bonds to be redeemed at the time registered, to the addresses that shall appear upon the registers thereof; but failure to mail such notice or any defect therein or in the mailing thereof shall not affect the validity of the call and redemption of any bonds so to be redeemed, and

RESOLVED FURTHER, That the signature of the President or a Vice president of this Corporation upon any of the bonds of said series, and/or the signature of the Secretary or Assistant Secretary of this Corporation, in attestation of its corporate seal, upon any of the bonds of said series, may be made by engraving, lithographing, or printing theron the facsimile signature of such President or Vice president and/or such Secretary or Assistant Secretary, in lieu of actual signature, and the corporate seal of this Corporation may be affixed thereto by engraving, lithographing, or printing thereon the same or a facsimile thereof, and

RESOLVED FURTHER, That the definitive bonds of said series shall be printed coupon bonds of the denomination of $1,000 numbered M1 and upward. At the election of this Corporation, coupon bonds of said series of the denomination of $500 or $100 may also be issued, numbered D1 and upward, and C1 and upward, respectively, and provision may be made therein for the exchange thereof for coupon bonds of said series of the denomination of $1,000 and/or $500 for the same aggregate principal amount, upon the terms and conditions specified in Sections ..... and ..... of Article ..... of said mortgage, and

RESOLVED FURTHER, That upon every exchange of bonds under the provisions of these resolutions, this Corporation may make a charge therefor sufficient to reimburse it for any tax or taxes or other governmental charges required to be paid by this Corporation, and, in addition, may charge a sum not exceeding ..... ($.....) Dollars for each new bond issued upon any such exchange, to be paid by the party requesting such exchange as a condition precedent for the exercise of the privileges conferred by these resolutions. All bonds executed, authenticated, and delivered in exchange for bonds so surrendered shall be valid obligations of this Corporation, evidencing the same debt as the bond surrendered, and shall be entitled to all the benefits and protection of said mortgage, as amended and/or supplemented, to the same extent as the bonds for which they were executed, authenticated, and delivered, and

RESOLVED FURTHER, That the .... Bank of the City of ...., is hereby appointed Bond Registrar and Transfer Agent of this Corporation with respect to the coupon bonds of said series, and the principal office of .... Bank of the City of ...., in the Borough of ...., City of ...., is hereby fixed as the office of this Corporation for the registration and transfer of the coupon bonds of said series, and

RESOLVED FURTHER, That the form of temporary bond of said series presented to this meeting, and each and every term, covenant, and provision therein contained, are hereby approved, and

RESOLVED FURTHER, That the officers of this Corporation are hereby authorized, empowered, and directed, in the name and for the account of this corporation, to take or cause to be taken, any and all such other and further action, and to execute, acknowledge, and deliver any and all such other instruments as in the judgment of such officers may be necessary, proper, or convenient in order to carry out the intent of these resolutions.

DIRECTORS' RESOLUTION AUTHORIZING ISSUE OF CONVERTIBLE BONDS, FIXING PRICE, AND CALLING MEETING OF STOCKHOLDERS TO CONSENT TO EXECUTION OF MORTGAGE AS SECURITY

RESOLVED, That the .... Company issue and dispose of its bonds or other obligations up to but not exceeding the sum of ..... ($.....)

Dollars, the bonds or other obligations to be sold at the present time not to exceed the sum of . . . . . ($ . . . . .) Dollars, such bonds or other obligations to bear interest at a rate not exceeding . . . . . (. . . . .%) percent per annum, payable semi-annually, and all and any part of said bonds or other obligations to become due and payable not more than . . . . . (. . . . .) years from the date thereof, and

RESOLVED FURTHER, That the stockholders, in conformity with the statute applicable thereto, be requested to consent that the . . . . Company execute a mortgage or a deed of trust mortgaging its property and franchises, to secure the payment of such bonds or other obligations, and that such mortgage or deed of trust shall be made to such corporation or person, and shall be in such form, and shall contain such provisions, as the Board of Directors of the Company may approve, and

RESOLVED FURTHER, That the stockholders be requested to consent that the Board of Directors, under such regulations as it may adopt, may confer on the holders of any of said bonds or obligations the right to covert the principal thereof after . . . . . (. . . . .) years, and not more than . . . . . (. . . . .) years from the date of such bonds, into First Preferred Seven (7%) Percent Cumulative Stock of the Company at the par value of said stock, said stock to be issued subject to the right of the Board of Directors of the Company to call in and retire said stock, or any part thereof, at one hundred ten (110%) percent and accumulated dividends.

RESOLUTION OF STOCKHOLDERS CONSENTING
TO ISSUE OF CONVERTIBLE BONDS

RESOLVED, That consent is hereby given to the creation of an issue of convertible debenture bonds of the Company, to be of an aggregate principal amount not exceeding . . . . . ($ . . . . .) Dollars, to bear such rate of interest, to mature at such date, and to contain such other terms and conditions as the Directors may determine, and to be offered to the stockholders for subscription, at such time or times and upon such terms and conditions as the Directors may determine, in proportion to their holdings of stock on a record date or dates to be designated by the Directors; and that consent is hereby given to the Directors, under such regulations as they may adopt, to confer upon the holders of said bonds the right to convert the principal thereof within such period and upon such terms and conditions as may be fixed by the resolutions of the Directors conferring said right of conversion, into capital stock of the Company.

RESOLUTION OF STOCKHOLDERS CONSENTING TO ISSUE OF
CONVERTIBLE BONDS AND EXECUTION OF MORTGAGE OR
DEED OF TRUST COVERING PROPERTY
AND FRANCHISE

RESOLVED, That the . . . . Company issue and dispose of its bonds or other obligations up to but not exceeding the sum of . . . . . ($ . . . . .)

Dollars (the bonds or other obligations to be sold at the present time not to exceed the sum of ..... ($.....) Dollars), such bonds or other obligations to bear interest at a rate not exceeding ..... (.....%) percent per annum, payable semi-annually, and all or any part of said bonds or other obligations to become due and payable not more than ..... (.....) years from the date thereof, and

RESOLVED FURTHER, That the stockholders, in conformity with the statute applicable thereto, do hereby consent that the .... Company execute a mortgage or deed of trust mortgaging its property and franchises, to secure the payment of such bonds or other obligations, and that such mortgage or deed of trust be in such form, and contain such provisions, as the Board of Directors of the Company may approve, and

RESOLVED FURTHER, That the stockholders do hereby consent that the directors, under such regulations as they may adopt, may confer on the holders of any of said bonds or obligations the right to convert the principal thereof after ..... (.....) years, and not more than ..... (.....) years from the date of such bonds, into First Preferred Seven (7%) Percent Cumulative Stock of the Company, at the par value of said stock, said stock to be issued subject to the right of the Board of Directors of the Company to call in and retire said stock, or any part thereof, at one hundred ten (110%) percent and accumulated dividends, and

RESOLVED FURTHER, That said mortgage or deed of trust provided to be executed for the purpose of securing said bonds shall be made to such corporation or person, shall be in such form, and shall contain such provisions as the Board of Directors of the Company may approve.

DIRECTORS' RESOLUTION AUTHORIZING DEPOSIT OF FUNDS WITH TRUSTEE OF MORTGAGE, IN ANTICIPATION OF USE OF AN EQUAL AMOUNT OF BONDS OR THEIR PROCEEDS FOR PURPOSES SPECIFIED IN THE MORTGAGE

WHEREAS, pursuant to the provisions of Section ..... of Article ..... of the Refunding and Improvement Seven Percent Mortgage of the .... Company to the .... Trust Company, at Trustee, dated ...., 19.., this Company is entitled to reimbursement out of bonds to be issued under said section of said mortgage, for expenditures or obligations made or incurred since ...., 19.., in the purchase of equipment and in improvements and betterments to its property and to the leased property mentioned in said section, and for the other purposes specified in said section, and

WHEREAS, in and by the terms of a certain order of the Public Service Commission, State of ...., made and entered at the Capital in the City of ...., State of ...., on ...., 19.., (Case No. .....), this Company was duly authorized to issue bonds under said mortgage to the par value of ..... ($.....) Dollars (of which ..... ($.....) Dollars have heretofore been issued, authenticated, and delivered), for the purpose mentioned in said order, and to be sold to provide funds for refunding car trust certificates maturing during the year 19.., and for expenditures made and to be made by this Company during the year 19.., for fixed capital, set forth in detail in Schedule A, attached to the petition filed by this Company with the said Public Service Commission, dated ...., 19.., and referred to in the Public Service Commission's order dated ...., 19.., or in the event of any necessary change or changes in the present plans of this Company, for expenditures for additions and betterments to its road and equipment, other than those listed in such schedule, which are properly capitalizable, and

WHEREAS, in and by the terms of a certain order of the Public Service Commission of the State of ...., dated ...., 19.. (Case No. .....), this Company was duly authorized to issue bonds under its Refunding and Improvement 7 Percent Mortgage, dated ...., 19.., as aforesaid, for the purpose of acquiring right of way for, and the construction and equipment of, an extension of the railroad of this Company to ...., of the par amount of ..... ($.....) Dollars, for the purposes mentioned in said order, which said ..... ($.....) Dollars par value of bonds, together with ..... ($.....) Dollars par value of bonds aforementioned, aggregate ..... ($.....) Dollars par value of bonds now available for authentication and delivery, and

WHEREAS, a petition is about to be presented to the Public Service Commission for permission to issue additional bonds to the amount of ..... ($.....) Dollars par value, which, when granted, together with ..... ($.....) Dollars of bonds aforementioned, aggregate ..... ($.....) Dollars of bonds available for authentication and delivery, and

WHEREAS, it is provided in Section ..... of Article ..... of said mortgage that, in anticipation of the use of certain bonds to be issued thereunder, this Company may become entitled to the authentication and delivery of bonds for any of the purposes specified in Section ..... of Article ..... of said mortgage, upon depositing with the Trustee an amount of money equal to the par value of said bonds to be so authenticated and delivered by the Trustee, and that the money so received by the Trustee shall be expended only for the purposes specified in Section ..... of Article ..... of said mortgage, and shall be paid to this Company, or upon its order, upon resolutions and certificates similar to those that would entitle it to the authentication and delivery of the bonds of which such case is the proceeds, but such resolutions and certificates shall be made in terms applicable to such payments of cash, instead of to the authentication and delivery of bonds, be it

RESOLVED, That pursuant to the provisions of Section ..... of Article ..... of the Refunding and Improvement Seven Percent Mortgage of this Company, the officers of this Company are hereby authorized, empowered, and directed forthwith to deposit, on or before ...., 19.., the sum of

..... ($.....) Dollars in cash, with the ..... Trust Company, as Trustee, in anticipation of the use of ..... ($.....) Dollars par value of bonds, or the proceeds thereof, for certain of the purposes specified in Section ..... of Article ..... of the said mortgage, there now being available for authentication and delivery, pursuant to orders issued by the Public Service Commission, ... ($.....) Dollars Seven Percent Mortgage Bonds of this Company, for estimated expenditures for additions and betterments during the calendar year 19.., as detailed in Schedule A, attached to the petition filed by this Company with the said Public Service Commission, dated ...., 19.., or, in the event of any necessary change or changes in the present plans of this Company, for expenditures for additions and betterments to its road and equipment, other than those listed in such schedule, which are properly capitalizable; and for the purpose of acquiring the right of way for the construction and equipment of the proposed extension of the railroad of this Company to ...., and for other purposes specified in Section ..... of Article ..... of said mortgage, and

RESOLVED FURTHER, That the .... Trust Company, as Trustee under said Refunding and Improvement Seven Percent Mortgage of this company, is hereby requested to authenticate and deliver to this Company, or upon its order, from time to time, bonds to the amount of ..... ($.....) Dollars, upon the deposit with it of an amount of money equal to the amount of bonds authenticated and delivered on orders duly signed by the proper officers of this Company, the said bonds or the proceeds thereof to be used to reimburse this Company for or to pay for the expenditures anticipated to be made by it only for purposes authorized by Section ..... of Article ..... of said mortgage as aforesaid.

DIRECTORS' RESOLUTION AUTHORIZING ISSUE OF EQUIPMENT BONDS IN ACCORDANCE WITH MORTGAGE CONDITIONS

WHEREAS, This Company is authorized, under the provisions of its mortgage to the .... Company of the City of ...., as Trustee, dated ...., 19.., to issue bonds under said mortgage, to an amount not exceeding ..... ($.....) Dollars per mile of continuous road, for the purchase of equipment (not exceeding, however, the actual cost thereof), and

WHEREAS, the railway of this Company is now ..... (.....) miles in length, and there has heretofore been issued, on account of equipment, ... ($.....) Dollars of said bonds, and

WHEREAS, this Company has expended since ...., 19.., in the purchase of additional equipment necessary for the transaction of its business as a common carrier, the sum of ..... ($.....) Dollars, be it

RESOLVED, That the President and the Secretary of this Company are hereby authorized and directed to execute, on behalf of this Company, its

First Mortgage 8 Percent Bonds, to the amount of ..... ($.....) Dollars, said bonds to be numbered from ..... (.....) to ..... (.....), inclusive, and to deliver the same to ...., Assistant Treasurer, and

RESOLVED FURTHER, That the .... Company, of the City of ...., is hereby authorized and requested to countersign, as Trustee, said bonds, to the amount of ..... ($.....) Dollars, namely, numbers ..... (.....) to ..... (.....), inclusive, and to deliver the same to ...., Assistant Treasurer.

DIRECTORS' RESOLUTION REQUESTING TRUSTEE TO COUNTERSIGN AND DELIVER MORTGAGE BONDS

RESOLVED, That ...., Trustee, is hereby requested by the Board of Directors to countersign, as Trustee, and to deliver to .... and ...., of .... (*Street*), ... (*City*), ... (*State*), in behalf of this Company, ... (.....) of the .... Company's First Mortgage Five Percent Bonds of One Thousand Dollars ($1,000) each, numbers ..... (.....) to ..... (.....) inclusive, and

RESOLVED FURTHER, That a certified copy if this resolution be sent to the said ...., Trustee.

DIRECTORS' RESOLUTION CANCELLING MORTGAGE UPON RECEIPT OF OTHER SECURITY

WHEREAS, a certain bond and mortgage were made, executed, and delivered to this Corporation by the .... Company, on ...., 19.., to secure the collection of certain securities in the amount of ..... ($.....) Dollars, transferred to this Corporation by the said .... Company, upon the purchase and sale of certain personal property, and

WHEREAS, it was resolved that such mortgage should not be recorded, but should be held only to keep alive the claim for any deficiency that might arise upon the collection of the aforesaid securities, and

WHEREAS, the said .... Company is desirous of selling the property covered by the said bond and mortgage, free and clear of the lien of the said mortgage, and

WHEREAS, the said .... Company has agreed to deliver to this Corporation, and this Corporation has agreed to accept from the said .... Company, certain additional securities, as collateral to secure the collection of the above amount in lieu of the bond and mortgage aforesaid, be it

RESOLVED, That the aforesaid bond and mortgage are hereby cancelled, released, and discharged, and ...., the Secretary, and ...., the Treasurer, of this Corporation, are hereby directed to cancel the same and to execute the necessary instruments therefor.

EXCERPT OF MINUTES OF DIRECTORS' MEETING AUTHORIZING LIMITED ISSUE OF DEBENTURES UNDER TRUST AGREEMENT, APPROVING AGREEMENT, APPOINTING A REGISTRAR, AUTHORIZING AUTHENTICATION OF DEBENTURES, APPOINTING OFFICERS TO EXECUTE DEBENTURES, APPOINTING PAYING AGENT, AND AUTHORIZING LISTING OF DEBENTURES

[Authorization of issue]

RESOLVED, That an issue, limited to the aggregate principal amount of ..... ($.....) Dollars, of 20-Year 7 Percent Debentures, is hereby authorized, the same to be issued under a trust agreement to be dated as of ...., 19.., to be made between this Company and the .... Trust Company of ...., as Trustee.

[Presentation of trust agreement]

The Chairman thereupon presented the form of trust agreement with the .... Trust Company of ...., as Trustee, to be dated as of ...., 19.., providing for said authorized issue of ..... (.....) Dollars, principal amount of 20-Year 7 Percent Debentures. The Chairman states that said form of trust agreement had been approved by counsel for the Company and for the .... Company and the .... Company of ....

Thereupon, upon motion of ...., seconded by ...., the following resolutions were unanimously adopted:

[Approval of trust agreement]

RESOLVED That the form, terms, and conditions of the trust agreement of this Company to be made with the .... Trust Company of ...., as Trustee, to be dated as ....., 19.., providing for an issue of ..... ($.....) Dollars, principal amount of 20-Year 7 Percent Debentures of the Company, together with the form, terms, and conditions of said debentures and the coupons to be attached thereto, and the certificate of authentication of the Trustee therein set forth, are hereby approved as presented to this meeting, and that the President or a Vice president and the Secretary or an Assistant Secretary of the Company are hereby authorized, empowered, and directed, for and in the name of the Company, and under its corporate seal, to execute, acknowledge, and deliver to the .... Trust Company of ...., as Trustee, a trust agreement in substantially the form presented to the meeting, with such changes therein as may be approved by the Chairman of the Board or the President.

[Authorization of officers to carry out trust agreement]

RESOLVED FURTHER, That the officers of the Company are hereby authorized, empowered, and directed to do or cause to be done all things deemed by them to be necessary or advisable and proper to comply with and carry out the terms of such trust agreement.

[Authentication by facsimile signature]

RESOLVED FURTHER, That the coupons to be attached to the 20-Year 7 Percent Debentures shall be authenticated by the facsimile signature of the present Treasurer of the Company, as provided in said trust agreement, and that the Company hereby adopts such signature as binding upon it.

[Appointment of Registrar]

RESOLVED FURTHER, That the ..... Trust Company of .... is hereby appointed the agent of this Company, with the title of Registrar, for the registration and transfer of ownership of said 20-Year 7 Percent Debentures, when said debentures shall be presented to said Registrar for that purpose.

[Authorization of temporary bonds and exchange for permanent bonds]

RESOLVED FURTHER, That the Chairman of the Board of Directors of the Company, or the President or one of the Vice presidents, and the Treasurer or one of the Assistant Treasurers, or the Secretary or one of the Assistant Secretaries, are hereby authorized and directed, for and in the name of the Company, and under its corporate seal, attested by the Secretary or an Assistant Secretary, to execute and deliver to the .... Trust Company of ...., as Trustee, a temporary debenture or debentures, to the aggregate principal amount of ..... ($.....) Dollars, in the form authorized by the said trust agreement, and in such denomination or denominations as are authorized thereby, and that said .... Trust Company of ...., as Trustee, be authorized and requested to authenticate and to deliver the same, pursuant to Section ..... of said trust agreement, to or upon the written order of the Company; and upon the preparation of the definitive 20-Year 7 Percent Debentures, said officers of the Company are hereby authorized and directed to execute and deliver the same to the .... Trust Company of ...., as Trustee, to an aggregate amount not exceeding ..... ($.....) Dollars principal amount in exchange, from time to time, for a like principal amount of temporary debentures, upon the surrender and cancellation of said temporary debentures.

[Effect of seal]

RESOLVED FURTHER, That the imprint of the seal of the Company upon the said temporary or definitive debentures shall have the same force and effect as though the corporate seal of the Company had been impressed thereon by the action of its proper officers.

[Appointment of officers with power to execute debentures]

RESOLVED FURTHER, That .... be appointed a Vice-President and .... be appointed an Assistant Secretary of this Company, with power limited to the execution of the temporary or definitive 20-Year 7 Percent Debentures of the Company, issued or to be issued under the proposed trust agreement to the .... Trust Company of ...., as Trustee, to be dated as of .... , 19.., to secure an aggregate principal amount of ..... ($.....) Dollars of said debentures.

[Appointment of paying agent]

RESOLVED FURTHER, That the . . . . Trust Company of . . . . , and the . . . . Bank of . . . . , and each of them, be appointed paying agents of this Company, for the purpose of paying the interest due and to become due on the said debentures and the principal amount thereof and any premium thereon, either at maturity of the said debentures or upon the redemption thereof prior to maturity.

[Listing of debentures]

RESOLVED FURTHER, That application be made to the New York Stock Exchange for the listing thereon of the 20-Year 7 Percent Debentures of the Company, and that the President, the Vice president, the Treasurer, or the Assistant Treasurer, each is hereby authorized and directed to appear before the Committee on Stock List of said Exchange with authority to make such application, as well as any changes thereof or agreements in regard thereto as may be necessary to conform to the requirements for listing.

DIRECTORS' RESOLUTION AUTHORIZING ISSUE OF NOTES AND EXECUTION OF COLLATERAL TRUST AGREEMENT

RESOLVED, That this Company issue its 8% One-Year Coupon Notes to the aggregate principal face amount of $ . . . . . , and

RESOLVED FURTHER, That to secure such notes, this Company execute and deliver to . . . . Trust Co., as Trustee, a collateral trust agreement, to be dated . . . . , 19. . , in substantially the form submitted at this meeting and hereby approved, and

RESOLVED FURTHER, That the officers of this Company are hereby authorized to sell to . . . . Trust Co., the $ . . . . . principal face amount of the said notes to be issued under and secured by the said collateral trust agreement, at a price equivalent to . . . . . percent thereof, less . . . . . percent of the said principal face amount thereof, the commission to be payable to said . . . . Trust Co.

DIRECTORS' RESOLUTION AUTHORIZING DELIVERY OF EQUIPMENT TO TRUSTEE UNDER TRUST AGREEMENT IN CONSIDERATION OF EQUIPMENT TRUST CERTIFICATES

RESOLVED, That the President and/or other proper officer be hereby authorized to sell, and by proper and sufficient bill of sale executed by such officers, with the seal of the Corporation thereto affixed and attested by the Secretary, to transfer, and make delivery of, to . . . . Bank of . . . . , Trustee, under the equipment trust agreement to be executed by . . . . Company with the . . . . Bank of . . . . , Trustee, the following-described equipment—to wit *(insert description of equipment)*—and to accept therefor from said Trustee, as full and complete consideration for said sale, transfer, and delivery of said equipment, and in full payment of the purchase price thereof, Equipment Trust Certificates, Series B (in temporary and/or definitive form), and to be issued by said Trustee to the aggregate principal amount of ..... ($.....) Dollars, under the terms of said equipment trust agreement, which said Equipment Trust Certificates, Series B, shall be in such form, and shall be payable on such terms and conditions and at such times as are set forth in said equipment trust agreement; and full authority and power is hereby conferred upon the President and/or other proper officer of the .... Company to agree upon the terms and conditions of the said equipment trust agreement and the form of said Equipment Trust Certificates, Series B, and the terms and conditions and the terms of payment thereof, as shall be set forth in said equipment trust agreement, and to execute the same in the name and in behalf of the .... Company.

DIRECTORS' RESOLUTION AUTHORIZING PRESIDENT TO SELL AND DELIVER EQUIPMENT TRUST CERTIFICATES

RESOLVED, That the President of this Company is hereby authorized to sell and deliver to the .... Bank certificates representing ..... ($.....) Dollars, face amount of .... Railways Equipment Trust, Series B, when the same are received by this Company, upon receipt of the purchase price of ..... ($.....) Dollars, with such adjustments for interest and other proper charges as he in his discretion shall see fit.

GUARANTY OF OBLIGATIONS

DIRECTORS' RESOLUTION AUTHORIZING OFFICER TO ARRANGE FOR GRANTING OF LINE OF CREDIT TO ANOTHER SUBSIDIARY CORPORATION AND TO GUARANTEE THE LOANS MADE THEREUNDER

RESOLVED, That the officers of this Corporation are hereby authorized, in the name of this Corporation, to arrange for the granting to the .... Company of a continuing line of credit with the .... Bank, to an amount not exceeding ..... ($.....) Dollars, or to such amounts as may hereafter be authorized by the Executive Committee of this Corporation; and any Vice president of this Corporation is hereby authorized to guarantee, in the name of this Corporation, and in such form as may be required by the bank making such loans, the payment of the principal and interest of all sums (not to exceed ..... ($.....) Dollars), which may be loaned by said bank to said .... Company, provided, however, that all loans, in order to come within the terms of any such guaranty, shall be authorized by the proper officer of said .... Company, and shall be approved by a Vice president of this Corporation.

RESOLUTION OF STOCKHOLDERS AUTHORIZING CORPORATION TO GUARANTEE OBLIGATIONS, AND EMPOWERING OFFICERS TO INDORSE NOTES OF SUBSIDIARY

WHEREAS, this Corporation is, and for many years past has been, the owner of all the shares of stock of the .... Company, and

WHEREAS, said .... Company is desirous of obtaining a loan of funds from the .... Bank, necessary for the operation of its business, and

WHEREAS, the said bank has agreed to advance the funds so required by the said .... Company, provided that payment of the indebtedness of the .... Company is guaranteed by this Corporation, and

WHEREAS, it is deemed for the best interests of the .... Company and for this Corporation that the said .... Company obtain the funds as aforesaid, be it

RESOLVED, That this Corporation is hereby authorized to guarantee the payment of any moneys advanced by the said .... Bank to the said .... Company, and ...., the President, and ...., the Treasurer of this Corporation, are hereby authorized and empowered to indorse, in the name of this Corporation, the notes or other obligations of the said .... Company, executed by it as evidence of the loans made by the .... Bank to it as aforesaid, and

RESOLVED FURTHER, That ...., Secretary of this Corporation, shall file with the .... Bank a certified copy of this resolution under the seal of the Corporation, and that this resolution shall be in full force and effect and binding upon this Corporation until it shall be repealed, and until written notice of such repeal shall be delivered to the said .... Bank.

RESOLUTION GUARANTEEING PAYMENT OF BILLS INCURRED BY SUBSIDIARIES

RESOLVED, That Mercantile Stores Company, Inc., guarantees the payment of all bills that may be incurred for merchandise and supplies by the following wholly owned subsidiaries: (*list*)

RESOLUTION GUARANTEEING BONDS OF SUBSIDIARY CORPORATION*

WHEREAS, this Corporation is, and for many years past has been, the owner of all the shares of stock of "B" Steel Company, hereinafter termed the

---

*See General Inv. Co. v. Bethlehem Steel Corp., (1918) 248 F. 303, in which a similar resolution appears.

Steel Company (except directors' qualifying shares), and the Steel Company, in the conduct of its manufacturing business, has received a large part of its supply of coke and of gas from the by-product coking plant formerly of "A" Company, situated at . . . ., ..., contiguous to the properties of the Steel Company, the said plant having been constructed primarily for the purpose of supplying coke and gas to the Steel Company, and

WHEREAS, the Steel Company has deemed it advantageous and essential, in the proper conduct of its business, that it acquire the entire control of the management and operation of said by-product coking plant, and for that purpose has purchased the entire capital stock of said "A" Company, and, in order to make part payment therefor, borrowed, upon its short-time collateral promissory note, the sum of seven million ($7,000,000) Dollars, which obligation the Steel Company and this Corporation are, each of them, desirous shall be promptly paid, and the indebtedness evidenced thereby funded, so that the same may be made payable over a series of years, and

WHEREAS, the Steel Company has caused or is about to cause said coking plant to be sold and transferred to said "C" Company, of which it owns all of the outstanding capital stock, in consideration whereof the Steel Company will acquire seven million ($7,000,000) Dollars of the First Mortgage 5% 14-Year Sinking Fund Bonds of "C" Company, secured by mortgage upon the properties and assets of said "C" Company, and the Steel Company has arranged with the holder of said collateral promissory note to accept payment of said note by the delivery to such holder, on or before . . . ., 19. ., of said seven million ($7,000,000) Dollars First Mortgage 5% 14-Year Sinking Fund Bonds of the "C" Company, on the condition, however, that the payment of the principal thereof and interest thereon shall be guaranteed by the Steel Company and by this Corporation, and

WHEREAS, the Board of Directors of this Corporation deems it advisable that payment of said indebtedness of 7 million ($7,000,000) Dollars, now owing by the Steel Company, be provided for, and that the arrangement proposed by the Steel Company is an advantageous one and to the best interests of the Steel Company and of this Corporation, and

WHEREAS, the form of said bonds and of the mortgage securing the same, and, as well, the form of guaranty to be executed by the Steel Company and by this Corporation, have been duly submitted to and considered by this Board, be it

RESOLVED, That, in order to provide for the payment of the seven million ($7,000,000) Dollars owing by the Steel Company, and to aid said Company advantageously to sell and dispose of said seven million ($7,000,000) Dollars First Mortgage 5% 14-Year Sinking Fund Bonds of the "C" Company, this Corporation guarantees the punctual payment of the principal and interest of said seven million ($7,000,000) Dollars of bonds, and

RESOLVED FURTHER, That the guaranty to be indorsed upon each of the permanent bonds of said issue of seven million ($7,000,000) Dollars of First Mortgage 5% 14-Year Sinking Fund Bonds of the "C" Company shall be substantially in the following form:

Guaranty

"B" Steel Corporation, a corporation created and existing under the laws of the State of ...., for value received, does hereby guarantee to the holder, or, if registered, to the registered owner of this bond the punctual payment of the principal of and interest on said bond, as the same shall become or be made due and payable according to the terms of said bond and of the indenture therein mentioned, dated ...., 19.., made by "C" Company to the .... Trust Company of ...., as Trustee, to secure the same.

IN WITNESS WHEREOF, said "B" Steel Corporation has caused its corporate seal to be hereunto affixed, and to be attested by its Secretary or an Assistant Secretary, and these presents to be signed by its President or a Vice president, as of the .. day of ...., 19..

"B" Steel Corporation

By ....

Attest:.....................

RESOLVED, That the President, or one of the Vice presidents of this Corporation, is hereby authorized and directed from time to time, as said bonds shall be authenticated by the Trustee, to execute said guaranty in the name and on behalf of the "B" Steel Corporation (not exceeding, however, the aggregate principal sum of seven million ($7,000,000) Dollars), and that the Secretary, or one of the Assistant Secretaries of this Corporation, is hereby authorized and directed, at the same time, to affix to every such guaranty the corporate seal of the "B" Steel Corporation, duly attested by the signature of such Secretary or Assistant Secretary, and

RESOLVED FURTHER, That, pending the preparation and execution of the permanent bonds, the officers of this Corporation, hereinbefore named, are hereby authorized and directed, whenever any temporary bond or bonds issued under said first mortgage of the "C" Company shall be authenticated by the Trustee, to execute on said bonds (not exceeding, however, the aggregate principal sum of seven million ($7,000,000) Dollars) said guaranty, substantially in the form hereinbefore set forth, with appropriate variations, omissions, and additions, in the name of and in behalf of "B" Steel Corporation and to affix to every such guaranty the Corporate seal of "B" Steel Corporation, duly attested by the signature of such Secretary or Assistant Secretary, and

RESOLVED FURTHER, That the proper officers of this Corporation are hereby authorized and directed to do such other acts and things as may be requisite to fully carry out and perform, upon the part of this Company, the terms and provisions of this resolution.

RESOLUTION OF STOCKHOLDERS AUTHORIZING DIRECTORS TO EXECUTE CONTRACT OF GUARANTY OF PRINCIPAL AND INTEREST ON BONDS AND MORTGAGE TO SECURE GUARANTY

RESOLVED, That the Board of Directors of the A Railroad Corporation is hereby authorized to cause a contract of guaranty to be indorsed upon each of the bonds of the B Railroad Company of its loan of 19.., amounting to ..... ($.....) Dollars, and to be duly executed under the corporate seal of this Corporation, which contract of guaranty shall be in the words following:

Form of Guaranty

For value received, the A Railroad Corporation hereby guarantees the punctual payment of the principal and interest of the within bond, at the time and in the manner therein specified and set forth, and covenants, in default of the payment of any part thereof by the obligor, to pay the principal and interest of the within bond and all taxes that may be assessed upon the same, or upon the mortgage securing the same, for national, state, or municipal purposes, as the same shall become due, upon the demand of the holders hereof. To secure said guaranty the A Railroad Corporation executed a mortgage, bearing even date herewith, to the .... Trust Company, Trustee, of all its property and franchises, including a traffic contract dated ...., 19.., between the A Railroad Corporation and the B Railroad Company. Reference is made to this mortgage for the terms thereof. This guaranty will not become obligatory until the certificate indorsed hereon shall have been signed by said Trustee.

IN WITNESS WHEREOF, the said Corporation has caused its corporate seal to be hereunto affixed, attested by its Secretary, and these presents to be signed by its Treasurer, at ....., on the .. day of ...., 19..

A Railroad Corporation,
By .... Treasurer

Attest: ....
            Secretary

RESOLVED FURTHER, That, for the purpose of securing the due performance of the contract of guaranty so to be indorsed upon each of said bonds, the Board of Directors of this Corporation is hereby authorized to cause to be executed under the corporate seal, a mortgage of all its railroad property and franchises, including the traffic contract made by this Corporation with B Railroad Company, and all the revenues to be derived therefrom, and

RESOLVED FURTHER, That, the Treasurer of this Corporation is hereby authorized to execute, in the name of the Corporation, under the corporate seal, duly attested by the Secretary, the contract of guaranty, which, by virtue of a resolution of the stockholders of this Corporation, has been indorsed upon ..... (.....) bonds of one thousand ($1,000) Dollars each, made by .... Corporation, and known as its loan of 19.., and

RESOLVED FURTHER, That the President of this Corporation is hereby authorized to execute a mortgage in the name of this Corporation, and to cause the corporate seal to be duly affixed thereto and attested by the Secretary, which mortgage shall in substance be in the form that is presented to this meeting and now approved.

DIRECTORS' RESOLUTION AUTHORIZING AGREEMENT TO ASSUME OBLIGATIONS OF ANOTHER COMPANY IF NECESSARY OR ADVISABLE

RESOLVED, That the officers of this Corporation are hereby authorized and directed to enter into an agreement with .... Trust Company, as trustee under the mortgage and deed of trust made by .... Co., dated ...., 19.., expressly assuming the obligations of said .... Co. if, under the terms of said mortgage and deed of trust, it shall be determined that such express assumption of the obligations of said .... Co. is necessary or advisable.

PAYMENT OF INTEREST

RESOLUTION OF EXECUTIVE COMMITTEE AUTHORIZING PAYMENT OF INTEREST DUE ON BONDS

WHEREAS, the semi-annual interest on Collateral Trust 7½% Bonds of this Company becomes due and payable on ...., 19.., be it

RESOLVED, That the proper officers of this Company are hereby authorized and instructed to pay such semi-annual interest falling due on said date, upon presentation and surrender of the interest coupon bonds, and in like manner to pay said interest so due upon the registered bonds, to the registered owners thereof at the close of business on ...., 19..

RESOLUTION OF EXECUTIVE COMMITTEE MAKING INTEREST ON BONDS PAYABLE THROUGH OFFICE OF COMPANY INSTEAD OF THROUGH AGENT

RESOLVED, That, until further action by this Executive Committee or by the Board of Directors, the interest on this Company's Collateral Trust 7½% Bonds, issued under a trust agreement between this Company and .... Trust Company, dated ...., 19.., be paid direct to the holders thereof, instead of through the .... Trust Company as heretofore, and

that the office of the Company is hereby designated as the office in the City of
. . . . for the payment of the interest on the above bonds.

RESOLUTION OF EXECUTIVE COMMITTEE DESIGNATING AGENT FOR PAYMENT OF INTEREST ON BONDS

RESOLVED, That, until further action by this Executive Committee or by the Board of Directors, the . . . . Trust Company, Trustee under the trust agreement between this Company and the said . . . . Trust Company, dated the . . day of . . . ., 19. ., under which said bonds were issued, be and the same hereby is designated the agent of this Company for the payment of the interest on its Collateral Trust 7½% Bonds issued under the said agreement, and that the office of the . . . . Trust Company, at . . . . (Street), ... (City), ... (State), be the office at which the said interest shall be payable.

DIRECTORS' RESOLUTION ACCEPTING UNPAID COUPONS FROM BONDHOLDERS FOR CANCELLATION

WHEREAS, by resolution passed at a meeting of the stockholders of the . . . . Company, on . . . ., 19. ., an issue of bonds amounting, in the aggregate, at par value thereof, to . . . . . ($. . . . .) Dollars, was authorized, and

WHEREAS, there is outstanding of said authorized issue of bonds . . . . . (. . . . .) bonds, amounting, in the aggregate, at par value thereof, to . . . . . ($. . . . .) Dollars, and

WHEREAS, the holders of said outstanding bonds of said authorized issue are likewise the holders of the shares of the capital stock of said . . . . Company, and

WHEREAS, for several good and valuable considerations, said holders of said outstanding bonds have surrendered, for the purpose of cancellation, all the overdue and unpaid coupons of said bonds so outstanding, up to and including the coupons maturing on . . . ., 19. .; provided, however, that said coupons so surrendered shall be cancelled by the said . . . . Company, or the Trustee under the deeds securing the payment of said authorized issue of bonds and coupons, and the said . . . . Company shall be discharged from the payment of said coupons so surrendered, be it

RESOLVED, That the directors, for the consideration aforesaid, accept from the holders of said outstanding bonds of said . . . . Company all the overdue and unpaid coupons attached to said bonds, up to and including the coupons maturing on . . . ., 19. ., and that the same shall be cancelled through the agency of the Trustee named in the deed securing the payment of said authorized issue of bonds and coupons, in such manner as will discharge the said . . . . Company from the payment of said coupons so surrendered, in accordance with the conditions imposed by the holders of said outstanding bonds.

DIRECTORS' RESOLUTION AUTHORIZING NONPAYMENT OF INTEREST COUPONS ON NOTES AND DEBENTURES, AND DIRECTING PUBLICATION AND MAILING OF NOTICE OF NONPAYMENT, AND PREPARATION OF INTEREST AND SINKING FUND ADJUSTMENT PLAN

RESOLVED, That the . . . ., 19. ., interest coupons on the Company's 10-Year 7½% Sinking Fund Notes, due . . . ., 19. ., and the Convertible 8% Sinking Fund Debentures, due . . . ., 19. ., not be paid at this time, and that the President is hereby instructed to publish a notice in the . . . . News Bureau, the . . . . *Journal,* and such other publications as he may deem advisable, in the form presented to this meeting, and that a copy of said notice be attached to the records of this meeting, and that they be mailed to all known note and debenture holders, to the Trustees under the respective indentures, and to the . . . . Stock Exchange, and

RESOLVED FURTHER, That the officers of the Company are hereby authorized and instructed, in collaboration with the Underwriters of the 10-Year 7% Sinking Fund Notes and the Convertible 8% Sinking Fund Debentures of the Company, to prepare a Note and Debenture Interest and Sinking Fund Adjustment Plan for the protection of the security holders of the Company and present such Plan to the directors at an early meeting.

REDEMPTION OF BONDS

DIRECTORS' RESOLUTION AUTHORIZING REDEMPTION OF ALL OUTSTANDING BONDS AND SETTING FORTH NOTICE OF REDEMPTION

RESOLVED, That this Company redeem and pay off, on . . . ., 19. ., the . . . . . ($. . . . .) Dollars principal amount of Collateral Trust 6% Bonds, Series A, of the Company, being all of the bonds now outstanding under the trust agreement dated . . . ., 19. ., between this Company and the . . . . Trust Company of . . . ., as Trustee, such redemption to be at the principal amount of said bonds and a premium of ten (10%) percent of such principal amount, together with accrued interest, pursuant to the provisions of Article . . . . . of said trust agreement, and

RESOLVED FURTHER, That, in accordance with the provisions of Article . . . . . of said trust agreement, this Company advertise in . . . ., ..., and . . . ., three (3) newspapers of general circulation in the City of . . . . once in each week for . . . . . successive weeks, beginning on . . . ., 19. ., that the Company has elected to redeem and pay off all of said bonds, and that, on . . . ., 19. ., there will become due and payable upon the bonds, at the principal office of the . . . . Trust Company of

.........., ... Street, City of ...., the principal thereof with a premium of ten (10%) percent of such principal, together with the accrued interest to such date, and that notice of such redemption to be so given shall be as follows:

(Here insert notice of redemption.)

RESOLVED FURTHER, That said notice be mailed on ...., 19. ., to the owners of all registered bonds at their addresses as the same shall respectively appear upon the bond register, and that the officers are hereby authorized, empowered, and directed to do any and all other acts necessary and proper to fully carry into effect the intent of the foregoing resolutions.

DIRECTORS' RESOLUTION AUTHORIZING REDEMPTION OF ENTIRE BOND ISSUE PRIOR TO MATURITY

WHEREAS, under a certain trust deed dated ...., 19. ., this Corporation did issue First Mortgage 7% Serial Bonds in the aggregate par value of ..... ($.....) Dollars, all of which bonds are now outstanding, and

WHEREAS, by the terms of the said trust deed, the aforesaid bonds were made redeemable in whole or in part at the option of this Corporation, at any time on thirty (30) days' notice, upon the payment of the principal amount of the aforesaid bonds and accrued interest thereon, together with a premium of ..... (.....%) percent of the principal thereof, and

WHEREAS, this Board of Directors believes it to be to the best interests of this Corporation to redeem the entire issue of the aforesaid bonds now outstanding, be it

RESOLVED, That this Corporation hereby declares its election to exercise the option aforesaid, and to redeem the entire issue of its First Mortgage 7% Serial Bonds outstanding as aforesaid, on the next interest payment date, to wit, ..., 19. ., and

RESOLVED FURTHER, That the President and the Secretary of this Corporation are hereby directed to cause a notice to be advertised in two daily newspapers in general circulation, one published in the City of ...., and one published in the City of ...., at least once a week for ..... (.....) successive weeks, the first publication to be not less than thirty (30), and not more than forty (40), days before the date of the redemption aforesaid, to wit, ..., 19. ., requiring the said bonds to be delivered for redemption at the office of this Corporation in the City of ...., State of ...., and

RESOLVED FURTHER, That the President and the Secretary of this Corporation are hereby authorized and directed to send a similar notice through the mails, at least thirty (30) days prior to the redemption date, to those who appear, on the bond register on . . . ., 19. ., to be the registered holders of the bonds aforesaid, and to do all other acts necessary and proper to carry the foregoing resolution into effect.

DIRECTORS' RESOLUTION AUTHORIZING REDEMPTION OF PART OF BOND ISSUE PRIOR TO MATURITY

WHEREAS, under a certain trust deed dated . . . ., 19. ., this Corporation did issue First Mortgage 7% Serial Bonds in the aggregate par value of . . . . . ($. . . . .) Dollars, all of which bonds are now outstanding, and

WHEREAS, by the terms of the said trust deed, the aforesaid bonds were made redeemable in whole or in part at the option of this Corporation, at any time on thirty (30) days' notice, upon the payment of the principal amount of the aforesaid bonds and accrued interest thereon, together with a premium of . . . . . (. . . . .%) percent of the principal thereof, and

WHEREAS, this Board of Directors believes it to be to the best interests of this Corporation to redeem . . . . . ($. . . . .) Dollars principal amount of the said bonds, be it

RESOLVED, That this Corporation hereby declares its election to exercise the option aforesaid, and to redeem . . . . . ($. . . . .) Dollars in principal amount of its aforesaid First Mortgage 7% Serial Bonds, on the next interest payment date, to wit, ..., 19. ., the bonds so to be redeemed to be determined by lot in any usual manner, in the presence of the President or a Vice president of this Corporation, or an officer of the . . . . Trust Company, Trustee under the aforesaid trust deed, and of a notary public, and

RESOLVED FURTHER, That the President and the Secretary of this Corporation are hereby authorized and directed to cause a notice to be published in a daily newspaper in the City of . . . ., and a daily newspaper in the City of . . . ., once a week for . . . . . (. . . . .) successive weeks, the first publication to be not less than thirty (30) days prior to the next interest payment date, to wit, ..., 19. ., stating the serial numbers of the bonds so drawn, that interest on such bonds shall cease on said . . . ., 19. ., and that, on such date, there will become and be due and payable on each of said bonds, at the office of this Corporation in the City of . . . ., State of . . . ., the principal thereof, together with the premium as aforesaid and accrued interest to such date, and requiring such bonds to be delivered for redemption, and

RESOLVED FURTHER, That the President and the Secretary of this Corporation, under the direction of the . . . . Trust Company, Trustee under the trust deed aforesaid, are hereby authorized and directed to send a similar notice through the mails, at least thirty (30) days prior to such redemption day to those who appear, on the bond register on . . . ., 19. ., to be the registered holders of the bonds so drawn by lot, and

RESOLVED FURTHER, That the President and the Secretary of this Corporation are hereby authorized and directed to execute all instruments and to do all other acts necessary and proper to carry the foregoing resolution into effect.

DIRECTORS' RESOLUTION APPROVING FORM OF AGREEMENT WITH TRUSTEE FOR REDEMPTION OF BONDS AT MATURITY, AND AUTHORIZING OFFICERS TO EXECUTE AND DELIVER AGREEMENT

WHEREAS, the contract dated ...., 19.., between this Company and the Trust Company, provides that all necessary steps shall be taken by this Company to redeem the Collateral Trust Series A Convertible 8% Bonds of the Company, dated ...., 19.., and to deposit with the .... Trust Company a sufficient sum in cash to redeem, on ...., 19.., all of said bonds, and authorizes notice thereof to be given in accordance with the terms of said bonds and the trust agreement securing the same, and

WHEREAS, a form of agreement with .... Trust Company, covering the deposit by this Company of the necessary funds for the redemption, on ...., 19.., of all of said Collateral Trust Series A Convertible 8% Bonds, has been presented to the meeting, be it

RESOLVED, That the form of agreement presented to the meeting for the deposit of funds sufficient to redeem all the Collateral Trust Series A Convertible 6% Bonds of the Company, dated ...., 19.., be hereby approved, and the officers of the Company are hereby authorized and directed to execute and deliver an agreement substantially in such form, and with such changes therein as may be approved by the Chairman of the Board or by the President, and to deposit thereunder the proceeds received from the sale of the ..... ($.....) Dollars worth of 20-Year 7% Debentures, dated as of ...., 19.., together with such further amount as may be required under the terms of said agreement, and

RESOLVED FURTHER, That the officers of this Company are hereby authorized, empowered, and directed to execute such documents, to take such steps, and to do all other acts as may by them be deemed necessary, advisable, or proper to comply with and carry out the terms of the contract of this Company with the .... Company and the .... Company of ...., dated ...., 19.., in connection with the issuance and sale of ..... ($.....) Dollars, principal amount of 20-Year 7% Debentures of this Company.

DIRECTORS' RESOLUTION AUTHORIZING TREASURER TO PURCHASE BONDS FOR SINKING FUND

RESOLVED, That the Treasurer is hereby authorized to purchase for the sinking fund of the 50-Year 8% Bonds of the Corporation, ... ($.....) Dollars, par value, of the ..... series 50-Year bonds, at 107 flat, on ...., 19..

RESOLUTION OF STOCKHOLDERS RATIFYING PURCHASE BY TRUSTEE OF BONDS FOR SINKING FUND PURPOSES OTHER THAN THOSE PRESCRIBED IN MORTGAGE

WHEREAS, by the terms of the first mortgage of the ....
Company to ...., Trustee, dated ...., 19.., it was provided that
the .... Company should pay over to said Trustee, or the successors in
trust, every six months, the sum of ..... ($.....) Dollars, which sums,
together with all accretions thereto, should immediately be invested by said
Trustee in the purchase, at the lowest market price or offer, not exceeding par
and accrued interest, of as many of the bonds secured by said first mortgage as
the funds in his hands for such purpose could buy, such bonds to be held for
purposes of the sinking fund, and

WHEREAS, the market price of the bonds secured by said first mortgage
greatly exceeds par and accrued interest, and it is therefore impossible for the
Trustee to invest the funds in his hands in said bonds in accordance with the
terms of said first mortgage, and

WHEREAS, ..., the successor in trust under said first mortgage,
has heretofore used a portion of said funds then in his hands in the purchase of
..... ($.....) Dollars of the Sinking Fund Collateral Trust Bonds of said
Company, and it is deemed advisable that the remainder of the funds now in
the hands of the acting Trustee under said first mortgage, and which may
hereafter accrue on account of said sinking fund, should be invested by the
Trustee in such other bonds of this Company, its successor or successors, as
the Board of Directors or the Executive Committee of this Company may
deem advisable, be it

RESOLVED, That the action of said ...., Trustee, in purchasing
said Sinking Fund Collateral Trust Bonds, on account of said sinking fund, is
hereby approved, ratified, and confirmed, and the acting Trustee under said
first mortgage is hereby authorized and requested to invest, from time to time,
such funds as may come into his hands on account of said sinking fund, in such
other bonds of this Company, its successor or successors, as may be approved
by the Board of Directors or the Executive Committee of this Company,
whenever said sinking fund cannot be invested in said first mortgage bonds in
accordance with the terms of said first mortgage.

EXCERPT OF MINUTES OF DIRECTORS' MEETING AUTHORIZING CANCELLATION OF DEBENTURES PURCHASED BY COMPANY, AND INSTRUCTING TRUSTEE TO CANCEL AND CREMATE DEBENTURES

The Treasurer reported that a total of $11,170,000 principal amount of
the Company's 20-Year 7½% Debentures due ...., 19.., together with
........, 19.., and subsequent interest coupons attached thereto had been
purchased by the Company and were held in the treasury of the Company as
of the close of business ...., 19... After full discussion of the
advisability, in view of the proposed redemption of a part of the Debentures

outstanding in the hands of the public, of the cancellation of all of said treasury Debentures, upon motion duly made, seconded, and passed, the following resolution was unanimously adopted:

RESOLVED, That the $11,170,000 principal amount of 20-Year 7½% Debentures due ...., 19.., of this Company, together with ...., 19.., interest coupon and all subsequent interest coupons attached thereto held in the treasury of this Company as of the close of business ...., 19.., be hereby cancelled, and the Treasurer of this Company is authorized and directed to deliver the same together with a certified copy of this resolution to The .... Bank of the City of ...., Trustee under the Indenture dated as of ...., 19.., under which said Debentures were issued, and to instruct said Trustee to note on its records the fact of such cancellation and to cremate said Debentures and interest coupons so cancelled and to deliver a certificate of cremation to this Company.

CONVERSION OF BONDS

DIRECTORS' RESOLUTION AUTHORIZING CONVERSION OF BONDS INTO STOCK

RESOLVED, That any and all holders of the First Mortgage 5% Bonds of the .... Corporation, duly authorized and about to be issued by the said Corporation, shall have the privilege of converting the said bonds into common stock of the Corporation without par value, on ...., 19.., ... (.....) shares of common stock without par value to be given in exchange for each bond of the face value of one thousand ($1,000) Dollars, and

RESOLVED FURTHER, That the said bondholders shall have the right to convert their bonds as aforesaid only upon condition that a written notice, stating the amount of the par value of the bonds that will be presented for conversion, shall be served by the holders thereof upon this Corporation, at its office at .... Street, on or before ...., 19...

RESOLUTION OF STOCKHOLDERS CONSENTING TO THE CONVERSION OF CONVERTIBLE DEBENTURES INTO STOCK

RESOLVED, That consent be hereby given to the Board of Directors of the Company, under such regulations as they may adopt upon authorizing the issue by the Company of not exceeding ..... ($.....) Dollars principal amount of convertible debentures, to confer upon the holders of such debentures the right to convert the principal thereof into common stock of the Company within such period and upon such terms and conditions as may be fixed by the resolutions of the Directors conferring said right of conversion.

REFUNDING—EXTENSION OF MATURITY

DIRECTORS' RESOLUTION AUTHORIZING ISSUE OF NEW OR EXTENDED NOTES IN EXCHANGE FOR MATURING NOTES, EXECUTION OF TRUST INDENTURE SIMILAR TO EXISTING INDENTURE RELATING TO MATURING NOTES, AND APPLICATION TO INTERSTATE COMMERCE COMMISSION FOR AUTHORITY TO ISSUE NEW OR EXTENDED NOTES

RESOLVED, That this Company issue new or extended three-year notes aggregating not more than $15,000,000, to be delivered in full payment of and in exchange for a like principal amount of its outstanding or issuable three-year 9% notes maturing ...., 19.., such new or extended notes to be dated .... , 19.., to bear interest at the rate of 9% per annum, to mature three years after date and to be redeemable as a whole or in part at any time prior to maturity at the principal amount thereof plus interest then accrued, and

RESOLVED FURTHER, That the President or any Vice president and the Treasurer of this Company are hereby authorized and directed to execute and deliver such new or extended notes and that said officers and also the Secretary or Assistant Secretary of this Company are hereby authorized to execute and deliver an indenture between this Company and .... Trust Company of New York, as trustee, providing for the authentication of such new or extended notes by the trustee and establishing the terms and conditions upon which they are to be issued (which indenture shall be in the general form of the Indenture, dated ...., 19.., and relating to said notes maturing ...., 19.., with such changes therein and additions thereto as may be necessary to conform to those resolutions, and with such further changes and additions as may be approved as necessary or advisable in the opinion of said officers, or of any of them, and of counsel for this Company), and to do each and every other act and thing necessary to accomplish the purposes of these resolutions; and that these resolutions are adopted subject to approval by the Interstate Commerce Commission of all matters under its jurisdiction, and

RESOLVED FURTHER, That application be made by this Company to the Interstate Commerce Commission for authority to issue said new or extended notes, and that ...., President, or ...., ..., or ...., Vice presidents, or ...., Treasurer is hereby designated and authorized to make, sign, verify, and file an application by this Company to the Interstate Commerce Commission in such form as may be approved by counsel for this Company, for any and all necessary authority and approval in the premises.

DIRECTORS' RESOLUTION AUTHORIZING OFFICER TO MAKE INQUIRY OF BONDHOLDERS CONCERNING REFUNDING

RESOLVED, That the President of this Company correspond with the present holders of the outstanding bonds, to ascertain whether or not they would be willing to accept bonds of a new issue, in amount equal to and in exchange for their present holdings (the total of the new issue to be .....($.....) Dollars, secured by a mortgage or deed of trust upon all the present property and future acquisitions of this Company, the proceeds to be used for the payment of the present indebtedness of this Company and for the cost of extension and equipment of its line).

RESOLUTION OF STOCKHOLDERS CONSENTING TO EXCHANGE OF NEW BONDS FOR OUTSTANDING BONDS

RESOLVED, That consent is hereby given to the Board of Directors of the Company, under such regulations as they may adopt, to issue new bonds aggregating not more than $5,000,000 to be delivered in full payment of, and in exchange for, a like principal amount of the Company's outstanding or issuable ten-year 7% bonds maturing ...., 19...

DIRECTORS' RESOLUTION EXTENDING MATURITY DATE OF BONDS, SUBJECT TO CONSENT OF STOCKHOLDERS AND BONDHOLDERS, AUTHORIZING APPLICATION TO THE INTERSTATE COMMERCE COMMISSION FOR EXTENSION OF MATURITY OF BONDS, AND AUTHORIZING PRESIDENT TO ENTER INTO EXTENSION AGREEMENT

WHEREAS, the first mortgage 7% bonds of the Company now outstanding in the principal amount of $..... mature and become due, according to their terms, on ...., 19.., and

WHEREAS, the Company will be unable to pay said bonds at their maturity date without selling the properties of the Company at a great loss, and it is, therefore, to the best interest of the Company that the maturity of said bonds be extended, and

WHEREAS, the holders of an overwhelming majority in amount of said bonds have signified their willingness to extend the maturity date of said bonds for a period of ten years from ...., 19.., be it

RESOLVED, That subject to the consent of the stockholders of this Company, and subject to the approval of the Interstate Commerce Commission, and subject to the consent of the owners and holders of said bonds, that the payment of the principal of said bonds be extended to ...., 19.., and

RESOLVED FURTHER, That subject to the consent of the stockholders, that the President of the Company, ..., is hereby authorized and directed to enter into an extension agreement with the owners and holders of said bonds, in substantially the form attached hereto as Exhibit "A", and

RESOLVED FURTHER, That, subject to the consent of the stockholders of this Company, that . . . . , the President, is hereby authorized and directed to sign, verify, and file with the Interstate Commerce Commission an application for authority on the part of the Company to extend the maturity date of its bonds to . . . . , 19 . . , and to file with the Interstate Commerce Commission such other instruments as may be necessary to comply with the requirements of the Commission with respect to such application, and

RESOLVED FURTHER, That a special meeting of the stockholders of this Company is hereby called to be held in the present office of the Company in . . . . City, ... , on . . . . , 19 . . , at . . . . . M., for the purpose of taking all such action in the premises as may be necessary, including approving all action of the Board of Directors in the premises, and

RESOLVED FURTHER, That the Board of Directors is further authorized to take, or cause to be taken, all such further actions or proceedings as may be necessary to carry into effect the foregoing resolutions.

DIRECTORS' RESOLUTION GIVING PROPER OFFICERS GENERAL POWER TO SECURE EXTENSION OF LOANS TO CORPORATION AND TO EXECUTE RENEWAL NOTES

RESOLVED, That the proper officers of this Company are hereby empowered and directed to do any and all acts, and to execute such instruments, as may be necessary to secure a renewal or extension of any loan heretofore made to this Company, and to execute such promissory notes upon such terms and conditions as they may deem proper in order to effect renewals of any existing loans, or to obtain further loans.

DIRECTORS' RESOLUTION AUTHORIZING EXTENSION OF PARTICULAR NOTES

RESOLVED, That the two notes executed by this Corporation on . . . . , 19 . . , for . . . . . ($ . . . . .) Dollars each, held by . . . . , be extended for a period of . . . . . (. . . . .) years from . . . . , 19 . . , with interest at the rate of . . . . . (. . . . . %) percent per annum, payable semi-annually, with a provision that this Corporation shall have the right to anticipate payment of the whole or any part of the said notes at any time, and

RESOLVED FURTHER, That . . . . , the President of this Corporation, is hereby authorized and directed to execute and deliver to the said . . . . the renewal notes as specified.

RESOLUTION OF STOCKHOLDERS TO RENEW NOTES
DISCOUNTED BY DIRECTORS AND AUTHORIZING OFFICERS
TO FURNISH COLLATERAL SECURITY

WHEREAS, ..., a Director of this Corporation, discounted the note of this Corporation dated ...., 19.., in the sum of ..... ($.....) Dollars, payable on ...., 19.., and

WHEREAS, said .... has agreed to renew said note provided the Corporation gives him as security for the payment thereof ..... ($.....) Dollars of first mortgage bonds of the .... Company, be it

RESOLVED, That the Company's note, in the sum of ..... ($.....) Dollars, discounted by ...., a Director of this Corporation, be renewed for ..... (.....) days, and that the Treasurer is hereby directed to deliver to the said ...., first mortgage bonds of the .... Company, in the amount of ..... ($.....) Dollars, as collateral security for the payment of said note, and

RESOLVED FURTHER, That the Treasurer obtain from the said .... a receipt and a stipulation to the effect that the said bonds shall be returned to this Company upon payment of the said note.

LOANS BY CORPORATION

EXCERPT OF MINUTES OF DIRECTORS' MEETING
AUTHORIZING LOAN TO DIRECTOR

Thereupon, the Chairman announced that since the next matter was a loan to ...., a Director, he would be asked not to participate in the vote.

........., a Director, having left the room, the following resolution was, on motion duly made and seconded, unanimously adopted.

DIRECTORS' RESOLUTION AUTHORIZING LOAN TO
DIRECTOR OUT OF SURPLUS FUNDS, AFTER DIRECTOR HAS
FURNISHED SECURITY

WHEREAS, ..., one of the directors of this Corporation, has applied to the Corporation for a loan in the sum of ..... ($.....) Dollars, and

WHEREAS, this Corporation has sufficient surplus funds to enable it to advance the said sum of ..... ($.....) Dollars to the said ...., and

WHEREAS, the said .... has offered to furnish good and sufficient security to guarantee the repayment of the said loan, be it

RESOLVED, That ...., the President, and ...., the Treasurer of this Corporation, are hereby authorized to issue a check to the said ...., for the said sum of ..... ($.....) Dollars, upon the receipt by them from the said ...., of a second mortgage, duly made and executed by the said .... in favor of this Corporation, covering his dwelling house located at .... (*Street*), in the City of ...., State of ...., which property is described as follows (*insert description of house to be mortgaged as security for loan to director*).

EXCERPT OF MINUTES OF STOCKHOLDERS' MEETING RATIFYING LOAN TO DIRECTOR

Thereupon the Chairman presented to the meeting the minutes of the special meeting of the Board of Directors held on ...., 19.., to pass upon the loan being made to ...., a Director, and in which meeting said loan was unanimously approved.

Upon motion duly made and seconded, it was unanimously

RESOLVED, That the action taken by the Board of Directors in its Special Meeting of ...., 19.., be hereby approved and ratified.

DIRECTORS' RESOLUTION RATIFYING LOANS BY TREASURER OF TREASURY STOCK TO BE USED AS COLLATERAL, AND AUTHORIZING FURTHER LOANS OF SECURITIES

WHEREAS, The Treasurer of this Corporation states that he has loaned to the .... Company, to be used as collateral by that Company, certain stocks from the treasury of this Corporation, be it

RESOLVED, That such loan by the Treasurer is hereby ratified and approved by this Board of Directors, and that the Treasurer is hereby authorized to make such further loans to .... Company of any or all securities now in the treasury of this Corporation as in his judgment seems proper.

DIRECTORS' RESOLUTION AUTHORIZING LOAN TO A SUBSIDIARY ON A NOTE, AND EXTENDING EXISTING LOAN

RESOLVED, That in order to enable the .... Co., Inc. to meet its fixed charges on ...., 19.., the proper officers of this Corporation are hereby authorized to loan to the .... Co., Inc. an amount not exceeding ..... ($.....) Dollars on the note of the .... Co., Inc., payable one year from date, with interest at the rate of nine (9%) percent per annum, secured by such collateral as the President of this Corporation may in his judgment deem proper and sufficient, and

RESOLVED FURTHER, That the existing loan of . . . . . ($. . . . .) Dollars from this Corporation to the . . . . Co., Inc. is hereby extended to and including . . . . ., 19. ., at the rate of interest which it now bears, and

RESOLVED FURTHER, That the proper officers of this Corporation are hereby authorized and directed to do and perform all acts and execute all instruments necessary or convenient to accomplish the purposes aforesaid, subject to the approval of counsel of this Corporation.

DIRECTORS' RESOLUTION AUTHORIZING RECONVEYANCE OF PROPERTY CONVEYED BY TRUST DEED GIVEN TO SECURE LOAN

WHEREAS, this Corporation did, on . . . ., 19. ., lend to the . . . . Company, a corporation organized and existing under and by virtue of the laws of the State of . . . ., the sum of . . . . . ($. . . . .) Dollars, and

WHEREAS, the said Company did, on the date aforesaid, execute and deliver a promissory note in the said sum to the order of this Corporation, payable on . . . ., 19. ., and did execute, acknowledge, and deliver to this Corporation a deed of trust to secure the payment of the said sum, with interest thereon at the rate of . . . . . (. . . . .%) percent per annum, as more fully appears in the said deed of trust now on record in the office of the County Recorder of the County of . . . ., State of . . . ., by which deed of trust the following described real property was conveyed to this Corporation (*insert description*).

WHEREAS, the said note mentioned has been fully paid, together with interest thereon to date, and all charges and claims under the note and trust deed have been fully satisfied, be it

RESOLVED, That this Corporation reconvey to the . . . . Company all the property conveyed by said deed of trust aforesaid, and that the trust created by said deed be declared fully discharged and satisfied, and

RESOLVED FURTHER, That . . . ., the President, and . . . ., the Secretary of this Corporation, are hereby authorized, empowered, and directed to execute, acknowledge, and deliver to the said . . . . Company, in the name of this Corporation and under its seal, a deed of grant, bargain, and sale in due form, conveying all the property described in said deed of trust.

DIRECTORS' RESOLUTION RATIFYING ACTION OF OFFICERS IN ACCEPTING BONDS OF SUBSIDIARY IN PAYMENT OF INDEBTEDNESS OF SUBSIDIARY TO PARENT COMPANY

RESOLVED, That the action of the officers of this Corporation in offering to cancel and discharge the indebtedness of . . . . . ($. . . . .) Dollars and any other indebtedness, except any accounts payable representing materials, supplies, and services owing this Corporation by . . . . & Company in consideration of the surrender by said Company to this Corporation of . . . . . ($. . . . .) Dollars principal amount of its 8% purchase money mortgage bonds issued under its deed of trust to . . . . & Company, dated . . . ., 19. ., is hereby ratified and confirmed, and

RESOLVED FURTHER, That the officers of this Corporation are hereby authorized and instructed, upon the surrender to this Corporation by . . . . & Company of . . . . . ($. . . . .) Dollars principal amount of the aforementioned 8% purchase money mortgage bonds, to execute and deliver to said . . . . & Company an instrument fully cancelling and discharging the said indebtedness of . . . . & Company to this Corporation amounting to . . . . . ($. . . . .) Dollars, and any other indebtedness except any accounts payable representing materials, supplies, and services.

Chapter 29

PURCHASE, SALE, AND LEASE OF ASSETS

Contents—Chapter 29

How corporations combine. Corporations that want to combine have a choice of several ways. Often the choice will depend on the tax consequences, so a tax adviser should be brought in at the very inception of the proposed transactions. Here are some of the common forms of combinations:

(1) Merger. In a merger, one or more corporations are absorbed by another, called the "surviving corporation." The absorbed corporations, called the "constituent corporations," go out of existence automatically.

(2) Consolidation. In a consolidation, two or more corporations, called the "constituent corporations," create a new corporation called the "consolidated corporation." The constituent corporations go out of existence automatically.

(3) Tender offers. In a tender offer, an offeror may acquire control of another corporation by buying its securities or exchanging them for securities of the offeror.

(4) Sale of assets. In a sale of assets, one corporation sells all or substantially all its assets for cash or stock in the buying corporation. The selling corporation may or may not go out of existence.

(5) Purchase of assets—or "combination." A purchase of assets (or "combination" as it is called in the statutes of at least one state) is an exchange of assets for stock in the buying corporation. Thus, it is basically the same transaction as 4, above—a sale of assets. But the terms "purchase of assets" and "combination" have been given special definition by the statutes of some states and, as so defined, the transactions are distinguishable from a sale of assets. The reason for the distinction is to make clearer the rights of stockholders dissenting from the transaction.[1]

A purchase of assets or combination can be defined broadly as the acquisition of assets of one corporation in exchange for a statutorily-defined percentage of the voting stock in the acquiring corporation. The stock of the acquiring corporation may be distributed to the corporation selling its assets or to its stockholders. There's a more detailed treatment of this type of transaction under "de facto mergers" on page 1139 in Chapter 31.

(6) Lease of assets. A lease of assets is a transfer of the possession of all or part of the corporate property, upon proper authority, with the right to use such property in exchange for rent to be paid to the

---

[1] Kemos, Inc. v Bader (CA-5 1977) 545 F2d 913 (distinguished from amalgamation, consolidation or merger).

lessor corporation or its stockholders. The obligations of the lessee are fixed in the lease.

(7) Purchase of stock. Another form of combination is the creation of a holding company. This results when one corporation acquires a controlling interest in the stock of another; the legal identity of each is preserved in the process. The acquiring corporation is known as the parent or holding company. The corporation whose stock is acquired is called the subsidiary corporation.

Power to dispose of corporate assets. *Outside regular cause of business:* Almost every state by statute authorizes corporations to sell, lease, exchange, mortgage, pledge or make other disposition of all or substantially all their corporate assets outside the regular course of business. However, the statutes vary considerably, they should be consulted before a sale or other disposition is authorized. For example, the statutes differ on such things as what kind of disposition needs stockholder consent (for example, only a few states say that mortgages need stockholder consent), whether consent must be obtained at a special meeting, what proportion of stockholders must approve, and what kind of notice must be given.

Ordinarily, neither directors nor a majority of stockholders, nor both together, have the power to sell or otherwise to transfer all the property of a going, prosperous concern, or even so much of it as renders the corporation unable to continue business and to carry out the purposes of its formation.[2] Unless there is statutory authority to the contrary, unanimous consent must be obtained. However, most states provide for sale of assets by less than unanimous vote, but more than a majority. Most often, they require a two-thirds or a three-quarter vote of the stockholders. The vote, of course, is of stock, not stockholders— thus where the statute calls for the approval of "two-thirds of the stockholders," the approval by one stockholder who owns more than two-thirds of the shares of stock is sufficient to carry the transaction.[3]

Note that the buyer of a radio station from its owner was entitled to specific performance of the contract to sell even though the seller had failed to comply with the technical requirement of the statute that two-thirds of the shares approve when both the majority stockholder and the corporate minority owner, through its president, gave

---

[2] Geddes v Anaconda Copper Mining Co., (1921) 254 US 590, 41 S Ct 209; Allied Chemical & Dye Corp. v Steel & Tube Co. (Del. Ch. 1923) 14 Del Ch. 1, 120 Atl 486; In re Leventall, (1934) 241 App. Div. 277, 271 N.Y.S. 493.
[3] Fredericks v Pennsylvania Canal Co., (1885) 109 Pa. St. 50, 2 Atl 48.

approval, since that was enough to achieve the primary purpose of the statute, protection of the stockholders' interests.[4]

If *all* the stockholders consent, corporations organized for private purposes and having no duty to the public possess a common law right to convey their entire property to an individual or to a corporation.[5]

Note that if a corporation is insolvent or unable profitably to execute the purposes for which it was created, it can sell or assign its property on the vote of a mere majority of the stock, provided that the sale is not (1) a fraud on creditors, or (2) contrary to statutory, charter or by-law requirements.[6] That exception doesn't apply if it's shown that the purpose is to continue the business through a new corporation; in that case the usual greater-than-majority consent set by the statute must be obtained.[7]

By statute in some states, the directors may dispose of corporate assets without stockholder consent when the corporation is unable to meet its liabilities or is in a "failing condition."

Also, it has been argued that, if the majority of stockholders of a private business corporation may sell to prevent greater loss, they may also sell to make greater gains.[8] The directors have no authority to sell all the property of the corporation without the consent of at least a majority of the stock.[9] While a majority of the stockholders may authorize the sale against the dissenting vote of the minority,[10] the minority is entitled to certain rights.

Disposition within the regular course of business: By statute in some states, a sale, lease, exchange, mortgage, pledge, or other disposition of corporate assets when made in the regular course of the corporation's business can be made by the directors without stockholder consent. But in some of these states, the statutes permit the charter or by-laws to require stockholder consent, and in other states a mortgage or pledge of corporate assets needs stockholder consent even though made in the regular course of business. However, a corporation cannot bring an action to invalidate a lease, on the ground it is void

---

[4] Wooster Republican Printing Co. v Channel 17, Inc. (WD Mo 1091) 533 F Supp 601.

[5] People ex rel Barney v Whalen, (1907) 119 App. Div. 749, 104 N.Y.S. 55, aff'd 189 N.Y. 560, 82 NE 1131; Johnson v Spartanburg County Fair Ass'n, (1947) 210 S.C. 56, 41 SE2d 599.

[6] Michigan Wolverine Student Co-op v Wm. Goodyear & Co., (1946) 314 Mich. 590, 22 NW2d 884; Hicks v Whiting, (1923) 149 Tenn. 411, 258 SW 784.

[7] Mills v Tiffany's, Inc., (1938) 123 Conn. 631, 198 Atl 185.

[8] Bowditch v Jackson Co., (1912) 76 N.H. 351, 82 Atl 1014.

[9] Solorza v Park Water Co., (1948) 86 Cal. App2d 653, 195 P2d 523; People v Ballard, (1892) 134 N.Y. 269, 32 NE 54. But see Union Trust Co. of Maryland v Carter (WD Va. 1905) 139 F 717; Beardstown Pearl Button Co. v Oswald, (1906) 130 Ill. App. 290.

[10] Hancock v Holbrook (ED La 1881) 9 F 353.

because not authorized by the stockholders, when the corporation had received benefits of the lease for four years.[11]

A buyer can compel a common carrier corporation to perform an agreement to sell its operating rights, even though not formally approved by the directors, when the sales agreement was signed by its president, who was the owner of all the corporation's outstanding stock.[12]

A successor board of directors cannot set aside the corporation's sale of corporate properties on the mere claim of waste and improvidence unless fraud or illegality is shown.[13]

When is a disposition in the "regular course" of business? This question arises most frequently in companies whose "inventory" consists of capital assets, for example, corporations dealing in real estate and corporations managing or liquidating estates.

A sale by a corporation of a parcel of real estate it was organized to liquidate is a sale in the regular course of business.[14] So too is a sale of the assets of a corporation organized to liquidate a decedent's estate,[15] and a sale of its real estate by a corporation organized to buy and sell real estate.[16]

Also held to be in the regular course of business is a sale of its assets by a corporation that wants to relocate in a more favorable economic environment.[17] At least one state by statute permits the directors to make a sale for that purpose without getting stockholder consent. Often the question that decides whether stockholders' consent is needed for a sale of a substantial part of the corporation's assets is whether the corporation will continue in the same business. If it will, stockholder consent is not needed.[18] A minority stockholder can bar the majority from transferring part of the corporation's assets to a subsidiary in exchange for the subsidiary's stock, even though the statute calling for two-thirds approval applies in terms only to the sale

---

[11]U-Beva Mines v Toledo Mining Co., (1970) 24 Utah 2d 351, 471 P2d 867.

[12]Beaufort Transfer Co. v Fischer Trucking Co. (S Ct Mo. 1970) 451 SW2d 40.

[13]Cross Properties, Inc. v Brook Realty (S Ct 1969) NYLJ 10–24–69, p. 18.

[14]In re Miglietta, (1942) 287 N.Y. 246, 39 NE2d 224.

[15]Jeppi v Brockman Holding Co., (1949) 34 Cal.2d 11, 206 P2d 847.

[16]Epstein v Gosseen, (1932) 235 A.D. 33, 256, N.Y.S. 49; Pollack v Atwood Corp., (1948) 321 Mich. 93, 32 NW2d 65; Thayer v Valley Bank, (1929) 35 Ariz. 238, 276 P 526.

[17]Matter of Avard, (1955) 5 Misc.2d 817, 144 N.Y.S.2d 204, app dism, (1956) 2 A.D.2d 647, 156 N.Y.S.2d 970; Matter of Hake, (1955) 285 A.D. 316, 136 N.Y.S.2d 817.

[18]Story v Kennecott Copper Corp., (1977) 90 Misc.2d 333, 294 N.Y.S.2d 353; Frankel v Tremont Norman Motors Corp., (1960) 8 N.Y.2d 901, 204 N.Y.S.2d 146, 168 NE2d 823.

of "all or substantially all the assets," when the transfer is not one in the ordinary course of business.[19]

What is a disposition of substantially all the assets? Substantially all the assets means those assets which are an integral part of and essential to carrying on the business, so that the sale of those assets would create a fundamental change in the nature or scope of the business. Thus, when the primary purpose of the corporation was to manufacture aluminum ware, the sale of all plants, tools, machinery, inventory, goodwill, and patents for $1,400,000 was a sale of "substantially all the assets," even though the corporation did not sell its stock in a subsidiary, and even though it had money in the bank, accounts receivable, and securities, of a total value over $760,000.[20]

Similarly when a corporation in the printing and lithographing business had an important, self-contained branch that manufactured calendars, its sale of the calendar branch, with its goodwill, meant that the corporation to that extent went out of business. The sale of the goodwill, therefore, deprived it of one of the powers conferred by the charter—the power to manufacture calendars.[21] But the sale of a small, experimental part of the business is not a fundamental change in the scope of the business.[22]

The decision of a conglomerate's board of directors to sell its oil and gas holdings did not amount to a sale of substantially all the corporation's assets so as to require shareholder approval, though the oil and gas business continued to be listed as the corporation's principal purpose and though oil and gas assets were substantial within the conglomerate; however, the sale was delayed to let a minority stockholder show $480 million sale price was grossly inadequate.[23] Similarly, one company's sale of a subsidiary didn't require stockholder approval, even though the subsidiary was the only part of the company that was making a profit.[24] And an acquisition plan by which a group including two key officers and directors bought 92.6 percent of the shares and used a cash-out merger to acquire the remaining 7.4 percent was not a sale of substantially all the assets so as to acquire approval by the directors and stockholders.[25]

---

[19] Aiple v Twin City Barge & Towing Co., (1966) 274 Minn. 38, 143 NW2d 374.
[20] Stiles v Aluminum Products Co., (1949) 338 Ill. App. 48, 86 NE2d 887.
[21] Matter of Timmis, (1910) 200 N.Y. 177, 93 NE 522.
[22] Klopot v Northrup, (1944) 131 Conn. 14, 37 A2d 700.
[23] Gimbel III v The Signal Companies, Inc. (Del. Ch. 1974) 316 A2d 599.
[24] Story v Kennecott Copper Corp., (1977) 90 Misc.2d 333, 394 N.Y.S.2d 353.
[25] Field v Allyn (Del Ch 1983) 457 A 2d 1091.

Sale or other disposition to stockholders, directors and officers. While a sale to the majority of stockholders that is fair and will serve the best interests of the corporation will be upheld,[26] the minority may always question the good faith of such a transaction.[27] Creditors also may challenge it.[28] In the same way, a sale to a director or officer that is made in good faith, for adequate consideration[29] and for the best interest of the corporation will be upheld by the courts,[30] but such transactions are always subject to the closest scrutiny.[31] For example, the sale of corporate property to interested directors who fail to make full disclosure to corporation of facts affecting value of property is voidable and can be set aside in stockholders' derivative action.[32] If a corporation conveys all its property to one of its stockholders, who is also a director, and is then dissolved, the grantee is not personally liable for the indebtedness of the corporation on a trust deed where the assets not subject to the trust deed were of trifling value.[33] A corporation's transfer of real property to a stockholder won't be set aside as an illegal preference, even though the corporation has unpaid outstanding debts, when the corporation has not refused to pay its debts, but merely fails to pay them on time.[34]

Adequacy of consideration. When a sale has the proper statutory consent of the stockholders, minority stockholders cannot attack it on the ground that the price was inadequate, if no fraud was committed and there was no collusion.[35] But minority stockholders can set aside a sale for a grossly inadequate price, where a secret interest or advantage is retained by those who authorize the sale, to the disadvantage of the minority stockholders.[36]

The provision in most of the statutes that dissenting stockholders shall receive the fair value of their shares after sale makes it incumbent

---

[26]Carrier v Dixon, (1919) 142 Tenn. 122, 218 SW 395.

[27]Jones v Missouri-Edison Electric Co. (CA–8 1906) 144 F 765; A stockholder can get a receiver appointed to preserve corporate assets when some stockholders-officers allegedly removed assets and took control of the corporation. Kramer v Margolis, S Ct, (1971) NYLJ, 4-27-71, p. 2.

[28]Bell Telephone Co. v Schwab, (1938) 33 Pa. D. & C. 270.

[29]Nipp v Puritan Mfg. & Supply Co., (1935) 128 Neb. 459, 259 NW 53.

[30]Ryan v Williams (Va. ED 1900) 100 F 172.

[31]Twin-Lick v Marbury, (1875) 91 US 586, Geddes v Anaconda Mining Co., (1921) 254 US 590, 41 S Ct 209, *reversing,* on other grounds (CA–9 1920) 245 F 225.

[32]Knudsen v Burdett, (1939) 67 S.D. 20, 287 NW 673.

[33]Life Ins. Co. of Virginia v Edgerton, (1934) 206 N.C. 402, 174 SE 96.

[34]Venice East, Inc. v Manno (Fla Dist. Ct of App 1966) 186 S2d 71.

[35]Koehler v St. Mary's Brewing Co., (1910) 228 Pa. 648, 77 Atl 1016.

[36]Cardiff v Johnson, (1923) 126 Wash. 454, 216 P 269, 222 P 902.

upon the stockholders to obtain an adequate price. If they do not and the minority stockholders exercise their rights under the statute, the corporation may be called upon to pay a larger sum to the minority stockholders, as the value of their interests, than their proportionate share of the amount realized on the sale.[37]

Although it is the duty of the directors and stockholders to obtain the highest price, what is the highest price cannot always be set on an absolute standard. Before interfering with any transaction, the courts give great weight to the honest judgment of those who managed the corporation successfully and to the wishes of those who own or represent the owners of nearly all the capital stock.[38] Here are some examples of the factors the courts will consider:

Examples: (1) Although the consideration offered on a sale of assets was substantially less than book value, the disparity was not so great as to be a violation of fiduciary duty by the directors and majority stockholders when earnings per share had dropped about 80% in four years and the outlook for continued profitable operation was dim.[39]

(2) Majority directors' approval of the sale was in good faith when they believed that the corporation would be unable to meet competition if it continued as a small family-held corporation and that the larger stockholders would be better prepared to meet estate taxes if the corporate assets were sold.[40]

(3) Buying corporation was not liable for personal injuries allegedly caused by a defective machine made by the selling corporation, when it was shown that the selling corporation continued business under a new name and the purchase price was more than adequate and paid in cash.[41]

(4) Voting trustees of all the corporation's stock violated their fiduciary duty to the corporation, when they accepted an offer from the corporation's chief financial backer to sell him all the corporation's assets, since they were dominated by the backer and their decision was made in his interest, not that of the corporation. However, the sale won't be set aside, but the price will be adjusted to reflect the corporation's value as a going business at the time the decision to sell was made.[42]

(5) An agreement by a corporation to transfer capital stock amounting to substantially all its assets in return for rights under a sublease was invalid when the sublease was subject to a contingency not yet in effect, so no property was actually received by the corporation for

---

[37] Matter of Bickerton, (1921) 196 App. Div. 231, 187 N.Y.S. 267.
[38] Lewisohn Bros. v Anaconda Copper Min. Co., (1899) 26 Misc. 613, 56 N.Y.S. 807.
[39] Baron v Pressed Metals of America, Inc., (1956) 35 Del. Ch. 581, 123 A2d 848.
[40] Cottrell v The Pawcatuck Co., (1956) 36 Del. Ch. 169, 123 A2d 848.
[41] McKee v Harris-Int. Corp., (1970) 109 N.J. Super. 555, 264 A2d 98.
[42] Stone v Massa, (1966) 351 Mass. 264, 218 NE2d 583.

the stock, and when there was no affirmative vote of the holders of two-thirds of the outstanding shares of stock.[43]

Consideration paid in stock of purchasing corporation. A corporation may sell its assets for the stock of the purchasing company, if it is authorized to acquire the securities of other corporations.[44]

A corporation that does not have the power to acquire stock in another corporation cannot sell its corporate property for stock of the purchasing company.[45] However, the sale will not be set aside if all the stockholders consent and creditors are not injured by the transaction.[46] Further, stockholders who have consented to the sale cannot later say the transaction was *ultra vires*.[47] Moreover, the statutory prohibition against the unauthorized purchase of stock, bonds, and securities only applies to a going concern, and sale that is made for the purpose of winding up the corporate affairs.[48] If, therefore, the transaction is for the purpose of winding up the business of the selling corporation, the corporation undoubtedly has the power to sell its property for stock; but if the purpose is not to wind up the corporation, but to continue the corporate life through the instrumentality of another corporation, the corporation cannot sell its assets for stock of the buying corporation unless the power is expressly conferred by the legislature.[49]

A statute that authorizes the sale of corporate property, but does not make provision for paying in cash to nonconsenting stockholders the appraised value of their shares, doesn't authorize a sale to another corporation, through an exchange of stock in the buying corporation for stock in the selling corporation, where the rights of the stockholders in the new corporation would differ from the rights of the stockholders in the old corporation.[50]

Under those statutes where the rights of nonconsenting stockholders are not protected, the right of sale given upon consent of a

---

[43] Vermillion Parish Peat Co. v Green Belt Peat Moss Co. (Tex. Civ. App. 1971) 465 SW2d 955.

[44] Erickson v Grande Ronde Lumber Co., (1939) 162 Or. 556, 92 P2d 170, reh'g den, (1939) 162 Or. 556, 94 P2d 139.

[45] Riker & Son Co. v United Drug Co., (1912) 79 N.J. Eq. 580, 82 Atl 930; Coler v Tacoma Railway & Power Co., (1903) 65 N.J. Eq. 347, 54 Atl 413, revg. 64 N.J. Eq. 117, 53 Atl 80; Germer v Triple State Natural Gas & Oil Co., (1906) 60 W.Va. 143, 54 SE 509.

[46] Read v Citizens' St. R. Co., (1903) 110 Tenn. 316, 75 SW 1056.

[47] Tryson v Southern Realty Corp. (D.C. Cir. 1921) 274 F 135.

[48] Metcalf v Amer. School Furniture Co. (WD N.Y. 1903) 122 F 115.

[49] McCutcheon v Merz Capsule Co. (CA–6 1896) 71 F 787.

[50] Murrin v Archbald Cons. Coal Co., (1921) 196 App. Div. 107, 187 N.Y.S. 606; affirmed 232 N.Y. 541, 134 NE 563.

percentage of the owners of the stock means the right of sale for cash at a fair valuation that would leave to the nonconsenting stockholders who did not agree to join the new corporation the right to their pro rata parts of the old corporation.[51] But, if arrangements are made whereby any stockholder can receive his share of the proceeds of the company's assets in money, his rights are not infringed by a stipulation that the stockholders may receive stock instead of money.[52]

Even if a corporation has authority to sell its property to another corporation for stock in the purchasing corporation, it cannot compel a minority stockholder objecting to the sale to take anything but cash for his interest.[53] The reason is that the minority stockholders may not lawfully be compelled to accept a change of investment made for them by others or to elect between losing their interests or entering a new company.[54] However, when the stock of the buying corporation taken in exchange for the corporation's property has an established market value, it can be treated as the equivalent of money, and if the sale is otherwise valid, it will be sustained.[55] Moreover, a minority stockholder cannot object to a sale of the corporate assets for stock of the buying corporation, if provision is made for cash payments to all the stockholders who do not want to take stock in the buying corporation.[56]

Procedure in disposing of assets. When a sale or other disposition of assets is made pursuant to a statute, the procedure outlined in the statute should be followed carefully. The usual steps are as follows:

(1) The board of directors of the selling company acts on the transaction.[57] A sale is valid when authorized by resolution of the stockholders and not by the directors as the stockholders are the parties vitally interested.[58]

Even an 88% stockholder and director acting alone can't bind a corporation to a sale of all its assets, when it's not approved by the board or by the stockholders at a stockholders' meeting; that the

---

[51] McCutcheon v Merz Capsule Co. (CA–6 1896) 71 F 787.

[52] Bowditch v Jackson Co., (1912) 76 N.H. 351, 82 Atl 1014.

[53] Metcalf v Amer. School Furniture Co. (WD N.Y. 1903) 122 F 115; Koehler v St. Mary's Brewing Co., (1910) 228 Pa. 648, 77 Atl 1016.

[54] Geddes v Anaconda Min. Co., (1921) 254 US 590, 41 S Ct 209.

[55] Metcalf v Amer. School Furniture Co. (WD N.Y. 1903) 122 F 115; Koehler v St. Mary's Brewing Co., (1910) 228 Pa. 648, 77 Atl 1016.

[56] Slattery v Greater New Orleans Realty & Development Co., (1911) 128 La. 871, 55 So 558.

[57] De Lamar Mines of Montana, Inc. v Mackay (CA–9 1939) 104 F2d 271.

[58] Merrion v Scorup-Sommerville Cattle Co. (CA–10 1943) 134 F 23 473.

stockholders later authorized the 88% stockholder to sell the corporate assets doesn't make its earlier agreement to sell enforceable against the corporation.[59] Neither was a minority's offer to sell a corporation's entire assets and its later ratification by a simple majority valid when the sale required three-fourths stockholder approval.[60] Even approval by all stockholders is not enough when done only individually.[61]

(2) A meeting of the stockholders is called upon proper notice, and a resolution authorizing the sale is passed. However, failure to give notice of the meeting will not necessarily bar a sale. For example, one court refused to bar a sale of a corporation's assets on the ground that no notice was given of a stockholders' meeting to act on the sale when (1) over 70% of the stock is in favor of the sale, (2) no wrongdoing was alleged, and (3) the dissenting stockholder would be granted an appraisal.[62] But a court will not set aside a transfer of assets once it has been made with the requisite stockholder approval, even though the statutory formalities for obtaining stockholder approval were not followed. The statutes are mandatory in requiring stockholder approval, but only directory in specifying the procedure for obtaining approval. Strangers dealing with the corporation don't have to inquire whether the directors complied with internal notification procedures.[63] Conversely, a close corporation cannot use its own failure to follow statutory requirement that the board of directors authorize and two-thirds of the stockholders approve the sale of assets as an excuse to evade the contract of sale, when it generally functioned informally and the stockholders did give informal approval.[64]

If the statute requires that the notice of meeting "contain a complete and specific statement of the proposal to be considered," and the notice sets out the proposal only in general terms, a stockholder can have the sale barred.[65]

But by court decision[66] and statute in many states, the stockholders can give advance consent to a sale in general terms, leaving it to the directors to fix the specific terms and conditions. However, another court has warned that if a corporation does this and

---

[59] Beall v Pacific Nat. Bank of Seattle, (1959) 55 Wash. 2d 210, 347 P2d 550.

[60] Kaufman v Henry (Mo. App. 1975) 520 SW2d 152.

[61] Carson v Isabel Apts. Inc. (Wash. App. 1978) 579 P2d 1027.

[62] Gottfried v Gottfried Baking Co., Inc., (1956) 1 AD 2d 793, 151 N.Y.S. 2d 583.

[63] McDermott v Bear Film Co. (Ore. law) (1963) 219 Cal. App. 2d 607, 33 Cal. Rptr. 486.

[64] Leslie, Semple & Garrison, Inc. v Gavit & Co., Inc., (1981) 81 App. Div. 2d 950, 439 NYS 2d 707.

[65] Schwartz v Inspiration Gold Min. (D. Mont. 1936) 15 F Supp 1030.

[66] Mattiello v Flagg, (1958) 14 Misc. 2d 597, 178 N.Y.S. 2d 179.

some stockholders dissent, the corporation will either have to go through with a sale, rescind the stockholders' resolution approving a sale, or pay off dissenters.[67]

(3) Any additional statutory requirements must be complied with, for example, that a copy of the contract of sale be filed in the office of the secretary of state.

(4) Delivery of a bill of sale to the purchasing company. Note that if stockholders may authorize the sale of a corporation's entire assets in accordance with contracts previously executed but they do not thereby validate those contracts; new contracts must be executed.[68]

(5) Any one of the following acts may now be required:

I. If the selling company has received cash only, it may distribute the cash and dissolve, or, if the sale is of a part only of the business, it may distribute or hold the cash and continue in existence, operating the remainder of its property.

II. If the selling corporation has received cash and stock of the purchasing corporation, or stock only, it may (a) distribute the stock, or cash and stock, to its stockholders and continue in existence; (b) distribute the new stock, or cash and stock, to its stockholders and dissolve; (c) distribute the consideration received and continue in existence nominally only; (d) exchange the stock acquired for its own stock and then turn over its own stock to the purchaser, thus becoming a subsidiary of the purchasing corporation; or (e) the corporation may hold the shares of the purchasing corporation, in which case it becomes a holding company.

(6) The selling company must satisfy the dissenting stockholders in accordance with the statutory provisions and the terms of agreement.[69]

Sale or other disposition of assets without statutory authority. If, without express statutory authority, the majority stockholders sell the property of the corporation against the will of the minority, thereby working a practical dissolution of the company,[70] the minority holders may, at their election within a reasonable time,[71] demand the market value of their stock at the date of sale, or their proportional value of the proceeds; or they may follow the property into the hands of the

---

[67] Hake v Hake Mfg. Co., (1955) 308 N.Y. 940, 127 NE2d 90.
[68] Gottfried v Gottfried Baking Co., (1956) 1 AD2d 993, 15 NYS2d 583.
[69] In re Independent Distillers of Kentucky (Ky. WD 1940) 34 F Supp 724.
[70] Levin v Pittsburgh United Corp., (1938) 330 Pa. 457, 199 Atl 332, s.c., (1939) 334 Pa. 107, 5 A2d 890, c.c., (1940) 338 Pa. 328, 12 A2d 430.
[71] Polans v Oreck's Inc., (1945) 220 Minn. 249, 19 NW2d 435.

purchaser[72] and share in the profits arising from its use in the same ratio that they would have shared if the sale had not been made.

However, the choice of following the property and demanding a pro rata share of the earnings after it has passed into other hands and has been put to use must be made under the supervision and approval of the equity court.[73]

An objecting stockholder can't just sit idly by when the majority has approved a sale of corporate assets and then later have it set aside.[74] However, he may be entitled to damages.[75]

If the transaction is in bad faith, the sale may be set aside and the corporation revived, provided the party asking for the rescission has not by his own delay allowed outsiders' rights to supervene.[76]

A court will not review the adequacy of the purchase price of corporate assets unless the disparity is so great as to shock the conscience of the court or warrant the conclusion that the majority was actuated by improper motives, thereby working injury to the minority; mere mistakes of judgment are not enough to justify interference in corporate transactions otherwise valid by law of the state of incorporation.[77]

But a stockholder can set aside a transfer of corporate assets if he can show bad faith, injury, or even that the transaction was not in the best interests of the corporation.[78] Even though a sale of assets made under the applicable statutory provision can be set aside for fraud, it's not also vulnerable merely because of failure to secure the unanimous consent of the stockholders that's required for statutory or common-law consolidation or merger.[79]

In selling corporate assets or franchises, directors, officers, and majority stockholders must not manipulate the stock to the detriment of minority stockholders.[80]

If the transaction is not yet consummated, the minority may secure an injunction to prevent the contemplated acts.[81] However, a

[72]Woods v Consolidated Newspapers, Inc, (1938) 275 Ky. 479, 122 SW2d 112.
[73]Tanner v Lindell R. Co., (1903) 180 Mo. 1, 79 SW 155. See also In re Leventall, (1934). 241 App. Div. 277, 271 N.Y.S. 493.
[74]Peterson v New England Furniture & Carpet Co, (1941) 210 Minn. 449, 299 NW 208.
[75]Finch v Warrior Cement Corp., (1928) 16 Del. Ch. 44, 141 Atl 54.
[76]Tanner v Lindell R. Co., (1903) 180 Mo. 1, 79 SW 155; Knudsen v Burdett, (1939) 67 S. D. 20, 287 NW 673.
[77]Massaro v Fisk Rubber Corp. (D. Mass. 1941) 36 F Supp 382.
[78]Citizens Bank & Trust Co. v Magnolia Sugar Co-op., Inc., (1942) La. App., 8 S2d 380.
[79]Argenbright v Phoenix Finance Corp., (1936) 21 Del. Ch. 288 186 Atl 124.
[80]Tanner v Lindell R. Co., (1903) 180 Mo. 1, 79 SW 155; Zabriskie v Railroad, (1867) 18 N.J. Eq. 178; Abbott v American-Hard Rubber Co., (1861) 33 Barg. (N.Y.) 589p; Weisbecker v Hosiery Patents, Inc., (1947) 356 Pa. 244, 51 A2d 811.
[81]Voigt v Remick, (1932) 260 Mich. 198, 244 NW 446.

minority stockholder who is present at the meeting at which the sale is authorized by the majority, and who participates in the meeting and assents to the action of the majority, cannot later repudiate the terms of the sale and decline to accept payment in accordance with conditions of the sale.[82] Nor may a stockholder who has ratified the acts of the majority stockholders, or acquiesced in the action, complain.[83] A court cannot rule on the validity of a proposed contract of sale or corporate assets, and a plan of dissolution, when the stockholders have not yet voted their approval of the sale or the dissolution as required by statute.[84]

The officers and directors of a corporation were liable for breach of duty when they transferred the corporation's assets to its wholly-owned subsidiary without stockholder approval.[85] However, even if a sale of corporate assets by the majority directors and stockholder amounts to a breach of their fiduciary duty to the minority, the latter can't bar the transaction unless they can show the price was inadequate.[86]

A court of equity won't bar a sale of corporate assets when the transaction is effected in full conformity to the applicable law.[87] But it will bar the sale if the notice of stockholders' meeting called to approve the sale of corporate assets is legally insufficient, or the resolution acted upon at the meeting is too vague and uncertain to amount to a valid contract.[88]

A corporation's sale of property to officers-stockholders for less than adequate consideration is not only voidable at the corporation's option, but an equity court can require them to pay the corporation the difference between the purchase price and the market price; especially when it's a family corporation that functioned informally, the court will tend to disregard the corporate shell.[89]

---

[82] In re Independent Distillers of Kentucky (WD Ky. 1940) 34 F Supp 724; Koehler v St. Mary's Brewing Co., (1910) 228 Pa. 648, 77 Atl 1016.

[83] Kimball v Success Min. Co., (1910) 38 Utah 78, 110 P 872.

[84] Escondido Mutual Water Co. v Georgia A. Hillebrecht, Inc., (1966) Cal. App. 2d 410, 50 Cal Rptr 495.

[85] Cambell v Vose (CA–10 1975) 515 F2d 256.

[86] Kaye v Kentucky Public Elevator Co., (1943) 295 Ky. 661, 175 SW2d 142.

[87] Meeks v Seawell, (1945) 198 Ga. 817, 33 SE2d 150.

[88] Loy v Lorm Corporation (N C App. 1981) 278 SE 2d 897; Schwartz v Inspiration Gold Min Co. (D Mont. 1936) 15 F Supp 1030.

[89] Warren v Warren (Del. S Ct 1983) 460 A 2d 526.

Note: If the sale of the assets has not been consummated, the majority stockholders may defeat the statutory right of dissenting minority stockholders by abandoning the sale of the assets, dissolving the corporation and compelling dissenters to take possibly lesser amounts as their distributive shares in liquidation.[90]

Liabilities of purchasing and selling corporations; rights of creditors. In a bona fide transaction of purchase and sale, where the selling corporation receives money to pay its debts, and there's no fraud or other ground to hold the buyer liable, the creditors of the selling corporation cannot subject the property in the hands of the purchaser to the payment of their claims, or have the sale set aside.[91] And the mere fact that at the time the transfer is authorized there are matured liabilities which seller is unable to meet will not prevent board of directors from authorizing the transfer.[92] In such a case, the consideration received by the seller takes the place of the assets sold and the creditors must look to the amount received for the satisfaction of their interests.[93] But if the only consideration is capital stock of the purchasing corporation, and the selling corporation, as a result of the sale has no property or assets of any kind that can be subjected to the payment of debts, the purchasing corporation will be liable.[94]

Just because one corporation has bought the property of another corporation does not make the buyer liable for the debts of the seller.[95] A purchaser, however, will be liable for the debts of the selling corporation, if any one of the following appears:

---

[90] Kirwan v Parkway Distillery, Inc., (1941) 285 Ky. 605, 148 SW2d 720.

[91] Lamp v Leroy Corp., (1969) 85 Nev. 276, 454 P2d 24; Chadwick v Air Reduction Co. Inc. (DC, ND Ohio 1965) 239 F Supp 247; Ozan Lumber Co. v Davis Sewing Machine Co. (D Del 1922) 284 F 161, affirmed (CA-3 1923) 292 F 134. Sale could not be set aside for tardiness in the formal transfer of assets when the statute had no time limit for compliance. Beccio v Tawnmoore Apartments, Inc., (1972) 265 Md. 297, 289 A2d 311.

[92] De Lamar Mines of Montana, Inc. v Mackay (CA-9 1939) 104 F2d 271; Chesher v Shafter Lake Clay Co., (1941) 45 N.M. 419, 115 P2d 636.

[93] Bryan, Griffith & Brunson, Inc. v General Newspapers Inc., (1935) 6 W. W. Harr. (Del.) 468, 178 Atl 645; Sinclair Refining Co. v Rayville Motor Co., (1935) La. App., 160 So 179; Everett v Carolina Mortgage Co., (1939) 214 N.C. 778, 1 SE2d 109.

[94] Valley Bank v Malcolm, (1922) 23 Ariz. 395, 204 P 207; Amer. Ry. Exp. Co. v Commonwealth, (1920) 190 Ky. 636, 228 SW 433; Goodwin & Jean v Amer. Ry. Exp. Co., (1927) 220 Mo. App. 695, 294 SW 100. But see McAlister v American Ry. Exp. Co., (1920) 179 N.C. 556, 103 SE 129. See, also, Bankers Trust Co. v Hale & Kilburn Corp. (CA-2 1936) 84 F2d 401; Seattle Investor Syndicate v West Dependable Stores of Washington, (1934) 177 Wash. 125, 30 P2d 956.

[95] Fairways of Country Lakes v Shenandoah Development Corp., (1983) 113 Ill. App. 3d 932, 447 NE 2d 1367; Anderson Lumber Co. v Meyers, Inc., (1973) 296 Minn. 33, 206 NW2d 365; Commercial Nat'l Bank v Newtson, (1976) 39 Ill. App. 3d 216, 349 NE2d 138; H.M. Chase Corp. v Idaho Potatoe Processors, Inc., (1974) 96 Ida. 398, 529 P2d 1270.

(1) *There is an agreement, express or implied, to assume the debts of the selling corporation.*[96]

Generally, a corporation purchasing the property of another company does not assume its obligations unless expressly required by agreement so to do.[97] Thus, a corporation that pays fair value for sole proprietor's business is not liable to his former employee for wages allegedly due him when it is unaware of and has not agreed to assume the debt.[98]

Similarly, the successor is not liable for an award against its predecessor based on employee discrimination.[99] However, a successor was held liable for alleged negligent failure by the predecessor to file an application for a patent, when, in buying the assets, it agreed to assume all its predecessor's "liabilities, obligations and covenants . . . except as specifically excluded."[100]

A corporation acquiring all the stock of another isn't bound by an oral agreement made by the selling corporation, of which it had no notice, that the selling corporation would press its claim against a third party only on certain conditions.[101]

Even though the president of a corporation did not have authority to make contracts on behalf of a successor corporation, the latter could accept and ratify the contract after it came into existence.[102]

A corporation that takes over assets of another corporation, and also, with full knowledge acts upon and accepts benefits of latter's contract, becomes liable on it.[103] Similarly, if a corporation buys another corporation's assets and expressly assumes seller's debts, it

---

[96] Wilson v Fare Well Corp., (1976) 140 N.J. Super. 476, 356 Atl 458; Bippus v Norton Co. (DC Ed. Pa. 1977) 437 F Supp 104; Pierce v Riverside Mortgage Securities Co., (1938) 25 Cal App 2d 248, 77 P2d 226; Kraft v Garfield Park Community Hospital, (1938) 296 Ill. App. 613, 16 NE2d 936; Nat. Cash Register Co. v Ness, (1938) 204 Minn. 148, 282 NW 827; Pankey v Hot Springs Nat'l Bank, (1941) 46 N.M. 10, 119 P2d 636; In re Lehrer-Howard, Inc., (1943) 181 Misc. 683, 44 N.Y.S.2d 494; St. Claire Lime Co. v Ada Lime Co., (1945) 196 Okla. 29, 162 P2d 547; East Texas Title Co. v Parchaman, (1938) Tex. Civ. App. 116 SW2d 497.

[97] Schwartz v McGraw-Edison Co. (181 Misc. 683, 1971) 14 Cal. App. 3d 767, 92 Cal. Rptr 776; Leach v Ross Heater & Mfg. Co. (WD N.Y. 1938) 25 F Supp 822.

[98] Pringle v Hunsicker, (1957) 154 Cal. App. 2d 789, 316 P2d 742.

[99] Kansas Commission on Civil Rights v Service Envelope Co., Inc., (1983) 233 Kan 20, 660 P 2d 549.

[100] Keller v Clark Equipment Co. (CA-8 1983) 715 F2d 1280.

[101] Pulsnation Enterprises, Inc. v Appliance Plan Company (Fla. Dist. Ct of App. 1962) 141 S2d 814.

[102] Interstate Folding Box Co. v La Mode Garment Mfg. Co., (1939) 301 Ill. App. 283, 22 NE2d 769.

[103] Maffi v O'Neil, (1940) Tex. Civ. App. 138 SW2d 134, aff'd Wellington Oil Co. of Del. v Maffi, (1941) 136 Tex. 201, 150 SW2d 60.

becomes liable to seller's creditors, who are considered as the beneficiaries of buyer's promise.[104]

It makes no difference that the buying company pays for the property of the selling corporation with stock—if buyer agrees to pay the liabilities and indebtedness of seller, the seller's creditors get a direct right to enforce the promise. Further, the provision applies even to contingent liabilities.[105] In this kind of situation, the creditor isn't limited to an action at law—he can proceed in an equitable action to have a trust impressed on the transferred assets, and have a receiver appointed.[106]

When a corporation buys the assets of another corporation and assumes its debts, with the seller then dissolving, the buyer is liable to a stockholder of the dissolved corporation for breach of its contract to buy his stock.[107]

The obligations and liabilities assumed include torts and liabilities of all kinds that might come to light, as well as those known to the parties at the time.[108]

(2) *The circumstances surrounding the transaction warrant the finding that there was a consolidation or a merger of the two corporations.*[109]

An agreement entitling an attorney to buy shares of a corporation in return for professional services, and letting him buy pro rata shares issued on an amalgamation, consolidation, or merger, did not apply to transaction in which the corporate assets were bought for adequate consideration and no stock was transferred; the attorney couldn't buy shares in the corporation that bought the assets.[110] On the other hand, a successor corporation was held liable for the entire debt of the transferor when it did not merely purchase the latter's assets but merged with it; the so-called "trust fund" theory that limited the damages to the property taken over did not apply in such a case.[111]

---

[104]Garey v Kelvinator Corp., (1937) 279 Mich. 174, 271 NW 723.
[105]Erickson v Grande Ronde Lumber Co., (1939) 162 Or. 556, 92 P2d 170, rehearing denied, (1939) 162 Or. 556, 94 P2d 139.
[106]Belle Isle v Moore, (1940) 190 Gd. 881,10 SE2d 923.
[107]Fox v Radel Leather Mfg. Co., (1937) 121 N.J. Eq. 291, 189 Atl 366. See also Bomanzi of Lexington, Inc. v Tafel (Ct of App. Ky. 1967) 415 SW2d 627.
[108]Marlin v Texas Co. (ND Tex. 1939) 26 F Supp 611.
[109]Knapp v North American Rockwell Corp. (CA-3 1974) 506 F2d 361; Hoche Productions, S.A. v Jayark Films Corp. (DC, SD N.Y. 1966) 256 F Supp 291; Pierce v Riverside Mortgage Securities Co., (1938) 25 Cal. App. 2d 248, 77 P2d 226; Pankey v Hot Springs Nat'l Bank, (1941) 46 N.M. 10, 119 P2d 636; Coline Oil Corp. v State, (1939) 184 Okla. 545, 88 P2d 897.
[110]Kemos, Inc. v Bader (CA-5 1977) 545 F2d 913.
[111]R.C. McEntire & Co. v Eastern Foods, Inc. (CA-4 1983) 702 F 2d 471.

(3) *The buying corporation is a mere continuation of the selling one.*[112]

When a corporation is substantially a continuation of an old business in new form, the corporation entity will be disregarded and continued liability will be imposed on the new business for obligations accrued before incorporation, at least to the extent of letting creditors of the old corporation follow after assets transferred to the new.[113] On this principle, a corporate successor to an individual proprietor is liable for payments due under the latter's contracts with a union, when it took over his business, hired his employees, and used his plant.[114] Similarly, a successor corporation is liable for the debts of its predecessor when both were wholly-owned by the same individual, operated the same business on the same premises, and had the same officers and directors.[115] On the other hand, a successor corporation was not liable for the debts of the selling corporation when the former was organized by secured creditors of the latter in order to help them achieve voting control, since in this situation there was no real continuity of enterprise between the seller and the successor.[116]

But one corporation is not liable for a judgment debt of another on the theory that it is merely a continuation of the other in reorganized form and has taken over properties of the other as the assignee of a purchaser at a mortgage foreclosure sale, when there was no fraud or breach of trust and the stockholders in the old corporation received stock in the new by virtue of a secured creditor position and not to the exclusion of the general unsecured creditors of the old corporation.[117] Nor is it liable for a predecessor's alleged wrongful termination of a franchise agreement when the successor bought for cash, and there was no assumption, no continuity of enterprise, and no showing of fraud.[118]

---

[112]Turner v Bituminous Casualty Co., (1976) 297 Mich. 406, 244 NW 2d 873; Alexander & Baldwin, Inc. v Peat, Marwick, Mitchell & Co. (S.D.N.Y. 1974) 385 F Supp 240; Cyr v B. Offen & Co., Inc. (CA-1 1974) 501 F2d 1145; Marine Oil Co. v Cutler Bros, Inc., (1938) La. App. 179 So 485; Avery v Safeway Cab, T.&S. Co., (1938) 148 Kan. 321, 80 P2d 1099; Ingram v Prairie Block Coal Co., (1928) 319 Mo. 644, 5 SW2d 413; Austin v Tecumseh Nat'l Bank, (1896) 49 Neb. 412, 68 NW 828.

[113]Miller v South Hills Lumber & Supply Co., (1939) 334 Pa. 293, 6 A2d 92.

[114]Misakawa Brass Mfg., Inc. v Milwaukee Valve Co., Inc. (Ind. App. 1983) 444 NE 2d 855.

[115]Audit Services, Inc. v Rolfson (CA-9 1981) 641 F 2d 757.

[116]State ex rel Donahue v Perkins & Will Architects, Inc., (1980) 90 Ill. App. 3d 349, 413 NE 2d 29.

[117]Calvin v Washington Properties, Inc. (CA-D.C. 1941) 12 F2d 19.

[118]Wine Imports of America, Ltd. v Gerolmo's Liquors, Ltd. (ED Wisc 1983) 563 F Supp 163.

A corporation's successor in interest can get the benefit of a release barring prosecution of claims in an anti-trust action.[119] Similarly, the buyer of a corporation's entire assets can sue for infringement of the selling corporation's copyright, even though the seller was dissolved immediately after the sale.[120]

When a successor corporation buys, takes over and runs the properties and assets of its predecessor, it impliedly assumes the latter's debts.[121]

(4) *The transaction is fraudulent in fact.*[122]

Unless the buyer of corporate assets buys in good faith and for value, it will be deemed to have taken on the seller's obligation under any bonds that were issued by the seller.[123]

A special facet of successor liability deals with whether the successor is liable for injuries from defects in products manufactured by its predecessor. In general the courts have used the same criteria as for liability to creditors of the predecessor: Was there any assumption of liability? Was the buyer essentially a continuance of the seller? Was there a merger or consolidation? Was the transaction a fraudulent attempt to evade responsibility? If these four questions are answered in the negative, generally there is no liability.[124]

Here are some other examples where the courts found no liability:

(1) The successor bought substantial assets from the receiver of its parent, but the parent continued to operate.[125]

(2) The successor bought some assets but it did not manufacture the same kind of machines as the seller had done.[126]

(3) The successor was a repair shop, not a manufacturer.[127]

---

[119] Marketing Assistance Plan, Inc. v Associated Milk Products, Inc. (DC SD Tex. 1972) 338 F Supp 1019.

[120] National Council of Young Israel, Inc. v The Felt Co., Inc. (DC SD N.Y. 1972) 347 F Supp 1293.

[121] Victoria Gravel Co. v Neyland (Tex. App. 1938) 114 SW2d 415; Trimper v Bruno Sherman Corp. (DC ED Mich. 1977) 436 F Supp 349; Andrews v John E. Smith's Sons Co. (Ala. S Ct 1979) 369 S2d 781. Cf. Hernandez v Johnson Press Corp, (1979) 70 Ill. App.3d 664, 388 NE2d 778.

[122] Luedecke v Des Moines Cabinet Co., (1918) 140 Iowa 223, 118 NW 456; Pankey v Hot Springs Nat'l Bank, (1941) 40 N.M. 10, 119 P2d 636; Hurd v N.Y. & Steam Laundry Co., (1901) 167 N.Y. 89, 60 NE 327; Coline Oil Corp. v State, (1939) 184 Okla. 545, 88 P2d 897.

[123] Coral Gables, Inc. v Mayer, (1934) 241 A.D. 340, 271 N.Y.S. 662.

[124] Gonzalez v Rock Wool Engineering and Equipment, Inc., (1983) 117 Ill. App. 3d 435, 453 NE 2d 792; Johnson v Ferrachute Press (ED Pa 1983) Civ. Act No 79–4166 11–23–83; Jones v Johnson Machine & Press Co., (1982) 211 Neb 724, 320 NW 2d 481, Bernard v Kee Mfg. Co., Inc. (Fla. S Ct 1981) 409 S 2d 1047; Jacobs v Lakewood Aircraft Services, Inc. (ED Pa. 1981) 512 F Supp 176.

[125] Tucker v. Paxson Machine Co. (CA–8 1981) 645 F 2d 620.

[126] Savine v Kent Machine Works, Inc. (ED Pa 1981) 525 F Supp 711.

[127] Cody v Sheboygan Machine Co., (1982) 108 Wisc. 2d 105, 321 NW 2d 142.

The sole stockholder of the successor had held no stock in the predecessor, and the predecessor continued its existence for some time after the successor bought its assets.[128]

Some courts, however, have found a possible liability under a "failure to warn" doctrine, which would make the successor liable if it knows of defects and fails to alert the purchaser about them.[129]

An exception to the theory that would impose liability also exists when the predecessor was not another corporation, but an individual proprietor.[130] Even though a successor corporation may be liable for a defective product, it is not therefore also entitled to indemnity from the employer of a workman injured by the defective machine, since the employer is liable only under workmen's compensation laws.[131]

A successor is not liable for *punitive* damages, even though it purchases the principal assets of its predecessor, when there was no clear showing of continuity of enterprise,[132] nor does the mere fact that a company takes over part of its predecessor's assets provide the basis for a Pennsylvania court to assume diversity jurisdiction over a Delaware corporation.[133]

Here are cases where the court did impose liability:

(1) The successor bought all its predecessors assets and continued manufacturing the same line of machinery.[134]

(2) The successor corporation maintained the same product, personnel, property, and apparently even the same customers.[135]

(3) The successor corporation assumed express and implied warranties; the court found an implied warranty against defective products.[136]

(4) A successor corporation became the parent of its predecessor, so that there was continuity of business enterprise.[137]

---

[128]Weaver v Nash International, Inc. (S.D. Iowa 1983) 562 F Supp 860.

[129]Schumacher v Richards Shear Co., Inc., (1983) 59 N Y 2d 239, 464 N Y S 2d 437.

[130]Meisel v M & N Modern Hydraulic Press Co., (1982) 97 Wash. 2d 403, 645 P 2d 689. *Contra:* Tift v Forage King Industries, Inc. (Wisc. S Ct 1982) 322 N W 2d 14.

[131]Langley v Harris Corp., (1982) 413 Mich. 592, 321 NW 2d 662.

[132]In re Related Asbestos Cases (N D Cal. 1983) 566 F Supp 818.

[133]McClinton v Rockford Punch Press & Manufacturing Co., Inc. (E D Pa 1983) No 81-2200, 8-25-83.

[134]Dawejko v Jorgensen Steel Co. (Pa. Super 1981) 434 A 2d 106.

[135]Amador v Pittsburgh Corning Corp. (E D Pa. 1982) 546 F Supp 1033.

[136]Valenta Enterprises, Inc. v Columbia Gas of New York, Inc. (NY S Ct 1982) 116 Misc 2d 536.

[137]Grant-Howard Association v General Housewares, (1982) 115 Misc 2d 704, 454 N Y S 2d 520.

(5) The successor continued the same business, even though it bought its predecessor's assets for cash.[138]

(6) The successor acquired all its (foreign) predecessor's assets in this country and was assigned all its contract rights and rights to trade names, even though it did not use its predecessor's plant and employees.[139]

Note that some courts have adopted the so-called "product-line" approach, which emphasizes the social desirability of holding the successor liable, and contends that the corporate entity is better able to assume the social cost and distribute it to the public.[140]

If all of a corporation's assets are disposed of without consideration or distributed among its stockholders, a creditor of the corporation is entitled to pursue those assets, on the theory that the assets to which he was entitled to look for satisfaction have gotten into other hands under such circumstances as to warrant the view that in equity they are burdened with a lien in his favor.[141] When a corporation transfers its property without consideration, the transferee is liable for the company's unpaid unemployment compensation contributions.[142] An employee of a corporation can collect a compensation award it owed him from the company to which it has transferred all its assets for less than adequate consideration, when the transfer amounted to a dissolution and so left the corporation unable to pay the debt.[143]

A corporation may not transfer all of its assets to other than a bona fide purchaser for value without making provision for paying off its creditors.[144]

A solvent corporation can prefer one creditor over another. A corporation's transfer of its property cannot be invalidated as in fraud of creditors, even though it is insolvent, so long as it has not suspended its ordinary business and the transferee, buying for a valuable consideration, had no notice of insolvency.[145]

Sole stockholders, directors and officers who, directly or indirectly, dispose of all the corporate assets are personally liable to

---

[138]Ramirez v Armsted Industries, (1981) 86 NJ 332, 431 A 2d 811.

[139]Rivers v Stihl, Inc. (Ala. S Ct 1983) 434 S 2d 766.

[140]Ray v Alad Corp., (1977) 136 Cal. Rptr 574, 560 P 2d 3.

[141]Berwick v Associated Gas & Electric Co., (1934) 20 Del. Ch. 265, 174 Atl 122; Studley, Inc. v Lefrah (App. Div. 1979) 412 NYS2d 901.

[142]Del. U.C.C. v George W. McCaulley & Son, Inc., (1942) 26 Del. Ch. 113, 22 A2d 862; South Chester Tube Co. v Naismith (CA-3 1934) 73 F2d 13.

[143]Jackson v Diamond T. Trucking Company, (1968) 100 N.J. Super. 186, 241 A2d 471.

[144]Everett v Carolina Mortgage Co., (1939) 214 N.C. 778, 1 SE2d 109.

[145]Checher v Shafter Lake Clay Co., (1941) 45 N.M. 419, 115 P2d 636.

unpaid creditors to the extent of consideration received for the property.[146]

Anyone who takes over the assets of a corporation without giving consideration and without notice to creditors will be deemed to have taken over its debts as well.[147] Obviously, if the transaction is tainted by fraud, a court will use its powers to set the matter right. Thus, where a corporation conveyed land as part of a fraudulent scheme, a court can appoint a receiver for the land, who will see that it will be used to satisfy the claims of creditors.[148]

A corporation acquiring the assets of another company with knowledge that the latter's stockholders and directors are planning to dispose of the assets and dissolve the company without paying its creditors, is liable to the creditors for the fair value of the assets received.[149]

Even if fraud is absent, bad faith may be sufficient to impose liability.

For example, a bad faith purchase for an inadequate consideration by one corporation of the assets of another can make the former liable for the debts of the latter even without an express assumption thereof.[150]

If stockholders strip a corporation of all of its assets, leaving it an empty shell, without taking the necessary steps to dissolve it legally, they may become personally liable for its debts.[151]

> **Caution:** Almost invariably, creditors of the selling corporation will include taxing authorities, both state and federal. Whenever there's a sale of corporate assets, be sure to look into the Internal Revenue Code provisions on the buyer's liability for unpaid income taxes due the government from the selling corporation.[152]

Sometimes the purchasing corporation is made liable for the debts of the selling corporation by the statute which authorizes the sale of the corporate assets.

---

[146]State v City of Greencastle, (1942) 111 Ind. App. 640, 49 NE2d 388; Southern Industries, Inc. v Geremias (N.Y. App. Div. 1978) 411 NYS2d 1945.

[147]Abeken v US (ED Mo. 1939) 26 F Supp 170.

[148]Irish v Bahner, (1937) Tex. Civ. App. 109 SW2d 1023.

[149]Cohen v Pavlick, (1938) 235 Ala. 289, 178 So 435.

[150]Payne-Baber Coal Co. Ky. v Butler, (1939) 276 Ky. 211, 123 SW2d 273.

[151]Reinfeld v Fidelity Union Trust Co., (1938) 123 N.J. Eq. 428, 198 Atl 220.

[152]Coca-Cola Bottling Co. of Tucson v I.R.C. (CA-9 1964) 334 F2d 285. See also P-H Federal Taxes.

Power of corporation to take property on lease. By statute in every state, corporations can acquire and hold property. But some states limit the time during which corporations may hold property that does not further the corporate purposes.[153] Also some states give corporation of foreign countries or with alien stockholders only limited rights to hold property.

As to leases the lessor of a corporation can hold both the corporation and a partnership lessee of the corporation liable on the lease.[154] But a lease for a purpose that is entirely foreign to the purposes for which the corporation was organized is not within the power of the corporation.[155]

Authority of officers to bind lessee corporation by lease. Primarily the power to lease property belongs to the board of directors, but the general manager,[156] or a president having the powers of a general manager,[157] may make leases of property necessary to the conduct of the business, and may adjust the rent.[158] A lease made by officers may be ratified expressly,[159] or impliedly from the use of the property by the corporation.[160]

Where the interests of a corporation are fully protected, the corporation may lease property from a director.[161] A director cannot (even where he has been removed from office) take a lease for himself when the interests of the company require that its lease should be renewed.[162] But he is free to act for himself when the corporation has definitely abandoned the lease or the landlord has indicated a definite decision not to renew the lease with the corporation.[163]

---

[153] Example: 5 years in Kentucky, 15 years in Texas.

[154] Pepper v Dixie Splint Coal Co., (1935) 165 Va. 179, 181 SE 406.

[155] Occum Co. v Sprague Mfg. Co., (1868) 34 Conn. 529.

[156] Georgia Casualty Co. v Massey, (1918) 20 Ala. 601, 79 So 33; Peninsular Savings & Loan Assn. v C. J. Breier Co., (1926) 137 Wash. 641, 243 P 830.

[157] Hawley v Gray Bros. Artificial Stone Paving Co., (1895) 106 Cal. 337, 39 P 609.

[158] Sherman, Clay & Co. v Buffum & Pendleton, (1919) 91 Ore. 352, 179 P 241.

[159] Bradford v Graham (CA–4 1923) 287 F 686.

[160] Jacksonville Etc., Railway v Hooper, (1895) 160 US 514, 16 S Ct 379; Patton v Texas Pac. Coal & Oil Co., (1920) Tex. Civ. App. 225 SW 857.

[161] Veeder v Horstmann, (1903) 85 AD 154, 83 N.Y.S. 99.

[162] Acker Merrall & Condit Co. v McGaw, (1907) 106 Md. 536, 68 Atl 17; Girard Co. v Lamoureux, (1917) 227 Mass. 277, 116 NE 572. See also Meinhard v Salmon, (1928) 249 N.Y. 458, 164 NE 545, (joint adventure.)

[163] Crittenden & Cowles Co. v Cowles, (1901) 66 AD 95, 72 N.Y.S. 701.

Power of corporation to become lessor. The statutory and other restrictions on the power of a corporation to lease its property are very similar to those for a sale of its property, discussed above.

Procedure in leasing total assets. The procedure in making a lease of assets is very similar to that outlined in making a sale of assets. What happens after the lease is made depends upon the terms of the lease. The corporation leasing its property may withdraw from all owning and operating activities or control, the lessee undertaking all the duties and obligations imposed upon the lessor; or the corporation leasing its property may continue to operate a non-leased part of the property. Even in the first event, the leasing corporation must remain in existence in order (1) to protect its corporate franchise, (2) to see that the terms of the lease are not broken, and (3) to afford a way to represent the stockholders in dealing with the lessee in matters concerning the terms of the lease, the financing of additions to property, and similar business. For example, a modification of a lease must be executed with the same formalities and with the same vote as required for an original lease.[164]

Rights of dissenting stockholders. The rights of stockholders who object to a lease of the corporation's entire property are often defined by statute. Generally, they are the same as the rights of stockholders who object to the sale of the corporate property. If no statute covers the rights of dissenting stockholders, their rights depend upon whether the lease may be entered into at all without their consent. Thus a stockholder could bar a lease of the corporation's entire property for a 25-year period, even though approved by a majority of the stockholders, since that amounted to a complete abdication of the corporation's function.[165]

Rights of creditors. In the absence of an agreement to assume the debts of the lessor, the lessee is not liable to pay the debts of the lessor.[166] If a corporation, by a lease of its property, in effect removes it as asset, the corporation's creditors can follow the property in the hands of the lessee.[167]

After a lease has been executed, the lessee is liable for all debts arising out of the operation of the property. Thus, a lessor cannot be

---

[164] Continental Ins. Co. v N. Y. & H. R. Co., (1907) 187 N.Y. 225, 79 NE 1026, aff'g 103 AD 282, 93 N.Y.S. 27.
[165] Small v Minneapolis Electro Matrix Co., (1891) 45 Minn. 264, 47 NW 797.
[166] Johnson v Western Union Telegraph Co., (1944) 293 N.Y. 379, 57 NE2d 721.
[167] Chicago, etc., Railway Co. v Chicago Bank, (1890) 134 US 276.

held liable for labor performed or material furnished the lessee company by others in the operation or maintenance of its property.[168]

Termination of lease. Corporate action is required for a surrender of a lease; generally it's the same action that's needed to execute the lease in the first place. Thus, when the president of the corporation has no power to authorize a lien, he similarly lacks power to surrender it.[169] On the other hand, an officer who has authority to sign a lease and who is charged with the duty of giving possession of the premises, looking after the making of repairs, collecting rents, and attending to other negotiations would also have the authority to effect a surrender of a lease.[170] A corporate lessee that transfers stock has not made an assignment of the lease so as to violate a lease provision forbidding an assignment of the lease without the lessor's prior consent.[171]

---

[168]Empire Trust Co. v Egypt Ry. Co. (ED N.C. 1910) 182 F 100.
[169]Laing v Price, (1914) 75 W. Va. 192, 83 SE 497.
[170]Commercial Hotel Co. v Brill, (1905) 123 Wis. 638, 101 NW 1101.
[171]Branmar Theatre Co. v Branmar, Inc., (1970) Del. Ch., 264 A2d 526.

Chapter 30

RESOLUTIONS RELATING TO

PURCHASE, SALE, AND LEASE

OF ASSETS

Contents—Chapter 30

Purchase and Sale of All Assets

PURCHASE AND SALE OF PART OF ASSETS

DIRECTORS' RESOLUTION AUTHORIZING PRESIDENT TO PURCHASE STOCK OF ANOTHER CORPORATION FROM AN INDIVIDUAL

RESOLVED, That the President of this Corporation is hereby authorized to purchase from ...., the stock of the .... Corporation, owned by said ...., amounting to ..... ($.....) Dollars of preferred stock and ..... ($.....) Dollars of common stock, at such price as he may deem advisable, not exceeding the sum of ..... ($.....) Dollars.

DIRECTORS' RESOLUTION AUTHORIZING ACCEPTANCE OF OFFER TO SELL PROPERTY; PAYMENT IN STOCK AND ASSUMPTION OF INDEBTEDNESS

WHEREAS, the .... Corporation has offered to sell and transfer to this Corporation all its machinery, tools, dies, stock on hand, furniture and fixtures used by it in connection with the manufacture of ...., which offer is more fully described in a written offer of sale presented to this meeting, and

WHEREAS, the .... Corporation is willing to accept as full consideration for the sale and transfer of said property ..... shares of fully paid and nonassessable common stock of this Corporation, having an aggregate par value of $....., and the assumption by this Corporation of the indebtedness of said Corporation not exceeding $.....; and

WHEREAS, it appears that the property described in said offer of sale has an actual value equal to the amount of consideration requested therefor, and that it is to the best interests of this Corporation to accept said offer, be it

RESOLVED, That the said offer is hereby accepted and the officers of the Corporation are directed to cause the issuance of ..... shares of fully paid and nonassessable common stock of this Corporation, having an aggregate par value of $....., and to assume the indebtedness of .... Corporation not exceeding $.....

DIRECTORS' RESOLUTION AUTHORIZING EXECUTION OF AGREEMENT WITH BANKERS TO ACQUIRE STOCK OF VARIOUS CORPORATIONS

WHEREAS, this Board of Directors deems it desirable for the business of this Corporation to acquire the stocks of the following-named companies, owning, mining, manufacturing, or producing materials or other property necessary for the business of this Corporation—to wit .... (insert names of companies)—and after careful investigation and appraisement, this Board has ascertained, adjudged, and determined, and hereby the directors do and each of them does ascertain, adjudge, and determine, that the value of such stocks, severally and respectively, is equal at least to the par value of the stock of this Corporation and the sums in cash to be issued and paid therefor if purchased or acquired by this Corporation on the terms of the proposed agreement authorizing . . . . *(insert name of banking firm)* to procure the sale thereof to this Corporation, a draft of such proposed agreement having been submitted to the Board of Directors and read, be it

RESOLVED, That such proposed agreement under the date of . . . ., 19. ., be executed in duplicate by the President for and in behalf of the Corporation, and that the corporate seal be thereunto affixed and attested by the Secretary, and that the draft of such agreement now submitted be filed with the Secretary.

NOTICE OF STOCKHOLDERS' MEETING CALLED TO APPROVE SALE OF REAL PROPERTY

Notice is hereby given that pursuant to call of the Board of Directors, a special meeting of the stockholders of . . . . Corporation, a . . . . *(insert state of incorporation)* corporation, will be held at the company's offices, ... *(address)*, on . . . ., 19. ., at . . . . . M., for the following purposes.

(1) To consider and act upon the recommendation of the Board of Directors that the property owned by the corporation consisting of the land and building commonly known as the . . . . Building, located at . . . ., together with all of the personal property owned by the corporation located and used in said building be sold to . . . . Company for the sum of $. . . . ., payable in cash, subject to customary adjustment and prorating of rentals, insurance, and other items;

(2) To approve the action of the Board of Directors in causing the offer of . . . . Company to be accepted, subject to the authorization of the shareholders of the corporation, and to authorize the Board of Directors to cause said accepted offer to be consummated and to adopt such method of effectuating the sale as the Board may deem proper;

(3) To consider and act upon the recommendation of the Board of Directors of the corporation that the corporation be voluntarily dissolved, in the event the proposed sale of said assets of the corporation be authorized by the affirmative vote of the requisite number of shareholders and said sale is actually consummated;

(4) To transact such other and further business as may come before the meeting.

You are further notified that at a special meeting held . . . . 19. ., the Board of Directors recommended said sale and, upon consummation, the voluntary dissolution of the corporation, and directed that the matters hereinabove set forth be submitted to a vote of the shareholders.

If you cannot be present in person at said meeting, kindly execute and return the enclosed proxy.

NOTICE OF STOCKHOLDERS' MEETING TO APPROVE INCREASE IN STOCK OF PURCHASING CORPORATION

NOTICE is hereby given that a special meeting of the stockholders of .... Corporation will be held at the office of the Corporation, ... *(address)*, on ...., 19.., at ..... M., for the following purpose:

To consider and take action upon a proposal to amend the Corporation's Articles of Incorporation so as to increase the authorized capital stock from ..... shares of Common Stock of the par value of $..... each to ..... shares of Common Stock of the par value of $..... each; and to authorize the Directors to issue ..... shares of the unissued authorized Common Stock of this Corporation to the .... Company, Inc. in full (on "impact") payment for all the assets and property (or "certain fixed assets and inventory") of that Company.

Stockholders unable to attend the meeting in person are requested to sign and date the enclosed proxy and mail it in the envelope provided for that purpose.

RESOLUTION OF STOCKHOLDERS APPROVING PURCHASE OF ASSETS AND INCREASE IN AUTHORIZED STOCK

WHEREAS, ... Company, Inc., has offered to sell certain of its fixed assets and inventory to this Corporation in exchange for shares, and

WHEREAS, it is necessary and desirable to authorize and issue additional shares for this purpose, be it

RESOLVED, That the authorized Common Stock of this Corporation be increased from ..... shares of $..... par value to ..... shares of $..... par value, and that the Articles of Incorporation of this Corporation are hereby amended by striking out Section ..... of Article ..... *(insert reference to appropriate article)* and substituting therefor the following:

"The total number of shares which this Corporation is authorized to issue is ..... shares of Common Stock of $..... par value, and ..... shares of Preferred Stock of $..... par value."

RESOLVED FURTHER, That the Board of Directors is hereby authorized to issue ..... shares of the unissued authorized Common Stock of this Corporation to the .... Company, Inc. in payment for certain fixed assets and inventory of the .... Company, Inc.

RESOLVED FURTHER, That the Board of Directors is hereby authorized and directed to take such steps and to do all acts and prepare, execute and deliver all documents that are necessary or advisable to carry the foregoing into effect.

RESOLUTION OF STOCKHOLDERS AUTHORIZING PURCHASE OF STOCK OF VARIOUS COMPANIES FOR STOCK AND BONDS OF PURCHASING CORPORATION

WHEREAS, ..., ..., and ...., as a committee acting in behalf of the several owners and holders of the stock of the corporations listed below, have offered to sell and transfer, or to cause to be transferred, to this Company, shares of capital stock of the following corporations *(insert name of corporation, amount of stock offered for sale, and proportion which amount offered for sale bears to total capital stock of each corporation),* in consideration of the issue of stock of this Company to the amount of ..... ($.....) Dollars par value and its seven (7%) percent bonds, secured by a collateral deed of trust or mortgage upon all of the above-mentioned stock, amounting in the aggregate to ..... ($.....) Dollars, and

WHEREAS, it appears to the stockholders of this Company that the above-mentioned property is necessary for the business of this Company, and that the same is of the value of ..... ($.....) Dollars, be it

RESOLVED, That the Board of Directors of this Company is hereby authorized and directed to purchase said property for said price, and to issue said stock and bonds in payment thereof, provided that, in the judgment of the Board of Directors, the said property is of the value above stated.

DIRECTORS' RESOLUTION AUTHORIZING SALE AND LEASEBACK OF REAL PROPERTY OWNED BY CORPORATION

RESOLVED, That this Corporation sell its real property located in ...., ..., which is more particularly described hereinafter, to the .... Insurance Company, at a price of not less than ....; that concurrently therewith the Corporation take back a lease thereof from said .... Insurance Company for a period of ..... years at a net annual rental of .....% of such purchase price; and that the proper officers of this Corporation be authorized in behalf of the Corporation to make, execute and deliver such deed, lease and other instruments as may be required or appropriate in connection therewith and to affix the corporate seal of this Corporation thereto. The said real estate is all that lot, tract or parcel of land lying in the City of ...., County of ...., and State of ...., and described as follows: *(insert a description of the property)* and

RESOLVED FURTHER, That the form of purchase and lease agreement with the form of lease annexed thereto as Exhibit "A" presented to this meeting, a copy of which is attached hereto, is hereby approved with such changes as the officers executing same on behalf of this Corporation may approve with the advice of counsel, such approval to be conclusively evidenced by the execution thereof.

[attach lease]

DIRECTORS' RESOLUTION AUTHORIZING SALE AND LEASEBACK AND EXPRESSING BUSINESS REASONS

WHEREAS, this Corporation has arranged to sell and convey its real estate holdings in the City of . . . . , exclusive of all buildings, machinery, fixtures, and other improvements thereon, to the . . . . Insurance Company, with a view to separating the real estate holdings of this Corporation in the City of . . . . from its other property and plant, it being the purpose and intention to secure other real estate in or near the City of . . . . , and ultimately to remove the plant of this Corporation to such new locations, and

WHEREAS, prior to . . . . , 19. . , this Corporation had arranged that the said . . . . Insurance Company should have an option on the real estate holdings of this Corporation in the City of . . . . , at the book value of such holdings as of . . . . , 19. . , and

WHEREAS, the book value of said real estate as of . . . . , 19. . , has been ascertained to be the sum of . . . . . ($. . . . .) Dollars, be it

RESOLVED, That the President and Secretary of this Company are hereby authorized and directed to execute to the . . . . Insurance Company, for and in behalf of this Company, a proper deed of conveyance conveying to the said . . . . Insurance Company all of the real estate holdings of this Corporation in the City of . . . . , for the consideration of the said sum of . . . . . ($. . . . .) Dollars, such conveyance to exclude all buildings, machinery, fixtures, and other improvements on the said property, with the right to remove the same within a reasonable time after the expiration of a lease to be made by the said . . . . Insurance Company to this Corporation; and

RESOLVED FURTHER, That this Corporation be authorized to accept from the said . . . . Insurance Company, a lease for the said real estate at an annual rental of . . . . . ($. . . . .) Dollars, plus all taxes accruing against the said property, the payment dates of such rental to be on the first day of each month beginning with . . . . . 1, 19. . for one month in advance; that such lease extend for a term of . . . . . year(s), and that the Corporation shall have the option, exercisable on or before . . . . . 1, 19. . , to enter into a lease for a term of . . . . . years beginning on January 1, 19. . , if in the Corporation's judgment appropriate real estate cannot be found elsewhere; and that the lessee be granted the privilege of removing all buildings, machinery, fixtures, and other improvements from the said premises within a reasonable time after the termination of the lease.

Comment: For sale and leaseback of corporate equipment or other personal property, the foregoing specimen directors' resolutions can readily be adapted to the factual situation. The important point is to make sure that the directors adopt a specific resolution authorizing each specific sale and leaseback transaction.

DIRECTORS' RESOLUTION OF RAILROAD COMPANY AUTHORIZING SALE OF LAND NOT REQUIRED FOR OPERATIONS

WHEREAS, the operating officers and the Chief Engineer of this Corporation have certified that the land hereinafter described is not required by this Corporation for railroad purposes, and

WHEREAS, in the opinion of the Board of Directors, said land is no longer required by this Corporation for railroad purposes, and is not now necessary for the maintenance, operation, or other purposes of this Corporation, and

WHEREAS, said land is not held for and used in the service of transportation, but, on the contrary, was expressly excepted and reserved from the property conveyed by this Corporation's mortgage dated . . . ., 19. ., to the . . . . Trust Company, be it

RESOLVED, That the President, or a Vice president, is hereby authorized, in the name and in behalf of this Corporation and under its corporate seal, to execute and deliver a quitclaim deed, conveying to . . . ., of . . . . City, ..., for the consideration of . . . . . ($. . . . .) Dollars, a certain parcel of land in said . . . ., as shown within the yellow lines on the map entitled . . . ., and bounded as follows . . . . (*insert description of property*).

RESOLVED FURTHER, That the proceeds from the sale of said land be deposited with the . . . . Trust Company of . . . ., under the terms of the mortgage hereinafter mentioned, until such time as new lands are to be purchased to which said proceeds are applicable, and

RESOLVED FURTHER, That the Treasurer of the State of . . . ., as Trustee under the general mortgage of the . . . . Company to the Treasurer of the State of . . . ., dated . . . ., 19. ., be requested, upon the written consent of the . . . . . Trust Company of . . . . ., to release said land from the lien and operation of said mortgage.

DIRECTORS' RESOLUTION AUTHORIZING SALE OF REAL PROPERTY OF CORPORATION TO SEPARATE REAL ESTATE HOLDINGS FROM OTHER PROPERTY, AND AUTHORIZING LEASE TO BE MADE WITH PURCHASER

WHEREAS, prior to . . . ., 19. ., this Company had arranged to sell and convey the real estate holdings of this Company in the City of . . . ., exclusive of all buildings, machinery, fixtures, and other improvements thereon, to . . . ., with a view to separating the real estate holdings of this Company in the City of . . . . from its other property and plant, it being the purpose and intention to secure other real estate in or near the City of . . . . , and ultimately to remove the plant of this Company to such new location, and

WHEREAS, prior to . . . . , 19. ., this Company had arranged that the said . . . . , for the use of himself and his associates, should have an option on the said real estate holdings in the City of . . . . , at the book value of such holdings as of . . . . , 19. ., and

WHEREAS, the book value of said real estate as of . . . ., 19. ., has been ascertained to be the sum of . . . . . ($. . . . .) Dollars, be it

RESOLVED, That the Vice president and the Secretary of this Company are hereby authorized and directed to execute to . . . . , for and in behalf of this Company, a proper deed of conveyance conveying to the said . . . . all of the real estate holdings of this Company in the City of . . . . , for the consideration of the said sum of . . . . . ($. . . . .) Dollars, such conveyance to exclude all buildings, machinery, fixtures, and other improvements on the said property, with the right to remove the same within a reasonable time after the expiration of a lease to be made by the said . . . . to this Company; that the said consideration be paid according to the terms of the vendor's lien note for the sum of . . . . . ($. . . . .) Dollars, payable . . . . . (. . . . .) years after date, with interest thereon at the rate of . . . . . (. . . . .%) percent per annum, the interest to be payable semi-annually, with the privilege of prepayment of the full amount, or of any multiple of . . . . . ($. . . . .) Dollars on . . . . or . . . . , of any year, upon . . . . . (. . . . .) days' written notice of such intention to prepay; that the vendor's lien be retained to secure the payment of the said note; and that the said . . . . execute, when requested, a deed of trust upon the said property, with power of sale, in the usual form, in order further to secure the payment of the said vendor's lien note, and

RESOLVED FURTHER, That this Company be authorized to accept from the said . . . . , a lease for the said real estate at an annual rental of . . . . . ($. . . . .) Dollars, plus all taxes accruing against the said property, the payment dates of such rental to be at the end of each six months, corresponding to the dates of interest payments on the said vendor's lien note; that such lease extend for the said term of . . . . . (. . . . .) years, but may be terminated prior to the expiration of said . . . . . (. . . . .) years if this Company shall secure and remove to a new location in or near the City of . . . . .; and that the lessee be granted the privilege of removing all buildings, machinery, fixtures, and other improvements from the said premises, within a reasonable time after the termination of the lease.

DIRECTORS' RESOLUTION OF CORPORATION ENGAGED IN BUYING AND SELLING REAL ESTATE, AUTHORIZING SALES TO BE MADE BY OFFICERS

RESOLVED, That the President and the Secretary of the . . . . Corporation are hereby authorized, empowered, and directed to sell, mortgage, lease, or convey any and all property of said Corporation, on such terms as they may deem advisable, and the said President and Secretary are hereby authorized, empowered, and directed to execute all deeds, mortgages, releases, leases, or other instruments necessary to carry into effect the sales, mortgages, or leases as herein provided.

DIRECTORS' RESOLUTION ACCEPTING OFFER TO SELL REAL PROPERTY IN CONSIDERATION FOR ENTIRE CAPITAL STOCK OF CORPORATION

WHEREAS, ... , Inc., has offered to sell, transfer, and convey the real property now owned by it at . . . . , Town of . . . . , ... County, ... , subject to a mortgage of . . . . , on the terms stated in a written proposal made to this Company by said . . . . , Inc., and forming part of the minutes of the first meeting of stockholders, and

WHEREAS, the incorporators and stockholders of this Company approved the said proposal and recommended that the Board of Directors accept the same, and

WHEREAS, in the judgment of this Board of Directors, the assets to be transferred to this Company are reasonably worth the amount of the consideration demanded therefor, and it is to the best interests of this Company to accept the said offer as set forth in said proposition, be it

RESOLVED, That the said offer of . . . . , Inc., as set forth in said proposition, is hereby approved and accepted, and that in accordance with the terms thereof, this Company shall, as full payment for said property, issue and deliver to said . . . . , Inc., or its nominees, the entire issue of the capital stock of this Company, and

RESOLVED FURTHER, That upon the execution and delivery of such proper instruments as may be necessary to transfer and convey the property aforesaid to this Company, the officers of this Company are authorized and directed to issue and deliver the shares of the capital stock of this Company in accordance with the said offer, and

RESOLVED FURTHER, That the acts of . . . . and . . . . , in engaging the . . . . Title Insurance Company to issue a title policy in the sum of $ . . . . . on the property at . . . . , ... County, ... at a cost of $ . . . . . , are hereby in all respects ratified, approved, and confirmed, as and for the acts and deeds of this Company.

DIRECTORS' RESOLUTION AUTHORIZING PURCHASE OF LAND AND BUILDING

WHEREAS, this Corporation has entered upon a policy of expansion and requires additional land for the purpose, and

WHEREAS, ... owner of the land and building immediately adjoining the property of this Corporation at .... Street, City of ...., State of ....., has offered to sell his land and the building thereon to this Corporation for the sum of ..... ($.....) Dollars, upon the terms hereinafter set forth, and

WHEREAS, the Board of Directors deems it advisable that the Corporation acquire said land and building from .... for the price aforementioned.

THEREFORE BE IT RESOLVED, That this Corporation purchase from .... the aforesaid land and building, more specifically described as follows (insert description).

RESOLVED FURTHER, That the President and Secretary of this Corporation are hereby authorized to enter into an agreement in behalf of this Corporation with said ...., to purchase the above-described property for the sum of ..... ($.....) Dollars, upon the following terms: ..... ($.....) Dollars to be paid upon the execution of the contract of sale; ..... ($.....) Dollars to be paid upon the closing of title and the delivery of a good and sufficient warranty deed conveying a good and marketable title to the premises, free from all encumbrances except a first mortgage in the sum of ..... ($.....) Dollars, now a lien upon the premises and held by the .... Trust Co.; the balance to be paid by the execution of a purchase money mortgage in the sum of ..... ($.....) Dollars, payable in semi-annual installments of ..... ($.....) Dollars, with interest at ..... (.....%) percent.

RESOLVED FURTHER, That the President and Secretary of this Corporation be and they hereby are authorized to execute all instruments to make all payments necessary to carry the foregoing resolution into effect, and to accept all documents, duly executed, which are or may be necessary for the transfer and conveyance to this Corporation of the aforesaid land and building.

RESOLUTION OF STOCKHOLDERS RATIFYING SALE OF REAL PROPERTY MADE BY DIRECTORS

RESOLVED, That the action of the Board of Directors in authorizing the sale of real property owned by this Corporation, described as follows .... (insert complete description), for the sum of ..... ($.....) Dollars, which said sum has been duly received and is now held in the treasury of this Corporation, and the action of the President and the Secretary in executing and delivering a deed to ...., dated ...., 19.., conveying the above-described real property, is hereby ratified, approved, confirmed, and accepted as the action of the Corporation.

RESOLUTION OF STOCKHOLDERS AUTHORIZING SALE OF BUSINESS CARRIED ON BY BRANCH OFFICE, TO NEW CORPORATION TO BE ORGANIZED AS SUBSIDIARY

RESOLVED, That the business, property, accounts, goodwill, and all other assets of this Corporation in the City of . . . . , State of . . . . , as now carried on by this Corporation's branch office in the City of . . . . , State of . . . . , be sold to a corporation now being organized under the laws of the aforesaid foreign state, in consideration of the issuance and delivery to this Corporation of . . . . . (. . . . .) shares of common stock with no par value and . . . . . (. . . . .) shares of the preferred stock with a par value of . . . . . ($ . . . .) Dollars each, the said stock to represent at least a majority of all the entire authorized capital stock of the said foreign corporation.

RESOLUTION OF STOCKHOLDERS AUTHORIZING SALE OF STOCK REPRESENTING HALF INTEREST IN ANOTHER COMPANY

RESOLVED, That this Corporation sell, transfer, and deliver to "A" Company and that the stockholders of this Corporation consent to the sale, transfer, and delivery to "A" Company of . . . . . shares, of the par value of $ . . . . each, of the capital stock of "X" Company, and . . . . . shares, of the par value of $ . . . . each, of the capital stock of "Y" Company (said shares representing this Corporation's one-half interest in "X" Company and "Y" Company) upon the terms and conditions set forth in the agreement dated . . . . , 19. ., between this Corporation and "A" Company, a copy of which has been submitted to this meeting, and that the execution of such agreement is hereby in all respects authorized, ratified, and approved, and

RESOLVED FURTHER, That the officers of this Corporation are hereby authorized and directed to take all action deemed by them necessary or proper to consummate the sale of said shares and to effect the purposes of the foregoing resolutions.

DIRECTORS' RESOLUTION AUTHORIZING SALE OF TREASURY STOCK AT AUCTION

WHEREAS, in the judgment of this Board, it is necessary and desirable for this Company to raise money for additional working capital and to meet the costs of improving the corporation's property, and to that end to sell shares of common stock of the Company now held in the treasury, be it

RESOLVED, That this Company offer to sell at public auction, as soon as possible, ... (. . . . .) shares of said common stock, giving to the general public the opportunity of making bids for all or any part of such stock, and

RESOLVED FURTHER, That all persons desiring to make bids for such stock be required to deliver the same in writing to .... Bank, Transfer Agent of this Company, specifying the number of shares desired and the price offered, and to deposit therewith ..... (..... %) percent of such price and that this company reserves the right to accept or to reject all or any of such bids, and

RESOLVED FURTHER, That the Secretary of this Company is hereby authorized and directed to prepare a form of circular containing the terms and conditions of said offer, and a form of bid, and to submit the same for approval at the next meeting of this Board.

DIRECTORS' RESOLUTION AUTHORIZING SALE OF COMPANY'S HOLDINGS OF GOVERNMENT BONDS

RESOLVED, That the President is hereby authorized to sell at the best price obtainable, a further amount of the Company's holdings of United States Government bonds, of any issue, up to an amount that will reduce the Company's holdings of United States Government bonds to ..... ($.....) Dollars.

DIRECTORS' RESOLUTION AUTHORIZING OFFICERS TO SELL OR ASSIGN SECURITIES AND TO RECEIVE MONEY OR PROPERTY THEREFOR

RESOLVED, That the Treasurer, with the approval of the President, is hereby authorized, for and in the name of this Corporation, to pledge, hypothecate, sell, or assign any stocks, bonds, participation receipts, bills receivable, or similar obligations standing in the name of or owned by this Corporation; and that he is further empowered to receive and to give receipt for all money or property proceeding from such pledge, hypothecation, sale, or assignment. The Secretary is hereby authorized to fix the seal of this Corporation to any such instruments as may be necessary and proper to carry out the terms of the foregoing resolution.

RESOLUTION OF STOCKHOLDERS AUTHORIZING SALE OF PROPERTY TO NEW CORPORATION TO BE ORGANIZED, AND DIRECTING OFFICERS TO FORM THE CORPORATION

RESOLVED, That this Corporation sell and convey the steamboats "X," "Y," and "Z" and the barge "S," subject to the deeds of trust, which now stand as security for the bonds issued thereunder, affecting the said vessels, to a corporation or corporations to be organized under the direction of the directors and officers of this Corporation, and that this Corporation accept as full consideration for such sale and conveyance the capital stock of such corporation or corporations so formed, and

RESOLVED FURTHER, That the Board of Directors and officers of this Corporation are hereby authorized and directed to cause to be formed a corporation or corporations, and, as in their judgment may seem proper, to purchase any or all of the above-named vessels from this Corporation, and to pay therefor with the capital stock of the corporation or corporations so formed as full consideration for the vessels sold by this Corporation to the new corporation or corporations, and

RESOLVED FURTHER, That the Board of Directors of this Corporation is hereby authorized and directed to execute and deliver any instrument or instruments and to do all things that may effectuate the sale and conveyance hereby authorized, and the payment of the consideration therefor, and the organization of a new corporation or new corporations for the purpose hereinbefore mentioned, in accordance with these resolutions, and they are hereby authorized to carry out these resolutions in such manner as to them may seem to the best interests of this Corporation, and to do all things necessary or incident to the carrying out of these resolutions.

DIRECTORS' RESOLUTION APPROVING OFFICERS' ACTION IN EXECUTING AND DELIVERING DEED OF PROPERTY

RESOLVED, That the action of ...., Vice president, and ...., Secretary, in executing and delivering a deed to ...., dated ...., 19.., conveying for a consideration of ..... ($.....) Dollars, all the following property *(insert complete description of the property),* is hereby in all respects approved, ratified, confirmed, and accepted as the action of the Company and of this Board of Directors.

PURCHASE AND SALE OF ALL ASSETS

RESOLUTION AUTHORIZING OFFICERS TO ACQUIRE OUTSTANDING CAPITAL STOCK OF ANOTHER CORPORATION

The Chairman stated that the purpose of the meeting was to consider and discuss methods by which .... Company might acquire the outstanding capital stock of the .... Corporation.

Upon motion, duly seconded and carried, it was

RESOLVED, That the officers of the Company are hereby authorized, by and with the advice of counsel, to take all steps necessary or in their opinion desirable to acquire the capital stock of .... Corporation, on a basis whereby two shares of the stock of .... Corporation will be received in exchange for one share of the common stock of .... Company.

RESOLUTION OF STOCKHOLDERS AUTHORIZING PURCHASE OF ASSETS AND CAPITAL STOCK OF ANOTHER CORPORATION FOR STOCK

WHEREAS, ..., Company has proposed, in writing, to sell, assign, transfer, convey, and set over all its rights to do business, its goodwill, stock in trade, office fixtures, assets, leases, licenses, privileges, benefits, advantages, and property, whether real, personal, or mixed; and "A," "B," and "C,"stockholders of the .... Company, have proposed, in writing, to sell, transfer, assign, and set over to this Corporation the stock of the .... Company, consisting of ..... (.....) shares of common stock, all of which are owned and controlled by them,

NOW, THEREFORE, in consideration of the amount specified in said proposal, which amount is of the fair value of the stocks, assets, etc., of the .... Company, be it

RESOLVED, That this Corporation purchase from "A,""B,"and "C"the ..... (.....) shares of common stock of the .... Company, and purchase from the .... Company all the goodwill, right to do business, stock in trade, assets, leases, licenses, privileges, benefits, advantages, and property, of any kind or character whatsoever, wheresoever located, for the sum of ..... ($.....) Dollars, to be paid for by issuing and delivering ..... (.....) shares of the common stock of this Corporation as follows: "A," ..... (.....) shares; "B," ..... (.....) shares; and "C," ..... (.....) shares, and

RESOLVED FURTHER, That these stocks are not to be delivered, and the transfer is not to be consummated, until "A," "B," and "C" execute to this Corporation their joint and several bonds, in and by virtue of the terms of which they each promise and agree to hold this Corporation, or its successor or successors, harmless from any debts, liabilities, obligations, liens, or incumbrances, of any kind or character, that may be outstanding against the .... Company or anyone claiming under or through it, and by which they each promise and agree to bind their heirs, executors, and assigns, and

RESOLVED FURTHER, That the President is hereby authorized and directed to execute such certificates of stock, and the Secretary is hereby authorized and directed to attest the same and to attach the official seal of the Corporation thereto.

DIRECTORS' RESOLUTION AUTHORIZING PURCHASE OF COPARTNERSHIP FOR STOCK AND OTHER CONSIDERATION

WHEREAS, this Corporation was incorporated under the laws of the State of ...., for the purposes set forth in the Certificate of Incorporation, and

WHEREAS, it was the intention of the incorporators, and it was one of the purposes set forth in the Certificate of Incorporation, among other things, to purchase, take over, and carry on the business now being carried on by "A" and "B" as copartners under the firm name of "A" & "B" Co., at .... Street, in the City of ...., State of .... and

WHEREAS, the purchase of said business and the assets thereof is authorized by the Certificate of Incorporation of this Corporation, and is necessary for the use and lawful purpose of said Corporation, and

WHEREAS, the said "A" and "B," copartners as aforesaid, have made a porposition, in writing, for the sale and transfer on their part, and the purchase on the part of this Corporation, of the said business as a going concern, including all the assets of said business, whether tangible or intangible, except certain accounts, the said transfer to be made on ...., 19. ., upon certain terms and conditions as more fully appear in the aforesaid proposal and offer that has just been read and spread upon these minutes, and

WHEREAS, it appears, after due consideration and investigation, that it is necessary and advantageous for the best interests of this Corporation that it acquire and purchase the said business and the assets thereof, and that it take over and carry on the said business, and

WHEREAS, in the judgment of this Board of Directors, after careful examination and fair appraisement, this Board is unanimously convinced that the said property is necessary and advantageous for the business of this Corporation, and the fair value thereof is the consideration mentioned in the said proposition, computing the stock of this Corporation at par, be it

RESOLVED, subject to ratification by the stockholders of this Corporation,

That this Board accept the aforesaid proposal and offer of "A" and "B," and purchase from them, the said business now conducted at .... Street, in the City of ...., State of ...., under the firm name of "A" & "B" Co., specified in said proposal, and pay for the same the sum of ..... ($.....) Dollars, to be paid over as follows: ..... ($.....) Dollars by the issuance of ..... (.....) shares of fully paid, nonassessable common capital stock of this Corporation at a par value of ..... ($.....) Dollars per share; ..... ($.....) Dollars by the issuance of ..... (.....) shares of fully paid, nonassessable preferred capital stock of this Corporation at a par value of ..... ($.....) Dollars per share; three notes of this Corporation, bearing interest at ..... (.....%) percent, for the sum of ..... ($.....) Dollars each, one of said notes to run for the term of one year from date, the second note to run for the term of two years from date, and the third to run for the term of three years from date, all payable to "B"; and three notes of this Corporation, bearing interest at ..... (.....%) percent, for the sum of ..... ($.....) Dollars each, one of said notes to run for the term of one year from date, the second note to run for the term of two years from date, and the third to run for the term of three years from date, payable to "A."

That this Corporation assume all obligations of said copartnership existing ...., 19.., not exceeding the sum of ..... ($.....) Dollars.

That all of said notes bear interest from ...., 19...

That the said stock and the said notes be issued and delivered on ...., 19.., to the said "A" and "B," copartners under the firm name of "A" & "B" Co., as set forth in said offer, upon the receipt by said Corporation of said bill of sale, the transfer to take effect on ...., 19...

That the President and the Treasurer of this Corporation, or either of them, are hereby authorized, empowered, and directed, upon the execution and delivery of the proper legal instrument or instruments necessary to convey and transfer said property as set forth in said proposition and offer, to issue and deliver, in accordance with this resolution, the stock and notes therein specified.

That the President and the Treasurer are hereby authorized and directed to deliver said certificates of stock and said notes at once to ...., Esq., in escrow, to be delivered by him to said "A" and "B" on ...., 19.., upon receipt by them of satisfactory proof that said bill of sale from said copartnership has likewise been delivered to said ...., in escrow, to be delivered by him to the said Corporation on ...., 19.., and provided that the said .... acknowledges in writing that he holds said certificates of stock, said notes, and said bill of sale to be delivered by him as herein provided on ...., 19..

DIRECTORS' RESOLUTION ADOPTING AGREEMENT ENTERED INTO BEFORE ORGANIZATION TO ACQUIRE ASSETS OF CORPORATION

RESOLVED, That the agreement heretofore made in behalf of this Corporation by .... & Co., with the Board of Directors and stockholders of "A" Corporation (a corporation organized under the laws of the State of ....), that this Corporation, when organized, should acquire all the property and assets of said "A" Corporation, in exchange for ..... (.....) fully paid and nonassessable shares of the preferred stock of this Corporation of the par value of ..... ($.....) Dollars each, and for ..... (.....) fully paid and nonassessable shares of the common stock of this Corporation without par value, is hereby approved and adopted for this Corporation, and

RESOLVED FURTHER, That the property and assets of "A" Corporation to be sold and transferred to this Corporation as aforesaid are, in the judgment of the Board of Directors of this Corporation, of the full and fair value of ..... ($.....) Dollars over and above the liabilities of said "A" Corporation, and

RESOLVED FURTHER, That the proper officers of this Corporation are hereby authorized and directed to issue and deliver to or upon the order of said "A" Corporation against a proper conveyance and delivery to this Corporation of all the assets and property of said "A" Corporation, certificates representing ..... (.....) fully paid and nonassessable shares of the preferred stock of this Corporation of the par value of ..... ($.....) Dollars each, and ..... (.....) fully paid and nonassessable shares of the common stock of this Corporation without nominal or par value.

RESOLUTION OF STOCKHOLDERS RATIFYING AGREEMENT TO PURCHASE ALL THE CAPITAL STOCK OF ANOTHER CORPORATION

WHEREAS, the Board of Directors, having considered it for the best interests of this Corporation to acquire the stock of the .... Company, entered into an agreement for the purchase of all of the capital stock of the .... Company, be it

RESOLVED, That the agreement heretofore made by this Corporation, providing for the purchase of stock of the .... Company at a price equal to the par value thereof, payable in capital stock of this Corporation, at a valuation or rate of .... ($.....) Dollars per share, is hereby ratified and approved, and that the officers and Board of Directors of this Corporation are hereby authorized to carry said agreement into effect by issuing and delivering new stock of this Corporation, authorized at this meeting, to holders of stock of the .... Company, in exchange for said stock, on the terms and conditions of the said agreement.

DIRECTORS' RESOLUTION RATIFYING AGREEMENT TO PURCHASE CORPORATE ASSETS FOR STOCK

WHEREAS, it is proposed to purchase the property and assets of .... Corporation by the issuance of ..... shares of the common stock of this Company, and

WHEREAS, the directors, after carefully considering the proposed agreement and after examining the reports and financial condition of .... Corporation as disclosed by its balance sheet, are of the opinion that the value of the property so proposed to be acquired is at least equal to what the stock proposed to be issued therefor is reasonably worth in money at a fair valuation, be it

RESOLVED, That the action of the officers in entering into said agreement of purchase whereby this company shall acquire all of the assets of .... Corporation in return for ..... shares of the common stock of this Company is hereby wholly ratified and approved, and

RESOLVED FURTHER, That the President and the other officers are hereby authorized and directed upon satisfactory conveyance to the Company of the assets of .... Corporation, pursuant to contract dated ...., 19.., approved by the directors this day, to cause to be issued to .... Corporation, for distribution to its common stockholders, ... shares of the common stock of this Company ŏf the par value of $ ....., and

RESOLVED FURTHER, That upon consummation of said transaction, the .... Trust Company, Transfer Agent of the shares of the common stock of this Company, is hereby directed to record in its transfer record, and countersign as Transfer Agent of the shares of common stock of this Company, and deliver to the .... Bank, Registrar, for registration, and, when countersigned by the Registrar, to deliver certificates of ..... shares of this Company's common stock not previously issued of the par value of $ ..... each to ..... Corporation, and

RESOLVED FURTHER, That said Transfer Agent is hereby authorized to make transfer of said certificates when presented to it for such purpose and to countersign and deliver new certificates accordingly when the same have been similarly executed, and

RESOLVED FURTHER, That the .... Bank , as Registrar of the common stock of this Company, is hereby directed to register and countersign certificates for common stock of this Company of the par value of $ ..... per share, to be issued in accordance with the foregoing resolutions.

RESOLUTION OF STOCKHOLDERS GIVING DIRECTORS AUTHORITY TO FIND BUYER AND DISPOSE OF ASSETS

RESOLVED, That full and exclusive authority is hereby conferred upon and vested in the Board of Directors of this Corporation, to sell, lease, or dispose of all the real estate, machinery, fixtures, and other assets of the Corporation, in whole or in part or parcels, for such price or prices and upon such terms as it may in its discretion and judgment deem to be most advantageous for the stockholders, and for these purposes to insert advertisements and to engage and authorize one or more real estate or other agents to effect such sales, hereby ratifying and approving all that said Board of Directors may do in the premises, and making it unnecessary to obtain further confirmation of the stockholders.

RESOLUTION OF STOCKHOLDERS AUTHORIZING DIRECTORS TO SELL PROPERTY OF CORPORATION

RESOLVED, That the Board of Directors is hereby authorized to sell or exchange all or any part of this Corporation's property and assets, including its goodwill and its corporate franchises, upon such terms and conditions and for such consideration, which may be in whole or in part shares of stock in any other corporation or corporations, as the Board of Directors shall deem expedient and for the best interests of the Corporation, and more especially, but without limitation of the foregoing, to sell or exchange its assets, including its goodwill and its corporate franchises, to "X" Corporation.

EXCERPT OF MINUTES OF STOCKHOLDERS' MEETING AT WHICH DIRECTORS ARE INSTRUCTED TO SELL ALL OF CORPORATION'S ASSETS AT PUBLIC SALE ON TERMS INDICATED; AMENDMENT OF RESOLUTION FIXING SALE PRICE, AND PROTEST OF OBJECTING STOCKHOLDERS

"A" offered the following resolution, which "C" seconded:

RESOLVED, That the Board of Directors is hereby instructed to proceed at once to sell at public sale the mills, premises, and entire property and plant of this Corporation, located at . . . . Street, in the City of . . . ., ..., on the following terms:

(Here insert such limitations as the stockholders wish to to place upon the terms.)

"X" offered the following amendment to the resolution:
Provided, That no bids for less than 75 cents on the dollar of stock be considered.

"A" refused to accept the amendment, and thereupon "X" moved and "Y" seconded the amendment.

"B" moved to amend the amendment by striking out the words "75 cents on the dollar of stock," and inserting the amount "$225,000." "C" seconded the amendment to the amendment. The amended amendment was carried, "X" and "Y" voting "no."

The resolution, as amended, was carried by the following vote:

Ayes	Nays
"A" . . . . . shares	"X" . . . . . shares
"B" . . . . . shares	"Y" . . . . . shares
"C" . . . . . shares	

The following protest of stockholders was, at the request of "X" and "Y," noted in the minutes:

The undersigned stockholders consider inadequate the minimum price of $225,000, fixed in the resolution offered by "A," as amended by "B," and adopted by a vote representing . . . . . (. . . . .) shares of stock, at a meeting of the stockholders held on . . . ., 19.., for the sale of the mills, premises, and entire property and plant of this Corporation at public sale on . . . ., 19.., and hereby protest against the said resolution.

. . . . ."X". . . . .
. . . . ."Y". . . . .

RESOLUTION OF STOCKHOLDERS AUTHORIZING DIRECTORS TO SELL AT PUBLIC OR PRIVATE SALE, ALL ASSETS OF A CORPORATION OPERATING AT A LOSS

WHEREAS, the mills and plant owned by this Corporation and located at .... Street, in the City of ...., ..., have remained idle since ...., 19.., because this Corporation has lacked the working capital necesary to operate the said mills and plant, and

WHEREAS, the said mills and plant have been depreciating in value because of idleness and will continue to depreciate if allowed to remain idle, and

WHEREAS, the officers and directors of this Corporation report that they are unable to raise the working capital necessary to put the mills and plant into operation, and are also unable to make any arrangement for operation by others under a contract that would net this Corporation a fair return upon its investment, be it

RESOLVED, That the Board of Directors of this Corporation is hereby directed and instructed to proceed at once to sell the mills, premises, and entire property and plant of this Corporation, at either public or private sale, upon the best terms obtainable, and that it is hereby authorized to make, execute, and deliver any and all necessary and proper deeds, contracts, and other instruments in order to consummate such sale, and

RESOLVED FURTHER, That the Board of Directors is hereby directed to report any action taken in this matter to the stockholders, at an adjourned meeting to be held on ...., 19.., and that no actual sale be made previous to that date.

RESOLUTION OF STOCKHOLDERS AUTHORIZING OFFICERS TO OFFER TO SELL CORPORATE ASSETS FOR STOCK OF ANOTHER CORPORATION, OFFER TO BE GOOD FOR LIMITED PERIOD

WHEREAS, negotiations have been carried on during a number of weeks prior hereto, between the officers of the "A" Company and the officers of the "X" Company, a corporation organized under the laws of the State of ...., relative to the purchase and sale of all the assets, business, goodwill, etc., belonging to the "A" Company, and

WHEREAS, an audit was made by ...., certified public accountants, of the books, records, papers, documents, stock, material, and finished product of the "A" Company as of ...., 19.., which said audit shows that the total assets of the "A" Company on said date has a value of .... ($.....) Dollars, and

WHEREAS, the stockholders of the "A" Company have carefully considered the value of said assets, and are satisfied that, on said ...., 19.., they were reasonably worth the sum of .... ($.....) Dollars, and

WHEREAS, the stockholders of the "A" Company have given careful thought and much consideration to the question of the advisability of selling and disposing of the assets of the "A" Company, and have come to the conclusion that it is for the best interests of the "A" Company that its assets and business should be merged, joined, and united with the business and assets of the said "X" Company, and that the consolidated business be conducted under one management, be it

RESOLVED, That the "A" Company offer to sell all its assets of every kind, nature, and description, tangible and intangible, and wherever situated, together with its goodwill, patent rights, trademarks, etc., to the said "X" Company of ...., for the following-described securities (*insert securities by name and amount*), and

That the "A" Company shall pay all its debts, liabilities, and obligations as they existed on ...., 19.., and that said "X" Company shall assume and agree to pay all debts, obligations, and liabilities incurred in connection with the operation of the "A" Company, on and after ...., 19.., and

That the "A" Company shall assign, transfer, and set over unto the said "X" Company all its contracts of every kind and nature, as they existed on said ...., 19.., or at the time of transfer, which it can legally assign, and the said "X" Company shall assume and agree to carry out and perform the same, and all obligations thereof agreed to be performed by said "A" Company, and

That the said "X" Company shall be entitled to receive and retain all profits or gains resulting from the operation of the business carried on by the said "A" Company from the close of business on ...., 19.., up to the date of this transfer, and said "X" Company shall, on or prior to ..... (.....) days from the date of the transfer of said assets, pay to the said "A" Company .... (.....%) percent upon the sum of .... ($.....) Dollars from ...., 19.., up to the date of the making of said payment, and

That the said assets shall be conveyed and transferred by good and sufficient conveyances, and

RESOLVED FURTHER, That the officers of the "A" Company are hereby authorized, instructed, and directed to put this offer into proper form, to deliver the said offer to the said "X" Company, and, upon acceptance thereof, to do every act reasonable, necessary, or proper in the premises to bring about, fully perform, and carry out the terms and conditions of said agreement and transfer, and

RESOLVED FURTHER, That this offer shall be good only for the period of ..... (.....) days from ...., 19.., and if not accepted within that time, shall be void and of no effect.

EXCERPT OF MINUTES OF MEETING OF STOCKHOLDERS AUTHORIZING DIRECTORS TO OFFER FOR SALE TO NEW COMPANY ASSETS OF COMPANY AND LICENSE TO MANUFACTURE UNDER PATENTS OWNED BY COMPANY

The President stated that the object of the meeting was to consider the granting of the sole and exclusive license to manufacture and sell safety razors and razor blades under the patents owned by this Corporation, to . . . . Company, a new company, which had been formed with an authorized capitalization of $500,000, of which $400,000 is common stock and $100,000 preferred stock, the proposed license fee to be $1 for the razor frame and 1¢ for each razor blade given in addition to those blades contained in each razor set. The President further stated that this Corporation was to receive, in consideration of the execution of the license agreement and the transfer to the new company of this Corporation's plant and materials on hand, the total issue of common stock, and the new company was also to assume all outstanding obligations of this corporation; and that, of the common stock so received by this Corporation in consideration of the transfer of its plant and other assets, and the signing of a license agreement, $50,000 par value is to be returned to the new company as treasury stock, to be used by the new company as a bonus in the sale of its preferred stock.

After full discussion, on motion duly made and seconded, it was unanimously

RESOLVED, That the President and Secretary of this Corporation are hereby authorized to formulate an offer to the . . . . Company to grant such Company a sole and exclusive license to manufacture and sell safety razors and razor blades, under the patents owned and controlled by this Corporation, and to transfer to such Company all its machinery, tools, dies, and stock on hand used by it in connection with the manufacture of safety razors and razor blades, for the consideration and in accordance with the terms stated by the President of this Corporation, the form of such offer to be approved by the Board of Directors, and

RESOLVED FURTHER, That, in the event that such offer be accepted, the President and the Secretary of this Corporation are hereby authorized to execute and deliver to the . . . . Company a license agreement, in a form to be approved by the Board of Directors of this Corporation.

MINUTES OF DIRECTORS' MEETING DISCUSSING METHODS OF SECURING A PURCHASER FOR THE ASSETS OF THE CORPORATION, AND AUTHORIZING EMPLOYMENT OF AGENT TO EFFECT SALE

The Treasurer reported to the Board of Directors concerning various persons whom he had contacted with a view to interesting them in purchasing the mills and all other assets of the Corporation, and described various methods that might be used to secure a purchaser. The question of employing a concern which made a business of selling manufacturing plants at private sale was duly considered, and after full discussion, it was

RESOLVED, That the President and Treasurer of the Corporation are hereby authorized to employ, for a period not exceeding six months, some reputable firm to undertake the sale of the mills and other assets of the Corporation, upon such terms and conditions as the President and Treasurer deem best for the interests of the Corporation.

DIRECTORS' RESOLUTION OFFERING TO TRANSFER PROPERTY TO NEW CORPORATION FOR STOCK AND ASSUMPTION BY NEW CORPORATION OF OBLIGATION TO ISSUE BONDS

WHEREAS, under date of . . . ., 19. ., the Board of Directors of this Corporation accepted a written offer of A Company, which offer provided, among other things, that the A Company would vest in this Corporation, free and clear of all encumbrances and obligations, the ownership and control of all the right, title, and interest of A Company in and to certain properties, known as ". . . . . Unit," of the B Company, which unit serves . . . . and vicinity with electrical service, A Company to pay any sums owing by it on the purchase of such properties, this Corporation to cause a corporation to be formed to acquire such properties, in which corporation this Corporation would own 100 percent of the authorized capital stock, and A Company to receive without additional consideration, ... ($. . . . .) Dollars par value of the First Mortgage 20-year 8% Bonds of said proposed corporation to be formed, which bonds were to be secured by a first mortgage on all of such . . . . properties, and

WHEREAS, this Corporation has now caused C Company, a . . . . corporation, to be formed with a total authorized capital stock of . . . . ($. . . . .) Dollars, represented by . . . . . (. . . . .) shares, all of one class, and of the par value of . . . . ($. . . . .) Dollars per share, and desires to vest the ownership and control of said properties in said C Company, now, therefore, be it

RESOLVED, That this Corporation offer to sell and transfer to C Company, free and clear of all encumbrances and obligations, all of its right, title, and interest in and to said . . . . properties, in consideration of the issuance to this Corporation of all the authorized capital stock of said Company, being . . . . . shares of the par value of . . . . ($. . . . .) Dollars per share, fully paid and nonassessable, and the assumption by said C Company of the obligation to issue and deliver to said A Company, without further consideration, ... ($. . . . .) Dollars of its First Mortgage 20-year 8% Bonds, to be secured by a mortgage on all of said properties, and that the officers of this Corporation execute and delivery to said A Company a written offer embodying the terms of this resolution.

DIRECTORS' RESOLUTION AUTHORIZING OFFICERS TO NEGOTIATE FOR SALE ALL THE CORPORATE ASSETS, PURSUANT TO RESOLUTION OF STOCKHOLDERS

WHEREAS, the stockholders of this Company, at a special meeting held on ...., 19.., by a resolution duly adopted, authorized and instructed the directors of this Company to proceed at once to sell the mills, premises, and entire property and plant of this Company, located at .... Street, in the City of ...., ..., at either private or public sale, and

WHEREAS, on account of the approach of winter, it is desirable to make this sale as early as possible, in order to enable the purchaser or purchasers to make necessary improvements and repairs, be it

RESOLVED, That the President and the Secretary of this Company are hereby directed and instructed to proceed at once to enter into negotiations for the sale of the mills, premises, and the entire property and plant of this Company, located at ...., in the City of ...., ..., and to advertise the sale of said property in at least two of the leading .... trade papers of this country, and

RESOLVED FURTHER, That the President and the Secretary are hereby directed to make a full report of the progress of said sale to this Board of Directors, at least ..... days prior to the adjourned meeting of the stockholders to be held on ...., 19...

DIRECTORS' RESOLUTION ACCEPTING OFFER TO PURCHASE ALL ASSETS OF CORPORATION, SUBJECT TO STOCKHOLDERS' APPROVAL, AND CALLING STOCKHOLDERS' MEETING TO CONSIDER EXECUTION OF AGREEMENT FOR SALE

WHEREAS, an offer has been made to this Corporation by the .... Company, to purchase the entire property and assets of this Corporation for the consideration and upon the terms and conditions set forth in the following proposed agreement (*insert copy of agreement*), and

WHEREAS, in the opinion of this Board of Directors, it is for the best interests of this Company that its entire property and assets be sold to the .... Corporation for the consideration and upon the terms and conditions named in the proposed agreement above, be it

RESOLVED, That the offer of said .... Corporation is hereby accepted, subject to the approval of the stockholders of this Company, and

RESOLVED FURTHER, That the President and the Secretary and hereby authorized and directed to make, execute, and deliver the aforementioned agreement upon the adoption of the same by the stockholders, and

RESOLVED FURTHER, That a meeting of the stockholders of this Company be called for the purpose of taking into consideration the execution of said proposed agreement, to be held at .... Street, ... City, ..., on ...., 19.., at ....M., and the Secretary is directed to give notice of the meeting to all the stockholders of the Company, as required by law and the By-laws of this Company.

DIRECTORS' RESOLUTION AUTHORIZING OFFICERS TO EXECUTE AGREEMENT FOR SALE OF ASSETS UPON CONSENT OF STOCKHOLDERS GIVEN AT MEETING

WHEREAS, on ...., 19.., the stockholders of this Corporation, by a vote of ..... of the stockholders, passed the following resolution:

WHEREAS, the .... Company, a corporation duly organized under the laws of the State of ...., has proposed to purchase and take over all the property, both real and personal, assets, business, and goodwill of this Corporation, and, in consideration therefor, to issue and deliver to the stockholders of this Corporation its total capital stock, amounting to .... ($.....) Dollars, and

WHEREAS, it is deemed advisable to accept said proposition, be it

RESOLVED, That the directors of this Corporation are hereby authorized and directed to make the following agreement (*insert copy of agreement*).

RESOLVED FURTHER, That said directors are hereby authorized and directed to do and perform all necessary acts and to make, execute, and deliver all necessary papers to carry said agreement into full force and effect.

THEREFORE, BE IT RESOLVED, That the President and Secretary of this Corporation are hereby authorized and directed to make, execute, and deliver the aforementioned agreement, to do and perform all necessary acts, and to make, execute, and deliver the necessary papers to carry the same into full force and effect.

DIRECTORS' RESOLUTION RATIFYING CONTRACT FOR PURCHASE OF ALL ASSETS OF ANOTHER CORPORATION FOR STOCK

WHEREAS, it is proposed to purchase the property and assets of "Y" Corporation by the issuance of ..... (.....) shares of the common capital stock of this Company, and

WHEREAS, the directors, after carefully considering the said proposed contract and after examining the reports and financial condition of said Corporation as disclosed by its balance sheet, are of the opinion and do adjudge that the value of the property so proposed to be acquired is at least equal to what the stock proposed to be issued therefor is reasonably worth in money at a fair bona fide valuation, be it

RESOLVED, That the action of the officers in entering into said contract of purchase whereby this Company shall acquire all of the assets of "Y" Corporation in return for . . . . . shares of the common capital stock of this Company is hereby wholly ratified and approved, and

RESOLVED FURTHER, That the President and the other officers are hereby authorized and directed, upon satisfactory conveyance to this Company of the assets of "Y" Corporation, pursuant to contract dated . . . ., 19. ., approved by the directors this day, to cause to be issued to "Y" Corporation, for distribution to its common stockholders, ... (. . . . .) shares of the common capital stock of this Company of the par value of . . . . ($. . . . .) Dollars, and

RESOLVED FURTHER, That upon consummation of said transaction, the . . . . Trust Company, Transfer Agent of the shares of the common stock of this Company, is hereby directed to record in its transfer record, and countersign as Transfer Agent of the shares of common stock of this Company, and deliver to the . . . . Bank, Registrar, for registration, and, when countersigned by the Registrar, to deliver certificates of . . . . . (. . . . .) shares of this Company's common stock not previously issued of the par value of . . . . ($. . . . .) Dollars each to "Y" Corporation, and

RESOLVED FURTHER, That said Transfer Agent is hereby authorized to make transfer of said certificates when presented to it for such purpose and to countersign and deliver new certificates accordingly when the same have been similarly executed, and

RESOLVED FURTHER, That the First National Bank of New York, as Registrar of the common stock of this Company, is hereby directed to register and countersign certificates for common stock of this Company of the par value of . . . . ($. . . . .) Dollars per share, to be issued in accordance with the foregoing resolutions—to wit: certificates for a total of . . . . . (. . . . .) shares.

RESOLUTION OF DIRECTORS OF SUBSIDIARY COMPANY APPROVING PLAN OF LIQUIDATION OF SUBSIDIARY AND TRANSFER OF ASSETS TO PARENT COMPANY, TO BE SUBMITTED TO STOCKHOLDERS

RESOLVED, That the "Plan of Liquidation, dated . . . ., 19. ., of the "A" Company, the "B" Company, and the "C" Company" is hereby approved, and

RESOLVED FURTHER, That the said Plan be submitted to the stockholders of the "A" Company at a special meeting to be held on . . . ., 19. ., ... Street, ... City, at . . . . M., and

RESOLVED FURTHER, That the "A" Company does hereby transfer, assign, and convey all of its property, real and personal, of every sort and description and wherever located, including specifically, but without being limited to, properties located in the States of . . . ., ..., ..., ..., ..., and . . . ., to the "AH" Company, Inc., and that the officers of this Corporation are hereby authorized and instructed to take all such action, and the President, or a Vice president, and the Secretary, or an Assistant Secretary, are hereby authorized and instructed to execute and deliver all such deeds, assignments, bills of sale, and other instruments as may be necessary or advisable to effect the foregoing transfer, assignment, and conveyance of its property, and

RESOLVED FURTHER, That this Corporation discontinue business as a corporation and surrender its charter and corporate franchises to the State of . . . ., and that this resolution be submitted to the stockholders of this Corporation at their special meeting to be held on . . . ., 19. . .

RESOLUTION OF STOCKHOLDERS OF SUBSIDIARY COMPANY APPROVING PLAN OF LIQUIDATION, AND TRANSFERRING ASSETS TO PARENT COMPANY

WHEREAS, the "AH" Company, Inc., by action of its directors and stockholders, has duly adopted the document presented to this meeting designated as "Plan of Liquidation, dated . . . ., 19.., of the "A" Company, the "B" Company, and the "C" Company," and

WHEREAS, the said Plan has been approved by the Board of Directors of this Company and has been submitted to the stockholders of this Company for action at the meeting, and

WHEREAS, by the terms of the said Plan, it shall be considered as adopted by this Company upon adoption by its stockholders of resolutions authorizing distribution of all of the assets of this Company in complete cancellation of all of its stock, and

WHEREAS, upon such adoption by the stockholders of this Company, the said Plan will become a binding agreement between this Company and the "AH" Company, Inc., be it

RESOLVED, That this Company distribute all of its assets in complete liquidation of all of its stock, upon the terms and conditions and in the manner specified in the said Plan, and that the adoption of this resolution shall effect and evidence the adoption of the said Plan by this Company, and

RESOLVED FURTHER, That this Company does hereby transfer, assign, and convey all of its property, real and personal, of every sort and description and wherever located, including specifically, but without being limited to, properties located in the States of . . . ., ..., ..., ..., ..., and . . . ., to the "AH" Company, Inc., and that the officers of this Company are hereby authorized and instructed to take all such action, and the President, or a Vice president, and the Secretary, or an Assistant Secretary, are hereby authorized and instructed to execute and deliver all such deeds, assignments, bills of sale, and other instruments as may be necessary or advisable to effect the foregoing transfer, assignment, and conveyance of its property, and

RESOLVED FURTHER, That this Company, the "A" Company, a corporation created and existing under the laws of the State of . . . ., do discontinue business as a corporation and surrender to the State of . . . . its charter and corporate franchises, and

RESOLVED FURTHER, That the President, or a Vice president, of this Company shall certify a copy of the foregoing resolution, under his hand and the seal of this Company, to the Secretary of State of the State of . . . ., and shall cause notice of the adoption thereof to be published once a week for at least two (2) successive weeks in a newspaper published or of general circulation in the County of . . . ., ..., being the county in which the principal office of this Company is located.

RESOLUTION OF STOCKHOLDERS CONSENTING TO SALE OF ENTIRE CORPORATE PROPERTY AND APPROVING AGREEMENT OF SALE

WHEREAS, ... Company has offered to purchase the entire property and assets of this Corporation, and to pay in consideration therefor the sum of . . . . Dollars ($ . . . . .) , upon the terms and conditions set forth in the proposed form of agreement submitted to this meeting, and

WHEREAS, the Board of Directors of this Corporation, at a meeting held on . . . ., 19.., by the affirmative vote of . . . . . of the directors, authorized the execution of said agreement, subject to the approval of the stockholders, be it

RESOLVED, That the stockholders of this Corporation consent to the sale of the entire property and assets of this Corporation to . . . . Company, in consideration of the payment of the sum of . . . . . Dollars ($ . . . .), upon the terms and conditions set forth in said proposed form of agreement, which form is hereby adopted and approved, and

RESOLVED FURTHER, That the President and the Secretary are hereby instructed and directed to make, execute, and deliver said agreement, to do and perform all necessary act, and to make, execute, and deliver all necessary papers to carry the sale herein authorized into full force and effect.

RESOLUTION OF STOCKHOLDERS ACCEPTING OFFER TO PURCHASE CORPORATE PROPERTY

WHEREAS, an offer was received from . . . ., at the public sale held on . . . ., 19.., to purchase the mills, premises, and entire property and plant of this Corporation, located at . . . . Street, in the City of . . . ., for the sum of . . . . ($. . . . .) Dollars, be it

RESOLVED, That the offer of said . . . . is hereby accepted, and the President and the Secretary are hereby authorized and directed to execute a proper deed to consummate the sale, and to deliver the said property to the said . . . ., upon receipt of payment therefor according to the terms of the sale—to wit, ... ($. . . . .) Dollars in cash, and a note for the balance of . . . . ($. . . . .) Dollars, payable six months from the date of the execution and delivery of a deed to the said property, with interest at . . . . . (. . . . .%) percent, secured by collateral satisfactory to the Board of Directors.

EXCERPT OF MINUTES OF MEETING OF STOCKHOLDERS CONSENTING TO SALE OF ENTIRE CORPORATE PROPERTY AND APPROVING AGREEMENT OF SALE

The Secretary presented and read a proposed form of agreement for the sale of the entire property and assets of this Company to . . . . Corporation. Upon motion duly made and seconded, the following resolution was adopted by the affirmative vote of all the stockholders:

WHEREAS, ... Corporation has offered to purchase the entire property and assets of this Company, and to pay in consideration therefor the sum of . . . . ($. . . . .) Dollars, upon the terms and conditions set forth in the proposed form of agreement submitted to this meeting, and

WHEREAS, the Board of Directors of this Company, at a meeting held on . . . ., 19. ., by the affirmative vote of . . . . . of the directors, authorized the execution of said agreement, subject to the approval of the stockholders, be it

RESOLVED, That the stockholders of this Company do hereby consent to the sale of the entire property and assets of this Company to . . . . Corporation, in consideration of the payment of the sum of . . . . ($. . . . .) Dollars, upon the terms and conditions set forth in said proposed form of agreement, which form is hereby adopted and approved, and

RESOLVED FURTHER, That the President and the Secretary are hereby instructed and directed to make, execute, and deliver said agreement, to do and perform all necessary acts, and to make, execute, and deliver all necessary papers to carry the sale herein authorized into full force and effect.

RESOLUTION OF STOCKHOLDERS AUTHORIZING OFFICERS TO ACCEPT OFFER TO PURCHASE ASSETS OF AN UNSUCCESSFUL CORPORATION FOR STOCK

WHEREAS, the officers of the "A" Mining Company have received a proposition as follows:

"Pursuant to a resolution duly adopted, the "B" Company, a .... corporation, does hereby offer .... (.....) shares of the capital stock of the "B" Company as the purchase price for the "A" Mining Claim, U.S. Lot No. ......, together with all other real and personal property owned by said "A" Mining Company.

The "B" Company

By ...., President

............, Secretary

WHEREAS, the "A" Mining Company is not a financial success, and is not a going concern, and has been unable to find any ore or valuable minerals on its ground, and, in order to conduct its business, it has been and will in the future be necessary to levy and collect assessments from its stockholders, and

WHEREAS, the stockholders are desirous of discontinuing operation of the Company's property, be it

RESOLVED, That the President and the Secretary are hereby authorized to accept ..... (.....) shares of the capital stock of the "B" Company, a .... corporation, as the full purchase price of the "A" Mining Claim, U.S. Lot No. ......, together with all other real and personal property owned by this Company, and that the President and the Secretary of this Company are hereby authorized and directed to make, execute, and deliver, for and in behalf of this Company, deeds of conveyance of all the real and personal property belonging to this Company, and to deliver the same to the "B" Company, upon receiving for the use and benefit of this Company ..... (.....) shares of the capital stock of the said "B" Company, and

RESOLVED FURTHER, That the Board of Directors of the "A" Mining Company is hereby requested, after it has received for the use and benefit of this Company the said ..... (.....) shares of the capital stock of said "B" Company, from the sale of real and personal property of this Company, to declare a dividend of all of said capital stock so received, and to pay the same to the stockholders of this Company pro rata, according to their holdings as shown by the books of this Company, upon delivery by said stockholders to the Secretary of this Company, for cancellation, of all their certificates of stock in the "A" Mining Company, properly indorsed.

RESOLUTION OF STOCKHOLDERS ACCEPTING OFFER TO PURCHASE ASSETS FOR CONSIDERATION OTHER THAN STOCK

WHEREAS, "A" and "B" have offered to purchase the entire mill plant of this Corporation, located at .... Street, ... City, and the sash and door plant located at .... Street, ... City, including therein all land, improvements thereon, fixtures, furniture, lumber, and all real and personal property of every kind, including all unassigned accounts receivable and choses in action, but not including the books of entry and accounts, which books, however, are to be open at all times for their use and inspection, with authority to take copies, and

WHEREAS, in consideration of this purchase, and "A" and "B" have offered to pay as follows:

(1) To transfer by indorsement log paper issued by .... Company, falling due within the next 90 days, in the amount of .... ($.....) Dollars;

(2) To execute their note to the Corporation in the sum of .... ($.....) Dollars, payable on or before ..... (.....) months from this date, with interest at the rate of ..... (.....%) percent per annum;

(3) To execute a note in the sum of .... ($.....) Dollars, payable on or before ..... (.....) years from this date, with interest at the rate of ..... (.....%) percent per annum, payable semi-annually, secured by a mortgage on the same property that is now covered by mortgage heretofore made by .... to ...., Trustee, making a total consideration to be paid to the Corporation of .... ($.....) Dollars; and said "A" and "B" have further agreed to assume and pay the present outstanding payroll of the Corporation, amounting to approximately .... ($.....) Dollars, and any other immediate expenses attached to the above plants, to assume and perform all obligations under the contract to furnish power between the Corporation and the .... Company, and to assume and pay any and all conditional sales contracts upon all machinery, including electrical machinery, and

WHEREAS, the Board of Directors considers that a fair valuable consideration has been offered for said property, and that it is for the best interests of the Corporation, its directors, and stockholders to accept said offer, be it

RESOLVED, That said offer is hereby accepted, and that the President and the Secretary of the Corporation are hereby authorized and directed to cause to be prepared and executed the necessary instruments conveying title to all the above-mentioned property, to "A" and "B" or to their order, and to deliver the same upon receiving said consideration, and

RESOLVED FURTHER, That as and when said consideration is converted into cash, the President and the Secretary are hereby authorized and directed to pay the creditors of the Corporation pro rata, after the payment of all secured and preferred claims. Pending the preparation of transfer papers, the President is hereby authorized to permit "A" and "B" to have joint equal possession of each of said mill plants, all operations thereof to be at their expense; provided, however, that, if the title to said real estate is in fact not marketable, "A" and "B" shall surrender, to the Corporation, the joint equal possession before referred to, on or before ...., 19...

RESOLUTION OF DIRECTORS (OR STOCKHOLDERS) AUTHORIZING EXECUTION OF BILL OF SALE OF ALL ASSETS BY OFFICERS

RESOLVED, That the President and Secretary of this Company are hereby authorized to execute and deliver to the . . . ., Inc., a Bill of Sale granting, conveying transferring, and assigning to the said . . . ., Inc., its successors and assigns, all its assets and property of every kind and character whatsoever, including (without limitation of the foregoing) fixtures, furniture, accounts and bills receivable, shares of stock, securities, cash in bank, moneys, patents, contracts, orders, trademarks, and other properties and assets of every kind, whether or not herein specified, belonging to the Company and/or pertinent to the business conducted by it and shown on its books and records as of . . . ., 19. .; and also said business as a going concern and the goodwill thereof, together with the right to the exclusive use of the name the . . . . Company; provided, however, that in said instrument, the . . . ., Inc., shall agree to take over and assume all the Company's outstanding contracts, to accept the foregoing assets, property, business, and goodwill subject to all the debts and liabilities of the Company as of . . . ., 19. ., including (but not by way of limitation) the obligations of the Company, to assume and agree to pay and discharge said debts and liabilities, and to perform the covenants agreed to be performed by the . . . . Company under the mortgage and deed of trust to . . . . Trust Company of . . . ., as Trustee, dated . . . ., . ., 19. ., securing an issue of $1,000,000 principal amount of First Mortgage Leasehold 8½% Sinking Fund Bonds, and under a certain indenture of lease from "X," to the . . . . Company, dated . . . ., 19. ., and

RESOLVED FURTHER, That the Secretary be authorized to attach the corporate seal of the Company to said Bill of Sale.

WRITTEN CONSENT OF MORE THAN MAJORITY OF STOCKHOLDERS TO SALE OF ALL ASSETS

. . . ., 19. .

We, the undersigned, constituting more than a majority of the holders of the voting stock of the "A" Company issued and outstanding, and the holders of more than a majority of such stock, do hereby authorize by our written consent, and do hereby ratify and approve of, the sale to "B" Corporation (made on . . . ., 19. .) of all the properties and assets of this Company in consideration for: (1) the assumption by the "B" Corporation of the Company's outstanding bonded indebtedness of six hundred thousand ($600,000) Dollars principal amount and all its other indebtedness and liabilities, and of all duties, obligations, and liabilities of "A" Company under the latter's deed of trust to . . . . Trust Company, dated . . . ., 19. ., ; (2) one million one hundred thousand ($1,100,000) Dollars par amount of the common stock of the "B" Corporation; and (3) the opportunity to the stockholders of the Company, during the period of forty-five (45) days from the date hereof, to purchase at par shares (in amounts proportionate to their respective holdings of the capital stock of the Company) of the "B" Corporation's preferred stock of the par value of one ($1) Dollar per share, all as is more fully set forth in the offer of "B" Corporation to the "A" Company, dated ...., 19.. (a copy whereof, marked Exhibit "A," is hereto attached).

We do hereby further authorize by our written consent, and hereby ratify and approve of, the sale (made on ...., 19..) of all of the properties and assets of the Company upon the terms and conditions, which we deem expedient for the best interests of the Company, set forth in the preambles and resolutions adopted by the Board of Directors at a meeting held ...., 19.. (a copy whereof, marked Exhibit "B," is hereto attached).

Name of Stockholder	*Number of Shares*
....	....
....	....
....	....
....	....

SECRETARY'S AFFIDAVIT VERIFYING NUMBER OF OUTSTANDING SHARES AND SIGNATURES

State of .... ⎱ ss:
County of .... ⎰

..........., being duly sworn, deposes and says:

(1) That he is the Secretary of the .... Company, a corporation duly created, organized, and existing under and by virtue of the laws of the State of ....

(2) That he is the custodian of the stock book of the said .... Company.

(3) That the total number of shares of the capital stock of the said .... Company issued and outstanding of ...., 19.., is ..... shares, and that the persons whose signatures are affixed to the foregoing consent are the holders of more than a majority of the said capital stock so issued and outstanding.

Sworn to before me
this ..... day of ...., 19..
....
    Notary Public

....
    Secretary

WRITTEN CONSENT OF ALL STOCKHOLDERS TO SALE OF ALL ASSETS OF CORPORATION

We, the undersigned, stockholders of the . . . . Corporation, of . . . . City, a corporation duly organized pursuant to the laws of the State of . . . ., and holders of stock therein of the number of shares set opposite our names and amounting in all to three hundred shares, the entire capital stock of said Corporation, hereby agree for value received, and in consideration of the same number of shares and of the same par value of the stock of the . . . . Company, Inc., hereby consent to the transfer of all the property of the . . . . Corporation to said . . . . Company, Inc., as existing on this date, subject, however, to the agreement of said . . . . Company, Inc. to assume and to pay at maturity all the debts and obligations of said . . . . Corporation of every name and nature, and consent to the exchange of the stock now held by us in the . . . . Corporation for the same par value of the stock of the . . . . Company, Inc.

Name of Stockholder	*Number of Shares*
. . . .	. . . .
. . . .	. . . .
. . . .	. . . .
. . . .	. . . .

DIRECTORS' RESOLUTION AUTHORIZING OFFICERS TO VOTE STOCK OWNED BY THE CORPORATION IN ANOTHER COMPANY IN FAVOR OF SALE OF ALL THE ASSETS OF THE COMPANY

RESOLVED, That the President, or a Vice president, of this Corporation is hereby duly authorized to vote, in behalf of this Corporation, at any meeting of stockholders of . . . . Company, all the shares of stock of said . . . . Company owned by this Corporation, in favor of a resolution to consent to the sale by . . . . Company of all of its assets to . . . . Co., Inc., or to consent in writing thereto.

OBJECTION BY STOCKHOLDER TO SALE OF ASSETS

The . . . . Corporation
. . . .
Gentlemen:

The undersigned shareholder of the . . . . Corporation hereby objects to and dissents from the following:

(1) The sale of the assets of said Corporation to . . . . Company.

(2) The approval and authorization of the agreement between . . . . Company and . . . . Corporation, and all actions taken at the shareholders' meeting of the . . . . Corporation held on . . . ., 19.., and all adjournments thereof, with respect to the matters hereinabove mentioned.

The undersigned, as the holder of . . . . . shares of common stock of the
. . . . Corporation hereby demands that said Corporation pay to him
the fair cash value of all of said shares, in accordance with Section . . . . . of the
General Corporation Law of . . . . . and hereby claims that the fair cash value
of such shares is $. . . . . per share.

Yours very truly,

. . . .

EXCERPT FROM MINUTES OF SPECIAL MEETING OF DIRECTORS AT WHICH ARE CONSIDERED STOCKHOLDERS' OBJECTIONS TO SALE OF ALL ASSETS OF CORPORATION AND DEMAND FOR FAIR CASH VALUE OF SHARES

The Chairman then made to the Board substantially the following statements:

Since the adjournment of the special meeting of the shareholders of this Company held on . . . ., 19. ., for the purpose, among others, of authorizing the assignment, transfer, and conveyance by this Company of all its property and assets, including its goodwill, to "P" Corporation, certain holders of common shares of this Company, purporting to act pursuant to the provisions of Section . . . . . of the General Code of . . . ., have in writing informed this Company of their objections to the transaction generally and have demanded that this Company pay to such holders certain amounts per share in the writings specified, which amounts such holders, respectively, have claimed in such writings to be the fair cash value of their shares. All except a few of such demands specified $. . . . . per share as the fair cash value of the common shares of this Company in respect of which such demands have been made. I submit to the meeting a copy of the form of writing by which most of such objections and demands have been made.

Counsel for the Company has not yet been able to determine the exact number of shares in respect of which the holders of common shares are entitled to make demands pursuant to the General Code of . . . ., but the number of shares in respect of which objections and demands have been received exceed . . . .

Counsel has advised me that under the provisions of the General Code of . . . . it is necessary that this Company, in writing, inform the holders of common shares of this Company who have made such objections and demands whether it will pay the amounts so demanded by them, and that, in case this Company is unwilling to pay the amounts so demanded, it is also necessary or advisable that this Company offer in writing to pay a specified amount per share for such shares. I herewith submit to the Board a copy of the form of writing which counsel has prepared for this purpose.

A copy of the form of demand and of the form of writing prepared to be sent by this Company to the holders of its common shares who have demanded payment for the common shares of this Company held by them in accordance with the statement that the Chairman made to the meeting, and which forms the Chairman submitted to the meeting, are, respectively, as follows:

(Here insert forms.)

Thereupon the following preamble and resolutions were offered and their adoption duly moved and seconded:

WHEREAS, certain holders of common shares of this Company have objected in writing to the action taken by the holders of the common shares of this Company at a special meeting thereof held on . . . ., 19.., and adjournments thereof, authorizing the assignment, transfer, and conveyance by this Company of all its property and assets, including its goodwill, to "P" Corporation, a . . . . corporation, and have demanded that this Company pay to such holders, respectively, the fair cash value of the common shares of this Company held by them, respectively, and have claimed that such fair cash value is in amounts varying from $. . . . . per share to $. . . . . per share, and

WHEREAS, counsel for this Company has advised that under the General Code of . . . . . it is necessary that this Company, within 10 days after the receipt of the aforesaid objections and demands, respectively, inform the holders of the common shares of this Company who have so objected to said action and have demanded payments as aforesaid whether it will pay the amounts so demanded by them, and that, if this Company shall refuse to pay such amounts, it is necessary or advisable that it offer to pay a specified amount as and for such fair cash value, be it

RESOLVED, That this Company inform such holders in writing that it will not pay the amounts so demanded by them, respectively, and that, pursuant to the General Code of . . . . . ., this Company in writing offer to pay to them, respectively, $. . . . . per share as and for the fair cash value thereof for all common shares of this Company in respect of which, they, respectively, have made the demands required by the provisions of said General Code and in respect of which, under the provisions of said General Code, they, respectively, are entitled to make such demands and to be paid, and

RESOLVED FURTHER, That the form of letter to be used in informing such shareholders as aforesaid be substantially in the form of the proposed letter that the Chairman has submitted to this meeting, except in cases where the demands have been made by writings in forms other than the form of objection and demand which the Chairman has submitted to the meeting, and that in such excepted cases the letters whereby this Company shall inform holders of common shares of this Company that it will not pay the amount or amounts demanded by them and whereby it offers to pay said price of $. . . . . per share be in such form or forms as counsel for this Company shall approve, and

RESOLVED FURTHER, That the Treasurer or Assistant Treasurer of this Company is hereby authorized, under the direction of counsel for this Company, to send letters in the name of this company in the form approved by or in the manner set forth in the foregoing resolution to each holder of common shares of this Company who has made an objection and demand in respect of common shares of this Company held by him, the blanks in such forms in each case being appropriately filled.

The aforesaid preamble and resolutions were thereupon discussed. Following the discussion a vote was taken upon the adoption of said preamble and resolutions, and the same were adopted, the vote being as follows:

. . . . ., ..., ..., ..., ..., ..., and . . . . ., voted "aye."
. . . . ., ..., and . . . . ., voted "nay."
. . . . ., and . . . . ., did not vote.

Mr. . . . . requested that the minutes show that some of the directors voted "nay," and he contended that in fixing the price, the directors should have before them the earnings of the Company, an appraisal of the physical properties of the Company, and the prices paid in sales of large blocks of shares, and that such dissenting directors consider the fair value of the shares to be far in excess of the amount fixed by the Board of Directors.

Said resolution was declared duly adopted by the directors, and there being no further business to come before the meeting, the same upon motion duly made, seconded, and adopted was adjourned.

DIRECTORS' RESOLUTION REJECTING STOCKHOLDERS' DEMAND AND OFFERING A LESSER SUM FOR DISSENTERS' SHARES

WHEREAS, certain holders of common shares of this Corporation have objected in writing to the action taken by the holders of the common shares of this Corporation at a special meeting thereof held on . . . ., 19. ., and adjournments thereof, authorizing the assignment, transfer, and conveyance by this Corporation of all its property and assets, including its goodwill, to . . . . Company, a . . . . (*insert state of incorporation*) corporation, and have demanded that this Corporation pay to such holders, respectively, the fair cash value of the common shares of this Corporation held by them, and have claimed that such fair cash value is in amounts varying from $. . . . . per share, to $. . . . . per share, and

WHEREAS, counsel for this Corporation has advised that under the General Corporation Law of . . . . it is necessary that this Corporation, within . . . . . days after the receipt of the aforesaid objections and demands, respectively, inform the holders of the common shares of this Corporation who have so objected to said action and have demanded payments as aforesaid whether it will pay the amounts so demanded by them, and that, if this Corporation shall refuse to pay such amounts, it is necessary or advisable that it offer to pay a specified amount as and for such fair cash value, be it

RESOLVED, That this Corporation inform such holders in writing that it will not pay the amounts so demanded by them, respectively, and that, pursuant to the General Corporation Law of . . . ., this Corporation in writing offer to pay to them, $. . . . . per share as the fair cash value thereof for all common shares of this Corporation in respect of which, they, respectively, have made the demands required by the provisions of said General Corporation Law and in respect of which, under the provisions of said General Corporation Law, they are entitled to make such demands and to be paid.

NOTICE BY CORPORATION TO DISSENTING STOCKHOLDER THAT AMOUNT DEMANDED AS FAIR CASH VALUE OF SHARES IS EXCESSIVE, AND INDICATING FAIR CASH VALUE OFFERED

Dear . . . .:

We acknowledge receipt of your communication, dated . . . ., 19. .., wherein you object to and dissent from the sale of the assets of the . . . . Corporation to . . . . Company, the approval and authorization of the agreement between . . . . Company and . . . . Corporation, and all actions taken at the shareholders' meeting of the . . . . Corporation held on . . . ., 19. .., and all adjournments thereof, with respect to the said sale of assets, and wherein you demand that this Corporation pay to you the fair cash value of the number of shares of the common stock of this Corporation set forth in such communication, and wherein you claim that the fair cash value of such shares is $. . . . . per share.

This Corporation considers that the amount claimed by you is excessive, and hereby informs you that it will not pay the amount so demanded by you; and, pursuant to the General Corporation Law of . . . . ., this Corporation hereby offers to you $. . . . . per shares as the fair cash value thereof for all the common shares of this Corporation in respect of which you have made the demand required by the provisions of said General Corporation Law, and in respect of which, under the provisions of said General Corporation Law, you are entitled to make such demand and to be paid.

Very truly yours,

. . . . Corporation

By . . . .

Treasurer

DIRECTORS' RESOLUTION ABANDONING PROPOSED SALE OF ASSETS AFTER DISSENTING STOCKHOLDER FILED OBJECTIONS AND PETITIONED FOR APPRAISAL OF STOCK

WHEREAS, at a special meeting of stockholders of the . . . . Corporation, held on . . . ., 19. .., the Board of Directors and officers of the Corporation were authorized to sell and convey to the . . . . Company all the assets of this Corporation, and to accept in payment thereof . . . . . shares of the capital stock of the purchasing corporation, and

WHEREAS, subsequently and within ..... days after the date of the aforementioned special meeting of stockholders, written notice was served on this Corporation in behalf of ...., objecting to the sale of the assets of this Corporation hereinbefore mentioned, and demanding that the Corporation purchase the stock of said person, and

WHEREAS, within ..... days of the date of the aforementioned special meeting of stockholders, the said ..... caused to be served on this Corporation a petition to the .... Court, ... County, and a notice of motion for that court to appoint three appraisers to appraise the stock of this Corporation and to direct the manner in which this Corporation should pay for the stock represented by the person so dissenting to the aforesaid sale, and

WHEREAS, this Corporation has not sufficient funds with which to purchase the stock of the person who has made the aforesaid petition to the .... Court, and cannot afford the necessary legal expense and the fees of appraisers incident to such a proceeding, and

WHEREAS, the .... Company has signified its willingness to permit this Corporation to withdraw its offer to sell all its assets to .... Company, be it

RESOLVED, That the Board of Directors and the officers of this Corporation take no action to carry out the resolution passed at the special meeting of stockholders held on ...., 19.., and

RESOLVED FURTHER, That the proposed sale and transfer of the assets of this Corporation to the .... Company, as outlined in the resolutions passed at the aforementioned special meeting of the stockholders held on ...., 19.., is hereby abandoned, and

RESOLVED FURTHER, That the President of this Corporation is hereby instructed to call a special meeting of stockholders to ratify and confirm the resolutions hereby adopted.

DISTRIBUTION OF PROPERTY UPON
SALE OF ASSETS

RESOLUTION OF STOCKHOLDERS APPROVING AGREEMENT FOR SALE OF ALL ASSETS, INCLUDING GOODWILL AND RIGHT TO USE CORPORATE NAME, FOR CASH AND STOCK; AUTHORIZING DISSOLUTION OF SELLING COMPANY AND DISTRIBUTION OF CONSIDERATION RECEIVED AMONG STOCKHOLDERS

RESOLVED, That the shareholders of this Company hereby approve the execution and delivery by this Company of the agreement dated ...., 19.., between this Company and .... Corporation, a ....

corporation, for the assignment, transfer, and conveyance by this Company of all of its property and assets, including its goodwill, to said .... Corporation, or its nominee or nominees, upon the terms and conditions set forth in said agreement, a copy of which has been submitted to this meeting; and that the shareholders of this Company hereby authorize the assignment, transfer, and conveyance of all of its said property and assets, including the goodwill of this Company and the right to the use of its corporate name, to said .... Corporation, or its nominee or nominees, upon the terms and conditions and for the considerations set forth in said agreement, and

RESOLVED FURTHER, That the minutes of the special meeting of the Board of Directors of this Company held on ...., 19.., which have been read to this meeting, are hereby in all respects approved; that the solutions therein set forth are hereby severally authorized, adopted, approved, ratified, and confirmed; and that all action therein or thereby taken or authorized by said Board of Directors and all action of every nature that has been or shall hereafter at any time be taken by an officer or officers of this Company in pursuance of said resolutions, action, or authorization of said Board of Directors be and it hereby is in all respects authorized, approved, ratified, and confirmed, and

RESOLVED FURTHER, That the Board of Directors of this Company is hereby authorized to take such further action and to authorize the execution and delivery of such further instruments in the name and in behalf of this Company and under its corporate seal or otherwise, and to do or authorize the doing of all such further acts and things as said Board of Directors shall deem necessary or proper in order to effect the assignment, transfer, and conveyance by this Company of all of its property and assets, including its goodwill and the right to the use of its corporate name, to said .... Corporation, or its nominee or nominees, in accordance with the terms and provisions of said agreement dated ...., 19.., and in order that this Company may perform all its obligations thereunder, and

RESOLVED FURTHER, That, in accordance with the agreement dated ...., 19.., between this Company and .... Corporation, a .... corporation, upon the assignment, transfer, and conveyance by this Company of all of its property and assets, including its goodwill and the right to the use of its corporate name, to said .... Corporation, or its nominee or nominees, this Company forthwith proceed to liquidate its affairs and to distribute among its shareholders the cash and shares of common stock of said .... Corporation that shall be received by this Company in exchange for all of its property and assets as aforesaid, and

RESOLVED FURTHER, That the holders of record of the common shares of this Company, the only class of shares of this Company that entitles the holders thereof to vote, declare that it is desirable to, and the Company does hereby elect to, wind up and dissolve as soon as possible after the assignment, transfer, and conveyance by this Company of all of its property and assets, including its goodwill and the right to the use of its corporate name, to said .... Corporation, or its nominee or nominees, shall have been accomplished as aforesaid, and

RESOLVED FURTHER, That said assignment, transfer, and conveyance having been accomplished as aforesaid, the President, or a Vice president, and the Secretary, or an Assistant Secretary, of this Company are hereby authorized and directed to execute and file in the office of the Secretary of State of the State of .... a certificate, verified by their oath as required by law, and to do or cause to be done all such other acts and things as shall be necessary or proper in order that the dissolution of this Company may be forthwith accomplished, and

RESOLVED FURTHER, That said assignment, transfer, and conveyance having been accomplished as aforesaid and the certificate for the dissolution of this Company having been made, verified, and filed as required by law, the Board of Directors of this Company is hereby authorized and directed to divide and distribute, or to cause to be divided and distributed, among the shareholders of this Company, in such manner as said Board shall deem expedient, the cash and shares of the common stock of said .... Corporation that shall have been received by this Company in exchange for all of its property and assets as aforesaid, all in accordance with the provisions of the Articles of Incorporation of this Company and of said agreement dated ...., 19.., to the end that this Company shall cease to do business and its affairs shall be liquidated forthwith upon the consummation of the transaction covered by said agreement.

DIRECTORS' RESOLUTION AUTHORIZING DISTRIBUTION OF CASH RECEIVED UPON SALE OF CORPORATE PROPERTY

RESOLVED, That the sum of ..... ($.....) Dollars per share be distributed to the stockholders of record of this Company, upon production to "X" & Co., Trustee, of the certificate therefor, in order that the amount of said payment may be indorsed thereon, and

RESOLVED FURTHER, That all such payments be made by check marked "on account of liquidation of this Company," and

RESOLVED FURTHER, That "X" & Co. be requested, upon presentation of the certificate for that purpose, to stamp upon each certificate an indorsement showing the amount paid per share and the date of such payment, and

RESOLVED FURTHER, That the President and the Treasurer of this Company be authorized, upon receipt of the remaining payment stipulated in the agreement with the "B" Company and of the other amount due this Company, to make, from time to time, further distribution to the stockholders of this Company in liquidation of its assets, in the same manner as provided in the foregoing resolutions, and

RESOLVED FURTHER, That the Board of Directors does hereby approve of the plan to send to the stockholders of this Company the following letter prepared by the President, announcing the liquidation, together with a letter to "X" & Co., and that it does hereby approve the form of receipt for the certificate:

Form of Letter Announcing Liquidation

...., 19..

Dear Sir:

The property of the Company has, pursuant to authority given at the stockholders' meeting held ...., 19.., been sold to the "B" Company for ..... ($.....) Dollars cash. Part of this amount has already been paid, and the balance is secured by bonds deposited with "X" & Co. as Trustee.

The Board of Directors has resolved that out of this sum there shall be distributed to the stockholders of record on the Company's books, in liquidation of the Company's affairs, as a first payment, the sum of ..... ($.....) Dollars per share, on presentation of the certificate of stock to "X" & Co., ... City, ... In order that the amounts now and hereafter to be paid may be noted thereon as made, please forward immediately your certificate of stock, with power of attorney properly signed and indorsed to "X" & Co., ... City, ...

Further distributions will be made from time to time as the balance of the purchase price is paid. These distributions should also be noted on the certificate. We therefore recommend that you authorize "X" & Co. to retain your certificate for this purpose and enclose a form of letter, to be filled in and signed by you to that effect. On receipt of the certificate of stock and the letter, "X" & Co. will give you a proper receipt.

Yours truly,
"A" Company
....
President

Form of Transmittal Letter

...., 19..

"X" & Co.
...., ...
Gentlemen:

In accordance with the instructions of the Company in its circular letter of ...., 19.., I herewith enclose certificates Nos. ..... and ..... for ..... (.....) shares of the capital stock of the "A" Company, the property of the undersigned, in order that payment of ..... ($.....) Dollars per share in liquidation, now authorized, may be noted thereon. You may retain the same in order that subsequent payments, in liquidation, may be noted on them as made.

Please acknowledge and forward receipt for the enclosed certificate, as mentioned in the Company's letter.

Yours very truly,

. . . .

Form of Receipt

RECEIVED, on . . . ., 19. ., from . . . ., certificate No. . . . . . for . . . . . (. . . . .) shares of the capital stock of the "A" Company standing in the name of . . . ., to be retained on deposit by the undersigned, in order that payments in distribution made on account of the liquidation of the affairs of the Company may be noted thereon, in accordance with the terms of the circular letter from the Company to its stockholders under date of . . . ., 19. ., and with the terms of the letter addressed to the undersigned by you, dated . . . ., 19. .

"X" & Co.

RESOLUTION OF STOCKHOLDERS AUTHORIZING SALE OF STOCK RECEIVED IN PAYMENT FOR SALE OF CORPORATE ASSETS, FOR CASH

WHEREAS, this Company has heretofore sold, transferred, conveyed, and disposed of all its assets to the "X" Company of . . . ., and has received in payment therefor certain of the fully paid, first preferred, second preferred, and common no par value shares of stock of said Company, which shares are now owned by this Company and held in its treasury, and

WHEREAS, this Company has received a written offer from . . . . Company, investment bankers, a corporation organized under the laws of the State of . . . ., to purchase . . . . . (. . . . .) shares of said first preferred stock at . . . . . ($. . . . .) Dollars per share and . . . . . (. . . . .) shares of said second preferred stock at . . . . . ($. . . . .) Dollars per share, said payments, however, to include, cover, and pay for . . . . . (. . . . .) shares of the said common no par value stock, and

WHEREAS, it is the opinion of those present at this meeting that it is for the best interests of this Company to accept said offer of said . . . . Company, be it

RESOLVED, That said offer of the said . . . . Company is hereby accepted, and that the officers of this Company are hereby authorized, instructed, and directed to do everything reasonably necessary and proper to carry out, bring about, or perfect said sale and transfer.

DIRECTORS' RESOLUTION AUTHORIZING DISTRIBUTION OF STOCK RECEIVED UPON SALE OF ASSETS

RESOLVED, That a dividend of the . . . . . (. . . . .) shares of the . . . . Corporation's stock, received as the purchase price for this

Company's real and personal property, is hereby declared; that the same be paid on the basis of ..... (.....) shares of said .... Corporation's stock for every ..... (.....) shares of this Company's stock; and that said dividend be paid by the Secretary to the stockholders of this Company pro rata according to their holdings as shown by the books of the Company, upon delivery by said stockholders to the Secretary of this Company, for cancellation, of all their certificates of stock in this Company, properly indorsed.

DIRECTORS' RESOLUTION AUTHORIZING PAYMENT FROM SURPLUS AS PART OF TOTAL AMOUNT TO BE PAID TO STOCKHOLDERS BY REASON OF SALE OF CORPORATION'S PROPERTY

WHEREAS, This Corporation has sold to the .... Company all of its property and assets except cash on hand and its claim or claims against the United States Government for a refund of taxes, and this Corporation has agreed to liquidate its affairs and to dissolve, and

WHEREAS, it is estimated that the sum paid by the .... Company for the property and assets of the Corporation, together with cash on hand and other assets, will be sufficient to pay all holders of the non par value common stock of the Corporation not less than eighty ($80) Dollars per share, and

WHEREAS, the Board of Directors of the Corporation has called a meeting of the stockholders, to be held ...., 19.., at ....M., to consider the question of the final dissolution of the Corporation and the distribution of its cash and the proceeds derived from its property and assets, after the payment of its debts, to its stockholders, and

WHEREAS, the Corporation now has on hand earned surplus and undivided profits sufficient to distribute therefrom, to each holder of shares of said no par value common stock, the sum of twenty-five ($25) Dollars, and

WHEREAS, the Board of Directors in its judgment deems it advisable and beneficial for the Corporation that such distribution be made as a part payment of the total sum to be paid to the holders of such stock by reason of the sale of the property and assets of the Corporation to the .... Company and the dissolution of the Corporation, be it

RESOLVED, That the Corporation distribute to the holders of its no par value common stock, from its earned surplus, the sum of twenty-five ($25) Dollars per share for each and every share thereof, upon condition, however, that such distribution shall constitute a part of the payment to be made to the holders of the no par value common stock of the Corporation by reason of the sale of its property and assets to the .... Company and the dissolution of the Corporation, and

RESOLVED FURTHER, That the President and Secretary of the Corporation prepare and mail to each holder of the no par value common stock of the Corporation at his or her last known place of residence, a written or printed notice stating the distribution to be made to the holders of such stock, and requesting such stockholders to forward their stock to the Corporation or to a specified bank or agent in the City of ...., ..., in order that it may be properly indorsed when payment is made, and

RESOLVED FURTHER, That all payments made to the stockholders by virtue hereof shall be a part of the total amount to be paid to such stockholders by reason of the sale of the property and assets of the Corporation, from which, together with cash on hand and the proceeds from other assets of the Corporation, it is estimated that the holders of no par value common stock will ultimately receive not less than eighty ($80) Dollars per share for each and every share of such stock; and that no payment shall be made to any person or persons except stockholders of record at the time or times payments are actually made, unless and until the certificate or certificates evidencing such stock ownership shall be presented to the Corporation, in order that proper indorsement of such payment or payments may be made thereon, and

RESOLVED FURTHER, That the President and Secretary of the Corporation are hereby authorized and directed to pay, or cause to be paid, to the holders of the no par value common stock of the Corporation, from its earned surplus, the sum of twenty-five ($25) Dollars per share, by reason of the distribution hereby ordered, when and not until the certificate or certificates evidencing such stock shall be presented to the Corporation and indorsed as follows:

There has been paid upon this certificate the sum of twenty-five ($25) Dollars for each and every share of no par value common stock of .... Corporation evidenced by such certificate, pursuant to a distribution ordered by the Board of Directors of said Corporation on ...., 19.., said distribution being a part of the total sum to be paid to the holders of common stock by reason of the sale of the Corporation's properties and assets to the .... Company and the final dissolution of the Corporation.

.... Corporation
By ....
Secretary-Treasurer.

NOTICE TO STOCKHOLDERS THAT STOCK RECEIVED UPON SALE OF ALL ASSETS OF THE COMPANY IS AVAILABLE FOR DISTRIBUTION AS FINAL DIVIDEND IN LIQUIDATION

To the Stockholders of .... Corporation:

At a special meeting of the stockholders of .... Corporation, held on ...., 19.., it was voted to accept the offer of .... Company to purchase the assets of .... Corporation.

In accordance with the terms of said offer, the assets of . . . .
Corporation have been transferred, and . . . . . shares of stock of . . . .
Company are available for stockholders of . . . . Corporation upon
surrender of their certificates representing shares of . . . . Corporation
stock now outstanding. Each stockholder of . . . . Corporation is
entitled to . . . . . shares of . . . . Company stock for each share of
. . . . Corporation stock held by him.

At adjourned meetings of the stockholders and directors of . . . .
Corporation, held on . . . ., 19. ., it was voted that the . . . . . shares of
. . . . Company be distributed as a final dividend in liquidation to
stockholders of . . . . Corporation of record on the books of the
Company at the close of business on . . . ., 19. .

Stockholders are now requested to forward their . . . . Corporation stock certificates, *properly indorsed,* for surrender and cancellation to
. . . . Corporation, ... (*address*).

Forthwith upon such receipt of . . . . Corporation stock certificates, but not prior to . . . ., 19. ., stock of . . . . Company will be
mailed to you.

Stock transfer stamps are not required unless stockholders of record
. . . ., 19. ., have assigned their interest.

. . . . Corporation

By . . . .

Treasurer

LEASE OF ASSETS

EXCERPT OF MINUTES OF MEETING OF DIRECTORS OF LESSOR, APPROVING FORM OF, AND AUTHORIZING OFFICERS TO EXECUTE AND DELIVER, LEASE

The Chairman referred to the special meeting of the Common and
Preferred Stockholders held on . . . ., 19. ., at which the Stockholders had
assented to this Company's leasing of its business and certain of its assets to
the "B" Company, and had empowered and directed this Board to take action
in connection therewith. He presented to the meeting the form of lease from
this Company to the "B" Company that had been presented to and approved
by the special Stockholders' meeting above referred to.

On motion duly made and seconded, the following preambles and
resolutions were unanimously adopted:

WHEREAS, the Stockholders of this Company at their special meeting
held on . . . ., 19. ., assented to the making of a lease by this Company of
its business and the assets, set forth in a form of lease presented to their
meeting, to the "B" Company, for the term of 99 years commencing at
midnight, December 31, 19. ., and empowered and directed this Board to
authorize and cause certain officers of this Company to execute, acknowledge,

and deliver a lease in the form presented to that meeting, or with limited changes therein considered advisable or appropriate by this Board or the officers executing such lease, and

WHEREAS, this Board deems it advisable and in the interest of this Company that such lease be consummated and carried into effect, be it

RESOLVED, That the form of lease presented to this meeting of the business and the therein-described assets of this Company to the "B" Company, for the term of 99 years commencing at midnight, December 31, 19.., in consideration, among other things, of a rental of ..... ($.....) Dollars per annum, plus the payment of taxes and insurance on the leased property, is hereby approved; and that the President or any Vice president, and the Secretary or an Assistant Secretary are hereby authorized and directed in behalf of this Company to execute, acknowledge, and deliver a lease in the form presented to this meeting, or with such additions thereto, omissions therefrom, or other changes therein as may be within the general purposes and intent expressed in the form of lease presented to this meeting, and as do not change the duration of the lease or decrease the rental below ..... ($.....) Dollars per annum, plus the payment of taxes and insurance on the leased property included therein, as the officers executing such lease shall consider advisable or appropriate; and such execution shall be conclusive evidence of such advisability or appropriateness, and

RESOLVED FURTHER, That any and all officers of this Company are hereby, and each of them hereby is, authorized and directed to do or cause to be done all such acts and things as may be necessary or advisable or convenient and proper in connection with the execution and delivery of the lease authorized at this meeting and in connection with or incidental to the consummation and carrying into effect during its full term of the lease so made, including, without limitation on the scope of the foregoing, the execution, acknowledgment, and delivery of any and all instruments and documents that reasonably may be required of this Company under such lease or may be considered supplemental thereto.

MINUTES OF DIRECTORS' MEETING RATIFYING ACTS OF OFFICERS IN EXECUTING AND DELIVERING LEASE

...., 19..

The President reported that on ...., 19.., pursuant to action taken by the stockholders of this Company at a special meeting of the stockholders held on ...., 19.., and pursuant to authority given by this Board at a meeting held on ...., 19.., the officers of this Company had executed and delivered to the "B" Company a 99-Year lease of the business and certain of the assets of this Company, and, pursuant to said lease, had delivered possession of the property included therein.

On motion duly made and seconded, it was unanimously

RESOLVED, That the acts of the officers of this Company in executing and delivering to the "B" Company said 99-Year lease and in delivering possession of the property included therein, are hereby approved, ratified, and confirmed.

RESOLUTION OF DIRECTORS (OR STOCKHOLDERS) AUTHORIZING EXECUTION OF LEASE OF PLANTS TO ANOTHER COMPANY

RESOLVED, That the officers of this Corporation are hereby authorized and directed to lease to the .... Co., ... plants Nos. 2, 3, and 4, at an annual rental of 80 percent of the net income of said .... Co., after it shall have paid all taxes and expenses in the maintenance and operation of all its plants, and after it shall have set aside, out of its profits, the quarterly sum of ..... ($.....) Dollars, for its own use, which said lease shall be in the form presented to this meeting and hereto appended.

(Insert copy of lease)

RESOLUTION OF STOCKHOLDERS OF LESSOR AUTHORIZING LEASE OF RAILROAD PROPERTY FOR 999 YEARS

RESOLVED, That the "B" Railway Company does lease its railroad, property, and franchises to the "A" Railroad Company, for the term of nine hundred and ninety-nine (999) years from ...., 19.., upon the terms and conditions set forth in the form of indenture of lease now submitted to this meeting, which form is hereby adopted and approved; that the President of the "B" Railway Company is hereby authorized and directed, for and in behalf of the "B" Railway Company, for and as its act and deed, to affix its corporate seal to the said indenture of lease, to sign the same as such President, to cause the same to be duly attested by the Secretary, and also to cause the said indenture of lease to be signed by any two directors and members of the Company other than the President and to be attested by witnesses; and that the President of the "B" Railway Company is hereby authorized and directed, when the said indenture of lease is so executed, to acknowledge the same, to cause the same to be acknowledged, to deliver and record the same, and to do and perform any act, matter, or thing that may be necessary to put the "A" Railroad Company into possession and operation of the railroad, property, and franchises of the "B" Railway Company under the terms of said lease.

(Insert copy of lease)

RESOLUTION OF LESSOR'S DIRECTORS APPROVING LEASE—RENT TO BE FIXED AMOUNT PLUS INSURANCE AND TAXES ON PROPERTY

WHEREAS, the stockholders of this Corporation at their special meeting held ...., 19.., assented to the making of a lease by this Corporation of its business and the assets, set forth in a form of lease presented to their meeting, to the .... Company, for the term of ..... years commencing at midnight, ..., 19.., and empowered and directed this Board to authorize and cause certain officers of this Corporation to execute, acknowledge, and deliver a lease in the form presented to that meeting, or with limited changes therein considered advisable or appropriate by this Board or the officers executing such lease, and

WHEREAS, this Board deems it advisable and in the interest of this Corporation that such lease be consummated and carried into effect, be it

RESOLVED, That the form of lease presented to this meeting of the business and the therein-described assets of this Corporation to the .... Company, for the term of ..... years commencing at midnight, ..., 19.., in consideration, among other things, of a rental of ..... ($.....) Dollars per annum, plus the payment of taxes and insurance on the leased property, is hereby approved; and that the President or any Vice president, and the Secretary or an Assistant Secretary, are hereby authorized and directed in behalf of this Corporation to execute, acknowledge, and deliver a lease in the form presented to this meeting, or with such additions thereto, omissions therefrom, or other changes therein as may be within the general purposes and intent expressed in the form of lease presented to this meeting, and as do not change the duration of the lease or decrease the rental below ..... ($.....) Dollars per annum, plus the payment of taxes and insurance on the leased property included therein, as the officers executing such lease shall consider advisable or appropriate; and such execution shall be conclusive evidence of such advisability or appropriateness; and

RESOLVED FURTHER, That any and all officers of this Corporation are hereby authorized and directed to do or cause to be done all such acts and things as may be necessary or advisable or convenient and proper in connection with the execution and delivery of the lease authorized at this meeting and in connection with or incidental to the consummation and carrying into effect during its full term of the lease so made, including, without limitation on the scope of the foregoing, the execution, acknowledgement, and delivery of any and all instruments and documents that may reasonably be required of this Corporation under such lease or may be considered supplemental thereto.

RESOLUTION OF LESSOR'S DIRECTORS OR STOCKHOLDERS AUTHORIZING EXECUTION OF LEASE— RENTAL BASED ON PERCENTAGE OF INCOME

RESOLVED, That the officers of this Corporation are hereby authorized and directed to lease to the .... Company plants Nos. 2, 3, and 4, at an annual rental of ..... percent of the net income of said .... Company, after it shall have paid all taxes and expenses in the maintenance and operation of all its plants, and after it shall have set aside, out of its profits, the quarterly sum of ..... ($.....) Dollars, for its own use. The lease shall be in the form presented to this meeting.

RESOLUTION OF LESSEE'S DIRECTORS
APPROVING LEASE

RESOLVED, That the lease by the .... Company, Inc., to this Corporation, of its entire properties as this day read, is hereby approved, subject to ratification by the stockholders, and that the President and the Secretary are hereby authorized, empowered, and directed to execute said lease in the name and under the seal of this Corporation substantially in the form as this day read to this Board of Directors, and generally to do all proper acts to carry the same into effect, upon ratification by the stockholders.

RESOLUTION OF LESSEE'S STOCKHOLDERS
RATIFYING LEASE

RESOLVED, That the lease of all the property of the .... Company, Inc., to this Corporation, dated ...., 19.., executed by the Presidents of the parties thereto under the authority of their respective Boards of Directors, which has this day been submitted to this meeting for ratification, is hereby approved.

DIRECTORS' RESOLUTION RATIFYING LEASE MADE
BY OFFICER (FOR USE BY LESSOR OR LESSEE)

RESOLVED, That the Board of Directors hereby confirms the action of its President, ..., in executing the lease of the property located at ...., dated ...., 19.., for the term of ..... (.....) years from ...., 19.., from (to) .... Company to (from) this Corporation, upon the terms mentioned in the lease.

DIRECTORS' RESOLUTION OF LESSOR CONSENTING TO
ASSIGNMENT OF LEASE

WHEREAS, the .... Company, Lessee under an instrument of lease between this Corporation as Lessor and the said .... Company, dated ...., 19.. (and recorded in ....), has requested the consent of this Corporation to an assignment of said lease, be it

RESOLVED, That this Corporation does hereby give and grant its consent to the .... Company for the assignment and transfer of said lease above-mentioned to ...., and the President and the Secretary of this Corporation are hereby authorized, empowered, and directed to prepare and execute, in the name and in behalf of this Corporation and under its corporate seal, a sufficient instrument, as required by the terms of said lease, giving the consent of this Corporation to the said assignment.

DIRECTORS' RESOLUTION OF LESSOR DEMANDING
ACCOUNTING FROM LESSEE

WHEREAS, by agreement of lease, duly executed and dated ...., 19.., this Company leased to ...., as Lessee, all the property of this

Company of whatever kind and wheresoever situated, then owned or that might thereafter be acquired, said property consisting principally of patents, drawings, office furniture, equipment, and all things incident to and necessary in the carrying on of the business of this Company, upon certain terms and conditions as therein set forth, and

WHEREAS, said .... has failed to account for and to pay to this Company the amounts due and owing to it under the terms of said lease, for a period since ...., 19.., and

WHEREAS, the stockholders of this Company have been dissatisfied with the accounts rendered by said .... prior to ...., 19.., under the terms of said lease, by reason of certain unauthorized payments and expenditures, such dissatisfaction having been expressed from time to time as such accounts were rendered, and

WHEREAS, this Company has been dissatisfied with the manner in which the said .... has been conducting said business under the lease agreement above mentioned, be it

RESOLVED, That said ...., as Lessee, under the terms of said agreement, be required to account forthwith to this Company for all dealings, transactions, expenditures, receipts, etc., pertaining to the business conducted by him under the terms of said lease from the date of said lease to the present time, and that he be further required to pay to this Company and to its stockholders, as provided by said agreement, on or before ...., 19.., all amounts found to be due and owing to this Company and to its stockholders, and

RESOLVED FURTHER, That, upon the failure of said .... so to account and pay, on or before ...., 19.., as above set forth, such steps as are necessary be taken to compel the said .... to account and pay as aforesaid, and for this purpose the following stockholders—namely, ..., ..., and ....—are hereby appointed a committee with full power to act in behalf of this Company and to take such steps as may be necessary to carry this resolution into effect, and

RESOLVED FURTHER, That the Secretary of this Company is hereby instructed to mail forthwith to said ...., by registered mail, directed to his business office at ...., a true and correct copy of this resolution, and

RESOLVED FURTHER, That the Secretary of this Company is hereby instructed to give formal notice to said ...., Lessee, of the action of this Board, and to make formal demand upon him for the accounting and the payment of the moneys due in accordance with the provisions of the above resolution.

RESOLUTION OF STOCKHOLDERS OF LESSOR RATIFYING ASSIGNMENT BY LESSEE OF AGREEMENT TO LEASE

WHEREAS, it appears that .... has assigned the agreement to lease, dated ...., 19.., between this Company and himself, to the "A" Company, a corporation organized under the laws of ...., be it

RESOLVED, That said assignment is hereby ratified and confirmed, and that the said "A" Company be hereafter treated as a party of said agreement to lease in place of ....

RESOLUTION OF DIRECTORS OF LESSOR AUTHORIZING NOTICE OF FORFEITURE TO BE SENT TO LESSEE UPON DEFAULT IN PAYMENT

WHEREAS, under an indenture made on ...., 19.., between this Company and the .... Traction Company, a lease was duly executed wherein the .... Traction Company, Lessee, agreed, among other things, to pay a rental or a compensation for the use of the property of this Company, certain amounts representing five (5%) percent of the bonds of the Company, and a dividend of five (5%) percent of the capital stock thereof, and

WHEREAS, under the same indenture, it was provided that, if the Lessee shall make default in the payments of said rental and such default shall continue for a period of thirty days after the time for such payment, it is the right of this Company to declare said lease forfeited and at an end, and if, within thirty days after notice of such intended forfeiture, the Lessee does not make the payments or perform the covenants in regard to which it has so defaulted, then this lease shall be ended and determined, and

WHEREAS, the payment of the semi-annual dividend of two and one-half (2½%) percent on the capital stock due and payable on the ...., 19.., was passed and default was made therein, and said default still exists, be it

RESOLVED, That this Company notify the Lessee that this default was made and still exists, and that, unless payment be made within thirty days from this date, the lease shall be and hereby is declared forfeited and at an end, and this Company shall enter in and retake possession of its property and make claim for such defaulted payments and such other damages as may have been sustained by reason of such lease and forfeiture.

RESOLUTION OF DIRECTORS OF LESSOR AUTHORIZING TERMINATION OF LEASE

WHEREAS, ..., Lessee under an instrument of lease between this Corporation as Lessor and the said ...., dated ...., 19.., relating to the premises at .... (*Street*), City of ...., State of ...., has defaulted in the payment of rent for the months of ..... and ...., 19.., and has defaulted in the performance of other terms and conditions of said lease, be it

RESOLVED, That the President of this Corporation is hereby authorized and directed to instruct . . . ., attorney for this Corporation, to serve a notice upon said . . . . to vacate the premises because of said defaults, and that the President is further authorized and directed to cause suit to be brought, and to take such proceedings as he may deem necessary to obtain possession of the said property and to collect any claims for damages or losses that may have been sustained by this Corporation by reason of said defaults and forfeiture of said lease.

EXCERPT OF MINUTES OF MEETING OF DIRECTORS OF LESSEE, APPROVING FORM OF AND AUTHORIZING OFFICERS TO EXECUTE LEASE

The Chairman referred to the discussions, particularly at the meeting of this Board on . . . ., 19. ., relating to the proposed lease to this Company of the business and certain of the assets of "A" Company, including its plants, equipment, and manufacturing facilities and real estate (with the exception of that located in the States of . . . . and . . . .) and all its brands, trademarks, business, goodwill, and certain other property used in connection with the business, for the term of 99 years commencing at midnight, December 31, 19. ., at an annual rental of . . . . . . ($. . . . .) Dollars, plus the payment of insurance and taxes on the leased property. The Chairman presented to the meeting a form of lease to give effect to the foregoing transaction.

On motion duly made, seconded, and adopted, it was unanimously

RESOLVED, That the form of lease presented to this meeting of the business and the therein-described assets of "A" Company to this Company for the term of 99 years commencing at midnight, December 31, 19. ., be approved; and that the President or any Vice president, and the Secretary or an Assistant Secretary, of this Company are hereby authorized in its behalf to execute, acknowledge, and deliver such lease, either in the forms in which the same has been presented to this meeting or with such additions thereto, omissions therefrom, or other changes therein as the officers executing such instruments shall consider advisable or appropriate; and such execution shall be conclusive evidence of such advisability or appropriateness, and

RESOLVED FURTHER, That any and all of the officers of this Company are hereby, and each of them hereby is, authorized to do or to cause to be done all such further acts and things as they or any of them shall deem necessary or advisable or convenient and proper in connection with the execution and delivery of the lease authorized at this meeting and in connection with or incidental to the consummation and carrying of the same into effect, including without limitation on the scope of the foregoing, the execution, acknowledgment, and delivery of any and all instruments and documents which may reasonably be required of this Company under such lease, or which may be considered supplemental thereto.

EXCERPT OF MINUTES OF MEETING OF DIRECTORS OF SUBSIDIARY COMPANY, AUTHORIZING TAKING OVER FROM PARENT COMPANY OF DEPARTMENT OF A BUSINESS AND CERTAIN ASSETS HELD BY PARENT COMPANY UNDER A LEASE

.... stated that the "B" Company, the sole stockholder of this Corporation, had arranged to lease the business and certain of the assets and to purchase certain other of the assets of the "A" Company, and in that Connection had suggested that this Corporation take over the business (other than the .... and foreign business) and certain of the assets of the .... Department of the "A" Company. He presented a communication to this Corporation from the "B" Company offering to transfer or cause to be transferred to this Corporation certain real estate located in the State of .... and certain other assets as the same would, except for transactions outside the ordinary and normal conduct of business on .... , 19.., be shown on the books of the .... Department of the "A" Company, on the basis of the depreciated cost thereof as so shown on the books of the "A" Company. He also stated that if this Corporation were to take over such business of the .... Department of the "A" Company, it would be advisable for this Corporation to take leases from the "A" Company of certain property located at (*insert list of locations*), and presented the proposed forms of leases to the meeting. He further stated that it would also be desirable for this Corporation to acquire the rights and assume the obligations of the "A" Company under certain contracts or agreements connected with such business of its .... Department, and also the rights and obligations of the "A" Company as tenant under certain leases.

On motion duly made and seconded, it was unanimously.

RESOLVED, That it is advisable and for the best interests of this Corporation that it take over the business (other than the .... and foreign business) of the .... Department of the "A" Company, and

RESOLVED FURTHER, That this Corporation accept the offer made to it by the "B" Company to transfer or cause to be transferred to it certain real estate located in the State of .... and certain other assets as the same would, except for transactions outside the ordinary and normal conduct of business on .... , 19.., be shown on the books of the .... Department of the "A" Company on the basis of the depreciated cost thereof as so shown on the books of the "A" Company, and

RESOLVED FURTHER, That this Corporation lease from the "A" Company its property located at (*insert list of locations*), and to that end execute leases in the forms presented to this meeting, with such additions thereto, omissions therefrom, or other changes therein as the officers executing the same shall consider advisable or appropriate, and

RESOLVED FURTHER, That this Corporation acquire the rights and assume the obligations of the "A" Company under such contracts or agreements connected with the business of its .... Department, and also the rights and obligations of the "A" Company as tenant under such leases, as the officers of this Corporation shall consider necessary or advisable, and

RESOLVED FURTHER, That the officers of this Corporation are hereby authorized, empowered, and directed to execute and deliver such agreements, leases, and other instruments and to do any and all such further acts and things as they, or any of them, shall deem necessary or advisable or convenient and proper in connection with or to effectuate the purpose and intent of the foregoing resolutions.

RESOLUTION OF STOCKHOLDERS RATIFYING LEASE OF RAILROAD TO CORPORATION

RESOLVED, That the lease of the railroad and property of the .... Railroad Co. to this Company, dated ...., 19.., executed by the Presidents of the parties thereto under the authority of their respective Boards of Directors, and this day submitted to this meeting for ratification, be hereby approved.

RESOLUTION OF DIRECTORS OF LESSEE APPROVING LEASE OF ENTIRE PROPERTIES, SUBJECT TO RATIFICATION BY STOCKHOLDERS

RESOLVED, That the lease by the .... Company to this Corporation, of its entire properties as this day read, is hereby approved, subject to ratification by the stockholders, and that the President and the Secretary are hereby authorized, empowered, and directed to execute said lease in the name and under the seal of this Corporation substantially in the form as this day read to this Board of Directors, and generally to do all proper acts to carry the same into effect, upon ratification by the stockholders.

DIRECTORS' RESOLUTION AUTHORIZING COMPANY TO TAKE LEASE OF PREMISES OCCUPIED BY IT

RESOLVED, That this company take a lease from the .... Corporation, of the premises now occupied by this Company at .... (*Street*), City of ...., State of ...., for a term of ..... (.....) years from ...., 19.., in accordance with the terms and conditions set forth and contained in the instrument of lease presented to and read at this meeting; that the President, the Vice president, and the Treasurer are hereby authorized in behalf of the Company to execute and deliver said lease presented at this meeting and a duplicate thereof, and to attach the seal of the Company thereto, and

RESOLVED FURTHER, That the rent to be paid by this Company to the .... Corporation for the use and occupancy of the premises described in the lease received from said .... Corporation, dated .... , 19.., for a period of ..... (.....) years from the said last named date, shall be ..... ($.....) Dollars per annum, payable in advance in installments of ..... ($.....) Dollars per month, the first payment to be made on .... , 19.., and that the President, the Vice president, and the Treasurer of this Company are hereby authorized in behalf of the Company to execute under the corporate seal an agreement to that effect.

DIRECTORS' RESOLUTION AUTHORIZING CORPORATION TO TAKE LEASE OF OFFICES

WHEREAS, an offer has been made to this Corporation to lease to it for a period of ..... (.....) years the offices located on the ..... floor of .... (*Street*), City of ...., State of ...., at a rental of ..... ($.....) Dollars per annum, and

WHEREAS, it is the opinion of this Board of Directors that said offices are suitable for the purposes of this Corporation, and that said rental is reasonable, be it

RESOLVED, That the President of this Corporation is hereby authorized and directed in behalf of this Corporation to execute a lease in duplicate for the offices above mentioned, for a period of ..... (.....) years, beginning on .... , 19.., and continuing up to and including .... , 19.., at a rental of ..... ($.....) Dollars per annum, the said lease to contain the usual covenants set forth in office leases in this city.

DIRECTORS' RESOLUTION AUTHORIZING PRESIDENT TO EXECUTE LEASE AND TO CONTRACT FOR OPTION TO PURCHASE LEASED PROPERTY

RESOLVED, That ...., President of this Corporation, is hereby authorized to lease from the .... Company, for the full term of ..... (.....) years, beginning on .... , 19.., and continuing up to and including .... , 19.., the following property (*insert full description*), and to contract with the .... Company for an option to purchase said property during the calendar year 19.., at such price and subject to such terms and conditions as he shall consider to be for the best interests of this Corporation, and

RESOLVED FURTHER, That said ...., President of this Corporation, is hereby authorized and empowered to sign and execute, in the name of this Corporation, such leasehold agreement and option contract as he may find necessary in carrying out the power above conferred, and to deliver the same for and in behalf of this Corporation.

RESOLUTION OF DIRECTORS OF LESSEE AUTHORIZING
SUBLEASE OF PREMISES

WHEREAS, this Corporation occupies the premises at . . . .
(*Street*), City of . . . ., State of . . . ., under a lease from the
. . . . Company as Lessor, dated . . . ., 19. ., which lease expires on
. . . ., 19. ., and

WHEREAS, said premises have become too small for the business
conducted by this Corporation, and

WHEREAS, an offer has been made to this Corporation by . . . . to
sublease the said premises during the remainder of the unexpired term, at the
rental fixed in said lease between this Corporation and the . . . .
Company, and subject to the covenants, conditions, and stipulations set forth
in said lease, and

WHEREAS, the . . . . Company, Lessor, has given its consent to the
subletting of the premises as aforesaid, be it

RESOLVED, That the offer of . . . . be hereby accepted; that the
Corporation sublease the premises now occupied by it at . . . . (*Street*),
City of . . . ., State of . . . ., under the above-mentioned lease, to
. . . ., from . . . ., 19. ., the termination of said lease—to wit,
. . . ., 19. ., at the same rental and subject to the covenants, conditions,
and stipulations set forth in the instrument of lease between this Corporation
and the . . . . Company, dated . . . ., 19. .; and that the President of
this Corporation is hereby authorized and directed to execute, in the name
and in behalf of this Corporation, an instrument of sublease in the form as
prepared by . . . . Esq., and as this day submitted to the Board of
Directors, and generally to do all things necessary to carry this resolution into
effect.

RESOLUTION OF DIRECTORS OF LESSEE ACCEPTING
SUBLEASE OF PREMISES

WHEREAS, "A" is the lessee of the premises located at . . . .
(*Street*), under a lease from . . . ., owner of said premises, and

WHEREAS, the said "A" has consented to sublease said premises to this
Corporation, be it

RESOLVED, That this Corporation, through its Board of Directors, does
hereby accept from said "A" a sublease, according to the terms mentioned in
the sublease, and does hereby authorize . . . ., President of this
Corporation, to sign and accept said lease for the use and benefit of this
Corporation.

RESOLUTION OF DIRECTORS OF LESSEE AUTHORIZING ASSIGNMENT OF LEASE OF PREMISES

WHEREAS, this Corporation occupies the premises at .... (*Street*), City of ...., State of ...., under a lease from the .... Company as Lessor, for a period of ..... (.....) years from ...., 19.., and

WHEREAS, the rental payable under said lease is considerably less than the current rental for other property in the neighborhood, and the lease has therefore become valuable, and

WHEREAS, it would be profitable for this Corporation to assign and transfer all its right, title, and interest in said lease for a money consideration, and to remove the offices of this Corporation to some other suitable location where rents are lower, and

WHEREAS, ... has offered to accept an assignment of said lease for and during the remainder of the term of ..... (.....) years mentioned in said lease, subject to rents, covenants, conditions, and stipulations therein mentioned, and to pay for the said assignment the sum of ..... ($.....) Dollars, be it

RESOLVED, That the offer of said .... be hereby accepted; and that the President is hereby authorized and directed to execute an instrument, for and in behalf of this Corporation, assigning, transferring, and setting over unto said .... all the right, title, and interest of this Corporation in the lease dated ...., 19.., between the .... Company as Lessor and this Corporation as Lessee (and recorded in ....), subject to rents, covenants, conditions, and stipulations therein contained, and to deliver said instrument of assignment upon receipt from said .... of the sum of ..... ($.....) Dollars.

RESOLUTION OF DIRECTORS OF LESSEE AUTHORIZING SURRENDER OF LEASE OF PREMISES

WHEREAS, this Corporation occupies the premises at .... (*Street*), City of ...., State of ...., under a lease from .... as Lessor, for a period of ..... (.....) years from ...., 19.., and

WHEREAS, said Lessor has offered to pay this Corporation the sum of ..... ($.....) Dollars for the surrender of said lease, and

WHEREAS, it is the opinion of this Board of Directors that said offer should be accepted, be it

RESOLVED, That the offer of said ...., Lessor under an instrument of lease between said .... and this Corporation as Lessee, dated ...., 19.., and expiring on ...., 19.., to pay to this

Corporation the sum of . . . . . ($. . . . .) Dollars for the surrender of said lease, be hereby accepted; that the President of this Corporation is hereby authorized and directed to execute an instrument surrendering and yielding up unto . . . ., the Lessor under said lease, the land and premises demised by said lease, and agreeing to waive any further notice to quit and vacate the premises on or before . . . ., 19. ., and to give full possession thereof to the said . . . .; and that the President hereby is authorized to deliver said instrument upon receipt from said . . . . of the sum of . . . . . ($. . . . .) Dollars.

RESOLUTION OF DIRECTORS OF LESSEE AUTHORIZING OFFICER'S COMPENSATION FOR SECURING LEASE AND PROVIDING CONDITIONAL PAYMENT

WHEREAS, at the request of this Corporation, ... has expended large sums of money and has rendered valuable services to this Corporation outside the line of his employment, in negotiating and securing for this Corporation that certain lease from the . . . . Company to this Corporation dated . . . ., 19. ., and set forth in these minutes on pages . . . . ., ..., and . . . ., and will render further valuable services to this Corporation by securing for this Corporation a continuation of said lease, thereby securing large profits to this Corporation, be it

RESOLVED, That this Corporation do pay said . . . ., as compensation for said services heretofore rendered and hereafter to be rendered, the sum of forty-five thousand ($45,000) Dollars in the manner following—to wit: eleven thousand ($11,000) Dollars forthwith, the further sum of ten thousand ($10,000) Dollars ninety days from this date, the further sum of twelve thousand ($12,000) Dollars five months from this date, and the further sum of twelve thousand ($12,000) Dollars six months from date; provided that, if the earnings of this Corporation shall not be sufficient to make said deferred payments at the respective times above provided, then said deferred payments shall be made to said . . . . when and as the earnings of this Corporation will permit. The President and the Treasurer are hereby authorized and directed to make the payments herein provided and to take receipts therefor as made.

DIRECTORS' RESOLUTION AUTHORIZING SALE AND LEASEBACK OF REAL ESTATE

RESOLVED, That this Corporation sell its real property located in . . . ., which is more particularly described hereinafter, to the . . . . · Company, at a price of not less than . . . . . ($. . . . .) Dollars and not more than . . . . . ($. . . . .) Dollars; that concurrently therewith the Corporation take back a lease thereof from said . . . . Company for a period of twenty-five (25) years at a net annual rental of . . . . . % of such purchase price; and that the proper officers of this Corporation be authorized in behalf of the Corporation to make, execute and deliver such deed, lease and other instruments as may be required or appropriate in connection therewith and to affix the corporate seal of this Corporation thereto. The said real estate is all that lot, tract or parcel of land lying in the City of . . . ., County of . . . ., and State of . . . ., and described as follows:

(Insert description of the property)

RESOLVED FURTHER, That the form of purchase and lease agreement with the form of lease annexed thereto as Exhibit "A" presented to this meeting, a copy of which is attached hereto, is hereby approved with such changes as the officers executing same on behalf of this Corporation may, with the advice of counsel, approve, such approval to be conclusively evidenced by the execution thereof.

(Attach form of agreement and lease)

DIRECTORS' RESOLUTION AUTHORIZING SALE AND LEASEBACK OF REAL PROPERTY (another form)

WHEREAS, this Company has arranged to sell and convey the real estate holdings of this Company in the City of . . . . State of . . . ., exclusive of all buildings, machinery, fixtures, and other improvements thereon, to the . . . . Company, with a view to separating the real estate holdings of this Company in the City of . . . . from its other property and plant, it being the purpose and intention to secure other real estate in or near the City of . . . ., and ultimately to remove the plant of this Company to such new location, and

WHEREAS, prior to . . . ., 19. ., this Company had arranged that the said . . . . Company should have an option on the said real estate holdings in the City of . . . ., at the book value of such holdings as of . . . ., 19. ., and

WHEREAS, the book value of said real estate as of . . . ., 19. ., has been ascertained to be the sum of . . . . . ($. . . . .) Dollars, be it

RESOLVED, That the President and Secretary of this Company are hereby authorized and directed to execute to the . . . . Company, for and in behalf of this Company, a proper deed of conveyance conveying to the said . . . . Company all of the real estate holdings of this Company in the City of . . . ., for the consideration of the said sum of . . . . . ($. . . . .) Dollars, such conveyance to exclude all buildings, machinery, fixtures, and other improvements on the said property, with the right to remove the same within a reasonable time after the expiration of a lease to be made by the said . . . . Company to this Company, and

RESOLVED FURTHER, That this Company be authorized to accept from the said . . . . Company, a lease for the said real estate at an annual rental of . . . . . ($. . . . .) Dollars, plus all taxes accruing against the said property, the payment dates of such rental to be on the first day of each month beginning with ...., 19.., for one month in advance; that such lease extend for a term of one year, and that this Company shall have the option, exercisable on or before ...., 19.., to enter into a lease for a term of ..... years beginning on ...., 19.., if in the Company's judgment appropriate real estate cannot be found elsewhere; and that the lessee be granted the privilege of removing all buildings, machinery, fixtures, and other improvements from the said premises within a reasonable time after the termination of the lease.

Chapter 31

CONSOLIDATION AND MERGER

Contents—Chapter 31

Consolidation or merger. Statutes in every state permit corporations to merge or consolidate. In a merger, one or more corporations are absorbed by another, called the "surviving corporation." The absorbed corporations called the "constituent corporations" go out of existence. In a consolidation, two or more corporations, called the "constituent corporations," create a new corporation called the "consolidated" or "new" corporation. The constituent corporations go out of existence.[1] However, a mere changing of the corporate name does not change a merger into a consolidation if a new corporation is not formed.[2] The merger and consolidation statutes may continue the constituent corporations in existence for limited purposes, for example, to permit creditors to sue them.

Once two corporations merge, they lose the power to rescind the merger and restore the separate identity of each.[3] Also, the merged corporation can no longer sue in its own name.[4] Nor can it be served with process even in a suit to challenge the merger itself—the challenge must be addressed to the surviving corporation.[5]

In most respects the procedure for a merger is like that for a consolidation. However, the distinction can be of some importance to creditors who seek satisfaction of unpaid claims, since the procedure may differ depending on whether there has been a merger or a consolidation.[6]

In every merger a sale of assets is involved.[7] Yet the converse is not true, viz., that in every sale of assets a merger or consolidation is involved.[8] The merger itself is neither a sale nor a liquidation of corporate property, but a melding together of the properties, powers and facilities of the constituent companies.[9]

When there has been a merger, the surviving corporation has the right to bring an action which its subsidiary, now merged into it, had against another company.[10] Similarly, the exclusive remedy provision

---

[1] Damon Alarm Corporation v American District Telegraph Co. (DC, SDNY 1969) 304 F Supp 83; Metropolitan Edison Co. v Commissioner (CA–3 1938) 98 F2d 807, affirmed 306 US 522, 59 S Ct 634; Freeman v Hiznay, (1944) 349 Pa. 89, 36 A2d 509.

[2] Millers National Ins. Co. v Iowa Kemper Mutual Ins. Co. (CA–8 1969) 408 F2d 534.

[3] Opinion of Attorney General to Secretary of State of Washington, 9-29-61.

[4] J. C. Peacock, Inc. v Hasko, (1960) 184 Cal. App. 2d 142, 7 Cal Rptr 490.

[5] Beals v Washington International, Inc. (Del. Ch. 1978) 356 A2d 1156.

[6] Chic., S. F. & C. Ry. Co. v Ashling, (1895) 160 Ill. 373, 43 NE 373; Syracuse L. Co. v Md. Casualty Co., (1919) 226 N.Y. 25, 122 NE 723.

[7] Cole v Nat'l Cash Credit Ass'n, (1931) 18 Del. Ch. 47, 156 Atl 183.

[8] Argenbright v Phoenix Finance Corp., (1936) 21 Del. Ch. 288, 187 Atl 124.

[9] King's Estate, (1944) 349 Pa. 27, 36 A2d 504.

[10] CBS, Inc. v Film Corporation of America (ED Pa 1982) 545 F Supp 1382.

of the state's Workmen's Compensation Act bars an action outside that act against an employer, so that a worker could not sue a corporation that, as a result of a merger, survived under a different name; that corporation was the same entity, not a different entity that a "consolidation" would have created.[11]

Note that a corporation that has been barred from selling to the state because of a conviction for fraud cannot avoid that bar by merging with another corporation—the survivor is likewise barred.[12] Also, the shareholders of a corporation that is contemplating a merger are not the intended beneficiaries of the merger and have no standing to insist that the merger must go through.[13]

Power to consolidate or merge. No matter how desirable or beneficial a combination may be, corporations cannot lawfully consolidate or merge unless the state gives them that authority.[14] The statute granting this authority may be one existing at the time of the organization of the combining corporations, or at the time of the consolidation or merger.[15] Each of the constituent companies must have the power to consolidate.[16] In some states, for example, a domestic corporation may not merge with a foreign corporation.[17] But the merger of two domestic corporations is proper even though the surviving corporation is domiciled in another state.[18]

Unless there is a statute or charter provision prohibiting it, the effect of a statutory merger can be produced by having one corporation buy all the property of another corporation and then having the selling corporation dissolve. Or it can be done by having one corporation buy all the stock of the other corporation. Some courts, though, have taken a dim view of this technique, seeing it a kind of subterfuge—the dissolution statute calls for a dissolution in good faith, they said, and shouldn't be used as a way to effect a consolidation.[19]

Public policy must be considered. Thus, an assignment of an antitrust claim made as part of a merger between New Jersey

---

[11] Handley v Wyandotte Chemicals Corp, (1982) 118 Mich. App. 423, 325 NW 2d 447.

[12] Okla OAG No. 83–250 1-30-84.

[13] Brooks v Land Drilling Co. (D Col. 1983) 564 F Supp 1518.

[14] Personal Credit Plan v Kling, (1941) 130 N.J. Eq. 41, 20 A2d 704; Levin v Mississippi River Fuel Corp. 386 US 162, 87 S Ct 927.

[15] Barnett v D. O. Martin Co., (1940) 191 Ga. 11, 11 SE2d 210; Brundage v New Jersey Zinc Co., (1967) 38 N.J. 450, 226 A2d 585.

[16] Louisville & N. R. Co. v Kentucky, (1896) 161 US 677, 16 S Ct 714; Imperial Trust Co. v Magazine Repeating Razor Co., (1936) 138 N.J. Eq. 20, 46 A2d 449.

[17] Riker & Son Co. v United Drug Co., (1912) 79 N.J. Eq. 580, 82 Atl 930.

[18] OAG Oregon, 7-29-69.

[19] In re Doe Rum Lead Co., (1920) 283 Mo. 646, 223 SW 600.

corporations doing business in New York, with the agreement to be governed by New York law, was void since such an assignment violated New York law against champerty; the merger agreement had to conform to the law of both states.[20]

Procedure in merger or consolidation. The procedure for accomplishing mergers or consolidations is substantially similar, but state statutes vary in detail and should be followed closely. Generally, here are the steps taken:

(1) *Negotiation of an agreement:* The directors of the corporations negotiate an agreement containing: the terms and conditions of the merger or consolidation; the manner of carrying the agreement into effect; and such details as the directors deem necessary to perfect the new organization and to meet the requirements of the statute.

The fact that an agreement failed to mention whether stock to be distributed in a "stock-for-assets swap" would be registered didn't invalidate the agreement.[21]

(2) *Directors' meeting to pass upon transaction:* The directors of each of the companies hold a meeting at which the agreement is approved. Authority is then given to the proper officers to execute the agreement after the stockholders give their approval. Meetings of the stockholders are then called to vote upon the transaction. The statutes generally call for a special meeting of the stockholders, and say that notice of the meeting indicating the time, place, and object of the meeting shall be given in writing to the stockholders a certain number of days before the meeting.

(3) *Stockholders' meeting to approve transaction:* The stockholders of each of the corporations vote at separate meetings of each corporation on a resolution authorizing the transaction and empowering the proper officers to execute and file the articles of merger or consolidation and to take whatever action is necessary to consummate the transaction. In some states, no meeting is necessary if the stockholders give their unanimous written consent.[22]

A corporation whose articles call for consent by a two-thirds vote of each class of stock to increase the number of shares, can enter into a merger agreement that provides for the surviving corporation to have an increased number of shares without first authorizing the change by

---

[20]Koro Co., Inc. v Bristol-Myers Co. (D Cal. 1983) 568 F Supp 280.

[21]Mid-Continent Tel. Corp. v Home Tel. Co. (DC ND Miss. 1970) 319 F Supp 1176.

[22]OAG Ariz., No. 70–3, 12–26–69. Consent was given to merge in accord with article in Paulek v Isgar (Col. App 1976) 551 P2d 213.

class vote; the statutory merger provisions for two-thirds vote of holders of all the stock applies.[23]

A shareholder can't bar a shareholders' meeting called to vote on a merger when (1) it was unlikely he would prevail on the merits, (2) a substantial premium over market price was offered to shareholders electing to participate in the merger, and (3) dissenters were entitled to a full hearing and to appraisal rights.[24]

When a statute requires approval by a two-thirds vote of the outstanding stock voted by class, the fact that the convertible stock could have been changed to common and voted as such did not void that requirement, since the conversion was not made when the vote was taken.[25] Nor will a court grant a preliminary injunction against a vote by a quorum, rather than a full majority of all outstanding shares, when the transaction did not amount to a de facto merger; even if it was, it could be unraveled later.[26]

(4) *Certification of results of meeting.* The consent of the required number of stockholders is certified upon the agreement by the secretary of each of the corporations and the agreement is filed in the office of the secretary of state, or some other place designated by statute. This constitutes the agreement or act of merger or consolidation of the combining corporations. The form that the articles of agreement of certificate of merger or consolidation take depends upon the wording of the statute and the official forms, if any, furnished by the state. Some states require the filing of a statement reciting that action has been taken, accompanied by certified copies of the resolutions adopted at the meetings of the stockholders.

As a procedural matter, the Kentucky Attorney General has ruled that a copy of the articles of merger or consolidation that is given to the county clerk for statutory recording must be returned to the surviving or new corporation after it has been recorded.[27]

(5) *Compliance with other requirements.* Be sure to check whether you must meet any additional requirements. If the surviving or new corporation intends to issue new securities, you may have to register the new issue under the Federal Securities Act, and comply with state securities ("blue sky") laws. In some states, you must publish notice of the consolidation.

---

[23] Moss Estate, Inc. v Metal & Thermit Corp., (1962) 73 N.J. Super. 56, 179 A2d 54.
[24] Weinberger v United Financial Corp. of California (Del. Ch. 1979) 405 A2d 134.
[25] Shidler v All American Life & Financial Corp. (Ia S Ct 1980) 298 NW 2d 318.
[26] Equity Group Holdings v DMG, Inc. (SD Fla 1983) No 83–8612 Civ–SMA 12–16–83.
[27] Ky OAG 83–18 1–12–83.

(6) *Payment of taxes:* State taxes and fees must be paid. Some states provide that a tax is payable only upon the amount of capitalization in excess of the aggregate capitalization of the constituent companies.

(7) *Exchange of securities:* Securities of the constituent companies are exchanged for securities of the surviving or new company, according to the terms of the agreement. And where the acquiring corporation is a subsidiary of another company, it is not improper for stockholders of the acquired corporation to receive stock in the parent company instead of the subsidiary.[28]

Takeovers and tender offers. Tender offers can be simply defined as proposals by one company (the acquiring company) to buy up all or part of the shares of another company (the target company) with the aim of taking the latter over. Such a takeover often will portend the installation of new management—so incumbent management is more than likely to put up a bitter fight to forestall the takeover. Nor is this always for selfish reasons—management may feel it is thereby also protecting the shareholders from measures it fears will hurt them too.

Before 1968, SEC did not regulate cash takeover bids, except that if the acquiring company planned to exchange its shares for those of the target company, the offered securities had to be registered. Congress became concerned about the number of attempted takeovers and the fierce battles that often ensued. So in 1968 it passed the Williams Act, which added new subsections 13d, 14d, 14e and 14f to the Exchange Act of 1934. As later amended, these sections in substance require any person or company that acquires a 5% beneficial ownership of any class of a company's securities to file certain schedules with SEC and the appropriate exchange. These schedules must disclose the potential acquiror's source of funds, the intent of the purchase, any planned changes in the structure of the business if acquired, and the like. The aim of the amendments, its sponsors emphasized, was not to tip the balance in favor of either target or raider. Rather, it was to assure that the tendering stockholders had enough information to make an informed decision on what action they should take in response to the offer. This point was emphasized by the United States Supreme Court in a landmark case denying relief to an unsuccessful tender offeror for alleged misstatements by the target

---

[28] Ia OAG No 13–A Corporations 3–4–70.

company and a competing tender offeror—the statute, said the High Court, was primarily intended for the benefit of the shareholders of the target company, not of tender offerors.[29] Note that a later decision by a district court applied the same reasoning to knock out a suit by a defeated tender offeror, even though this suit was brought not under Section 14, but under the antifraud laws and rules.[30]

The mere fact that two companies considered becoming partners in tender offers didn't mean they were involved in a conspiracy to take over the target company; the talks ended before the tender offer was made, so failure to disclose the plan didn't violate this section.[31] Nor can a target company get a preliminary injunction against a cash tender offeror on the ground that the offeror represented that any stock not purchased or tendered might be delisted, when there was a possibility that many small holders would accept the offer, so that delisting was in fact a distinct possibility.[32] Of course, if no tender offer is in fact made, there is no cause of action under the Williams Act, though there may be a common law claim for breach of fiduciary duty.[33]

What is a tender offer? A mere solicitation to buy shares is not a tender offer (under a state takeover act) when the terms of the offer were negotiable, it was not contingent on the tender of a fixed number of shares, it was not limited in time and there was no pressure to sell the stock.[34] Nor was a letter asking owners of bonds to approve the sale of some collateral supporting the bonds, since there was no offer to sell the bonds themselves.[35]

Does the Williams Act authorize an injunction at the suit of the offeror, if it feels that the takeover is willfully being thwarted by the target company? The United States Supreme Court in the landmark *Chris Craft* case left this question open;[36] but lower courts have given an affirmative answer. For example, courts have barred a target company from selling its authorized but unissued stock to an affiliate when the sole purpose of the sale is allegedly to thwart a possible takeover,[37] and

---

[29]Piper v Chris Craft Industries, (1977) 430 US 1, 97 S Ct 926.

[30]Crane Co. v American Standard, Inc. (DC SD N.Y. 1977) 439 F Supp 945.

[31]Texasgulf v Canada Development Corp. (DC SD Tex 1973) 366 F Supp 374; Staffen v Greenberg (ED Pa 1981) 509 F Supp 825.

[32]Missouri Portland Cement Company v H.K. Porter Company, Inc. (CA–8 1976) 535 F2d 388.

[33]Lewis v McGraw (CA–2 1980) 619 F 2d 192, cert den, (1980) 449 US 951, 101 S Ct 354.

[34]Matter of CTS Corporation (Ind. App. 1981) 428 NE 2d 794.

[35]E.H.I. of Florida, Inc. v Insurance Co. of North America (CA–3 1981) 652 F 2d 310.

[36]Piper v Chris Craft Industries, (1977) 430 US 1, 97 S Ct 926.

[37]Applied Digital Data Systems, Inc. v Milgo Electronic Corp. (DC, SD N.Y. 1977) 425 F Supp 1145.

from trying to sell off the assets and destroy the charter, with that same aim.[38]

Some other cases where the courts have found violations by the target company:

It made statements that the offer was "inadequate" and an attempt to seize control at "bargain prices" when these statements were without material foundation; however the court did not enjoin the target company since the tender offeror had itself been barred from going ahead with the offer.[39]

It granted one tender offeror an irrevocable option to purchase certain corporate stock as well as the target's interest in valuable oil resources if a competing offeror won.[40]

Courts have frequently granted injunctions when the offeror made false or misleading claims. Here are some examples:

(1) A cash tender offer can be enjoined for failure to disclose material information; but the offeror can correct the information and give the target company shareholders the opportunity to rescind their tenders.[41]

(2) A corporation's tender offer containing a material omission as to control persons warrants a preliminary injunction; however, the offeror can cure the deficiencies before the offer is consummated.[42]

(3) A target company can enjoin a tender offer for its shares when the offer fails to disclose merger rights that dissenting shareholders have and fails to disclose prior antitrust litigation, since the target company showed that irreparable harm would result in the form of decline in employee morale and the loss of customer confidence.[43]

(4) Investors of company located in State A can get preliminary injunction barring wholly-owned subsidiary in State B from soliciting tender of company's shares in exchange for its stock when the prospectus allegedly fails to disclose that major result of merger would be surrendering their one vote per share right and getting "scale voting" (one vote per share for first X shares and then one vote for every additional Y shares), invalid in State A, in exchange.[44]

---

[38]Joseph E. Seagram & Sons, Inc. v Abram (SD NY 1981) 510 F Supp 860.

[39]Emhart Corp v USM Corp. (D Mass.) 404 F supp 660.

[40]Mobil Corp. v. Marathon Oil Company (CA-6 1981) 669 F 2d 366. See also Jewel Companies, Inc. v Pay Less Drug Stores Northwest, Inc. (ND Cal. 1981) 510 F Supp 1006; Conoco, Inc. v Seagram Co., Ltd. (SD NY 1981) 517 F Supp 1279.

[41]Sonesta International Hotel Corp. v Wellington Associates (CA-2 1973) 483 F2d 247.

[42]Ronson Corp. v Aktiengesellschaft (CA-3 1973) 483 F2d 846. See also Pabst Brewing Co. v Kalmanowitz (D Del. 1982) 551 F Supp 882.

[43]Boyertown Burial Casket Company v Amedco, Inc. (DC, ED Pa. 1976) 407 F Supp 811.

[44]Blanchette v Providence & Worcester Company (DC, Del. 1977) No. 76–411, 1/17/77.

On the other hand, a court will not enjoin a tender offer when it adequately and accurately informed the target's shareholders of the "control" relationship between the offeror and its parents; there was no showing of irreparable harm to the target.[45] Even if an offeror's SEC filing did not disclose the offeror's intention to take over the target, a court will not enjoin the tender offer when a subsequent filing corrected the omission.[46] Nor will the court enjoin a target corporation from amending its charter to require 80 percent approval for a business combination, since there was no showing of irreparable harm, and damages can be sought later.[47]

The president of a target corporation cannot be held liable on his alleged promise to an unsuccessful tender offeror that it would be given an opportunity to match or increase another offeror's bid, since there was no proof of reliance on the alleged statement.[48]

A successful tender offeror does not have the right to rescind the corporation's sale of treasury stock to the unsuccessful bidder, when there was no showing the sale was in bad faith or was misleading or manipulative.[49]

The fact that a successful tender offeror later sold his shares to a corporation controlled by his uncle does not make the tender offer itself invalid, since there was no reliance on that non-disclosed fact.[50]

Note that purchasers of stock have no duty to disclose details of their offer to target company stockholders who sold their stock before the offer, since the purchasers were not insiders who had any fiduciary duty to the stockholders during preliminary negotiations.[51] Nor did a bank have any duty to return to the stockholders shares it held as depository under a tender offer when the stockholders did not give the guaranteed signatures required under the agreement.[52]

What happens when there has been a failure to disclose and rescission is not practicable? What is the measure of damages? Answer: The difference between the price paid and the actual value of the stock.[53]

---

[45]Gray Drug Stores, Inc. v Simmons (ND Okl. 1981) 522 F Supp 961.

[46]Raybestos-Manhattan, Inc. v Hi-Shear Industries, Inc. (ED NY 1980) 503 F Supp 1122.

[47]FMC Corp. v R.C. Sherer Corp. (D Del 1982) 545 F Supp 318.

[48]Liberty Leather Corp. v Callum (CA-1 1981) 653 F 2d 694.

[49]Buffalo Forge Co. v Ogden Corp. (CA-2 1983) 717 F 2d 757 cert den 104 S Ct 550.

[50]Lynch v Cook, (1983) 148 Cal. App. 3d 1072, 196 Cal. Rptr 544.

[51]Moss v Morgan Stanley, Inc. (CA-2 1983) 719 F 2d 5.

[52]Smith v Mobil Corp. (CA-5 1983) 719 F 2d 1313.

[53]Lynch v Vickers Energy Corp. (Del. S Ct 1981) 429 A 2d 497.

A tender offeror has a wide latitude on how it structures its offer. For example, it can cut off its offer by sending an individual notice to each shareholder saying that its offer is fully subscribed or it can do so by a general public announcement.[54] However, if a particular kind of notice is promised, it must be given.[55] And sometimes, too, direct notice may be required when that's needed for the protection of unsophisticated investors.[56]

But it was not only the federal government that regulated tender offers. Concerned about takeovers in companies within their own boundaries, many states adopted statutes aimed at hindering corporate takeovers. For example, Virginia[57] and Nevada[58] adopted legislation closely paralleling the Williams Act, but providing for advance notice of an intended tender offer. Ohio[59] adopted a highly restrictive statute—it calls for extensive information to be filed with the Division twenty days in advance of the commencement of the tender offer; also the Division may on its own initiative or at the request of the target company order hearings on the adequacy of the disclosures proposed to be made to the shareholders of the target company.

Many of these laws, however, must now be considered invalid. In a landmark case, the United States Supreme Court struck down the Illinois Takeover Law. It was, the court said, unconstitutional under the Supremacy Clause because the act interfered with Congress' objectives and therefore was preempted by the Supremacy Clause in these areas: (1) the "precommencement notification" provision frustrated Congressional intent to strike a balance between investor, management, and offeror; (2) the hearing requirement introduced extended delay in the take-over process since there wasn't any deadline for completion of the hearing; and (3) the requirement that the Secretary of State pass on the substantive fairness of a takeover frustrated the Congressional intent to have the investor make his own decisions. The law was also found unconstitutional under the Commerce Clause because it directly regulated and could prevent interstate tender offers and the burden it imposed on interstate

---

[54]The Indiana Nat'l Bank v Mobil Oil Corporation (CA–7 1978) No. IP 75–195C, 6/19/78. See also: Kroeze v Chloride Group, Ltd. (CA–5 1978) 572 F2d 1099; Peterson v Federated Development Co. (DC SD N.Y. 1976) 416 F Supp 466.

[55]Becke & Co. v International Controls Corp. (DC SD N.Y. 1971) 324 F Supp 998 aff. (CA–2 1972) 409 F2d 696.

[56]Van Gemert v Boeing Co. (CA–2 1975) 520 F2d 1373, cert den, (1975) 423 US 947.

[57]S.C.A. §13.1–528 et seq.

[58]G.C.L. §78–346 et seq.

[59]G.C.L. §1707.041.

commerce was excessive compared to the local interest the act was supposed to further.[60]

"Short merger." The term "short merger" refers to the abridged procedure for merging parent and subsidiary corporations sanctioned by the statutes of some states. Under these statutes, a parent can merge into itself a wholly-owned or, in some states a largely owned, subsidiary without the consent of the stockholders of either corporation. In most states, the directors of the parent simply adopt a resolution containing the plan of merger and assuming the subsidiary's obligations. In some states, the directors of both corporations must approve the merger.

The statutes vary on procedural details, such as filing procedures, notice to stockholders, and the effective date of the merger.

Short merger statutes are not an unconstitutional interference with the rights of minority stockholders of the subsidiary.[61] The minority can be compelled to take cash for their shares; they do not have a vested right to a continuation of their investment.[62] One state court has held the merger can't be set aside for fraud.[63]

Dissenting minority stockholders in the subsidiary have the right to payment for their shares,[64] but normally must make a demand before they will be entitled to an appraisal.[65] Dissenting stockholders in the parent do not have the right to payment when the merger is with a wholly-owned subsidiary, unless the charter is amended or new stock is issued.

Once the majority has enough stock to carry through a short-form merger, must it justify the merger by showing a "business purpose"? Most courts seem to say that it doesn't have to, that the minority gets all it is entitled to when it is accorded its appraisal rights.[66] However, a New York court did grant the state Attorney General a right to bar a merger when he showed there was no real corporate purpose for the merger other than the reacquisition of

---

[60]Edgar v Mite Corporation, (1982) 457 US 624, 102 S Ct 2629, 73 L Ed 2d 269.

[61]Alpren v Consolidated Edison Co., (1938) 168 Misc. 381, 5 N.Y.S.2d 254.

[62]Coyne v Park & Tilford Distillers Corp., (1959) 38 Del. Ch. 514, 154 A2d 893; Bove v Community Hotel Corp. of Newport, (1969) 105 R.I. 36, 249, A2d 89.

[63]Stauffer v Standard Brands, Inc., (1962) 41 Del. Ch. 7, 187, A2d 78.

[64]Joseph v Wallace-Murray Corp., (1968) 354 Mass. 477, 238 NE2d 360.

[65]Carl Marks & Co. v Universal City Studios, Inc. (S Ct Del. 1967) 233 A2d 63.

[66]Beloff v Consolidated Edison Co., (1949) 300 N.Y. 11, 87 NE2d 569; Willcox v Stern, (1966) 18 N.Y. 2d 195, 273 NYS2d 38, 219 NE2d 401; David J. Greene & Co. v Schenley Industries, Inc. (Del. Ch. 1971) 281 A2d 30.

control by the original insiders, to their great profit.[67] Other states also seem to be tending in this direction.[68]

Even when a freeze out ordinarily would be a breach of majority's duty to the minority, when the minority was an employee who was to return his stock to the corporation when he left, and he did leave, there was no fiduciary duty to him.[69] Also, a deal under which investors first bought 92.6 percent of the shares, then another 5 percent by a tender offer and the rest by a short-form merger did not amount to a sale of all the assets requiring approval by the board and a vote by shareholders, even though that may have been its effect.[70]

If the majority does have to show a business purpose, when does it meet that burden?

(1) When it shows that the aim of the merger is to combine management and resources and to remove certain restrictions on intercompany transactions.[71]

(2) When it shows that the aim is to achieve economies by centralized procurement of raw materials; joint distributions, warehousing and marketing; greater diversity of products so as to even out cyclical demands; and a strengthened financial position.[72]

(3) When it shows it wanted to eliminate a minority stockholder whose main interest was short-term profits, as against the growth objectives of the majority.[73]

Note that under Delaware law a short-form merger cuts off a stockholder's right to continue a pending derivative action, when there's no taint of fraud or illegality.[74] Also a diversity action brought in New York but based on Delaware's short-form merger is governed by New York's six-year statute as to fraud claims and its three-year statute for breach of fiduciary duty.[75]

These cases arose under state law. Some minority shareholders attempted to stymie short-form mergers by claiming they violated the antifraud provisions of the securities laws. The United States Supreme Court refused to go along. It said that even if a short-form merger had

---

[67] People v Concord Fabrics, Inc., (1975) 83 Misc. 2d 120, 371 N.Y.S.2d 550, aff'd 50 A.D. 2d 787, 377 N.Y.S.2d 84.

[68] Roland International Corp. v Napper (Del. S Ct 1979) 153–1978, 8-6-79.

[69] Coleman v Taub (CA-3 1981) 638 F 2d 628.

[70] Field v Alleyn (Del. Ch 1983) 457 A 2d 1089 aff (Del. S Ct 1983) 467 A 2d 1274.

[71] Schulwolf v Cerro Corp., (1976) 86 Misc. 2d 292, 380 N.Y.S. 2d 957.

[72] Tanzer Ec. Assoc., Etc. v Universal Food Sp., (1976) 87 Misc. 2d 167, 383 N.Y.S. 2d 472 (Me. law).

[73] Cross v Communications Channels, Inc., (1982) 116 Misc 2d 1019, 456 NYS 2d 971.

[74] Rubinstein v Catacosinos, (1983) 91 A D 2d 445, 459 NYS 2d 286.

[75] Loengard v Santa Fe Industries, Inc. (SD NY 1983) 573 F Supp 1355.

no business purpose and was aimed solely at "freezing out" the minority, that did not amount to a deceptive or manipulative device that violated the antifraud law and rules; further, the court said, it was reluctant to interfere in state policies on corporate regulation.[76]

De facto mergers. Under merger statutes, stockholders dissenting from the merger must be paid for their shares. So if the corporation doesn't have enough cash to pay them, the merger can't go through. To avoid this result, corporations sometimes try to accomplish what is in fact a merger by having one corporation sell all its assets to the other in exchange for stock in the other, followed by a dissolution of the selling corporation. (Although the dissenting stockholders in a corporation that *sells* all its assets can get payment for their shares, the dissenters in the *buying* corporation usually can't.) Here's an example of how it works:

> Holding Corp. wants to take over Manufacturing Corp. But if the statutory merger procedure is followed, there won't be enough cash to pay the dissenting stockholders in Manufacturing Corp.
> So Holding Corp. and Manufacturing Corp. agree that Manufacturing will *buy all the assets* of Holding Corp. in exchange for stock in Manufacturing; that Holding will then distribute the stock to its stockholders and dissolve. Manufacturing gives Holding enough of its stock so that Holding's stockholders become the majority stockholders in Manufacturing. Result: A merger, in practical effect.
> However, since Manufacturing *bought* the assets of Holding, Manufacturing's dissenting stockholders can't get payment for their shares.

That technique may not always work. For example, in one case with similar facts, the court enjoined the transaction, called it a merger in fact. It said since Manufacturing Corp.'s stockholders were not notified of their right to dissent and be paid, their approval of the transaction was void.[77] And in another similar case, the directors of Manufacturing were held personally liable to the corporation for $118,000 damages for waste of funds spent in preparing the merger and in defending the litigation.[78]

---

[76]Santa Fe Industries v Green, (1977) 430 US 462, 97 S Ct 1292. See also Marshel v AFW Fabric Corp., (1977) 429 US 881, 97 S.C. 228, remanded and dismissed as moot (CA–2 1977) 552 F2d 471.

[77]Farris v Glen Alden Corp., (1958) 393 Pa. 427, 143 A2d 25; Bloch v Baldwin Locomotive Works, (1951) 75 Pa. D. & C. 24.

[78]Gilbert v Burnside (S Ct 1959) 197 N.Y.S.2d 623.

However, the cases aren't uniform. Thus another court said that a corporation's purchase of all the assets of another corporation in exchange for stock isn't a de facto merger, though the sale agreement required the selling corporation to dissolve and distribute the buying corporation's stock.[79] But a so-called "reorganization plan" having the approval of a shareholder majority may be enjoined by a stockholder if it really amounts to a merger requiring two-thirds approval.[80]

When the buying company (1) assumes all contractual liabilities of the seller, (2) absolves its officers, directors and personnel, and (3) gives shares of stock in surviving company as payment, that amounts to a merger; the buyer can be liable for sellers alleged fraud even though it has disclaimed tort liability in the purchase agreement.[81]

More and more states are denying appraisals to stockholders of corporations the shares of which are listed on a national stock exchange. *Reason:* The value of the shares is easily ascertainable— there's a constant market.

Important questions can arise as to when a transaction amounts to a merger, say so as to trigger the right to an appraisal. For example, a partnership arrangement between corporations with interlocking directorates and controlled by the same family was held to be a de facto merger when the management, sales and bookkeeping functions of the corporate partnership were unified under the directors of the partnership; minority stockholders of a constituent corporation were entitled to an appraisal.[82]

Rights given by statute to dissenting stockholders. Statutes in almost every state (so-called appraisal statutes) give stockholders[83] who dissent from certain corporate transactions the right to be paid[84] for their shares. Most states give this right to dissenters from a merger

---

[79]Hariton v Arco Electronics Inc. (Del. St Ct 1963) 188 A2d 123; Applestein v United Board and Carton Corp., (1960) 331 N.J. 72, 161 A2d 474. See also Orzeck v Englehart (Del. Ch. Ct 1963) 192 A2d 36.

[80]Rath v Rath Packing Co., (1965) 257 Iowa 1277 136 NW2d 410.

[81]Western Resources Life Ins. Co. v Gibhardt (Tex. Civ. App. 1977) 553 SW2d 783.

[82]Pratt v Ballmen-Cummings Furniture Co. (Ark. S Ct 1977) 549 SW2d 270.

[83] As to who are stockholders, see Lewis v Corroon & Reynolds Corp., (1948) 30 Del. Ch. 200, 57 A2d 632; Salt Dome Oil Corp. v Schenck, (1945) 28 Del. Ch. 433, 41 A2d 583, (1944) 28 Del. Ch. 54, 37 A2d 64; Era Co. Ltd. v. Pittsburgh Consolidated Coal Co., (1946) Pa. 49 A2d 332; Martin v Same, (1946) 355 Pa. 223, 49 A2d 344.

As to choice of statutory remedies given stockholders, see Anderson v Int. Min. & Chemical Corp., (1946) 295 N.Y. 343, NE2d 573.

[84]Chicago Corp. v Munds, (1934) 20 Del. Ch. 142, 172 Atl 452; Ahlevius v Bunn & Humphreys, Inc., (1934) 358 Ill. 155, 192 NE 824; American General Corp. v Camp, (1937) 171 Md. 629, 190 Atl 225.

or consolidation, a lesser number to dissenters from a sale of assets, with only a small number giving this right to dissenters from such things as an extension of corporate existence. The statutes vary as to the procedure[85] to be followed by the dissenting stockholders to obtain payment, the time in which demand for payment must be made, the manner of making the demand,[86] the method of appointing appraisers[87] or a commission to determine the value of each stockholder's distributive share,[88] and the procedure to be followed in case of disagreement as to the value of the shares.

Here are some examples of how courts have interpreted statutes that prescribe a procedure to be followed by dissenting stockholders who want payment for their shares:

(1) Court will not let a stockholder dissenting from a sale of the entire assets have his stock appraised if he bought it after the directors had approved the sale and publicized that fact.[89]

(2) Dissenters can have appraisal even though they made their demand through an agent who did not show his authority to the corporation, when they later confirmed the agency by complying with the corporation's request to surrender their shares.[90]

(3) Beneficial owner of stock registered in a broker's name can't sue for an appraisal of the stock upon dissenting from a merger; only the registered owner can sue.[91]

(4) Dissenting stockholder's right to payment is lost for want of written dissent when a brokerage firm, as the record owner of stock owned by the dissenter, sends in a proxy but in its letter of transmittal says only that (a) the proxy is a dissenting one and (b) it reflects the customer's instructions.[92]

---

[85] Milner v Van Higgins, (1933) 227 Ala. 333, 149, So. 872; In re Standard Coated Products Corp., (1944) 183 Misc. 736, 50 N.Y.S.2d 521; Apartment Properties, Inc. v Luley, (1969) 252 Ind. 201, 247 NE2d 71, 74.

[86] Zeeb v Atlas Powder Co., (1952) 32 Del. 486, 87 A2d 123.

[87] Meade v Pacific Gamble Robinson Co., (1944) 21 Wash. 2d 866, 153 P2d 686, c.c., Grant v Pacific Gamble Robinson Co., (1944) 22 Wash. 2d 65, 154 P2d 301 (Wash. state court held without power to appoint third appraiser under Del. statute).

[88] Scott v Arden Farms Co., (1942) Del. Ch., 28 A2d 81; Roselle Park Trust Co. v Ward Baking Corp., (1939) 177 Md. 212, 9 A2d 228.

[89] Matter of Corwin (S Ct 1960) 199 N.Y.S.2d 866.

[90] Clarke v Rockwood & Co., (1959) 110 Ohio App. 38, 168 NE2d 592.

[91] Raynor v LTV Aerospace Corp. (Del. Ch. 1975) 331 A2d 393; Dollard v Barker Bros. Corp. (Circuit Ct 1959) Balto. Daily Rec. 4–28–59. Contra: Bohrer v US Lines Co., (1966) 92 N.J. Super 592, 224 A2d 348; Raab v Villager Industries, Inc. (Del. 1976) 355 A2d 888 (corporation knew of record owner's intent to dissent); Matter of Bowman (N.Y. 1978) 98 Misc.2d 1028.

[92] F.S. Mosely & Co. v Midland-Ross Corp. (Del. S Ct 1962) 179 A2d 295.

(5) Dissenting shareholder who has begun appraisal proceedings does not thereby waive his right to examine corporation records.[93]

(6) Dissenters from a corporate recapitalization can refuse the corporation's appraisal offer, even if the value set by an outside appraiser is not materially greater than the corporation's offer, so long as the refusal is in good faith.[94]

(7) A dissenting shareholder cannot sue for payment of shares when the corporation has not taken any of the proposed actions the dissenter objected to; nor does the dissenter's dismissal as officer, director, and employee entitle her to relief.[95]

(8) Dissenting shareholders to a merger can file a petition for appraisal in the county where the survivor's registered office was located, when the survivor has not filed required valuation petitions nor told dissenters that there had been a change in the registered office.[96]

(9) Dissenters to a merger cannot get payment of an advance on the value of their shares pending a formal appraisal on the basis (a) of mere conjecture that the surviving corporation won't ultimately be able to pay or (b) that they should not have to subsidize the corporation while the appraisal goes on.[97]

(10) A dissenter to a merger cannot have his appraisal rights determined within the 20-day period allowed corporations to begin an action to determine the rights of all dissenters; he remains a dissenter though the corporation questions his appraisal rights within that period, and as a dissenter, his right to petition the court for an appraisal runs for 30 days after that 20-day period.[98]

(11) Dissenter from merger could not get payment for lost option rights, since the sole issue in statutory appraisal is the value of merged corporation's stock; he cannot dissent as to only part of his shares.[99]

(12) A surviving corporation could not, by settling at a premium with a handful of dissenting stockholders who filed an appraisal petition, defeat the rights of those other dissenting shareholders who had perfected a right to an appraisal but had not filed individual petitions; only one petition was needed to require a hearing for valuation.[100]

[93] E.I.F.C., Inc. v Atnip (Ky. 1970) 454 SW2d 351.
[94] Lipe-Rollway Corp. v Seligson, (1969) 59 Misc. 2d 805, 300 N.Y.S.2d 478.
[95] Application of Valando, (1971) 67 Misc. 2d 515, 232 N.Y.S.2d 608.
[96] Matter of Hamburg Knitting Mills, Inc. (Com Pls 1971) *Berks County (Pa.) L.J.*
[97] Loeb v Schenley Industries, Inc. (Del. Ch. 1971) 285 A2d 829.
[98] Petition of Gruntal & Co. (S Ct 1972) 328 N.Y.S. 2d 141.
[99] Lichtman v Recognition Equipment Inc. (Del. Ch. 1972) 295 A2d 771.
[100] Raynor v LTV Aerospace Corp. (Del. Ch. 1974) 317 A2d 43.

(13) Pre-vote objection notice signed by one spouse of a pair of joint tenants is enough notice for the corporation and entitles holders to an appraisal; but a pre-vote payment demand by dissenting joint tenants must be signed by both; claimants must prove receipt of written payment demand by the corporation when controverted, but corporate objections to appraisal rights based on mere technicalities of signatures will be rejected.[101]

(14) A dissenting stockholder has an absolute right to an appraisal even though the corporation's offer was for more than the stock was worth and even though the stockholder's purpose was to harass the corporation.[102]

(15) A dissenting stockholder made an election when, after being offered $55 a share, she sent a letter asking for $150, and so could not later sue to block the merger.[103]

(16) Under the Delaware statute, a stockholder who does not accept the merger can petition for appraisal, but after 60 days he cannot withdraw his election and resume his rights as a shareholder without the corporation's consent.[104]

(17) Amending the corporate articles to change its duration from 30 years to perpetual existence is not the kind of change that triggers appraisal rights; there's no violation of the constitution, since limited duration is not a vested right.[105]

(18) Under Pennsylvania law, the stockholders of a parent corporation do not get any appraisal rights when their corporation's wholly-owned subsidiary merges with another corporation.[106]

(19) The violation of a stockholder's preemptive rights does not give rise to any right of appraisal.[107]

(20) A dissenter must actually vote against the merger in order to be paid for his shares; a letter to the corporate secretary objecting to the merger was not enough.[108]

Caution: Statutory appraisal procedures are detailed and technical. A dissenting stockholder should follow them to the letter if he wants to avoid losing his rights for failure in a matter of technique. *Examples:* A dissenter to a merger cannot get an appraisal, when he doesn't file a petition on time though he mails it to the clerk of the

[101] Raab v Villager Industries, Inc. (Del. 1976) 355 A2d 888.
[102] Kaye v Pantone, Inc. (Del. Ch 1978) 395 A 2d 369.
[103] Deutsch v Blue Chip Stamps (Cal. App. 1981) LA Daily Journal 2-27-81 p. 56.
[104] Dofflemeyer v W.F. Hall Printing Co. (Del. S Ct 1981) 432 A 2d 1198.
[105] Miller v Magline, (1981) 106 Mich. App. 413, 306 NW 2d 533.
[106] Terry v Penn Central Corp. (CA-3 1981) 668 F 2d 188.
[107] Breniman v Agricultural Consultants, Inc. (Col. App. 1982) 648 P 2d 165.
[108] Waite v Old Tucson Development Co., (1974) 22 Ariz. App. 517, 528 P 2d 1276.

proper court on the last day allowed under the statute.[109] However, when dissenting stockholders filed the dissent on time, but submitted the certificates 15 days late, they were excused, since there was no prejudice to the corporation from the delay.[110] Note, also, that a corporation discharged its statutory duty when it deposited a notice of dissenters' rights in the mail; the failure to receive the notice did not excuse the dissenters' failure to comply with the requisites for exercising their appraisal rights.[111]

Exclusiveness of statutory remedy. In some states the statute expressly declares that the statutory remedy of payment for his shares is the dissenting stockholder's exclusive remedy. And in some states whose statutes are silent on the point, courts have held the statutory remedy to be exclusive.[112] However, say some courts, if the terms of the merger or other transaction to which the stockholder dissents are actually or constructively fraudulent, oppressive to minority stockholders or otherwise illegal, a stockholder can always enjoin the transaction or get other relief, regardless of whether the statutory remedy is "exclusive."[113] Thus, the minority stockholders can block a proposed merger of their corporation with a second, the sole asset of which was stock in the first, though the merger met the state law's technical requirements, when its purpose was to return the corporation to the majority's private control and freeze out the minority; the majority also breached its fiduciary duty of fairness to the minority by decreasing the market value of the stock through self-dealing.[114] But if the transaction is "merely unfair" to the minority stockholder and does

---

[109]Hochberg v Schick Investment Co. (Tex. Civ. App. 1971) 469 SW2d 474. Time ran out also in Endicott Johnson Corp. v Bade, (1973) 42 AD2d 236, 346 N.Y.S. 33, and in Schneyer v Shenandoah Oil Corp. (Del. Ch. 1974) 316 A2d 570. See also McGowan v Grand Island Transit Corp., (1981) 80 AD 2d 731, 437 NYS 2d 158.

[110]Greco v Tampa Wholesale Co. (Fla. App. 1982) 417 S 2d 994.

[111]Meadows v Microdyne Corp (N D Cal. 1983) 573 f Supp 1030.

[112]Cole v Nat'l Cash Credit Ass'n (Ch. Ct 1931) 18 Del. Ch. 47, 156 Atl 183; Adams v United States Distributing Corp., (1945) 184 Va. 134 34 SE2d 244, cert den, (1946) 327 US 788, 66 St Ct. 807; Anderson v Int. Mineral & Chemical Corp., (1946) 295 N.Y. 343, 67 NE2d 573. *Contra:* Miller v Steinbach (DC S.D.N.Y 1967) 268 F Supp 255.

[113]Mullen v Academy Life Insurance Co. (CA–8 1983) 705 F 2d 971; Cole v Nat'l Cash Credit Ass'n (Ch. Ct 1931) 18 Del. Ch. 47, 156 Atl 183; Eisenberg v Central Zone Property Corp., (1953) 306 N.Y. 58, 115 NE2d 652; Porter v C.O. Porter Machinery Co., (1953) 336 Mich. 437, 58 NW2d 135; Krantman v Liberty Loan Corporation (ND Ill. 1956) 152 F Supp 705, affirmed (CA–7 1957 246 F2d 581, cert den 78 S Ct 332; Clark v Pattern Analysis & Recognition Corp., (1976) 87 Misc. 2d 385, 384 N.Y.S.2d 660; Gabhart v Gabhart (Ind. S Ct 1977) 370 NE2d 345. But see In re Jones & Laughlin Steel Corp. (Pa. Super Ct 1979) No. 703, 2–7–79.

[114]Berkowitz v Power Mate Corp., (1975) 135 N.J. Super. 35, 342 A2d 566; Lerosi v Elkins, (1982) 89 AD 2d 903, 453 NYS 2d 718; Flum Partners v Child World, Inc. (SD NY 1983) 557 F Supp 492; Klurfeld v Equity Enterprises, Inc. (1980) 79 AD 2d 124, 436 NYS 2d 303.

not amount to actual fraud, the stockholder's only remedy may be under the appraisal statute.[115]

For example, a stockholder dissenting from a sale of all his corporation's assets can get the fair value of his stock, but he can't get damages from the majority stockholder for claimed fraud in squeezing him out by sale to a new corporation set up for that purpose, so long as the 80% stockholder consent called for by the statute was obtained.[116] Dissenters cannot use the survivor's share exchange offers to show the value of the tendered shares in figuring the damages for their alleged loss of appraisal rights, since the survivor never offered to pay cash for the shares and the dissenters did not show what actual damage the exchange caused them.[117]

Once you dissent you can only get payment and not shares in the new corporation.[118]

Abandonment of reorganization: The Model Business Corporation Act conditions a dissenter's right to be paid for his shares on the merger or other reorganization going through and the statutes of some states follow the Model Act on this point. Such a provision is constitutional.[119]

Valuing dissenters' shares. Appraisal statutes describe the basis of value of a dissenter's shares in varying terms, "fair value," "fair cash value," and "fair market value," being some examples; and in the statutes of some states, these and other terms are used interchangeably.

Precisely what each of these terms means and what, if any, difference there is among them is hard to say. One court put it this way:

> "While there is no legal formula which can be enunciated or applied in valuation proceedings, the appraisal remaining a matter of judgment on the facts in each case, the court can reiterate accepted principles which, simply stated, are that the appraisal should take account of market value, investment value, and net asset value. The weight to be attached to each factor will naturally vary in accordance with the facts of each case. . . ."[120]

---

[115]Matteson v Ziebarth, (1952) 40 Wash. 2d 286, 242 P2d 1025; David J. Greene & Co. v Schenley Industries, Inc. (Del. Ch. 1971) 281 A2d 30; Lessler v Dominion Textile, Ltd. (DC SD N.Y. 1976) 411 F Supp 40 (merging corporation provided full disclosure of business prospects—which did not have to include predictions of future profitability—and business reasons existed for merger).

[116]Farnsworth v Massey (Tex. S Ct 1963) 365 SW2d 1.

[117]LeLandais Co. Inc. v MDS-Atron, Inc. (CA–2 1976) 543 F2d 421.

[118]Aaren Rents v Corr, (1974) 133 Ga. App. 296, 211 SE2d 156.

[119]Goldberg v Arrow Electronics, Inc. (CA–2 1975) 512 F2d 1258.

[120]Appliction of Behrens (S Ct 1946) 61 N.Y.S.2d 179, affirmed, (1947) 271 A.D. 1007, 69 N.Y.S.2d 910.

Other courts have stated these rules:

The market price of the stock being appraised is entitled to considerable weight but it is not the controlling factor. Only after book value, earnings, market price to earnings ratio, future prospects, management policies, the value of stock in similar companies and many other factors have been taken into account can appraisers arrive at an intelligent decision.[121]

Market value should be the *controlling* factor "where there is a free and open market on a recognized stock exchange and the volume of transactions and conditions make it a fair reflection of the judgment of the buying and selling public."[122] However, if the market price is "infirm," for example, when the stock is traded over-the-counter and the quotations used reflect depreciation in the stock as a result of the action dissented from, the appraisers should also consider investment value and asset value.[123]

Market value should be given no weight when the surviving corporation had maintained the market in the constituent's stock for two years prior to the merger.[124]

One case gives a vivid example of how widely appraisal experts "of high standing" can differ in evaluating stock, and what elements of value courts and appraisers will sometimes consider:

> The corporation offered the stockholder $8,000 for his shares which was the net asset, or liquidating, value. At the appraisal proceeding the corporation's experts valued the stock as low as $21,000. On the other hand, the stockholder's experts placed the value at from $2.2 to $2.6 million. The appraiser finally fixed the value of the dissenter's stock at $1.1 million, *fifty* times its liquidating value. In approving the appraiser's award, the court noted that the following elements of value were properly considered: The company's favorable position in its industry, a phenomenal growth in its sales and income, an expanding market for its product, favorable prospects for increasing its share of that market, skillful management, and its stock shares the current popularity of growth stocks.[125]

---

[121] Austin v City Stores (Com. Pls. Phila. Co. 1953) 89 Pa. D. & C. 57; Tri-Continental Corp. v Battye, (1950) 31 Del. Ch. 523, 74 A2d 71; Poole v N. V. Deli Maatschappij (S Ct Del. 1966) 224 A2d 260.

[122] Marcus v Macy, (1951) 303 N.Y. 711, affirming without opinion, (1948) 273 A.D. 725, 79 N.Y.S.2d 76; General Grain, Inc. v Goodrich (Ind. App. Ct 1966) 221 NE2d 696; Multitex Corp. of America v Dickinson (CA-11 1982) 683 F 2d 1325 683 F 2d 1325 (what willing buyer would give willing seller).

[123] Matter of Silverman, (1953) 282 A.D. 252, 122 N.Y.S.2d 312.

[124] Sporborg v City Specialty Stores, Inc. (Del. Ch. Ct 1956) 123 A2d 121.

[125] Application of The Tabulating Card (Co. Inc. 1961) 32 Misc. 2d 720, 223 N.Y.S. 2d 652.

The court noted that courts have consistently refused to lay down hard and fast rules for valuing stock, holding that an appraiser must use his own judgment and give such consideration to the various elements of value as he may deem proper. In another case, a court decreased the appraised value of a dissenter's shares from about $44, as set by the court's own appraiser, to about $34, though the former majority stockholder got $53 for his controlling block of stock; the court's new appraisal formula excluded the value of an isolated unusually profitable sale of the merged corporation's subsidiary and the value of the merged corporation's assets and included only the stock's market value at the time of the merger, the average earnings for the past five years and interest.[126]

Here are some more examples of rules for valuing dissenters' stock that have been announced by various courts:

(1) Fair value of stock is weighted at: asset value 50%, reconstructed value 25%, and investment or earnings value 25%.[127]

(2) Appraisal was proper when based on (a) corporation's earning capacity, (b) investment value of stock, (c) corporation's dividends policy, and (d) price on previous sales.[128]

(3) Appraisal at 100% of net asset value was reasonable when asset mainly in securities and corporate goal was appreciation.[129]

(4) A court did not err when it considered market value, earnings value, and net asset value in an appraisal and then applied a marketability discount of 25 percent, as long as the discount is not based solely on the dissenter's minority status.[130]

(5) Appraiser need give no weight to investment value when the corporation had no earnings and could assign 40% weight to reconstructed market value of the stock when there was no established market for it.[131]

(6) Sum included for "negative good will" was properly excluded in valuing shares as it duplicated value determined earlier.[132]

(7) Movie company's earnings were properly averaged over 5-year period to find multiplier for capitalizing its earnings in appraising

---

[126]Gibbons v Schenley Industries, Inc. (Del. Ch. 1975) 339 A2d 640. See also Forglesong v Thurston Nat'l Life Ins. Co. (Okl. 1976) 555 P2d 606 in which appraised value didn't reflect price paid for control block but only asset and market value and earnings.

[127]Brown v Hedahl's—Q B & R, Inc. (N.D. 1971) 185 NW2d 249.

[128]General Securities Corp. v Watson, (1972) 251 Ark. 1066, 477 SW2d 461.

[129]King v Southwestern Cotton Oil Co. (Okla. App. 1978) 585 P2d 385.

[130]Ford v Courier-Journal Job Printing Co. (Ky. App. 1982) 639 SW 2d 553.

[131]Tome Land & Improvement Co., Inc. v Silva, (1972) 83 N.M. 549, 494 P2d 962.

[132]Endicott Johnson Corp. v Bade, (1974) 45 A.D.2d 407, 357 N.Y.S. 2d 738, aff'd, (1975) 37 N.Y.2d 585, 338 NE2d 614.

its stock, when a 5-year period was representative of its earnings experience in the broader context of its industry and none of those years was extraordinary.[133]

(8) Appraiser's valuation of $12.50 per share of dissenter's preferred stock will be upheld though its liquidating value was $21 and it cost the dissenter $20, when the corporation had not paid a dividend on it for the past 3 years.[134]

(9) Book value and previous arm's length transactions are relevant in valuing stock of close corporation.[135]

(10) Appraisal can be based on investment, asseet, and market value and not on market value alone.[136]

(11) Appraisal based 60% on earnings and 40% on assets was proper, even though company was natural resources (lumber) company and not in manufacturing.[137]

(12) A premium of 29% to stockholders of a listed company who are forced out in a merger is reasonable.[138]

The dissenter must accept the value that the appraiser fixes, even though the net asset value alone is greater than the appraised value, which included market value, investment value and the corporation's earning capacity, in addition to net asset value,[139] even if it is less than the corporation's offer.[140]

Under such a statute, a 6% interest rate on a dissenter's award was held excessive and was reduced to a 2% rate when the stock paid annual dividends of less than one-fourth of 1% of its appraised value for the three years before the merger.[141] Another court held a 6% rate equitable.[142]

In some states, interest may be denied if the dissenter does not act in good faith. What a dissenter does after refusing to surrender his stock doesn't affect his right to get interest on its appraised value.[143]

---

[133] Gillette Co. v Williams (DC D Conn. 1973) 360 F Supp 1171.

[134] Fitzgerald v Investors Preferred Life Ins. Co., (1975) Ark. 530 SW2d 195.

[135] Stewart v D.J. Stewart & Co., (1976) 37 Ill. App. 3d 848, 346 NE2d 475.

[136] Matter of Sheridan (S Ct 1977) NYLJ, 2-9-77, p. 6. See also, In re Valuation of Common Stock, of Libby, McNeill & Libby, (1979) 406 A2d 54.

[137] Bell v Kirby Lumber Corp. (Del. Ch. 1978) 395 A2d 730.

[138] Tanzer v International General Industries (Del. Ch. 1979) 402 A2d 382.

[139] Lucas v Pembroke Water Co., (1964) 205 Va. 84, 135 SE2d 147.

[140] Re Watt & Shand (Pa. Com. Pls. 1972) 63 Lanc. L.R. 127.

[141] Clark v Rockwood & Co., (1961) 18 O.O. 2d 414, 181 NE2d 59. (Supplemental opinion in the case: Appellate court can change the rate of interest allowed by the trial court when the latter abused its discretion in setting the rate.)

[142] Endicott Johnson Corp. v Bade, note 132 supra.

[143] Dimmock v Reichhold Chemicals, Inc., (1977) 41 N.Y.S. 2d 273, 360 NE2d 1079.

One more important point to note: Dissenters' shares are to be appraised as of the time just before the merger, not at a value resulting from it.[144]

Right to enjoin or set aside consolidation. Under certain conditions, a dissenting stockholder has the right to enjoin a proposed consolidation, or, if accomplished, to have it set aside, whether or not the statute makes provision for this remedy.[145] If, for example, there is no statutory authority for merging or consolidating, a dissenting stockholder may have the proposed consolidation or merger enjoined.[146] Or, if a proposed consolidation violates the rights of minority stockholders, they can bring an action to bar it.[147]

If a proposed consolidation or merger is illegal, for example, if it violates the antitrust laws, dissenting stockholders can bar it even though there is statutory authority permitting it.[148] Furthermore, if fraud has been committed against the minority stockholders in effecting the consolidation, the minority may have the consolidation set aside and the property restored to the constituent companies.[149]

However, objecting stockholders may be barred by negligence from attacking a consolidation,[150] or they may be estopped by acquiescence in it.[151] A minority stockholder cannot enjoin the merger of his corporation with another corporation unless (1) he shows fraud, and (2) acts promptly.[152]

The mere fact that directors of a merged corporation received premiums for their influence in assisting the merger was not a ground for rescinding it, when there was full disclosure of this fact at all times.[153]

---

[144] Perlman v Permonite Mfg. Co. (ND Ind 1983) 568 F Supp 222.

[145] Alpren v Consolidated Edison Co., (1938) 168 Misc. 381, 5 N.Y.S.2d 254.

[146] William B. Riker & Son Co. v United Drug Co., (1912) 79 N.J. Eq. 580, 82 Atl 930. Concerning refusal of court to assume jurisdiction, see Bichart v Kelly-Springfield Tire Co., (1934) 243 App. Div. 72, 276 N.Y.S. 372.

[147] Hubbard v Jones & Laughlin Steel Corp. (WD Pa. 1941) 42 F Supp 432; Federal United Corp. v Havender, (1940) Del. S Ct 11 A2d 331; Outwaters v Public Service Corp., (1928) 103 N.J. Eq. 461, 143 Atl 729; Zobel v Am. Locomotive Co., (1943) 183 Misc. 323, 44 N.Y.S.2d 33.

[148] De Koven v Lake Shore & M. S. Ry. Co. (SD N.Y. 1914) 216 F 955; Ramsburg v American Investment Co. of Illinois (CA-7 1956) 231 F2d 333.

[149] MacCrone v Am. Capital Corp. (D Del. 1943) 51 F Supp 462; Porges v Vadsco Sales Corp., (1943) 27 Del. Ch. 127, 32 A2d 148. See also cases cited in footnote 147 above.

[150] Clarke v Gold Dust Corp. (CA-3 1939) 106 F2d 598; cert den, (1940) 309 US 671, 60 S Ct 614; Jones v Missouri-Edison Electric Co. (CA-8 1906) 144 F 765; Windhurst v Central Leather Co., (1927) 101 N.J. Eq. 543, 138 Atl 772.

[151] Drake v N.Y. Suburban Water Co., (1898) 26 A.D. 499 50 N.Y.S. 826.

[152] Rankin v Interstate Equities Corp., (1935) 21 Del. Ch. 39, 180 Atl 54; Voege v Smith (DC S.D.N.Y. 1971 329 F Supp 180; Tanzer Economic Assoc., Inc. v Masoneilan Intl. Inc. (S Ct 1977) *NYLJ* 5-26-77; p. 6; Low v Weltner, (1966) *NYLJ* 10-20-66, p 15.

[153] Nelson v Gammon (CA-6 1981) 647 F 2d 710.

Objecting stockholders may not sit idly by and, when the merger or sale of corporate assets has been accepted by a great majority of stockholders, come into court to have it set aside, especially where there has been laches.[154] ("Laches" is a failure to do a thing at the proper time to the detriment of another). Thus, a stockholder who waits until a consolidation has become effective can't have it set aside even though (1) the directors didn't formally vote for it, (2) notice of the stockholders meeting that approved it was void because not properly signed, (3) a beneficial owner's proxy from the record owner that made up the two-thirds vote needed at the stockholders' meeting wasn't valid, and (4) the proxy was false and misleading because it stated that the directors had approved the consolidation and it set forth a combined balance sheet of the subject companies instead of separate ones.[155]

Suit to enjoin stockholders meeting to vote on a merger is moot after the meeting is held and the merger approved, and can't be continued as one to rescind the merger when no effort is made to bring both parties to the merger into court.[156]

A court will annul the merger of two corporations when the wrong corporation is named as the survivor if, as a result, the sole stockholder would suffer much loss due to tax consequences of that mistake.[157]

Rights of creditors. Corporations don't need the consent of their creditors to consolidate or merge. But every state has statutes providing that the consolidation or merger can't impair the corporation's property, and that all debts and liabilities of the former corporation shall attach to the new and surviving corporation, just as if they had been originally incurred by it. There is no reason, however, why the parties to the agreement who hold claims against the constituent corporations cannot bind themselves in such a way that they bar themselves from proceeding against the consolidated corporation for their claims.[158]

Rights of local creditors of the consolidating corporation are entitled to protection where the consolidated company is a foreign corporation and it is proposed to transfer the consolidating company's

---

[154] Peterson v New England Furniture & Carpet Co., (1941) 210 Minn. 449, 299 NW 208.
[155] Andrews v Precision Apparatus, Inc. (SD N.Y. 1963) 217 F Supp 679.
[156] Sawyer v Pioneer Mill Co. (CA–9 1962) 3–14–62, No. 17, 223.
[157] In re Ryback (S Ct 1971) *NYLJ* 10-4-71, p. 2.
[158] In re Utica Nat'l Brewing Co., (1897) 154 N.Y. 268, 48 NE 521. See also Utley v Standard Magnesium & Chemical Co. (Okl. 1970) 478 P2d 953.

assets to the home state of the consolidated corporation. Before that can be done, it has been held, the assets must be subjected to the satisfaction of the claims of local creditors of the consolidated corporation.[159] Notice of the proceeding, of course, must be given to the creditors.[160]

Claims against the surviving or new corporation may include federal and state taxes, like income taxes and social security taxes. Whether a tax liability will survive against a new or surviving corporation depends on the law and practice in this regard in the taxing jurisdiction. Thus, the surviving corporation in a merger assumed a constituent's obligations under a mutual aid fund agreement though the agreement had no specific clause to that effect.[161]

A federal court has held that an injured longshoreman can go after a consolidated shipping corporation if he has a claim against a constituent corporation.[162]

Instead of an equity action to follow the assets of the constituent corporation, a creditor may bring an action at law against the new or surviving corporation to enforce its liability for the debts of the constituent corporation.[163]

Note also that creditors of a post-merger corporation that goes into bankruptcy cannot hold the directors of the pre-merger corporation for allegedly impairing its stated capital; only the creditors of the pre-merger corporation who extended credit to it based on that capital have such standing.[164]

---

[159] Gauss v Lloyds Ins. Co. of America, (1940) 295 Mich. 199, 294 NW 153.
[160] Laco X-Ray Systems, Inc. v Fingerhut, (1982) 88 AD 2d 425, 453 NYS 2d 757.
[161] Western Airlines v Allegheny Airlines, Inc. (Del. Ch 1973) 313 A 2d 145.
[162] Duris v Erato Shipping, Inc. (CA-6 1982) 684 F 2d 352.
[163] Wolf v Shreveport Gas, Etc Co., (1916) 138 La 743, 70 So 789.
[164] Johnston v Wolfe (Del. Ch 1983) No. 6682, 2-24-83.

Chapter 32

RESOLUTIONS RELATING TO

CONSOLIDATION AND MERGER

Contents—Chapter 32

DIRECTORS' RESOLUTION AUTHORIZING OFFICERS TO ENTER INTO NEGOTIATIONS FOR A MERGER OR CONSOLIDATION

WHEREAS, it has been proposed to this Corporation by the . . . . Company to consolidate [or merge] the two corporations into a single corporation, and

WHEREAS, this Board of Directors deems it advisable that this Corporation enter into negotiations with the . . . . Company with a view to consolidating [or merging] the two corporations; be it

RESOLVED, That the President and the Secretary of this Corporation are hereby authorized and directed to enter into negotiations with the . . . . Company with a view to consolidating [or merging] the two corporations, and also to prepare a proposed form of Agreement of Consolidation or Merger prescribing the terms and conditions of consolidation, and the mode of carrying the same into effect, as well as the manner of converting the shares of each of the constituent corporations into shares of the new [or surviving] corporation, with such other details and provisions as may be necessary; and

RESOLVED FURTHER, That the proposed form of Agreement be presented to the Board of Directors at its next regular meeting, or at a special meeting called for the purpose of considering the proposed Agreement on the stockbook of this Corporation on the record date, at least . . . . . days prior to the date of said special meeting.

RESOLVED FURTHER, That in the event said Agreement and Plan shall be approved and adopted at said special meeting or at any adjournment thereof by the stockholders of this Corporation in accordance with the applicable requirements of the laws of the State of . . . . and shall also be approved and adopted by the stockholders of . . . . Company in accordance with the requirements of the laws of the State of . . . ., then the Secretary of this Corporation is hereby authorized to certify on said Agreement and Plan the fact that said Agreement and plan has been so approved and adopted, which certification shall be under the seal of this Corporation, and the President or any Vice president and the Secretary or any Assistant Secretary of this Corporation are hereby authorized in the name and on behalf of this corporation and under its corporate seal, to execute said Agreement and Plan and to cause the same to be filed in the Office of the Secretary of State of . . . . and to be recorded in the Office of the Recorder of the County of . . . ., ..., and

RESOLVED FURTHER, That wherever in these Resolutions any director or officer of this Corporation is authorized to take any action that he deems necessary, proper, advisable or required, the signing or execution by such director or officer of any instrument or the taking of any such action by him shall be conclusive evidence that he deems the same to be necessary, proper, advisable or required.

DIRECTORS' RESOLUTION AUTHORIZING MERGER OF PARENT AND SUBSIDIARY

WHEREAS, this Corporation now owns all the stock of .... Company, a stock corporation organized under the laws of the State of ...., and engaged in business similar and incidental to that of this Corporation, and

WHEREAS, it is deemed advisable that this Corporation merge with said .... Company in order that all the estate, property, rights, privileges, and franchises of said Company shall vest in and be possessed by this Corporation; be it

RESOLVED, That said .... Company be merged into this Corporation, and that this Corporation assumes all its obligations; and [see Comment]

RESOLVED FURTHER, That the President or any Vice president and the Secretary or the Treasurer of this Corporation, are hereby authorized and directed to make and execute, in the name and under the corporate seal of this Corporation, a certificate of ownership of all the stock of said .... Company, and of the adoption and date of adoption of these resolutions, and to file such certificate in the Office of the Secretary of State of the State of ...., and to do all other acts and things that may be necessary to carry out and effectuate the purpose of these resolutions.

Comment: If it is desired that the surviving corporation use the name of the absorbed company, the following may be inserted here:

"RESOLVED FURTHER, That this Corporation relinquish its corporate name and assume in place thereof the name of the merged Company, namely, '............ Company.' "

DIRECTORS' RESOLUTION ADOPTING MERGER OR CONSOLIDATION AGREEMENT

RESOLVED, That this Board of Directors hereby recommends, approves and adopts the proposed Agreement and Plan of Merger between this Corporation and .... Company, a .... (*insert state of incorporation*) corporation, substantially in the form presented to the meeting with such changes therein as the directors and officer, or officers, of this corporation executing said Agreement and Plan deems necessary and proper, and the Directors and the President of this Corporation are hereby authorized to enter into said Agreement and Plan by executing, under the corporate seal of this Corporation, and delivering said Agreement and Plan with such changes therein as they may deem necessary and proper.

RESOLVED FURTHER, That said Agreement and Plan as entered into by the directors and officers of this Corporation be submitted to the holders of the Preferred and Common Stock of this Corporation at a special meeting thereof hereby called to be held on . . . ., 19. . at . . . . M., at the offices of the Corporation, ... (*address*), for the purpose of considering and voting by ballot upon the approval and adoption of said Agreement and Plan.

RESOLVED FURTHER, That . . . ., 19. ., is hereby fixed as the record date for the determination of the holders of the Preferred and Common Stock of this Corporation entitled to notice of, and to vote at, such special meeting.

RESOLVED FURTHER, That notice of the time, place and object of said special meeting shall be given by publication at least once a week for four successive weeks in a newspaper published in . . . . County, ..., and that a copy of such notice be mailed to the last known post office address of each stockholder, as shown on the stockbook of this Corporation on the record date, at least . . . . . days prior to the date of said special meeting.

RESOLVED FURTHER, That in the event said Agreement and Plan shall be approved and adopted at said special meeting or at any adjournment thereof by the stockholders of this Corporation in accordance with the applicable requirements of the laws of the State of . . . . and shall also be approved and adopted by the stockholders of . . . . Company in accordance with the requirements of the laws of the State of . . . ., then the Secretary of this Corporation is hereby authorized to certify on said Agreement and Plan the fact that said Agreement and Plan has been so approved and adopted, which certification shall be under the seal of this Corporation, and the President or any Vice president and the Secretary or any Assistant Secretary of this Corporation are hereby authorized in the name and on behalf of this corporation and under its corporate seal, to execute said Agreement and Plan and to cause the same to be filed in the Office of the Secretary of State of . . . . and to be recorded in the Office of the Recorder of the County of . . . ., ...

RESOLVED FURTHER, That wherever in these Resolutions any director or officer of this Corporation is authorized to take any action that he deems necessary, proper, advisable or required, the signing or execution by such director or officer of any instrument or the taking of any such action by him shall be conclusive evidence that he deems the same to be necessary, proper, advisable or required.

DIRECTORS' RESOLUTION AUTHORIZING EXECUTION OF ARTICLES OF CONSOLIDATION

RESOLVED, That the "A" Railroad Company has agreed and hereby does consent to the consolidation and merger of the capital stock, franchises, privileges, and properties of the "B" Railroad Company, the "C" Railroad Company, and the "D" Railroad Company, with and into the capital stock, franchises, privileges, and properties of the "A" Railroad Company, on the terms and conditions set forth in the Articles of Consolidation and Merger now submitted to the Board of Directors, and the President of the Company is authorized, in behalf of the Company, to execute the said Articles of Consolidation and Merger under its seal, attested by the Secretary, and to acknowledge and deliver the same.

DIRECTORS' RESOLUTION AUTHORIZING EXECUTION OF ARTICLES OF CONSOLIDATION UPON RATIFICATION BY STOCKHOLDERS

RESOLVED, That the President and the Secretary of this Company are hereby authorized to execute the Articles of Consolidation with the .... Company, which have been read at this meeting, when said Articles of Consolidation shall have been duly approved and authorized by the stockholders of said Companies.

DIRECTORS' RESOLUTION APPROVING PROPOSED AGREEMENT OF MERGER, AND CALLING STOCKHOLDERS' MEETING FOR RATIFICATION

RESOLVED, That the merger of .... Company and .... Company with this Corporation, in accordance with the terms and conditions of the Merger Agreement submitted to this meeting, with such changes therein as counsel may approve, is hereby approved; and that a majority of the Board of Directors of this Corporation is hereby authorized and directed to enter into an agreement, in the form submitted to this meeting, with such changes therein as counsel may approve, with a majority of the Board of Directors of the .... Company, providing for the merger of the three corporations into one corporation under the chapter of this Corporation and under the name of "The .... Corporation" in accordance with the provisions of the .... Law.

RESOLVED, That a copy of said Merger Agreement, when so executed, be attached to the minutes of this meeting.

RESOLVED, That a special meeting of the shareholders of the .... Corporation be called to convene at the principal office of this Corporation, ... (*Street*), ... City of ...., State of ...., on ...., 19.., at ....M., for the purpose of voting upon the ratification and confirmation of the terms and conditions agreed upon by a majority of the Board of Directors of the .... Company, by a majority of the Board of Directors of the .... Company, and by a majority of the Board of Directors of this Corporation, for the merger of said three corporations under the charter and name of "The .... Corporation," and for the transaction of such other business as may properly come before said meeting.

RESOLVED, That the books for the transfer of the shares of the capital stock of this Corporation be closed at the close of business on . . . ., 19. ., and, unless otherwise ordered by this Board, be reopened at the opening of business on . . . ., 19. . .

RESOLVED, That the Secretary of this Corporation be authorized and directed to give notice of said meeting to the shareholders of this Corporation in accordance with the provisions of the by-laws of this Corporation and of the provisions of law applicable thereto.

RESOLVED, That it is the judgment of this Board that if such Merger Agreement shall be ratified and confirmed and an increase of the capital stock of this Corporation from . . . . . (. . . . .) shares to . . . . . (. . . . .) shares shall be authorized as therein provided, (1) . . . . . (. . . . .) of the new or additional shares of this Corporation shall be allotted to the shareholders of the . . . . Company on the effective date of the merger, as provided in said Merger Agreement, (2) . . . . . (. . . . .) of said new or additional shares of this Corporation shall be allotted to the shareholders of the . . . . Company on the effective date of the merger, as provided in said Merger Agreement, and (3) . . . . . (. . . . .) of said new or additional shares of such authorized capital stock shall be issued and sold at the fair value, but at not less than the par value thereof, in such manner and to such parties as the Board of Directors of this Corporation shall approve, as provided in said Merger Agreement.

RESOLVED, That . . . . and . . . . be appointed as representatives of this Corporation upon the Committee of six provided for in the Merger Agreement, with full power and authority to pass upon the assets to be contributed by each of the merging corporations, and to take any and all further action that may be required on the part of said Committee in order to carry out the true intent and purpose of said Merger Agreement and of the resolutions heretofore adopted by this Board at this meeting.

RESOLVED, That if any shareholder of the . . . . Company or any shareholder of the . . . . Company shall, in connection with the allotment of shares of this Corporation provided for in said Merger Agreement, be entitled to receive fractional shares of the capital stock of this Corporation, one or more scrip certificates in respect of such capital stock expressed in one hundredths shall be issued in the name of such shareholder; that the scrip certificate so to be issued shall be in such form as the Chairman of the Board, or the President, or any Vice president, and counsel may approve; and that the proper officers of this Corporation be authorized to execute, under its corporate seal or otherwise as they shall deem proper, and deliver scrip certificates substantially in such form when required as aforesaid.

RESOLVED, That the officers of this Corporation are authorized and directed from time to time to take all proceedings, execute and deliver all instruments, and do and perform all acts necessary, convenient, or proper, as advised by counsel, to carry into effect the full intent and purpose of the resolutions heretofore adopted by this Board at this meeting with respect to said merger.

RESOLVED, That the officers of this Corporation are authorized and directed to send to the shareholders of this Corporation a circular letter briefly summarizing the matters authorized by the resolutions heretofore adopted at this meeting with respect to said merger, together with a formal notice of said special meeting of shareholders.

DIRECTORS' RESOLUTION TO MERGE CORPORATION, WHERE MERGING CORPORATION OWNS ALL OF CAPITAL STOCK OF OTHER CORPORATION

WHEREAS, this Company now owns all the stock of .... Corporation, a stock corporation organized under the laws of the State of ...., and engaged in business similar and incidental to that of this Company, and

WHEREAS, it is deemed advisable that this Company merge with said .... Corporation in order that all the estate, property, rights, privileges, and franchises of said Corporation shall vest in and be possessed by this Company, be it

RESOLVED, That this Company merge with said .... Corporation and assume all its obligations, and

RESOLVED FURTHER, That this Company relinquish its corporate name and assume in place thereof the name of the said merged Corporation—to wit, the name "............ Corporation"—and

RESOLVED FURTHER, That the President or the Vice president, and the Secretary or the Treasurer of this Company, are hereby authorized and directed to make and execute, in the name and under the corporate seal of this Company, a certificate of ownership of all the stock of said .... Corporation, and of the adoption and date of adoption of these resolutions, and to file such certificate in the office of the Secretary of State of the State of ...., and to do all other acts and things that may be necessary to carry out and effectuate the purpose of these resolutions.

DIRECTORS' RESOLUTION AUTHORIZING OFFICERS TO ENTER INTO MERGER AGREEMENT

RESOLVED, That the merger agreement providing for the merging of "A" Corporation with this Company, hereinafter in these resolutions set forth, is hereby approved, and that the President or a Vice president of this Company is hereby authorized and directed to make, in the name of this Company and in its behalf, under its corporate seal, duly attested by its

Secretary or an Assistant Secretary, a written agreement in duplicate between this Company and "A" Corporation, in substantially the following form (*insert a full copy of the merger agreement*).

RESOLVED FURTHER, That a special meeting of the stockholders of this Company is hereby called to be held at the principal office of the Company at .... (*Street*), in .... (*City*), on ...., 19.., at .... M., for the following purpose or purposes: (1) to vote upon the proposition to merge "A" Corporation with this Company; (2) to approve the merger agreement to be submitted at said meeting pursuant to the authority hereinabove contained; (3) to vote upon the increase in capital stock of this Company from ..... ($.....) Dollars, consisting of ..... (.....) shares of the par value of ..... ($.....) Dollars each, to ..... ($.....) Dollars, consisting of ..... (.....) shares of the par value of ..... ($.....) Dollars each, as provided in said Merger Agreement, in order to provide shares issuable when the merger becomes effective; and (4) to act upon any and all matters connected with or incidental to said merger which may properly come before said meeting.

RESOLVED FURTHER, That .... and .... are hereby appointed Inspectors of Election to act at the above-mentioned special meeting of the stockholders to be called as aforesaid.

RESOLVED FURTHER, That when the merger hereinabove referrred to becomes effective, the number of directors of this Company shall be increased to ....

RESOLVED FURTHER, That the officers of this Company are hereby each authorized and directed, in behalf of this Company, to take all such steps and to do and authorize to be done all such acts and things as may be necessary or advisable or convenient and proper for the purpose of carrying out the foregoing resolutions and the intent thereof, and for the purpose of fully effectuating and carrying out the merger referred to in the foregoing resolutions.

EXCERPT OF MINUTES OF STOCKHOLDERS' MEETING, SHOWING RESOLUTION AUTHORIZING CONSOLIDATION

The Secretary presented and read a proposed Certificate of Consolidation. After consideration thereof, upon motion duly made and seconded, the following resolutions were adopted by the affirmative vote of the holders of record of ..... (.....) shares, representing more than (*insert fraction required by statute*) of the outstanding stock of this Corporation entitled to vote thereon:

RESOLVED, That this Corporation be consolidated with the .... Corporation, under the name of ...., and

RESOLVED FURTHER, That the terms and conditions of such consolidation, the mode of carrying the same into effect, and the manner of distributing the shares of the new corporation among the shareholders of the constituent corporations shall be as set forth in the proposed Certificate of Consolidation, submitted to this meeting, and

RESOLVED FURTHER, That the President or the Vice president, and the Secretary or an Assistant Secretary of this Corporation, are hereby authorized and directed to execute and file in the proper offices a Certificate of Consolidation, in the form presented to this meeting, and to do all things that may be essential to effectuate such consolidation, and

RESOLVED FURTHER, That the Secretary is hereby directed to spread a copy of the proposed Certificate of Consolidation, in the form presented to this meeting, upon the minutes of this meeting (*insert Certificate of Consolidation*).

RESOLUTION OF STOCKHOLDERS APPROVING AGREEMENT OF MERGER ADOPTED BY DIRECTORS

RESOLVED, That the stockholders of ...., Inc., hereby approve the adoption of a certain Agreement of Merger, approved on ...., 19.., by the respective Boards of Directors of ...., Inc., and .... Corporation, a corporation of the State of ...., and entered into by a majority of the directors of each of such corporations, respectively, on such date, in which Agreement of Merger are prescribed the terms and conditions of the proposed merger of .... Corporation into ...., Inc., and the mode of carrying the same into effect, and

RESOLVED FURTHER, That the said Agreement of Merger and the terms and conditions therein set forth and provided are hereby in all respects approved, adopted, authorized, and agreed to, and

RESOLVED FURTHER, That if and in the event that said Agreement of Merger shall have been duly executed, acknowledged, and certified, and all other action in regard to the execution and adoption of said Agreement of Merger shall have been duly and properly taken by ...., Inc., and by .... Corporation, the proper officers of this Corporation are hereby authorized and directed to file said Agreement of Merger, so executed, acknowledged, and certified, in the office of the Secretary of State of the State of ...., as and for the agreement and act of merger of ...., Inc., and .... Corporation, and

RESOLVED FURTHER, That a copy of said Agreement of Merger submitted to this meeting is hereby ordered to be filed with the minutes of this meeting.

RESOLUTION OF STOCKHOLDERS RATIFYING AGREEMENT TO PURCHASE ALL THE STOCK OF ANOTHER CORPORATION

WHEREAS, the Board of Directors, having considered it for the best interests of this Corporation to acquire the stock of the .... Company, entered into an agreement for the purchase of all of the capital stock of the Company, be it

RESOLVED, That the agreement heretofore made by this Corporation, providing for the purchase of stock of the .... Company at a price equal to the par value thereof, payable in capital stock of this Corporation, at a valuation or rate of ..... ($.....) Dollars per share, is hereby ratified and approved, and the officers and Board of Directors of this Corporation are hereby authorized to carry said agreement into effect by issuing and delivering new stock of this Corporation, authorized at this meeting, to holders of stock of the .... Company, in exchange for said stock, on the terms and conditions of the said agreement.

RESOLUTION OF STOCKHOLDERS AUTHORIZING MERGER AND RETENTION OF NAME OF ACQUIRED CORPORATION

RESOLVED, That the stockholders of this Corporation do hereby authorize the merger of the .... Company with this Corporation, and that to that end the officers of this Corporation are hereby empowered to acquire the entire capital stock, assets, and goodwill of the said .... Company; to issue in exchange therefor, ... ($.....) Dollars par value of preferred stock, and ..... ($.....) Dollars par value of common stock of this Corporation; to assume the debts and liabilities of said .... Company; and either wholly to discontinue said .... Company and organize a new corporation of that name with nominal capitalization, or to reduce the capitalization of said .... Company to a nominal amount, and retain control of said name by continuing the nominal corporate existence of said Company.

RESOLUTION OF STOCKHOLDERS' COMMITTEE TO EXTEND TIME TO MAKE DEPOSITS OR TAKE ACTION UNDER AGREEMENT OF MERGER

The Stockholders' Committee constituted under the Agreement of Deposit, dated ...., 19.., providing for the deposit of stock of .... Company, does hereby adopt the following resolution as of ...., 19..;

RESOLVED, That the Committee extend the time for the making of deposits of stock, for delivering proxies or consents, or for taking any further action or proceeding under the plan and agreement or merger, to and including ...., 19...

....
By ....
Proxy

. . . .
By . . . .
                                                        Proxy

. . . .
By . . . .
                                                        Proxy

RESOLUTION OF STOCKHOLDERS APPROVING MERGER OR CONSOLIDATION

RESOLVED, That the agreement for the merger of the . . . . Company with this Corporation, dated . . . ., 19. ., in the form submitted to this meeting, is hereby approved, and the directors and officers of this Corporation are hereby authorized and directed to take whatever action and to execute and deliver whatever instruments may be necessary to consummate and carry out said agreement.

WRITTEN CONSENT OF STOCKHOLDERS TO MERGER OR CONSOLIDATION

We, the undersigned, holders of the number of shares of the capital [or "Common" or "Preferred"] stock of . . . . Corporation set opposite our respective names, which shares in the aggregate constitute the entire outstanding stock of the Corporation, do hereby consent to the merger of . . . . Corporation and . . . . Company, the resulting corporation to be known as . . . ., upon the terms and provisions of the Agreement of Merger dated . . . ., 19. . .
Dated: . . . ., 19. . .

Name of Stockholder	Number of Shares	Signature
. . . .	. . . .	. . . .
. . . .	. . . .	. . . .
. . . .	. . . .	. . . .
. . . .	. . . .	. . . .

NOTICE OF STOCKHOLDERS' MEETING CALLED TO APPROVE MERGER

NOTICE is hereby given that a special meeting of the stockholders of . . . . Corporation will be held at the offices of the Corporation at . . . . (*address*) on . . . ., 19. ., at . . . . M., for the following purposes:

(1) To consider the question of increasing the authorized Common Stock of the Company from . . . . . shares of the par value of . . . . . Dollars each to . . . . . shares with the same par value.

(2) To consider and act upon the adoption of the Agreement of Merger between ...., Inc., and .... Corporation providing for the merger of ...., Inc. into .... Corporation on the terms and conditions contained in the agreement, a copy of which is set forth in Exhibit A attached hereto.

(3) To transact such other business as may properly come before the meeting.

Only stockholders of record at the close of business on ...., 19.., will be entitled to vote at the meeting. With respect to the matter referred to in item (1) of this notice, the holders of Common Stock will be entitled to vote as a class, and with respect to the matter referred to in item (2), the holders of both the Common and the Preferred Stock will be entitled to vote as a class. [*Insert this last sentence only if different classes have different voting rights.*]

By order of the Board of Directors,
............, Secretary

NOTICE OF STOCKHOLDERS' MEETING CALLED TO APPROVE CONSOLIDATION

NOTICE is hereby given that a special meeting of the stockholders of .... Corporation will be held at the offices of the Company at .... (*address*) on ...., 19.., at ....M., for the following purposes:

(1) To consider and vote upon the adoption of an Agreement of Consolidation dated ...., 19.., providing for the consolidation of .... Corporation, ... Company, and ...., Inc., into a single new corporation to be known as .... Corporation.

(2) To transact such other business as may properly come before the meeting.

Only stockholders of record at the close of business on .... 19.., will be entitled to vote at the meeting.

DIRECTORS' RESOLUTION AUTHORIZING MERGER TO CHANGE STATE OF INCORPORATION

Resolutions of Board of Directors of Ecks, Wye Corp., ..., 19... Meeting with respect to Merger with Eks, Wye Corp. of ....
(state)

WHEREAS, this Board of Directors, by resolutions adopted at its regular meeting on ...., 19.., directed the officers of the Company to form a .... corporation with an organizational and capital structure
(state)

substantially the same as that of the Company and to prepare a plan to be submitted for approval to this Board of Directors and to the stockholders of the company for merging the Company and the . . . . corporation
(state)
so that the . . . . corporation would be the surviving corporation;
(state)
and

WHEREAS, a . . . . corporation was so formed on . . . .,
(state)
19. ., under the name "Ecks, Wye Corp. of . . . .," and the officers
(state)
of the Company have presented to this meeting as directed a plan of merger embodied in proposed "Articles of Merger and Joint Agreement," it is

RESOLVED, That the merger of Ecks, Wye Corp. of . . . .,
(state)
a . . . . corporation, with this Company, in accordance with the
(state)
terms and conditions of the Articles of Merger and Joint Agreement submitted to this meeting, with such changes therein as counsel may approve, be and the same hereby is approved; and that a majority of the Board of Directors of this Corporation is hereby authorized and directed to enter into and execute said Articles of Merger and Joint Agreement in the form submitted to this meeting, with such changes therein as counsel may approve, providing for the merger of the two corporations into one corporation under the charter of . . . . Corporation of . . . ., all in accordance
(state)
with the provisions of the General Corporation Law of the State of . . . . and of the Business Corporation Act of the State of . . . .; and

RESOLVED FURTHER, that a copy of said Articles of Merger and Joint Agreement, when so executed, be attached to the minutes of this meeting; and

RESOLVED FURTHER, that the Articles of Merger and Joint Agreement as approved by this Board of Directors, and all the terms and conditions thereof, be submitted to the stockholders of the Corporation for the purpose of voting upon the approval, ratification and confirmation thereof; and

RESOLVED FURTHER, that, subject to approval, ratification and confirmation by the stockholders, the officers of the Corporation be and they hereby are authorized and directed from time to time to take all proceedings, execute and deliver all instruments, and do and perform all acts necessary, convenient, or proper, as advised by counsel, to carry into effect the full intent and purpose of these resolutions, including, but not by way of limitation, the preparation and filing of such applications for approval of the merger as shall be required by law, and the preparation and filing of all such agreements or other documents as shall be required by the . . . . Stock Exchange and the Securities and Exchange Commission.

RESOLUTION OF STOCKHOLDERS AUTHORIZING MERGER
TO CHANGE STATE OF INCORPORATION

Resolution of Stockholders of Ecks, Wye Corp. Approving Articles of Merger and Joint Agreement with Respect to Merger of Ecks, Wye Corp. and Ecks, Wye Corp. of ....
(state)

RESOLVED, That the stockholders of the Company hereby approve the adoption on ...., 19.. by the Board of Directors of the Company of that certain Articles of Merger and Joint Agreement, in which are prescribed the terms and conditions of the proposed merger of the Company into Ecks, Wye Corp. of ...., and the mode of carrying the same into effect; and

RESOLVED FURTHER, That the said Articles of Merger and Joint Agreement and the terms and conditions therein set forth and provided be and the same hereby are in all respects approved, adopted, authorized, and agreed to; and

RESOLVED FURTHER, That the officers of the Company be and they are hereby directed to execute, acknowledge and certify said Articles of Merger and Joint Agreement on behalf of the Company and to take all other action in regard to the carrying into effect of said Articles of Merger and Joint Agreement as shall be necessary or advisable, including the filing of said Articles of Merger and Joint Agreement, so executed, acknowledged, and certified, in the office of the Secretary of State of the State of .... and of the Secretary of State of the State of ...., as and for the agreement and act of merger of the Company and Ecks, Wye Corp. of ....; and

RESOLVED FURTHER, That a copy of said Articles of Merger and Joint Agreement submitted to this meeting be and same hereby is ordered to be filed with the minutes of this meeting.

PROXY STATEMENT FOR MERGER OF
A WHOLLY OWNED SUBSIDIARY

Proxy Statement

Able, Baker Corp.

Enclosed Proxy is solicited by management of Able, Baker Corp. for use at a special meeting of shareholders to be held on ...., 19... A proxy may be revoked at any time before it is voted by notice in writing to the Secretary, and if not revoked, will be voted as directed by the shareholder. As of ...., 19.., the record date for determination of shareholders entitled to vote at the special meeting, there were outstanding ..... shares of the capital stock of Able, Baker Corp.; each share entitling the holder to one vote.

Proposed Merger

The purpose of the special meeting is to consider and take action upon a merger agreement providing for the merger of Zed Corp., a wholly-owned subsidiary of Able, Baker Corp., into Able, Baker Corp., which will be the surviving corporation. The merger will be accomplished under the laws of the State of ...., in which both corporations are incorporated (or the states in which each is incorporated, if different).

The boards of directors of both corporations have carefully considered this merger and have concluded that such merger will permit certain operating economies, and that the transfer of Zed Corp.'s property to Able, Baker Corp. by merger will effect material savings in taxes otherwise payable on such conveyance (add any other reasons that are pertinent).

In addition to the approval by the boards of directors of both companies, which has already been obtained, the merger requires the approval of the shareholders of at least .....% of the shares of Able, Baker Corp., and its consent as the sole shareholder of Zed Corp. Financial statements are not furnished with this proxy because they are not deemed necessary for the exercise of prudent judgment with respect to the merger.

Comment: SEC Regulations say that proxy statements must include certain information about the merger, but they except mergers involving wholly owned subsidiaries from some requirements [SEC Rule X–14A–11].

When the merger becomes effective, all the business, property and assets of Zed Corp. will become those of Able, Baker Corp., which will in turn assume responsibility for the debts, liabilities and obligations of .... The outstanding stock of Zed Corp. (all owned by Able, Baker Corp.) will be cancelled and no securities will be issued in its place.

The merger may be abandoned by mutual consent of the board of directors of both parties to the merger, and without action of shareholders, at any time before it becomes effective.

The directors and officers of Able, Baker Corp. in office immediately prior to the effective date of the merger will continue as such until the next annual meetings of shareholders and directors in 19...

If the merger agreement is approved by the shareholders of Able, Baker Corp., and consented to by Able, Baker Corp. as sole stockholder in Zed Corp. the agreement will be filed and recorded as required by law, at which time the merger will be deemed effective.

Comment: If articles of incorporation are to be amended by the shareholders that fact and the reasons for the amendment should be included.

Federal Tax Status

In the opinion of counsel, the merger will constitute a tax-free reorganization and, for federal income tax purposes, neither gain nor loss will result to the corporations or the shareholders of either corporation from the merger.

Comment: If a tax ruling has been obtained from the Internal Revenue Service prior to mailing of the proxy statement, tell the stockholders what the ruling is and how it affects their tax position.

Rights of Dissenting Stockholders

[Insert here the verbatim text of the state(s) statute section(s) applicable, if such verbatim statement is required under such laws. Otherwise you can summarize the provisions of the statute(s). If there's doubt as to whether a vote against the merger constitutes sufficient objection to it under the merger statute, state that fact here, as follows:

In the opinion of counsel, a vote against the merger or direction in the proxy to vote against the merger does not constitute the objection required by the statute.]

Expenses of Solicitation

The cost of the solicitation of proxies will be borne by . . . . In addition to use of the mails, proxies may be solicited personally, by telephone or telegraph, by regular employees of Able, Baker Corp. Such services will not be paid for. However, Able, Baker Corp. will reimburse brokers and other persons holding stock in their names, or in the names of nominees, for their expenses in sending proxy material to principals and obtaining their proxies.

Other Business

The board of directors is not aware of any other matters that are to be presented for action at the meeteing other than set forth herein.

By order of the Board of Directors
. . . . Secretary

(City, State)

. . . .

(Date)

. . . .

NOTICE TO STOCKHOLDERS OF MERGER
OF WHOLLY OWNED SUBSIDIARY

Able, Baker Corporation

Notice, pursuant to Section . . . . . of . . . . General Corporation Law, of proposed merger of wholly owned corporation into parent corporation

To the Stockholders of Able, Baker Corporation:

Please take notice that the Board of Directors of Able, Baker Corporation (parent corporation), at a meeting held on . . . ., 19 . ., duly approved proposed Articles of Merger under which the following wholly-owned subsidiary of the parent corporation is to be merged into the parent corporation:

Cee Dee Sales Co. Inc. (a . . . . corporation)
Under the proposed Articles of Merger:

   (a) No amendment of the charter of the parent corporation is to be effected thereby; and

   (b) No shares of the parent corporation are to be issued for shares of the merged subsidiary, but on the effective date of the Articles of Merger, the shares of stock of the merged subsidiary are to be surrendered for cancellation to the parent corporation.

This Notice is sent to you pursuant to the requirements of Section . . . . .
of the General Corporation Law of . . . .

By order of the Board of Directors.

John Able, Secretary

Dated: City of . . . ., State of . . . ., ..., 19. . .

DIRECTORS' RESOLUTION APPROVING PROXY STATEMENT AND AUTHORIZING FILING OF LISTING APPLICATION WITH STOCK EXCHANGE

RESOLVED, That the form of notice for the special meeting of stockholders, the proxy statement and form of proxy to be sent to the stockholders of this Corporation in connection with the special meeting called for . . . ., 19. ., in the respective forms submitted to this meeting of the Board of Directors, are hereby approved, subject to such changes therein as the Secretary of this Corporation shall determine to be proper and as shall be necessary to satisfy the requirements of the Securities and Exchange Commission.

RESOLVED FURTHER, That the President, any Vice president, the Secretary and Treasurer of this Corporation, and each of them, be authorized and directed in the name of and on behalf of, this Corporation to execute and file with the . . . . Stock Exchange an application for listing on such Exchange of the shares of common stock issuable to holders of the common stock of . . . . Company surrendered in exchange for stock of this Corporation pursuant to the Agreement and Plan of Merger dated . . . ., 19. ., and each of the officers designated above is hereby authorized to appear before any committee or department of said Exchange with authority to make changes in such application or in any Agreement relative thereto as may be necessary to conform with the requirements for listing and to take any and all other actions deemed necessary to conform with the requirements for listing.

Chapter 33

REORGANIZATION, LIQUIDATION,

AND DISSOLUTION

Contents—Chapter 33

Definition and purpose of reorganization. Reorganization is a rearrangement of a company's capital structure—its outstanding stock and debt—required or suggested by an actual or impending failure to meet its financial obligations. The broad purpose of a reorganization in this case is to avoid collapse of the business. By keeping the corporation alive you preserve the greater value its assets would have as assets of a going business than they would have on a forced sale in liquidation. Specific objectives usually include:

(1) Reduction of fixed or contingent charges, for example, of interest charges or of preferred dividend obligations, especially when the preferred dividends are cumulative.

(2) Extension of time to pay, or readjustment of, early maturing debts.

(3) Acquisition of new capital.

(4) Finding and eliminating management weaknesses causing the difficulty.

Reorganization may take place under state law usually without resort to the courts, or under the federal Bankruptcy Act (U.S. Code Title 11).

Extension of maturity date of loans. Usually, both the debtor corporation and its creditors are anxious to avoid legal proceedings. The expense of the proceedings, the bad publicity and the reduction in the value of the debtor's assets that follow when a debtor is taken to court may simply add to the creditors' losses.

When the business is small, with few creditors, and when the financial problem is temporary, the creditors may agree to postpone the due date of their obligations.

However, all creditors must agree to the extension of the obligation. Those who don't are not bound and can start bankruptcy proceedings. Because of this, the larger creditors will sometimes not object if small creditors are paid in full.

Composition of creditors. When the business is insolvent or if insolvency is imminent, it may be necessary for the creditors to agree to accept only a percentage of their claims in full payment. The creditors may well feel that they will profit more in the long run by taking notes for, say, 50¢ on the dollar rather than by forcing the debtor into liquidation and getting 20¢ in cash. If the business can be rehabilitated, future profitable business may more than make up creditors' present losses.

In practice, a composition of creditors is usually available only to the smaller firms with few creditors. All creditors must agree to the plan; a dissenter can force the debtor into bankruptcy.

This type of composition is accomplished under state law. It is similar to an "arrangement" under Chapter XI of the federal Bankruptcy Act except that a Chapter XI arrangement is binding on nonassenting minority creditors.

Assignment for the benefit of creditors. An assignment for the benefit of creditors is an assignment of all its property by a debtor corporation to a trustee. The trustee is usually selected by the corporation or a credit or trade association. The trustee liquidates the assets and distributes the proceeds to the creditors in proportion to their claim.

All creditors must agree to the plan because an assignment for the benefit of creditors is an act of bankruptcy and a dissenting creditor has the right to institute bankruptcy proceedings. However, since all creditors share alike, and since the assignment spares the expense and complications of a bankruptcy proceeding, there is little reason for a creditor to object.

The assignment is usually made under state common law. However, in some states, an assignment for the benefit of creditors is governed by statute. These statutes must be carefully followed.

Other methods of reorganizing a corporation. Other methods of reorganization under state law are sale of assets, and merger or consolidation.

The federal Bankruptcy Act also provides detailed procedures for the rehabilitation or liquidation of corporations in financial difficulties.

Reorganization under federal law. A new National Bankruptcy Act was enacted by Congress, effective Oct. 1, 1979, to provide reorganization procedures for businesses in financial distress [U.S. Code Title 11]. Chapter 11 of the Act is the most important for corporations.

The essential purpose of Chapters X and XI is to preserve and continue a going business; but in cases where going concern values have been wholly or practically eliminated, the case is one for liquidation rather than reorganization.[1]

Jurisdiction of federal bankruptcy court over reorganization proceedings is exclusive and cannot be defeated by assumption by state

---

[1] In re Dutch Woodcraft Shops, Inc. (WD Mich. 1935) 14 F Supp 467.

court of jurisdiction of suit for fraud against debtor corporation in which state court is about to render or has rendered a judgment not dischargeable in bankruptcy.[2]

The new Chapter 11 takes a new approach to corporate reorganization, consolidating subjects dealt with under several chapters of the old Bankruptcy Act. The new consolidated Chapter 11 has no special procedure for companies with public debt or equity security holders. Instead, factors like the standard to be applied to solicitation of acceptances of a plan of reorganization are left to be determined by the court on a case-by-case basis. To ensure that an adequate investigation of the debtor will be conducted to determine fraud or wrongdoing on the part of present management, an examiner must be appointed in all cases in which the debtor's fixed, liquidated and unsecured debts exceed $5 million. Also, SEC and any party in interest who is creditor, equity security holder, indenture trustee or any committee representing creditors or equity security holders can raise any issue in a case under Chapter 11; they also have the right to appear and be heard. This lets the bankruptcy court evaluate all sides of a position and find the public interest. The advisory role of SEC lets the court balance the needs of public security holders against equally important public needs relating to the economy like employment and production, and other factors like the public health and safety and the protection of the national interest.

Chapter XI of the former Bankruptcy Act had two drawbacks that Chapter 11 of the new Act overcomes. First, Chapter XI did not let a debtor "affect" secured creditors or shareholders, unless they consented. Second, a debtor corporation in Chapter XI often could not get a discharge in respect of certain kinds of claims including fraud claims, even in cases where the debtor was being run by new management. The new Chapter 11 solves these problems and so has greater utility and flexibility than the old Chapter XI.

A state court cannot enjoin a corporation from filing a petition for reorganization,[3] and a dissolved corporation, during time the state statute continues its existence for winding-up purposes, may file a petition for reorganization under the Bankrupty Act;[4] but not thereafter.[5]

---

[2] In re Cloisters Bldg. Corp. (CA-7 1935) 79 F2d 694.
[3] De Kalb Trust & Savings Bank v De Paul Educational Aid Society, (1934) 278 Ill. App. 102.
[4] In re International Sugar Feed Co. (D Minn. 1938) 23 F Supp 197.
[5] Chicago Title & Trust Co. v Forty-one Thirty-six Wilcox Building Corp., (1937) 302 US 120, 58 S Ct 125.

Also, a corporation reinstated after dissolution for non-payment of taxes can file a voluntary petition in bankruptcy.[6]

A stockholder not given notice of a stockholders' meeting to authorize the filing of a petition and the transfer of corporate assets to a new corporation reorganization plan can recover damages against the directors and others responsible for the proceedings for loss of the proportionate interest in the new corporation that he would have received had hc bccn treated on the same basis as other stockholders.[7]

Protective committee arrangements. The committee may invite stockholders to deposit their securities in the custody of a trust company under a "deposit agreement." This agreement establishes the terms on which securities may be deposited and defines the powers of the depositors and of the committee.[8]

Certificates of deposit, which are issued to the security holders to evidence their interest in the committee assets, may have to be registered with the Securities and Exchange Commission under the Securities Act of 1933.[9]

Usually persons who were interested in the flotation of the issue and whose reputations guarantee earnest and effective effort will make up the committee; the members, however, are not required to have any direct interest either in the security or the corporation.[10] A corporation can have as one of its powers, the power to act as a committee for bondholders in a reorganization.[11]

The committee must act fairly and cannot contract for secret profits.[12] In general it may be said that a protective committee has the same power as the holders of the deposited securities.[13] The committee members are trustees and have full right to act as provided in the agreement.[14]

Bondholders' protective committee is entitled to compensation for its services in the reorganization of a corporation and does not forfeit its right to compensation by effort to sustain, against desire of majority bondholders, resale of corporate property.[15]

---

[6] McClung v Hill (5 Cir. 1938) 96 F2d 235.
[7] Mills v Tiffany's, Inc., (1938) 123 Conn. 631, 198 Atl 185.
[8] See, for example, Tracy, "Corporate Foreclosure" pp. 490, et seq; Dewing, "Financial Policy of Corporations" pp. 939–40; Cravath, "Reorganization of Corporations" in "Some Legal Phases of Corporate Financing, Reorganizations and Regulations."
[9] See Prentice-Hall Securities Regulation.
[10] Haines v Kinderhook & Hudson Ry., (1898) 33 App. Div. 154, 53 N.Y.S. 368.
[11] Jewett v Com. Bond Corp., (1934) 241 App. Div. 522, 271 N.Y.S. 522.
[12] Marshall v Lovell (CA–8 1927) 19 F2d 751; cert den 276 US 616, 48 S Ct 207.
[13] Trustees System Co. of Pa. v Payne (3 Cir. 1933) 565 F2d 103.
[14] Bullard v City of Cisco, (1933) 290 US 179, 54 S Ct 177.
[15] Lewis v Fisher, (1938) 174 Md. 41, 197 Atl 571.

Dissolution—definition. A corporation is said to be dissolved when its existence is terminated, its charter extinguished,[16] its affairs wound up, and its assets distributed among creditors and stockholders.

A dissolution of a corporation has been defined as the death of the corporation, a disintegration, a separation, a going out of business.[17]

While dissolution is not effected merely by failure of a corporation to exercise the powers granted by its charter, nor by suspension of business and abandonment of the corporate enterprise,[18] such inaction may be grounds for forfeiture of the charter by the state in a proper proceeding.

Similarly, dissolution does not take place simply by reason of a sale of all the corporation's assets,[19] by the appointment of a receiver,[20] or by purchase of all the stock by one person.[21] But dissolution may result from proceedings under the federal Bankruptcy Act.

Dissolution of a corporation is governed by the law of the state of its incorporation.[22]

Classification of methods of dissolution. Dissolutions may be broadly classified as (1) voluntary and (2) involuntary. Voluntary dissolution, as the term implies, is the result of some action on the part of the corporation itself, generally prescribed by statute, evidencing a surrender of the corporate charter. Involuntary dissolution, on the other hand, may be brought about by, for example, (a) expiration of the corporation's period of existence, (b) failure to pay annual taxes or file its annual report, (c) failure to appoint or maintain a registered agent or office, or (d) a suit in equity by a minority stockholder or creditor.

Voluntary dissolution. All states by statute permit a corporation to dissolve voluntarily by one or more of the following methods:

---

[16]Parker v Bethel Hotel Co., (1896) 91 Tenn. 252, 34 SW 209.

[17]Moore v Los Lugos Gold Mines, (1933) 172 Wash. 570, 21 P2d 253.

[18]Wall and Beaver Street Corp. v Munson Line, Inc. (D Md 1943) 58 F Supp 101; Graham-Newman Corp. v Franklin Distilling Co., (1942) 26 Del. Ch. 233, 27 A2d 142; Coleman v Woodland Hills Co., (1945) 72 Ga. App. 92, 33 SE2d 20.

[19]Hunn v United States (CA–8 1932) 10 F2d 430; Schneider v Schneider, (1941) 347 No. 102, 146 SW2d 584; In re Clark's Will, (1931) 257 N.Y. S. 487, 178 NE 766; Levin v Pittsburgh United Corp., (1938) 330 Pa. 457, 199 Atl 332, s.c., (1939) 334 Pa. 107, 5 A2d 890, c.c., (1940) 338 Pa. 328, 12 A2d 430.

[20]Standard Roller Bearing Co. v Hess-Bright Mfg. Co. (CA–3 1921) 275 F916; In re Beaver Cotton Mills (ND Ga. 1921) 275 F 498.

[21]Coleman v Woodland Hills Co., (1945) 72 Ga App. 92, 33 SE2d 20; Kentucky Harlan Coal Co. v Harlan Gas Coal Co., (1932) 245 Ky. 234, 53 SW2d 538.

[22]U.S. Truck Co. v Pa. Surety Corp., (1932) 259 Mich. 422, 242 NW 311.

(1) By the incorporators before the corporation has begun business and before it has issued shares. The incorporators simply file a certificate of dissolution containing certain required information with a designated state official.

(2) By written consent of all the shareholders without a meeting.

(3) By the consent of some specified majority of the shareholders given at a meeting.

All formalities prescribed by these statutes must be strictly complied with to bring about a legal dissolution.[23] Details of the procedure vary among the states. The most common procedure is by resolution of the board of directors recommending dissolution followed by adoption of a stockholder's resolution dissolving the corporation.

In voting for dissolution, the majority stockholders must exercise the utmost good faith, and the courts will interfere to prevent fraud and oppression of the minority.[24] If the dissolution is used as a device for the majority to appropriate the business, the directors, officers and stockholders responsible cannot be liable in damages to the minority stockholders for the value of their shares.[25]

Also, the majority stockholders, directors, and officers cannot override the rights of a minority stockholder by dissolving the corporation pending his derivative action.[26]

Dissenters' right to appraisal: Shareholders dissenting from a voluntary dissolution have no statutory right to payment for their shares, except in special circumstances in some states; for example, if on liquidation assets are to be distributed in kind. A complaint as to the manner in which the assets are distributed, however is not itself grounds for a derivative action, since payment for shares is the proper remedy.[27]

Stockholders, directors and officers can abandon the corporation and thereby effect, a *de facto* dissolution. They are then entitled, if

---

[23]Underwood v Comm. of Int. Rev. (CA–7 1932) 56 F2d 64. See also Chorpenning v Yellow Cab Co., (1933) 113 N.J. Eq. 389, 167 Atl 12; Moore v Los Lugos Gold Mines, (1933) 172 Wash. 570, 21 P2d 253.

[24]J. H. Lane & Co. v Maple Cotton Mills (CA–4 1915) 226 F 692; Reade v Broadway Theatre Co., (1926) 99 N.J. Eq. 282, 132 Atl 477; Kavanaugh v Kavanaugh Knitting Co., (1919) 226 N.Y. 185, 123 NE 148. See also Stevenson v Sicklesteel Lumber Co., (1922) 219 Mich. 18, 188 NW 449; Elston v Elston & Co., (1932) 131 Me. 149, 159 Atl 731.

[25]Lebold v Inland Steel Co. (CA–7 1941) 125 F2d 369, cert den 316 US 675 62 S Ct 1045; see also 136 F2d 876.

[26]Welt v Beachcomber, Inc., (1937) 166 Misc. 29, 1 N.Y.S.2d 177; Matter of Garay (S Ct N.Y. 1970) NYLJ, 10–8–70, p. 2.

[27]Gartenberg v Rosen (S Ct 1967) *NYLJ* 10–26–67, p. 16. cf. Independent Investor Protective League v Time, Inc., (1980) 50 NY 2d 259, 406 NE 2d 486.

interests of creditors do not intervene, to the conveyance and equitable ownership of corporate property (to which they did not receive legal title from the corporation) sufficient to allow them to insure the property and collect insurance proceeds thereon.[28]

An insolvent corporation may be voluntarily dissolved and trustees in dissolution may sell its property.[29]

Voluntary dissolution of a corporation will be converted into involuntary dissolution by appointment of receiver, where interests of company and stockholders require it.[30]

The courts will generally not inquire into the motives of a majority of the stockholders for authorizing dissolution.[31] Nor will it consider the voluntary dissolution of a tenant corporation as a breach of obligations under the lease when the lease was assigned to a strong new tenant and the landlord suffered no damage from the breach; the landlord won't be able to enjoin the dissolution.[32]

Court will entertain the petition of the majority stockholders to dissolve and wind up a corporation, despite a provision in the articles barring a disposition of all assets without the approval of all the stockholders.[33] But a one-third stockholder can't get dissolution despite the breach of a unanimity agreement.[34] Nor can a minority stockholder have a corporation dissolved on the ground that internal dissension has hampered its activities.[35]

When a corporation dissolves while a suit against it and its president is pending, the trustee in dissolution needn't be brought in as a party.[36] However, dissolution revokes the authority of an agent for the service of process to accept such service.[37]

Trustees winding up a dissolved corporation couldn't be surcharged even though they were negligent in relying on only one broker to sell the corporation's land, when there was no loss to the trust

---

[28] Dunning v Firemen's Ins. Co. of Newark, N.J., (1940) 194 S.C. 98, 8 SE2d 318.

[29] Beach v Wharton Min. Co., (1940) 128 N.J. Eq. 192, 15 A2d 605.

[30] Masterson v Lenox Realty Co., (1940) 127 Conn. 25, 15 A2d 11, c.c., (1940) 127 Conn. 35, 15 A2d 15.

[31] J.H. Lane & Co. v Maple Cotton Mills (CA-4, 1915) 226 F 692; Rossing v State Bank, (1917) 181 Iowa 1013, 165 NW 254; Major v American Malt & Grain Co., (1920) 110 Misc. 132, 181 N.Y.S. 152. See also In re Security Finance Co. (Cal. Dist. Ct of App. 1957) 308 P2d 531; Escondido Mutual Water Co. v George A. Hillebrecht, Inc., (1966) 241 Cal. App. 2d 410, 50 Cal. Rptr. 495.

[32] Rauch v Circle Theatre (Ind. App. 1978) 374 NE2d 546.

[33] In re Mayellen Apartments, Inc., (1955) 134 Cal. App. 2d 298, 285 P2d 943.

[34] Matter of Danzig (S Ct 1971) *NYLJ*, 12-7-71, p. 17.

[35] Horne v Radiological Health Services, (1975) 83 Misc. 2d 446, 371 N.Y.S. 2d 948.

[36] Chapman v L. & N. Grove, Inc. (Fla. Dist. Ct App. 1972) 265 S2d 725.

[37] Custom Shop Associates v Minskott (S Ct 1977) *NYLJ*, 5-24-77, p. 4.

corpus or any showing of self-dealing, since the cash terms of the sale were reasonable and consistent with the main trust purpose.[38] However, when the majority dissolve a corporation, sell its assets and force the minority to accept worthless promotional shares, the minority can sue for breach of fiduciary duty.[39] And damages can be awarded against a liquidator who breaches his duty by selling the corporation's assets to his own corporation for too little, even though the sale couldn't be rescinded, when subsequent buyers of the assets didn't get timely notice of the stockholder's suit.[40] And a liquidation plan providing for payment of "book value" to minority stockholders will be revised by a court to "fair value" when that is more.[41] A liquidator of corporation must retain corporate assets till tax liabilities are determined; he can't pay consulting fees till then.[42]

Dissolution procedure. The usual procedure for dissolution is as follows:

(1) The board of directors adopts a resolution recommending that the corporation be dissolved voluntarily, and directing that the question of dissolution be submitted to a vote at an annual or special meeting of shareholders.

The directors in determining whether dissolution is advisable cannot consider their personal wishes, comfort, or advantage.[43] And in the absence of fraud or bad faith a court will not interfere with directors, backed by majority stockholders, who refuse to initiate proceedings for dissolution of corporation.[44]

(2) Notice of a meeting to consider the advisability of voluntarily dissolving the corporation is given to the stockholders within the time and in the manner provided by statute.

However, shareholders may waive publication of notice of a proposed voluntary dissolution when there's unanimous written consent to such action.[45]

(3) A resolution to dissolve the corporation is adopted at the meeting duly called and held, by the required proportion of the stockholders.

---

[38] Lockwood v OFB Corp. (Del. Ch. 1973) 305 A2d 636.
[39] Grain v Electronic Memories & Magnetics Corp., (1975) 50 Cal. App. 3d 509, 123 Cal. Rptr. 419.
[40] Noe v Rousse (La. 1975) 310 S2d 806.
[41] Kirtz v Grossman (Mo. App. 1971) 463 SW2d 541.
[42] Berger v Berger Miller, Inc. (S Ct 1979) NYLJ 1–22–79, p. 11.
[43] Kavanaugh v Kavanaugh Knitting Co., (1919) 226 N.Y. 185, 123 NE 148.
[44] Hayman v Brown, (1941) 176 Misc. 176, 26 N.Y.S.2d 898.
[45] OAG Ariz., No. 70–3, 12–26–69.

Unless it is shown that a legal meeting of stockholders, the requisite proportion of stockholders voted to voluntarily dissolve corporation, court is without jurisdiction to order dissolution.[46]

(4) A certificate evidencing the fact that the proper consent of stockholders to a voluntary dissolution has been obtained is executed by the proper officers of the corporation and is filed with a designated state official. The form of certificate will vary from state to state.

Dissolution proceedings may be insufficient if the certificate of dissolution fails to contain the consent of the stockholders as required by statute.[47]

(5) Notice of dissolution is given to creditors by publication of the certificate of dissolution, or by mailing a copy of it to each known creditor, or in some other manner. Failure to notify creditors could impose personal liability on the shareholders after dissolution.[48]

In some states the shareholders, creditors, or the corporation may apply to the courts for supervision of the dissolution.

Creditors may oppose the dissolution,[49] but in the absence of fraud or injury to the rights of creditors, a court will not undo, by means of a liquidating receivership, what the parties have done in winding up a corporation and distributing its assets, although what was done was not authorized by law.[50]

One dentist-stockholder in a professional corporation can't bar the other three dentist-stockholders from dissolving the corporation on the ground that he was no longer "carrying his weight," since the majority could liquidate the assets of the corporation; his only right was to have his stock appraised.[51]

In some states, a corporation can amend its articles to shorten its period of duration, and thus terminate its existence without dissolution proceedings.[52] One advantage of this method could be the smaller stockholder vote needed to amend the articles than is needed to dissolve. However, this advantage has been eliminated in those states

[46]Farmers Union Coop. Brokerage v Palisades Farmers Union, (1943) 69 S.D. 126, 7 NW2d 293, c.c., State v Farmers Union Coop. Brokerage, (1944) 70 S.D. 14, 13 NW2d 809.

[47]Chorpenning v Yellow Cab Co., (1933) 113 N.J. Eq. 389, 167 A 12; Escondido Mutual Water Co. v George A. Hillebrecht, Inc., (1966) 241 Cal. App. 2d 410, 50 Cal. Rptr. 495.

[48]Elmhurst Stamping & Mfg. Co. v Amax Plating, Inc., (1978) 67 Ill. App. 3d 257; Standard Financial Corp. v Automatic Foods Corp. (CA-7 1967) 382 F2d 1; Sears v Weissman, (1962) 6 Ill. App. 3d 827, 286 NE2d 777.

[49]State ex rel New First Nat'l Bank v White, (1928) 223 Mo. App. 36, 7 SW2d 475.

[50]Salembier v Great Neck Bond & Mortgage Corp., (1937) 22 Del. Ch. 183, 194 A 35.

[51]Leavitt v Cantor (S Ct 1976) *NYLJ,* 12–14–76, p. 6.

[52]OAG W.Va. No. 34, 10–30–56; OAG Ohio No. 77–089, 12–12–77.

that by statute require the same proportion of stockholder vote to amend the articles to *shorten* the period of existence as is needed to dissolve.

Revocation of dissolution. Statutes in some states permit the revocation of voluntary dissolution proceedings after they have been begun. Revocation can be by written consent of all the shareholders without a meeting, or by resolution of the board of directors recommending revocation followed by adoption of a shareholder's resolution revoking the dissolution. A "statement of intent to dissolve" or similar document may have to be filed with a designated state official.

When the dissolution proceedings have been revoked, the corporation can again carry on its regular business.

Involuntary dissolution by expiration of charter. The articles of most corporations now generally provide for perpetual existence, but if they fail to do so, that existence ends at the expiration of whatever term is specifically fixed in the articles.[53] However, a corporation does not become so extinct by expiration of a specific term as to permit a tenant to block the corporation's suit to recover possession of its property by claiming no such corporation exists.[54]

No adjudication of a court is necessary to terminate the corporate life.[55] If, after the expiration of its existence a corporation continues to conduct its corporate business it may be liable as a *de facto* corporation[56] for property and services furnished it, even though the property and services were furnished to it under a name different from the name it used as a corporation.[57] However, when a corporation's charter expires, it ceases to exist for all purposes except winding up; after expiration, it's not even a de facto corporation even though it continues its business for 10 years after termination and the state recognizes its existence.[58]

---

[53] In re F. H. Koretke Brass & Mfg. Co., Ltd., (1940) 195 La. 415, 196 So 917; Grand Rapids Trust Co. v Carpenter, (1925) 229 Mich. 582, 201 NW 882.

[54] West v Flynn Realty Co., (1936) 53 Ga. App. 594, 186 SE 753. See also, West v Flynn Realty Co., (1936) 54 Ga. App. 523, 188 SE 468; Black River Associates, Inc. v Goehler, (1967) 126 Vt. 394, 233 A2d 175.

[55] In re Friedman, (1917) 177 App. Div. 755, 164 N.Y.S. 892.

[56] See Elson v Schmidt, (1941) 140 Neb. 646, 1 NW2d 314, c.c., Brown v Price, (1941) 140 Neb. 644, 1 NW2d 319.

[57] Hall v Kimsey, (1934) 48 Ga. App. 605, 173 SE 437.

[58] Opinion of Attorney General of Florida, No. 059-104, 6-4-59.

Trustees in dissolution who violate their duties by continuing corporation instead of winding it up may be personally liable in damages at suit of individual stockholder for injury to trust estate.[59]

In some states, the statute permits an extension of the term of existence, either by amendment of the articles or by filing of a certificate of renewal with designated authorities.

In some states, renewal must be applied for before expiration of existence; in other states, it may be requested after expiration.

Petition for revival of charter of corporation is properly brought in the name of the corporation; it's not defective because it's not brought in the names of the persons who procured the original charter.[60]

The consent of stockholders or of directors to such renewal is generally required. And once the corporation has gone out of existence with shareholder approval, a stockholder can't compel the corporation to furnish a list of stockholders for the purpose of calling a meeting to renew the corporate charter.[61]

Under a statute that didn't provide for renewal of corporate existence, new articles of incorporation filed after a corporate charter elapsed didn't revive the old corporation; the new one had no right to the property of the old corporation, absent a formal conveyance, and so couldn't sue for trespass on it.[62]

The existence of the corporation is in some instances extended for a limited time after the charter has expired in order to enable the corporation to wind up its affairs.[63]

One way of winding up its affairs is for the corporation to sell all its assets to new company formed for that purpose.[64]

A dissolved corporation during the time a state statute continues its existence for winding up purposes may file a petition for reorganization under the National Bankruptcy Act.[65] It may not do so thereafter.[66]

---

[59] Word v Union Bank & Trust Co., (1940) 111 Mont. 279, 107 P2d 1083, c.c., State v Dist. Ct., (1941) 112 Mont. 458, 117 P2d 494.

[60] Atlanta Trust Co. v Oglethorpe University, (1939) 187 Ga. 766, 2 SE2d 403.

[61] Willard v Harrworth Corporation (Del. 1970) 267 A2d 577.

[62] Eagle Pass Realty Co. v Esparza (Tex. App. 1971) 474, SW2d 624.

[63] M. H. McCarthy Co. v Central Lumber & Coal Co., (1927) 204 Iowa 207, 215 NW 250; Kash v Lewis, (1928) 224 Ky. 679, 6 SW2d 1098; Grand Rapids Trust Co. v Carpenter, (1925) 229 Mich. 582, 201 NW 882.

[64] Greene v Stevenson, (1943) 295 Ky. 832, 175 SW2d 519.

[65] In re International Sugar Feed Co. (D Minn 1938) 23 F Supp 197.

[66] Chicago Title & Trust Co. v 4136 Wilcox Building Corp., (1937) 302 US 120, 58 S Ct 125.

Also a corporation reinstated after dissolution for nonpayment of taxes can file an involuntary petition in bankruptcy.[67]

Action of directors as trustees of corporation, charter of which has expired, in transferring assets of dissolved company to newly formed corporation constitutes settlement of dissolved company's affairs; does not constitute conversion of dissenting stockholder's shares in old company.[68]

Involuntary dissolution by equity suit of stockholder or creditor. Formerly the general rule was that a minority stockholder had no right to bring a suit to wind up the affairs of a solvent corporation, unless a statute specifically authorized it.[69] That's now changed—even without a statute, an equity court can dissolve a corporation if it's shown that dissolution is needed to protect the interests of stockholders or creditors.[70]

Such protection may be required in the event of fraud on the part of majority stockholders,[71] mismanagement on the part of directors or officers,[72] or such dissension among stockholders as to render impossible a continuation of the business.[73] The last situation may result in a deadlock dissolution. However, adoption by the corporate management of a policy of gradual liquidation of the corporation does not result in a nonuser of corporate functions authorizing the

---

[67] McClung v Hill (CA-5 1938) 96 F2d 235.

[68] Tenison v Wilson (Tex. Civ. App. 1941) 151 SW2d 327.

[69] Bleck v East Boston Co., (1939) 302 Mass. 127, 18 NE2d 536; Flemming v Heffner & Flemming, (1933) 263 Mich. 561, 248 NW 900; Schneider v Schneider, (1941) 347 Mo. 102, 146 SW2d 584.

[70] National Benefit Life Ins. Co. v Shaw-Walker Co. (D D.C. 1940) 111 F2d 497; Masterson v Lenox Realty Co., (1940) 127 Conn. 25, 15 A2d 11, c.c., (1940) 127 Conn. 35, 15 A2d 15; Specialty Furniture Co. v Rusche, (1937) 212 Ind. 184, 6 NE2d 959; Dorf v Hill Bus Co., (1947) 140 N.J. Eq. 444, 54 A2d 761; Lennan v Blakeley, (1947) 72 N.Y.S.2d 901, aff'd 273 App. Div. 767, 75 N.Y.S.2d 331, leave to appeal denied, 273 App. Div. 846; Ward v Colcord, (1969) 110 Ill App. 2d 68, 249 NE2d 137; Leibert v Clapp, (1963) 13 N.Y.2d 313, 247 N.Y.S.2d 102.

[71] Stott Realty Co. v Orloff, (1933) 262 Mich. 375, 247 NW 698; Rugger v Mt. Hood Electric Co., (1933) 143 Or. 193, 20 P2d 412; Lowder v All Star Mills, Inc. (NC S Ct 1981) 273 SE 2d 247.

[72] Ashley v Keith Oil Corp. (D Mass. 1947) 73 F Supp 37; Burnham v Arcola Sugar Mills Co. (SD Tex. 1932) 2 F Supp 738; Altoona Warehouse Co. v Bynum, (1942) 242 Ala. 540, 7 S2d 497; Loney v Consol. Water Co. of Pomona, (1932) 122 Cal. App. 350, 9 P2d 888; Barnett v International Tennis Corp., (1978) Mich. App. 263 NW2d 908 (dissension among stockholders, lack of formality in accounting and carelessness in running a corporation didn't justify its dissolution absent a showing that leaving its management in office would lead to its ruin).

[73] Cowin v Salmon, (1947) Ala. 28 S2d 633; Merlino v Fresno Macaroni Mfg. Co., (1944) 64 Cal. App2d 462, 148 P2d 884; Olechny v Thadeus Kosciuszko Soc., (1942) 128 Conn. 534, 24 A2d 249; Lush'us Brand Distributors, Inc. v Ft. Dearborn Lithograph Co., (1947) Ill. App. 70 NE2d 737; Petition of Petters, (1982) 117 Misc 2d 21, 457 NYS 2d 170; Matter of Ronan Paint Corp. (NY 1984) 98 AD 2d 413.

appointment of a receiver, at the suit of a stockholder, to wind up the company under applicable state law.[74] Also, majority shareholders are not proper parties to a suit alleging unfairness brought by the minority, since the corporation is the real party in interest.[75] And a guarantor of a corporation's promissory notes can't have a receiver appointed for a corporation, when the guarantor didn't make the corporation a party to the suit; nor will the court appoint a receiver, since the petition didn't allege the statutory or equitable grounds on which it was based.[76] Similarly, the issuance of no par instead of $1 par stock is not a ground for dissolution, since the issuance of stock is not a condition precedent to corporate existence.[77]

Oppression of the minority by the majority can be ground for dissolution. Some examples where the courts found oppressive tactics:

Two stockholders discharged a third equal owner as officer and as employee.[78]

Majority completely excluded the minority from any voice in the operation of the business.[79]

Alleged conspiracy by two stockholders to oust the third on false charges of dishonesty.[80]

Some examples where no oppression was found:

Majority paid themselves somewhat high salaries, retained earnings (plausible business reasons) and removed the complaining shareholder from the board.[81]

Majority discharged minority for inadequate management.[82]

Directors of a medical corporation that was the lessor of a medical building failed to reelect two doctors to the board after they withdrew from the corporation's clinical practice, thus affecting their deferred compensation.[83]

A corporation will not be dissolved at the suit of a stockholder when there has been no fraud, the corporation's object appears attainable and it owes no debts of any consequence, even though

---

[74] Orman v Bransford Realty Co., (1934) 168 Tenn. 70, 73 SW2d 713; Bergman v Johnson (S Ct Wash. 1965) 405 P2d 715.

[75] Weisman v Odell, (1970) 83 Cal. Rptr. 563.

[76] Associated Bankers Credit Co. v Meis (Tex. App. 1970) 456 SW 2d 744.

[77] Drury v Abdullah (Mass. App. 1980) 401 NE 2d 154.

[78] Application of Topper (N Y S Ct 1980) 433 NYS 2d 359.

[79] Goben v Barry, (1984) 234 Kan 721, 676 P 2d 90; Gooding v Millet (La. App. 1983) 430 S 2d 742; Skierka v Skierka Bros., Inc. (Mont. S Ct 1981) 629 P 2d 214.

[80] Notzke v The Art Gallery, Inc., (1980) 84 Ill. App. 3d 294, 405 NE 2d 839.

[81] Iwasaki v Iwasaki Bros., Inc., (1982) 58 Or. App. 543, 649 P 2d 598.

[82] Capital Toyota, Inc. v Gervin (Miss. S Ct 1980) 381 S 2d 1038.

[83] Kisner v Coffey (Miss S Ct 1982) 418 S 2d 58.

financing to date may have been imprudent.[84] Nor will a court dissolve a farming corporation that is earning little profit and won't sell its highly appreciated land for industrial purposes, in the absence of proof, as required by statute, that the corporate objectives were unattainable.[85]

On the other hand, dissolution won't be denied merely because profit is possible.[86] When the majority stockholder-director didn't loot, diminish, or waste the corporation's assets, a minority stockholder seeking to have the corporation dissolved on that ground will lose.[87] Likewise, a 40% stockholder can't get a dissolution on the ground that the 51% stockholder misappropriated the corporate assets by increasing his own salary and making corporate loans to a debtor corporation in which he had a one-third interest, when the majority stockholder's pay wasn't above that of competitors and the corporation didn't lose on the loans.[88] Minority stockholder can't sue to force dissolution if he bought his stock knowing the facts he complains of and with the purpose of starting suit.[89]

Generally, a receiver is appointed by the court to take the corporate property into his possession, to wind up the affairs of the corporation, and to make distribution among creditors and stockholders.[90] A receivership is, however, recognized as a radical remedy and is invoked only when no other relief would be adequate.[91] Thus, minority stockholders couldn't get a receiver appointed for a corporation for "gross mismanagement" by the majority stockholders

---

[84]Rose Theater Inc. v Jones, (1955) 224 Ark. 951, 278 SW2d 105.

[85]Gruenberg v Goldmine Plantation Inc. (La. App. 1978) 360 S2d 884.

[86]Taulin v Munsey Candlelight Corp. (App. Div. 1979) 415 NYS2d 438.

[87]Sandfield v Goldstein, (1977) 71 Misc. 2d 735, 336 N.Y.S. 2d 881.

[88]Baker v Commercial Body Builders, (1973) 264 Or. 614, 507 P2d 387.

[89]Gerstein v Tudor City Second Unit, Inc. NYLJ 4-11-58, p. 6.

[90]See Nat'l Ben. Life Ins. Co. v Shaw-Walker Co. (D D.C. 1940) 111 F2d 497; Masterson v Lenox Realty Co., (1940) 127 Conn. 25, 15 A2d 11, c.c., (1940) 127 Conn. 35, 15 A2d 15; Tri-City Electric Service Co. v Jarvis, (1933) 206 Ind. 5, 185 NE 136; Matter of Kaplan *NYLJ* 1-23-68, p. 16; Jones v Free, (1967) 83 Nev. 31, 422 P2d 551.

[91]Lichens Co. v Standard Commercial Tobacco Co., (1944) 28 Del. Ch. 220, 40 A2d 447; Stott Realty Co. v Orloff, (1933) 262 Mich. 375, 247 NW 698; Schneider v Schneider, (1941) 347 Mo. 102, 146 SW2d 584; Bowman v Gum, Inc., (1936) 321 Pa. 516, 184 Atl 258; Matter of Neldin v J.J.R. Realty Corp., (1969) 25 NY2d 543, 255 NE2d 713; Cumberland Publishing Co. Inc. v Adams Real Estate Corp. (Ct of App. Ky. 1968) 432 SW2d 808; McMunn v ML & H Lumber, Inc., (1967) 247 Ore. 319, 429 P2d 798; Porta-Drill, Inc. v R.M. Hall Corp., (1967) 423 Pa. 637, 223 A2d 526; Halpin v Marson, (1964) 20 A.D. 564, 245 N.Y.S. 2d 857; Dulsorth & Burress Tobacco Warehouse Co. v Burress (Ct of App Ky. 1963) 369 SW2d 129; Lafayette Realty Corp. v Moller, (1966) 247 Ind. 433, 215 NE2d 859; Texarkana College Bowl, Inc. v Phillips (Ct of Civ. App. Tex 1966) 408 SW2d 537; Cohen v Financial Acceptance Co., (1965) 56 Ill. App. 2d 359, 206 NE2d 308; Kruger v Gerth, (1975) 16 NY2d 802, 210 NE2d 355.

as officers-directors based on these allegations: (1) failure of the corporation to hold regular stockholders' meeting, (2) payment of loans or advance dividends to stockholders (the corporation was solvent at the time), (3) continued payment of salaries to corporate employees who became disabled and were no longer doing their work, (4) reduction of dividends because of the institution of a policy whereby 20% of profits was placed in capital reserves, (5) employment of the president's children by the corporation, (6) acquisition of an executive airplane.[92]

And stockholders couldn't have a receiver appointed or bar a corporation from selling assets, though it was suffering large losses, since the stockholders didn't show probable success in a derivative suit against the directors for securities law violations and mismanagements; showing only financial difficulty wasn't enough.[93] But a court will appoint a receiver for two corporations that hadn't held stockholders meetings for several years, hadn't filed corporate tax returns, and had made out checks to the president for his personal expenses.[94] And the minority stockholders can have a receiver appointed for their corporation when the directors fraudulently loaned the corporation's money to another corporation they controlled,[95] or, pending the resolution of a dispute over an employment contract of a minority stockholder, when the majority stockholder's sale of the corporation's property to a third party meant the corporation abandoned its business.[96] However, if a statute makes dissolution or appointment of a custodian for a corporation the sole remedy of minority stockholders against oppressive conduct by the majority, a court won't grant alternative remedies like directing dividend payments, disallowing the majority stockholder's rent claim and granting minority stockholders severance pay.[97]

Dissolution is not the proper remedy when an action is brought primarily to compel the corporation to declare dividends.[98] Nor can a stockholder who dissents from a sale of assets use it as the remedy, especially when she knew of the sale; appraisal is the exclusive remedy.[99] Similarly, it was error for the lower court to appoint a

[92] Fincher v Clairborne Butane Co. (La. App. 1977) 349 S2d 1014.
[93] B & B Investment Club v Kleinert's Inc. (ED Pa. 1974) 381 F Supp 569.
[94] Leeds v Billig (S Ct 1976) NYLJ 10-14-76, p. 6.
[95] Ross v 311 North Central Avenue Building Corp., (1970) 130 Ill. App. 336, 264 NE2d 406.
[96] Nishon's Inc. v Kendigian, (1975) 91 Nev. 504, 538 P2d 580.
[97] White v Perkins, (1972) 213 Va. 129, 189 SE2d 315.
[98] Muller v Silverstein, (1983) 92 AD 2d 455, 458 NYS 2d 597.
[99] Jones v Highway Inn, Inc. (Fla. App. 1983) 424 S 2d 944.

receiver for a mining company when one stockholder allegedly was interfering with another stockholder's access to the mining property, since an injunction was the proper remedy.[100]

When an insolvent corporation has made a preferential payment of a debt to its officers a creditor seeking to recover that preference must sue on behalf of all the corporation's creditors.[101] Similarly, an action to collect unpaid stock subscriptions must be brought on behalf of all the creditors of a corporation.[102]

In absence of fraud, illegality or *ultra vires,* a federal court sitting in equity and applying state corporation law cannot interfere with the internal management of a corporation by wholly or partially liquidating it, nor can it accomplish the same result by indirection by appointing a receiver, except in extraordinary cases.[103]

Although a combination of long-term management contracts to controlling stockholders, large corporate losses, and salary hikes to those in control, came close to amounting to oppressive or illegal conduct on the part of the controlling stockholders, that conduct wasn't serious enough to compel dissolution under a statute authorizing that relief for "illegal, oppressive, or fraudulent conduct" on the part of those in control.[104]

Likewise, none of the following was illegal, oppressive or fraudulent so as to justify dissolution of a professional corporation sought by an ex-employee-minority stockholder: (1) contributing $17,000 to a profit sharing and pension plan after an employee left— because that was within limits allowed by the Internal Revenue Service and to maintain employee morale, (2) lending money to the president and his wife—because the loan was repaid with 7% interest, and (3) paying a $20,000 bonus to the president—although entered on the books before it was earned, it wasn't drawn on till the end of the fiscal year and was based on overtime work.[105]

Under such a statute, income beneficiaries of a testamentary trust couldn't petition for dissolution of a corporation in which the trust owned shares since only holders of shares with voting rights could file such a petition.[106] Under still another such statute, a family

---

[100] Hines v Plante (Nev. S Ct 1983) 661 P 2d 880.
[101] Portage Insulated Pipe Co. v Coatanzo, (1971) 114 N.J. Super. 164, 275 A2d 452.
[102] Davis v Olson, (1971) 4 Wash. App. 390, 482 P2d 795.
[103] Wall and Beaver Street Corp. v Munson Line, Inc. (D Md. 1943) 58 F Supp 101. See also Williams v Green Bay & Western R.R. Co., (1946) 326 US 549, 66 S Ct 284; Ashton v O'Carroll (D Pa. 1946) 66 F Supp 585.
[104] Fix v Fix Material Co. Inc. (Mo. App. 1976) 538 SW2d 351.
[105] Lynch v Buchanan, (1977) 37 Md App. 413, 377 A2d 592.
[106] Turner v Elynn & Emrich Co. of Balto. City, (1973) 269 Md. 407, 306 A2d 218.

corporation was dissolved at the request of one of three stockholders who broke off contact with the corporation after a management dispute and was denied salary and dividends; the court granted the dissolution though it found no deadlock or mismanagement, since the statute permitted that to protect minority stockholders' rights.[107] A minority stockholder will be refused an involuntary dissolution of a corporation that ousted him from its presidency and raised the salary and bonuses of all other officers; a narrow construction of the applicable statute didn't include that situation as a basis for dissolution; other remedies existed.[108]

The co-owner of all of a corporation's stock could sue to liquidate the corporation on the ground the second co-owner allegedly misused corporate funds and mismanaged the corporation, though the second co-owner offered to buy the suing stockholder's shares under a by-law requiring a stockholder who wanted to sell his shares to give the corporation or the remaining stockholders the first chance to buy those shares; that by-law didn't bar the suit as the suit wasn't an offer to sell the shares but was a separate remedy for alleged violations of the stockholder's rights.[109] Only a bona fide shareholder can bring a suit to dissolve; a self-styled "vice president" can't.[110]

In the absence of such a statute, many courts refuse to decree a dissolution (although they will order a liquidation without a dissolution) on the theory that corporate life can only be extinguished under the authority of a statute.[111] Some courts will dissolve the corporation.[112]

The distinction is more formal than real. When all the assets have been sold and the proceeds distributed, the corporation is a mere shell without the means of pursuing its purposes—itself a ground for involuntary dissolution under some state statutes. Furthermore, the court may dissolve the corporation in effect by ordering the directors to petition for a dissolution under the voluntary dissolution statute.[113]

Involuntary dissolution through forfeiture of charter. The state that gave the corporation life may declare its existence at an end if the

---

[107]Stumpf v C.E. Stumpf & Sons, Inc., (1975) 47 Cal. App3d 230, 120 Cal. Rptr. 671.
[108]King v Coulter, (1976) 113 Ariz. 245, 550 P2d 623.
[109]Baylor v Beverly Book Co., (1975) 216 Va. 22, 216 SE2d 18.
[110]Concrete Construction Systems v Jensen (App. Div. 1978) 410 NYS2d 460.
[111]See, for example, Lichens Co. v Standard Commercial Tobacco Co., (1944) 28 Del. Ch. 220, 40 A2d 447.
[112]Flemming V Heffner & Flemming, (1933) 263 Mich. 561, 248 NW 900.
[113]Kroger v Jaburg, (1931) 231 A.D. 641, 248 N.Y.S. 387.

corporation abuses the powers given to it (misuser),[114] or if it fails to exercise them (nonuser).[115]

> *Example:* A state could have an insolvent corporate collection agency's charter forfeited and have a receiver for its assets and records appointed without notice, when the corporation illegally kept student loan funds owed to schools and its officers co-mingled those funds with their own and might, if notified, destroy corporate records.[116]

Unless a statute requires that the corporation be dissolved, a dissolution usually will not be decreed for acts merely in excess of the corporate powers. The interest of the public is to be considered, and there must be a willful abuse of power to justify a forfeiture.[117] Nor will a charter be forfeited merely because the corporation adopts an unauthorized method of prosecuting its authorized business when it did not engage in a business not authorized by its charter. Thus, although a corporation may not have power to enter into a partnership, its entry into joint venture with another company, without deviation from the business for which it was organized, will not warrant forfeiture of its charter.[118]

The state may also repeal a charter without cause if the right to do so has been reserved by the state either by law in force at the time the charter was granted or by the terms of the charter itself.[119] Where the State Corporation Commissioner revoked a bankrupt corporation's certificate of authority for failure to file reports and pay fees, a court couldn't order it reinstated.[120]

Statutes in the various states generally enumerate the grounds for which forfeiture of the charter may be declared by the state. These include, in addition to misuser and non-user for a fixed number of years, fraud practiced on the state in procuring the franchise, failure to

---

[114]In re Opinion of the Justices, (1921) 237 Mass. 619, 131 NE 29; N.Y. v Saksnit (S Ct 1972) NYLJ, 4–21–72, p. 15; State v Gamble-Robinson Fruit Co., (1919) 44 N.D. 376, 176 NW 103.

[115]Geinsendorfer v Rainbow Mill & Lumber Co., (1945) 70 Cal. App. 2d 705, 161 P2d 561; Graham-Newman Corp. v Franklin County Distilling Co., (1942) 26 Del. Ch. 233, 27 A2d 142; J. & I. Block, Inc. v Hi-Lo Corp., (1944) 182 Misc. 414, 48 N.Y.S.2d 894; State v Farmers Union Coop. Brokerage, (1944) 70 S.D. 14, 13 NW2d 809.

[116]Collegiate Recovery & Credit Assistance Programs, Inc. v State (Tex. Civ. App. 1975) 525 SW2d 900.

[117]State v Retail Credit Men's Ass'n of Chattanooga, (1931) 163 Tenn. 450, 43 SW2d 918. See also Burnham v Arcola Sugar Mills Co. (SD Tex. 1932) 2 F Supp 738.

[118]Com. v United Warehouse Co., (1943) 293 Ky. 502, 169 SW2d 300.

[119]See Greenwood v Union Freight R.R. Co., (1881) 105 US 13.

[120]Matter of Dolly Madison Industries (CA–3 1974) 504 F2d 499 (Va. law).

file annual reports,[121] failure to pay franchise taxes,[122] and failure to maintain a statutory agent.

In most states, failure to pay taxes suspends the charter, but the charter is revived upon payment of back taxes plus penalties and interest.[123] While its charter was suspended for nonpayment of taxes, a corporation could still buy property at a foreclosure sale and sell it to a third party; a deed executed for that conveyance was valid.[124] When a statute limiting the time in which a corporation can reinstate its charter merely authorizes, but doesn't require, cancellation of the charter after that time, the state can reinstate the charter after that time.[125]

Once a forfeited charter has been revived, only the State can void it on the ground that the parties applying for revival were not authorized to do so.[126] The revival of a corporate charter validates all conveyances or other contracts made between forfeiture and revival except where it would be inconsistent with action taken by surviving directors as trustees during that period.[127] A minority stockholder can't have a receiver appointed and the corporation liquidated on the ground its charter had been forfeited for nonpayment of franchise taxes so as to end the corporation's existence and vest its assets in its stockholders, when the charter had been reinstated by the payment of back taxes and penalties.[128]

Note that it is not a defense to a corporation's forfeiture of its charter for failure to file reports and nonpayment of franchise taxes that the Secretary of State failed to issue a warning notice to the corporation.[129]

"Informal dissolution." In most states, forfeiture of the charter for failure to file an annual report or pay annual taxes is brought about by a proclamation of some state official, for example, the secretary of state.[130] This may look like a good way to avoid the expense of formal

---

[121]State v A.B. Collins & Co. Inc. (WD Mo. 1940) 34 F Supp 550; Fidelity Metals Corp. v Risley, (1946) 77 Cal. App2d 377; 175 P2d 592.

[122]Trademen's Nat'l Bank & Trust Co. v Johnson (D Md. 1931) 54 F2d 367; A.R. Young v Dunne, (1927) 123 Kan. 176, 254 P 323; Bergerow v Belisle, (1931) 256 Mich. 225, 239 NW 277; OAG S.C., No. 1783, 1–15–65.

[123]Okla OAG, No. 66–335, 10–24–66; Sustain, Ltd. v Montgomery Ward & Co., (1966) 17 N.Y.2d 776, 217 NE2d 674.

[124]Parker v Life Homes, Inc., (1974) 22 NC App 297, 206 SE2d 344.

[125]Iowa OAG, 3–13–73.

[126]Engstrum v Paul Engstrum Associates, Inc., (1956) 36 Del. Ch. 19, 124 A2d 722.

[127]Cloverfield Improvement Ass'n, Inc. v Seabreeze Properties, Inc., (1977) Md. App. 374 A2d 906. To same effect, Mo. OAG, No. 210, 12–12–75.

[128]McGown v Kittel (Tex. Civ. App. 1972) 480 SW2d 47.

[129]Kans. OAG, No. 80–39, 2–11–80.

[130]Mo. OAG, No. 317, 9–27–70.

dissolution: Simply withhold filing the report or paying taxes until the state proclaims the corporation dissolved. Then, sell the assets, pay off creditors, and distribute the remainder among the stockholders.

But note that this procedure can have serious drawbacks. *Examples:*

(1) In some states, the taxes continue to accrue and the stockholders or directors may be personally liable for them.

(2) The directors may be personally liable on claims, known and unknown, that existed against the corporation at the time it was "dissolved."

A court may hold the directors personally liable, for example, if they sell the assets for less than they might have got, although they acted in good faith and derived no personal profit from the sale.[131]

Results of forfeiture for nonpayment of taxes. Interest and penalties can mount rapidly, of course. But the following consequences can be even more serious:

(1) In some states, forfeiture frees the corporate name for use by others. When this happens, the good will built up after years of effort can be lost completely.

(2) The right of the corporation to sue or to seek affirmative relief in the courts may be suspended,[132] and it may be deprived of its right to appeal from an adverse judgment.[133] However, the corporation can interpose a defense purely negative in character based on matters that arose while it was lawfully engaged in business.[134] Payment of back

---

[131]New York Credit Men's Adjustment Bureau v Weiss, (1953) 305 N.Y. 1, 110 NE2d 397.

[132]Stephens County v J.M. McCammon, Inc., (1932) Tex. 54 SW2d 880; Sulphur Spgs. Rec. Pk. v City of Camden, (1969) 247 Ark. 713, 447 SW2d 844; R.V. McGinnis Theatres v Video Independent Theatres, Inc. (CA-10 1967) 386 F2d 592; Rodar Leasing Corp. of Colo. v Wholesome Dairy, Inc. (Tex. Civ. App. 1969) 442 SW2d 467; Nelson v Miller (Dist. Ct of App. Fla. 1968) 212 S2d 66. See also Schwab v Schlumberger Well Surveying Corp., (1946) 145 Tex. 379, 198 SW2d 79; Jesse A. Bland Co. v Knot Concrete Products, Inc., (1960) 207 Tenn. 206, 338 SW2d 605; Reese Sales Co. Inc. v Gier, (1977) Wash. App. 557 P2d 1326; Kupski v Bal Investment Co., (1971) 35 Mich. App. 680, 192 NW2d 519 (corporation couldn't foreclose mortgage acquired while its charter was suspended); Mather Construction Co. v U.S. (Ct Cl. 1973) 475 F2d 1152 (contract claim against U.S. barred); Mackay Knobel Enterprises, Inc. v Teton Van Gas, Inc., (1969) 23 Utah 2d 200, 460 P2d 828; M.A.S. Inc. v Van Curler Broadcasting Corp. (D.C. 1973) 357 F Supp 686 (corporation could continue suit begun before revocation of its charter for failure to pay fee, without first paying the fee); Raleigh Swimming Pool Co. v Wake Forest Country Club, (1971) 11 NC App. 715, 182 SE2d 273 (suspension didn't bar suit begun less than five years later).

[133]Ocean Park Bath & Amusement Co. v Pac. Auto Park Co., (1940) 37 Cal. App. 2d 158, 98 P2d 1068; Gar-Lo, Inc. v Prudential S. & L. Ass'n, (1974) 41 Cal. App. 3d 242, 116 Cal. Rptr. 389; Laurel Crest, Inc. v Vaughn, (1969) 272 Cal. App. 2d 363, 77 Cal. Rptr. 538; Peacock Hill Ass'n. v Peacock Lagoon Constr. Co., (1972) 100 Cal. Rptr. 742.

[134]Bryan v Cleveland Sand & Gravel Co., (1940) Tex. Civ. App. 139 SW2d 612; Diverco Constructors, Inc. v Wilstein, (1970) 4 *CA* 3d 6, 85 Cal. Rptr. 851.

taxes may permit the corporation to continue or defend a suit begun prior to suspension.[135] Some states provide a grace period, like five years after suspension.[136] Also, even when a corporation couldn't bring the suit because it had failed to file required reports, dismissal with prejudice was too harsh—the court should allow the default to be cured.[137]

However, distinguish this from a case where the contract itself was entered into during the period of default—in that case, the corporation can't enforce the agreement.[138]

(3) Stockholders, directors, officers and agents of the corporation may be personally liable on debts contracted by the corporation while its charter was forfeited.[139] In some cases, later payment of the back taxes, and restoration of existence, etc., may absolve these persons from personal liability.[140]

How forfeiture is effected. Generally the statutes specify how forfeiture is effected. In some cases, the statutes prescribing forfeiture are self-executing, that is, a forfeiture automatically results upon breach of the conditions enumerated and the charter is lost without further proceedings.[141] In order to have this effect, however, the

---

[135]Rush Street Rugby Shop, Ltd. v Maryland Casualty Co. (CA-7 1969) 409 F2d 540; Duncan v Sunset Agricultural Minerals, (1969) 273 Cal. App. 2d 489, 78 Cal. Rptr. 339; The Traub Co. v Coffee Break Service, Inc., (1967) 66 Cal. 2d 368, 57 Cal. Rptr. 846, 425 P2d 790; Urich Oil Co. v Crown Discount Department Stores, (1973) 34 Cal. App. 2d 743, 110 Cal. Rptr. 316; Kaybill Corp. Inc. v Cherne, (1974) 24 Ill. App. 3d 309, 320 NE2d 598; York & York Constr. Co. v Alexander (DC App. 1972) 296 A2d 710; Stutzman Feed Service, Inc. v Todd & Sargeant, Inc. (SD Iowa 1972) 336 F Supp 417; Dept. of Highways v Martin (Okl. App. 1977) 574 P2d 611; La France Enterprises v Van Der Linden, (1977) 70 Cal. App. 3d 375, 138 Cal. Rptr. 690 (that corporation paid taxes only after indication of favorable result in case didn't deny it judgment); Spieier Tire Co., Inc. v Tony Benson Chevway Rental & Leasing, Inc. (Tex. App. 1982) 643 SW 2d 772.

[136]Philbin Investments, Inc. v Orb Enterprises, Ltd., (1978) 35 NC App. 622, 242 SE2d 176; Levey v Roosevelt Fed. S. & L. Ass'n (Mo. App. 1973) 504 SW2d 241.

[137]Central Contracting Co. Inc. v Goldman, (1973) 48 Mich. App. 604, 210 NW2d 901.

[138]Hearth Corp. v C-B-R Development Co. Inc. (Iowa 1973) 210 NW2d 632; D & W Central Station Alarm Co., Inc. v Copymasters, Inc. (N Y C Civ. Ct 1983) 471 NYS 2d 464.

[139]Matter of Hare (DC Md. 1962) 205 F Supp 881; Moore v Rommel, (1961) 233 Ark. 989, 350 SW2d 190; Vlasic Foods Co. v Russek, (1967) 7 Mich. App. 359 151 NW2d 872; Pepi, Inc. v Heclar Corp. (CA-3 1972) 458 F2d 1062; Mobil Oil Corp v Thoss (Fla. App. 1980) 385 S 2d 726; Nichols-Homeshield, Inc. v Mid-American Construction Supply, Inc. (Okl. S Ct 1982) 643 P 2d 309; Kessler Distributing Co. v Neill (Ia. App. 1982) 317 NW 2d 519; In re Estate of Plepel, (1983) 115 Ill. App. 3d 803; Chatman v Day, (1982) 7 Ohio App. 3d 281, 455 NE 2d 672; Mullenax v Edwards Sheet Metal Works, (1983) 279 Ark. 247, 650 SW 2d 582.

[140]Spector v Hart (Fla. App. 1962) 139 S2d 923; Marsh Furniture Co. v Solomon (Balto. City Ct 1958) Balto. Daily Record, 12–4–58, p. 2; Frederic G. Krapf & Son, Inc. v Corson (Del. 1968) 243 A2d 713; Contra: Lents, Inc. v Borstad, (1968) 251 Ore. 296, 445 P2d 597; Bergy Brothers, Inc. v Zeeland Feeder Pig, Inc., (1982) 415 Mich. 286, 327 NW 2d 305; Barker-Chadsey Co. v W.C. Fuller Co., Inc., (1983) 16 Mass. App. 1, 448 NE 2d 1283.

[141]California Nat. Supply Co. v Flack, (1920) 183 Cal. 124, 190 P 634.

statutes must clearly so provide.[142] In most cases no forfeiture occurs unless the state brings a direct proceeding for that purpose and a court decrees the forfeiture.[143] Such a proceeding by the state is known as a proceeding in *quo warranto.*

In a quo warranto proceeding the court in its discretion may declare a forfeiture of the corporate franchise or it may declare an ouster only of the corporation's right to continue the illegal acts shown.[144]

The proceeding may be instituted by the state solicitor or attorney general of his own accord or at the instance of an individual, called a relator, in his own name or in the name of the state.[145] Some states also provide for the revival of a charter or the reinstatement of a corporation dissolved for failing to file reports, pay taxes, and the like.[146]

After the involuntary dissolution of a corporation for one or more of the reasons set forth above, its power to engage in its ordinary business and the authority of others to act for it is terminated,[147] although technically its existence may continue.[148] Thus, a corporation whose charter had been revoked couldn't continue business by contracting to repair a house, since the statute allowed it only to wind up its affairs; a note and a deed of trust given in connection with the repairs were void and were not validated even by the later reinstatement of the corporate charter.[149] Statutes may provide, however, that suits may be started against such dissolved corporations,

---

[142] Four-S Razor Co. v Guymon, (1922) 110 Kan. 745, 205 P 635. See also Kaiser Land & Fruit Co. v Curry, (1909) 155 Cal. 638, 103 P 341; New York & L. I. Bridge Co. v Smith, (1896) 148 N.Y. 540, 42 NE 1088.

[143] Bergerow v Belisle, (1931) 256 Mich. 225, 239 NW 277; Julius J. Olson, J., In Trustees of Hamline University v Peacock, (1944) 217 Minn. 399, 14 NW2d 773.

[144] See State v Portland Natural Gas & Oil Co., (1899) 153 Ind. 483, 53 NE 1089.

[145] See People v Dashaway Ass'n, (1890) 84 Cal. 114, 24 P 277.

[146] See also Bates v Mitchell, (1948) 67 Ariz. 151, 192 P2d 720; Arnold v H. Piper Co., (1943) 319 Ill App 91, 48 NE2d 580; Stott v Stott Realty Co., (1939) 288 Mich. 35, 284 NW 635; Poritzky v Wachtel, (1941) 176 Misc. 633, 27 N.Y.S.2d 316.

[147] Arnold v Streck (CA-7 1939) 108 F2d 387; Glenman v Lincoln Inv. Corp. (D D.C. 1940) 110 F2d 130; Arnold v H. Piper Co., (1943) 319 Ill App 91, 48 NE2d 580; Black v Sivalls & Bryson, Inc. v Connell, (1939) 149 Kan. 118 86 P2d 545; Atlantic Mill & Lumber Realty Co. v Keefer, (1941) 179 Md. 496, 20 A2d 178; Studerus Oil Co. v Bienfang, (1939) 122 N.J. Law, 238, 4 A2d 787; Poritzky v Wachtel, (1941) 176 Misc. 633, 27 N.Y.S.2d 316.

[148] Cohn v Dowling (CA-6 1941) 123 F2d 408; Benton Harbor Federation v Nelson, (1942) 301 Mich. 465, 3 NW2d 844; Stensvad v Ottman, (1949) 123 Mont. 158 208 P2d 507 (Del. law).

[149] Accurate Construction Co. v Washington, D.C. (D.C. App. 1977) 378 A2d 681. To same effect on first point, see Cloverfields Improvement Assoc. Inc. v Seabreeze Properties, Inc., (1976) 32 Md. App. 421, 362 A2d 675. See also, on second point, (1977) 378 A2d 681.

generally for specific purposes, designating the persons upon whom service of process may be made, like the last directors or officers.[150]

Note also that a suit brought by a dissolved corporation does not abate; the court should merely substitute its proper legal successor as the plaintiff.[151]

Effect of dissolution. *Common law:* The common law rule is that, in the absence of a statute to the contrary, a dissolved corporation ceases to exist for any purpose;[152] it cannot sue or be sued,[153] it cannot hold[154] or convey property,[155] it cannot make contracts,[156] nor can it exercise any other powers granted by its charter.[157] However, merely as an incident to settling and closing its affairs, it can enter into a continuing obligation, like renewing a lease of its property.[158]

Dissolution does not impair remedies against the corporation, its stockholders, directors, or officers for liabilities incurred previous to dissolution.[159]

State statutes: To obviate the inconveniences and inequities resulting from the common-law rule, many states' statutes now provide that a dissolved corporation shall have a qualified existence for a limited time after dissolution for prosecuting and defending suits,[160]

---

[150]Seaboard Terminals Corp. v Standard Oil Co. (SD N.Y. 1940) 35 F Supp 566; Quigley v William M. Rideout & Co., (1939) Mo. App. 127 SW2d 37; In re S. M. & J. Eisenstadt, Inc., (1939) 256 App. Div. 488, 10 N.Y.S.2d 868, aff'd 283 N.Y. 578, NE2d; Wilner Friends Credit Ass'n, Inc. v Scheffres, (1941) 175 Misc. 909, 25 N.Y.S.2d 664; Carpenter & Carpenter, Inc. v Kingham, (1941) 56 Wyo. 314, 109 P2d 463 reh'g den, 110 P2d 824.

[151]River Cities Construction Co., Inc. v Barnard & Bush, Inc. (La. App. 1982) 413 S 2d 666.

[152]See Black, Sivalls & Bryson, Inc. v Connell, (1939) 149 Kan. 118, 86 P2d 545; Barrowman Coal Corp. v Kentland Coal & Coke Co., (1946) 302 Ky. 803, 196 SW2d 428; In re F. H. Koretke Brass & Mfg. Co., Ltd., (1940) 195 La. 415, 196 So 917, Elchinger v F. H. Koretke Brass & Mfg. Co., (1941) 196 La. 962, 200 So 314.

[153]National Labor Relations Board v Southport Petroleum Co. (5 Cir. 1941) 117 F2d 90, aff'd, (1942) 315 US 100 S Ct 452; Woodbury Granite Co. v US, (1945) Ct. of Cl., 59 F Supp 150; Trounstine v Bauer, Pogue & Co. (SD N.Y. 1942) 44 F Supp 767, aff'd (CA–2 1944) 144 F2d 379, cert den, (1944) 323 US 777 65 S Ct 190; Atkinson v Reid, (1932) 185 Ark. 301, 47 SW2d 571; Katenkamp v Super Ct., (1940) 16 Cal.2d 969, 108 P2d 1; Shore Management Corp. v Erickson Bros., (1942) 314 Ill App 571, 41 NE2d 972; Parkside Terrace Apartments, Inc. v Lindner, (1969) 252 Md. 271, 249 A2d 717.

[154]Klorfine v Cole, (1927) 121 Oreg. 76, 252 P 708.

[155]Bradley v Reppell, (1895) 133 Mo. 545, 32 SW 645.

[156]Van Landingham v United Tuna Packers, (1922) 189 Cal. 353, 208 P 973. See Stentor Electric Mfg. Co. v Klaxon Co. (CA–3 1940) 115 F2d 268, rev'd on other grounds, (1941) 313 US 487, 61 S Ct 1020; Laning v Nat. Ribbon & Carbon Paper Mfg. Co. (ND Ill. 1940) 40 F Supp 1005; Trounstine v Bauer, Pogue & Co. (SD N.Y. 1942) 44 F Supp 767, aff'd (CA–2 1944) 144 F2d 379, cert den, 323 US 777, 65 S Ct 190; Arnold v H. Piper Co., (1943) 319 Ill. App. 91, 48 NE2d 580.

[157]Bowe v Minnesota Milk Co., (1890) 44 Minn. 460, 47 NW 151.

[158]Kay Furniture Co. v Rovin, (1945) 312 Mich. 290, 20 NW2d 194.

[159]Gonzalez v Progressive Tool & Die Co. (ED N.Y. 1978) No. 77C–892, 8–10–78. See, however, Dick v Petersen, (1931) 90 Col. 83, 6 P2d 923.

[160]Gassert v Commercial Mechanisms, Inc. (N.M. S Ct 1979) 277 NW2d 392; Covington v Robinson, (1942) 242 Ala. 337, 6 S2d 421; Northwest Development, Inc. v Dunn, (1971) 29 Col.

disposing of and conveying its property,[161] settling and closing its affairs,[162] and dividing its assets, but not for the purpose of continuing its existence.[163] Statutes extending corporate life for specified periods for winding up purposes should be liberally construed.[164] But a corporation can't be sued after the statutory wind-up period.[165] However, note that an employee cannot hold the president of a dissolved corporation liable after the statutory wind-up period terminates for alleged failure to adequately provide for the corporation's prospective product liability, since that termination extinguishes all claims.[166] There is an exception, though: A minor's action can be brought even after the wind-up period.[167]

Whether a foreign corporation can be sued after its dissolution depends on the law of the state where it is incorporated.[168]

Here are some discriptions courts have given of the status and powers of dissolved corporations:

App 364, 483 P2d 1361; Feldesman v Chase, Harris, Forbes Corp., (1942) 179 Misc. 10, 37 N.Y.S.2d 143, modified and aff'd, (1942) 265 App. Div. 848; Berger v Levin (Dist. Ct of App. Fla 1970) 231 S2d 875; Goodsons & Co., Inc. v Federal Republic of Nigeria (S D N Y 1983) 558 F Supp 1204; Igbara Realty Corp. v New York Property Insurance Underwriting Ass'n, (1983) 94 2d AD 79, 463 NYS 2d 211; Jourdan v Missouri Valley Investment Co. (Mo. App. 1983) 651 SW 2d 169; Don Rich Corp. v Rossini, (1983) 1 Conn. App. 120, 468 A 2d 1273.

[161] Porter-Wadley Lumber Co. v Bailey (CA-5 1940) 110 F2d 974, cert den, (1940) 311 US 680, 61 S Ct 48 (La. Law); Markus v Chicago Title & Trust Co., (1940) 373 Ill. 557, 27 NE2d 463; Porter v Tampa Min. & Mill. Co., (1939) 59 Nev. 332, 93 P2d 741.

[162] Ohio OAG No. 77-089, 12-12-77; Underwood v Comm. of Internal Revenue (CA-7 1932) 56 F2d 64; Tradesmen's Nat'l Bank & Trust Co. v Johnson (D Md 1931) 54 F2d 367. See also Kimball v Cedars B. & L. Ass'n, (1942) NJLJ, 11-12-42, p. 5, col. 1; City of New York v New York & S.B.F. & S.T. Co., (1921) 231 N.Y. 18, 131 NE 554; Clayton v Southwestern Life Ins. Co., (1942) Tex. Civ. App. 158 SW2d 820 rev'd, McBridge v Clayton, (1942) 140 Tex. 71 166 SW2d 125; Tenison v Wilson, (1941) Tex. Civ. App. 151 SW2d 327.

[163] Duval v Commissioner of Internal Revenue (CA-5 1932) 57 F2d 496; Willard v Kimball, (1931) 277 Mass. 350, 178 NE 607; Houston v Utah Lake Land Water & Power Co., (1919) 55 Utah 393, 187 P 174; Lewis v Schwartz (N Y S Ct 1983) NYLJ 10-19-83 p 5.

[164] Kay Furniture Co. v Rovin, (1945) 312 Mich. 290, 20 NW2d 194; cf MBC, Inc. v Engel (N.H. S Ct 1979) 397 A2d 636; Midland Financial Corp. v Wisconsin Dep't of Revenue (Wis. App. 1982) 328 NW 2d 866; In re Citadel Industries, Inc. (Del. Ch 1980) 423 A 2d 500; Pollock v T&M Investments, Inc. (Fla. App. 1982) 420 S 2d 99.

[165] Johnson v Helicopter & Airplane Services, Corp. (D Md 1975) 404 F Supp 726; Patterson v Missouri Valley Steel, Inc., (1981) 229 Kan. 481, 625 P 2d 483; Hunter v Fort Worth Capital Corp. (Tex. S Ct 1981) 620 SW 2d 298; River Cities Construction Co., Inc. v Barnard & Burk, Inc. (La. App. 1982) 413 S 2d 666; Farmers Union Cooperative Ass'n v Mid-States Construction Co., (1982) 212 Neb. 147, 322 NW 2d 373; Showers v Cassier Asbestos Corp., Ltd (E D Pa 1983) 574 F Supp 322. cf Kennedy v Strand Radio Sales & Services, Inc., (1982) 14 Mass. App. 935, 437 NE 2d 241; Devlin Construction Corp v Drifway South Construction Corp., (1982) 14 Mass. App. 954, 437 NE 2d 1069; Bonsall v Piggly Wiggly Helms, Inc. (S. Car. S Ct 1981) 274 S. E. 2d 298.

[166] Blankenship v Demmler Mfg Co., (1980) 89 Ill. App. 3d 569, 411 NE 2d 1153.

[167] Moore v Nick's Fine Foods, (1984) 121 Ill. App. 3d 923, 460 NE 2d 420.

[168] Casselman v Denver Tramway Corp., (1978) Col. 577 P2d 293; Advance Machine Co. v Berry (Fla. App. 1979) 378 S 2d 326; North American Asbestos Corp. v The Superior Court of Alameda County, (1982) 128 Cal. App. 3d 138, 179 Cal. Reptr. 889; Gross v Hougland (CA-6 1983) 712 F 2d 1034.

Indictment of a corporation for a federal law violation does not abate on the corporation's dissolution when the state dissolution statute continues the dissolved corporation's existence for purposes of defending "suits" and "proceedings" against it.[169] This is true even if indictment follows completion of dissolution.[170] This question has had a controversial history,[171] apparently settled by the *Melrose* case.[172]

Closing up business includes the adjustment of taxes due and the execution of waivers extending the period for assessment of federal income taxes.[173]

After revocation of charter of corporation for failure to pay taxes directors as trustees have power to settle and close corporate affairs.[174]

Failure to file report and pay taxes does not disable corporation from conveying its property through duly elected officers in the course of winding up its affairs.[175]

Dissolved corporation can file voluntary petition in bankruptcy.[176] And a petition in bankruptcy can be filed against a dissolved corporation.[177]

Dissolved corporation can compel arbitration.[178]

Assignee of a corporation can sue in the corporation's name even though the corporation had voluntarily dissolved after the assignment.[179]

Dissolved foreign corporation can continue to remove standing timber it had bought since a statute of its state of incorporation permits it to exist for a period of years after dissolution to wind up its affairs.[180]

Statute providing for survival of remedies against a dissolved corporation does not apply to a contingent liability of a corporation that does not become actionable until after dissolution.[181]

A note given to a corporation after its dissolution is valid.[182]

---

[169]Melrose Distillers, Inc. v US, (1959) 359 US 271, 79 S Ct 763.

[170]US v San Diego Grocers Ass'n, Inc. (SD Cal. 1959) 177 F Supp 352.

[171]US v Brakes, Inc. (SD N.Y. 1958) 157 F Supp 916.

[172]Melrose Distillers, note 169 supra.

[173]Continental Oil Co. v US, (1936) US Ct of Cl. 14 F Supp 533.

[174]Byrnes v Hudson Valley Lumber Co., (1937) 294 N.Y. Supp. 978.

[175]Bruun v Cook, (1937) 280 Mich. 484, 273 NW 474; Honnegger's & Company, Inc. v Frog Valley Farm Services, Inc., (1980) 94 Mich. App. 568, 296 NW 2d 314.

[176]Partan v Niemi, (1934) 288 Mass. 111, 192 NE 527.

[177]In re Thomas (6 Cir. 1935) 78 F2d 602.

[178]Matter of Milton L. Ehrlich, Inc., (1959) 5 N.Y.S. 2d 275, 157 NE2d 495.

[179]Lapham Motors v Rutland Railway Corp., (1958) 121 Vt. 24, 146 A2d 242.

[180]Elk River Mill & Lumber Co. v Georgia Pacific Corp., (1958) 164 Cal. App. 23 459, 330 P2d 404.

[181]Pine Manor Homes, Inc. v Duval (Pa. Com. Pls. 1958) 75 Montg. Co. L.R. 255.

[182]Means v Norwood (Tex. Civ. App. 1958) 319 SW2d 817.

A foreign corporation cannot assert a counterclaim after its certificate of authority to do business was forfeited, even though the counterclaim arose prior to the forfeiture.[183]

An antitrust action brought by former stockholders of a dissolved corporation is barred when brought after the expiration of the statutory wind-up period, just as a suit by the corporation itself would be.[184]

Dissolution does not so thoroughly extinguish the existence of a corporation as to bar a corporation from restoration of its custom license when it paid its taxes and was reinstated.[185]

A dissolved corporation can't bring an action alleging monopolization, price fixing and price discrimination more than two years after it had been dissolved, though the corporation claimed it didn't know it had a cause of action, due to its fraudulent concealment.[186]

A corporation, dissolved on the death of its sole shareholder after the filing and removal of the case, can continue a suit for breach of contract.[187]

A foreign corporation whose charter was suspended for failure to pay state taxes can have a default judgment entered against it.[188]

Officers can execute consents to extend a tax audit after dissolution though no suit was begun against the corporation within the statutory period when the consents were given to preserve the interests of the corporation.[189]

A derivative action will be dismissed after the dissolution of a corporation.[190] So will an action in the name of a dissolved corporation, whose existence wasn't continued.[191]

The majority stockholder of a dissolved corporation can't sue for breach of contract after the winding-up period by saying that the action was for the shareholders, not for the corporation's, benefit.[192]

Directors-officers can't vote themselves large pay raises when the corporation had forfeited its charter for failure to file required reports

---

[183]Luna v Iowa-Mo. Enterprises, Inc. (Mo. App. 1980) 597 SW 2d 278.

[184]Canadian Ace Brewing v Joseph Schlitz Brewing Co. (CA-7 1980) 629 F 2d 1183.

[185]Bar Bea Truck Leasing Co., Inc. v United States (US Ct of Intern Tr 1982) 546 F Supp 558.

[186]Canadian Ace Brewing Co. v Anheuser-Busch, Inc. (ND Ill. 1978) 445 F Supp. 769.

[187]Froning's Inc. v Johnson Food Service, Inc. (CA-8 1978) 568 F2d 108.

[188]Weinstock v Sinatra (CD Cal. 1974) 379 F Supp 274.

[189]Associates Investment Co. v Comm. of Int. Rev., (1972) 59 TC 42.

[190]Katz v Aspinwall (CA-5 1972) 459 F2d 1045, cert den 409 US 1000, S Ct 316 (Ala. law).

[191]Gary Furniture & Appliance Co. v Skinner, (1972) 288 Ala. 617, 264 S2d 174.

[192]Koepke v First Nat. Bank of DeKalb, (1972) 5 Ill. App3d 799, 284 NE2d 671; cf Jainchill v Citibank, N.A. (App. Div. 1983) 469 NYS 2d 12.

and pay taxes, absent a strong showing of justification for the increases.[193]

A corporation's mortgages are invalid when given to continue its business after its charter was repealed for non-payment of taxes.[194]

The statutory two-year bar against actions against a dissolved corporation does not apply to an action against an individual stockholder who, when the corporation dissolved, agreed to assume its liabilities.[195]

Dissolution does not automatically sever the agency relationship, so service upon the corporation's registered agent within the wind-up period was a valid service.[196]

A corporation can bring a suit after its charter is restored, even though the suit was filed during the period of forfeiture, since the restoration validates all acts done.[197]

A corporation that executed articles of dissolution and had its certificate cancelled still has the obligation to pay delinquent license fees and file annual reports, whether or not it seeks reinstatement.[198]

Status of directors: Directors of a corporation in dissolution are frequently said to be trustees of the corporation,[199] and are made liable for failure properly to perform their duties. (However, statutes in some states expressly say they are not to be considered trustees).

Thus, the directors of dissolved corporation, as trustees in dissolution, are liable to former stockholder for damages for breach of contract, partially performed, for purchase of his stock by dissolved corporation.[200] Directors and officers engaged as trustees in winding up affairs of dissolved corporation are personally liable for transactions in the name of the company that are not in settlement of its affairs.[201] But directors and officers cannot be held personally liable to

---

[193]Blake v Nat'l Research Associates, Inc. (CA–4 1972) 466 F Supp 570 (Md. law).

[194]Higi v Elm Tree Village, (1971) 114 N.J. Super. 88, 274 A2d 845.

[195]Great American Insurance Co. v Byrd & Watkins Construction, Inc. (CA–6 1980) 630 F d 460.

[196]Vogel v Missouri Valley Steel, Inc., (1981) 229 Kan. 492, 625 P 2d 1123.

[197]A.R.D.C., Inc. v State Farm Fire & Casualty Co. (Mo. App. 1981) 619 SW 2d 843.

[198]Iowa OAG, No 83–9–4(L) 9–12–83.

[199]See Chorpenning v Yellow Cab Co., (1933) 113 N.J. E.q. 389, 167 Atl 12; Marine Trust Co. v Tralles, (1933) 147 Misc. 426, 263 N.Y.S. 750. See also Krueger v US (D N.J. 1940) 33 F Supp 102, rev'd, US v Krueger (CA–3 1941) F2d; Smith v Steele Motor Co., (1933) 53 Idaho 238, 22 P2d 1070; Wortham v Lachman-Rose Co. (Ct of App. Tex. 1969) 440 SW2d 351.

[200]Fox v Radel Leather Mfg. Co., (1937) 121 N.J. Eq. 291, 189 Atl 366.

[201]Trower v Stonebraker-Zea Live Stock Co. (ND Okla. 1937) 17 F Supp 687; Young v Blandin, (1943) 215 Minn. 111, 9 NW2d 313; Todd Shipyards Corp. v Lomm (Ct of App. La. 1966) 190 S2d 125; Kelly Broadcasting Co. v Sovereign Broadcast, Inc. (Nev. S Ct 1980) 606 P 2d 1089.

judgment creditor of corporation for moneys received from sales of remaining corporate assets to third persons; moneys were applied to back salaries due them and to expenses of winding up company, after creditors had been paid pursuant to a composition agreement to which plaintiff judgment creditor was a party.[202]

Trustees in dissolution who violate their duties by continuing corporation instead of winding it up may be personally liable in damages at suit of individual stockholder for injury to trust estate.[203]

The directors are charged with the duty of collecting debts due the corporation,[204] liquidating the assets, paying the corporate debts, and distributing the proceeds to the stockholders.[205] They act as fiduciaries for the corporation and the stockholders, and they cannot use their office to further their personal interests.[206] So a trustee in dissolution who speculates with corporate funds in his hands with resulting loss is personally liable to a shareholder to whom distribution should have been made.[207] But officers aren't personally liable for running the business of a distributor after its charter was forfeited but before the manufacturer ended the distributorship, absent a showing the officers hadn't acted for the corporation's best interests.[208]

Executory contracts: Executory contracts are not extinguished by dissolution. For example:

(1) When a parent corporation dissolves its subsidiary, taking over its property, the parent must execute the subsidiary's contracts.[209]

(2) The forfeiture of the corporate charter does not revoke a previously given power and assignment to collect debts due the corporation.[210]

(3) The corporation may exercise an option to purchase real estate after dissolution.[211]

---

[202]Chelsea Sales Corp. v A. Jacobs Co., Inc. (La App. 1940) 193 So 402.

[203]Schulz, Davis & Warren v Marinhovich (Mont. S Ct 1983) 661 P 2d 5; Word v Union Bank & Trust Co., (1940) 111 Mont. 279, 107 P2d 1083.

[204]See Hewson v Charles P. Gillen & Co., (1928) N.J. Eq., 142 Atl 250. Wyoming-Indiana Oil & Gas Co. v Weston, (1932) 43 Wyo. 526, 7 P2d 206.

[205]Wiseman v Sierra Highland Min. Co., (1941) 17 Cal. 2d 690, 111 P2d 646.

[206]Bisbee v Midland Linseed Products Co. (CA-8 1927) 19 F2d 24.

[207]Young v Blandin, (1943) 215 Minn. 111, 9 NW2d 313.

[208]Eaton, Yale & Towne v Sherman Industrial Equipment Co. (ED Ma. 1970) 316 F Supp. 435.

[209]Hughes Tool Co. v Comm. (CA-5 1945) 147 S2d 967.

[210]Sager v State Highway Commission, (1939) Mo. App. 125 SW2d 89.

[211]Nardis Sportswear v Simmons, (1949) 147 Tex. 608, 218 SW2d 451. See also Chestnut v Master Laboratories, (1947) 148 Neb. 378, 27 NW2d 541.

While the corporation may not be compelled to perform the contract, it may be compelled to pay damages for breach of contract.[212] Thus, a corporation that dissolves voluntarily must perform its obligation to pay for advisory services to be rendered over a specified period though that period extends beyond the dissolution date.[213] And an attorney retained by a corporation for a definite period at a definite minimum fee can recover the total amount due under the retainer from the corporation's liquidator when it later dissolves during the life of the retainer.[214] But when a stockholder-employee consents to and participates in the dissolution proceedings, this is tantamount to abandonment of his employment contract.[215]

A corporation is not liable for damages for alleged negligence when the accident that caused the injury occurred after dissolution.[216] But a manufacturer of a crop harvester couldn't escape a product liability suit, though the accident sued on occurred after the corporation's dissolution, when the machine that caused it was made and sold before then.[217]

Dissolution of a corporation does not terminate a lease.[218] A dissolved corporation may foreclose on a mortgage even if the winding up period has expired, since only the debt and not the securing mortgage is extinguished.[219]

Revival of existence: Some states have statutes that allow you to renew or revive the existence of a corporation that has been dissolved. The revival of a suspended corporation's existence won't retroactively validate the timeliness of a suit brought by it when the limitation period expired during the suspension.[220]

Distribution of assets of dissolved corporation. The assets of a dissolved corporation belong to the stockholders.[221] They can, for

---

[212]Okmulgee Window Glass Co. v Frink (CA–8 1919) 260 F 159; Napier v People's Store Co., (1923) 98 Conn. 414, 120 Atl 295; Wyoming-Indiana Oil & Gas Co. v Weston, (1932) 43 Wyo. 526, 7 P2d 206.

[213]Martin v Star Publishing Co., (1956) 50 Del. 181, 126 A2d 238.

[214]In re Mosquito Tawks, Inc. (La. Ct of App. 1959) 100 S2d 815.

[215]In Leak v Halaby Galleries, Inc., (1932) Tex. Civ. App. 49 SW2d 858.

[216]Bishop v Schield Bantam Co. (ND Iowa 1968) 293 F Supp 94; Contra; Chadwick v Air Reduction Co. Inc. (ND Ohio 1965) 239 F Supp 247.

[217]Naugher v Fox River Tractor Co. (ND Miss. 1977) 446 F Supp 1281.

[218]In re Mullings Clothing Co. (CA–2 1916) 238 F58, 252 F 667; Downtown Athletic Club, Inc. v Brown (N H S Ct 1982) 448 A 2d 402.

[219]Security National Bank v Cohen, (1966) 31 Wis. 2d 656, 143 NW2d 454.

[220]Welco Construction, Inc. v Modulux, Inc., (1975) 47 Cal. App. 3d 69, 120 Cal. Rptr. 572.

[221]Jones v Peck, (1923) 63 Cal. App. 397, 218 P 1030; Barrowman Coal Corp v Kentland Coal & Coke Co., (1946) 302 Ky. 803, 196 SW2d 428; Munn v Wadley, (1939) 192 La. 874, 189 So 561; Sale v Ambler, (1939) 335 Pa. 165, 6 A2d 519; Cohen v L. & G. Inv. Co., (1936) 186 Wash. 308, 57 P2d 1042; Commonwealth v Passell (S Ct Pa. 1966) 233 A2d 24.

example, sue to collect the balance due on a note given the corporation.[222] However, the corporate note debts must be paid and its obligations discharged before the proceeds obtained in liquidating the assets may be distributed among the stockholders.[223] But neither the directors of an insolvent corporation who authorized the transfer of corporate assets to discharge a secured debt nor the stockholder to whom the transfer was made were liable to creditors for unlawfully distributing those assets when that stockholder was a secured creditor.[224]

The property of the corporation being a trust fund for the creditors, no distribution of assets upon liquidation can be made to stockholders until all debts are paid.[225] If distribution to stockholders is made before debts are paid, a liability in favor of unpaid creditors is imposed not only upon the stockholders who have received the assets, but upon the directors and officers who were charged with the duty of making proper distribution.[226] Stockholder's liability has been held to attach although the corporation did not formally dissolve.[227]

Neither the last board of directors nor the statutory trustees of an expired corporation have any duty or obligation to pay up company's debts and taxes with their personal funds to protect the assets of the company for stockholders.[228] Directors of a voluntarily dissolved corporation may be liable for their corporation's contingent liabilities

---

[222]Thomas v Harper, (1971) 14 Ariz. App. 140, 481 P2d 510.

[223]See Underwood v Comm. of Internal Revenue (CA–7 1932) 56 F2d 64; O. G. Orr & Co. v Fireman's Fund Ins. Co., (1932) 235 App. Div. 1, 256 N.Y.S. 79, rev. 141 Misc. 330, 253 N.Y.S.2 See also Novo Trading Corp. v Comm., (1940) 113 F2d 320; Guilford Const. Co. v Biggs (CA–4 1939) 102 F2d 46; Horn & Hardart Baking Co. v U.S., (ED Pa. 1940) 34 F Supp 89; Burton v Bowers, (ED S.C. 1948) 79 F Supp 418; Wilson v Lucas, (1932) 185 Ark. 183, 47 SW2d 8; In re Pac. Coast B. & L. Ass'n, (1940) 15 Cal.2d 134, 99 P2d 251; Brooks v Saloy, (1948) 334 Ill. App. 93, 79 NE2d 97; Steinhardt Import Corp. v Levy, (1940) 174 Misc. 184, 20 N.Y.S.2d 360; Bell Telephone Co v Schwab, (1938) 33 Pa. D.&C. 270; Adler v Dickstein, (1940) 139 Pa. Super. 447, 12 A2d 489; Duncan v Jones (Ind. App. 1983) 450 NE 2d 1018.

[224]Franklin Press, Inc. v National Diversified Corp. (La. App. 1973) 286 S 2d 469. See also Henry I Siegel Co., Inc. v Holliday (Tex. S Ct 1984) 663 SW 2d 824.

[225]In re Pac. Coast B. & L. Ass'n, (1940) 15 Cal.2d 134, 99 P2d 251; City of Newark v Joseph Hollander, Inc., (1945) 136 N.J. Eq. 539, 42 A2d 872, aff'd, (1946) 138 N.J. Eq. 112, 46 A2d 786; Steinhardt Import Corp. v Levy, (1940) 174 Misc. 184, 20 N.Y.S.2d 360; In re F. E. Schundler Feldspar Co. Inc., (1945) 70 S.D. 513, 19 NW2d 337; Spokane Merchants Ass'n v Lobe, (1975) 13 Wash. App. 68, 533 P2d 133; In re Merrick Dairy Co., (1946) 249 Wis. 295, 24 NW2d 679.

[226]U.S. v Snook (ND Ga. 1928) 25 F2d 844; Rochell v Oates, (1941) 241 Ala. 372, 2 S2d 749; Cohen v Pavlik, (1938) 235 Ala. 289, 170 So 435; James Talcott, Inc. v Crown Industries, Inc. (Fla. Dist. Ct App. 1976) 323 S2d 311; Chelsea Sales Corp. v A. Jacobs, Co. Inc., (1940) La. App. 193 So 402; N.J. Title Guarantee & Trust Co. v Berlkner, (1945) 136 N.J. Eq. 162, 40 A2d 790p Reinfeld v Fidelity Union Trust Co., (1938) 123 N.J. Eq. 428, 198 Atl 220; Griffin v Dyett, (1941) 262 App. Div. 368, 29 N.Y.S.2d 488; Zinn v Bright, (1970) 9 Cal. App. 3d 188, 86 Cal. Rptr. 736; Ficor, Inc. v McHugh (Col. S Ct 1983) 639 P 2d 385.

[227]Hunn v US (CA–2 1932) 60 F2d 430.

[228]Santa Anita Corp. v Walker, (1940) 106 Col. 465, 106 P2d 459.

to known creditors if the directors did not (1) notify the creditors of the dissolution nor (2) provide for payment of the liability in the articles of dissolution.[229] When a creditor got past payment of a judgment against a corporation that had dissolved, a director that didn't notify the creditor of the dissolution, as the statute required, wasn't liable for the rest of the judgment because (1) the creditor's failure to get paid in full wasn't due to lack of notice, and (2) the part payment he got equalled what he would have gotten if he had received statutory notice.[230]

Creditors with unliquidated claims that arose before the dissolution of a corporation can sue its dissolution trustees on the claims after the dissolution.[231]

A pledgee of stock can recover liquidating dividends from the officer of a dissolved corporation who paid the dividends to the pledgor without requiring surrender of the stock certificates.[232]

The directors of an insolvent corporation who liquidated at public auction and by selling the assets at a price far below cost, and without giving creditors notice of the proposed sale, are liable to the creditors for their failure to get "full value" for the assets. That the directors committed no fraud and made no personal profit from the sale is immaterial.[233]

A dissolution trustee can buy the corporation's stock at a pledgee's sale if he can prove that his purchase of the stock is fair and involves no misuse of his office.[234]

Shareholders of an insolvent corporation did not make an invalid distribution when they gave a promissory note and mortgage to two corporations they controlled to secure a preexisting debt, since (1) giving a creditor security for a preexisting debt is not an unlawful distribution, and (2) there is a real question whether, if it was a distribution, it was the distribution to shareholders that the statute forbids.[235]

Minority stockholders can set aside a dissolution sale of assets consisting of mineral rights that can be distributed in kind and the value of which cannot be easily ascertained for a public auction sale.[236] And the liquidation sales must be fair to minority stockholders. Thus a

---

[229]Pine Manor Homes v Duval (Pa. Com. Pls. 1959) 76 Montg. Co. L.R. 296.
[230]State Bank of Lombard v Segovia, (1977) 49 Ill. App. 3d 682, 364 NE2d 688.
[231]Wewoka Petroleum Corp. v Gilmore (Okla. S Ct 1957) 319 P2d 285.
[232]Bogardus v Kentucky State Bank (Ky. Ct of App. 1955) 281 SW2d 904.
[233]N.Y. Credit Men's Adj. Bureau v Weiss, (1953) 305 N.Y. 1, 110 NE2d 397.
[234]Miller v Wahyou (CA–9 1956) 235 F 2d 612.
[235]AMP Service Corp v Richard (La. S Ct 1982) 419 S 2d 911.
[236]Blanchard v Commonwealth Oil Co. (Fla. Dist. Ct of App. 1959) 116 So2d 663.

sale was set aside when (1) three brothers owned three-fourths of the corporate assets, (2) they appointed a cousin to liquidate the corporation, and (3) the liquidator, after an appraisal by one of the brothers, sold the assets at under their market value to a partnership consisting of those three brothers, since the liquidator has a fiduciary duty to represent all the stockholders.[237] The interests of the various classes of stockholders in the proceeds remaining after debts have been paid are equal, unless there's some contrary provision in the charter or in the contract of the stockholders.[238]

Creditors of a dissolved corporation can follow distributive assets into the hands of stockholders and hold each of them liable for each one's distributive share.[239] But not a creditor who becomes one more than three years after dissolution.[240] Also, general creditors can bring an action to recover preferential payments made before dissolution, even though such an action ordinarily belongs solely to the liquidating trustee, when the court's final order releasing the trustee assigned any remaining claims to the creditors.[241]

However, if there has been no fraud and no injury to creditors' rights, a court will not undo, by means of a liquidating receivership, what the parties have done in winding up a corporation and distributing its assets even though what was done was not authorized by law.[242]

Stockholders may be personally liable for corporate taxes, when no provision is made for them before dissolution.[243]

In some states, the statutes fix the time within which distribution after dissolution is to be made, and indicate the order in which debts shall be paid.

---

[237] Drenning v Kuebel, Inc. (La. App. 1976) 327 So2d 571; Levy v Billeaud (La. S Ct 1984) 443 S 2d 539.

[238] Williams v Henshaw, (1927) 220 App. Div. 39, 220 N.Y.S. 432.

[239] John Julian Constr. Co. v Monarch Builders, Inc. (Del. Super Ct 1973) 306 A2d 29; Koch v US (10 Cir. 1943) 138 F2d 850; Gaskins v Bonfils (CA-10 1935) 79 F2d 352; US v Markowitz (SD Cal. 1940) 34 F Supp 827; Cafritz v Corporation Audit Co. (D.C. 1945) 60 F Supp 627, aff'd in part and rev'd in part. (D.C. Cir 1946) 156 F2d 839; US v Friedman (ND N.Y. 1941) 29 AFTR 1359; Rademacher v Daniels, (1943) 64 Idaho 376, 133 P2d 713; Stock v E.A. Fabacher, Inc., (1938) La. App. 185 So 48; Steinhardt Import Corp. v Levy, (1940) 174 Misc. 184, 20 N.Y.S.2d 360; Fruth v Gaston, (1945) Tex. Civ. App. 187 SW2d 581; Bankers Pocahontas Coal Co. v Monarch Smokeless Coal Co., (1941) 123 W.Va. 53, 14 SE2d 922.

[240] Gonzales v Progressive Tool & Die Co. (EDNY 1979) 463 F Supp 117.

[241] Geroux v Fleck, (1982) 33 Wash. App. 424, 655 P 2d 254.

[242] Salembier v Great Neck Bond & Mortgage Corp., (1937) 22 Del Ch 183, 194 Atl 35.

[243] Cosden Mfg. Co. v US (E.D. Ky. 1972) 340 F Supp 1204; Drew v US (Ct of Cl Ariz. 1966) 367 F2d 828.

Chapter 34

RESOLUTIONS RELATING TO REORGANIZATION, LIQUIDATION, AND DISSOLUTION

Contents—Chapter 34

1205

RECAPITALIZATION

DIRECTORS' RESOLUTION AUTHORIZING
A SPLIT-UP OF CORPORATION

WHEREAS, this Corporation has certain assets which now have a net fair market value of two hundred forty thousand ($240,000) Dollars, and which are used in the manufacturing of women's hats, and

WHEREAS, this Corporation is, and has been for many years, primarily in the business of manufacturing women's dresses, and the net fair market value of the assets of this Corporation devoted to the manufacture of women's dresses is three hundred thousand ($300,000) Dollars, and

WHEREAS, substantial amounts of additional equity capital are required to utilize the opportunities for expansion of the manufacturing of women's dresses, and

WHEREAS, investors interested in the manufacturing of women's dresses do not necessarily wish to also invest in the women's hat business, and

WHEREAS, as a consequence of this situation this Corporation is experiencing difficulty in obtaining needed equity capital, be it

RESOLVED, That the President and Secretary of this Corporation are hereby authorized and directed to do all acts necessary and proper to establish two corporations pursuant to the corporation laws of this state, one of which corporations shall have the purposes and powers necessary to conduct the business of manufacturing women's hats, and to do any other things incidental to the proper operation of a hat manufacturing business, and the other of which corporations shall have the purposes and powers necessary to conduct the business of manufacturing women's dresses, and to do any other things incidental to the proper operation of a dress manufacturing business, and

RESOLVED FURTHER, That the Corporation which shall be engaged in the manufacture of hats shall be named "Top Fashion Corporation" (hereinafter called TOP), and the Corporation which shall be engaged in the manufacture of dresses shall be named "Smart Fashsion, Inc." (hereinafter called SMART), and

RESOLVED FURTHER, That the capitalization of TOP shall be two hundred forty thousand ($240,000) Dollars consisting of 2,400 shares of common stock each with a par value of one hundred ($100) Dollars and that the capitalization of SMART shall be three hundred thousand ($300,000) Dollars consisting of 3,000 shares of common stock each with a par value of one hundred ($100) Dollars, and

RESOLVED FURTHER, That following the creation of TOP, this Corporation shall transfer and convey to said TOP all of the assets, property and documents relating to the hat manufacturing operations of this Corporation (and subject to the liabilities thereof) in exchange for all of the common stock of said TOP, and that following the creation of SMART, this Corporation shall transfer and convey to said SMART all of the assets, property and documents relating to the dress manufacturing operations of this Corporation (and subject to the liabilities thereof) in exchange for all of the common stock of said SMART, and

RESOLVED FURTHER, That immediately after the transfers have been completed pursuant to the requirements of the immediately preceding Clause, or as soon thereafter as is practicable, the Board of Directors shall take the steps necessary to liquidate this Corporation, and, as part of such liquidation, the TOP and SMART common stock received by this Corporation in exchange for its assets shall be distributed pro-rata to the stockholders of this Corporation upon the surrender of their stock in this Corporation, and

RESOLVED FURTHER, That the President and Secretary of this Corporation are hereby authorized and empowered to do all acts and sign all documents necessary and proper to execute the orders of this Board of Directors as expressed in this Resolution, and

RESOLVED FURTHER, That . . . . , counsel for this Corporation, be instructed to make application to the United States Treasury Department requesting a ruling that the distribution described hereinbefore qualifies as a tax-free transaction pursuant to Section 355 of the Internal Revenue Code of 1954, and that the effectuation of this resolution be made subject to the obtaining of such ruling.

RESOLUTION OF DIRECTORS AUTHORIZING A SPIN-OFF

WHEREAS, the Corporation owns all the outstanding shares of the capital stock of its subsidiary, Ecks—Wye Corp., and

WHEREAS, in the opinion of the Board of Directors of the Corporation, it is in the best interests of the Corporation to dispose of its holdings in said subsidiary, and

WHEREAS, counsel for the Corporation has obtained a ruling from the U.S. Treasury Department that no gain or loss will result, for income tax purposes, to the stockholders of the Corporation as a result of the distribution to them of the shares in Ecks—Wye Corp., be it therefore

RESOLVED, That the outstanding shares of the capital stock of Ecks—Wye Corp. be distributed to the holders of record of the Common Stock of the Corporation at the rate of . . . . . share(s) of Ecks—Wye Corp. for each . . . . shares of the Corporation held on the record date indicated below; and

RESOLVED FURTHER, That no fractional shares of Ecks—Wye Corp. or scrip will be issued and that stockholders of the Corporation entitled to fractional share interests may, at their option, either (1) purchase for their respective accounts the additional fractional shares needed to make up a full share, at the market price prevailing on the date of purchase, or (2) sell for their accounts the fractional interests they respectively own and receive the cash proceeds therefor, and

RESOLVED FURTHER, That . . . ., 19. . is hereby fixed as the record date for determining the holders of the Corporation's Common Stock entitled to share in said distribution, and

RESOLVED FURTHER, That a notice be sent to all holders of the Common Stock of the Corporation advising them of the action taken by the Board of Directors, and setting forth the options with respect to fractional interests, and the instructions as to how and when such options may be exercised.

LETTER TO STOCKHOLDERS ADVISING OF SPIN-OFF

To the Stockholders of Able, Baker Corp.:

The Board of Directors of your Corporation, at its meeting held on . . . ., 19. ., voted to distribute to the holders of its issued shares of Common Stock all of the outstanding shares of the capital stock of Corporation's wholly-owned subsidiary, Ecks—Wye Corp. The distribution will be made on . . . ., 19. ., to holders of record of the Common Stock at the close of business on . . . ., 19. . .

Each Common Stockholder will receive . . . . . share(s) of Ecks—Wye Corp. stock for each . . . . . shares of Able, Baker Corp. owned.

In lieu of the issuance of fractional shares or scrip certificates to stockholders who would otherwise be entitled to the same, the Board of Directors has adopted Order Forms that stockholders should use to direct . . . . Bank, as agent for the stockholders entitled to fractional share interests, to sell their fractional share interests and remit the proceeds to them, or to purchase the additional fractional share interests required to entitle them to a full share of the Common Stock of Ecks—Wye Corp. Full instructions with respect to the use of said Order Forms will accompany the Stock Certificates to be mailed on or about . . . ., 19. . .

The Corporation has received a ruling from the United States Treasury Department that the distribution of the shares of Ecks—Wye Corp. will not result in income, for Federal income tax purposes, to the stockholders of Able, Baker Corp.

Respectfully,

. . . .
Benjamin Baker, Chairman

. . . .
Arthur Able, President

DIRECTORS' RESOLUTION AUTHORIZING SPLIT-UP OF STOCK AND CALLING STOCKHOLDERS' MEETING TO APPROVE IT

RESOLVED, That it is advisable to amend the Agreement of Consolidation under which this Corporation was formed by:

(1) Changing the number of the issued and outstanding shares of the capital stock, without par value, of the Consolidated Corporation, from 263,860 to 1,055,440, each of such 263,860 shares being thereby changed into four shares, such change to be effective at the close of business . . . ., 19. ., without the capital of the Consolidated Corporation being increased or decreased by the transfer of surplus to capital account or the transfer of capital to surplus, or otherwise.

(2) Changing Article III of the Agreement of Consolidation, under which this Corporation was formed, to read as follows:

"The number of shares of the total authorized capital stock of the Consolidated Corporation shall be one million five hundred thousand (1,500,000) shares without par value, all of one class."

"All the stock of the Consolidated Corporation without par value, whether now authorized or authorized by subsequent increase of capital pursuant to any amendment of this Agreement of Consolidation, may be issued from time to time for such consideration as may be fixed from time to time by the Board of Directors, and authority so to fix such consideration is hereby granted to the Board of Directors by the stockholders."

RESOLVED FURTHER, That . . . . Bank, as Transfer Agent of the shares of the capital stock of the Corporation, is hereby authorized and directed to issue and, when countersigned and registered by . . . . Bank & Trust Company, as Registrar, to deliver from time to time after the close of business on . . . ., 19. ., in accordance with the order or orders of this Corporation evidenced by a writing or writings signed by its President or a Vice president, and countersigned by its Secretary or Treasurer, certificates for not exceeding 791,580 shares, without par value, of the capital stock of the Corporation, subject to the effective amendment of the Agreement of Consolidation under which the Corporation was formed, so as to permit the issuance of such shares as aforesaid, and

RESOLVED FURTHER, That . . . . Bank & Trust Company, of the City of . . . ., as Registrar of the shares of the capital stock of the Corporation, is hereby authorized and directed to countersign and register the certificates for not exceeding 791,580 shares, without par value, of the capital stock of this Corporation, referred to in the next preceding resolution, when issued by . . . . Bank, as Transfer Agent, and

RESOLVED FURTHER, That action be taken upon the foregoing proposals to amend the Agreement of Consolidation at a special meeting of the stockholders to be held on . . . ., 19. ., at . . .M., at the principal office of the Corporation, ... (*Street*),. . . . (*City*),. . . ., which meeting is hereby called for that purpose and for the transaction of such other business as may properly come before the meeting, and

RESOLVED FURTHER, That the date for the determination of the stockholders entitled to notice of and to vote at said meeting of the stockholders to be held on . . . ., 19. ., is hereby fixed as . . . ., 19. ., at the close of business on that day, and

RESOLVED FURTHER, That the Secretary be instructed to send to the stockholders entitled thereto appropriate notices and forms of proxies for use at the said stockholders' meeting, such notices and proxies to be in such form as the Secretary may with the advice of counsel deem necessary or advisable, and

RESOLVED FURTHER, That if the stockholders at the meeting of stockholders on . . . ., 19. ., determine to change each share of the issued and outstanding shares of the capital stock without par value of this Corporation into four shares of such capital stock without par value, it is advisable that such change be made effective on . . . ., 19. ., and that stockholders of record at the close of business on that date receive certificates for three additional shares for each share held, in effectuation of such change.

DIRECTORS' RESOLUTION APPROVING PLAN OF RECAPITALIZATION AND AMENDMENT OF ARTICLES

RESOLVED, That the Board of Directors of the Corporation hereby proposes, adopts, and approves the following plan providing for a revision of the capital structure of the Corporation, and the issuance and exchange of shares of the capital stock of the Corporation, as follows:

(1) Increase the present authorized capital stock to . . . . . shares, and reclassify all of said authorized shares into 3 classes, to consist of . . . . . shares of common stock without nominal or par value, ... shares of 4% convertible preferred stock of the par value of $100 each, and . . . . . shares of 5% cumulative second preferred stock of the par value of $100 each;

(2) Exchange all of the presently issued and outstanding shares of common stock exclusive of treasury stock for shares of the new common stock, in the ratio of 1 share present common stock for . . . . . shares of new common stock;

(3) Exchange each share of the presently issued and outstanding 6% cumulative preferred stock, exclusive of treasury stock, with accrued dividends thereon, amounting to $. . . . . per share, for . . . . . shares of the new 5% cumulative second preferred stock, and 1 share of the new common stock;

(4) The amount of capital that will represent the aggregate number of shares of new common stock to be issued pursuant to this plan shall be $.....;

(5) Amend the Articles of Incorporation of the Corporation to provide for said 3 classes of stock in lieu of the present common stock and the 6% cumulative preferred stock;

(6) Further amend the Articles of Incorporation with respect, among other things, to the preemptive rights of the holders of all classes of stock, the powers of the Board of Directors, and the objects, purposes, and powers of the Corporation; and

(7) Declare a dividend of $..... per share on account of the arrears in dividends on the 6% cumulative preferred stock conditional upon the approval of the plan by the stockholders.

(8) If the stockholders approve the foregoing plan and the amendments to the Articles of Incorporation, all rights appertaining to the present common stock and the present 6% cumulative preferred stock, or accruing by virtue of the ownership thereof, shall cease and terminate, and the holders thereof shall surrender the certificates therefor to the Corporation for cancellation, and receive and accept in lieu thereof certificates of new stock in exchange for and in substitution of the present stock as above provided; and

RESOLVED FURTHER, That if the stockholders of the Corporation at a meeting to be called for that purpose approve the aforesaid plan for the revision of the capital structure of the Corporation and the amendments to the Articles of Incorporation of the Corporation in connection therewith and the Corporation receives $..... for the ..... shares of convertible preferred stock to be issued under said plan:

(1) There be appropriated and set aside out of the surplus of the Corporation the sum of $..... as and for a dividend at the rate of $..... per share on the present 6% cumulative preferred stock of the Corporation in part payment of accumulated dividends thereon, payable on or before ...., 19.., to holders of record of such stock on ...., 19..; and

(2) The ..... shares of common stock and ..... shares of preferred stock owned by the Corporation as treasury stock be cancelled and retired, and the Treasurer of the Corporation be authorized to make all necessary entries in connection therewith on the books of the Corporation; and

RESOLVED FURTHER, That the Board of Directors of .... Corporation declare it advisable and for the benefit of the Corporation that the capital stock of the Corporation be increased and reclassified so that in lieu and instead of the present authorized capital stock of ..... shares consisting of ..... shares of common stock, without any nominal or par value, and ..... shares of preferred stock of the par value of $100 each, the capital stock shall consist of ..... shares divided into ..... shares of common capital stock without any nominal or par value, ... shares of convertible preferred stock of the par value of $100 each, and ..... shares of second preferred stock of the par value of $100 each, and that the preferences, rights, qualifications, limitations, and restrictions of said classes of stock shall be as set forth in the next following resolution, and that it is advisable and for the benefit of the Corporation that the Articles of Incorporation of the Corporation be amended as set forth in the next following resolutions; and

RESOLVED FURTHER, That it is proposed to amend the Articles of Incorporation of the Corporation by striking out Article ..... in its entirety and inserting in lieu and instead therefore the following Article ......

(Insert capital stock clause.)

RESOLVED FURTHER, That a special meeting of stockholders of the Corporation be called to be held on ...., 19.., at ....M., for the purpose of voting in respect to the foregoing resolutions and of considering the amendments to the Articles of Incorporation.

DIRECTORS' RESOLUTION APPROVING STOCK SPLIT AND AMENDMENT OF CERTIFICATE

WHEREAS, The Board of Directors of this Company deems it advisable and therefore proposes and recommends to the stockholders of this Company that the Certificate of Incorporation of the Company be amended so as to change the authorized Capital Stock of the Company from one million (1,000,000) shares of Capital Stock of the par value of seventy-five ($75.00) Dollars each into three million (3,000,000) shares of Capital Stock of the par value of twenty-five ($25.00) Dollars each, and that each share of Capital Stock presently issued and outstanding be changed into three shares of Capital Stock of the par value of twenty-five ($25.00) Dollars each, so as to effect a three-for-one stock split of said issued and outstanding shares; be it

RESOLVED, That, subject to the requisite approval of the stockholders at the Annual Meeting to be held ...., the Certificate of Incorporation of this Company be amended by decreasing the par value of the shares of its Capital Stock from seventy-five ($75.00) Dollars to twenty-five ($25.00) Dollars, and that the Capital Stock of this Company shall consist of three million (3,000,000) shares of Capital Stock of the par value of twenty-five ($25.00) Dollars per share; and

RESOLVED FURTHER, That each share of Capital Stock of the par value of seventy-five ($75.00) Dollars each of the Company issued and outstanding at the close of business on the date of the taking effect of said amendment, being the date of the filing and recording of said amendment in the Office of the Secretary of the State of ...., be changed into three fully paid and nonassessable shares of Capital Stock of the par value of twenty-five ($25.00)

Dollars each of the Company; that all certificates for shares of Capital Stock of the par value of seventy-five ($75.00) Dollars each that are then issued and outstanding shall thereupon and thereafter be deemed to be certificates for the same number of shares of Capital Stock respectively of the par value of twenty-five ($25.00) Dollars each; and that each holder of record of said certificates at the close of business on the effective date of said amendment shall be entitled to receive additional certificates representing two additional shares of Capital Stock of the par value of twenty-five ($25.00) Dollars each for each outstanding share of Capital Stock; and

RESOLVED FURTHER, That upon approval by the stockholders at the Annual Meeting of Stockholders on . . . . of the proposed amendment and stock split, the certificate of amendment of the Certificate of Incorporation of the Company shall be filed in the Office of the Secretary of the State of . . . . , and that the stock certificates for the additional shares to be issued shall be mailed on or about . . . . to the stockholders of record at the close of business as of the date of said filing with the Secretary of State, such stock certificates to represent two additional shares for each share held; and

RESOLVED FURTHER, That the proposed stock split shall not result in any increase or decrease in the aggregate amount of the capital account or the surplus accounts of the Company; and

RESOLVED FURTHER, That the forms of stock certificates representing shares of the Capital Stock of the par value of twenty-five ($25.00) Dollars each of the Company submitted to this meeting be and the same hereby are adopted and approved as the forms of stock certificates representing shares of the Capital Stock of the par value of twenty-five ($25.00) Dollars per share of the Company, effective upon the close of business on the date of the filing of the aforesaid amendment; and

RESOLVED FURTHER, That the proper officers of the Company, and any of them, be and they hereby are authorized, empowered and directed to take any and all such actions as in their discretion they deem necessary or expedient to effectuate the purposes of the foregoing resolutions.

STOCKHOLDERS' RESOLUTION APPROVING PLAN OF RECAPITALIZATION

RESOLVED, That the plan of recapitalization approved and recommended by the Board of Directors is hereby adopted and the offer of exchange made to the holders of the preferred stock and therein outlined, be approved, so that the Corporation shall offer to the holders for each share of preferred stock deposited under the plan:

(1) 1 share of common stock

(2) $ . . . . . in cash; and

(3) an additional amount in cash equal to the dividends accrued and accruing on such share of preferred stock to .... 19.., ... ($.....) Dollars per share and remaining unpaid at the date of exchange.

NOTICE OF SPECIAL MEETING OF STOCKHOLDERS TO VOTE ON PLAN OF RECAPITALIZATION

NOTICE is hereby given that a special meeting of the stockholders of .... Corporation will be held at the office of the Corporation, ... (*address*), on ...., 19.., at ....M., for the purpose of voting upon a proposed plan of recapitalization, and upon the adoption of an amendment of the Articles of Incorporation relating to said proposed plan of recapitalization, copies of which are attached hereto.

The Board of Directors has fixed ...., 19.., as the record date for the determination of stockholders entitled to notice of and to vote at said special meeting of stockholders, or any adjournments thereof, and only stockholders of record at the close of business on the date so fixed will be entitled to notice of and to vote at said meeting or adjournments thereof. The stock transfer books will not be closed.

Any stockholder who does not expect to attend the meeting in person is requested to date and sign the accompanying proxy and assent and return the same in the accompanying envelope.

....
Secretary

LETTER ACCOMPANYING NOTICE OUTLINING PLAN OF RECAPITALIZATION

To the Stockholders of .... Corporation:

Enclosed herewith is a notice of a special meeting of stockholders to be held on ...., 19.., at the offices of the Corporation, ... (*address*).

The principal matter to be discussed at the meeting is: A plan of exchange of preferred stock for cash and common stock according to which plan each holder of preferred stock will be entitled to receive for each share of preferred stock deposited under the plans, (1) 1 share of common stock, (2) $..... in cash, and (3) an additional amount in cash equal to the dividends accrued and accruing on such share of preferred stock to ...., 19.., .. ($.....) Dollars per share and remaining unpaid at the date of exchange.

Favorable action on this proposal is a matter of vital concern to the Corporation and to the stockholders. Speedy action is particularly necessary if the full benefit of this readjustment is to be realized. To delay putting these plans into effect beyond the end of this calendar year may defeat the desired purpose.

....
President

NOTICE TO STOCKHOLDERS OF ADOPTION OF PLAN OF RECAPITALIZATION WITH REQUEST TO DEPOSIT CERTIFICATES

To the Stockholders of the .... Corporation:

We are pleased to report that at the special meeting of the stockholders of the .... Corporation held on ...., 19.., the entire plan of recapitalization proposed to the stockholders in the letter of the chairman of ...., 19.., was adopted by a large majority of the capital stock outstanding and entitled to vote.

The Board of Directors has declared this plan effective in every respect and pursuant to such plan urges holders of preferred stock of the Corporation who desire to avail themselves of the benefits of the plan to deposit the certificates thereof at or before ....M., ..., 19.., with the .... Trust Company, depositary, Corporate Trust Department, ... (*address*) together with the letter of transmittal sent to preferred stockholders on ...., 19... Additional letters of transmittal may be obtained either from the depositary or from the offices of this Corporation.

Certificates for preferred stock deposited must be duly indorsed in blank for transfer or accompanied by proper assignments in blank for transfer duly executed, in each case with signatures witnessed and guaranteed by a bank or trust company in the City of .... or by a brokerage firm having membership in the .... Stock Exchange or by a bank or trust company having a correspondent in the City of .... Transferable deposit receipts of the corporation in form approved by the Board of Directors will be issued to depositors.

The .... Corporation

By ....

President

Dated: ...., 19...

STATEMENT TO BE SENT TO STOCKHOLDERS GIVING REASONS FOR STOCK SPLIT

The Board of Directors is of the opinion that the proposed split of each common share into three common shares is in the best interests of the Company and its stockholders. It feels that making a larger number of shares available will broaden the market for the Company's stock and will increase the public's interest in the Company's business. Such increased interest is expected to materially aid the sales of Company products. It is also hoped that the availability of more shares will stabilize the market price of the Company's stock and result in a broader distribution of the Company's shares.

The Company is advised by counsel that, under existing Federal income tax law, the proposed stock split and amendment of Certificate of Incorporation to reflect such recapitalization by tripling the shares of capital stock while decreasing the par value to one-third, will not result in taxable income or in gain or loss to the holders of shares of capital stock in the Company.

RESOLUTION OF STOCKHOLDERS ASSENTING TO PROPOSAL TO READJUST CORPORATION IN ORDER TO SEGREGATE ACTIVITIES AND TO ORGANIZE HOLDING COMPANY TO CONTROL SUBSIDIARIES

WHEREAS, the Board of Directors of this Corporation has declared it desirable to place under the control of a separate corporate body the property of this Corporation devoted to the business of manufacturing television and radio sets and other electronic equipment, in order to ascertain definitely and accurately the separate results of the electronic equipment manufacturing operations and the cabinet making activities of this Corporation, and

WHEREAS, the Board of Directors of this Corporation has further declared that the best interests of the Corporation and its stockholders require a readjustment of the corporate capital structure, and

WHEREAS, the stockholders of this Corporation approve the plan to carry into effect the foregoing readjustment, submitted to them by the Board of Directors, be it

RESOLVED:

(1) That a new corporation be organized as a holding company under the laws of the State of . . . . , with a capital stock of not less than 200,000 shares without par value.

(2) That the name . . . . , under which this Corporation has been operating, be included in the name of the new corporation.

(3) That this Corporation sell to the aforesaid new corporation the stock of the "A," "B," and "C" Corporations, owned by this Corporation, and any other assets not required in the business of manufacturing electronic equipment.

(4) That the stockholders of this Corporation accept in lieu of and in exchange for the shares of stock of this Corporation held by them, the shares of stock of the new corporation on the basis of two shares of new no par value stock for each share of the stock of this Corporation with a par value of $100.

RESOLVED FURTHER, That . . . . . , ... , and . . . . . , be appointed a Readjustment Committee to do all things and to perform all acts necessary to carry the foregoing resolution into effect.

RESOLUTION OF STOCKHOLDERS AUTHORIZING DIRECTORS TO ORGANIZE NEW COMPANY TO TAKE OVER BUSINESS OF OLD CORPORATION AND TO CONDUCT ADDITIONAL ENTERPRISE

RESOLVED, That the Board of Directors is hereby authorized to do all things necessary for the formation of a new corporation under the laws of the

State of . . . ., with a capital of $1,000,000, divided into 10,000 shares of common stock of the par value of $100 each, with the object of purchasing or otherwise acquiring the entire undertaking and business of this Corporation and the property and liabilities thereof, and to carry on the business of advertising contractors and agents and any other business that may be usefully carried on in connection with such business, and

RESOLVED FURTHER, That the Board of Directors is hereby authorized to enter into any agreements necessary to transfer the business of this Corporation to such new corporation, for a consideration to be determined by the directors, and to do all other things and to perform all acts necessary to carry the foregoing resolution into effect.

RESOLUTION OF STOCKHOLDERS AFTER EXPIRATION OF CHARTER, AUTHORIZING OFFICERS TO TAKE STEPS NECESSARY FOR ORGANIZATION OF NEW COMPANY AND TO TRANSFER ALL ASSETS AND LIABILITIES OF OLD COMPANY TO NEW COMPANY

WHEREAS, the charter of this company has expired, and

WHEREAS, the shareholders of the Company have unanimously requested the directors and officers to take such action as may be necessary to organize a new corporation for the purpose of continuing the business of the Company and taking over its assets, such new corporation to have a capital stock of . . . . . ($. . . . .) Dollars and a duration of . . . . . (. . . . .) years, and

WHEREAS, application has already been made to the Secretary of State of the State of . . . . for a charter for such new corporation, be it

RESOLVED, That the President and the Secretary of this Company are hereby authorized and directed to take such steps as counsel may advise as necessary for the purpose of completely vesting in the proposed new corporation, when organized, the title to all the assets of every description belonging to this Company, and for the purpose of enabling said new corporation to continue the business of this Company, and

RESOLVED FURTHER, That a full, true, and just inventory of the assets of this Company be made for the purpose of determining the question of the value thereof in excess of all liabilities, in connection with the proposed transfer of said assets to said new corporation.

RESOLUTION OF SUBSCRIBERS OF NEW CORPORATION ACCEPTING ASSETS AND LIABILITIES OF FORMER COMPANY OF SAME NAME AND AUTHORIZING ISSUANCE OF STOCK AS SOON AS PROPERTY IS TAKEN OVER

WHEREAS, this Company was organized by the assent of all the subscribers to its stock, and also by the assent of the holders of all the shares of the stock of the former Company of the same name, for the purpose of acquiring the assets of said former Company and continuing its business, and

WHEREAS, the written statement, dated . . . . , 19. ., of the assets and liabilities of said former Company, which statement has been transferred to this Company and is now on file in its principal office, has been heretofore thoroughly examined by the directors of this Company, and they have also examined and are familiar with such changes in the assets and liabilities as have taken place since said statement of . . . ., 19. ., and they are fully informed as to the value of the assets of said former Company as the same existed on . . . ., 19. ., and today, and believe that the same then were and now are of greater value than . . . . . ($. . . . .) Dollars, be it

RESOLVED, That the proposition of the subscribers to the stock of this Company, which has been presented to the meeting, be hereby accepted, and that the assets and business of said former Company be taken over as of . . . ., 19. ., as shown by the inventory above mentioned, and

RESOLVED FURTHER, That the President and the Secretary of this Company are hereby authorized to issue to each of the subscribers to the stock of this Company certificates for the number of shares subscribed, as soon as proper transfers, assignments, and conveyances shall have been made to this Company of all the assets of every description of said former Company, as mentioned in said proposition, and

RESOLVED FURTHER, That this Company assume and agree to pay all the liabilities of said former Company, and that the President and the Secretary are hereby authorized to enter into such written agreement with the old Company as counsel may advise, covering the transactions referred to in these resolutions.

RESOLUTION OF STOCKHOLDERS RATIFYING BOARD'S ACTION IN APPROVING PLAN OF READJUSTMENT

RESOLVED, That the stockholders of the . . . . Railroad Company hereby ratify the action of the Board of Directors in approving the Plan of Readjustment of . . . . Company and the . . . . Company, dated . . . ., 19. ., as modified by the Modifications dated . . . ., 19. ., which Plan and Modifications are now submitted to this meeting.

REORGANIZATION THROUGH PROTECTIVE COMMITTEES

RESOLUTION OF EXECUTIVE COMMITTEE AUTHORIZING OFFICERS TO EXECUTE REORGANIZATION AGREEMENT AND MANAGEMENT CONTRACT

WHEREAS, it has become necéssary, in order to reorganize the affairs of the . . . . Company, for the Company to be reorganized as a . . . . corporation, known as . . . ., Inc., and

WHEREAS, in order to insure the proper reorganization, it seems advisable for this Corporation to become a party to such Reorganization Agreement, including, as an exhibit thereto, the form of agreement that this Corporation will execute with said reorganized corporation for services in connection with the reorganization of said corporation, be it

RESOLVED, That the President or a Vice president of this Corporation is hereby authorized and directed to execute and deliver, to . . . ., Inc., in as many counterparts as may be required, the Reorganization Agreement of the . . . . Company, dated . . . ., 19.., and the Secretary or an Assistant Secretary of this Corporation is hereby authorized and directed to attest such signature and the seal of this Corporation to such Reorganization Agreement, and

RESOLVED FURTHER, That the President or a Vice president of this Corporation is hereby authorized to execute and deliver an agreement in the form of Exhibit "K," attached to and made a part of said Reorganization Agreement, covering the service of this Corporation to . . . ., Inc., and the Secretary or an Assistant Secretary of this Corporation is hereby authorized and directed to attest such signature and the seal of this Corporation to such service agreement in the form of Exhibit "K," attached to and made a part of said Reorganization Agreement, and

RESOLVED FURTHER, That a copy of said reorganization Agreement, with all exhibits attached thereto, be entered in the minute book immediately following the minutes of this meeting.

RESOLUTION OF BONDHOLDERS' PROTECTIVE COMMITTEE AMENDING PROTECTIVE AGREEMENT

RESOLVED, That the Bondholders' Protective Agreement under which this Committee was organized is hereby amended by adding an additional paragraph at the end of Section . . . . . of said Agreement as follows:

(Here insert new paragraph.)

RESOLVED FURTHER, That the Committee hereby determines that said amendment herein made materially affects the rights of the bondholders, and that notice be given in the manner provided by Section . . . . . of said Agreement.

RESOLUTION OF COMMITTEE TO EXTEND TIME FOR DEPOSIT OF SECURITIES

WHEREAS, considerably more than a majority of the preferred stockholders of the . . . . Company has assented to the Plan of Reorganization of the said . . . . Company, submitted by this Committee, dated . . . ., 19.., and only a comparatively small number of the common stockholders has assented thereto, be it

RESOLVED, That the time for receiving assents to the aforesaid plan be extended until ....M., ..., 19.., and that the Secretary of the Committee is hereby authorized and directed to give notice to the stockholders that this will be the last extension of time for participation in the benefits of the plan made by this Committee, and that the Committee will endeavor promptly, at the expiration of the aforesaid period, to have underwritten the full amount that may be required to carry out said plan for the benefit of the assenting stockholders.

EXCERPT OF MINUTES OF DIRECTORS' MEETING RESCINDING PRIOR APPROVAL OF REORGANIZATION AGREEMENT, AND APPROVING MODIFIED REORGANIZATION AGREEMENT

The chairman stated that the Reorganization Agreement approved by the Board of Directors on ...., 19.., had been modified and, as modified, had been executed by all of the parties thereto, and that an executed copy thereof had been delivered to each of the parties thereto. The Secretary thereupon presented a copy of the Reorganization Agreement as modified and executed. After full discussion, and upon motion duly made and seconded, it was unanimously

RESOLVED, That the resolutions adopted by this Board on ...., 19.., approving the form of Reorganization Agreement submitted to this Board at such time, are hereby rescinded, and

RESOLVED FURTHER, That the action of the officers of this Corporation in executing the Modified Reorganization Agreement, Dated ...., 19.., is hereby ratified, confirmed, and approved, and that a copy of said Modified Reorganization Agreement presented to this meeting be initialed by the Secretary and held in the records of the Corporation, and

RESOLVED FURTHER, That the officers of this Corporation are hereby authorized to do all acts and things necessary, convenient, or expedient in the performance of said Agreement and in carrying out the intent of said Agreement and the foregoing resolutions.

RESOLUTION OF COMMITTEE DECLARING PLAN OF REORGANIZATION OPERATIVE

WHEREAS, the assent of the holders of all of the Preferred Stock of "A" Company, Inc., and of all of the stock of "B" Company to the plan of reorganization of "A" Company, Inc., dated ...., 19.. (hereinafter called the "Plan") has been obtained, and

WHEREAS, the assent of the holders of 22,192 shares of Common Stock of "A" Company, Inc., has been obtained, and

WHEREAS, in the opinion of the undersigned members of the Committee formed under the Plan, it is desirable to declare the Plan operative, be it

RESOLVED, That the undersigned members of the Committee formed under the Plan of ...., 19.., hereby declared said Plan operative, and

RESOLVED FURTHER, That in compliance with the requirements of the New York Stock Exchange, the undersigned members of said Committee hereby extend the time for deposit by the stockholders of the Common Stock of "A" Company, Inc., of such stock under such Plan to and including ...., 19...

MINUTES OF COMMITTEE DECLARING PLAN OPERATIVE IN PART ONLY

The Stockholders' Committee constituted under the Reorganization Plan and Agreement hereby declares the Plan operative so as to embrace only the features of the Plan set forth in Articles I, II, and III thereof, reserving the right, however, hereafter to declare the Plan operative so as to provide for the distribution of cash and common stock of the "New Corporation," as provided in Article IV of the Plan.

....

....

....

Stockholders' Committee

...., 19..

RESOLUTION OF DIRECTORS (OR STOCKHOLDERS) AUTHORIZING SALE OF ASSETS PURSUANT TO TERMS OF REORGANIZATION AGREEMENT

RESOLVED, That the .... Company sell, assign, transfer, exchange, grant, and convey unto The ...., Inc., its successors and assigns, all its assets and property of every kind and character whatsoever, including (without limitation of the foregoing) its business as a going concern and the goodwill thereof, together with the right to the exclusive use of the name The .... Company, and also its interest in the leasehold from "X," dated ...., 19.., and recorded in Deed Book ....., page ....., of the Deed Records of ..... County, ..., a description of the real estate included in said lease being as follows (*insert description*), in consideration for the issuance and delivery, in the manner and form set forth in paragraph .. of the Reorganization Agreement dated ...., 19.., by and between this Company, the Stockholders' Committee of The ..... Company, ... & Co., Inc., ... Service Corporation, ... Management, Inc., The ...., Inc., and others, of ..... shares of the no par capital common stock of said The ...., Inc., as follow:

(1) ..... shares shall be issued by The ...., Inc., to .... Management, Inc., provided that .... Management, Inc., enters into the agreement with The ...., Inc., at the request of The .... Company, as provided in paragraph .. of said Reorganization Agreement dated ...., 19...

(2) .....shares shall be issued by The ...., Inc., to .... & Co., as nominee for certain persons named in Exhibit .., attached to said reorganization Agreement, in consideration of the entering into certain agreements by certain of the parties to said Reorganization Agreement for the purchase of notes, as provided in said Reorganization Agreement.

(3) ..... shares shall be issued by The ...., Inc., in the name of .... & Co., and shall be deposited with .... Trust Company, as Escrow Agent under the escrow agreement annexed to the Reorganization Agreement as Exhibit ....., to be delivered by said Escrow Agent, together with notes, pursuant to the terms of said escrow agreement, at the rate of ..... shares for each $..... principal amount of said notes.

(4) ..... shares shall be issued and delivered to the Stockholders' Committee of The .... Company, to be deposited by them in accordance with the Reorganization Agreement dated ...., 19.., hereinabove referred to.

DIRECTORS' RESOLUTION OF CREDITOR CORPORATION APPOINTING ATTORNEY IN FACT TO CARRY OUT TERMS OF REORGANIZATION AGREEMENT

WHEREAS, the "A" Company is indebted to this Corporation for materials sold and delivered in the sum of fifty thousand ($50,000) Dollars, secured by eighty (80) bonds of the said "A" Company of the par value of one thousand ($1,000) Dollars each, and

WHEREAS, the said "A" Company has entered into a certain agreement dated ...., 19.., with the .... Trust Company, the bondholders, certain creditors, and the receivers of the said "A" Company, for the purpose of reorganizing the said "A" Company, and

WHEREAS, it is advisable that this Corporation appoint an attorney in fact to do such things as may be necessary, for and in behalf of this Corporation, to carry out the terms and provisions of said agreement, be it

RESOLVED, That ...., Vice president of the .... Trust company, is hereby appointed attorney in fact of this Corporation for it and in its name to:

(1) Assign to the "B" Company, under the provisions of said agreement dated ...., 19.., all the right, title, and interest of this Corporation in and

to a certain bid dated . . . ., 19. ., made by the bondholders of the "A" Company to the receivers of the said Company.

(2) Assign to said "B" Company, subject to the terms and conditions of said bid, all the right, title, and interest of this Corporation in and to said eighty (80) bonds of the "A" Company.

(3) Receive from the said "B" Company the shares of its capital stock to which this Corporation is entitled.

(4) Execute the voting trust agreement provided for in said agreement, dated . . . ., 19. ., to transfer and deliver to the Trustee thereunder said shares of stock, and to receive and transmit to this Corporation the receipts therefor, and

RESOLVED FURTHER, That the President of this Corporation is hereby authorized, for and in behalf of this Corporation, to execute a proper form of power of attorney to the said . . . ., Vice president of the . . . . Trust Company, authorizing him to do and perform all things above mentioned.

RESOLUTION AUTHORIZING PAYMENT OF CHARGES AND EXPENSES IN CARRYING OUT PLAN OF REORGANIZATION

RESOLVED, That the proper officers of this Corporation are hereby authorized and directed to pay or cause to be paid any and all taxes, assessments, or other charges, printing bills, and other expenses of whatsoever kind and nature incurred in connection with the carrying out of the Plan and Agreement of Reorganization of . . . . Company, dated . . . ., 19. ., and of the resolutions adopted by the stockholders and directors of this Corporation, including any and all taxes required to be paid in connection with the issue and transfer of bonds, notes, and stocks of this Corporation, and transfer of stocks acquired by this Corporation in such reorganization or otherwise.

RESOLUTION OF REORGANIZATION COMMITTEE PROVIDING FOR EXCHANGE OF BONDS FOR STOCK OF NEW CORPORATION

RESOLVED, That the holders of the . . . . Company's 6 Percent First Mortgage Bonds, who sign underwriting papers for exchange of their bonds for shares of stock in the proposed . . . . Company, shall receive for each bond of one thousand ($1,000) Dollars, one thousand ($1,000) Dollars of preferred stock and one hundred and fifty ($150) Dollars of common stock of the new company.

RESOLUTION OF STOCKHOLDERS' COMMITTEE APPROVING PLAN OF REORGANIZATION AND ACTION TAKEN IN CARRYING OUT PLAN

The undersigned Committee under the Plan and Agreement for Reorganization of . . . ., Inc., dated . . . ., 19. ., hereby, on . . . ., 19. ., with the concurrence of both of its members, adopts the following written resolutions:

[Approval of Plan and Agreement]

RESOLVED, That the above-mentioned Plan and Agreement, dated . . . ., 19. ., a copy of which is annexed hereto as Exhibit "A," said Agreement having been executed in triplicate by the members of this Committee and one executed counterpart having been deposited with each of the Depositaries and one with this Committee's counsel, ..., is hereby approved, and that the manner of carrying out said Plan as stated in detail in said Plan is hereby approved.

[Approval of letter from Committee to security holders]

RESOLVED, That the letter from this Committee to holders of common stock of . . . ., Inc., dated . . . ., 19. ., a copy of which is annexed hereto as Exhibit "B," and which was executed in triplicate by the members of this Committee and an executed counterpart thereof deposited with each of the Depositaries and with this Committee's counsel, ..., is hereby approved.

[Approval of assent and proxy]

RESOLVED, That the form of assent to the Plan and of the stockholders' proxy and power of attorney, which is hereto annexed as Exhibit "C," is hereby approved.

[Confirmation of appointment of counsel]

RESOLVED, That the action of this Committee in appointing as its counsel . . . ., of the City of . . . ., is hereby approved and confirmed.

[Ratification of counsel's action in mailing Plan and Agreement to stockholders]

RESOLVED, That the action of this Committee's counsel in mailing, on . . . ., 19. ., to each of the holders of common stock of the . . . ., Inc., residing in the State of . . . . at the close of business, on . . . ., 19. ., as certified to said counsel by . . . . Company, ... City, ..., transfer agent for said stock, a copy of the above-mentioned Plan and Agreement, letter and assent, and proxy is hereby approved, adopted, ratified, and confirmed.

[Approval of instructions to Depositaries]

RESOLVED, That the form of written instructions for this Committee to the Depositaries, annexed hereto as Exhibit "D," is hereby approved, and that the Committee sign written instructions in said form, in duplicate, and deliver one duplicate original thereof to each of the Depositaries.

[Confirmation of extension of time for deposits]

RESOLVED, That the action of the Committee in extending from time to time the period within which deposits of . . . . , Inc. common stock might be made under said Plan and Agreement to noon . . . ., 19.., and in declaring the time for making such deposits closed and terminated at that time, is hereby approved and confirmed.

[Election to direct transfer of deposited stock to another corporation]

RESOLVED, That the Committee hereby elects to direct the transfer of all of the deposited stock into the name of . . . . Corporation, the . . . . (*insert state*) corporation referred to in said Plan and Agreement.

[Ratification of Depositaries' action in furnishing list of depositors to counsel]

RESOLVED, That the action of the Depositaries in furnishing to the Committee's counsel lists of the depositors under said Plan and Agreement showing the number of shares deposited by each, is hereby approved, adopted, ratified, and confirmed.

[Approval of instructions from Committee to transfer agent]

RESOLVED, That the form of written instructions from this Committee to . . . . Trust Company as transfer agent for the common stock of . . . . , Inc., hereto annexed as Exhibit "E," is hereby approved, and that the Committee sign written instructions in said form and deliver the same to said transfer agent.

[Approval of offer for acquisition of stock deposited under plan]

RESOLVED, That the form of offer, dated . . . ., 19.., from this Committee to . . . . Corporation, hereto annexed as Exhibit "F," said offer providing among other things for the acquisition by said Corporation of the common stock of . . . . , Inc., deposited under said plan, and the issuance by it in exchange therefor, share for share, in the names of the several depositors under said plan (a list of whom is attached to said offer), of the common stock of said . . . . Corporation, is hereby approved, and that the Committee execute said offer in duplicate and deliver the same to . . . . as its agent, to be held and delivered by him in accordance with written instructions to be given to him by this Committee.

[Approval of appointment of agent for Committee]

RESOLVED, That the form of written instructions from this Committee to . . . . , ... (*Street*), ... (*City*), ..., constituting him this Committee's agent and attorney for the purposes and with the authority therein set forth, which form is annexed hereto as Exhibit "G," is hereby approved, and that this Committee execute and deliver to said . . . . written instructions in said form.

[Call of meeting of stockholders of corporation which is to acquire stock deposited]

RESOLVED, That the form for the call of a special meeting of the stockholders of . . . . Corporation, hereto annexed as Exhibit "H," to be signed by this Committee as the agent and attorney in fact, and proxy for the depositors under the Plan and Agreement (who are to become stockholders of said . . . . Corporation), is hereby approved, and that this Committee sign a call in said form and deliver the same to . . . ., Vice president and Assistant Secretary of said . . . . Corporation, the same to become effective forthwith upon the issuance of the stock of . . . . Corporation in the names of the depositors under said plan; and that said . . . . and/or said . . . ., as the agents and attorneys of this Committee, are hereby authorized to sign any such further or substitute call for a stockholders' meeting in or substantially in said form, and to take all such further action for the purpose of holding a stockholders' meeting of said . . . . Corporation or of evidencing the written consent of the stockholders thereof as they or either of them shall deem necessary or desirable in connection with the carrying out of the said Plan and Agreement.

[Execution of substitute proxies by Committee members]

RESOLVED, That the form of substitute proxy, hereto annexed as Exhibit "I," to be signed by the members of this Committee for the purpose of substituting, in place of each such member, under the proxies and powers of attorney given to them by the depositors, is hereby approved, and that each member of this Committee sign a substitute proxy in said form and deliver the same to the said . . . . . and . . . . ., to be used by them or either of them for the purpose of voting or taking other action as therein provided.

[Approval of organization records of new corporation]

RESOLVED, That the Certificate of Incorporation of . . . . Corporation, the records of the first meeting of its incorporators held on . . . ., 19. ., including the By-laws that are a part thereof, the records of the special meeting of the Board of Directors of said Corporation held on . . . ., 19. ., and the draft of records for a special meeting of said Board to be held on . . . ., 19. ., and for an adjourned session thereof to be held on the same day, and the records of the special meeting of the stockholders of said Corporation to be held on . . . ., 19. ., and of an adjourned session thereof to be held on the same day, all of the foregoing being annexed hereto as Exhibit "J," are hereby approved as being in proper form for the carrying out of said Plan and Agreement in the manner determined by this Committee.

[Written consent to sale of assets]

RESOLVED, That the form of written consent to the sale of all the assets of said . . . . Corporation, hereto annexed as Exhibit "K," to be signed by this Committee as agent and attorney in fact for all of the stockholders, is hereby approved, and that this Committee sign a written consent in said form and deliver the same to . . . ., Assistant Secretary of said Corporation, to be filed by him with the records of said Corporation.

[Approval of letter to depositors]

RESOLVED, That the form of letter, dated ...., 19.., from this Committee to the depositors under said Plan and Agreement, hereto annexed as Exhibit "L," is hereby approved, and that the action of counsel to this Committee in making arrangements for the mailing of the latter in said form to each such depositor with the .... Company stock (and scrip, if any) to which he shall be entitled under said Plan and Agreement, is hereby approved, adopted, ratified, and confirmed.

[Consent to dissolution of Corporation]

RESOLVED, That the form of written consent to the dissolution of said .... Corporation, hereto annexed as Exhibit "M," to be signed by this Committee as agent and attorney in fact for all of the stockholders of said Corporation, is hereby approved, and that this Committee sign consent in said form in duplicate, and deliver the same to ...., Assistant Secretary of said Corporation, one duplicate to be filed by him with the records of said Corporation and the other to be filed in the office of the Secretary of State of ....

IN WITNESS WHEREOF, the members of said Committee have hereunto set their hands this ..... day of ...., 19...

....
....
Committee

DIRECTORS' RESOLUTION ACCEPTING OFFER PURSUANT TO PLAN AND AGREEMENT OF REORGANIZATION TO SELL ASSETS OF REORGANIZED COMPANY IN CONSIDERATION FOR STOCK

WHEREAS, The .... Company, a .... corporation, has by written offer contained in the Plan and Agreement of Reorganization submitted to this meeting, offered to sell and deliver to this Corporation all of the assets of said Company, including its goodwill and corporate name, subject, however, to its liabilities, in consideration for the issuance and delivery in manner and form as provided in the Plan and Agreement of Reorganization, of 250,000 shares of the common stock of the Corporation, and

WHEREAS, The Stockholders' Committee of The .... Company has, in said Plan and Agreement of Reorganization, offered, in consideration of the said offer of The .... Company being accepted by this Corporation, to vote all of the preferred and common stock of the Company which has been deposited with it pursuant to the deposit agreement dated as of ...., 19.., in favor of the sale by said Company to the Corporation as hereinabove mentioned and for the consideration hereinabove mentioned, and generally to use its best endeavors to carry out all of the purposes of the Plan and Agreement of Reorganization, be it

RESOLVED, That the offer of The .... Company is hereby accepted, and

RESOLVED FURTHER, That it is the judgment of the Directors of this Corporation that the personal and real property and/or leases to be acquired by this Corporation from The .... Company, subject to its liabilities, have a value equal to or in excess of the 250,000 shares of common stock without nominal or par value of this Corporation to be issued therefor pursuant to the following resolutions, and

RESOLVED FURTHER, That the 250,000 shares of said common stock when so issued are hereby declared and shall be taken to be fully paid stock and not liable to any further call, nor shall the holder thereof be liable for any further payments therefor, and

RESOLVED FURTHER, That the offer of The Stockholders' Committee of The .... Company hereinabove mentioned is hereby accepted, and

RESOLVED FURTHER, That the proper officers of this Corporation are hereby authorized and directed to issue fully paid and nonassessable common stock of this Corporation pursuant to the terms of said Plan and Agreement of Reorganization—to wit:

(A) 127,500 shares of said common stock to or upon the order of ...., Inc., upon the execution and delivery to this Corporation of the agreement Exhibit .., annexed to said Plan and Agreement of Reorganization, in the names and denominations requested by .. .., Inc., all necessary Federal and State original issue and transfer stamps having been duly affixed and cancelled;

(B) 37,500 shares of said common stock to .... & Co. as nominees for certain persons named in Exhibit ....., annexed to said Plan and Agreement of Reorganization, all necessary Federal and State original issue and transfer stamps having been duly affixed and cancelled, said shares to be deposited in escrow under the escrow agreement, said Exhibit .....;

(C) 62,500 shares of said common stock to or upon the order of The Stockholders' Committee of The .... Company, with all necessary Federal and State original issue and transfer stamps duly affixed and cancelled, against the receipt of said Stockholders' Committee containing the following provisions:

(1) That said Stockholders' Committee shall tender to each of the stockholders of The .... Company, who was the record holder of shares of the preferred stock of said The .... Company on ...., 19.., and who dissented at a special meeting of the stockholders of The .... Company held on ...., 19.., that number of shares of common stock of this Company which bears the same proportion to the total

number of shares of common stock of this Company to be delivered to said Stockholders' Committee—namely, 62,500 shares—as the total number of shares of preferred stock of The . . . . Company standing in the name of such dissenting stockholder on . . . ., 19. ., bears to the total number of shares of preferred stock of said The . . . . Company issued and outstanding on . . . ., 19. . .

(2) That the number of shares of common stock of this Company not accepted by such dissenting stockholders pursuant to the offer mentioned in (1) of this subdivision (C) will be held for the account of this Company and returned to the treasury of this Company by said stockholders' Committee forthwith upon the expiration of the twenty-day period after . . . ., 19. ., provided in the Statutes of the State of . . as a period during which said dissenting stockholders may file notice of protest and demand for appraisal of their stock.

(3) The said Stockholders' Committee shall retain for the account of the stockholders of said The . . . . Company depositing with said Committee the balance of said 62,500 shares of common stock of this Company—to wit: the balance after deliveries to dissenting stockholders pursuant to the offer mentioned in subdivision (1) of this subdivision (C), and after returning to this Company the number of shares of common stock of this Company not so delivered to such dissenting stockholders pursuant to said offer, for distribution to said depositing stockholders of said The . . . . Company on a basis deemed equitable by said Stockholders' Committee and in accordance with the authority conferred upon said Stockholders' Committee.

(D) 22,500 shares shall be issued in the name of . . . . & Co. and shall be deposited with . . . . Trust Company of New York as escrow agent under the escrow agreement attached to and made a part of the Plan and Agreement of Reorganization and designated as Exhibit . ., subject, however, to the approval of the execution of Exhibit . . . . . by this meeting, to be delivered by said escrow agent after registration in the appropriate name or names at the rate of 18 shares for each $1,000 principal amount of notes of this Corporation sold pursuant to said Plan and Agreement of Reorganization.

RESOLUTION OF STOCKHOLDERS AUTHORIZING SALE OF ASSETS AND ASSIGNMENT OF LEASE TO NEW CORPORATION PURSUANT TO REORGANIZATION AGREEMENT

RESOLVED, That The . . . . Company sell, assign, transfer, exchange, grant, and convey unto The . . . ., Inc., its successors and assigns, all its assets and property of every kind and character whatsoever, including (without limitation of the foregoing) its business as a going concern and the goodwill thereof, together with the right to the exclusive use of the name The . . . . Company; and also its interest in the leasehold from . . . ., dated as of . . . ., 19. ., and recorded in Deed Book . . . . ., page ..... of the Deed Records of .... (*County*), ..., a description of the real estate included in said lease being as follows—to wit:

(Here follows description.)

in consideration for the issuance and delivery in the manner and form set forth in Paragraph Fourth of the Reorganization Agreement dated ...., 19.., by and between this Company, The Stockholders' Committee of The .... Company, ... & Co., Inc., ... Corporation, ..., Inc., and others, of 250,000 shares of the no par capital common stock of said The ...., Inc., as follows—to wit:

(A) 127,500 shares shall be issued by The ...., Inc., to ...., Inc., in consideration of ...., Inc., entering into the agreement with The ...., Inc., at the request of The .... Company, as provided in Paragraph Eleven of said Reorganization Agreement dated ...., 19...

(B) 37,500 shares shall be issued by The ...., Inc., to .... & Co. as nominee for certain persons named in Exhibit .... attached to said Reorganization Agreement, in consideration of the entering into certain agreements by certain of the parties to said Reorganization Agreement for the purchase of notes, as provided in said Reorganization Agreement.

(C) 22,500 shares shall be issued by The ...., Inc., in the name of .... & Co., and shall be deposited with .... Trust Company of .... as escrow agent under the escrow agreement annexed to the Reorganization Agreement as Exhibit .. to be delivered by said escrow agent together with notes pursuant to the terms of said escrow agreement at the rate of 18 shares for each $1,000 principal amount of said notes.

(D) 62,500 shares shall be issued and delivered to The Stockholders' Committee of The .... Company to be deposited by them in accordance with the Reorganization Agreement dated ...., 19.., hereinabove referred to.

RESOLVED FURTHER, That the Board of Directors of this Company is hereby authorized to empower the President and Secretary of this Company to execute and deliver to The ...., Inc., a Bill of Sale granting, conveying, transferring, and assigning unto said The ...., Inc., its successors and assigns, all its assets and property of every kind and character whatsoever, including (without limitation of the foregoing) fixtures, furniture, accounts and bills receivable, shares of stock, securities, cash in bank, moneys, patents, contracts, orders, trademarks, and other properties and assets of every kind, whether or not herein specified, belonging to the Company and/or pertinent to the business conducted by it and shown on its books and records as of ...., 19..; and also said business as a going concern and the goodwill thereof, together with the right to the exclusive use of the name The .... Company; provided, however, that in said instrument The . . . ., Inc., shall agree to take over and assume all the Company's outstanding contracts and accept the foregoing assets, property, business, and goodwill subject to, and assume and agree to pay and discharge, all the debts and liabilities of the Company as of . . . ., 19. ., including (but not by way of limitation) the obligations of the Company, and perform the covenants agreed to be performed by The . . . . Company under the mortgage and deed of trust to . . . . Trust Company of . . . ., as Trustee, dated . . . ., 19. ., securing an issue of $1,000,000 principal amount of First Mortgage Leasehold 6½% Sinking Fund Bonds, and under a certain indenture of lease from . . . . to The . . . . Company, dated . . . ., 19. . .

RESOLVED FURTHER, That the Board of Directors of The . . . . Company be fully authorized to empower the President and Secretary of this Company to execute and deliver to The . . . . Inc., a deed and/or assignment of the lease of . . . ., lessor, to The . . . . Company, dated as of . . . ., 19. ., recorded in Deed Book . . . . . page . . . . . of the Deed Records of . . . . (*County*), ..., substantially in accordance with the Reorganization Agreement between this Company, The Stockholders' Committee of The . . . . Company, ... & Co., Inc., ... Corporation, ..., Inc., and others, dated . . . ., 19. . .

RESOLVED FURTHER, That the Board of Directors of The . . . . Company empowers the President and Secretary of this Company to perform and carry out all matters incident or pertinent to the matters and things adopted at this meeting and/or incident or pertinent to the Reorganization Agreement between this Company, The Stockholders' Committee of The . . . . Company, ... & Co., Inc., ... Corporation, and others, dated . . . ., 19. ., approved at this meeting, including the execution and delivery of all instruments in writing deemed by said officers, or either of them, to be necessary or desirable to carry into effect the matters and things hereinbefore set forth and/or adopted at this meeting and/or said Reorganization Agreement.

RESOLVED FURTHER, That any and all action heretofore taken by any of the officers of this Company, including the execution and delivery of all instruments in writing deemed by said officers, or any of them, to be necessary or desirable to carry into effect the matters and things hereinbefore set forth and/or adopted at this meeting and/or said Reorganization Agreement, is hereby ratified, confirmed, and approved.

RESOLUTION OF STOCKHOLDERS OF NEW CORPORATION RATIFYING AND ADOPTING AGREEMENT MADE BY REORGANIZATION COMMITTEE

WHEREAS, ... and . . . . were on . . . ., 19. ., duly appointed by the bondholders, the creditors, and the stockholders of the . . . . Corporation as a Committee to effect a reorganization of the said corporation, and were duly clothed with full power to do all things deemed necessary and advisable by them to that end, and

WHEREAS, pursuant to the power so conferred upon them, the said Reorganization Committee did cause all the assets of the said corporation to be transferred to this corporation, organized for the purpose of taking over the business and undertaking of the said . . . . Corporation, and did effect a reorganization of the said . . . . Corporation as authorized, and

WHEREAS, the said Reorganization Committee, in effecting the said reorganization, did enter into a certain agreement with the B Corporation to purchase all the machinery of the said B Corporation now located in the City of . . . . , State of . . . . , in exchange for . . . . . (. . . . .) shares of the common stock without par value of this corporation, be it

RESOLVED, That the said agreement entered into between the said Reorganization Committee and the B Corporation is hereby in all respects adopted, ratified, and confirmed, and that . . . . , the President, and . . . . , the Treasurer, of this corporation are hereby authorized and directed to purchase the machinery aforesaid and to issue in exchange and as payment of the purchase price thereof . . . . . (. . . . .) shares of the common stock without par value of this corporation.

DISSOLUTION

DIRECTORS' RESOLUTION AUTHORIZING APPLICATION FOR REINSTATEMENT AFTER EXPIRATION OF DURATION OF EXISTENCE

WHEREAS, this Corporation is actually engaged at the present time in business within the State of . . . . , and

WHEREAS, the articles of the Corporation, granted on . . . ., 19. ., for a period of . . . . . (. . . . .) years, did expire on . . . ., 19. ., and

WHEREAS, this Corporation has inadvertently allowed its articles to be forfeited and cancelled by lapse of time, but without any intention to surrender its corporate privileges or retire from business, and

WHEREAS, this Corporation has been continuously engaged in carrying on the purposes of its incorporation since the forfeiture and cancellation of its articles as aforesaid, be it

RESOLVED, That the present President and Secretary be and they hereby are authorized and directed to make application to the . . . . (*insert proper authority*) of the State of . . . . , to set aside the said forfeiture and cancellation, to renew the articles for a period of . . . . . (. . . . .) years, and to accompany the same with a certified copy of this resolution, with the payment of all corporate fees owing to the state, and with the report as required by the laws of the State of . . . .

DIRECTORS' RESOLUTION RECOMMENDING DISSOLUTION
AND CALLING MEETING OF STOCKHOLDERS TO
TAKE ACTION UPON RESOLUTION

RESOLVED, That in the judgment of this Board of Directors, it is deemed advisable and for the benefit of the .... Corporation that said Corporation should be dissolved; and to that end, as required by law, it is ordered that a meeting of those stockholders of said Corporation having voting power, to take action upon this resolution, is hereby called, to be held at the principal office of said Corporation, at .... (*Street*), in the City of ...., County of ...., State of ...., on ...., 19.., at ....M., and that the Secretary of this Corporation is hereby authorized and directed, within ..... (.....) days after the adoption of this resolution, to cause notice of the adoption of this to be mailed to each stockholder of this Corporation residing in the United States, and also within ..... (.....) days after the adoption of this resolution, to cause a like notice to be inserted in a newspaper published in the County of ...., State of ...., once a week, for at least ..... (.....) successive weeks next preceding the time appointed for said meeting of stockholders.

NOTICE OF STOCKHOLDERS' MEETING
TO ACT ON DISSOLUTION

NOTICE is hereby given that at a special meeting of the directors of .... Corporation, duly held on ...., 19.., a resolution was adopted recommending the dissolution of the Corporation and calling a special meeting of stockholders to consider and act upon said resolution.

Pursuant to said resolution of the Board of Directors, notice is hereby given that a special meeting of the stockholders will be held at the office of the Corporation, ... (*address*) on ...., 19.., at ....M., for the purpose of acting upon said resolution for the dissolution of said Corporation, and for the purpose of transacting such other business as may properly come before the meeting.

Stockholders of record at the close of business ...., 19.., will be entitled to vote at this meeting. ...., 19...

....

Secretary

RESOLUTION OF STOCKHOLDERS CONSENTING TO
DISSOLUTION OF CORPORATION, DIRECTING OFFICERS TO
FILE NECESSARY PAPERS, AND EMPOWERING DIRECTORS TO
WIND UP AFFAIRS

RESOLVED, That the .... Corporation surrender its charter to the State of .... and that it cease to be and exist as a corporation, and

RESOLVED FURTHER, That ...., the President, and ...., the Secretary, of the said .... Corporation, are hereby authorized and directed to file the necessary certificate of dissolution of this Corporation with the Secretary of State of the State of . . . . , and with the County Clerk of the County of . . . . . , and

RESOLVED FURTHER, That the Board of Directors of this Corporation is hereby authorized, empowered, and directed to do all things necessary and requisite to settle the affairs of the Corporation, to collect the outstanding debts, to provide for the payment of the liabilities and obligations of the Corporation, to distribute its assets, and to do all other things necessary to carry into effect the foregoing resolution.

DIRECTORS' RESOLUTION TO DISSOLVE CORPORATION ON WRITTEN CONSENT OF ALL STOCKHOLDERS

WHEREAS, the . . . . Corporation has completely discontinued and closed its business, and has paid all its debts, obligations, and liabilities, and

WHEREAS, all the stockholders of the . . . . Corporation having voting power have consented in writing to a dissolution of the said Corporation, be it

RESOLVED, That the . . . . Corporation abandon its corporate authority, surrender its charter, and dissolve; and that . . . . , the President, ... , the Secretary, and . . . . , the Treasurer, are hereby authorized to file in the office of the Secretary of State of the State of . . . . the written consent of the stockholders as aforesaid, together with a list of the names and residences of directors and officers of this Corporation, duly certified, to record in the office of the Recorder of the County of . . . . the certificate of dissolution to be issued by the Secretary of State of the State of . . . . , and to do all other things necessary to carry into effect the foregoing resolution.

RESOLUTION OF STOCKHOLDERS AUTHORIZING OFFICERS TO FILE PAPERS FOR DISSOLUTION, THE CONSENT OF MORE THAN TWO-THIRDS IN INTEREST OF STOCKHOLDERS HAVING BEEN OBTAINED

WHEREAS, more than two-thirds in interest of the stockholders of . . . . Corporation having voting power have consented in writing to a dissolution of the said Corporation, be it

RESOLVED, That . . . . Corporation abandon its corporate authority, surrender its charter, and dissolve, and that . . . . , the President, ... , the Secretary, and . . . . , the Treasurer, are hereby authorized to file in the office of the Secretary of State of the State of . . . . the written consent of the stockholders to the dissolution of said Corporation as aforesaid, together with a list of the names and residences of directors and officers of this Corporation, duly certified, and that said officers

be further authorized to record in the office of the Recorder of the County of
........., State of ...., the certificate of dissolution to be issued by
the Secretary of State of the State of ...., and to do all other things
necessary to effect the dissolution of said Corporation, and

RESOLVED FURTHER, That the Board of Directors of this Corporation
is hereby authorized and empowered, without further action by the
stockholders of this Corporation, to take any and all action and to do any and
all acts and things that may, in the judgment of said Board, be necessary or
proper to wind up the affairs of said Corporation, and to distribute in cash
among its stockholders ratably, according to their respective interests, the
remaining assets of the Corporation.

RESOLUTION OF STOCKHOLDERS DISSOLVING CORPORATION, AUTHORIZING DIRECTORS TO CONVERT PROPERTY INTO CASH AND TO DISTRIBUTE IT, AND DIRECTING OFFICERS TO PUBLISH NOTICE OF DISSOLUTION

RESOLVED, That this Corporation forthwith discontinue business as a
corporation and surrender its charter and corporate franchises to the State of
........., and

RESOLVED FURTHER, That the property and assets of this Corporation
shall, under the order and direction of the Board of Directors of this
Corporation now in office, be subject to the payment of the liabilities of this
Corporation and the expenses of winding up its affairs; and that the surplus, if
any, then remaining shall be distributed among the stockholders according to
their respective interests, provided that no distribution is made to the
stockholders until after the publication of the notice hereinafter referred to,
and

RESOLVED FURTHER, That the property and assets of this Corporation
so to be distributed to the stockholders of this Corporation shall be
distributed in cash, or in property, or partly in cash and partly in property, as
said Board of Directors may in its sole discretion determine, and

RESOLVED FURTHER, That the Board of Directors of this Corporation
is hereby authorized and empowered, without further action by the
stockholders of this Corporation, to convert all or any part of the property
and assets of this Corporation into cash, and to take any and all action and to
do any and all acts and things which may, in the opinion of counsel or in the
judgment of said Board, be necessary or proper to dissolve this Corporation
and wind up its affairs, and carry out the intent and purposes of the foregoing
resolutions, and

RESOLVED FURTHER, That the President or a Vice president of this
Corporation is hereby authorized and directed to cause notice of the adoption

of the foregoing resolutions to be given immediately by advertisement in some
newspaper of general circulation, published near the principal office or place
of business of this Corporation, once in each week for at least . . . . . (. . . . .)
successive weeks; to certify a copy of the foregoing resolutions to the Secretary
of State of the State of . . . . ; and to deliver to said Secretary of State a
certificate showing the publication of said notice as required by law.

RESOLUTION OF STOCKHOLDERS DISSOLVING CORPORATION WHICH HAS FULFILLED PURPOSES FOR WHICH IT WAS INCORPORATED

WHEREAS, the . . . . Company has fulfilled the purposes for which
it was incorporated, and

WHEREAS, the said Company has paid all its indebtedness and has no
liabilities whatsoever outstanding against it, be it

RESOLVED, That the . . . . Company be dissolved, and that the
Board of Directors of said Company immediately take all necessary steps, by
proceedings in court and otherwise, to consummate the dissolution of the
Company.

DIRECTORS' RESOLUTION AUTHORIZING PETITION FOR DISSOLUTION OF CORPORATION

WHEREAS, the directors of the . . . . Corporation have discovered
that the property and effects of the Corporation have been reduced to such an
extent by losses that the said Corporation will be unable to pay all just
demands against it or to offer a reasonable security to those who deal with it,
and

WHEREAS, all the directors deem it beneficial to the interests of the
stockholders that the said Corporation be dissolved, be it

RESOLVED, That this Corporation be dissolved, and that the directors,
or a majority of them, are hereby authorized to petition to the . . . .
Court for the dissolution of the Corporation, and to do all other things
necessary to carry the foregoing resolution into effect.

DIRECTORS' RESOLUTION RECOMMENDING THAT APPLICATION FOR DISSOLUTION BE ADDRESSED TO COURT, AND CALLING MEETING OF STOCKHOLDERS

WHEREAS, the Board of Directors of this Corporation deems it to be to
the best interests of this Corporation and its stockholders that the said
Corporation be dissolved, it is

RESOLVED, That a special meeting of the stockholders of this
Corporation be called to convene on . . . ., 19. ., at . . . . . M., at the office

of the Corporation at . . . . (*Street*), in the City of . . . ., State of
. . . ., to consider and pass upon the advisability of petitioning to the
. . . . Court for the dissolution of the Corporation, and

RESOLVED FURTHER, That the Secretary of this Corporation is hereby
directed to send notices of the aforesaid meeting forthwith to all the
stockholders, in the manner provided by the By-laws of this Corporation.

RESOLUTION OF STOCKHOLDERS AUTHORIZING OFFICER TO EMPLOY ATTORNEY TO PREPARE AND FILE PETITION IN COURT FOR DISSOLUTION OF CORPORATION

WHEREAS, all the indebtedness, liabilities, and obligations of this
Corporation have been paid, satisfied, and discharged, and

WHEREAS, the Corporation has ceased to carry on the business for
which it was organized, and

WHEREAS, the stockholders of this Corporation deem it to be for the
best interests of this Corporation that the said Corporation be dissolved, and
that its assets be distributed among its stockholders, be it

RESOLVED, That . . . ., the President of this Corporation, is
hereby authorized and directed to employ a competent attorney to prepare
and file in the proper court (*or, insert the words* "in the . . . . Court of the
County of . . . ., State of . . . . . ") a petition requesting the dissolution of
this Corporation, and to carry on all proceedings and to do all things and to
perform all acts necessary to prosecute the said application to final judgment.

DIRECTORS' RESOLUTION AUTHORIZING EMPLOYMENT OF COUNSEL TO OPPOSE CREDITOR'S APPLICATION FOR DISSOLUTION

WHEREAS, the . . . . Company, a creditor of this Corporation, has
instituted an action in the . . . . Court, praying for the dissolution of this
Corporation on the ground of its insolvency, and

WHEREAS, this Corporation is not insolvent and is fully able to pay all
just claims against it, and

WHEREAS, it is the belief of the directors of this Corporation that the
said action is without foundation in law and in fact, be it

RESOLVED, That . . . . ., the President of this Corporation, is hereby
authorized and directed to employ . . . . as counsel to interpose a
defense in behalf of this Corporation to the action aforesaid, to do all things
necessary to carry on the proceedings to oppose the said creditor, and to
defeat its aforesaid application for the dissolution of this Corporation, the
compensation of the said attorney to be agreed upon between him and

........., the President of this Corporation, subject to the approval of this Board of Directors.

RESOLUTION OF DIRECTORS AUTHORIZING APPLICATION TO RENEW CHARTER AFTER EXPIRATION OF EXISTENCE

WHEREAS, this Corporation is actually engaged at the present time in business within the State of ....., and

WHEREAS, the charter of the Corporation, granted on ...., 19.., for a period of ..... (.....) years, did expire on ...., 19.., and

WHEREAS, this Corporation has inadvertently allowed its charter to be forfeited and cancelled by lapse of time, but without any intention to surrender its corporate privileges or retire from business, and

WHEREAS, this Corporation has been continuously engaged in carrying on the purposes of its incorporation since the forfeiture and cancellation of its charter as aforesaid, be it

RESOLVED, That the present President and Secretary are hereby authorized and directed to make application to the .... (*insert proper authority*) of the State of ....., to set aside the said forfeiture and cancellation, to renew the charter for a period of ..... (.....) years, and to accompany the same with a certified copy of this resolution, with the payment of all corporate fees owing to the state, and with the report as required by the laws of the State of ....

NOTICE OF STOCKHOLDERS' MEETING TO APPROVE DISSOLUTION AFTER SALE OF ASSETS

To the Stockholders of .... Corporation:

Pursuant to a plan for the reorganization of your Corporation, the Corporation, under authority given by its stockholders at a special meeting held ...., 19.., has transferred its assets to the ..... Company and has received in return .. shares of .... Company Common Stock. The plan referred to requires that the Corporation shall now be dissolved. Consequently, the Board of Directors has adopted a resolution to dissolve, subject to a vote of the stockholders to be held at a special meeting.

Notice is hereby given that the special meeting of the stockholders to vote on the dissolution of the Corporation will be held at the office of the Corporation, ... (*address*) on ...., 19.., at ...M. If you do not expect to attend this meeting, please sign the enclosed proxy and return it in the enclosed envelope.

It is expected that dissolution will be effected by ...., 19.., so that on and after that date the ..... shares of .... Company Common Stock above-mentioned may be distributed to you by way of a liquidating

dividend in final liquidation of the Corporation, in the proportion of
...../.....th of a share of such stock for each share of ....
Corporation Capital Stock then registered in your name on the stock transfer
books of the Corporation.

You will shortly receive a letter of transmittal with instructions as to the
place and manner of presenting your stock as evidence of your right to receive
the liquidating dividend. Please do not present your stock without the letter of
transmittal.

The stock transfer books of your Corporation will be closed after the
close of business on ...., 19.. ...., 19..

....
[President or Secretary]

EXCERPT OF MINUTES OF STOCKHOLDERS' MEETING
AUTHORIZING SALE OF ASSETS AND DISSOLUTION
UPON REORGANIZATION

Upon motion of .... seconded by ...., the following
resolutions were unanimously adopted:

RESOLVED, That the President and the Secretary of this Company are
hereby authorized and empowered to sell all the assets of the Company of
whatsoever kind and wheresoever situated, including all accounts receivable,
patents, machinery, equipment, stock of merchandise, and goodwill, to .....,
....., and ....., of ....,at a price equal to the net value of all the
assets of this Company, said net value to be determined by the books of this
Company as of ...., 19.., and

RESOLVED FURTHER, That the President and the Secretary of this
Company are hereby authorized to make such arrangements as to the time
and manner of payment upon the sale aforesaid as they in their judgment shall
deem advisable, and to execute and deliver, in behalf of this Company, any
and all agreements, bills of sale, and other instruments necessary to effectuate
the said sale, and

RESOLVED FURTHER, That the President and the Secretary of this
Company are hereby authorized and empowered to take all necessary steps to
wind up its affairs, to pay all its debts and obligations, to distribute the
remaining assets among the stockholders in proportion to their holdings in the
Company, and to execute and file all instruments and to do all things
necessary to dissolve this Company in the manner provided by law.

RESOLUTION OF STOCKHOLDERS AUTHORIZING
DISSOLUTION ON CONSUMMATION OF SALE
OF ENTIRE ASSETS

WHEREAS, this Company has this day, by resolutions passed and
adopted by this meeting, authorized and approved the giving of an option of
sale of all the assets of this Company, and has likewise authorized the

distribution of the proceeds of such sale among the stockholders, as a liquidation distribution of the assets of this Company, be it

RESOLVED, and voted by the stockholders of the .... Company, at a special meeting duly called and held, that if said option shall be exercised, and if and when said sale shall be consummated, it is the desire of the stockholders to surrender the charter and to dissolve the Company, and the President and the Secretary of the Company are authorized and directed to file in the office of the Secretary of State a sworn certificate showing the adoption by the stockholders of such resolution aforesaid; and that the expense incident to preparing and filing such certificate be paid out of the treasury of this Company.

RESOLUTION OF STOCKHOLDERS APPROVING AGREEMENT SETTING FORTH PLAN FOR COMPLETE LIQUIDATION OF CORPORATION

RESOLVED, That the stockholders of the Corporation hereby approve the dissolution of this Corporation, and

RESOLVED FURTHER, That the stockholders of this corporation hereby approve the Agreement dated as of ...., 19.., between this Corporation and ...., a .... corporation, setting forth the Plan for the Complete Liquidation of this Corporation, in the form presented to this meeting, and

RESOLVED FURTHER, That the proper officers of this Corporation are hereby authorized and directed to do or cause to be done all such acts and things and to file or cause to be filed all such documents as, with the advice of counsel, they may deem necessary or advisable in order to carry into effect the dissolution of this Corporation, the Plan for the Complete Liquidation of the Corporation (as set forth in the Agreement dated as of ...., 19.., between the Corporation and .. ..), and, generally, the purposes and intent of these resolutions.

RESOLUTION OF STOCKHOLDERS APPOINTING LIQUIDATORS ON DISSOLUTION AND PROVIDING FOR COMPENSATION

RESOLVED, That .... and .... are hereby appointed liquidators for the purpose of winding up the business of this Corporation, and

RESOLVED FURTHER, That the compensation of the said liquidators for their services in the winding up of the business as aforesaid shall be fixed (*insert either one of the following*):

(1) at the sum of ..... ($.....) Dollars, in addition to their disbursements and expenses.

(2) at a sum equal to ..... (.....%) percent of the amount of assets recovered by them in winding up the business during their period of office.

RESOLUTION OF STOCKHOLDERS APPOINTING LIQUIDATOR ON EXPIRATION OF CHAPTER

WHEREAS, the charter of the .... Corporation will expire on ...., 19.., and

WHEREAS, it has become necessary to have all the assets of the Corporation, of every character, sold for the purpose of paying its debts and distributing the surplus, if any, among the stockholders, and

WHEREAS, it is impossible properly to advertise and sell said property by the .... of .... next, be it

RESOLVED:

First. That the .... Trust Company is hereby appointed liquidator of the affairs of the Corporation, with directions to operate, for the use of the stockholders, the affairs and business of said Corporation as they have been operated, until the property can be properly advertised and sold and the possession thereof delivered to the purchaser.

Second. That, prior to the said sale, the liquidator shall cause to be made, for the use of the stockholders, a comprehensive statement of the assets and liabilities of the Corporation, and shall furnish said stockholders with a copy of said statement.

Third. That the said liquidator shall, in its advertisement, specify the nature of the articles to be sold, shall make such sale for cash, to be paid on the delivery of possession, and shall require the purchaser to deposit a certified check for an amount equal to one-third of the total purchase price, which the liquidator shall hold and credit upon the purchase price when the sale is consummated, or, if for any reason it shall be set aside, the liquidator shall return it to the bidder. If the said bidder to whom the property is knocked down shall fail at once to deliver to the liquidator the certified check as herein provided, the liquidator shall immediately resell the property and refuse to receive bids from said former bidder.

Fourth. Said liquidator may, in his discretion, employ an auctioneer or other agent necessary or proper to be used in the sale of the property.

Fifth. Until said sale, and during the operation of said property, said liquidator is given full authority and permission to employ such agents and persons as may be necessary properly, conveniently, and economically to operate the property, to keep an account of all its expenses, and to take vouchers therefor. After the property has been fully administered, said liquidator shall make out a comprehensive account of its acts and doings, and shall furnish a copy thereof to each of the stockholders.

Sixth. The said liquidator shall, from the proceeds of the sale of the property, pay all debts of the Corporation, and the balance, if any, shall be distributed among the stockholders according to their legal rights.

RESOLUTION OF STOCKHOLDERS DIRECTING TRUSTEES IN DISSOLUTION TO SELL REMAINING ASSETS TO NEW CORPORATION IN EXCHANGE FOR STOCK

WHEREAS, a resolution was duly adopted by the directors and stockholders of the . . . . Corporation, on . . . ., 19. ., to dissolve the said Corporation, and

WHEREAS, ... and . . . . were duly appointed trustees to wind up the business of the said . . . . Corporation, and

WHEREAS, all the debts of the said Corporation have now been paid, and there are no liabilities whatsoever outstanding against it, be it

RESOLVED, That . . . . and . . . . ., trustees as aforesaid, are hereby authorized to sell all the remaining assets of this Corporation, both real and personal, of whatsoever kind and nature, and wheresoever the same may be located, to . . . . Company, a corporation organized on . . . ., 19. ., under and by virtue of the laws of the State of . . . ., and to accept in full payment thereof, ... (. . . . .) shares of the common stock of the said Company having a par value of . . . . . ($. . . . .) Dollars each, amounting in the aggregate to . . . . . ($. . . . .) Dollars, and

RESOLVED FURTHER, That the said trustees are hereby authorized and empowered to make, execute, and deliver, for and in behalf of the . . . . Corporation, all deeds of conveyance and other instruments, and to do all other things necessary to transfer the property aforesaid to the said . . . . Company, upon receipt of the stock as aforesaid, and

RESOLVED FURTHER, That said stock to be received in payment for the sale of assets hereinabove authorized be distributed upon receipt thereof among the stockholders of the . . . . Corporation, in proportion to their respective holdings in the Corporation.

RESOLUTION OF TRUSTEES IN DISSOLUTION TO PROCEED TO WIND UP AFFAIRS

RESOLVED, That, immediately upon the completion of the publication of the certificate of the Secretary of State, issued on . . . ., 19. ., in the matter of the voluntary dissolution of this Corporation, pursuant to the laws of the State of . . . ., this Board of Trustees shall proceed to adjust and

wind up the affairs of the Corporation; and that, beginning with ....,
19. .., no contracts or agreements of any kind shall be entered into, except such
as shall be necessary to liquidate the affairs of the Corporation.

RESOLUTION OF TRUSTEES IN DISSOLUTION AUTHORIZING OFFICERS TO CONTINUE IN OFFICE

RESOLVED, That the present officers of the Corporation continue in
their respective offices during the liquidation and winding up of the
Company's affairs, and that their salaries be continued during the liquidation
at the same rates as heretofore.

RESOLUTION BY TRUSTEES IN DISSOLUTION AUTHORIZING APPRAISAL OF PROPERTY AND ARRANGING FOR CONFERENCE WITH APPRAISERS

RESOLVED, That an appraisal of the real and personal property of the
.... Company be made immediately, and that the following-named
persons be invited to appear before the Board of Trustees of the ....
Company, at its next meeting, to be held on ...., 19, at ... .
(*Street*), in the City of ...., State of ...., to confer with the said
Board in regard to the qualifications of said persons as appraisers and in
regard to the compensation to be paid them for the appraisal of the property
of the .... Company, now in the process of liquidation:

(Here insert names and addresses of appraisers.)

RESOLVED FURTHER, That ...., the Chairman of this meeting, is
hereby authorized and directed to cause notice of the adoption of this
resolution to be mailed forthwith to the aforementioned appraisers.

RESOLUTION OF TRUSTEES IN DISSOLUTION AUTHORIZING PAYMENT FOR LEGAL SERVICES

WHEREAS, ..., a member of this Board of Trustees, who is an
attorney and counselor at law, has conferred with this Board since ....
.., 19. .., when the dissolution of .... Company was proposed, in regard
to important questions of law and procedure relative to the liquidation of said
Company's business and affairs, and

WHEREAS, the opinions and advice of said ...., communicated to this Board of Trustees, have proved of great assistance and value to
the Board in winding up the affairs of this Company, and

WHEREAS, this Board of Trustees is of the opinion that the said ....
should receive compensation for his services, be it

RESOLVED, That ...., the Treasurer of this Company, is hereby
authorized and directed to pay to the said .... the sum of ..... ($.....)

Dollars, as compensation for such professional services as he has rendered to the Trustees of this Company in connection with the dissolution of this Company and the liquidation of its affairs.

DIRECTORS' RESOLUTION ACCEPTING OFFER OF TRUST COMPANY TO ACT AS DEPOSITARY OF ASSETS FOR PAYMENT OF CREDITORS ON DISSOLUTION

WHEREAS, the stockholders of the . . . . Corporation have duly resolved to dissolve the Corporation after payment of the claims of all creditors, and

WHEREAS, the . . . . Trust Company has offered to act as depositary of the assets of the . . . . Corporation, to be distributed among the creditors of the Corporation on dissolution, free of charge, be it

RESOLVED, That the said offer is hereby accepted, it being agreed and understood that the said . . . . Trust Company is acting solely as agent and trustee for the . . . . Corporation and its creditors, and that it does not assume any responsibility for the accuracy or validity of the claims against the Corporation, and

RESOLVED FURTHER, That the said . . . . Trust Company is hereby expressly authorized to accept the list, furnished by the Treasurer of the . . . . Corporation, of the names of the creditors of the Corporation and the amounts due to each as accurate and complete, without further inquiry on the part of the said . . . . Trust Company, and

RESOLVED FURTHER, That . . . . , the Treasurer of the . . . . Corporation is hereby authorized and directed to convert forthwith into cash all the assets of the Corporation, to collect all the outstanding accounts of the Corporation, and to deposit with the said . . . . Trust Company all sums received through such conversion of the assets into cash, through collection of the accounts due the Corporation, or in any other manner, said sums to be held in trust for the creditors of the . . . . Corporation, and

RESOLVED FURTHER, That distribution of the amount so placed on deposit with the . . . . Trust Company be made by it pro rata among the creditors of the . . . . Corporation, on . . . ., 19 . . ; that subsequent distributions be made on the first day of each and every month thereafter among the creditors pro rata, until the full amount of the claims with interest at the rate of 6 percent per annum shall have been paid; and that, when the full amount of the creditors' claims, with interest as aforesaid, has been paid, the officers of the . . . . Corporation are hereby authorized to execute all papers and to do all other acts and things necessary to effect a dissolution of the Corporation.

LIQUIDATION

STOCKHOLDERS' RESOLUTION AUTHORIZING DIRECTORS TO CONVERT PROPERTY INTO CASH AND DISTRIBUTE IT

RESOLVED, That the property and assets of this Corporation shall, under the direction of the Board of Directors of this Corporation now in office, be subject to the payment of liabilities of this Corporation and the expenses of winding up its affairs; and that the surplus, if any, then remaining shall be distributed among the stockholders according to their respective interests, and

RESOLVED FURTHER, That the property and assets of this Corporation so to be distributed to the stockholders of this Corporation shall be distributed in cash, or in property, or partly in cash and partly in property, as the Board of Directors may in its sole discretion determine, and

RESOLVED FURTHER, That the Board of Directors of this Corporation is hereby authorized, without further action by the stockholders of this Corporation to convert all or any part of the property and assets of this Corporation into cash, and to do all acts that, in the opinion of counsel or in the judgment of the Board may be necessary or proper to dissolve this Corporation and wind up its affairs, and carry out the intent and purposes of the foregoing resolution.

RESOLUTION OF STOCKHOLDERS APPOINTING LIQUIDATORS TO WIND UP BUSINESS ON DISSOLUTION

RESOLVED, That .... and .... are hereby appointed liquidators for the purpose of winding up the business of this Corporation, and

RESOLVED FURTHER, That the compensation of the liquidators for their services in winding up the business of the Corporation shall be fixed at the sum of $....., in addition to their disbursements and expenses.

RESOLUTION OF STOCKHOLDERS APPOINTING TRUST COMPANY AS LIQUIDATOR

WHEREAS, in pursuance of the action of the stockholders dissolving this Corporation, it has become necessary to have all the assets of the Corporation, of every character, sold for the purpose of paying its debts and distributing the surplus, if any, among the stockholders, and

WHEREAS, it is impossible properly to advertise and sell said property by ...., 19.., be it

RESOLVED:

First. That the .... Trust Company is hereby appointed liquidator of the affairs of the Corporation, with directions to conduct, for the use of the stockholders, the affairs and business of said Corporation as they have been conducted, until the property can be properly advertised and sold and the possession thereof delivered to the purchaser.

Second. That, prior to the sale, the liquidator shall cause to be made, for the use of the stockholders, a comprehensive statement of the assets and liabilities of the Corporation, and shall furnish the stockholders with a copy of the statement.

Third. That the liquidator shall, in its advertisement, specify the nature of the articles to be sold, shall make such sale for cash, to be paid on the delivery of possession, and shall require the purchaser to deposit a certified check for an amount equal to .... (*insert fraction*) of the total purchase price, which the liquidator shall hold and credit upon the purchase price when the sale is consummated or, if for any reason the sale shall be set aside, the liquidator shall return the deposit to the bidder. If the bidder to whom the property is knocked down shall fail at once to deliver to the liquidator the certified check as herein provided, the liquidator shall immediately resell the property and refuse to receive bids from said former bidder.

Fourth. The liquidator may, in his discretion, employ an auctioneer or other agent necessary or proper to be used in the sale of the property.

Fifth. Until said sale, and during the operation of said property, the liquidator is given full authority to employ such agents and persons as may be necessary to the economic operation of the property, to keep an account of all its expenses, and to take vouchers therefor. After the property has been fully administered, the liquidator shall make out a comprehensive account of its acts and doings, and shall furnish a copy thereof to each of the stockholders.

Sixth. The liquidator shall, from the proceeds of the sale of the property, pay all debts of the Corporation, and the balance, if any, shall be distributed among the stockholders according to their legal rights.

NOTICE OF LIQUIDATING DIVIDEND WITH LETTER FOR TRANSMITTAL OF STOCK CERTIFICATES

NOTICE is hereby given that at a special meeting of stockholders of .... Corporation held on ...., 19.., pursuant to a resolution adopted by the Board of Directors on ...., 19.., the holders of more than two-thirds in interest of the stock of the corporation voted in favor of its dissolution and signed their consent in writing to such dissolution. The consent of the stockholders, together with the required certificate of the proper officers of the Corporation will be filed with the Secretary of State of the State of ..... on ...., 19.., and the dissolution completed on ...., 19..

Pursuant to action of the Board of Directors, the stock transfer books of the Corporation will be closed permanently on ...., 19.., at the close of business on that day.

The assets of the Corporation, verified by audit of ...., Certified Public Accountant, dated ...., 19.., consist of $..... cash in banks. Of this amount there will be reserved for payment of miscellaneous liabilities and expenses of dissolution the sum of $....., leaving $....., being the equivalent of $..... per share of outstanding stock.

Distribution in final liquidation will be made on and after ...., 19.., at the office of the .... Trust Co., ... (*address*), to stockholders of record at the close of business on ...., 19.., upon delivery at said office by the stockholder of all his certificates of stock of the Corporation for surrender and cancellation, each certificate to be indorsed, witnessed, and signature guaranteed by a bank having a .... (*name of city or state*) correspondent or by a brokerage firm which is a member of the .... Stock Exchange. The words "For Surrender and Cancellation" should also be written on the back of each certificate. Stock transfer tax stamps need not be affixed.

For your convenience, there is enclosed a form of letter of transmittal for use in sending stock certificates to the .... Trust Company.

Very truly yours,

...., 19...   ....
Secretary

Letter of Transmittal

...., 19..

.... Trust Company

....

Gentlemen:

Pursuant to notice received from .... Corporation, dated ...., 19.., the undersigned encloses herewith for surrender and cancellation the following stock certificates of .... Corporation.

Certificate No.	For number of shares
....	....
....	....

Yours very truly,
Name: ....
Address: ....

NOTICE TO STOCKHOLDERS OF DISTRIBUTION OF CASH RECEIVED UPON SALE OF BUSINESS TO BE MADE IN INSTALLMENTS, WITH LETTER OF TRANSMITTAL AND RECEIPT FOR STOCK CERTIFICATE DEPOSITED

. . . . City, ..., 19 . .

Dear Sir:

The property of this Corporation has, pursuant to the authority given at the stockholders' meeting held . . . ., 19 . ., been sold to the . . . . Company for $ . . . . . cash. Part of this amount has already been paid, and the balance is secured by bonds deposited with . . . . Trust Co., as trustee.

The Board of Directors has resolved that out of this sum there shall be distributed to the stockholders of record on the Corporation's books, in liquidation of the Corporation's affairs, as first payment, the sum of $ . . . . . per share on presentation of the certificates of stock to . . . . Trust Co., ... (*address*). In order that the amounts now and hereafter to be paid may be noted thereon as made, please forward immediately your certificate of stock, with power of attorney properly signed and witnessed, to . . . . Trust Co.

Further distributions will be made from time to time as the balance of the purchase price is paid. These distributions will also have to be noted on the certificate. We therefore advise you to authorize . . . . Trust Co. to retain your certificate for this purpose, and enclose a form of letter to be filled out and signed by you to that effect. Upon receipt of your certificate of stock and letter, you will be given a proper receipt.

Yours truly,

. . . . Corporation

By . . . .

President

Letter of Transmittal

. . . ., 19 . .

. . . . Trust Co.

. . . ., ...

Gentlemen:

In accordance with the instructions of . . . . Corporation in its circular letter of . . . ., 19 . ., I herewith enclose Certificate No. . . . . . . for . . . . . shares of the capital stock of . . . . . Corporation, the property of the undersigned, in order that payment of $ . . . . . per share, in liquidation, now authorized, may be noted thereon. You may retain the same in order that subsequent payments, in liquidation, may be noted on them as made.

Please acknowledge and forward receipt for the enclosed certificates, as mentioned in the Company's letter.

Yours very truly,

. . . .

Receipt

Received . . . ., 19 . ., from . . . . . Certificate No. . . . . . for . . . . . shares of the capital stock of . . . . Corporation, standing in the name of ...., to be retained on deposit by the undersigned in order that payments in distribution made on account of the liquidation of the affairs of that Corporation may be noted thereon, in accordance with the terms of the circular letter from the Corporation to its stockholders under dated of ...., 19.., and of the letter addressed to the undersigned by you, dated ...., 19...

.... Trust Company

ARTICLES OF DISSOLUTION BY INCORPORATORS

Pursuant to provisions of Section ..... of the .... Business Corporation Act, the undersigned, being a majority of the incorporators of the corporation named below, adopt the following Articles of Dissolution:

First. The name of the corporation is ....

Second. The date of issuance of its certificate of incorporation was ...., 19...

Third. None of its shares have been issued.

Fourth. The corporation has not commenced business.

Fifth. The amount, if any, actually paid in on subscriptions to its shares, less any part thereof disbursed for necessary expenses, has been returned to those entitled thereto.

Sixth. No debts of the corporation remain unpaid.

Seventh. A majority or all of the incorporators elect that the corporation be dissolved.
Dated: ...., 19...

[Signed:] ....
....
....
Incorporators

STATEMENT OF INTENT TO DISSOLVE
BY WRITTEN CONSENT OF STOCKHOLDERS

Pursuant to the provisions of Section ..... of the .... Business Corporation Act, the undersigned corporation submits the following statement of intent to dissolve upon the written consent of the holders of record of all its outstanding shares:

First. The name of the corporation is ....

Second. The names and addresses of its officers are:

Name	*Address*	*City,*	*State*
President:	. . . .	. . . ,	. . . .
Vice presidents:	. . . .	. . . ,	. . . .
	. . . .	. . . ,	. . . .
Treasurer:	. . . .	. . . ,	. . . .
Secretary:	. . . .	. . . ,	. . . .

Third. The names and addresses of its directors are:

Name	*Address*	*City,*	*State*
. . . .	. . . .	. . . ,	. . . .
. . . .	. . . .	. . . ,	. . . .
. . . .	. . . .	. . . ,	. . . .

Fourth. The following consent to the dissolution of the corporation has been signed by all the stockholders of the corporation, or signed in their names by their duly authorized attorneys:

[Insert copy of consent]

Dated: . . . ., 19. .

            . . . . Corporation
            By its authorized officers:
            . . . ., President
            . . . ., Secretary

STATEMENT OF INTENT TO DISSOLVE
ADOPTED BY STOCKHOLDER VOTE

Pursuant to the provisions of Section . . . . . of the . . . . Business Corporation Act, the undersigned Corporation submits the following statement of intent to dissolve by act of the corporation:

[Insert the paragraphs entitled *First, Second,* and *Third* in the "Statement of intent to dissolve by written consent of stockholders."]

Fourth. The following resolution authorizing the dissolution of the Corporation was adopted by the stockholders of the Corporation on . . . ., 19. .;

[Insert copy of the resolution]

Fifth. The number of shares of the Corporation outstanding at the time of such adoption was . . . . The number of shares entitled to vote on the above resolution was:

Class	*Number of Shares*
. . . .	. . . .
. . . .	. . . .

Sixth. The number of shares voted for such resolution was ..... The number of shares voted against was .....

Seventh. The number of shares of each class entitled to vote on the resolution as a class voted as follows:

	Number of Shares Voted	
Class	*For*	*Against*
....	....	....
....	....	....

Dated: ...., 19...

.... Corporation
By its authorized officers:
................, President
................, Secretary

(*Note:* If there is only one class of stock, only the first sentence of paragraph *Fifth* is needed and paragraph *Seventh* may be omitted altogether.)

STATEMENT OF REVOCATION OF VOLUNTARY DISSOLUTION PROCEEDINGS BY WRITTEN CONSENT OF STOCKHOLDERS

Pursuant to the provisions of Section ..... of the .... Business Corporation Act, the undersigned corporation submits the following statement of revocation of the voluntary dissolution proceedings previously instituted:

[Insert paragraphs entitled *First, Second,* and *Third* in the "Statement of intent to dissolve by written consent of stockholders."]

Fourth. The following consent of the corporation revoking its voluntary dissolution proceedings has been signed by all the stockholders of the corporation, or signed in their names by their duly authorized attorneys:

[Insert copy of consent]

Dated: ...., 19...

.... Corporation
By its authorized officers:
................, President
................, Secretary

STATEMENT OF REVOCATION OF VOLUNTARY DISSOLUTION PROCEEDINGS ADOPTED BY STOCKHOLDER VOTE

Pursuant to the provisions of Section ..... of the .... Business Corporation Act, the undersigned corporation submits the following statement of revocation of the voluntary dissolution proceedings previously instituted:

[Insert paragraphs entitled *First*, *Second*, and *Third* in the "Statement of intent to dissolve by written consent of stockholders."]

Fourth. The following resolution was adopted by the stockholders on ...., 19.., revoking the previously instituted dissolution proceedings:

[Insert copy of the resolution; then follow with paragraph *Fifth* of the "Statement of intent to dissolve adopted by stockholder vote."]

NOTICE TO STOCKHOLDERS OF PLAN FOR TAX-FREE LIQUIDATION UNDER I.R.C. §337

To the Stockholders of .... Corporation:
Pursuant to a plan of liquidation adopted by your Board of Directors on ...., 19.., and a resolution adopted on that date that it be submitted for approval to the stockholders of the Company, notice is hereby given that the plan will be offered for adoption at a special meeting of Stockholders to be held on ...., 19.., at the office of the Company .... at ....M. of that day.

Stockholders of record at the close of business on ...., 19.., will be entitled to vote at this meeting.

Outline of the plan:

This plan for complete liquidation (the "Plan") of .... Corporation (the "Company"), a ..... (State) corporation, is intended to accomplish the complete liquidation of the Company in conformity with Section 337 of the Internal Revenue Code of 1954; the Plan is as follows:

(1) The Plan shall be and become effective upon the approval and adoption thereof by the affirmative vote of the holders of at least ..... % of the outstanding shares of the Company.

(2) After approval and adoption of the Plan by the shareholders, the Company shall sell, exchange or otherwise dispose of or reduce to cash all of its assets, properties and rights (exclusive of such thereof as may be distributed in kind, pro rata, to the shareholders of the Company from time to time), and ascertain, pay or make provision for the payment and discharge of all obligations of and claims against the Company, including unascertained or contingent liabilities and expenses.

(3) After the approval and adoption of the Plan by the shareholders, the aforesaid sales, exchanges and other dispositions of the assets, properties and rights of the Company shall be consummated as expeditiously as practicable

and, in any event, within the twelve months' period beginning on the date of the adoption of the Plan by the shareholders of the Company.

(4) After the approval and adoption of the Plan by the shareholders, and after such sales, exchanges or other dispositions, and as expeditiously as may be practicable thereafter, and in any event within the twelve months' period beginning with the adoption of the Plan by the shareholders, the Company shall:

(a) Cease doing business as a going concern and continue its activities merely for the purpose of winding up its affairs;

(b) Withdraw from all jurisdictions, other than ..... (State of incorporation), in which it is qualified to do business; and

(c) Make to its shareholders, pro rata, one or more distributions of its assets, including the proceeds of such sales, exchanges and other dispositions of its assets, properties and rights (less any assets retained to meet claims, including unascertained or contingent liabilities and expenses, and specifically set aside for that purpose), in full and complete cancellation, liquidation and redemption of all outstanding shares of the Company.

(5) Upon the completion of all of the foregoing acts and things, the Company shall be formally dissolved in accordance with the appropriate laws of the State of ....

Dated, ..., 19.., ...
                                                              Secretary

ARTICLES OF DISSOLUTION (TO BE FILED AFTER LIQUIDATION)

Pursuant to the provisions of Section ..... of the .... Business Corporation Act, the undersigned adopts the following Articles of Dissolution:

First. The name of the corporation is ....

Second. A statement of intent to dissolve [by written consent *or* by stockholder vote] was filed with the Secretary of State on ...., 19..

Third. All debts, obligations, and liabilities of the corporation have been paid and discharged, or adequate provision has been made therefor.

Fourth. All the remaining property and assets of the corporation have been distributed among the stockholders, in accordance with their respective rights and interests.

Fifth. There are no suits pending against the corporation in any [or, if there are suits pending, "Adequate provision has been made for the satisfaction of any judgment, order or decree which may be entered against the corporation in any pending suit."].

Dated: ...., 19...

.... Corporation

By its authorized officers:

.........., President

.........., Secretary

NOTICE OF CREDITORS TO PRESENT CLAIMS AGAINST DISSOLVED CORPORATION

Notice to Creditors

TO ALL CREDITORS OF AND CLAIMANTS against ...., Inc., a dissolved corporation, and all other interested persons:

PLEASE TAKE NOTICE that ...., Inc., under the provisions of Section ..... of the Laws of the State of ...., on ...., 19.., duly filed a certificate of dissolution in the office of the Secretary of State.

ALL CREDITORS OF AND CLAIMANTS against ...., Inc., its assets and directors and shareholders, are hereby required to present all claims and demands that have arisen or that may arise against ...., Inc., in writing, giving full details to the directors thereof, at the office of ...., Inc., at ...., on or before ...., 19..

THIS NOTICE does not constitute recognition of the claim of any person receiving it; nor is it intended to, nor does it operate to recognize, revive or make valid claims barred by the lapse of time or for any other reason.

Dated: ...., 19...

.........., Inc., a corporation

in dissolution

ASSIGNMENT FOR BENEFIT OF CREDITORS AND RECEIVERSHIP

DIRECTORS' RESOLUTION ASSIGNING PROPERTY TO TRUSTEE FOR BENEFIT OF CREDITORS

WHEREAS, This Coporation has contracted liabilities and obligations to numerous persons, firms, and corporations, in large amounts, some of which are past due and remain unpaid, and

WHEREAS, although this Corporation is wholly solvent, its property consists mainly of slow assets, with the results that it is unable immediately to discharge the aforesaid liabilities and obligations without material loss to the Corporation, and

WHEREAS, it is the opinion of the Board of Directors of this Corporation that the interests of the creditors and the stockholders of this Corporation would best be served by conveying all the produce, income, and assets of the Corporation of every kind and nature and wheresoever situated, to . . . ., of the City of . . . ., as Trustee, to operate and control the business, and out of the proceeds to pay the said liabilities and obligations of this Corporation, and thereupon to reconvey the said property and assets to the Corporation, be it

RESOLVED, That the President, or the Vice president, and the Secretary of this Corporation are hereby authorized and directed to execute and deliver to . . . ., of . . . . (*Street*), in the City of . . . ., as Trustee, in the name and in behalf of this Corporation and under its corporate seal, a deed of trust in substantially the form submitted to the Board of Directors at this meeting.

(*If the statute requires the consent of the stockholders to effect an assignment for the benefit of creditors, omit the last paragraph and add the paragraphs given below.*)

RESOLVED, That a special meeting of the stockholders of this Corporation be called, to be held on . . . ., 19. ., at . . . . . M., at the office of the Corporation at . . . . (*Street*), in the City of . . . ., State of . . . ., to consider and act upon the advisability of authorizing the officers of this Corporation to execute and deliver to . . . ., of . . . . (*Street*), City of . . . ., as Trustee, in the name and in behalf of this Corporation and under its corporate seal, a deed of trust in substantially the form submitted to the Board of Directors at this meeting, and

RESOLVED FURTHER, That the Secretary of this Corporation is hereby authorized and directed to send notices of the aforesaid special meeting forthwith to each of the stockholders appearing on the books of this Corporation.

RESOLUTION OF STOCKHOLDERS CONSENTING TO GENERAL ASSIGNMENT FOR THE BENEFIT OF CREDITORS AND AUTHORIZING ITS EXECUTION BY THE OFFICERS

WHEREAS, this Corporation is in financial difficulties and is unable to meet its obligations in the ordinary course of business, and

WHEREAS, the Board of Directors has recommended that it would be to the best interests of this Corporation to execute a general assignment for the benefit of creditors, it is

RESOLVED, That the stockholders do hereby consent to the execution of such assignment, and it is further

RESOLVED, That the President or the Vice president and the Secretary of this Corporation be and they hereby are authorized and directed, to execute and deliver, in the name of and on behalf of this Corporation and under its corporate seal, a general assignment for the benefit of creditors to .... as assignee, assigning all the corporate assets of whatsoever kind and wherever situated and authorizing said assignee to take all steps necessary to sell and otherwise dispose of such assets under the procedure authorized by the State of .... and to pay over the proceeds to creditors as provided by the laws of the State of ...., 19...

DIRECTORS' RESOLUTION AUTHORIZING ASSIGNMENT OF ALL CORPORATE ASSETS TO CREDITORS' COMMITTEE TO SELL AND LIQUIDATE

WHEREAS, this Corporation is indebted to divers persons for considerable sums of money, which sums it is presently unable to pay in full, and

WHEREAS, the creditors have heretofore held a meeting among themselves at which were present the President, Treasurer and Secretary of this Corporation, and

WHEREAS, after due deliberation and discussion with the creditors, the directors are of the opinion that the interests of the Corporation would best be served by conveying all the assets of the Corporation to a creditors' committee that shall continue to operate the business, collect outstanding indebtedness and sell the assets at the best price obtainable in the open market, it is therefor

RESOLVED, That the officers of this Corporation are authorized to execute an assignment to a creditors' committee of .... of .... Corp., ..., and .... of .... Inc., as a committee representing all the creditors of this Corporation and duly elected by the creditors on ...., 19..; said assignment to be of all the assets and property of this Corporation of any description, and it is

RESOLVED FURTHER, That said creditors' committee shall operate and control said business for such time as it deems necessary and in which it feels it can realize a sum equivalent to 60% of the total amount due all the creditors of this Corporation and to that end may sell or dispose of any and all assets necessary in the process, and it is

RESOLVED FURTHER, That in the event that the creditors' committee realizes more than 60% of the total required as aforesaid, then the balance after deduction of administration expenses shall be turned back to the Corporation.

(*Note:* This resolution can of course provide for payment of any sum up to 100% of the indebtedness and if sum desired is not realized nothing will be returned to the Corporation.)

DIRECTORS' RESOLUTION AUTHORIZING ASSIGNMENT OF ALL CORPORATE ASSETS TO CREDITORS' COMMITTEE TO OPERATE, PAY DEBTS AND RECONVEY TO CORPORATION

WHEREAS, this Corporation has contracted liabilities and obligations to persons, firms and corporations, in varied amounts, some of which are past due and remain unpaid, and

WHEREAS, although this Corporation is wholly solvent, its property consists mainly of assets which cannot be speedily liquidated, with the result that the Corporation is unable to immediately discharge the aforesaid liabilities and obligations without material loss of the Corporation, and

WHEREAS, the directors have met with a duly authorized creditors' committee and after such discussion and deliberation the Board of Directors are of the opinion that the interests of the creditors and the stockholders of this Corporation would best be served by assigning and conveying all the income and assets of this Corporation of every kind and nature and wherever situated, to the creditors' committee composed of ...., ..., and ...., to operate and control the business of the Corporation and out of the income and proceeds from the sale of such assets as are set forth on the attached Exhibit "A," pay 100% of the liabilities and obligations due said creditors, and thereafter to reconvey any remaining assets and property of this Corporation to it, be it therefore

RESOLVED, That the officers of this Corporation are hereby authorized and directed to execute and deliver to the creditors' committee above named, in the name of the Corporation and under its seal, an assignment in substantially the form submitted to the Board of Directors at this meeting.

DIRECTORS' RESOLUTION RECOMMENDING APPOINTMENT OF RECEIVER

WHEREAS, this Corporation is unable to meet its obligations as they mature, and it is the opinion of this Board of Directors that a receiver is to preserve and administer its assets for the benefit of all concerned, be it

RESOLVED, That ...., Secretary of the Corporation, is hereby authorized and directed to interpose an answer in any suit that may be filed in the United States District Court for the .... District of ...., to have a receiver appointed for the property of this Corporation, all of which property is situated in said ..... District of ....., to consent to the immediate appointment of such suitable person as the Court may appoint to take charge of, administer, and sell the property of this Corporation, and to do any other act necessary for the immediate appointment of a receiver by the United States District Court.

DIRECTORS' RESOLUTION RECOMMENDING
APPOINTMENT OF RECEIVER (another form)

RESOLVED, That it is the opinion of the Board of Directors that it would be for the best interests of the creditors of this Company that either a receiver in equity or a receiver in bankruptcy be appointed therefor.

BANKRUPTCY

DIRECTORS' RESOLUTION AUTHORIZING FILING
OF A VOLUNTARY PETITION FOR REORGANIZATION

RESOLVED, That this Corporation file a voluntary petition under and in pursuance of the National Bankruptcy Code for a reorganization, and

RESOLVED FURTHER, That this Corporation employ the law firm of . . . . as counsel to represent this Corporation in the reorganization proceedings, and

RESOLVED FURTHER, That the President of this Corporation is hereby authorized and directed to deliver to said legal counsel the necessary filing fees of the Court of Bankruptcy.

DIRECTORS' RESOLUTION AUTHORIZING OFFICER TO
FILE PETITION FOR REORGANIZATION UNDER THE
BANKRUPTCY CODE AND REQUESTING ATTORNEYS
TO REPRESENT THEM IN THE PROCEEDINGS

RESOLVED, That in the judgment of the Board of Directors, it is desirable and in the best interests of this Corporation, its creditors, stockholders, and other interested parties, that a petition for reorganization of this Corporation be filed under the provisions of the Bankruptcy Code, and

RESOLVED FURTHER, That the form of petition for reorganization under said Code presented to this meeting is hereby approved and adopted; that . . . ., Executive Vice president of this Corporation, is hereby directed, on behalf of this Corporation, to execute and file a petition in the Bankruptcy Court, and

RESOLVED FURTHER, That the law firm of . . . . is hereby authorized to represent this Corporation before the Bankruptcy Court in connection with the foregoing, and

RESOLVED FURTHER, That the officers of the Corporation are hereby authorized to execute and deliver all such instruments and do such other acts as they may deem desirable in furtherance of the purpose of the foregoing resolutions.

DIRECTORS' RESOLUTION ADMITTING CORPORATION'S INABILITY TO PAY DEBTS AND WILLINGNESS TO BE ADJUDGED BANKRUPT

WHEREAS, an involuntary petition in bankruptcy was filed against this Corporation on ...., 19.., in the Bankruptcy Court, and

WHEREAS, this Board of Directors believes that this Corporation is insolvent and wholly unable to pay its debts, and that it is in the best interest of the Corporation and its stockholders that the petition in bankruptcy be unopposed; be it

RESOLVED, That the .... Corporation hereby declares its inability to pay its debts and obligations and its willingness to be adjudged a bankrupt.

(*Note:* If the corporation prefers a reorganization to a liquidation, the directors' resolution would substitute "its willingness to seek and accept a Plan of Reorganization to be negotiated and confirmed by the Bankruptcy Court.")

DIRECTORS' RESOLUTION AUTHORIZING OFFICERS TO ADMIT ALLEGATIONS OF INVOLUNTARY PETITION FOR REORGANIZATION, EXCEPT AS TO INSOLVENCY

WHEREAS, a petition for reorganization of .... Corporation under the Bankruptcy Code was made by .... as trustee for the 5% Convertible Bonds of this Corporation under the trust indenture dated ...., 19.., and

WHEREAS, said petition was duly filed in the Bankruptcy Court, on ...., 19.., and

WHEREAS, a copy of the said petition and subpoena was duly served upon ...., President of the Corporation, on ...., 19.., and

WHEREAS, in the opinion of this Board of Directors, a reorganization of the .... Corporation is advisable, be it

RESOLVED, That the officers of this Corporation are hereby authorized to admit the jurisdiction of the Bankruptcy Court and the allegations of the petition of the Indenture Trustee filed in said court on ...., 19.., except as to insolvency, and

RESOLVED FURTHER, That the officers of this Corporation are hereby authorized to join in a prayer for approval of the aforesaid petition of the Indenture Trustee, and to take such steps in the proceeding for reorganization of the .... Corporation under the Bankruptcy Code, and to execute

and deliver all such instruments, and to do such other acts and things as may be necessary and proper.

STOCKHOLDERS' RESOLUTION RATIFYING ACT OF DIRECTORS IN ADMITTING INABILITY TO PAY DEBTS AND WILLINGNESS TO SEEK AND ACCEPT A PLAN OF REORGANIZATION

WHEREAS, the Board of Directors of this Corporation did on ...., 19. ., adopt a resolution admitting that this Corporation is unable to pay its debts and declaring the willingness of this Corporation to seek and accept a Plan of Reorganization, and

WHEREAS, the creditors of this Corporation did, on ...., 19. ., file a petition in bankruptcy against it; be it

RESOLVED, That the aforesaid action of the Board of Directors in admitting the Corporation's inability to pay its debts is hereby ratified and confirmed, and the officers of this Corporation are hereby authorized and directed to file a schedule of the property and a list of creditors of the Corporation, to execute all necessary instruments, and to do all things required by law in connection with such bankruptcy proceedings, and to seek and accept a Plan of Reorganization to be negotiated and confirmed by the Bankruptcy Court.

RESOLUTION OF STOCKHOLDERS RECOMMENDING THAT DIRECTORS FILE PETITION IN BANKRUPTCY

WHEREAS, legal proceedings have been instituted by some of the creditors of the .... Corporation, which will in all likelihood result in lengthy and expensive litigation, and

WHEREAS, it is deemed to be to the best interests of the said .... Corporation and its creditors to wind up the affairs of the said Corporation as speedily as possible, and sell the property of the said Corporation within the next few months, be it

RESOLVED, That the stockholders of the .... Corporation do hereby acknowledge that said Corporation cannot pay its debts, and that it is willing to be adjudged a bankrupt, and

RESOLVED FURTHER, That the directors are hereby authorized and directed to take the necessary steps to file a petition in bankruptcy and to have the affairs of the .... Corporation wound up forthwith.

DIRECTORS' RESOLUTION AUTHORIZING OFFICERS TO EMPLOY COUNSEL TO INTERPOSE ANSWER TO PETITION IN BANKRUPTCY AND TO OPPOSE PROCEEDINGS

WHEREAS, an involuntary petition in bankruptcy was filed against this Corporation on . . . ., 19. ., in the United States Bankruptcy Court for the . . . . District of . . . ., upon the ground that this Corporation did, within four months of the filing of the petition, and while it was insolvent, transfer property to creditors, with intent to prefer such creditors, and

WHEREAS, it is the opinion of the directors that this Corporation is wholly solvent and is fully able to meet all its obligations and pay all just claims against it, and

WHEREAS, the Corporation did not transfer property to any creditors with intent to prefer them, within four months of the filing of the aforesaid petition or at any other time, be it

RESOLVED, That an answer to the aforesaid petition in bankruptcy be interposed in behalf of this Corporation, denying the allegations contained therein, and that the officers of this Corporation are hereby authorized and directed to employ . . . ., an attorney, of . . . . (*Street*), City of . . . ., to represent this Corporation in the aforesaid proceeding, to do all things necessary to defend this Corporation, to oppose the proceedings brought against it as aforesaid, and to pay all reasonable expenses thereof and disbursements therefor.

INDEX